THE
HINDI
PADĀVALĪ
OF
NĀMDEV

फिरिब्रह्मावै॥ऐकादसीसहतसंजमकरै॥तमोऽहिसुयिनैकंधनयां

THE HINDI PADAVALĪ OF

NĀMDEV

A critical edition of Nāmdev's Hindi songs
with translation and annotation

WINAND M. CALLEWAERT
MUKUND LATH

Motilal Banarsidass Publishers Pvt. Ltd.
Delhi

First Published: 1989

Also available at
MOTILAL BANARSIDASS
Bungalow Road, Jawahar Nagar, Delhi 110 007
Chowk, Varanasi 221 001
Ashok Rajpath, Patna 800 004
24 Race Course Road, Bangalore 560 001
120 Royapettah High Road, Mylapore, Madras 600 004

ISBN: 81-208-0607-7

Produced on the laser at the K.U. Leuven, Belgium. Printed in India at the Saraswati Printing Press, A-95, Sector V, Noida (U.P.), India and published by Narendra Prakash Jain for Motilal Banarsidass Publishers Pvt. Ltd., Delhi 110 007.

CONTENTS

ABBREVIATIONS

For the sigla of the manuscripts see Ch. 2.4. Bibliographical references (like e.g. Kāmaṭ:1970j) are found in Ch. 1.2 or in the short Bibliography (App. 3).
GG stands for *Guru Granth*

LIST OF ILLUSTRATIONS (Appendix 7)

PREFACE

This book does not give the answers some may be looking for. It is not definitive about Nāmdev's date and place of birth or of his *samādhi,* about the exact number of poems sung by him (in Hindī), or about 'his' language, when and if he travelled through North India. Perhaps we should not even be interested in these facts, convinced that the grapes are sour.

Very illuminating, however, is the historical 'exercise' presented in Chapter 1. Starting with a brief enumeration of miracles in the earliest written source (Anantadās:1588), the hagiographical writings eventually mention his exact date of birth (Singh:1906) and even give a description of his previous birth (Marāthī *abhaṅga* 1245). Of course, there is one 'early' source which cannot be properly classified in our chronological list: the Marāṭhī *abhaṅgas* attributed to Nāmdev and his servant-disciple, Janābāī (edited in Āvaṭe:1908 or even earlier in Tātyā:1894). If all *abhaṅgas* relating to Nāmdev's life were also composed by him, we would be out of the woods. But most *abhaṅgas* probably are not; quite a few certainly are not. Till we see a critical edition of the Marāthī *abhaṅgas,* we cannot date the information found in them. We suggest that there is a relation between the oral tradition from which Mahīpati:1762 drew his information and the period when, e.g., the *Tīrthāvalī* was written. But that remains a challenging topic for manuscript hunters and text-editors.

The personality of Nāmdev has constantly eluded us, from the day we started to copy manuscripts with his Hindī poems in 1973, through our initiation period into the computer age in 1980, up to the present when 125 poems are presented in English translation, selected from our critical edition of 258 poems. Seventy-five poems are not even critically edited, because they occur only in the *Guru Granth* (36) or only in one manuscript (39).

In Chapters 2 and 3 we describe the Rājasthānī manuscripts in which we found the 258 Hindī poems attributed to Nāmdev. Even if we do not go beyond this question of attribution 'to Nāmdev', around 1600 AD when the scribal tradition started, we do get close to early musical repertoires. Relying on our feeling for the way in which musical repertoires were handled and on a mathematical analysis made by the computer, we selected poems which we know were certainly popular around 1550 AD and probably even before that.

This was only the first thrill in the often dreary task of editing the texts: we caught scribes tampering with the text as well as musicians adjusting the lines to their mood, genius or audience. And in the forest of doubts in all books about Nāmdev, we know this for certain: the poems attributed to Nāmdev in the manuscripts (dated·1582 AD and later), have not survived unchanged during the 250 years of musical transmission. The variants we find in the manuscripts are to a great extent musical, and often of minor importance. And, the mixture of both musical and scribal variants make all attempts to construct a classical stemma futile. Note that in the discussion about *rāgas, rāmkali* and *rāmgiri, gaud* and *gunḍ* are identical.

We give in Chapter 4 a selection of 125 poems in English translation. Specialists have read in Nāmdev's Hindī poems the experience of a mature mystic, who "must have come to the Panjāb at a later age". We see in them some of the earliest Hindī *bhakti* poetry, sung in Rājasthān and Panjāb. These songs greatly influenced later trends and poets, including Kabīr. When, in the Dādūpanth, there was a need to go back to the sources and the idea of a *Pañcavāṇī* came up, it was Nāmdev who was presented as the earliest poet. This mystical poetry is now for the first time available in English translation, based on a critical edition of the earliest Rājasthānī manuscripts.

In Chapter 5 we give the 'critical' edition with apparatus, based on the 'musical' and 'scribal' versions at hand. The critical apparatus is the result of a computer programme. After the initial input and revision of each manuscript and the establishment of the 'critical' lines, there was no further scribal interference, and no opportunity for later generations to detect scribal errors. It may be that computer errors will be the next quarry.

Nāmdev's poems published here have been handled by many singers before they were written down and this publication owes a lot to many people who have contributed to its form.

First we thank the custodians of the institutions where, since 1973, we have been allowed to study and copy manuscripts: Dr. A. Das and Mr. G.N. Bahura, City Palace, Jaipur; the Mahants of the Dādū Mahāvidyālay, Jaipur; the Directors of the Oriental Research Institute at Jaipur, Jodhpur and Bikaner. The English rendering of Nāmdev's terse songs has kept improving with the valuable suggestions of Richard Barz of Canberra, Francine Krishna of Jaipur and Ila Dalmia of Delhi. The computer programmes have been developed especially for this study by Herman Swinnen and Paul Bijnens of the University of Leuven, Belgium. We owe the fine laser print-out to the patience and expertise of Erik Van Eynde, University of Leuven and we are obliged to Ken Bryant, Vancouver, for the design of the Devnāgarī font. Generous funding by the University of Leuven has enabled us to pursue our intercontinental co-authorship both in India and in Belgium. For the input of the Hindī material we thank Vinay Jain and Anuradha Patni, Delhi, and Bart Op de Beeck, Leuven, for his very meticulous care in the production of the final copy.

INTRODUCTION

One sometimes wonders whether looking for manuscripts isn't a waste of time and energy. One peers through catalogues and handwritten lists, corresponds for years, travels in buses, drinks tea again and again, finds temples and institutions open but the person-in-charge absent. Eventually one can copy old manuscripts on film and spend hours at the reading machine. The editors of the New Oxford Complete Shakespeare (1986) define the task of editing as "a total waste of time which periodically reconstructs our image of the past". Of course they did prepare a new edition, leaving out even very popular passages.

But why bother? Why do we engage in the 'waste of time' of re-editing songs sung in the 14-16th centuries and committed to writing after a long period of oral transmission? Certainly, it does no harm periodically to stir up the academic or sectarian complacency and to remind ourselves that the *bhajans* we hear and read have been mediated by unknown singers and known scribes. Very few such transmitters passed on the songs of a poet-mystic without changing them. Musicians adjusted the poetic line to suit the rhythm and adapted the language for the convenience of the audience, as they went from village to village, from one region to the other. And then the scribes took over, while the oral tradition too continued, adding and changing.

Studying the songs of a poet like Nāmdev is quite different from the study of Shakespeare or Kālidāsa. It is the ambition of a text-critic studying Shakespeare to bring out the text 'written' by the author, looking at the various versions available in manuscripts. The text-critic soon realizes that this is impossible in the case of a Namdev or a Kabir. There is no way by which we can reach beyond the oral tradition to the poets themselves. This oral tradition, unlike that of the Vedas, did not shun variety and creativity. Consequently, the oeuvre of Nāmdev (and other Sants?) has come to us in a multiplicity of forms, changing over both space and time. We should look for an analogy in the Purāṇas, rather than in Shakespeare or Kālidāsa.

Fortunately, the manuscript tradition allows us to reach the threshold of this oral tradition, or the moment when it started to be written down, some time before 1600 AD (while the oral tradition continued). Our textual study is an attempt to study the *tradition* of Nāmdev's Hindī songs. We try to reproduce Nāmdev's oeuvre as it existed in great diversity around 1600 AD. Unable to give up our *samskār* as text-critics we also look for uniformities in the multiplicity, slender threads which might lead us beyond the oral maze to Nāmdev himself. We cannot claim that we have succeeded in going beyond the songs of *bhakti* to Nāmdev the individual *bhakta*. But we certainly have gone deep into the rain forest of oral traditions, beyond the borderline between the oral and written traditions. The key to the nebulous past was the musical traces in the manuscripts: the *rāg* pattern and the *geyavikāras*.

What do we know about Nāmdev?

Rarely have critical questions been asked about the authenticity of the biographical data now so abundantly available in editions of Santa literature. Written material giving information about a Santa results from oral traditions which continue, up to the present day, after the written tradition had started. The oral traditions kept growing as time went on and were regularly written down in ever more elaborate versions. We do not suggest that these versions are 'incorrect'. For millions deriving inspiration from oral traditions the written word is less important. And inspiration is as important a value as historical 'authenticity'. But when we look at the biography of Nāmdev (and other Sants) from the historical point of view, we have to admit that there is very little we know for certain.

What do we know about Nāmdev? The earliest hagiography, the *Parcaī* of Anantadās, was written in 1588 AD, more than 200 years after Nāmdev had died, and reflects a rich and well-formulated oral tradition[1]. For Anantadās the date of birth of Nāmdev and many now 'well-known' facts were either not available or of no importance. He only briefly refers to a few miracles (ch. 1.5-8):

5. The first *bhakta* who lived in this Kali age was Nāmdev,
he had God in his hands:
he gave God milk, made the temple turn around
and settled a quarrel with the Sultan.

6. He surrendered mind and body to the ultimate Brahma,
reanimated a cow and scared an elephant.
He retrieved a bed dry from a river:
the king and all the people were witnesses.

7. With His own hands Hari repaired the roof of his hut,
He took the form of a dog to eat the bread offered by Nāmdev.
Nāmdev also reanimated a bullock,
so that the bullock cart could move again.

8. Hari did everything for the sake of his *bhakta* Nāmdev,
whose miraculous deeds cannot be counted.
Bringing an image of stone to life,
he even made Hari speak[2].

---

(1) The date '1350' for Nāmdev's death is found for the first time in references published by Āvaṭe (1908). In Mahīpati:1762 we read for the first time that 'Nāmdev and Dñyāndev were contemporaries'. Are there earlier, dated sources for this work in Marāṭhī? For Nāmdev's guru lineage via Visoba Khecar to Gorakhnāth and Ādināth, see Kāmat:1976 (for all these references, see below, Ch. 1).

(2) See below, Ch. 1.3.

It is due to an ever-growing and continuing oral tradition that we have so many details about a Santa who certainly had a great appeal, even 400 years after his death.

For Anantadās it was important to stress the superiority of *bhakti* above ritual practices: 'The Santa has power even over God who is in love with him. Like a yogī mastering his body and attaining liberation, the *bhakta* has power over God'. In his *Parcaī* Anantadās basically tells only two stories connected with Nāmdev in order to emphasize this message. He records what he found important for true devotees to know about Nāmdev[3], assuming that they would be familiar with the details of other 'events'. He wrote a didactic essay, not a historical biography.

Now we turn to our manuscripts. The earliest manuscript with Hindī songs of Nāmdev is dated 1582 AD[4]. It was written more than 200 years after Nāmdev's death. Its source was an oral tradition which did not shun change or mutation. The biographical historicity of its material may be doubtful, but it may in its own way be a reflection of true events. In song 231 from this manuscript we read that Nāmdev's mother asks him not to go to the temple, and in song 234 we read about problems with Brahmans and about a temple incident[5]. The miracle of the dry bed in the river' (see below, Ch. 1.1;E14) is first found in Nāmdev's song 195, which is given only in two manuscripts. It should be ascertained whether any Marāṭhī manuscript with autobiographical data is dated before 1582 AD.

We do not deny that it is possible that songs edited and translated in our book were really composed by Nāmdev, and that autobiographical hints may have been given by him. What we know for certain is that these songs giving autobiographical information were sung in Rājasthān or in Panjāb around 1600 AD. Manuscripts dated around 1600 AD are records of an oral tradition as it existed 250 years after Nāmdev's death. Songs recorded in later manuscripts contain more details. Each later version is often like a new miniature painting of an old scene, recording more people in the background and packing more events into the scene. Whatever the historical value of the pictures we find in the songs recorded in our manuscripts, we should not forget that they are the *only dated* early material about Nāmdev's life. The manuscripts with the ever-expanding hagiographical accounts (see below Ch. 1) postdate the early manuscripts with songs.

The songs of Nāmdev

Let us imagine we are travelling through Northwest India in 1550 AD, on sandy tracks or on bumpy roads after the rainy season. We spend the nights on the floor in temples and watch the audiences drawn by travelling singers singing songs of *bhakti*. These singers, like the Purānic bards, received extended hospitality depending on the quality

(3) For the same reason he wrote the biographies of Kabīr, Raidās, Pīpā, Senā, Dhanā etc. (edition forthcoming).

(4) Fatehpur Manuscript; see below, Ch. 2.4.

(5) Both songs are found *only* in this earliest manuscript giving songs of Nāmdev.

and depth of their performance. We are on the way to Rājasthān after a visit to Banāras, where a few years before Raidās had died and where the grandfather of one of the singers had heard a person called Kabīr. And this grandfather's great-grandfather, in this family of travelling musicians, may have been to Mahārāshtra where he had heard a poet called Nāmdev[6].

The singers sang the songs that were most in demand, such as those of Nāmdev and Kabīr, which they had learned from their fathers. They also kept enlarging their repertoire when, during their travels, they heard a new song by a famous *bhakta*. Inspired by a particular environment, they added new songs to the repertoire. Memory was their only way of recording, but as the repertoires grew bigger, some musicians started to keep little (or big) notebooks as an aid to their memory. The earliest manuscripts seem to have had these notebooks as their basis. The manuscripts of the 17th century that have been preserved are *copies* of these early manuscripts now lost. Scholars of the 20th century have to rely on 17th century manuscripts which are copies of the scribbled notes of singers in order to reconstruct and edit what the singers were singing, We do not say: 'to reconstruct what Nāmdev or Kabīr had sung'.

Musicians classified the songs according to the *rāg*. Scribes kept the *rāg* tag of each song. Eventually, more 'message'-oriented compilers like Rajab and Gopāldās classified them in chapters, roughly according to theme (see below, Ch. 2.4.V). But this was a later phenomenon. It is on the early manuscripts with the *rāg* classification that we must rely if we hope to get close to what the original songs of a Santa might have been.

In these early, *rāg* oriented Mss. of the Dādūpanth, Nāmdev's songs are part of a larger corpus called *Pañcavāṇī,* literally the 'songs of the five'. These are the *Vāṇīs* of the five highly-respected poets in the Dādūpanth: Dādū, Kabīr, Nāmdev, Raidās and Hardās.

The six Mss. which give the Nāmdev repertoire in a *Pañcavāṇī* group can be classified in two groups, depending on the first song they give and on the sequence of songs: group I with Mss. *d a v* and group II with Mss. *h m p* (see below, Ch. 2.7).

Looking at the consistent order (Dādū, Nāmdev, Kabīr, Raidās and Hardās) in all the *Pañcavāṇī* Mss., we might be tempted to imagine that the numerous *Pañcavāṇī* manuscripts we have today all go back to a single archetype, compiled by one of the learned disciples of Dādū, perhaps even under the guru's direct inspiration. It might seem to us that this archetypal exemplar served as the basis for all later copies, the earliest now extant being dated 1636 AD.

Such an idyllic thought, cherished by text-critics up till the present, must be given up. The *Pañcavāṇī* manuscripts now at hand cannot go back to one archetype or to any single compiler.

With the hypothesis that the *Pañcavāṇī* tradition in the Dādūpanth started around 1600 AD, we face the amazing fact that there must have been several *Pañcavāṇī* compilers, each working separately either from

(6) For the 102 'Hindusthānī' songs of Nāmdev in the Mahārāshtrian collections, see below Ch. 2.4.IX.

existing manuscripts or in direct contact with the oral tradition. We can no longer speak of *one* Rājasthānī *Pañcavāṇī* recension or Western *pāṭh* tradition.

Because of a plainly direct link with different musical traditions, we find in our manuscripts variants which were *introduced during the musical transmission*, along with those produced by scribes. To keep both the oral and the scribal variants in mind and clearly distinguish between these two streams is a gigantic task for unaided human memory which has to collect its data over a span of several years. Our hypothesis about musical repertoires could be formulated only with the help of computer programmes developed to count and compare variants, making a distinction between those that are oral and those that are scribal[7].

A consideration about 'musical' variants in the text (see below, Ch. 2.3) is not the only clue pointing to a development of Nāmdev's songs in different 'recensions' during the oral period. Indian musicians used to sing clusters of songs according to particular modes, called *rāg*. It appears that first the singers sang a particular *pad* in a particular *rāg;* then they grouped together the *padas* which were to be sung in the same *rāg*. Consequently, a *rāg* is like an identity-card for the earliest period of oral transmission. It was only later, when compilers took over, that *padas* were classified in *aṅgas*, according to the main theme. The same song, however, could be sung to different *rāgas*. As a result we find songs classified under different *rāgas* in different manuscripts. This variation in classification is obviously not due to a scribe's intervention, but stems from the oral period itself, when the songs were in the hands of the singers. Subsequently, the songs were transmitted under different *rāgas* and appeared as such also in the manuscripts. Thus, looking at the *rāg* pattern we are able to make a preliminary classification of the musical recensions. The statistical computer count corroborates this classification, adding nuances.

Not all our Rājasthānī 'musical' manuscripts (see Ch. 2.4ff.) are of the *Pañcavāṇī* type. Ms. *u* is Dādūpanthi but not *Pañcavāṇī* and Ms. *c* (and *j*) may be defined as 'Nāth-siddha'. Ms. *c* is a huge compilation of the songs and sayings of the Siddhas, which includes along with Nāmdev other *nirguṇ* poets like Kabīr and Raidās, who seem to have been popular in 17th century Nāth circles. Like the *Pañcavāṇī* collections, these Nāth collections are of a musical kind, classifying songs according to *rāg*. Although postdating the Dādūpanthī collections, they are independent repertoires, relying on an independent source. Again, although they are sometimes quite different, the songs of Nāmdev in these Nāth collections often have much in common with the versions we find in the Dādūpanthī collections.

This suggests the hypothesis that the singers walking on the Rājasthānī roads around 1550 drew their repertoires from a common source. But this source is different from the source which gave us the *Guru Granth* repertoires. When we compare the *rāg* structure in the *Guru Granth* with that in the Rājasthānī repertoires, we find considerable differences. The Panjābī singers handled a text which was

(7) For a detailed analysis, see below Ch. 3.

musically and morphologically different from what their colleagues in Rājasthān had[8]. We are tempted to propose that the *padas* which have the same *rāg* in the *Guru Granth* and in the Rājasthānī Mss. are likely to have belonged to a very early common source. Perhaps we should resist the temptation.

One important point can be made at this stage: we can no longer call the *Guru Granth* the oldest available version of, for example, Kabīr's *padas.* What we find in the 17th century Rājasthānī Mss. is a variant musical version which may well be as old as the musical version from which the Panjābī singers drew their inspiration, if not older. At what muddy or sandy crossroads did singing families go their own way, and at what point in history? We do not know, but the division certainly set in quite early.

Of the 61 songs of Nāmdev in the *Guru Granth,* only 25 are found in the Rājasthānī manuscripts. When we look at the (only) 11 songs of Nāmdev which are classified under the same *rāg* in the *Guru Granth* and in the Rājasthānī Mss., we notice that these songs are found in *all* the Rājasthānī recensions (with only one exception), and we see that these songs have exactly the same *rāg* in all these recensions. On the other hand, when we look at those songs which do *not* have the same *rāg* in all Rājasthānī Mss., they are also the songs which are not given in all the Mss., often occurring in a few Mss. only.

We looked at the *first 150 songs* in the present corpus from the viewpoint of variation in *rāg* and inversion of *antarās,* and were surprised not to find a consistent correlation. Of the 10 songs in this set, common to the *Guru Granth* and the Rājasthānī manuscripts, and with the same *rāg,* six (60%) have an inversion of *antarās.* Of the remaining 10 common songs, with a different *rāg,* again six (60%) have an inversion of *antarās.*

In these first 150 songs, 130 are found only in the Rājasthānī manuscripts. Of these, 106 have the same *rāg* in all the manuscripts and 27 (25%) have an inversion of *antarās.* Of the 24 having a different *rāg* in one manuscript or more, six (25%) have an inversion of *antarās.* We conclude that both the changes in the *rāg* and the inversion of *antarās* are brought about by singers, not scribes, but in the songs of Nāmdev there is no relevant correlation between these two kinds of changes. We do not find more inversions in the songs which are found under a different *rāg* in some manuscripts[9].

Traditionally, language has been considered a reliable clue for arriving at the authentic version of a text. Many text-critics have used it to define the genuineness of an expression, a line or a whole song. They

(8) For his critical edition of the *pad bhāg* of Kabīr, P.N. Tivārī finally selected 200 *padas.* Of these, 121 are found in the *Guru Granth* also, and of these only 55 are classified under the same *rāg* as in the Rājasthānī tradition. Out of the 35 common *padas* under *gauḍī* in the Rājasthānī tradition, 31 are under *gauḍī* in the *Guru Granth.* Further, *āsāvarī:* 8 out of 23; *rāmkalī:* 3 out of 6; *kedārau:* 1; *bhairū:* 8 out of 11; *vasant:* 4 out of 5. For the other *rāgas,* nothing is common.
On the other hand, most *padas* of Kabīr we looked at in 3 Rājasthānī Mss. (one *Pañcavānī* manuscript, Ms. *u* and Ms. *c)* are there classified under the same *rāg.*

(9) We arrived at a similar conclusion when preparing the critical edition of Raidās.

have also used it as a norm for modifying a text. The linguistic test, however, is often contradicted by the musical *(rāg)* pattern in which the songs of Nāmdev were arranged. Songs which are found under the same *rāg* in all our manuscripts, and presumably belong to an old layer in the oral tradition, are linguistically quite a mixed bag: we have songs in almost pure Gujarātī, others in a kind of Marāṭhī-Rājasthānī and still others in Braj.

Must the text-critic stick to the assumption that the poet sang in his own dialect *only?* As is the case even today, musical repertoires were not language-oriented. To take one example, Dādū --whose works survive without much change because they were almost immediately written down-- has left us songs in more than one language. In the musical tradition too it was common to compose in more than one language. Certain kinds of songs are traditionally associated with certain dialects (for example *ṭhumrī* with Eastern Hindī), and musicians composed in those dialects, whatever their 'own' language was. It is also likely that certain *rāgas* or certain ways of singing were associated with a particular dialect. Language was not a reliable clue for our text-edition.

When we construct a tentative stemma on the basis of the similarity in the order in which the songs were arranged under the heading of a *rāg*, or on the basis of the order of lines in the different manuscripts, then our effort will continually be contradicted by the dissimilarity of the oral and scribal variants. The result is a totally blurred and confused pattern, if any pattern appears at all. If --after having the computer count the variants and compare the variants that are identical in only particular manuscripts-- we draw the proper conclusions, we despair of ever finding a classical stemma and an archetype[10]. There seems to be no scribal stemma and no scribal archetype.

The computer count establishes that, in the case of Nāmdev's songs, there is no consistent relation between two manuscripts of the same *Pañcavāṇī* group. No consistent relation between manuscripts is seen throughout. This suggests a very nebulous *interaction* between singing traditions. If we seek to establish an 'original text' on the basis of stemmatic clues, we deceive ourselves for the simple reason that a scribal *'critical text'* perhaps never existed.

So, if Nāmdev once sang his poems, very soon they became the property of singers who handled them according to their own inspiration, musical genius and particular dialect. Singers may well have combined several versions they had heard, and passed on to their students new textual combinations. We may assume that it was mostly the capable singers, those who were more poetic and creative, who prevailed; we notice the consequences in the stemmatic chaos before us.

What then have we looked for? We have looked for a text which is found in many musical traditions. We have tried to isolate an old Rājasthānī core, without suggesting that the songs of this core are in any

(10) See below, Ch. 3. For a study on the same line, see John G. Griffith, 'Non-stemmatic Classification of Manuscripts by Computer Methods', in: *La Pratique des ordinateurs dans la critique des textes*, eds. Jean Irigoin and Gian Piero Zarri, Paris, CNRS 1979, 73-86.

way closer to the poet. It is our translation that accords them a special status, in the hope that what we selected for translation forms the oldest Rājasthānī layer.

If there is no stemma and no justified 'critical' text, then what do we have? We have the conviction that, possibly for centuries, a Nāmdev enthusiasm had gripped people in Rājasthān and Panjāb, and that this enthusiasm was linked somehow to Nāmdev's songs of the 14th century. Full of enthusiasm for Nāmdev's songs, poets and musicians sang and recited his verses, adding songs or lines of their own or changing the lines according to their own taste and genius. This *Santa-enthusiasm theory* may well apply to many more *nirguṇ* and *saguṇ* mediaeval poets than has hitherto been believed.

Still, even if we cannot get to Nāmdev himself, our search is worthwhile. We discover poetry that is often very beautiful and a mystical literature which has influenced the religious life of thousands, from the beginning of the 15th century until the present day.

Nāmdev in Panjāb?

The traditional 'Panjābī' view handed down orally suggests that Nāmdev[11] sang *abhaṅgas* in Mahārāshtra and that he spent his latter days in Panjāb. In Ghumān (Panjāb) we find his *samādhi*[12].

There is more than one problem in this view. With due respect for oral traditions, it should be noted that the first documents referring to Nāmdev's presence in Panjāb are W. Crooke, *The Tribes and Castes of the Western Provinces,* 1896, and M.A. Macauliffe, *The Sikh Religion,* 1909[13]. So far we have found no reference to Nāmdev's presence in Rājasthān[14]. The Mahārāshtrian oral tradition reflected in Mahīpati:1762 speaks of Nāmdev's journey to Banāras. Isn't it even today a respectable reference to be able to say you have studied in Banāras? Mahīpati makes no mention of Rājasthān or Panjāb.

It is hard to explain how a Panjābī influence could have caused so many and so varied musical repertoires of Nāmdev's songs to be popular in Rājasthān around 1550. We pointed out earlier that 61 songs of Nāmdev are given in the *Guru Granth.* Of these only 25 are found in the Rājasthānī Mss, and only 11 are found under the same *rāg.* This suggests a weak rather than a strong connexion between Panjāb and Rājasthān.

---

(11) For the 'six' persons called Nāmdev, see P. Caturvedī:1951, p. 105. For the argument that the 'Panjābī' Nāmdev and the Mahārāshtrian Nāmdev are *not* identical, see Ādkar:1972, p. 59f.

(12) Another '*samādhi*' is found in Pandharpur, Mahārāshtra. See below, Ch. 1.1,G1; especially N.Singh:1981.

(13) Even in N. Singh:1981 we find no mention of earlier Panjābī references.

(14) In interviews in Jaipur, in 1986, tailors and *chīmpīs* claimed to be of the *vamsha* of Nāmdev. Should this be rendered as 'in family-lineage linked to Nāmdev'? They also stated that originally they were not from Rājasthān, but from Gujarāt. There are two distinct groups, apparently not inter-marrying, in Cār Pol Bāzār, Thākur Bagru kā rāstā, near Raghunāth kā Mandir, Jaipur. There are also clans in the South which claim a connexion with Nāmdev (see below, Ch. 1.2;I3). For the genealogical table from Nāmdev, 'via Bohddasa to the present day descendants in Panjāb', see Ch. 1, N. Singh:1981, p. 73-75.

If we suppose, as we have done, that the presence of Nāmdev's songs in Panjāb and in Rājasthān is explained by a transmission through wandering musicians, and not by Nāmdev's physical presence, we still have problems. How can we envisage the relation between the quite different Rājasthānī and Panjābī repertoires? It is hard to argue that the abundant material in Rājasthān is a later offspring of an original corpus in Panjāb. There are too few songs in common, considering the abundant material found in Rājasthān, presumably going back to repertoires of pre-Nānak times. One may perhaps explain the phenomenon by supposing that Nāmdev travelled through Rājasthān, spending time in temples and villages so that his songs and message became popular. He then went on to Panjāb and from the repertoire which developed there independently of Rājasthān 61 songs found their way into the Sikh tradition. No other repertoire is now found there.

But is the presence of Nāmdev at all necessary to explain the popularity of his songs? Kabīr and Raidās are not said to have been to Panjāb and Rājasthān; yet we find a large number of their songs too in both the *Guru Granth* and in the Rājasthānī manuscripts[15]. What evidence do we have to believe that Nāmdev was in Panjāb, while Kabīr and Raidās were not? Perhaps we should not forget that Kabīr lived around 1500 and Nāmdev around 1300 AD. Two centuries, at that time, may have been sufficient to allow devotees (in the 18th century?) to 'know' that the great Santa Nāmdev had actually been in their region. Of course, there is no point in 'proving' that Nāmdev did *not* go to Panjāb. The point is that not enough importance has been given to travelling singers and their repertoires. *They* spread the *nirguṇ* message and the traces of their handling of songs are seen in our manuscripts. We reached this conclusion early in our study when we realized that looking for a scribal archetype or the hypothesis of a mammoth scribal contamination could not bring clarity to the material in the 17th century manuscripts.

Singers are responsible both for the spreading of the message and for the stemmatic chaos.

We have to question the traditional *saguṇ-nirguṇ* label when we read the songs of Nāmdev. The following names for God are used by him.

keshav, nārāyaṇ, rām, narhari, hari, viṭṭhal, paṇḍarīnāth, gusāī, krishna, gopāl, govind, banvārī, murārī;
keval brahma, param tat, pārbrahma;
bhuvanpati, prān nāth, samrath, tribhuvan nāth;
sarbaṅg, syambha dev (svayambhū), ātma rām, antaryāmī, nirañjan;
svāmī, prabhu, thākur, sāhab, dev, devā, nāth, bhagvant;
dīndayāl, sadguru;
alakh, abhev, ākulā;
baikuṇṭhanāth, garuḍāgāmī, sāraṅgapāni;
bābā, bāp, bābulā.

---

(15) In the *Guru Granth* we find 225 songs of Kabīr, 61 of Nāmdev and 40 of Raidās; in the Rājasthānī Mss. we find ca. 350 of Kabīr, 258 of Nāmdev and ca. 80 of Raidās.

Many of these names are clearly Vaiṣṇav, *saguṇ*. We also find that the legendary Vaiṣṇav *bhaktas* Dhruv and Prahlād are the ideals of Nāmdev. A good *bhakta* is indeed called a Vaiṣṇav[16] and Viṣṇu himself preaches to Nārad the essence of *bhakti* (song 95).

In several songs, which could belong to both a *saguṇ* and a *nirguṇ* collection, we feel the mystic expressing his personal love (see song 5, 88, 89, 90).

The main idea of the Anantadās *Parcaī* is to preach *bhakti* above all paths, including faith in ritual practices. Both *saguṇ* and *nirguṇ* poets believed this, although the message in Nāmdev sounds more *nirguṇ* (e.g. song 91). Other songs show a strong Nāth-Siddha influence, for which the poet supposes a knowledge of esoteric language (64, 74, 77, 97, 111). The fear of *saṃsār,* common to all religious seekers in India, is a frightening obsession (84, 124). Nāmdev gives a clear definition of detachment, to be distinguished from meaningless asceticism (92).
Clear examples of *ulaṭbānsī* usage are seen in songs 76 and 101. Songs with Viṣṇudās[17] in the *bhaṇitā* generally appear at the end of the collection in each manuscript. Several of these 'Viṣṇudās' songs are also found in the Marāthī *Abhaṅga Gāthā*, in the name of Viṣṇudās. Other songs found in the *Gāthā* are our song 240 *(Gāthā,* p. 255), 148 (p. 729) and 224 (p. 236). In manuscript *v* 3 songs, all under *rāg toḍī,* are marked as 'Dakkhinī *pad*' (148, 226 and 224).
Nāmdev has produced many beautiful songs in Hindī. For sheer delight one may read songs 62, 71, 73 and 112.

(16) The Gujarātī poet Narsī Mehtā (15-16th centuries) has a famous song *(vaiṣṇav jan to tene kahiye),* in which a *vaiṣṇav* is described as one who should practice compassion, humility, tolerance, control of passions and who avoids lying, stealing or adultery. Devotion to Viṣṇu does not figure among the essential characteristics. In stanza 4 we read that the 'vaiṣṇav remains absorbed in the contemplation of the name of Rām This is not Rām the *avtār* of Viṣṇu, but the Rām of the Sants.

(17) For Viṣṇudās, see below, Ch. 1.1; A6.

CHAPTER 1

DO WE KNOW NĀMDEV?

It is not our intention to add another biography of Nāmdev to the long list of existing accounts[1]. That would be easy, but useless. We would then quote all existing (contradictory) opinions and at best we would produce a few concluding remarks to express our own opinion about certain (delicate) issues. Worse still, we could simply make a list of quotations from learned scholars. In most studies about the history of Hindī literature we find biographies of Sants written in a simple way: biographical information is copied from works published earlier and arranged chronologically. As a result we learn most about a poet in the most recent works, because nobody has bothered to distinguish the early sources from the later ones.

It is however a very useful exercise to study the sources which mention Nāmdev, classify them chronologically, and study the relationships among the data about him. As a result, one notices not only that there are no written sources preserved which antedate the end of the 16th century, or roughly 300 years after Nāmdev, but also that in the earliest sources very little is said. What is said is generally of a miraculous order. In a chronological list we clearly see in what source a particular piece of information was first formulated and began to be copied. In recent biographies, we are even told on what particular day of the month Nāmdev was born, as "mentioned by Nāmadeva himself in one of his *abhangas* (77 in the 1931 Poona edition)"[2] or what happened in his previous birth.

As a first part of the exercise in historical criticism, we give all biographical data about Nāmdev found in the literature, along with the earliest 'written' source we found. In section 1.2 we give a detailed bibliographical list. This exercise is based on written material, taking for granted that an oral period of creative composition and transmission took place before the songs and stories were written down. About the length of this creative, oral period we can only make guesses, but from this exercise we can at least note the following:

The earliest dated sources --all Hindī (Anantadās:1588, Nābhādās:1600 and *Guru Granth:* 1604)-- mention only the miracles.

(1) For a recent study, see N.N. Relekar et alii, *Śrī Nāmdev darshan,* 1970; this is an edition of 84 articles (1078 p.), dealing with a broad variety of topics and questions around Nāmdev. Plenty of information is brought together, but at times a critical analysis is lacking. A detailed and critical study is H.V. Ināmdār, *Santa Nāmdev* (Marāṭhī), Pune, 1970, 302p. For detailed references to the sources about Nāmdev, see below, Ch. 1.2.

(2) N. Singh:1981, p. 45.

The *padas* of Nāmdev in the *Guru Granth*[3] which give this information are *not* found in the Hindī manuscripts written in Rājasthān. Raidās and Dhanā in the *Guru Granth* (and Rajab:1620) state that Nāmdev was of a low caste and a *chīmpī.* Again, the Priyādās *Commentary* (1712) and the Rājasthānī Rāghavadās *Bhaktamāl* (1720) refer only to the miracles when eulogizing Nāmdev. Other information still seems to be of no importance to these hagiographers. Out of the 15 biographical 'items' referred to in the Marāṭhī *abhaṅgas* (Āvaṭe:1908), only two (E1: 'Nāmdev feeds milk to God' and E5: 'the turning of the temple') are of the miraculous kind. Might these two *abhaṅgas* also belong to the earlier period, and the others to the second wave of biographical writing?

The second wave of biographical *writing* may be roughly placed in the second half of the 18th century (Mahīpati:1762, who "wrote from books before him, and from the oral tradition"). We might perhaps presume that the 'books' before Mahīpati were existing manuscripts which already contained the *abhaṅgas* modern biographers like to quote (e.g. *Tīrthāvalī;* see Āvaṭe:1908).

A third wave of publications started after the Marāṭhī *abhaṅgas* were edited and reprinted. The first printed edition was published by R.S. Gondhalekar, in 1849. For other editions, see Ch. 1.2, H.V. Ināmdār:1987 (pp. 181-182; 17 entries). The final word about Nāmdev's life can only be said when the earliest, dated manuscripts with his *abhaṅgas* are collected and critically edited. It is puzzling that writers go on quoting 'autobiographical' *abhaṅgas* by Nāmdev as part of their biographical essays about him. Unless we find early manuscripts or strong arguments to date the *abhaṅgas* as early evidence, we cannot give historical value to quotations from the *Nāmdev Abhaṅga Gāthā.*

Several interesting facts also emerge from the Panjābī oral sources, written down by Crooke:1896 and Macauliffe:1909. In these we read for the first time that Nāmdev was born 'on the 26th Oct. 1270'. The date of birth 1443 proposed by Crooke and the suggestion that Nāmdev met Kabīr (Mahīpati:1762) or that he was a disciple of Rāmānanda (Singh:1949), only increase the confusion and controversy about Nāmdev.

Finally, until we find more and earlier sources, it should be noted that the first mention of Nāmdev's association with Dñyāndev is in Mahīpati:1762. This again, of course, emphasizes that we shall find conclusive evidence only in a critical edition of the Marāṭhī *abhaṅgas*[4].

Some Marāṭhī writers argue that the Nāmdev of the *abhaṅgas* has to be different from the Nāmdev of the Hindī songs found in Rajasthan and in the *Guru Granth.* We should point out that in oral traditions and hagiographical writings in North-India around 1600 AD we find the same miracles told in connexion with Nāmdev as in Maharashtra. The biographical references in songs (Fatehpur Ms. and *Guru Granth),* in the Anantadās *Parcaī* and in the song of Vyās (1580) are the earliest written sources about Nāmdev in North-India. In the song attributed to Vyās (1580), clear reference is given to a Nāmdev who worships

(3) Songs 151,213, 216, 218, 209. See below, Ch. 5 and Ch. 1.2:1604.

(4) P. Caturvedī:1951, p. 106 refers to *abhaṅgas* in which Nāmdev's association with Dñyāndev is referred to.

Viṭṭhal, who must be the deity of Pandharpur *(jākī jāti-pānti-kul biṭhal)*. It is noteworthy that this Nāmdev (and in a previous song Kabīr) is quoted by Vyās as a *sācobhakta*. The same Nāmdev is quoted as a highly respected Santa in the Dādūpanthī *Pañcavāṇī*. Who defined the distinction between *saguṇ bhaktas* and *nirguṇ* Sants?

Frequently in hagiographies we find biographical data which are also, it is said, reflected in Nāmdev's songs. Sometimes however the relationship between the songs and the biography is farfetched. Obviously, biographical data do not have more historical value because a (vague) reference to them is thought to be found in Nāmdev's songs. As an illustration we quote a fine example from Macauliffe:1909. Many stories can in fact be read between the lines of this song, which is numbered 23 in our edition. I invite the reader to try to find the purse.

> "This hymn was addressed to a reputedly holy man who had stolen a merchant's money, and falsely imputed the offence to Nāmdev. The merchant had gone to bathe, and while doing so the hypocrite seated in a religious attitude stole his purse. The merchant missed it on returning. He could not think of attributing the theft to the man in religious garb, so he charged Nāmdev with it. The merchant would not accept Nāmdev's denial, and had him flogged. While Nāmdev was being punished a storm arose which lifted the cloth on which the reputed holy man sat. The missing purse was then found under the cloth. Upon that, Nāmdev addressed the following verses to the hypocrite:
>
> 'The serpent casteth its slough, but not its poison:
> Since thy heart is not pure,
> Why perform mock meditation and repetition of God's name?
> Thou art as the crane watching for fish in the water.
> The man who eateth the food of lions,
> Is called the god of thieves.
> Nama's Lord hath settled the quarrel;
> Drink God's elixir, O double-faced one' "
> (Macauliffe, Vol. 6., p. 43).

This translation by Macauliffe of Nāmdev's song in the *Guru Granth*, is *slightly* different from ours. In the *Guru Granth* we often find the first stanza before the refrain (see below, Ch. 2.3, on *geyavikāras)*.

Why meditate?
Why mutter prayers,
When you are blind
  to your self?

The serpent
  sloughs its skin,
but not its poison.
The heron
  stands meditating,
a *yogī* only in looks.

But can the prey hide
  from the lion?
This is all a worship
  of false gods.

Nāmdev's Lord has
  silenced all strife.
Drink the medicine *Rām*,
  you hypocrite. (song 23).

Another example of 'reading into a text' is the interpretation of *khecar* in *pad* 209 of the *Guru Granth*[5].

1.1. Biographical data.

The following data have been collected from biographical sources. As a rule we have given the references only to the first (and the most important) source(s) where a biographical item is mentioned. It is evidently also found in many later biographies and studies. In section 1.2 we have tried to give all the data each author refers to.

Identity of Nāmdev

A1: Nāmdev is a contemporary of Dñyāndev.
  Mahīpati:1762 (see also A9),
  Āvaṭe:1908
 In 1291 he met Dñyāndev.
  Mar. Enc.:1985[6]
A2: Nāmdev was *not* a contemporary of Dñyāndev.
  Bhardvāj:1898
  Caturvedī:1951 (p. 104)[7]
A4: Nāmdev of the *abhaṅgas* is Nāmdev in the *Guru Granth.*
  Sen:1930
A6: Nāmdev and Vishnudās are *not* identical
  Ranade:1933c (p. 187ff.)[8]
A7: Kabīr is an imitator of Gorakh and Nāmdev.
  Caturvedī:1951, (p. 105)
A8: Nāmdev is a disciple of Rāmānanda.
  Singh:1949
A9: Nāmdev met Kabīr.
  Mahīpati:1762 (see also A1)[9]
A10: Nāmdev's maternal grandfather is Vāmdev.

(5) See below, Ch. 1.2, Āḍkar:1972, and Ch. 1.3, Anantadās *Parcaī*, v. 1.12, note.
(6) For a good analysis of the chronology of Dñyāndev and Nāmdev, see Vaudeville:1969d, p. 5-7.
(7) Entries A3 and A5 appeared to be doubles when the list was nearly complete. For convenience, we omitted them to avoid disturbance in the cross-references.
(8) See also N. Singh:1981, p. 54.
(9) See Vaudeville:1969d, p. 6, n.1.

Nābhādās:1600

A11: Dāmodar Paṇḍit and Nāmdev.
Smriti-sthal 1432
Āḍkar:1972

Occupation and caste

B1: Nāmdev was a *chīmpī* or tailor.
Guru Granth: 1604 Dhanā, Nāmdev
Rajab:1620
Āvaṭe:1908

B2: Nāmdev was low-caste.
Guru Granth: 1604 Raidās
Prem Ambodh Pothī: 1693

B3: Nāmdev was a Kshatriya.
Varmā:1926b

B4: Nāmdev's father was Dāmā Shet[10].
Mahīpati:1762
Āvaṭe:1908
'His forefather was Yadushet'
Mule:1952

B5: Nāmdev's father went frequently to the Kāshirāj Shiv Mandir.
Āvaṭe:1908
Macauliffe:1909

B6: Nāmdev's mother was Gonā Bāī, daughter of a tailor.
Āvaṭe:1908 (Janābāī *abhaṅga)*
Deshmukh:1970b
'He is the son of a 12 year old widow'
Nābhādās:1600
Pūrandās:1888

B7: Nāmdev Dāmāsetī (surname Relekar).
Āvaṭe:1908
Mule:1952

B8: Nāmdev was miraculously born from a shell[11] *(sīp)*.
Mahīpati:1762

B9: Nāmdev was an *avtār*.
'of Uddhav' Mahīpati:1762
'of Vishnu' Garcin de Tassy:1839 (also Caturdās:1800)
'of Sanatkumār' *Bhakta Kathāmrit,* quoted in Āḍkar:1972, (p. 84, n. 7).

Date of birth

C1: 1270 AD *(śak* 1192)[12].

(10) For the 'complete family' of Nāmdev, see H.V. Ināmdār:1970, p. 52 and 59.

(11) See also N. Singh:1981, p. 97.

(12) This date is based on *abhaṅga* 1254 (Āvaṭe edition; 16 in the Dhere ed., 1983) in Nāmdev's 'autobiographical' *Nāmdev caritra.* We have no indication about the date of the manuscripts in which this set of *abhaṅgas* was first found. For a discussion about the meaning of this *abhaṅga,* see S.K. Āḍkar:1972, p. 65 and 75.

Singh:1906
Āvaṭe:1908
Macauliffe:1909
Ranade:1933c
26th Oct. 1270
Mar. Enc.:1985
C2: 1309 AD.
Bhardvāj:1898 (see Vaudeville:1969d, p. 5, n.2)
C3: 1390 AD.
Sarva Bhakta Paricay:1696 (?)
1370 AD.
Bhagat Rām:1936b
1364 AD.
Pūranadās:1888[13]
C4: 1443 AD.
Crooke:1896 ('in Marvar')
Farquhar:1920
C5: *Shanivār*, 11th *Kārtik sudi, śak* 1192.
Macauliffe:1909
Joshī:1940
an.:1970c
C6: "Nāmdev will write a hundred thousand abhaṅgas".
Āvaṭe:1908
Macauliffe:1909
Ranade:1933c
C7: Born in Narasi Vamani, near the Krishna river[14].
Barthvāl:1936
Joshī:1940
Sharmā:1957c
Dīkshit:1970d
C8: Born in Paṇḍharpur.
Āvaṭe:1908 (*Janābāī abhaṅga*)
Bhandarkar:1913b
C9: Nāmdev was born in Narasi Brāhmanī[15].
Dattātrey:1723 (?)
Koratkar:1926
Pāngarkar:1933
Mar. Enc.:1985[16]
C10: Nāmdev was born of a virgin widow, daughter of Vāmdev.
Priyādās:1712
Caturdās:1800

(13) For more dates (1423, 1363) see S.K. Āḍkar:1972, p. 73.

(14) See Āḍkar:1972, p. 78. For the arguments and the *abhaṅgas* supporting the theory that Nāmdev was born near Bārsī in Sholāpur Dt., see *Ibidem*, p. 79. For an evaluation of the different opinions about Nāmdev's birthplace, see p. 77f.

(15) Parbhani Dt (Marāṭhvāḍā)

(16) 'Born in Narasī, in Marāṭhvāḍā, where there is a *samādhi* and a temple in his name'; an *abhaṅga* is quoted. 'Narasī and Bamaṇī are 2 different villages'.

Family

D1: Nāmdev married at the age of 9.
Sharmā:1957c

D2: Nāmdev married Rāj Bāī, daughter of Govinda Shet.
Vānakhande:1964b
Deshmukh:1970b
Mar. Enc.:1985 ('Rajāī')

D3: Nāmdev had a son and God brought gifts.
Mahīpati:1762

D4: Nāmdev had four sons[17].
Mahīpati:1762
Āvaṭe:1908 (Janābāī *abhaṅga*)
Vānakhande:1964b
Deshmukh:1970b
'His sister was Āūbāī'.
Sharmā:1957c

D5: Nāmdev had no interest in business.
Deshmukh:1970b
'and God sent gold'
Mahīpati:1762

D6: Krishna wrote down the verses of Janābāī.
Mahīpati:1762

Miracles

E1: Nāmdev feeds milk to God while his father is absent.
Vyās:1580
Anantadās:1588
Nābhādās:1600
Guru Granth: 1604 (song of Namdev and of Raidās)
Nāmdev threatens to kill himself.
Caturdās:1800

E2: Nāmdev was a robber.
Macauliffe:1909
Ājagānkar:1927 (with lengthy description); see Pātaskar:1935, who doubts the authenticity.
Ranade:1933c (one *abhaṅga*)

E3: Nāmdev abandons robbery, goes to the Shiva Mandir in Aundhī, near Paṇḍharpur.
Macauliffe:1909
Ranade:1933c

E4: Nāmdev and the widow.
Ranade:1933c
N. Singh:1981

E5: The turning of the temple.
Vyās:1580
in 'Kabīr'; see Caturvedī:1951

(17) Nārāyan, Govinda, Viṭṭhal, Mahādev, and a daughter called Limbā Bai.

Nāmdev's song in the Fatehpur Ms.:1582 (?)[18]
Anantadās:1588
Nābhādās:1600
Guru Granth: 1604 (song of Nāmdev)
Prem Ambodh Pothī'

...at Nāgnāth'
Mahīpati:1762

E6: Miracle near Bikaner.
Mahīpati:1762

E7: Nāmdev reanimates a cow.
Vyās:1580
Anantadās:1588
Nābhādās:1600; see also Priyādās:1712 and Caturdās:1720

E8: Nāmdev reanimates a cow for the Governor of Bīdar.
Caturvedī:1951

E9: Nāmdev reanimates a cow for Firoz Sultān of Bahmani.
Guru Granth: 1604 (?)

'for a Muslim king'
Caturdās:1800

E10: The dog and the bread.
Vyās:1580
Anantadās:1588
Prem Ambodh Pothī: 1693

E11: Ranka and Banka.
Prem Ambodh Pothī: 1693
Mahīpati:1762

E12: Construction of Nāmdev's hut by God.
Vyās:1580
Anantadās:1588
Nābhādās:1600
Guru Granth Nāmdev):1604

E13: Nāmdev reanimates a dead Brāhman (see also below E18).
Prem Ambodh Pothī: 1693
Priyādās:1712

E14: Nāmdev retrieves a bed from the river.
Nāmdev's song 195 (in two manuscripts only)
Anantadās:1588
Nābhādās:1600

E15: Nāmdev receives gold for half the name of Rām.
Anantadās:1588

E16: He makes an image of stone speak.
Anantadās:1588

E17: The house of the emperor burns down.
Rāghavadās:1720
Caturdās:1800

(18) In song 231 we read that Nāmdev's mother asks him not to go to the temple, and in song 234 we read about problems with Brāhmans and about a temple incident. Nothing is said about the miracle of the 'turning of the temple', which is elaborately described in later hagiographies. Both songs are found only in this earliest manuscript. In N. Singh:1981 *dehurā* is explained as 'human body'.

E18: God comes as an old Brāhman on an *ekādaśī* day.
Anantadās:1588
Mahīpati:1762
E19: Nāmdev turns pebbles into touchstones.
Mahīpati:1762
E20: Nāmdev and the missing purse.
Macauliffe:1909

Nāmdev and his guru

F1: Nāmdev finds his guru Visobā after the incident with the potter Gorobā.
Mahīpati:1762
Pāngarkar:1933
Deshmukh:1970b
F2: Nāmdev finds his guru Visobā Khecar.
Āḍkar:1972 ('Nāmdev *pad* 209 in the *Guru Granth'*)
with his feet on the *linga'*[19].
Mahīpati:1762
Āvaṭe:1908
Deshmukh:1970b
F3: Nāmdev's guru lineage goes back to Ādināth.
Sharma:1957c
Kāmat:1976
His guru is Khecarnāth Nāthpanthī.
Viyogī Hari:1957e
F4: Nāmdev meets Visobā in Dvādasi (Barasi).
Bhandarkar:1913b
F5: Nāmdev meets Visobā at Audi.
Kāmat:1976
F6: Nāmdev is initiated at Auḍyanāganātha.
Bhai Gurdās:1700
F7: Nāmdev's guru is Sopāndev.
Āvaṭe:1908 (Janābāī *abhaṅga)*

The travels of Nāmdev

G1: Nāmdev travels around Panjāb, (at the age of 50).
Macauliffe:1909
Sen:1930
N. Singh:1981
G2: Nāmdev settles in Ghumān.
Crooke:1896
Rose:1914
G3: Nāmdev settles in Bhatawal, near a pond.
Macauliffe:1909
G4: Nāmdev travels to Banāras (with Dyñāneśvar).
Mahīpati:1762

(19) For more *abhaṅgas* 'related' to this meeting with Khecar, see Āḍkar:1972, p. 87.

Cauhān:1969b[20]

G5: disciples of Nāmdev.
Macauliffe:1909
Mar. Enc.:1985

Date of death

H1: 1350 AD.
Āvaṭe:1908
Mar. Enc.:1985 (3rd July 1350)

H2: 1372 AD.
Bharadvāj:1931

H3: 1450 AD.
Sarva Bhakta Paricay 1696 (?)

H4: 1464 AD.
Sen:1930

H5: Nāmdev takes *samādhi* in Paṇḍharpur.
Viyogī Hari:1957e
Singh:1981

H6: 1350 AD. (*śak* 1272 *āsāḍha krishna* 13).
Mar. Enc.:1985

H7: Nāmdev is buried at the door of the Paṇḍharpur temple.
Ranade:1933c

H8: Nāmdev takes *samādhi* at Ghumān.
Macauliffe:1909
Bh. Mishra:1964

H9: Nāmdev takes *samādhi* at Narsī (Marāṭhvāḍā)
Koratkar:1926

His descendants

I1: The descendants of Nāmdev's successor Bohardās still live in Ghumān today.
Sen:1930
N. Singh:1981

I2: The present priest in Paṇḍharpur is a descendant of Nāmdev.
Vānakhande:1964

I3: Tailors in the south...
Mar. Enc.:1985

(20) For doubts about the authenticity of Nāmdev's *Tīrthāvalī*, see Pendse:1969b.

1.2. The sources

In this section we give, in chronological order, the important English, Hindī, Marāṭhī and Panjābī sources in which biographical data about Nāmdev have been found. As was stated earlier, we do not know where to classify the Marāṭhī *abhangas* attributed to Nāmdev until we see a critical edition. For the 'item' listed with each source (e.g. E1), refer to Ch. 1.1. In the later sources many items are usually mentioned and discussed. We have listed an item with the source in which it occurs for the first time; only occasionally have we also given later sources.

JANĀBĀĪ (?)
(maidservant and first disciple of Nāmdev); see below, Āvaṭe:1908, *Sakal Santa Gāthā.*

1423 NARSĪ MEHTĀ mentions Nāmdev as an 'earlier poet'; see Sharmā:1957c, p. 107.

1432 *Smritisthal.* This Mahānubhāv work, written in 1432 AD, is edited by V.N. Deshpande (1939), 2nd ed. 1960, based on four manuscripts; the earliest manuscript is dated 1601 AD. In *smriti* 244 (p. 74) reference is made to the meeting between Nāmdev[21] *simpā* and Dāmodar.

A11

EKNĀTH (1533-1599); ca. 1574: *Eknāthī Bhāgvat.*
See below, Mahīpati:1762 and ĀVAṬE:1908, *Sakal Santa Gāthā,* Dhere ed., vol. 3 (3554-3635).

1532 GYESHĀNANDA

A8 as argued by Singh:1949, p. 74-75[22].

1580 HARIRĀM VYĀS is one of the *kavitrayī,* along with Haridās and Hit Harivamsha (Orcchā, floruit 1510-1600 AD?). In *Bhakta-kavi Vyās jī,* Vāsudev Gosvāmī, ed. (Mathura, 1952, 448p.) gives 787 songs and 148 distichs attributed to Vyās The oldest manuscript in which some songs of Vyās are found are dated 1582 AD (Fatehpur Ms.) and 1658 AD (Ms. *v;* see below, Ch. 2.4). One song (p. 195) is about Nāmdev. Calling Nāmdev a *sāco bhakta* and a devotee of Viṭṭhal, Vyās mentions several miracles: E1, E5, E7, E10, E12. Interestingly, in a song in the same context, entitled *kuṭumbha hamārau,* Vyās enumerates Sain, Dhanā, Nāmā, Pīpā, Kabīr, Raidās, the *camār,* along with Sūr, Mīrā etc. (p.196).

1582 NĀMDEV *padas* in the Fatehpur Manuscript (1582)

E5[23]

1588 ANANTADĀS (1588) *Nāmdev kī Parcaī,* written in 1588 AD (see below, Ch. 1.3, v.1):

C8? Āḍkar:1972 (p. 76), quotes a verse from a handwritten copy of this *Paricaī* (preserved in the Jaykar Granthālay, Pune; no date), in which Anantadās is supposed to state that Nāmdev was born in

(21) The word 'nāmdev' is missing in two of the four manuscripts.

(22) Quoted in Sharmā:1957c, p. 105, who criticizes Singh's arguments.

(23) See below, Ch. 2.4,VIII. In song 234 we read about a 'problem with the Brāhmans'. This may be a reference to the incident of the turning of the temple. In song 231, Nāmdev's mother asks him not to go to the temple.

Paṇḍharpur. This verse was *not* found in the ancient Mss. we consulted (see below, Ch. 1.3).
E1, E5
E7 (a cow *and* a bullock);
E9, E10, E12, E14
E15 The story "of the gold for half the name of Rām" takes 22 verses of the total of 49 verses in the biography written by Anantadās.
E16
For all these data we quote from our translation (below, Ch. 1.3):
"5. The first *bhakta* who lived in this Kali age was Nāmdev,
he had God in his hands:
he gave God milk, made the temple turn around
and settled a quarrel with the Sultān.
6. He surrendered mind and body to the ultimate Brahma,
reanimated a cow and scared an elephant.
He retrieved a bed dry from a river:
the king and all the people were witnesses.
7. With His own hands Hari repaired the roof of his hut,
He took the form of a dog to eat the bread offered by Nāmdev.
Nāmdev also reanimated a bullock,
so that the bullock cart could move again.
8. Hari did everything for the sake of his *bhakta* Nāmdev,
whose miraculous deeds cannot be counted.
Bringing an image of stone to life,
he even made Hari speak".

E18 The *ekādaśī* story takes 17 verses in the account of Anantadās. It is not clear how Singh:1981 (p. 66, n. 47) found the reference in the biography written by Anantadās, "who records Nāmadeva's coming from Mahārāstra to Panjāb"; see Ms. no. 398, Jaikar Library, Pune University, Pune. It should be interesting to examine the *lipikāl* of that manuscript. For the dates of the manuscripts we used for our edition and translation of the *Nāmdev kī Parcaī*, see below, Ch. 1.3.
KRISHNĀNANDA: In the Introduction to his *Santa Nāmdev kī Hindī Padāvalī*, (p. 11-12), Bh. Miśra:1964 refers to a Manuscript in the Nāgarī Pracāriṇī Sabhā, Banaras collection (number 1400; no date) in which a *Parcaī* is preserved, by 'Krishnānanda'. Several additional biographical data about Nāmdev are given in this *Parcaī*, but since the manuscript is not dated and we have no further information about this work, we cannot include these data in our chronological chart.
For the text of this *Parcaī*, see below Vānakhande:1970h.
KABIR (?): *Kabīr Granthāvalī*, S.S. Dās ed. (NPS), Banaras, 1928, p. 117.
E5[24]
1600 NĀBHĀDĀS, *Bhaktamāl*, ca. 1600, ed. R.K. Garg, Śrī Vrindāban Dhām, 1960 (p. 286f.). A Commentary in 4 vols. was prepared by Śhrī Gaṇeshdās Bhaktamālī, Vrindāban, 3rd. ed., 1986 (Nāmdev on II, p. 193-248).
E1, E5, E7, E12, E14
1604 RAIDĀS in the *Guru Granth*

(24) See Caturvedī:1951, p. 111.

B2 Nāmdev is low-caste;

E1 Nāmdev feeds milk to the deity *(Guru Granth,* p. 1104).

1604 DHANĀ in the *Guru Granth*

B1 Nāmdev was a *chīmpī (Guru Granth,* p. 487).

1604 NĀMDEV in the *Guru Granth.* Interestingly, many biographical data in 'Nāmdev's songs' are found in songs which appear *only* in the *Guru Granth,* and not in any of the Hindī manuscripts we consulted.

B1 *chīpe ke ghari janmu dailā gur updesu bhailā* (151 in our list; see also 160).

E1 The song *dūdhu katorai* (p. 1163-64, vol.2; song 213 in our list) refers to the legend of Nāmdev feeding the idol during his father's absence.

E5 *Hasat khelat* (turning of the temple), p. 1164 (song 216 in our list).

E9 *Sulatānu puche,* p. 1165 (song 218 in our edition; R.N. Maurya doubts the authenticity of this song)[25].

E12

F2 Āḍkar:1972 (p. 87) quotes a line from a song in the *Guru Granth (khecar bhūcar tulsī mālā parsādī pāiā;* 209 in our list) as literary evidence that Nāmdev accepted Khecar as his guru. *Khecar* ('one flying in the air') is the opposite of *bhūcar* or 'one who stays on earth'.

RAJAB (ca. 1620?),

Sarvāṅgī, Sādh māhima kau aṅg (which follows Chapter 22 *Bhajan Pratāp kau aṅg),* verse 12 (on fo. 161b in Ms. E, dated 1744 AD)[26].

B1 *Chīmpī grabhe utapanno nāmdev mahāmunī.*

TUKĀRĀM (1608-1650)

In one *abhaṅga* Tukārām is said to "be asked by Nāmdev, in a dream, to compose poetry"[27].

MOHSIN FĀNI, *Dabistān-i-Mazāhib* or *School of Manners* was "written in the mid-seventeenth century and generally attributed to Mohsin Fāni. It appears that the author was personally acquainted with Gurū Hargobind, the sixth Gurū, and he explicitly claims a close acquaintance with Gurū Hari Rāi, the seventh Gurū,... and it is clear that Mohsin Fāni relied largely upon Sikh informants"[28].

According to Blochmann[29] the work was written around 1665 AD. Amazingly, no reference to Nāmdev is given, although e.g. Dādū is referred to.

1693 *Prem Ambodh Pothī,* in Gurmukhī[30].

B2 "Nāmdeva came of a low caste of calicoprinter, but people called him a wise man".

(25) See *'Hindustānī',* Jan.-March 1962, p. 112.

(26) See W.M. Callewaert, *The Sarvāṅgī of the Dādūpanthī Rajab,* Leuven, 1978, p.81 and 99.

(27) Courtesy of G.S. Tulpule, Pune; see Ranade:1933c.

(28) H. McLeod, *Gurū Nānak and the Sikh Religion,* p. 9, n. 1. The book is anonymous according to V. A. Smith, *Akbar,* (Indian repr. 1966), p. 343. The work was translated from the original Persian, with Notes and Illustrations, by D. Shea and A. Troyen, 3 vols, Paris, 1843.

(29) See W.G. Orr, *A Sixteenth-century Indian Mystic,* London, 1947, p. 47.

(30) Singh:1981, p. 89ff.

E5 Singh:1981 explains *dehurā* in the anecdote as 'the human body, the person who turns' (p. 91).

E7

E10 "A dog runs away with a bread without ghee applied on it. Nāmdeva chases the dog with a pot of ghee in his hand persuading the dog to take ghee along with the dry bread. After some distance the dog assumed the form of Bithala."

E11, E12, E13

Sarva Bhakta Paricay (1696?), quoted in Mohan Singh:1949 (p. 3) and Caturvedī:1951, who doubts the reliability of this information (p. 108).

C3, H3 1390-1450

BHĀI GURDĀS(II), (Nābhādās) *Bhaktamāl Ṭīkā,* in Gurmukhī, ca. 1700; the second "Bhāī Gurdās was a contemporary of the ninth and tenth Sikh Gurus"[31].

F6 "This commentary (of the second Gurdās) was the first to make mention of Nāmadeva's initiation at Auḍyanāganātha", (N. Singh:1981, p. 99).

1712 PRIYĀDĀS, *Bhakti Ras Bodhini Ṭīkā,* Commentary on the *Nābhādās Bhaktamāl,* ed. R.K. GARGA, Śrī Vrindāban Dhām, 1960, p. 286ff.

C10, E1, E5

E7 "for the king of the Mlecchas, he revived a cow"

E12, E13, E14, E15

1720 RĀGHAVADĀS, *Bhaktamāl,* This Dādūpanthī *Bhaktamāl,* written probably in 1720 AD[32] is a gigantic work dealing with about 1200 saints. A Commentary was written by Caturdās:1800. This 'Northern' biography mentions quite a few details about Sants not noted down elsewhere.

Edited by A. Nāhaṭā, Jodhpur, 1965, p. 1-248, mainly based on two manuscripts dated 1804 and 1829 AD. Another edition was prepared by Svāmī Nārāyan Dās[33] "because the first edition appears to be full of mistakes *(bahut aśuddha)*". Nārāyanadās used 9 manuscripts, dated between 1783 and 1879 AD. Both editions give also the Commentary by Caturdās (q.v.), dated 1800 AD. We quote from the former edition:

E1 *pratimā kar pay pāy*

E5 *deval pheryau dvār*

E7 Nāmdev revives *both* a calf and a cow

E12 God constructs his house

E14 He retrieves a bed from the river

E15 He receives gold in exchange for half the name of Rām

---

(31) N. Singh:1981, p. 99, n. 37. There was also a commentary on the Nābhādās *Bhaktamāl* written by an earlier Gurdās: "It may be noted that Nābhādās was contemporary of Anantadās, Guru Arjunadev and Bhai Guradās", Singh.1981, p. 96. The second "Bhai Guradas's *Vāras* are based on the *Parcais* of Anantadās and the Bhaktamāl of Nābhājī" (ibidem).
For an edition, see Cakar Amar Singh, ed., *Vārām Giāna Ratnāvalī* Bhāī Gurdāsjī, SGPC, Amritsar, 1977. Also S.B. Singh:1975.

(32) See Callewaert:1978, p.24-25.

(33) Nārāyandās, Svāmī, *Śrī Rāghavdās jī viracit Bhaktamāl,* (Hindī), *(Svāmī Caturdās jī krit padya ṭīkā tathā bhaktacaritra prakāshikā gadya ṭīkā sahit),* Pushkar, 1969, p.283f.

E17 The palace of the emperor burns down

1723 DATTĀTREY, *Nāmdevācī Ādi Samādhi*, (Marāṭhī manuscript, dated 1723 AD); see *Pandharpur Sandesh, Sant Nāmdev Viśeṣānk*, Pandharpur, 1970, p. 78-80. I could not examine the manuscript during my 1988 visit to Pandharpur.

C9

1762 MAHĪPATI, *Bhaktavijaya*, 1762, tr. by J.E. Abbott and N.R. Godbole, 1933 (2 vols); *The Poet Saints of Maharasthra*, No. 9 (vol. I, 499p.) and No. 10 (vol. II, 507p).

In this voluminous work Mahīpati describes at length the lives of about 30 saints: "He wrote from books before him, and from oral tradition" (p. xxiv)... " He mentions some of the books, such as the work of Nabhaji and Chidghan. He possessed the Gathas (songs) of one Nama Vishnudas. For if we compare the stories told by that Nama we find indisputable evidence that Mahīpati used them in writing his own account. Whether the stories of the different saints are real or legendary, matters little, but from them we learn what was popularly considered their conception of God, and their way of approach to Him" (Preface, p. xix).

"The faithfulness of Mahīpati in recording the traditions received by him, either through books or oral sources, does not ensure the truth of these traditions, which must be established on other grounds,..." (xxvii). For the biography of Mahīpati by Dās Gaṇu in *Arvāchīn Bhaktalīlāmrita*, see J.E. Abbott, *Stotramālā, The Poet-Saints of Mahārāshtra*, No. 6, 1929, p. 155f. The following quotations are from the *Bhaktavijaya*, vol. I. No diacritics are given by Mahīpati. In the text below, the figures between brackets refer to the page in Mahipati).

A1 Dñyandev entered into the house of Nāmdev, who prostrated himself before him and lovingly embraced him (159). See further p.159-170. ..."Such were their daily and occasional discussions, as they walked along full of joy. Suddenly in their wanderings to sacred places they arrived at Hastanapur (Delhi)" (170).

A9 G4 Nāmdev visited all sacred bathing places and finally came to Banaras (178). " Nāmdev heard of the very extraordinary reputation of Kabir. He told Dñyandev of it and the two came to visit Kabir. When Kabir saw Dñyandev..., " (185).

B8, B9 Narayan asked Shuka (for Kabir) and Uddhav to become avatars. He turned him into an infant, put him in a shell[34] and dropped him in the Bhimarathi river (57-58).

B4 Damaji, the tailor and his wife Gonai had no child of their own. He went to the bank of the Bhima and Nāmdev came floating down (58-59).

D3 "When Nama was growing up he had a son. For the naming of the child on the twelfth day, God Himself brought the gifts" (62).

D4 For the incident of Nāmdev's daughter and Vanka, see below under E11.

---

(34) The story of the shell *(sīp)* seems to be based on an *abhaṅga* (294), attributed to Janabai in: *'Ādi'* of Vishnudas Nama. Quoted in Inamdar:1970, p. 13ff. See also Eknāth in Āvaṭe:1908, *abhaṅgas* 3554-3635.

D5 Because of the complaints of Nāmdev's wife (Rajai) that he left her in great poverty, Krishna appeared in the form of a merchant, called Keshava and sent gold to his house (65).
Jani, Nama's maidservant, tells the story of the visit of Krishna to Nama's house, with the bag of gold (75). See also p. 338f.
D6 Krishna writes down the verses of Jani (351).
Mahīpati further relates how Jani was introduced to the saints, at the request of the Lord of the world (354). "Dñyaneshwar said to Jani, Nāmdev has assumed four avatars (sic): Prahlad, Angad and Uddhav, and made Krishna subservient to him'" (355).
E1 Nāmdev feeds "an offering" to God in the temple (no threat of suicide; see below, Caturdās:1800), (60-61).
E5 "After visiting Rameshvar..., both arrived at Nagnath (193). Nāmdev stood before the great door of the temple and began kirtan...A great crowd of people came with the desire to listen,...and all good listeners became happy,...Brāhmans just then came from bathing,... and shouted at the crowd: 'Look out or you will touch us; get off to one side',..' Why are you singing here uselessly, clapping your hands and shouting aloud? Such doings are acceptable at Pandari only'...'We have already been delayed in our worship of Shiva and there is no way for us to go into the temple. Beat out Nama at once. If anyone of these people touches us, we shall have to go again and take a bath with our clothes on'...They retired behind the temple of Shiva and nine hundred thousand banners came down from heaven like lightning... The temple that had faced the east, suddenly turned around to the west", (passim, till p.203).
E6 On the way back from Dwarawati, Dñyandev and Nāmdev passed through the desert of Marwad. Dñyandev got water from a deep well through his yogic powers and Nāmdev got water because Krishna made the well overflow for him (187-190).
They visited many places (191-192).
E7 In Delhi, the Muhammadan king killed a cow "And he said to Nama:' What is it you are singing, you heretic? If you will raise this cow again to life I shall regard your songs as true. If you do not bring the cow to life, I shall kill you with my own hand'" (171-175).
Nāmdev visited Gayā, Allahābād, Ayodhyā, Mathurā, Gokul (187-191).
E11: While washing clothes on the bank of the Bhima, the daughter of Nāmdev disturbed Vanka (283).
E12 Krishna repairs Nāmdev's hut (340-341).
E18 God came in the form of an old Brāhman begging for food. As Nāmdev was observing a fast that day, he refused to give him cooked food and the Brāhman died. Nāmdev reanimated him (334-337).
E19 Nāmdev's wife had borrowed a touchstone, in order to do away with her poverty. Nāmdev threw it in the Chandrabhag river for "gold and clay seem the same in value". Later on, he turned all the pebbles into touchstones (305-310).
F1/F2 Mahīpati only mentions that, after having travelled all over India in the company of Dñyandev, on their return to Paṇḍharpur, "some noble Vaishnavas came to see Him: Nivritti and Dñyaneshvar, Sopan, Visobā Khechar and Narahari the goldsmith"

(207). Later on, Krishna tells Nāmdev to take Visobā Khecar as guru, after the incident with Gora the potter (295): "As Nāmdev himself lifted up Visobā's feet, the whole place seemed to take the form of the emblem of Shiva" (301).
There also, Nāmdev gives a feast to the Brāhmans and Krishna eats from his plate, to the great scandal of the Brāhmans (209f.).
G4
1800 CATURDĀS, *Commentary* on the Rāghavadās *Bhaktamāl:1713* (q.v.), dated 1800 AD.
C10
E1 ...and Nāmdev threatens to kill himself if God does not drink the milk.
E5
E9 he reanimates a cow for a Muslim king *(bhūp turak)*.
E12, E14, E16
E17 (lengthy description).
E18
1839 DE TASSY Garcin, *Histoire de la littérature Hindoui et Hindoustani*, Paris, 1839.
B9 Nāmdev was an *avatār* of Vishnu[35].
E14 Vol. II., p. 436.
1849 GONDHALEKAR R.S., *Nāmadevakrita jñānadevācyā samādhice abhaṅga* (lithogr.), Jagaddhitecchu Press, Poona, 1849.
1860 JANĀRDAN R.C., *Kavi caritra*, (Marāṭhī), Bombay, 1860.
B9 'Nāmdev is an *avatār* of Uddhav' (p. 152).
1888 PŪRANADĀS, *Janam sākhī śrī svāmī Nāmdevjī kī*.
B7 Nāmdev was born in *samvat* 1420 or 1364 AD, as the son of a 12 year old widow (quoted in Āḍkar:1972, p. 71-72).
1892 GONDHALEKAR R.S., ed., *Nāmdevācī Gāthā*, Pune, (1892, 1st ed), 1896.
1894 TĀTYĀ T., ed., *Nāmdevāñcī āṇi tyāñcyā kutumbāntīl va saṁkālīn sādhūñcyā abhaṅgāñcī Gāthā*, (Marāṭhī), Bombay, (1894), 1972.
This edition gives the *abhaṅgas* attributed to Nāmdev, his family members and contemporaries. On p. 645-677 we find 106 *'Hindustānī bhāṣent abhaṅga'* (2345-2450).
1896 CROOKE W., *(The Tribes and Castes of the Western Provinces and Oudh*, Calcutta, 1896), *The Tribes and Castes of the North-Western India*, Cosmo Publications, Delhi, 1974.
C4 "The Dhuniyas have one Namadeo Bhagata, a tribal saint, who is much respected by them. He is said to have been born in Marwar in AD 1443 and to have flourished in the time of Sikander Lodhi (1488-1512). According to one account he was born at Paṇḍharpur in the Dakkhin" (p. 299).
G2 " After a considerable amount of travelling to and fro, he at last settled in the village of Ghuman" (p. 144).
1898 BHĀRADVĀJ R., *Dyñāndev va Nāmdev samkālīn hote kāy?*, in: *'Sudhārak'* (Marāṭhī), 5th Dec. 1898 AD, quoted in Āḍkar1972 (see below 1931), p. 66.

(35) Narhari Mālū, in his *Bhakta Kathāmrit*, calls Nāmdev an *avtār* of Sanatkumār, one of the four sons of Brahmā; quoted in Āḍkar:1972, p. 84, n.7.

A2
C2 Nāmdev was *not* a contemporary of Dñyāndev[36].
1900 BHINGARKAR P., *Śrī mahāsādhu Dyñāneśvar mahārāj yāñcā kāl nirṇay va saṃkṣipta caritra,* (Marāṭhī), Pune, 1900.
1906 Singh G.B., *Bhagat Nāmdevjī dā jīvan caritra,* (Panjābī), Khalsā Tract Society, Amritsar, 1906.
C1
1908 ĀVAṬE T.H., ed., *Sakal Santa Gāthā* or *Gāthāpañcak,* Pune, 1908 AD; repr. in 5 vols, by R.C. Dhere, Pune, 1983.
Vol. 2 (804p. and 32p.) is only about Nāmdev, without any reference to a manuscript or to the sources from which the information was collected. On p. 678-700 the author quotes 102 'Hindustānī' songs, again without referring to any manuscript. On p. 606-637 we find 'as a work of Nāmdev' the biographies of Sants like Kabīr and others, who lived centuries later. S.G. Tulpule[37] finds it difficult to define with certainty which of the 2500 *abhaṅgas* may be attributed to Nāmdev. See also Pendse:1969c, who doubts the authenticity of Nāmdev's *Tīrthāvalī.*
A1 Nāmdev and Jñāndev travelled together in North and South India (*Tīrthāvalī, abhaṅg as* 612-670, p. 151ff.).
B1 *abhaṅga* 1407 (quoted in Miśra:1969, p. 64)[38].
B4 according to an *abhaṅga* attributed to Janābāi (Āḍkar:1972, p. 82f.).
B5
B6 according to an *abhaṅga* attributed to Janābāi (Āḍkar:1972, p. 82f.).
B7
C1
C6 100 *koṭi* and eventually only 84 *koṭi abhaṅgas;* 1404ff.[39].
C8 according to an *abhaṅga* attributed to Janābāī (136 in the Āvaṭe ed.).
D4 according to an *abhaṅga* attributed to Janābāi (Āḍkar:1972, p. 82f.).
E1
E5 described at length in *Tīrthāvalī,* p. 1033ff.
F2
F7 Sopāndev is Nāmdev's guru, according to an *abhaṅga* attributed to Janābāi[40].

---

(36) For the controversy about this issue, see Āḍkar:1972, p. 66.
(37) *Pāñca santa kavi,* p.138-139.
(38) Or *abhaṅga* 1243 as quoted in Āḍkar:1972, p. 84. For more references see *Ibidem,* p. 84.
(39) Miśra:1969, p. 64, or *abhaṅga* 162, p. 317 in Āḍkar:1972, p. 97.
There is a discrepancy in the numbering between the Āvaṭe:1908 edition of 1983 and the editions used by Miśra:1969: 1) Indira Press, Pune, 1924 and 2) Santa Vāṅgmay Prakāshan Mandir, Pune, 1967. References to the *Sakal Santa Gāthā* can be found in Miśra:1969, p. 83f.
For the Table giving the numbers of the Hindī songs in the *Guru Granth* and in the *Sakal Santa Gāthā,* see *Ibidem,* p. 90f.
It is interesting to note that Sūr Dās also "composed a lakh and a quarter songs", see J.S. Hawley, *Sūr Dās. Poet, Singer, Saint,* Seattle, 1984, p. 36.
(40) See Aḍkar:1972, p. 8.

H1 *abhaṅga* 977.

"All these facts are also found in the 'Hindustani pad' in the *Sakal Santa Gāthā*"[41].

In Vol. 3 (3554-3635) is given the *Nāmdev Caritra* attributed to Eknāth. Until we see a more critical edition of the *abhaṅgas* of Nāmdev, we cannot accept *abhaṅgas* in these editions as 'early evidence'.

1909 MACAULIFFE M.A., *The Sikh Religion*, vols 1-6, 1909.[42].

B5, C1, C5, C6, E2; E3 (p. 20),
E20

G1,G3,G5 "Nāmdev visited the district of Gurdaspur in the year when he was fifty-five years of age. He first went to Bhattivala and dwelt beside a tank there which is called Namiana in memory of him. He had two disciples (Ladha and Jalla, a carpenter) who settled down with followers of their own in the villages of Sukhovala and Dharivala respectively. Nāmdeva moved from Bhattivala and took up his abode near another tank in a lonely forest where he hoped for more leisure for prayer and meditation on God." (p. 39)[43].

H8 (p. 35).

1909b *Srī Nāmdev Māsik*, monthly, from 1909 AD onwards.

1910 MOODALIAR K., *Nāmadev an Indian Saint*, Triplicane, 1910.

1913 PATWARDHAN W.B., *Wilson Philological Lectures*, Fergusson College Magazine, Vol. III, 4 (Jan. 1913).

1913b BHANDARKAR R.G., *Vaisnavism, Saivism and Minor Religious Systems*, K.J.Trubner, Strasbourg, 1913.

C3 Nāmdev, therefore, probably lived about or after the end of the 14th century' (p. 97).

C8 (p. 89), F4 (p. 9).

1914 ROSE H.A., *A Glossary of the Tribes and Castes of the Punjab and North-West Frontier Province*, Lahore, Civil and Military Gazette Press, 1914.

G2 (p.152).

1918 NATESAN G.A., *Shri Dñyaneshvar, a sketch of his life and teachings*, Madras, 1918.

1915 MACNICOL N., *Indian Theism*, 1915.

F2 (p. 114).

1920 FARQUHAR J.N., *An Outline of the Religious Literature of India*, Oxford, 1920.

C4 '1430 AD'[44].

1925 DESHPĀNDEY Y.K., *Mahānubhāvīya Marāṭhī Vāṅgmay*, Yavatmāl, 1925.

---

(41) Miśra:1969 p. 89.

(42) In a footnote (VI, p. 17), Macauliffe states that "the accounts of Nāmdev current in different provinces and languages of India are, for the most part, incorrect. The most trustworthy materials for his life are contained in the *Gāthā*, compiled by Mr. Tukaram Tatya." "The author is indebted to ..., in the Sholapur Dt, for inquiries made regarding the lives of Nāmdev and other saints of the Dakhan."

(43) Based on Dane, L.W. and Douglas, M.W., *Settlement Report of the Gurdaspur District*.

(44) See *JRAS of Great Britain and Ireland*, April, 1920, 'Historical Position of Rāmānand'.

1925b SHARMĀ P.R., *Nāmdevācā Nirṇay,* in: *'Bhāratīy Itihās saṃshodhak Maṇḍal',* 3,1(1925).
1925c JOG V.H., ed., *Śrī Nāmdevācā Gāthā,* Pune, 1925. In vol. 4, p. 455-473, we find 102 *'Hindustānī pad'.*
1925d KULKARNI P.D., *Were Jñāneśvara and Nāmadeva contemporaries?* in: 'ABORI' VI, Pt 2 (1925), p. 67f.
1926a KORATKAR K.R., *Nāmdevācī Narsī,* (Marāṭhī), in: *'Bhārat Itihās Saṃshodhak Mandal',* 7 (1926), 1-4 (quarterly), Pune, 1926.
C9 "Koratkar was the first to establish that Nāmdev's birthplace Narsī Brāhmanī was situated in the Parbhani Dt of Marāṭhvāḍā"[45].
H9
1926b VARMĀ N.L., *Śrī Nāmdev Vanshāvalī,* (Hindī), Jabalpur, 1926.
B3 "Nāmdev was a Kshatriya and his ancestors took up the profession of a *chīmpī* in order to hide their caste-affiliations" *(bhūmikā,* p. 2ff.)[46].
1927 AJAGĀNKAR J.R., *Santa Śiromaṇi Nāmdev mahārāj āṇi tyānce saṃkālīn santa,* 1927.
E2 (described at length on p. 21-24).
1927 P.D. KULKARNI, 'Historical Position of Namdeva', in Annals of BORI, Poona, 1927, 335-341.
1929 ABBOTT J.E., *Stotramala, A Garland of Hindu Prayers,* (The Poet-Saints of Mahārāshtra 6), Pune, 1929.
1930 SEN K.M., *Mediaeval Mysticism of India,* (Calcutta, 1930), tr. by Manmohan Ghosh, (Luzac), London, 1936; *(Mysticism of Mediaeval India,* Munshiram Manoharlal, Delhi, 1974).
A4 Nāmdeva's sayings have been included in the Grantha Sahib. This famous person has two less known namesakes. One of them was a calicoprinter by profession and had his place in Bulandshehar. Nāmdeva of Marwar was a cotton-carder by birth. Both these were reputed as bhaktas and have numerous devoted followers" (p.56).
G1 "In his fiftieth year he renounced the world and travelled all over India and made acquaintance of saints and holy men. For sometime he stayed in Hardvar, but left the place afterwards for Ghoman in the Punjab where he passed his last days.", p. 56).
H4 Nāmdev dies in 1464 AD, "after meeting Firoz Shah Tuqluq who donated land for a monastery" (p. 56).
I1: The descendants of Nāmdev's disciple Bohardās still live in Ghuman today.
1931 BHARADVĀJ R., *Jñānadeva va Jñāneśvara,* in 'Sudhārak' 1898-99, collected and publ., Poona, 1931 (see above, 1898).
H2
1932 PŪRAN SINGH Bābā, *Janamsākhī Śrī Svāmī Nāmdevjī,* (Panjābī), Amritsar, 1932.
1932b PĀNGARKAR L.R., *Marāṭhī Vāṅgmay Itihās. Dñyāneśvar Nāmdevācā Kāl,* Bombay, 1932.
1933 PANGARKAR L.R., *Śrī Dyñāneśvar Caritra,* Gorakhpur, 1933.
C9, F1 (p. 131-34f.).

(45) See Āḍkar:1972, p. 79.
(46) Caturvedī:1951, p. 107.

A1 "Jnanadeva and Nāmdeva thereupon have been reported to have wandered throughout the length and breadth of Upper India" (p.147).

A6

1933b KEDĀR B.V., *Śrīnāmdev Vanshāvalīcā vād,* in: *'Vijayo Nāmdev Māsik'*, 1933.

1933c RANADE R.D., *Mysticism in Maharashtra,* vol. 7, Aryabhushan Press, Poona, 1933; (repr. as *Pathway to God in Marathi Literature,* Bharatiya Vidya Bhavan, Bombay, 1961); repr. Delhi, 1982.

A6, C1,

C6 p.185f. Ranade refers to "abhangas" in which Nāmdev is supposed to say that "a certain Brahmin, Babaji by name, had cast his horoscope, foretelling that Nāmdeva would compose a hundred crores of Abhangas" (p. 185).

E2-E4 (the 'story of the widow' is slightly different in Singh:1981)

F2 (p. 149).

H7 Nāmdev is buried at the great door of the temple of Viṭhobā... "The priests in Vithoba's temple say that the bones of their Nāmdev who was buried at the front door are the bones of a Brahmin Nāmdeva (Vishnudās Nāmā), and not of the tailor Nāmdeva" (p.190).

Singh:1981 comments: "The tradition of a samādhi of brahmana Nāmdeva in the temple of Vitthala at Paṇḍharpur, is most probably introduced by the Vaisnava priests in the first half of the sixteenth century AD or it was concocted in the later centuries" (p.147).

1935 PĀṬASKAR P.N., *Śrī santa Shiromaṇi bālbhakta Śrī Nāmdev mahārāj he daroḍekhor hote kāy?,* Pune, 1935.

E2 (the author doubts the authenticity of this *abhanga*, p. 20).

1936 BARTHVĀL P.D., *The nirguṇa School of Hindī Poetry,* Banaras, 1936 (Hindī ed. 1950).

C7

1936b BHAGAT RĀM, Bābā, *Śrī Svāmī Nāmdev,* (Panjābī), Ghuman, 1936.

C3 Nāmdev is born in 1370 AD.

1938 PRIYOLKAR A.K., *Shikhāncyā Ādigranthāntil Nāmdev,* Bombay, 1938, gives a Marāṭhī translation of the 61 songs of Nāmdev in the Guru Granth.

1939 PARALKAR L., *Nāmdevācī Panjābvar svārī,* in: *'Dyñānprakāsh'*, 15 July, 1939.

1940 JOSHI S.P., *Panjābāntīl Nāmdev,* Bombay, 1940 (with a Marāṭhī translation of the 61 songs of Nāmdev in the Guru Granth).

C5 '11th *kārtik shak* 1185', i.e. 1263 AD (p. 15).

C7 (p. 126).

1941 EDWARDS J.F., *Dñyāneshwar, the Out-caste Brāhmin,* Poona, 1941.

1944 RĀNOJĪ RAO B.S., *Santa Śiromanī Śrī Nāmdev mahārājāncī Vanshāval,* 1944.

1947 RANADE R., *Jñāneśvara āṇi Hindī santa-kavi,* in: *'Prasād'*, Aug. 1947.

1948 TULPULE S.G., *Pāñc Santa kavi,* Pune, 1948 (1962 2nd ed.).

1949 SINGH Mohan 'Dīvānā', *Bhakta Śiromaṇī. Nāmdev kī nayī jīvanī, nayī padāvalī,* (Hindī), Ambālā, 1949.

A8: see Sharmā:1957c, p. 105.

1949b SUBANDH P.S., ed., *Śrī Nāmdevarāyāñcī sārth Gāthā,* (5 vols), from 1949 onwards. Marāṭhī ed. with commentary.

1950 RAE Balvant Bābā, *Uc te uc Nāmdev samdarshī,* (Hindī), Ghuman, 1950.

1951 CATURVEDĪ P., *Uttarī Bhārat kī Santa paramparā,* Ilāhābād, (1st ed. 1951), 1964 (p. 103f.).

A7, E5 (p.111), E8 (p. 112).

1951b SINGH Bhāī Nidhan, *Prasaṅg Dhane Bhagata te Nāmdevajī dā ate Bārām Māhā,* (Panjābī), Lahore, 1951.

1952 MULE M.A., *Śrī Nāmdev caritra,* Pune, (repr. 1952).

B4 'Nāmdev's forefather *(mūl purush)* was Yadushet' (p. 27).

B7 His sub-caste was 'Relekar'.

1952b RAE Balvant Bābā, *Janamsākhī Śrī Svāmī Nāmdevjī,* (Panjābī), Ghuman, 1952.

1956 BAHIRAT B.P., The Philosophy of Jnanadeva, Bombay, (1st ed. 1956), 1961.

1957 DIKSHIT A.P., *Paricayī Sāhitya,* Lucknow, 1957.

1957b ŞHRĪVĀSTAV B.D., *Rāmānand Sampradāy tathā Hindī Sāhitya par uskā Prabhāv,* Prayāg, 1957.

1957c SHARMĀ V.M., *Hindī ko Marāthī santoṅ kī den.* (Hīndi), Paṭnā, 1957 (p.101-132).

C7, D1, D4, F3

1957d SINGH Bhāī Jodh, *Bhagata Bāṇāṇī Saṭīk,* (Panjābī), Ludhiana, (Lahore Bookshop), 1957.

1957e VIYOGĪ HARI, *Saṁkṣipta Santa Sudhāsār,* (1953), Delhi, 1957 (p. 21-28).

F3, H5

1958 SINGH Giānī Khazān, *Śrī Nāmdevjī de Jivan Prasaṅga,* (Panjābī), New Delhi, 1958.[47]

1960 DELEURY G.A., *The Cult of Viṭhobā,* Poona, 1960.

1960b SHEDE S., *Vishnudās Nāmyācyā Mahābhāratācā vivecanātmak Abhyās,* Bombay Vidyāpīṭh Granthālay (unpubl.), 1960.

1960c SINGH Gandā, *Early Maratha-Sikh Relations,* in: *'The Sikh Review',* vol. X,1(1960), p. 44-48.

1962b MAURYA R.N., *Santa mat ke ādi pravartak: santa Nāmdev,* in: *'Hindustānī',* Jan.-March 1962.

1962c MACHVE P., *Hindī aur Marāṭhī kā santa kāvya,* Vārāṇasī (Chowkhambā), 1962.

1963 BHAVE Vinobā, *Nāmdevāñcī Bhajane* (Marāṭhī), Pavnar, Vardhā, 1963.

1963b MACHVE P., *Nāmdeva. Life and Philosophy,* Patiala, Panjābī Un., 1963.

1964 MIŚRA Bh. and R.N. MAURYA, *Santa Nāmdev kī Hindī Padāvalī,* Pune, 1964 (see below, Ch. 2.5).

H8 (p. 39).

(47) For more works of this author, see Singh:1981, p. 302.

1964b VĀNAKHANDE K.G., *Bhagat Rāj Śrī Nāmdev jī*, (Panjābī), (Śrī Nāmdev Sahit Prakāśan), Ludhiana, 1964.

D2, D4

12: "The genealogical table indicates that the present priest is a descendant of Nāmdev[48]."

1965 SINGH Khaḍag Ranjit, *Bhagat Nāmdev. Ek Adhyayan*, in: *'Panjābī Dhuniā' (bhagat aṅka)*, Patiala, Bhāshā Vibhāg, Sept.-Oct. 1965.

1968 BĀRATAKKE M.G., *Śrī Santa Nāmdevāncī sārth Hindī pade* (Marāṭhī), Pune, 1968.

1969 MIŚRA R.C., *Santa Nāmdev aur Hindī Pad Sāhitya*, (Hindī), Farrukhābād, 1969. Gives a Hindī translation of the 61 *padas* in the *Guru Granth* (p. 127f.); see Miśra:1976b.

1969b CAUHĀN D.S., 'Dyñānobāncī Kāshī yātrā shake 1216' (or 1294 AD) in: *'Itihās āṇi sanskriti'* (Marāṭhī thri-monthly), Jan. 1969.

G4

1969c PENDSE S.D., *Dyñāndev āṇi Nāmdev*, (Marāthī), Pune, 1969 (1st ed.), 1972. The author doubts the authenticity of Nāmdev's *Tīrthāvalī* (p. 335).

1969d VAUDEVILLE Ch., *L'Invocation. Le Haripāṭh de Dñyāndev*, Paris, 1969.

A9 (?)

1970 INĀMDĀR H.V., *Santa Nāmdev*, (Marāṭhī), Pune, 1970; this is a recent, detailed and critical study. See below, Dikhsit:1970d.

1970b DESHMUKH M.G., *Nāmadeva*, (Marāṭhī), Sahitya Academy, Delhi, 1970, with Hindī translation by P. Machve (1970) and Panjābī translation by Harbhajan Singh (1970).

B6 (p.15, *abhaṅga* 2233): "Janabai, a maidservant in Nāmdeva's family writes in her *abhaṅga* that Nāmdeva's mother Gonabai prayed to Kanha (i.e. Vitthal) in Paṇḍharpur for blessing her with a godly son. Her prayer was granted. Damaseti was happy and Janabai had a bliss at that moment".

D2

D4 (*abhaṅga* 2376).

D5 (*abhaṅga* 966); p.17f.

F1 "*abhaṅgas* 1063,1064", p. 24-26.

F2 "*abhaṅga* 1092" (p.28).

1970c an., *Śrī Nāmdev Gāthā*, Govt. of Maharashtra Publ., Bombay, 1970, 1152 p. No specific mention of manuscripts is made for each set of *abhaṅgas* attributed to Nāmdev and we do not know where to classify this source.

C5 '26th Oct. 1270'.[49]

1970d DĪKSHIT A.P., *Nāmdev kā krititva*, in: *'Rāshtravāṇī'. Santa Nāmdev viśeṣāṅk* (Oct.-Nov. 1970).

(48) Singh:1981, p. 37.

(49) Quoted in Āḍkar:1972, who doubts the authenticity of the *abhaṅga* (1254, Āvaṭe ed.), which is usually quoted in support of this precise date (p. 64). See also Ājagānkar:1927, p. 2.

C7 Dīkshit rejects Ināmdār's (1970) argument about the location of Nāmdev's birthplace "because the *abhaṅga* quoted is most probably not authentic" (p. 112).

1970e KARANDIKAR M.A., *Nāmdev*, (Govt. of Maharashtra Publ.), New Delhi, (1970), 2nd ed. 1985; (30 p.).

1970f KAVITKAR G.V. et alii, *Śrīnāmdev*, (Marāthī), Bombay 1970 (168p.).

1970g RELEKAR N.N. et alii, eds., *Śrī Nāmdev Darshan*, (Marāthī), 1970 (1078p.).

This is an edition of 84 articles (1078 p.), dealing with a broad variety of topics and questions around Nāmdev. Plenty of information is brought together, but one misses at times a critical analysis.

1970h VĀNAKHANDE K.G., *Santa Nāmadev tathā unkā Hindī sāhitya*, Delhi, (Publ. Div. of Govt. of India), 1970.

Gives in an Appendix the text of the undated *Nāmdev kī Paricayī* of Krishnānanda.

1970i KASEL K. Singh, *Jīvan te Darshan Bhagata Nāmadev*, (Panjābī), (Bhāshā Vibhāg), Patiala, 1970.

In Appendix a *Nāmdev-Trilochan Dialogue* is given, quoted from a *Gosati Saṅgrah* in Patiala (access. No. 354)[50].

1970j KĀMAT A.P., *Śrī Nāmdev. Ek Vijay-yātrā*, (Marāthī) Poona, 1970.

1970k SINGH Vilkhu Surain, *Ādi Santa Śrī Nāmdevjī mahārāj*, Ghuman, 1970.

1970l SINGH Khaḍag Ranjit, *Santa Nāmadeva. A study in the life and thought*, New Delhi, 1970.

1971 TALIB G.S., *Bhagat Nāmadev*, in: *'The Journal of Religious Studies'*, Patiala, Panjābī Un., 1971.

1972 ĀDKAR S.K., *Hindī nirguṇ-kāvya kā Prārambh aur Nāmdev kī Hindī kavitā*, (Hindī), Allahabad, 1972.

A11 'Dāmodar initiates (a third) Nāmdev in the Mahānubhāv sect, in 1276 AD'[51].

B9

F2? On p. 87, the author quotes a line from a song in the *Guru Granth: 'khecar bhūcar tulsī mālā parsādī pāiā'* (209 in our list) as literary evidence that Nāmdev accepted Khecar as his guru. *Khecar* ('one flying in the air') is the opposite of *bhūcar* or 'one who stays on earth'.

1972b BAHIRAT B.P., and P.G. BHĀLERĀV, *Vārkarī sampradāy. Uday va vikās*, (Marāṭhī), Pune, 1972.

1973 MAURYA R.N., *Santa Nāmdev. Bhakti aur Kāvya*, Pune, 1973.

1973b SINGH Dardi Prītam, *Śrī Nāmdevajī mahārāj dī Panjāb num den*, Ghuman, 1973.

1974 SINGH Sāheb, *Bhagat Bāṇi Saṭik. Bāṇī Bhagat Nāmdev*, Amritsar, 1974.

1975 SINGH Sabja Balwant, *Sromani Bhagat Nāmdev*, Ghuman, 1971.

---

(50) Singh:1981, p. 306.

(51) The author (p. 58) quotes Y.K. Deshpāndey, *Mahānubhāvīy Marāṭhī Vāṅgmay*, Yavatmāl, 1925.

1976 KĀMAT A.P., *Mahārāṣtra ke Nāth Pamthīy Kāviyon kā Hindī Kavya,* Javahar Pustakalaya, Mathura, 1976. Quotes Derejī, R.C., *Satsthal. Ek Sānskritik Abhyās, n.d.,* (p.140), which deals with the Manuscript of *Satsthal* of Visobā Khecar.

F3 according to the study made by Dereji of Visobā's *Satsthala* (Ms.), Nāmdev's guru lineage goes via Visobā Khecar, Krishnanath, Çangavateshvar, Muktābāi, Gorakhanāth and Matsyendranāth to Ādināth.

F5 (p. 138).

1976b MIŚRA R.C., *The Padas of Bhagat Nāmdev. A Comparative Study based on 'Śrī Guru Grantha Sāhib and Gāthā Pañcak',* in: *'The Journal of Sikh Studies',* Amritsar, Guru Nanak Dev Un., vol. III, 2, Aug. 1976: see Miśra:1969.

1977 TULPULE S.G., *Mahānubhāv Panth āṇi Nāmdev,* in: 'Navbhārat', Wai, Oct., 1977, pp. 51-53.

1977b KHĀNOLKAR G.D., ed., *Marāṭhī Vāngmay Kos,* I, Bombay, 1977; on Nāmdev, pp. 157-163.

1977c an., *Saint Namdev,* Radha Soami Satsang Beas, 1977; gives an English translation of 27 songs from the *Marāṭhī Abhaṅga Gāthā,* 37 from the *Guru Granth* and 26 from Miśra:1964.

1981 SINGH Nirbhai, *Bhagata Nāmdeva in the Guru Grantha,* Panjābī University Patiala, 1981.

E4 "As the local tradition goes there was a widow named Aḍoḷi. She had one little boy. One day the boy expired owing to illness. Baba Nāmdeva could not tolerate the touching cries of the bereaved mother. It is said that he went to her house and revived the child with a japa of the rama-nama and a sprinkle of water. The widow gifted the child to Baba Nāmdev.

After some time Nāmdeva left Bhutavinda village and passing through Bakala, Satniala, Dukoha, came to a place called Bhattivala (1 km. north of Ghuman)" (p.67). The 'story of the widow' in Ranade:1933c is slightly different.

G1 "Our survey of Gurdaspur and Amritsar districts reveals that Nāmdeva proceeded from Hardwar to Kolayat near Bikaner in Rājasthān and first came to a village Bhutavinda, tehsil and district Amritsar. (Now it is called Rampur)" (p.67).

Singh comments: "The tradition of a samādhi of brahmana Nāmdeva in the temple of Vitthala at Paṇḍharpur, is most probably introduced by the Vaisnava priests in the first half of the sixteenth century AD or it was concocted in the later centuries" (p.147).

It is not clear how Singh:1981 (p. 66, n. 47) found the reference in the biography written by Anantadās, "who records Nāmadeva's coming from Mahārāstra to Punjab"; see Ms. no. 398, Jaikar Library, Pune University, Pune. It should be interesting to examine the *lipikāl* of that manuscript. For the dates of the manuscripts we used for our edition and translation of the *Nāmdev kī Parcaī,* see below, Ch. 1.3.

G5 Three disciples: Baba Jallo, Baba Ladha, Baba Keso Kaladhari (p.73).

H5 Singh refers to the "powerful local tradition in Maharashtra that he took samādhi in Paṇḍharpur at the feet of Vitthala" (p.36).

"According to the local tradition the rest of the fourteen members of the family wilfully drowned in the River Bhima when Nāmdeva took samādhi" (p.36)[52].

I1 For the genealogical table from Nāmdev, "via Bohddasa to the present-day descendants", see p. 73-75.

1983 DHERE R.C., *Sakal Santa Gāthā*, 1983, see above, Āvaṭe:1908.

1984 TULPULE S.G., *Mysticism in Mediaeval India*, Wiesbaden, 1984.

1985 JOSHI L.S. ed., *Marāṭhī Vishva-Kosh*, 'Nāmdev', p. 493-495.

A1 He was one of the great poets of the Vārkarī sect. In 1291 he met Dñyāndev. He went with him on *tīrth-yātrā* all over India.

C1 26th Oct. 1270.

C9 Born in Narasī, in Marāṭhvāḍā, where there is a *samādhi* and a temple in his name (an *abhaṅga* is quoted). Narasī and Bamaṇī are two different villages.

D2

G5 Visnusvāmī, Bohardās or Bahordās, Jāllo (or Jālhan), Ladhā, Keso Kalandar (see I3).

H1 Died on the 3rd July 1350.

H6 He died in front of the main door of the Viṭṭhal temple in Paṇḍharpur. Janābāi took *samādhi* on the same day.

I3 Tailors in the south and a Mallāh caste started to adopt 'Nāmdev' as an alternative name, after his visit there (see Kavitkar:1970). Keso Kaldhāri established a *maṭh* at Bhāvalpur.

1985b JAUHARĪ P., *Santa Nāmdev kā Kāvya aur Sangīt Tattva*, (Hindī), New Delhi, 1985.

1987 INĀMDĀR H.V., ed., *Santa Nāmdev. Kāvyasambhār āṇi Santaparivār*, Pune, 1987; 10 articles and a bibliography of 236 titels.

(52) See also Mate, M.S., *Temples and Legends of Maharasthra*, Bombay, Bharatiya Vidya Bhavan, 1970, p. 201. For Dāmodar's giving spiritual knowledge to 'a Nāmdev', see p. 55.

1.3. The *Nāmdev Parcaī* written by Anantadās

Anantadās wrote a biography of several Sants: Trilochan, Kabīr, Pīpā, Raidās and Dhanā[53]. In 1588 AD (see v. 1.1) he wrote the *Nāmdev kī Parcaī,* with a clear message: the superiority of Vaiṣṇav *bhakti* above rituals. He gives none of the biographical data which are so abundantly available in 20th century publications. Only briefly does he refer to a few miracles (v erses 1.5-8), but he expands on the miracle of the *ekādaśī* fast, the revival of a Brāhman (verses 1.9-2.5) and the miracle of the *tulsī* leaf (verses 2.6-end).

Until late in the 19th century, many copies continued to be made of the *parcais* of Anantadās traditions. From the 15 manuscripts at hand[54] we selected four for collation[55]:

k: VBJ 34; 1658 AD; fo. 579-580.
b: CPJ 1843; 1665 AD; fo. 14-16.
c: DMVJ 2; 1676 AD; fo. 364f.
d: CPJ 3321; 1687 AD; fo.1-4.

As a rule we have closely followed the version of Ms. *k*. An analysis of the variants and of the omissions and inversions of lines suggests that we deal here not only with copied manuscripts, but especially with repertoires which underwent changes at the hand of the narrators. The *parcaīs* were basically narratives and did not form a part of the *kīrtan* singing of *padas*. Yet, they seem to have been part of a performance and as a result we have different repertoires reflected in the manuscripts. Many variants cannot be explained as mere scribal changes. Consequently, we have opted for one repertoire (reflected in manuscript *k*) --even if the line occurs only in that manuscript--, instead of 'reconstructing' the 'original' version. That would in fact have been the redaction of yet another repertoire. On account of the changes brought about during the period of narrative performance, there is no way to 'reconstruct' the version written or narrated by Anantadās.

The lines which are *not* found in *all* manuscripts are indented, except for 1.1a and 1.2b (in *b c k*), 1.12b, (in *k*), 2.13a, 2.15a and 2.19b, (in *d k*).

We note the following omissions:
Only in *b c k:* 1.1a and 1.2b.
The first half of line 1.10b is missing in *b c.*

(53) A critical edition and English translation of the complete, biographical work of Anantadās should appear in 1989.
(54) See Callewaert:1980,1.
(55) The following abbreviations are used
VBJ: Vidyā Bhūshan Saṅgrah, Jaipur.
CPJ: City Palace, Jaipur.
DMVJ: Dādū Mahāvidyālay, Jaipur.

Only in *k:* 1.12b and 1.18b1-2.
Only in *b c d:* 13.b1, 1.18a1.

There are more variants in chapter 2.

Only in *k:* 2.1b1-2, 2.2a1, 2.6a1-4, 2.7a1, 2.7b1-2, 2.8b1 (half in *b c*) *and 2.21b1.*
Only in *b c d:* 2.6b1 and 2.25b1.
Only in *c:* 2.18b1.
Only in *b c:* 2.9a.
Only in *b d:* 2.21a1.
Only in *k d:* 2.15a and 2.19b.

We note a pairing off of *b c* versus *d k* in the variant lines 1.9b, 1.10a, 2.1a, 2.9ab, 2.12a, 2.20a, 2.23a and a distinction in ***K*** versus ***b c d*** in the variant lines 1.3a, 1.7b, 1.8a, 1.11a, 1.17a, 2.1b, 2.4b, 2.7a, 2.18a, 2.25a, 2.26b and 2.27ab. Manuscript *d* is quite variant from Mss. *b c k* in lines 1.5a, 1.17b, 2.3a.

These 'variant lines' cannot be due to a scribe's intervention; they point at the creativity of narrators.

For an interesting variant, see v. 1.18: 'The people blamed Nāmdev'; in Mss. *b* and *d* we read instead: 'The people blamed the shaved' *(muḍiyā)*.

1.3a English translation

Chapter one

1. I bow to you, Indefinable and Pure God,
grant me the company of good people.
It is now the year 1645 of the *vikram* era[56].
let me speak sweet and moving words.

2. The Indweller gave a command
and I, Anantadās, recite my story.
I ask for *bhakti* and the knowledge of the Supreme,
while I speak of the prominent *bhaktas* of earlier days.

3. I sing the praises of God, hoping to acquire *bhakti:*
may I reach the ultimate goal with the guru's help.
Immersed in their incomparable devotion,
I tell the stories of *bhaktas.*

4. Numberless *bhaktas* have lived
in the earlier ages of Satya, Dvāpar and Tretā,
but I know nothing of their real lives.
I speak only of some who lived in the present Kali age.

5. The first *bhakta* who lived in this Kali age was Nāmdev,
he had God in his hands[57].

(56) 1588 AD.
(57) Lit.: 'He held Keshav in his power'.

he gave God milk, made the temple turn around
and settled a quarrel with the Sultān.

6. He surrendered mind and body to the ultimate Brahma,
reanimated a cow and scared an elephant.
He retrieved a bed dry from a river:
the king and all the people were witnesses.

7. With His own hands Hari repaired the roof of his hut,
He took the form of a dog to eat the bread offered by Nāmdev.
Nāmdev also reanimated a bullock,
so that the bullock cart could move again.

8. Hari did everything for the sake of his *bhakta* Nāmdev,
whose miraculous deeds cannot be counted.
Bringing an image of stone to life,
he even made Hari speak.

9. Nāmdev was a strict observer of the *ekādaśī* fast:
for one full day twice a month he took no food.
One day, Hari visited him as a Brāhman
and asked for grains, insisting to find satisfaction.

10. Nāmdev refused to give grains, but
offered all the milk and yoghurt the Brāhman wanted, saying: I
do not take cereals on an *ekādaśī* day
and I cannot give such food to anyone.

11. Further, I should not direct you to another house:
that would be a sin, it brings no good".
The Brāhman answered: "Well, listen, tailor,
I have travelled all over Jambudvīp.

12. Are you trying to fool me with a new theory[58].
What is the point in dying of hunger?
Worship the Master with all your feelings
and give up your *ekādaśī* fast".

13. Nāmdev replied: "Why do you undermine the *ekādaśī* fast?
Have you not heard the story of Rukmāṅgad,
or of Ambarīṣ of Ayodhyā,
or of the numberless *bhaktas* who observed the *ekādaśī?"*
    If you decide to observe a total fast,
    the whole town will go to heaven *(b c d)*.

14. The Brāhman replied: "Listen to me, fool.
Believe me, I am telling the truth:
As long as Rām is not in a man's heart,

(58) *Khecarī* is the name of an occult skill by which a person could fly in the air.

He lays down all kinds of rules.

15. The fire-fly can only shine
till the sun appears, and
if a buffalo lives in an oilman's house,
you get only milk smelling of oil.

16. Till one day you taste clarified butter,
without the smell of oil.
Likewise, these observances are inferior:
who has ever reached salvation without Rām?"

17. The Brāhman really spoke words of truth,
but Nāmdev did not give up his *ekādaśī* fast.
Then the Brāhman lay down at the door,
pretending to be dead.

18. The people blamed Nāmdev:
"Who has ever gained *bhakti* by killing a Brāhman?
    In confusion the devotees are running away,
    for great is your sin *(b c d)*.
You are a sinner, who still wants to keep your company?
How can this ever remain hidden?"

19. Nāmdev put all his trust in Hari,
while his *bhakta* friends fled in confusion.
He decided to be cremated along with the Brāhman,
there was nothing else he could do.

20. *'If you are good, the world is good to you*[59]
there is no other way to be good.
You know within yourself you are good
or you know it from people of experience.

Chapter two

1. Nāmdev announced: " I too shall die,
I will enter the fire with the Brāhman."
He sat down on the pyre, the Brāhman's head in his lap,
his life ebbing away[60].
    The fire was lit on all sides,
    but Nāmdev had no fear.
    When He saw the trust of Nāmdev,

(59) These lines are not part of the story; they seem to be the poet's reflection on the situation. The change in the metre also indicates that the poet has stepped out of the story and is commenting on it.

(60) Lit.: 'his vital spirits entering a state of emptiness', *ṣoḍi,* meaning 'inferiority, deficiency'.

Hari came into life.

2. As the fire began to burn them both,
Hari jumped down the pyre and ran away, laughing.
Taking his hand He dragged Nāmdev along
and appeared to all people present *(k)*.
Praised be Nāmdev the true *bhakta*,
he gave up his *ekādaśī* fast and became truly liberated.

3. Ritual observances are fetters shackling the world.
Can anyone cross *samsār* without Rām?
Can salt be mixed with sugar
or vinegar with milk?

4. One should not follow any rule of conduct except *bhakti:*
it does not go together with delusion.
From that day Nāmdev gave up the *ekādaśī* fast and
as the days passed his *nirguṇ bhakti* intensified.

5. People do not know the real *ekādaśī*[61].
they are lost in delusion.
Their mind is shackled by *dvādaśī;*
they cannot find liberation.

6. There was a big merchant in Paṇḍharpur;
Everyone knew he wanted to donate his own weight in gold.
For the sake of *dharma* he distributed wealth,
giving away to people even without their asking it.
Everyone came,
eager to collect money
and everyone returned home satisfied.
Only Nāmdev stayed at home.
The rich merchant asked
if anyone was left without a gift *(k)*.
It was said that only Nāmdev had not come and
the merchant gave instructions to fetch him.
I am disappointed if I cannot give *(bcd)*.

7. One man went to call him, and then a second;
only with the third messenger Nāmdev came along.
The merchant said: "Why have you come late;
You give joy to all devotees?" *(k)*.
"Please accept something", the merchant pleaded,
"your acceptance will give me religious merit".
"Take home some of the gold
and give it to the Sants.
Even if nothing serves your purpose,
you will give me religious merit" *(k)*.

---

(61) The 'real' *ek-ādaśī* seems to be a pun for 'The One'. *Dvā-daśī* then refers to the ambiguity of ritual worship.

8. But Nāmdev refused: "I have no desire for money".
This greatly distressed the merchants.
"Please, do not say you don't accept,
your refusal will cost me my honour.
"If you take a little I'll be satisfied:
if you take nothing I shall be distressed *(k)*.

9. Take a little if you do not care for much,
take something and my reputation will be safe in town".
Nāmdev answered: "Listen, merchant,
you have donated gold to everyone.

10. Do not bother about me.
Besides, if I do accept, there will never be enough;
but if you really insist, give me something
equal in weight to a leaf.

11. Only do what I ask you. Get a leaf of the *tulsī* plant
and weigh it against gold.
I will accept that
and you will have religious merit".

12. The merchant, called Vimal, insisted:
"What is the point in asking so little, friend?
Take twenty or thirty *tolās*[62] and
do not blame me afterwards for giving little".

13. Nāmdev said: "God is great,
just wait and see what will happen.
I accept only because you insist;
whatever comes on the scale will be mine".

14. A *tulsī* leaf was brought and
the whole town turned up to watch.
On the leaf Nāmdev wrote *R*
for Rām, who has the weight of the whole world.

15. The leaf was placed on the scale and the weighing began.
Greatly surprised, the merchant woke up as from a sleep.
He had to pile up gold, silver and coins on the scale,
rushing to fetch also pearls and rubies.

16. He then placed the leaf on a heavier scale,
but still his precious gifts could not lift it.
Whatever he had he finally put it on the scale,
running to other merchants to borrow more.

17. The entire Baniyā community assembled,

(62) One *tolā* is equivalent to the weight of 216 grains.

and placed their wealth on the scale,
but the side with the leaf would not leave the ground:
the scale ridiculed traditional religion[63].

18. Then the merchant called his wife,
and made her remove all her jewelry.
She cried and cursed him:
"You have no son and now you make us bankrupt as well"
"We have given all because our master asked us,
but it is useless against half the Name" *(c)*.

19. The merchant asked to stop the music
and to silence the girls singing auspicious songs.
Nāmdev said: "Do not lose courage,
add the weight of your rituals too to the scale".

20. They accepted his suggestion and
took water in their hands, symbolizing their rituals.
Some served food to a hundred thousand Brāhmans,
while others arranged for various Vedic sacrifices.

21. They performed sacrifices, asceticism and vows,
and rituals difficult to identify.
The merit of 64 ritual baths
or of innumerable pilgrimages *(k bc)*.
The merchant lost face, totally embarrassed,
the Brāhmans were furious.
'Nothing can equal half the Name,
all rituals vanish before it *(k)*.

22. *'There is nothing one can give
in exchange for even half Rām's name.
All rituals, all power and wealth
are worthless before it'.*

23. The merchants prostrated before Nāmdev and asked humbly:
"We do not know your secret, but
please, accept now something from us:
what is offered to you reaches Rām Himself".

24. Nāmdev refused: "You are not giving for the sake of Rām,
inflated with your own greatness you do not recognise Rām.
If you had given something really equal to the leaf,
I would have gladly accepted your wealth.

25. Why should I accept something worthless?
Your wealth, you can keep".
Nāmdev picked up his leaf:

(63) *Lok bed kā dharma*, lit: 'the religion of the world and of the Vedas'.

Viṭṭhal was always ready to help him.
The merchants picked up their things:
they had experienced half the Name *(bcd)*.

26. How can I describe all the occasions,
when God became manifest[64] to Nāmdev?
Wherever Nāmdev went to find Hari,
there Hari came immediately.

27. Anantadās here ends his tale,
full of the glory of Nāmdev.
I am a slave of all Sants,
I sit at their feet'.

1.3b Hindī text

The following signs are used in the critical apparatus:

2: Ms. *b*
3: Ms. *c*
4: Ms. *d*
11: Ms. *k*
- : word is missing in the manuscript
-- : line is missing in the manuscript

For the Hindī concordance of the *Nāmdev parcaī*, see Appendix 5.

१ अलष निरंजन बिनउं सोई । मांगौ साध संगति दे मोही ।
संबत सोला सै पैंताला । बाणी बोलै बचन रसाला ।
२ अंतरजांमी आग्या दीन्ही । दास अनंत कथा कहि लीन्ही ।
मांग्यौं भगति अरु ब्रह्म गियांनां । कथौं भगत जन आदि पुराना ।
३ भगति हेत हरि के गुन गांऊं । गुर परसादि परमपद पांऊं ।
बिन उनमानि भगति ल्यौ लांऊं । भगतन की परचई सुनांऊं ।
४ सतजुग त्रेता द्वापर भइयौ । उन भगतनि कै अंत न लहियौ ।
उनकौ मरम कछू नहीं जांनौं । कलिजुग के कछु भगत बषांनौं ।
५ कलिजुगि प्रथमि नामदे भईयौ । केसौ अपनैं बसि करि लीयौ ।
दूध पिवाइ र देवल फेरयौ । पातिसाह स्यूं झगरौ नबेरयौ ।
६ तन मन पारब्रह्म कूं अरप्यौ । गाइ जिवाई हाथी डरप्यौ ।
सूकी सेज जलां तैं आंनीं । राजा परजा सबही जांनीं ।

१;१ अलष। -- ४; बिनउं। बिनऊं ३; बिनउ ११; बनऊं २; सोई। तोहि २ ३; मांगौ। साध २ ३; साध। संगति २ ३; संगति। मांगी २ ३; दे। दै २ ३; मोही। मोहिं ३; माहिं २

१;२ संबत। संवत ४; सोला। सोरह ४; पैंताला। पंताला २ ३; पैताला ४; बाणी। बांणी २; वाणी ४; बोलै। बोलैं २; बोले ४ ११; बचन। वचन ४

२;१ दीन्ही। दीन्हीं ११; दीनी ४; दास। दासि २ ३; कहि। करि २ ३ ४; लीन्ही। लीनी ४

२;२ मांग्यौं। -- ४; माग्यौं २; भगति। ब्रह्म ३; ब्रह्म २; ब्रह्म। भगति २ ३; गियांनां। ग्ययांनां २ ३; कथौं। जहा २; जहां ३; भगत। देषौं २ ३; जन। तहां २ ३; आदि। पेषौ २ ३; पुराना। पुंरांनां ११; रांमां २ ३

३;१ भगति। गुर २ ३ ४; हेति। पग्रादे ३; परसाद ४; परसादे २; के। - २ ३ ४; गुन। गुण २ ३; गांऊं। गाऊ ४; परसादि। परसाद २ ३ ४; परमपद। पर्मपद २ ३; पांऊं। पांऊ २ ४

३;२ बिन। बिनि २ ३; बिन ४; उंनमानि। उनमानि २; इनमांन ४; भगति। - २ ३ ४; ल्यौ। अकलि २ ३ ४; लांऊं। उपजांऊं २ ३; उपजाऊ ४; भगतन। अहरि भगतनि ४; परचई। परच २ ३ ४; सुनांऊं। सुनांऊ ४

४;१ त्रेता। द्वापर ४; द्वापर। त्रेता ४; भइयौ। भईयौ २ ११; गये ४; उन। तिन ४; भगतनि। भगतन २ ३; महि ४; कै। भगत ४; का २ ३; अंत। अनंत ४; न। ही ४; लहियौ। भयें ४; पईयौ २ ३

४;२ उनकौ। तिन ४; उन २ ३; मरम। भगतन ३; भगतन कौं ४; भगतन का २; कछू। अंत ४; मरम २ ३; नहीं। न २ ३ ४; कलिजुग। कलियुग २ ३; के। की २ ३ ४; भगत। कथा २ ३ ४; बषांनौं। वषांनौं ४

५;१ कलिजुगि। प्रथम ४; कलि में २ ३; प्रथमि। नांमदेव ४; प्रथम ३; थम २; नामदे। नांमदे ११; नामदेव २ ३; कलिजुग ४; भईयौ। भयउ ४; भइया २ ३; केसौ। जिनि ४; तिनि २ ३; अपनैं। केसौ २ ३ ४; बसि। अपने २ ४; अपनैं ३; करि। बसि २ ३; वसि करि ४; लीयौ। किया २ ३; लयऊ ४

५;२ पिवाइ। पिवायौ ४; र। - ४; दे २ ३; देवल। दूरौ २ ३; स्यूं। स्यौं २ ३; सौं ४; झगरौ। झगरो ११; नबेरयौ। निबेरयौ २ ३; नीवेन्यौ ४

६;१ तन। तंन ११; पारब्रह्म। पारबम्ह ४; कूं। कौ ४; कौं २ ३; गाइ। गाई ११; जिवाई। जिवाइ २ ३; जीवाइ ४; हाथी। हसति २ ३

६;२ सेज। सेझ २; जलां। जला २ ३ ४; तैं। स्यौ २ ३; सौ ४; आंनीं। आंनी २ ४; आनी ३; परजा। परिजा २ ३ ४; सबही। सवही ४; जांनीं। जांनी २ ३ ४

७ अपणै हाथी छांनि हरि छाई । स्वांन रूप धरि रोटी षाई ।
बलद जिवाई रू रथ चलायौ । नांमैं कह्यौ तहां हरि आयौ ।
८ भगत हेति हरि कारिज सारा । परचा पुरे अनंत अपारा ।
हठ करि हरि पैं बात कहाई । पांहन की प्रतिमां बिगसाई ।
९ ग्यारसि ब्रत नांमदे करता । कसट दिनां दोई दूभर भरता ।
तब हरि कीया बिप्र का भेषा । मांगै अन न करै संतोषा ।
१० नांमौ कहै अन नही दीजै । दूध दही बहुतेरो लीजै ।
ग्यारसि कै दिनि अन नहि लेऊं । आपण पांउं न औरै देऊं ।
११ और द्वार नहीं दैंउ बताई । लागै पांप न होइ भलाई ।
बांभण बोलै सुणि रे छीपा । हौं फिरी आयौ जंबूदीपा ।
१२ तैं मोस्यूं षेचरी चलाई । भूष मूवा कौणैं गति पाई ।
भाव सहित भगवंत कूं भजिये । ग्यारसि ब्रत बेगि अब तजिये ।

७;१ अपणै। अपर्णैं ११; आपनै ४; हाथी। हाथि २ ३ ४; छांनि। हरि २ ३; हरि। छीन्हि २ ३; छाई। छवाई २; छवाइ ३; स्वांन। स्वान २; धरि। ह्वै ३ ४; रोटी। रौटि २ ३; षाई। षांई ४

७;२ बलद। बलध २ ३; वलध ४; जिवाई। जिवाया २ ३; जीवायौ ४; रू। गाडी २ ३ ४; रथ। चाली २ ३ ४; चलायौ। हरि २ ३ ४; नांमैं। स्यौं २ ३; जी ४; कह्यौ। बात २ ३; वात ४; तहां। कहि २ ३; कही ४; हरि। सौ २ ३; सो ४; आयौ। पाली २ ३ ४

८;१ भगत। एक २ ३ ४; हेति। लगन २ ३ ४; हरि। ह्वै ४; दोइ २ ३; कारिज। काज ४; सारा। सवारया ४; सारया २ ३; परचा। अपर्णैं २ ३; अपाना ४; पुरे। डालि हरि ३; दल हरि ४; दालि हरि २; अनंत। न्रिपति ४; अनत ११; नृप २ ३; अपारा। निवारया २ ३ ४

८;२ पैं। पै ४; बात। - ३; वात ४; कहाई। कहांइ ४; कहाइ ११; पांहन। पांहण २ ३; प्रतिमां। मूरति २ ३; मरति ४; बिगसाई। विगसांई ४

९;१ ग्यारसि। ग्यारिसि २ ३; ब्रत। उपासौं ४; पासा २ ३; नांमदे। नांमौ ४; नामा २ ३; करता। रहिता २ ३; रहतौं ४; कसट। क ४; कष्ट २ ३; दिनां। दिना २ ३; दोई। ह्वै २ ४; द्वै ३; दूभर। भारी २ ३ ४; भरता। सहिता २ ३; सहतौं ४

९;२ तब। - २ ३ ४; हरि। किश्नि २ ३; कीया। कीनौ ४; कर्या २ ३; बिप्र। बांम्हन २ ३; बांह्मण ४; का। कौ ४; मांगै। मांगैं ३ ११; अन। अंन ४; अनं २ ३; न। - ११

१०;१ नांमौ। नांमदेव ४; नामौं ११; कहै २ ३; कहै। नामदेव २ ३; अन। दोस २ ४; दोष ३; नही। जिनि ४; न २ ३; दीजै। देहु ३; देहू २; देही ४; बहुतेरो। भावै सो २ ३; बहूतेरौ ४; लीजै। लैही ४; लेहु ३; लेहू २

१०;२ ग्यारसि। - २ ३; कै। - २ ३; दिनि। - २ ३; अन। - २ ३; नहि। - २ ३; न ४; लेऊं। - २ ३; दैऊ ४; लेउ ११; आपण। और ४; पांउं। ही ४; षांउ २; षांउं ३; न। औरै ३; दैउ ४; औरै। औरै २; आपन ४; न ३; देऊं। देहू २ ३; लैऊ ४

११;१ और। पर २ ३ ४; द्वार। उपगार २ ३ ४; नहीं। न २ ३ ४; नही ११; दैंउ। दैऊ ४; देहू २ ३; बताई। ब्हताई ११; वताई ४; होइ। होई ११

११;२ बांभण। बांभन ३; बाभन २; बाह्मण ४; बोलै। वोलै ४; सुणि। सुनि २ ३ ४; रे। से ४; छीपा। छींपा ११; छीपां ४; हौं। हू ४; फिरी। फिरि ४; परि २ ३; जंबूदीपा। जंवुदीपा ४

१२;१ मोस्यूं। मोस्यौं २ ३; मोसौ ४; मूवा। मुवां ४; मूवां २ ३; कौणैं। कौनै ४

१२;२ भाव। -- २ ३ ४

१३ नार्मौं कहै ग्यारसि क्यूं नाषी । रूकमांगद की सुणि लै साषी ।
अंबरीष साकेता आर्णौं । और भगता कौ अंत न जांर्णौं ।
जे तन मन दे ग्यारसि दिढवाई । सकल पुरी बैकुंठां जाई ।
१४ बांभण बोलै सुणि रे भोरा । साचा सबद मांनि लै मोरा ।
जब लग हिरदै रांम न आवै । तब लग धम अनेक दिढावै ।
१५ जब लग नांहिन रवि परकासा । तब लग उडगंण करै उजासा ।
तेली कै घरि महषी होई । तेल षीर मैं जीमै सोई ।
१६ ऐक दिनां भई घीई स्यूं भेटा । पायौ स्वाद तेल जब मेटा ।
ये सब है वैले ब्यौहारा । रांम बिना को उतरचौ पारा ।
१७ बिप्र बात साची सब भाषी । तउ न नांमदे ग्यारसि नांषी ।
मिस करि मुवौ परचौ दिज द्वारै । नग्र मांहि भयौ हैहैकारै ।
१८ लोग कहैं नार्मौं अपराधी । बांभण मारि भगति किंनि साधी ।

१३;१ नार्मौं। नांमदेव २ ३ ४; क्यूं। क्यौ ४; क्यौं २ ३; नाषी। नांषी ४; रूकमांगद। सुणि २ ३; रूकमांगद ४; की। लै २ ३; सुणि। सुनि ४; रूकमागद २ ३; लै। की २ ३

१३;२ अंबरीष। अंबरिष ३; अमरीष ४; अबरिष २; साकेता। सेके २ ३; आर्णौं। आंनौ २; आणौ ४; भगता। भगत २ ३; भगतनि ४; कौ। का २ ३; अंत। मरम २ ३; जांर्णौं। जांनौं २ ३ ४

१३;३ जे। - २ ३; -- ११; तन। तम २ ३; दे। सहित २ ३; दिढवाई। डिढाई २ ३; बैकुंठां। बैकूंठें ३; बैकूठें २

१४;१ बांभण। बांभन ३; बाभन २; ब्रांह्मन ४; बोलै। वोलै ४; सुणि। सुनि २ ३ ४; रे। रै २ ३; साचा। सांचां ४; सबद। सवद ४; मांनि। मानि २

१४;२ जब। जव ४; लग। लगि ४; हिरदै। हीरदै ४; रांम। राम २; आवै। आवैं ४; तब। तव ४; लग। लगि ४; धम। ध्ररम २ ३ ४; अनेक। अनेक ३ ११

१५;१ जब। जव ४; लग। लगि ४; नांहिन। नांहि ४; नाही २ ३; रवि। रबि २ ३; परकासा। प्रकासा। २ ३; परकांसा ४; तब। जव ४; लग। लगि ४; उडगंण। ससिगण २ ३; ससिगन ४; उजासा। प्रकासा ४

१५;२ महषी। मैहषि ४; तेल। जीवैं २ ३; मैं। सौ ४; तेल २ ३; जीमै। सौं २ ३; जीमैं ११; जीवै ४; सोई। साई २ ३

१६;१ ऐक। एक ४; येक २ ३; दिनां। दिना २ ३; भई। भइ ४; भइया २ ३; घीई। घी ४; घीरत २; धीरत ३; स्यूं। स्यौं २ ३; सौ ४; पायौ। विसरयौ ४; पाया २ ३; स्वाद। स्वांद ४; तेल। ते तेल २ ३; जब। तव ४

१६;२ ये। ऐ ११; अैसै ४; सब। सव ४; है। - ४; हैं २ ३; वैले। वैला २ ३; वोले ४; ब्यौहारा। ब्यौहारा ४; रांम। हरि २ ३ ४; बिना। विनि ४; बनि २ ३; को। कौंन २ ३ ४; उतरचौ। उतारै २ ३ ४

१७;१ बिप्र। कहै २ ३; कहत ४; बात। नामदे २ ३; नामदेव ४; साची। बाद २ ३; वांद ४; सब। न २ ३ ४; भाषी। कीजै २ ३ ४; तउ। अन २ ३ ४; नांमदे। दैउ ४; दैउं २ ३; ग्यारसि। और कछु २ ३; और सव ४; नांषी। लीजै २ ३ ४

१७;२ मिस। ब्राह्मण ४; करि। मिस ४; मुवौ। मुवौं ११; मुवो २ ३; करि ४; परचौ। पडौ २ ३; पारियौ ४; दिज। - ४; द्वारै। द्वारैं ४; द्वारा २ ३; नग्र। भयो २ ३; नगर ४; मांहि। मांऊ ४; नगर २ ३; भयौ। मै २ ३; हैहैकारै। हैहैकारा २ ३

१८;१ कहैं। कहै ४ ११; नांमौं। मुढिया २ ३ ४; अपराधी। अपंराधी ११; उपराधी २ ३; बांभण। बांभन २ ३; ब्राह्मण ४; भगति। भंगति २ ३; किंनि। किनि ४; कहा २ ३

भरमी भगत सवै उठि भागा । यह्या अपराध वडा तोहि लागा ।
तेरौ मुष को देषै पापी । अैसी बात रहै क्यूं छापी ।
नांमां का मन हरि स्यूं लागा । भरमीं भगत सबै उठि भागा ।
नांमैं कै मंनि ऐसी आई । जरिये साथि न और उपाई ।
१९ आप भला तौ जुग भला । नांतर भला न कोई ।
कै जीव जांणैं आपणों । कै जामैं बीती होई ।

२

१ कहत नांमदे हूं पण मरिहौं । बांभण साथि अगनि मैं जरिहौं ।
गोद सीस धरि नांमौं बैठा । तब जाई जीव षोडि मै पैठा ।
दसौं दिसा तैं पावक दीया । नांमैं कै मंनि भै नही कीया ।
नांमैं का मन देष्या धीरा । तब हरि चेतनि भया सरीरा ।
२ बांभण साथि जरण जब लागा । हसत हसत हरि उतरि भागा ।
कर धरि बाथ नांमदे लीया । प्रगट जंन कूं दरसण दीया ।

१८;२ भरमी। -- ११; भमि २ ३; सवै। सबै २ ३; यह्या। नामा २ ३; अपराध। तोहि २ ३; वडा। उपराध २ ३; तोहि। जु २ ३

१८;३ तेरौ। तेरो ११; तौरा २ ३; को। कौ २ ३ ४; बात। वात ४; क्यूं। क्यौ ४; क्यौं २ ३; छापी। छापी। २ ३

१८;४ नांमां। -- २ ३ ४; भरमीं। बरमीं ११; भागा। भागा ११

१८;५ नांमैं। -- २ ३ ४; ऐसी। अैसी ११

१९;१ आप। आपण २; नांतर। नातस २ ३; भला। भले २ ३; भलौ ४

१९;२ जीव। जिव २ ३; जपि ४; जीवं ११; जांणैं। जांनै ४; आपणों। आपणौं २ ३ ११; आपनौं ४; जामैं। जामै ४; बीती। बिति २ ३; वीती ४; होई। होय ४

१;१ कहत। बांभन २ ३; नांमदे। मुवो २; मूवो ३; नांमदेव ४; हूं। तो मै २ ३; पण। पणि ११; हु २ ३; फूनि ४; मरिहौं। मरौं ४; बांभण। बांभन २ ३; ब्राह्मण ४; साथि। सहित २ ३; अगनि। उगनि ११; मैं। मै ४; जरिहौं। जरौं ४

१;२ गोद। रचि २ ३; रची ४; सीस। सनेती ४; सनाती २ ३; धरि। उपरि २ ३ ४; नांमौं। - २ ३; वै ४; बैठा। स्यौ ४; तब। तव ४; जाई। जिव २ ३; जय ४; जीव। आंनि ४; आइ २ ३; षोडि। मरे २ ३; मरा ४; पैठा। पैस्यौ ४

१;३ दसौं। -- २ ३ ४

१;४ नांमैं। -- २ ३ ४

२;१ बांभण। बांभन २ ३; ब्राह्मण ४; साथि। संगि ४; सहित २ ३; जरण। जरन २ ३ ४; जब। जव ४; हसत। हस्त ४; हसत। हस्त ४; उतरि। ऊठि र २ ३

२;२ कर। -- २ ३ ४; बाथ। साथ ११

धनि धनि नामदेव साचा भगता । ग्यारसि छाडि होई रहूं मुकता ।
३ करम धरम बांध्यौ संसारा । रांम बिनां को उतरचौ पारा ।
मिसरि मांहि मीठौं क्यूं मिलई । दूध मांहि क्यूं काजी मिलई ।
४ दूजौ धरम करै मति भाई । भगति मांहि क्यूं भरंम समांई ।
तब तें नांमदे ग्यारसि छाडी । त्रिगुन भगति निरंतरि बाढी ।
५ ऐकादसी न जांणही । भरम भुलांणीं लोइ ।
मन लें बांध्यौ द्वादसी । तातैं मुक्ति न होई ।
६ साह एक पंडरपुर मांहै । चढचौ तुला जांन्यौं सब काहूं ।
धंम हेति धंन बांटनं लाग्यौ । सब काहू दे अनही मांग्यौ ।
पुरबासी सबही तहां आये । द्रब लेन कूं आतुर धाये ।
लै लै गये आपणैं धांमां । त्रिहचल एक रह्यौ जंन नांमा ।
बडे साह पूछे तब जाई । अब को रह्यौ नग्र मैं भाई ।

२;३ धनि। धंनि ११; धनि। धंनि ११; नामदेय। नांमदेव ११; तु ४; तू २ ३; साचा। सांचा ४; साचौ २ ३; ग्यारसि। ग्यारिसि २ ३; छाडि। छाडिसि २ ३ ?; होई। होईसी २ ३; होय ४; रहूं। - २ ३; लै ४

३;१ करम। करंम ११; करमि २ ३; रांम ४; धरम। भरमि २ ३; सुमरि ४; बांध्यौ। बाध्यौ २ ३; लै ४; संसारा। त्यागि ४; रांम। पसारा ४; राम २; बिनां। करम ४; सुमिर २ ३; को। धरम ४; लै २ ३; उतरचौ। छाडि २ ३; लागा ४; पारा। पसारा २ ३; संसारा ४

३;२ मिसरि। मिश्री ४; मिश्रि २ ३; मांहि। मांहिं ११; मांझि ४; माहिं २ ३; मीठौं। अंन २ ३; अन ४; मीठौ ११; क्यूं। क्यौ २ ३ ४; मांहि। मांहिं २; मांझि ४; क्यूं। - ४; कांजि २; कांजी ३; काजी। क्यौं २ ३; कांजी ४

४;१ दूजौ। दूजा २ ३; धरम। धरंम ११; करै। करहि २ ३ ४; मति। जिनि २ ३ ४; मांहि। मांझ ४; माहि २ ३; क्यूं। क्यौ ४; क्यौं २ ३; भरंम। षोट २ ३ ४; समांई। षिटाई ४; संमाई ११; षटाई २ ३

४;२ तब। तव ४; तें। तैं २ ३ ११; ते ४; नामदे। नामैं २ ३; नामदेव ४; ग्यारसि। ग्यांरसि ११; ग्यारिसि २ ३; त्रिगुन। जन तैं २ ३; जव ते ४; भगति। किश्न २ ३ ४; निरंतरि। निरतरि ११; गए है ३; गए हैं २; गहें ४; बाढी। षांडी २ ३ ४

५;१ ऐकादसी। ऐकादसि ३; एकादसि २; एकादसी ४; जांणही। जांनही २ ३ ४; भरम। भरंमि ११; भरमि २ ३; भुलांणीं। भूली ४; रहि २ ३; लोइ। सब लोग २ ३; सव लोई ४; लोई ११

५;२ बांध्यौ। बाध्यौ ११; वांध्यौ ४; द्वादसी। द्वादसि २ ३; तातैं। मुकति २ ३ ४; मुक्ति। कहां २ ३ ४; न। की २ ३; ते ४

६;१ एक। ऐक ११; पंडरपुर। पुडरपुर ४; पांडरपुर २ ३; मांहै। मांहैं ११; मांही २ ३ ४; चढचौ। तुला ४; तूला २ ३; तुला। ढाचहो २ ३; चटचौ ४; जांन्यौं। जान्यौं २ ३; जानैं ४; सब। सव ४; काहूं। कांही २ ३; काही ४

६;२ धंम। -- २ ३ ४

६;३ पुरबासी। -- २ ३ ४; लेन। लीन ११

६;४ लै। - २ ३ ४; लै। - २ ३ ४; गये। - २ ३ ४; आपणैं। - २ ३ ४; धांमां। - २ ३ ४; त्रिहचल। टिया २; दिया ३; दीयौ ४; एक। दरवि ४; दरबै २ ३; रह्यौ। सब २ ३; जैसौ ४; जंन। कोई २ ३; जहि ४; नांमा। जानां २ ३ ४

६;५ बडे। पीछै २ ३; वहूस्यौ ४; साह। बोल्या २ ३; तुझ्यौ ४; पूछे। साह २ ३ ४; तब। सयांनां २ ३ ४; जाई। - २ ३ ४; अब। अव ४; रह्यौ। है २ ३; रहै ४; नग्र। नगर २ ३ ४; मैं। मै ३ ४; भाई। भांई ४

कहै रह्यौ ऐक नांमदेव दासा । साह कहै आंणौं मो पासा ।
बिन दिन्हां वो रहै निरासा ।
७ ऐकै कहैत उभै उठि धावैं । तीजै बोलि नांमदेव आवै ।
साह कहै क्यूं बिलब लगाई । तुम सेवग सब के सुषदाई ।
लेहु द्रब यूं उचरै साहूं । हंमारौ धरम सुफल करि जाहूं ।
सोनां ले घर भीतरि धरिहूं । संता की सेवा तुम करिहू ।
नांही कछू तुम्हारै कांमां । हंमारा धम सुफल ह्वै नांमां ।
८ हंम तौ नहीं द्रब के भुषे । इतनी कहत साह सब दूषे ।
यूं जिनि कहौ न ल्यां हंम भाई । बिन लीया मेरी पति जाई ।
लेहुं कछू तौ हौं भल मांनौं । लीयें बिनां भलौ जिनि जांनौं ।
९ जे तुमहु बहूत भावै थोरा । तौ जस रहै नग्र मैं मोरा ।
नांमौं कहै सुनौं हो साहूं । तैं सोनां दीन्हां सब काहू
१० मेरैं लीयें न पुरौ होई । मेरै ष्यालि परै मति कोई ।

६;६ कहै। तब २ ३; तव ४; रह्यौ। नांमदेव ४; नामा २ ३; ऐक। की २ ३ ४; नांमदेव। सुरति ४; षबरी २ ३; दासा। कराई ४; सुनाई २ ३; साह। ल्यावो २ ३; आनहू ४; कहै। भगत २ ३ ४; आंणौं। बेगि २ ३; वेगि ४; मो। मोहि २ ३

६;७ बिन। -- ११; बिण २; विनि ४; दिन्हां। दीया ४; वो। वह ४

७;१ ऐकै। एक २ ३ ४; कहैत। कहत ११; बुलाया २ ३; वुलार्यौ ४; उभै। - २ ३ ४; उठि। देय ४; दोइ २ ३; धावैं। पठाए ४; पठाया २ ३; बोलि। वोलि ४; नांमदेव। नांमदे २ ३; आवै। आए ४; आया २ ३

७;२ साह। -- २ ३ ४

७;३ लेहु। लेहू २ ३ ४; द्रब। दरबि २ ३; दरवि ४; यूं। आदर २ ३ ४; उचरै। करि २ ३; करै ४; साहूं। साहू २ ३ ४; हंमारौ। धरम ४; हंमारा २ ३; धरम। हमारौं ४; सुफल। सफल २ ३; जाहूं। जाहू २ ३ ४

७;४ सोनां। -- २ ३ ४

७;५ नांही। -- २ ३ ४

८;१ हंम। हम ४; नहीं। नही २ ३; नांही ४; द्रब। धरम ४; दरब २ ३; के। का २ ३; भुषे। भुषा २ ३; भूषे ४; इतनी। ईतनी ११; इतनौं २ ३; सब। सव ४; दूषे। दूषा २ ३

८;२ यूं। यौं २ ३ ४; कहौ। करौ २ ३; करौं ४; न। - २ ३ ४; ल्यां। रामजन २ ३ ४; हंम। - २ ३ ४; भाई। भांई ४; बिन। ब़िण २ ३; विन ४; लीया। दीन्हां २ ३; दीनां ४; मेरी। मैरी २ ३

८;३ लेहुं। -- २ ३ ४

९;१ जे। जौ ४; लेहू २ ३; तुमहु। द्रबि २ ३; तुम लेहू ४; बहूत। बहूंत ११; बहौत २ ३; वहोत ४; भावै। अर ४; अरु २ ३; तौ। ज्यौं २ ३: तो ४; जस। जुग २ ३; रहै। माहि २ ३; नग्र। जगत ४; रहै २ ३; मैं। मै ४; जस २ ३; मोरा। मोरां २ ३

९;२ नांमौं। कहत ४; जो न २ ३; कहै। नांमदेव ४; रहौ २ ३; सुनौं। सुनि ४; तौ २ ३; हो। हौ ४; इतनि २ ३; साहूं। करहू २ ३; सांहु ४; तैं। तुम ४; रंचिक ३; रंचित २; सोनां। मेरै २ ३; सौनौ ४: दीन्हां। हू २ ३; दीनौ ४; सब। कर २ ३; सव ४; काहू। धरहू २ ३

१०;१ मेरैं। मेरै ४; हमारे ३; हमारैं २; लीयें। दीयें ४; दाथां ३; दायां २; पुरौ। पूरा २ ३; होई। होय ४; मेरै। हंमारै २ ३; ष्यालि। ष्याल ४; परै। परौ ४; मति। जिनि २ ३

जौ न रहौ तौ इतनी कीजै । दल संमि तुलि हमकु दीजै ।
११ जो हूं कहूं सोई तुम मांनौं । पात ऐक तुलसी कौ आंनौ ।
पात बराबरि जोषौ सोनां । सो हंम लेहि होई तुम पुनां ।
१२ बिमल सेठ बोलै समझाई । इतनैं कौं का माग्यौ भाई ।
तोला बीस तीस किन लैहू । पीछैं हंम कूं दोस न देहू ।
१३ कहत नांमदेव हरि है ऐसा । देषि तमासा करिहै कैसा ।
इतनौं राषौं बोल तुम्हारा । चढै तुला सो होई हंमारा ।
१४ तब तुलसी कौ पात मंगायौ । देषन लोग नगर कौ आयौ ।
पात मांहि लिष्यौ ररंकारा । जामैं सकल बिस्व कौ भारा ।
१५ घालि तराजु तोलन लागा । भयौ अचंभौ सोवत सा जागा ।
सोनां रूपा आनि चढाया । माणिक मोती ले ले धाया ।
१६ बडी तुला मैं ले दल धरिया । तउ न होइ पात समसरिया ।

१०;२ जौ। -- २ ३ ४

११;१ जो। जैसी ४; हूं। बिधि २ ३; विधि हू ४; कहूं। कहो ४; कहौं २ ३; सोई। सोइ २ ३; समांन ४; तुम। बिधि २ ३; हु ४; मांनौं। मानौं २ ३; तौ ४; पात। एक ४: ऐक। पात ४: येक २ ३; तुलसी। तुरसी २ ३; कौ। का २ ३; आंनौ। आंनौं ११; आंनहू ४; आनौं २ ३

११;२ बराबरि। वरावरि ४; जोषौ। जोषहू ४; तोलौ २ ३; सोनां। सौनां ४; सोना २; सो। हंम २ ३: हंम। हम ४; लैहैं २ ३; लेहि। तुम २ ३; लेह ४; होई। कौं २ ३; तुम कौ ४; तुम। ह्वै २ ३; होई ४; पुनां। पुंनां २ ३

१२;१ बिमल। विमल ४; दरब २ ३; सेठ। लेहु २ ३; बोलै। मागि २; मार्गि ३; बोलै ४; समझाई। समझांई ४; बौहताई २ ३; इतनैं। एता ४; ईतनैं ११; इतना २ ३; कौं। कौ ४; का २ ३; का। क्या २ ३; कहां ४; माग्यौ। मागौ ४; माग्या २ ३

१२;२ तोला। तौला २ ३; बीस। पांच २ ३; चारि ४: तीस। पांच ४; सात २ ३; किन। क्यौं न २ ३; किनि ४. लैहू। लेहू २ ३; लेही ४; पीछैं। पीछै ४; हंम। हम २ ३ ४; कूं। कौं २ ३ ४; दोस। दास २ ३; देहू। देहि ४

१३;१ कहत। -- २ ३; ऐसा। अैसा ४ ११; तमासा। तमांसा ४

१३;२ इतनौं। अतनां ११; इतनौ ४; राषौं। राषौ २ ४; बोल। वोल ४; तुम्हारा। तुम्हारौ ४; तुमारौ २ ३; चढै। तुला २ ३; तुला। न सिव ४; चढै २ ३; होई। होइ ४; दरब २ ३; हंमारा। हमारौ २ ३; हमारौं ४

१४;१ तब। तव ४; तुलसी। तुरसी २ ३: कौ। को ११; मंगायौ। मगायौ २ ३ ४; देषन। देषत २ ३; नगर। सहर २ ३; आयौ। आयौं ४

१४;२ मांहि। मै २ ३; मांझ ४; लिष्यौ। लिक्षा २ ३; लीष्यौ ४; जामैं। तामै ४; तामैं २ ३; सकल। तिनि २ ३; तीनि ४; बिस्व। लौक २ ३; लोक ४; कौ। का २ ३

१५;१ घालि। -- २ ३; भयौ। अचिरज ४; अचंभौ। भयौ ४; सा। सव ४

१५;२ सोनां। सोनौ ४; सोना २; रूपा। रूपौ ४; आनि। आंनि ४; ले २ ३; चढाया। चढावा ४; लें २ ३; माणिक। धावैं २ ३; मांणिक ४; मोती। माणिक २ ३; ले। मोति २ ३; ले। आणि ३; आपि २; धाया। धावा ४; चढावै २ ३

१६;१ बडी। वडी ४; मैं। मांहि ४; ले। - ४; जब २ ३; दल। द्रब २ ३; होइ। हो ३; होई ११; होय ४; ही २; समसरिया। समरिया २ ३; सरभरिया ४

दरब चढाया जो घर मांही । पर घर लैंन उधारौ जांही ।
१७ जेता बाण्या न्यूतैं आया । तिनि सब अपणा दरब चढाया ।
दल का पला न धरती छाडै । लोक बेद कौ धरमहि षांडै ।
१८ ता पीछै बोलाई सब नारी । आभुषंण सब लीये उतारी ।
गारी दे दे नारी रोवै । कहा निपूता तूं घर षोवै ।
ये सब दियां साह कैं मागै । झूठा अरध नाम कै आगैं ।
१९ बाजा बाजत बरजैं बनिंयां । मंगल जिनिं गावौ कामनिया ।
कहत नांमदे मन न डुलावो । अपनां अपनां धंम चढावो ।
२० नांमदेव कहि स सबही मांनी । धरम सकल पैं कर धरि पांनी ।
काहूं बांभण लाष जिमाया । काहूं होम पचास कराया ।
२१ काहूं होम नेम ब्रत कीनां । धरम अनेक न जांही चीन्हां ।
काहूं अठसठि तीरथ न्हाया । केई नग्र कोटि ह्वै आया ।

१६:२ दरब। घर २ ३; दरव ४: चढाया। मै २ ३; चढायौ ४; जो। दरब २ ३; घर। सु २ ३; मांही। आंणि २ ३; पर। चढाया २ ३; वहू ४; घर। स्यौ ४; बाहरि २ ३; लैंन। लैन ४: उधारौ। उधारो ४: जांही। धाया २ ३

१७;१ जेता। जित ४; बाण्या। नैवनियां ४; बणियां २ ३: न्यूतैं। न्यूंतें ११; न्यौंतैं २ ३; न्योते ४; तिनि। तिन २ ३ ४; सब। हू ४; तौ २ ३; अपणा। द्रबि २ ३: दरवि ४; दरब। अनत २ ३; वहोत ४

१७;२ का। कौ २ ३; पला। पलौ २ ३; पलान ११; न। धरती ११; धरती। धरति २ ३: न ११; बेद। वेद ४; कौ। कै २ ३, का ४; षांडै। षांडैं ४; षाडै ११

१८;१ ता। तव ४; पीछै। पाछै ३; पाछैं २: बोलाई। बोली २ ३; वाली ४; सब। - ११; सव ४: नारी। नांरी ४; आभुषंण। तिनके ४; अनका ३; उनका २; सब। आभरण २ ३: आभरण सव ४: लीये। धरे ४: धरचा २ ३

१८;२ गारी। गाली २ ३; दे। दै ४; दे। दै ४: नारी। नांरी ४: रोवै। रोवैं २ ३ ४; कहा। कांय २ ३; काहि ४ तूं। तू २ ३ ४; षोवै। षोवैं २ ३

१८:३ ये। -- ११; ए ४; सब। सव ४; दियां। दीया ४: कैं। कै ३ ४; मागै। नागैं ४: अरध। धरम ४: नाम। नांम ४; कै। कैं ४; आगैं। आगै ३

१९;१ बाजा। वाजा ४; बाजत। वाजत ४; बरजैं। वरजे ४; बनिंयां। बंनियां ११; वनिया ४; गंगल। मगल २ ३; जिनिं। जिनि २ ३ ४; गावौ। गावो २ ३ ४; कामनिया। कांमनिंयां २ ३; कांमनिया ४; कामनियां ११

१९;२ कहत। -- २ ३; नांमदे। नामदेव ४; न। मति ४; डुलावो। डुलावों ४; अपनां। अपनौ ४; अपनां। अपनौ ४; धंम। धरम ४; चढावो। चढायौ ११; चढावौ ४

२०;१ नांमदेव। कहै २ ३; कहि। नामदेव २ ३; कही ४; स। सो २ ३; सव ४; सबही। बिधि २ ३: ही ४; मांनी। मानौं २ ३; धरम। करहि ४; करौ २ ३; सकल। संकलप ४; सकलप २ ३; पैं। पानी २ ३: जु ४; कर। - २ ३; लै ४; धरि। - २ ३; लै ४; पांनी। आंनौं २ ३; पांनीं ११

२०;२ काहूं। कांहूं २ ३; काहू ४; बांभण। बांम्हण २: बांभन ३; वाह्मण ४; लाष। लाषं २ ३; जिमाया। जिवांए ४; काहूं। कांहूं २ ३; काहू ४; कराया। कराए ४

२१;१ काहूं। - २ ३; काहू ४, होम। - २ ३; तप ४; नेम। - २ ३; तीरथ ४; ब्रत। - २ ३: दत ४; कीनां। - २ ३; कीना ४, अनेक। अनक ११; न। परै २ ३ ४; जांही। नहि २ ३: नही ४; चीन्हां। चिन्हा ४; चीन्ही ३

२१;२ काहूं। - ४; कांहूं २ ३; अठसठि। - ४; जपतप २ ३; न्हाया। कोन्ही २ ३; केई। - २ ३; नग्र। - २ ३; कोटि। - २ ३; ह्वै। - २ ३; आया। - २ ३

गई कला तब साह षिसांणां । तिन परि बांभण षरा रिसांणां ।
अरध नांऊ समि होई न कोई । धरम सकल पै देषि वै जाई ।
२२ अरध नांउ कै पटंतरै देबै कूं कछु नांहि ।
सकल धरंम रीधि सिधि जिती सब झूठे ह्वै जांई ।
२३ करै डंडौत बहूत मनुहारी । हंम न गति कछू लषी तुम्हारी ।
लेहूं दरब पुनि ह्वै नांमां । तुमकूं चढचौ सु पहुच्यौ रांमां ।
२४ रांम हेति तुम नांही दीन्हां । करो बडाई राम न चीन्हां ।
जे तुम पात बराबरि देता । तौ हंम दरब तुम्हारौ लेता ।
२५ अब वोछा काहे कूं लीजै । दरब तुम्हारा तुम्ह कूं दीजै ।
नांमदेव दल लिया उठाई । जाकै बीठल सदा सहाई ।
बनियां अपना दरब उठाया । अरध नाम का परचा पाया ।

२१;३ गई। गइ २ ३ ४; कला। तुला २ ३; तब। सब २; जव ४; साह। साहं २; षिसांणां। षिसांनां २ ३ ४; तिन। ता २ ३; परि। सौ ४; बांभण। बांभन २ ३; बाह्मन ४; षरा। बहौत २ ३; वहौत ४; रिसांणां। रिसांना ४; रिसांनां २ ३

२१;४ अरध। -- २ ३ ४

२२;१ अरध। -- ४; नांउ। नाम २ ३; पटंतरै। पटतरै २; देबै। देबे २ ३; कूं। कों २ ३; कछु। कछू ११; नांहि। नाहि २ ३

२२;२ सकल। -- ४; धरंम। धरंम अरु ३; धरम अरु २; रीधि। रिधि २ ३; सिधि। सिद्वि २, जिती। सब २ ३; सब। ठि २; झूठी ३; झूठे। ह्वै ३; झूटे २; जांई। जांहि २ ३

२३;१ करै। करि ४; डंडौत। दंडोवत ४; दंडबत २; दंडवत ३; बहूत। मनि ४; मानैं २ ३; बहूंत ११; मनुहारी। मांनीहारी ४; हारी २ ३; हंम। हम ४; न। कछु ४; तौ २ ३; गति। सति २ ३; कछू। न २ ३ ४; लषी। जानी २ ३; तुम्हारी। तुमारी २ ३

२३;२ लेहूं। लेहू ४; दरब। उठाइ ४; द्रबि २ ३; पुनि। उठाइ २ ३; दरव ४; ह्वै। योह २ ३; यह ४; नांमां। नामां २ ३; तुमकूं। जो २ ३ ४; चढचौ। कछु २ ३ ४; सु। पुरयौ सु २ ३; दीजु ४; पहुच्यौ। पुरवै ४; दीयौ २ ३; रांमां। रांमा ४ ११; रामा २ ३

२४;१ रांम। राम २ ४; हेति। दिवायौ २ ३ ४; तुम। कब २ ३; कव ४; नांही। तुम २ ३ ४; दीन्हां। दीन्हौं २ ३; दीनौं ४; करो। करौ २ ३ ४; बडाई। बडाइ २ ३; वडाई ४; राम। रांम ४ ११; चीन्हां। चिन्हौ ४; चीन्हौं २ ३

२४;२ जे। जौ २ ४; जो ३; तुम। तु ४; बराबरि। वरावरि ४; देता। देतौं ४; हंम। हू ४; दरब। दरवि ४; तुम्हारौ। तुमारौ २ ३; लेता। लेतौ ४

२५;१ अब। अव ४; वोछा। वोछौ २ ३; वोछो ४; काहे। काहै ४; कूं। कौ ४; कौं २ ३; लीजै। लेहैं २ ३; लेव ४; दरब। तातै ४; तातैं २ ३; तुम्हारा। तुमरौ ४; तुमारौ २ ३; तुम्ह। तुमही २ ३ ४; कूं। - २ ३ ४; दीजै। देहैं २ ३; देव ४

२५;२ नांमदेव। नामदेव २ ३; तव नांमै ४; लिया। लियौ २ ३; लीयौ ४; उठाई। ऊठाई ११; जाकै। ताकै २ ३; बीठल। केसौ २ ३ ४

२५;३ बनियां। -- ११; वनिये ४; अपना। अपनौ ४; दरब। दरव ४; उठाया। उठायौं ४; नाम। नांम ४; का। कौ ४; परचा। परचौ ४; पाया। आयौं ४

२६ ऐसा परचा बरणौं केता । नांमदेव कूं हरि दीन्हां जेता ।
जहां जहां नांमदेव हरि ध्यायौ । तहां तहां हरि तबही आयौ
२७ दास अनंत कथा कही नांमदेव जस गाइ ।
चेरौ सबही संत कौ चरणां रह्यौ संमाइ ।

२६;१ ऐसा। कैसा २ ३ ४ ११; बरणौं। बरंनौं २ ३; वरनौ ४; केता। कैता २ ३; नांमदेव। नांमां ४; नामा २ ३; कूं। कौ २ ३ ४; हरि। - ११; दीन्हां। दिया २ ३; दीया ४

२६;२ जहां। जे ४; जेता २ ३; जहां। श्रवणा २; मै ४; प्रवण ३; नांमदेव। कांन ४; सुण्ण २; सुण्णा ३; हरि। सुनै ४; तेता २ ३; ध्यायौ। कह्या २ ३; ते ४; तहां। - २ ३; कहै ४; तहां। - २ ३; और ४; हरि। विनां ४; अणसुण्या २ ३; तबही। अबरण्या ३; अबरण्यां २; बर ४; आयौ। नैही ४; रह्या २ ३

२७;१ दास। अनंत ४; दासि २ ३; अनंत। विचार ४; अंनत ११; अनंति २ ३; कथा। करि ४; कही। भगतन ४; नांमदेव। भगतन कौ २ ३; कौ ४; गाइ। गाई २ ३ ११; गाय ४

२७;२ चेरौ। -- २; नांमां ४; नामा ३; सबही। की ३ ४; संत। कीरति ३ ४; कौ। कहि ३; कही ४; चरणां। आगै ४; आगैं ३; चरंणां ११; रह्यौ। और ३ ४

CHAPTER 2

MUSICIANS AND SCRIBES

2.1. *Pad* literature in musical performance

It has been the ambition of modern scholarship to sift the 'authentic' *padas* or songs by the major Sants from the large corpus of manuscripts. The time-honoured method to achieve this has been to trace the ancestry of a corpus in the manuscripts. This method creates many frustrating problems for there was a considerable period of oral transmission before the earliest manuscripts were written down, in cases like those of Kabīr[1] or Nāmdev.

The *padas* of Nāmdev --and other Sants-- have come down to us as songs, to be sung as *bhajans*. We are mistaken if we study them only as poems.

Singing traditions

The early, oral transmission of *padas* probably took place within a tradition of singing, a tradition which was oral in a distinct sense, with characteristics of its own. It is essential that we realize this and look for traces of the singing tradition surviving in the written corpus we have before us. Such traces can be spotted. They give us clues that can help in discovering a pattern, where the traditional method of stemmatic text-editing can see nothing but chaos.

Before we take up an enquiry into what may be called 'musical traces in the written corpus', we outline the history and nature of the singing tradition in India, within which the early *nirguṇ padas* were composed and handed down in the earliest stage of their transmission. An idea of the song tradition in India will be useful for a student of these *padas*, because the song tradition was in many important ways different from the purely literary, poetic tradition: it was, and still is, more oral in its mode of transmission than the poetic tradition.

The affiliation of the *padas* with the singing tradition, which was itself part of a larger musical tradition, is indicated by the following factors:

(a) the connexion of the *padas* with a *rāg*,

(b) the use of a *bhaṇitā*, i.e. the inclusion of the composer's name in the text of the song, usually in the last stanza,

---

(1) At the beginning of Volume I of P. Tivārī's *Kabīr Granthāvalī* (pp. *a,i)*, we find the baffling statement that not even a single *pad* was common to the seven different manuscript traditions of the Kabīr-corpus Tivārī had identified. And only one *pad* was common to six different traditions, though the total number of Kabīr *padas* he found in different manuscripts amounted to 1579.

(c) the use or indication of the *ṭek* (the *dhruva* of older songs) or repeated refrain,
(d) a metrical usage different from that in poetry.

The bhaṇitā

The use of the *bhaṇitā*, or the *chhāp* as it is often called, was peculiar to songs. In old Hindī poetry, however, the *bhaṇitā* was not only used in sung *padas*. It was also given in *muktakas* or poems like the *dohā*, the *kabitta*, the *savaiyā*, etc. These *muktakas* were meant to be poems rather than songs, even though they were, it seems, sometimes sung[2]. How then can we say that the *bhaṇitā* is peculiar to songs? We suggest that the use of the *bhaṇitā* came into Hindī poetry from the singing tradition, where it had been established for centuries, as is testified by Saṅgīta texts. Sanskrit and Prākrit *muktaka* poems never used a *bhaṇitā*. Even the Apabhraṁśa *muktaka*, closer in time to that of Hindī, did not use it. *The Svayambhū-chanda*[3] of Svayambhū and the later *Kavidarpaṇa*[4] quote many *muktakas* in Apabhraṁśa as illustrative of different metres. The poet's name is always given separately.

In the musical tradition, on the other hand, the use of the *bhaṇitā* was an old, established practice. Song composers in this tradition were known as *vāggeyakāras*, literally, 'the creators of texts and music'. A *vāggeyakāra* was expected to enter his name in the body of his text. Manuals of Saṅgīta, (written for *vāggeyakāras* and musicians in general), lay this down as a rule[5].

Nāmdev's padas: prabandhas and the repertoires of gharānās

The musical style or genre in which the *vāggeyakāras* composed was the *prabandha*. It was a rich and flourishing genre from at least the Gupta age down to the 13th or 14th centuries AD. Then it continued in a more or less decaying form till the emergence from it of *dhrupad* and the later *khyāl* styles of current classical music. The *prabandha* was a very large genre, ranging over a wide variety of forms. The distinct forms like *dhrupad, khyāl, ṭhumrī, tappa, ghazal, gīt* and *bhajan* of modern musical practice would in older Saṅgīta usage have all been categorised as different types of *prabandha*.

---

(2) The 17th century *Rāgadarpan* (in Persian) of Faqīrullah lists *kabitta*, along with *khyāl* and *dhrupad*, as one of the major forms of classical songs sung by the musicians of Shāhjahān's court. See *Rāgadarpan*, (published by the Dept. of Persian, Univ. of Delhi), 1981, p. 72 and p. 76. Musicians of the next century, during the days of Muhammad Shah were also fond of singing *kabitta;* see *Muraqq-e-Dehlī*, a contemporary account written by Dargah Qulī Khān (published by the Dept. of Urdu, Univ. of Delhi), pp. 172-203.
Kabitta singing is no longer current. Thus it is difficult to know what connexion the music had with the poetic form.

(3) *Svayambhū-chanda*, (unknown authorship, 10th cent.), ed. by H. D. Velankar and publ. by Rājasthān Oriental Research Institute, Jodhpur, 1962.

(4) *Kavidarpaṇa*, (13th cent.), ed. by H. D. Velankar (publ. by Rājasthān Oriental Research Institute), Jodhpur, 1962.

(5) The Saṅgīta manuals we refer to date from the 8th to the 13th centuries and were obviously written in a tradition going further back.

The old *prabandha* clearly included what today is called *pakkā gānā*, such as the more classical singing of *dhrupad* and *khyāl*, as well as the more popular varieties of songs. The main difference, from a textually-biased point of view, between 'classical' and 'popular' songs is the different kind of attention paid to the *pada*, using the term *pada* in the Paninian sense of 'a meaningful word'. In classical singing, words are a peg on which to hang the music. It is not important that meanings be carefully conveyed to the audience. In popular music, on the other hand, the melody is used as an aid to the text.

The tradition being oral, it is hardly surprising that of the literally thousands of songs that must have been composed over the centuries in the various *prabandhas*, only a handful have come down to us. Examples that survive are either stray quotations or songs which were appreciated for their content as well as for their music[6].

The *padas* of Nāmdev must also have been composed as *prabandhas*, though of a less 'classical' variety, being more word-dominated. Nāmdev lived towards the end of the heyday of the *prabandha*, but the tradition outlived him and was certainly alive in the 15th century when Mahārānā Kumbha wrote his extensive treatise on music, the *Saṅgītarāja*. The *Kānhaḍde Prabandha*, a historical romance in old Rājasthānī or Gujarātī, written in 1445 AD speaks of the singing of *pāṭ-prabandha;* the context makes it clear that the *prabandha* genre is meant *(jānai jeha bhārahasaṅgīta pāḍaprabaṅdha te gāi gītā)*[7]. Nāmdev himself says in a *pad: nāmadeva chīmpyau caupāī gāī* or 'Nāmdev the tailor sings a *caupāī*'[8]. The *caupāī* here is clearly the *catuśpadī*[9], a kind of *prabandha*, distinct from the metrical *caupāī* of Tulsī's *Rāmāyaṇ*. A similar reference to the *ṣaṭpadī*, another *prabandha*, is to be found in a song attributed to Gorakh: *śatapadī bhaṇimlai gorasa avadhūta*[10].

Transmission of songs in the oral tradition --the *guru-śiṣya-paramparā*-- is itself a major institution in India, working at various levels and involving families, even clans, of professional musicians and their *śiṣyas*. There are many *gharānās* of classical musicians, but there are also *gharānās* of traditional *bhajan* or *kīrtan* singers that still exist in certain parts of India.

We suggest that the *padas* of Nāmdev and the early Sants were handed down by such *gharānās* before being recorded in manuscripts. What the

---

(6) Some of the oldest *prabandhas* that survive are the *Caryāgītis* of the Buddhist Tantrika Siddhas. They were recorded for their value as religious-mystic tracts. We have also the *aṣṭapadīs* of Jayadeva's *Gītagovinda*. These were recorded for their poetic value and because they happened to be part of a larger poetic context.
For more information about the *prabandha* links of the *Gītagovinda*, see M. Lāth:1975.

(7) Padmanābha, *Kānhaḍde prabandha*, ed. by Kāntilāl Baidevrām Vyās; Rājasthān Purātattva Mandir, Jaipur 1953, 4, 55 (p. 173).

(8) See below, Ch. 4, poem 105.5a. Other Marāṭhī saints too perhaps contemporary with Nāmdev, had sung *caupadīs* in Hindī. We thus have the Hindī and Marāṭhī *caupadīs* of Ācārya Dāmodar Paṇḍit. For details, see (Dāmodar Pandit,) *Ādya mahārāstrīya hindī kavi Ācārya Dāmodar Paṇḍit aur unkī kavitā*, ed. by Asok Prabhākar Kāmaṭ, Mahārāṣṭra Rāṣṭrabhāṣā Sabhā, Poona, 1967.

(9) Only Ms. *v* reads *copadī* instead of *caupāī*.

(10) *Gorakh-bānī*, Barathvāl:1950, *pad* 2 (p. 88).

earliest manuscripts record are the repertoires of *gharānās*, with songs arranged according to *rāgas*, as is natural in a musical repertoire.

2.2. *Bhajan* singing in the Bhakti milieu

Bhajan as sādhanā

Bhajan and *kīrtan* singing was a great and popular institution during the Bhakti age. Literature speaks again and again of *bhajan* singing lasting throughout the night, for days on end. There is also an indication that there were groups of professional *bhajan* singers. *Bhaktavijaya*, the well-known 18th century Marāṭhī work of the *Bhaktamāl* genre (see above, Ch. 1.2; Mahīpati:1762), speaks of *haridāses*, who appear to have been a class of professional *bhajan* singers.

'I am where my devotees sing', says Viṣṇu to Nārad in a celebrated statement from the Purāṇas. *Bhajan* or singing songs about God or to God was a major mode of *upāsanā* in the Bhakti period. The word *bhajan* is used in two senses, meaning 'song of devotion' as well as 'devotion' itself. Both these meanings are intimately connected with each other. Singing *bhajans* was a vital part of a *bhakta's sādhnā*[11].

As the *bhakti* ideal became more deeply rooted in the social consciousness, institutions were established to uphold, preserve and propagate the ideal. There were numerous *bhakti sampradāyas* and orders, each with its own body of followers. *Bhajan* was cherished by them all. Each had a favourite set of *bhajans* which were closest to their hearts and to their particular kind of *bhakti*. Many *sampradāyas* made written collections of their favourite *bhajans* in order to propagate and preserve them in a more lasting form. It is to this zeal that we owe our earliest records of Santa songs. The process of making written records probably started in the second half of the 16th century. By this time Nāmdev had become one of the most popular among the earlier Sants. In his *Parcaī*, written in 1588 AD. Anantadās notes that Nāmdev is 'the first among *nirguṇ* Sants' (see above, Ch. 1.3).

The *Parcaīs* of Anantadās (written around 1588 AD) are a valuable source for a glimpse into this milieu. The *Parcaīs* describe the lives of Sants celebrated as ideal *bhaktas* in *nirguṇ* circles during or before the days of Anantadās. He gives us many interesting details that can help us to visualize the various activities which *bhakti* circles of his time engaged in or considered worth engaging in. *Bhajan* was one of these. Almost all the *bhaktas* he speaks of are extolled for their *bhajan* singing[12].

Pīpā, the famous *bhakta*, was --in Anantadās's *Pīpā kī Parcaī*-- a king who had given up his kingdom to become a disciple of Rāmānand. He lived as a poor man with his wife Sītā and is often described as singing

(11) The concept of *navadhā-bhakti* (the nine progressive steps on the path of *bhakti)* was common to all *bhaktas, nirguṇ* or *saguṇ*. The first two steps were *śravaṇ* or 'listening to the Lord's greatness' (his deeds, his glory, his grace) and *kīrtan* or 'singing of the Lord'.

(12) For details about the other *Parcaīs* by Anantadās, see our forthcoming edition and English translation of these hagiographies.

bhajans ('*kīrtan*' is the word used by Anantadās). Below we summarize the story of Pīpā.

Once as Pīpā and Sītā walked through a forest "they sang *bhajans*, a lovely pair whom no one would hurt".

They walked to the city of Āvā where they met a man who was in military service. He invited them to his house and "they sang *kīrtans* there".

Later in the story we find Pīpā and Sītā travelling again. They travelled to Divālau where "both of them sang *kīrtans* to a large gathering of merchants, enthralling them with their songs".

One day Pīpā went to see Śrīrang, a *bhakta* who lived in Dausā. He stopped in a park near the town. As news of his arrival reached Śrīrang and the other *bhaktas* living in Dausā, they all decided to meet him and "carrying their drums and their *viṇās* they proceeded towards the park, dancing and singing all the way". What they sang were surely, *bhajans*.

In a later episode we find Pīpā in a village where he was not welcome. He was allowed to live in a ruined hut. There he and his wife Sītā began to sing *bhajans*, rapt in God. Their singing attracted one of the villagers who, being accused of murder, had run away from the village and lived in hiding. He became a *bhakta*.

Similarly,Kabīr, Dhanā and Raidās too were fond of *bhajan* singing, as is evident from the biographical accounts written by Anantadās.

Mahotsav

Socially, one of the most important expressions of *nirguṇ bhakti* was the *mahotsav*. This was a huge celebration, spread sometimes over a number of days, in which feasts and festivities were arranged for *sādhus* and *bhaktas*. *Bhajan* singing was essential in a *mahotsav*. Nothing can illustrate better the importance given to such a festivity than this episode from Raidās's life, as told by Anantadās. We summarize the account.

Raidās was a simple man, a devoted *bhakta* since childhood. When he grew to manhood, his family gave him his share of the joint property and asked him to set up a separate home for himself. He had to live at the back of the small family house *(bakhari)*. He began practising his ancestral trade as a cobbler and continued his worship of Hari with great devotion and purity of soul. Moved by his poverty, Hari Himself came to him in the guise of a *bhakta* and offered him a *pāras* stone which could turn base metal into gold. Raidās refused to accept it, arguing that wealth destroys *bhakti*. Hari pointed out that wealth was necessary for organizing *mahotsavas*. Raidās was not convinced and asked 'why don't you organise *mahotsavas* yourself?' Hari persisted and, finally, as he left, he hung the *pāras* stone to a beam that supported the thatching over Raidās's cottage. Raidās did not refuse the *pāras* stone, but he never used it. A year later, Hari came back in the same guise, and rebuked Raidās for his stubbornness. 'Hari's name is my *pāras* stone' was

Raidās's answer. Hari was forced to take back His *pāras* stone. However, He did not give up and He appeared to Raidās in a dream, offering to give him five hundred gold coins every day. The money was for the service of *bhaktas*. This time, Raidās accepted the gift and with his miraculously acquired wealth, he made arrangements for a continuous *mahotsav*. He erected spacious buildings where numerous *bhaktas* were lavishly lodged and feasted. *Kīrtans* were held continuously. The whole town flocked to see the wondrous spectacle.

Pīpā too was fond of arranging *mahotsavas*. Anantadās speaks of one for which messengers were sent to invite *bhagats* from far and wide. The *mahotsav* he organised seems to have been a large *bhakti* fair, spread over a huge area: there were many groups singing *bhajans* 'in different corners'.

Even Kabīr is said to have organised a great *mahotsav*, where many *bhaktas* gathered. Some 'danced and some sang'[13]. No doubt they sang *bhajans*.

We also find interesting references to *mahotsavas* in the *Dādū Janma Līlā* of Jangopāl, written soon after Dādū's death (in 1603 AD), i.e. a few decades after the *Parcaīs* of Anantadās. Jangopāl was a disciple of Dādū and he stayed in close contact with the saint during the latter part of his life, which was spent in Rājasthān. The *Janma Līlā* is available in two versions. The earlier version is much less legendary than the *Parcaīs* of Anantadās. Jangopāl tells us of many *mahotsavas*, organised by Dādū's followers to welcome him, as he travelled to meet his disciples living in different towns and villages of Rājasthān[14].

Jangopāl reports an old story *(ādu kathā)* recording, apparently, an incident he had heard from other followers of Dādū, but which occurred long before he himself joined their number. It is said that Dādū had been present at seven different *mahotsavas*, organised simultaneously in his honour by different *bhaktas*[15].

The celebrated saint-poet Rajab, who lived as a *sanyāsī* before he became a disciple of Dādū, urged Dādū to visit him at his village and he too arranged a big *mahotsav*[16].

The biggest *mahotsav* described by Jangopāl was the one organised by Garībdās, Dādū's son and successor, soon after Dādū's death. It lasted for a whole month. Every Dādū follower attended it. The house-holders contributed whatever they could. Lavish meals were served to everyone present. *Bairāgis* who preferred to cook their own meals were given as much rice, lentils, wheat, ghee and sugar as they desired. Jangopāl adds that during the *mahotsav*, '*bhajan* singing continued incessantly, day and

(13) We find a reference to *mahauchā* in the *Kabīr Parcaī*, vv. 2.11; 3.1; 10.4; 10.10-11.

(14) The quotations are from the new edition of the *Dādū Janma Līlā*, Callewaert:1988 Jangopāl speaks of many *mahotsavas* organised by his disciples, including those by Govindadās, 13.13; Raisingh Kacchvāhā, 13.22; the younger Gopāl, Tīlā and Chītar, 14.6; the Rāthorī queen Kanaksutā 14.7-8; the seven-day *mahotsav* organised by Kārū, Kūmbhā and Nārāyan 14.14; Cain, 14.16; Jagjīvan, 14.24; Dāmodar of Andhi, 14.28; and Caturbhuj, Rāmdatt and Khemdās 14.32.

(15) *Ibidem*, 3. 18-21.

(16) *Ibidem*, 13.7f.

night *(rāti divas kīratan hoī)*'[17]. Garībdās himself must have participated in the *bhajan* singing for he is described as a fine musician. an expert in singing and playing the *vīṇā*. Dādū too was fond of singing *bhajans*. When he was young, he often sang *padas* in a temple. He appears to have attracted large crowds of listeners; this angered the Qāzī and other Muslims of his town.

Professional musicians

Jangopāl describes an interesting episode during one of Dādū's journeys through Rājasthān:

> As he travelled he met a band of singers *(gāin)* who showed him great respect. Bowing low with reverence they stood around him in a group. Dādū too responded to their attention and, as Jangopāl says, 'made them happy *(svāmī sukh dīnau)*'. 'They walked with him for a long way, stopping and revering him whenever he rested.' (9.14)

These were, obviously, professional musicians, belonging to one of those hereditary clans of musicians still numerous in Rājasthān. Jangopāl speaks of their meeting with Dādū as a fleeting one, such as those of wayfarers: they were, he reports, quite spontaneously enchanted by Dādū's personality and could not help following him for some distance, paying their respect to his saintliness.

This particular meeting between Dādū and a band of travelling musicians may have been a fleeting one, but, certainly, their role as professional musicians was important in the life of Dādū and his followers. They must have been invited often by Dādū and his followers to sing *bhajans* for them, especially on the occasion of *mahotsavas*.

Professional musicians are experts in moulding their art and their repertoire to suit the demands of the audience. It is reasonable to imagine that their services were called for -and paid for- in many of the *mahotsavas* which, from the evidence noted above, seem to have been so common during the days of Anantadās and Jangopāl. Yet these writers do not actually mention the presence of any professional class of *bhajan* singers.

Such a class is explicitly mentioned by Mahīpati, the late 18th century author of the *Bhaktivijaya*, a well-known Marāṭhī collection of the lives of saints (see Ch. 2.2, Mahīpati:1762). Mahīpati speaks of the institution of *haridāses*, professional musicians who sang *kīrtans* for payment. Mahīpati strongly disapproved of the practise of accepting payment for performing *kīrtan* and he has expressed his disapproval in a story about Kamāl, Kabīr's son, who is said to have been a great *kīrtan* singer.

> At the age of seven Kamāl set out on a pilgrimage, visiting sacred places. Whenever he came to a town the townspeople, seeing him, would take him into the town with marks of honour. He would

(17) *Ibidem*, 16.11.

remain there all night and perform *Hari-kīrtan*[18]. Once during his journeys, he came to the town of Chitrakut, where a merchant, a pious devotee of God called Viṣṇudās, invited him to his home, gave him a good meal and 'for the night a *Hari-kīrtan was* arranged, and all the people of the town assembled.' At the end of the *kīrtan*, the merchant wanted to make an appropriate present to Kamāl. Since he knew Kamāl would not accept money, he offered him a diamond. Kamāl, like any wealth-shunning *bhakta*, naturally refused to accept it. The merchant tied the diamond to a corner of Kamāl's garments as he left. Kamāl was unaware of his rich possession and when he returned home, the diamond was discovered by Kabīr, who accused his son of 'selling the name of Rām' for personal profit. A greater sin than this does not exist. Kamāl at once went back to the merchant and returned the diamond[19].

Such a strong disapproval of one who accepts money for singing *kīrtans* certainly implies that there were people who did make a living in this manner. Why else such strong censure? In fact, Mahīpati does speak of professional *bhajan* singers, the *haridāses*, though sometimes in ways that belittle them. He relates one exemplary story.

> Once there was a *haridās* from Pandharpur who wanted to go to Lohagaon for a month-long festival to be held in that town so that he could make money singing *kīrtans*. But as he was preparing for his journey, a merchant told him that the famous *bhakta* Tukā was in Lohagaon and had been singing *kīrtans* every day, for a month. The *haridās* was disheartened and said, 'I must not go into Lohagaon at all. Where the *kīrtan* of the God-loving (Tukā) is being performed, there the people will not like my skill. A patient will never accept a medicine when he can obtain divine nectar.'
> Later in the story, Tukā sees to it that a good sum of money is donated to the *haridās* and that he is properly honoured, but not before Mahīpati has made his point[20].

Although the *haridāses* were less respected, when compared to true, disinterested *bhaktas*, Mahīpati did commend them as an institution. For, after all they sang praises of Hari and if what they offered was not 'nectar', it was good 'medicine'. It was something that created the right atmosphere for *bhakti* and helped to spread the message of *bhakti*.

We may, in this context, quote the story about Uddhav Chidghan, a *bhakta* from Dharur, who 'went from country to country lovingly performing *kīrtans*'. Chidghan was not a *haridās*. One day, he was invited to be present at the Rāmanavamī festival; for the performance of the *kīrtan* so-called 'Vaiṣṇav performers' were invited. They were *haridāses*. These *haridāses*, Mahīpati relates, moved in a procession singing their songs and passed a mosque on the way. This enraged some Muslims who beat the *haridāses* and broke their musical instruments.

(18) Mahipati:1762, Vol.I, p. 95.
(19) *Ibid.*, Vol.I, pp. 98-99.
(20) *Ibid.*, Vol. II, pp. 283-288.

This ill-treatment of the *haridāses* angered Hanumān, the great *bhakta* and companion of Lord Rām Himself. He pulled the mosque down; the Muslim culprits were buried under the ruins. This miracle was reported to the Muslim king who apologized to Chidghan, asking him to proceed with the performance of his festival without any fear[21].

Even more than his predecessors, Mahīpati considered *bhajan* (or *kīrtan*, the word which he, like Anantadās, uses) as an essential part of a life devoted to *bhakti*. There is a well-known story about Nāmdev, in which the power of his *bhakti* is said to have made a temple --and the Lord's image installed in it-- turn towards him when some Brahmans, despising Nāmdev for his caste, forced him to sit at the back of the temple. Mahīpati has a similar story. He speaks of Nāmdev's visit to the Shaiva temple of Nāganātha where early in the morning he began to sing *kīrtans* before the image of Lord Shiva. The Brahman priests of the temple forced him to stop his 'infernal noise' and he had to retire to the back of the temple. A large audience of rapt listeners followed him there and, in the words of Mahīpati:

> 'Just then a most extraordinary thing happened. Nine hundred thousand banners came down from heaven like lightning and suddenly stood upright where the *kīrtan* was being performed. They were not merely nine hundred thousand flags; they were the fruit of the nine forms of *bhakti;* or as if the nine *rasas* becoming personified entered the *kīrtan* performance'.
> Even the temple which had been facing east turned towards Nāmā, for 'hearing Nāmā's *kīrtan* the Husband of Pārvatī, together with the temple, turned their faces to the west and listened with love'.
> In another story, Krishna Himself joins Nāmdev's *kīrtan* as a cymbal-player, since Nāmdev was without a helper on that day[22].

Almost every *bhakta* in Mahīpati's story is a devoted and accomplished *kīrtan* singer. Mahīpati valued *kīrtan* so highly that he lets Raidās justify his 'low' profession of working with leather with these words: 'musical instruments and drums are used in the praise-service of Hari. One has never seen any of them without their being connected with leather'[23].

2.3. The *geyavikāras*

The term *geyavikāra* (or 'change brought about by a singer') is modelled after *sāmavikāra* of Vedic times; it was coined in a tradition which gave much attention to textual transformations due to singing. *Vikār* or *vikriti* ('transformation' or 'modification') implies a knowledge of *prakriti* or the 'unmodified form'. In the case of the songs of Nāmdev we only know the 'modified forms'. The true form, the words originally

(21) *Ibid.*, Vol. II pp. 362-366. Other references to *haridāses* in Mahīpati are: Vol.I, p. 21; p. 261; Vol.II, p. 208.

(22) *Stories of the Indian Saints*, Mahīpati:1762, Vol.I, p. 385.

(23) *Ibid.*, Vol.I, p. 403-404.

uttered by the poet, remain unknown. Yet we manage to define certain forms as modified, because they differ from what the similarity in many manuscripts suggests. Also, these modifications are *geya* or introduced by the singers, not by scribes.

We noted several kinds of singer's modifications: inversion of *antarās*, addition of short phrases or syllables, fillers, 'additions' and the different approaches to the refrain *(ṭek)*. Since the musical tradition in Panjāb was different from that in Rājasthān (see below, Ch. 2.6 and 2.7), these *geyavikāras* are most obvious when we compare these two traditions. We shall also demonstrate (Ch. 2.8) how the Nāth manuscripts *c* and *j* are distinct from the other repertoires. This distinction is clearly seen also in the *antarā* order of many songs quoted in them. Especially manuscripts *c* and *j*, and the *Guru Granth*, stand apart when compared with the 'standard' Rājasthānī Mss. In several songs the *Guru Granth* has an *antarā* (like an *udgrāha)* before the refrain or *rahāv*.

a) *Inversion of antarās and lines*

Each single song (of Nāmdev) is a musical and textual unit and this unit is the basis for textual considerations. 'Language' cannot be a satisfactory basis, as in traditional text-editions. The songs are often found in collections, but these collections cannot form a satisfactory basis for drawing 'textual' conclusions. Further, the order in which these songs are classified differs immensely in the records now at hand. The only factor which binds songs together is the classification under a particular *rāg*. But even this often varies. Consequently each individual song has to be considered as a separate unit.

Performed as music, the formal structure of a song is musical. It consists of a *ṭek* or *rahāv*, which is followed by *antarās* In the *Guru Granth* the *antarās* are called *pade*, like *dupade, cauṗade, asaṭpadī* etc. We do not use this term because *pad* also refers to a *bhajan*[24].

One of the most common *geyavikāras* is the (dis)order of the *antarās*. Only a few illustrations of variations are discussed here. For more details we refer to Appendix I.

Song 58 (all under *rāg gaur*, except Rajab *Sarvāṅgī.: ṭoḍī)*

standard	c/j	*GG*	Raj. *Sarvāṅgī*
		2a[25]	
ṭek	*ṭek*	*rahāv*	*ṭek*
1	2	2	1
2	1	1	2
3	3	3	2b
			3

(24) The term *antarā* is not a recent term, although it is not frequently used in Santa manuscripts and not at all in the *Guru Granth.* We find it on p. 119-120 of the Fatehpur Manuscript (see Ch. 2.4). In that manuscript the *ṭek* is not always marked as such, although the *antarā* section is at times separated from it.

(25) The numbers 2a and 2b indicate that *different antarās* have been added in the two repertoires.

Although an *antarā* is 'added' in the *Guru Granth* and in the Rajab *Sarvāṅgī*, we find the *bhaṇitā* or poet's name in the *antarā* which comes in the last position. This last *antarā* seems to function like an *ābhoga*. This last part of the composition in old *prabhandhas* was supposed to give the name of the composer[26]. The association of the composer's name with the *ābhoga* was so strong that in the *gadyaprabandha* where Sāraṅgadeva does not explicitly say that the part where the composer was to be named was the *ābhoga*, his commentator Kallinātha assumes this to be the case[27].

Song 91 is one of the oldest of Nāmdev's songs. It has many recensions, including one in the *GG*. The relations among the recensions are complex. It is difficult to decide on a specific order of *antarās*, because there is such a variety in the order of semantic units. In order to illustrate the five different recensions, we quote in Hindī.

c/j

छाडि छाडि रे मुगध नर कपट न कीजै ।
गोबिद नारायण नाम मुषांह लीजै ।। टेक
बनारसी तप करे। पलटि तीरथ मरै ।
काया साधि अग्नि कलेस करै ।
असमेद जगि कीजै ।
रांम रांम रांम समि तउ न तुलै ।। १
कोटि जौ तीरथ करै। तन जो हिवालै गलै ।
गोमती संगम गउ सहस्र दीजै ।
गया जो कुरूषेत न्हइये ।
स्यंघ जो गोदावरी जइये ।
रांम रांम रांम सगि तउ न तुलै ।।२।।
असुदान गजदान (/) कन्यादान भोमिदान ।
नारी सहित ग्रिहदान दीजै ।
तन तुला तोलि दीजै ।
मन जो निरमल कीजै ।
रांम रांम रांम सरि तउ न तुलै ।।३।।
जम्महि न दीजै दोस । मनुहं न कीजै रोस ।
निरषि निरबाण पद मुषा लीजै ।
रांम नाम निज सार ।
जन भजि पावै पार ।
भनत नामदेव अम्रित पीजै ।।४।।

छाड़ि छाडि रे मुगध नर कपट न कीजै ।
गोबिन्दा नारायण नाम मुषा लीजै ।। टेक
कोटि जो तीरथ करै। तन जौ हिवालै गले ।
प्रिथी सकल प्रदछन दीजै। करवत कासी में लीजै
सिव कूं जे सीस दीजै ।
राम राम राम सरि तउ न तुलै ।।१।।
बाणारसि तप करे। पलटि तीरथ फिरै ।
काया जे अगनि मुषि कलेस कीजै ।।
हिरणग्रभ दान दीजै। अस्वमेद जज्ञ कीजै ।
राम राम राम सरि तऊ न तुलै ।।२।।
मान जौ सरोवर जइये गया जौ कुरषेत न्हइये ।
गोमती सनान गऊ कोटि दान दीजै ।
सिघहस्त गोदावरी न्हइये ।
राम राम राम सरि तऊ न तुलै ।।३।।
अस्वदान गजदान (/) भोमिदान कन्यादान ।
ग्रिहदान सिज्यादान दान दीजै ।
तन तुला तोलि दीजै। मन जो नृमल कीजै ।
राम राम राम सरि तऊ न तुलै ।।४।।
जमहि न दीजै दोस। मनहि न कीजै रोस ।
निरषि निब्रांण पद रामनाम लीजै ।
आतमां अंगि लगाइ। सेविलै सहज भाइ ।
भणत नामंइयौ छीपौ अम्रित पीजै ।।५।।

r/g/p

छाडि छाडि रे मुगध नर कपट न कीजै ।
गोबिंदा नारायण नाम मुषां लीजै ।

a/m

छाडि छाडि रे मुगध नर कपट न कीजै ।
गोब्यंद नारायण नाव मुषां लीजै ।। टेक

---

(26) Such was the rule in the large body of *prabandhas* called *Elā: ..'ābhogastadantaram / geyo vāggeyakāreṇa svābhidhānavibhuṣitaḥ*. See *Saṅgīta Ratnākara*, 4,38; Adyar ed., vol. 11, p. 217. In *Karaṇa*, another large body of *prabandhas*, a similar rule was followed: *ābhogstatra nāma syādgātrnetroḥ* .. *Ibidem*, 4,134; see also 4,201; 5,226; 4,262-263.

(27) See Kallinātha on *Saṅgīta Ratnākara*, 4, 184-198; Adyar edition vol. 11, p. 274.

d/v

कोटि जो तीरथ करे। तन जौ हिवालै गले ।
रांम रांम रांम सरि तऊ न तुलै ।। टेक
कोटि जो तीरथ करै ।
वाराणसी तप करै। पलटि तीरथ मरै ।
काया जे अगनि मुषि कलेस कीजै ।
हिरण्यगरभ दांन दीजै। अस्वमेधा जगि कीजै ।
रांम रांम रांम समि तऊ न तुलै ।।१।।
मान सरोवरि जाइये। गया जो कुरषेत न्हइये ।
गोमती अश्नांन गउ कोटि दीजै ।
कुंभ जो केदारि जइये। सिंघहस्त गोदावरी न्हइये ।
रांम रांम रांम समि तउ न तुलै ।।२।।
अस्वदांन गजदांन (/) भोमिदांन कन्यांदांन ।
ग्रिहदान सिज्या दीजै। तन तुला तोलि दीजै ।
मन जौ त्रिमल कीजै ।
रांम रांम रांम सरि तउ न तुलै ।।३।।
जमहि न दीजै दोस। मनहि न कीजै रोस ।
निरषि त्रिबाण पद रांम लीजै ।
आतमां अंगि लगाई। सेविलै सहज भाइ ।
भणत नांमइयौ छीपौ अम्रित पीजै ।।४।।

कोटि जौ तीरथ करे। तन जौ हिवाले गले ।
राम राम राम समि तउ न तुलै ।।१।।
बानारसी तप करै। पलटि तीरथ फिरै ।
काया जे अगनि मुषि कलेस कीजै ।
हिरनगर्भ दान दीजै। असुमेद जगि कीजै ।
राम राम राम समि तउ न तुलै ।।२।।
मांन जौ सरोवर जइये गया जौ कुरषेत न्हाइये ।
गोमती अस्नांन गउ कोटि दीजै ।
कुंभ जौ केदार जइये। सिंघहस्त गोदावरी न्हइये
राम राम राम सरि तउ न तुलै ।।३।।
अस्वदांन गजदांन (/) भोमिदान कन्यांदान ।
ग्रिहदांन सिज्यादान दीजै ।
तन तुला तोलि दीजै। मन जौ नृमल कीजै ।
राम राम राम सरि तउ न तुलै ।।४।।
जमहि न दीजै दोस। मनहि न कीजै रोस ।
निरषि त्रिबांण पद राम लीजै ।
आतमां अंगि लगाइ। सेविलै सहज भाइ ।
भणत नामंइयौ छीपौ अम्रित पीजै ।।५।।

GG

बनारसी तपु करै उलटि तीरथ मरै
अगनि दहै काइया कलपु कीजै ।
असुमेध जगु कीजै सोना गरभ दान दीजै
राम नाम सरि तऊ न पूजे ।।१।।
छोडि छोडि रे पाखंडी मन
कपट न कीजै ।
हरि का नाम नित नितहि लीजै ।। रहाव
गंगा जौ गोदावरी जाइये। कुंभि जौ केदार न्हाइये।
गोमती सहस गऊ दानु कीजै ।
कोटि जौ तीरथ करै। तनु जौ हिवाले गरै ।
राम नाम सरि तऊ न पूजै ।।२।।
असुदान गजदान सिहजा नारी भूमिदान ।
ऐसो दान नित नितहि कीजै ।
आतमच जौ निरमाइल कीजै ।
आप बराबरि कंचनु दीजै ।
राम नाम सरि तऊ न पूजै ।।३।।
मनहि न कीजै रोसु। जमहि न दीजै दोसु
निरमल निरबाण पदु चीन्हि लीजै ।
जसरथ राइ नन्दु राजा मेरा रामचन्द्र प्रणवै नामा
ततु रसु अम्रितु पीजै ।।४।।

Song 99 is found in all repertoires, and under the same *rāg;* it has 4 four-line *antarās*. In the B. Miśra:1964 edition it has 7 *antarās*, copied from later manuscripts. Interestingly, the additional *antarā* after *antarā* 1 in the Miśra edition is also found in Ms. *a* and *c/j*, with slight variations. The order of *antarās* too is not uniform, although the readings are quite similar in all repertoires:

standard	a, c/d	GG
-	-	2
ṭek	*ṭek*	*rahāv*
1	1	3
2	1a	-
3	2	1
4	4	4

Song 131, in which a miracle by Nāmdev is mentioned, seems to be old in the tradition. It is found in all repertoires, except for the Rajab *Sarvāṅgī (rāg kānaḍā;* and *malār* in the *Guru Granth).* The *GG* has a different text for the first 2 lines of the third *antarā.* This song is also found in the Fatehpur Ms., where these two lines have a text similar to the *GG.* The whole song in the Fatehpur Ms. is close to the reading in the *GG.*

In the manuscripts of the 18th c., quoted in Miśra:1964, we find an additional *antarā* in song 138, not found in any of the 17th century Mss. In song 140 we find *antarā* 1 as *udgrāha* in the *Guru Granth.* Further, *antarā* 3 is revealing: it is missing from Ms. *m,* while the other Rājasthānī Mss. give two different readings. One of these readings (in Ms. *p)* is similar to the version in the *Guru Granth.*

Being an *ārati,* song 144 (with 5 *antarās)* must have been an old song, performed on many occasions when Nāmdev's songs were sung. The difference in order --when compared with our 'standard'-- is remarkable because it is seen in two *Pañcavāṇī* Mss. *and* in the *Sarvāṅgīs.* Mss. *c/j* drop *antarā* 3 and the order of *antarās* is: 2, 1, -, 4, 5. In Ms. *p* too *antarā* 3 is omitted but the standard order is maintained. The order in the Gopāldās *Sarvāṅgī* is 1, 3, 2, 4, 5 and in the Rajab *Sarvāṅgī* it is 1, 2, 4, 3, 5. Indeed one wonders if we can speak of a 'standard' order here.

Song 145 is another *ārati.* In the manuscripts which are recorded in Miśra:1964, two additional *antarās* are given; in Ms. *d,* --the oldest Dādūpanthi manuscript,1636 AD-- *antarā* 3 is omitted.

b) *Tāl and āvarta*

The evidence in the section above suggests that each *antarā* in a Santa song could have a life of its own. Within the song it could be moved about, dropped or added as an independent unit. This does not surprise us, for it happens even today in both classical performances and in lighter forms like the *bhajan.* An important question for the text-critic dealing with various versions of the same song is: was the *antarā* the smallest unit that could be moved about?

In songs 94 and 136 --songs with four-line *antarās*-- we see that half *antarās,* consisting of two lines, have been moved about. In other songs half *antarās* were dropped or replaced by an entirely different reading. In songs 91[28] and 206 even smaller units --of a single line-- have been moved about.

Since we are dealing with songs we have to ask: what is it in the musical structure that makes the movement of these textual units possible? For this we must consider the notions of *tāl* or rhythmic cycles and of *āvarta* or 'the single *tāl* cycle', which is the smallest unit of the *tāl.* In our manuscripts only the *rāg* is given, not the *tāl,* although it must be assumed, since *bhajans* are always sung to *tāl.* Usually a simple

(28) See above, p. 65.

tāl is used, one which is suitable for songs where the words dominate rather than the music.

The emergence of *tāl* in Indian music seems to be contemporary with the beginning of *prabandhas;* since then it has remained a dominant feature in all Indian music, both light and classical, profane or devotional. *Tāl* is especially important in text-oriented forms, like *bhajans.* A *tāl* is a patterned cycle of beats repeated again and again for the entire duration of a song. Changing the number of beats in a *tāl* or the pattern of arrangement, also changes the *tāl.* Changing the *tāl* during the performance of a song is rare, especially in the performance of *bhajans.* This is clearly seen in Hindī *bhajan* singing today.

The number of beats to which different *tāl* cycles can be patterned is theoretically limitless. In practice, however, we find only a few *tāls,* those with 5, 6, 7, 8, 10, 12, 14 or 16 beats. The reason is that *tāl* is not mere rhythm, although it is built upon it. Rhythm is inherent in the way we group a series of beats; *tāl* is not. *Tāl* uses basic rhythmic structures for more complex formations. Our sense of rhythm distributes beats into two simple and basic clusters: clusters of 2 --or more often 4-- beats and clusters of 3 beats. These are known in Indian musicological literature as *yugma* (even) and *ayugma* (odd) clusters.

We can have a *tāl* of 5, 6 or 8 beats, a combination of two *yugmas* or of a *yugma* and an *ayugma,* put together in such a way as to give a complex structure appearing as a whole. This can be done in a number of ways. On a drum it can be done through a skilful patterning of the beats. A simple, common way is to achieve it through accentuation: if two clusters are combined, one is stressed, the other is not. In the jargon of modern Hindustānī music, this is to render one cluster *bhari* (heavy) and the other *khālī* (light, empty). Stress can be obtained through light or heavy strokes on the drum, by clapping the hands or on a cymbal, a *jhānjh* or *majīrā,* through the use of 'closed' or 'open' sounds. A *tāl* of 8 beats can be obtained by combining two clusters of 4 beats, making one *bhari* and the other *khālī.* Clusters of 2 beats are used only to combine *yugma* with *ayugma* structures, as in a *tāl* of 5 beats, which can be patterned either as a combination of 3+2 or as 2+3, one of these clusters (either 2 or 3) being *bhari,* the other *khālī.* The simpler *ayugma tāl* of 6 beats can be similarly obtained by combining two *ayugmas* (3+3 beats), keeping one *bhari* and the other *khālī.* Larger *tāl* structures are obtained by combining more than two *yugma* or *ayugma* units (or a mixture of these). A 16 beat *tāl* --very popular in North-Indian practice and evidently the most common with our singers-- of Santa songs is obtained by combining 4 clusters of 4 beats[29] each. The third cluster is

(29) In his Introduction to the *Chandonnuśāsana of Hemacandra* (Bhāratīya Vidyā Bhavan, Bombay, 1961), p. 16, H.D. Velankar has appropriately named such clusters of 4 beats *'tāl-gaṇas'.*
Bhola Śaṅkar Vyās (see *Prākṛt Paiṅgalam,* publ. by the Prākrit Grantha Pariṣad, 1962; Part II, p. 336f.) discusses Velankar's notion of *tāl-gaṇa* and speaks also of *tāl-gaṇas* of 5, 6 and 7 beats, associating them with the *tālas* to which they are sung. Most prosodists do not mention *tāl-gaṇas.* Vyās (pp. 349, 447) refers to one exception: *Dalapata Piṅgala* (Gujarātī), in which the connexion between *tāl* and metre are described in detail.

made *khālī*. This still leaves room for ambiguity and does not tell us where the *tāl* begins. The ambiguity can be removed by adding extra stress on the first beat, which is called the *sam*. After every full cycle, the *tāl* returns to this very important beat. The *sam* is not only the first beat; it is important to note that it is also the final beat to which all other beats lead. A complete movement, from one *sam* to the next is called an *āvarta*.

This full cycle of a *tāl* is the smallest unit in a song and we argue that we are able to discover the *āvarta* in the text of a song, even without having access to the singing tradition in which it was sung. The texts often reveal the *tāl* appropriate for it.

Let us look at song 7. Almost every line of the song has a 16 *mātrā* structure, easily to be divided into *yugma* clusters of 4 *mātrās*. If we take one *mātrā* to indicate one beat, every line can smoothly fit in an *āvarta* of 16 *mātrās*. Thus every line is a semantic and meaningful unit and the *āvarta* seems to be a unit that can be repeated on its own.

S I I/S S/S I I/S S
रांम स नांमां नांमही रांमां ।
S S/I I S/S I I/ S S
तू साहिब मैं सेवग स्वांमां ।
I I I I/I I I I/I I I I/S S
हरि सरवर जन तरंग कहावै ।
S I I/I I I I/I I I I/S S
सेवग हरि तजि कहु कत जावै ।

However, we cannot be certain that song 7 was actually sung to an *āvarta* of 16 *mātrās*. It could have been 8 or even 4 *mātrās*. All we can say is that it has a dominant 4 *mātrā* pattern, called *caturasra* or a 'square pattern' --the dominant pattern in most of Nāmdev's songs. But we cannot conclude that the *line* was the unit of an *āvarta*.

This takes us to the importance of the phenomenon found in songs 91 and 206, where single lines are given in different places in the different repertoires. They correspond to the minimum length of an *āvarta*, the smallest unit that can be repeated on its own. Musicians *can* --if they feel that this does not really change the song, its sentiment or message-- move it from one place to another. And this *has* happened in some --not many-- of our songs, as the variant readings preserved in the manuscripts demonstrate. In song 91, we clearly see the independence of single-line units, although the metric structure of the 'independent' lines does not give an insight into the beat-structure of the *āvarta*. For this we should look at the structure, not from the *varṇa-mātrika*, but from the *akṣara-mātrika* viewpoint, counting every *varṇa* as a beat. This should give a coherent *āvarta.*

The three versions of song 206 (see Ch. 5) reveal the independence of the line as a unit. The song has a clear *caturasra* division of 4 *mātrā* clusters, although most lines have a total of 15 *mātrās,* the fourth cluster having 3 instead of 4 *mātrās.* The line must have been sung to 16 and not 15 *mātrās.* The last 2 *mātrā* syllable -- a long vowel-- can easily be stretched to a *pluta* (a syllable stretched to 3 *mātrās),* making it a smooth 16 *mātrā* line. The *caturasra* flow of the lines requires a 16 *mātrā āvarta,* as the metre seems to suggest. In singing, a *pluta* is a common phenomenon; it does not disturb the meaning of a word and gives variety in the cadence. We find it in quite a few songs of Nāı .dev.

Song 231 is found in the repertoires reflected in Ms. *a* and in the Fatehpur manuscript (see below, Ch. 5). Only 2 lines have changed places, without disturbing the song. If these segments could be moved from one place to another by a singer, they must have formed an independent *āvarta.* The lines which give the *āvarta* here are 13 *mātrā* lines, distributed in a *caturasra* pattern. In the song as a whole we see that the 13 *mātrā* lines are followed by 12 *mātrā* lines. If the *āvarta* had 14 *mātrās,* distributed as 4+4+4+2, then the small gap of 1 or 2 *mātrās* could be filled by a *varṇa-prakarṣa,* or 'stretching of a syllable', in this case the final syllable. The *varṇa-prakarṣa* needed is so slight that it can embellish the song without in the least disturbing the meaning and the metric structure of the lines. We suggest, however, that the song was sung to a 16 *mātrā āvarta,* with a slightly greater *varṇa-prakarṣa,* for both the 14 and the 13 *mātrā* line.

c) *Fillers*

A large number of Nāmdev's songs appear in a *'sār'* pattern: a succession of 16 *mātrā* lines followed by a 12 *mātrā* line, both in *caturasra* clusters[29]. In such cases, what was the length of the *āvarta?* We cannot imagine in *tāl* singing that an *āvarta* of 16 *mātrās* alternates with an *āvarta* of 12 *mātrās* throughout a song. An *āvarta* of 28 *mātrās* is rather unlikely: *sār* is abundantly available in *bhajan* singing and the *āvarta* used has 16 *mātrās.* An *āvarta* of 28 *mātrās* is rare, even in classical Hindustānī singing. The question with *sār* is: how are the 4 empty *mātrās* filled in?

---

(29) Many *sār* songs do not have the 16-12 pattern. We also see a 16-14 pattern (songs 16, 48, 50, 61, 67, 68, 99, 131, 144, 174, 179), a 16-10 pattern (songs 8, 29, 70, 234) or even a 16-8 pattern (song 164). Many songs have a mixed pattern, with some lines having the 16-12 pattern, others the 16-14 or 16-10 pattern (songs 53, 63-65, 118, 136). The question --how the empty *mātrās* are to be filled-- remains the same. In a 16-8 pattern we can imagine an *āvarta* of 8 *mātrās,* but in other lines the problem is the same as with the 16-12 pattern.
In the songs of Sūr and others too we find the same phenomenon: *'sār'* songs with lines of 16-12 alternating with lines of 16-14 or 16-10. See e.g. *Pad Sūrdāsjī kā,* p. 33, song 48 (16:10 alternating with 16:12, 16:11); p. 67, song 94 (16:12 alternating with 16:10 and 16:11); p. 78, song 110, *rāṣi lai...* (16:11 alternating with 16:13); p. 81, song 115, *man re bhūlyo...* (16:12 alternating with 16:14 and 16:16), etc.

One can certainly make use of music to fill up the empty space in *tāl*, this must have been done earlier, as it is done today. With text-dominated songs like *bhajans*, singers often added a short phrase or word, or a meaningless string of syllables. These were neutral additions and served as a *stobha* or filler, as a support for the music. For a *bhajan*, it would appear, a mere musical filler was not enough: a text was required.

How can we discover the additions of this kind? Fortunately, we have at our disposal all the variants of the repertoires, reflected in the manuscripts. These variant readings are distinguished from the variants we consider to have been brought about by scribes (see below, Ch. 3.1).

Rupert Snell has described one way in which the empty *mātrās* of a *sār* song (sung to a 16 *mātrā caturasra āvarta* of *tāl*-- most commonly *tīn tāl)* can be filled in. His study is based on an analysis of the actual singing practice of the *Caurāsi Pad* of Hit Harivaṃśa[30]. His approach does away with fillers as an addition to the song and uses an appropriate part of the *ṭek* itself for the purpose. In such a treatment of the *ṭek* --common to classical 16 *mātrā tīn tāl* compositions--, the *ṭek* does not start with a *sam*, but at a strategic point near it, the point being suggested by the text itself, as is shown by Snell. As a result, the short 4 *mātrā* phrase with which the *ṭek* is begun in singing can act both as a textual and musical 'anacrusis' *(uṭhāv)*, leading dramatically up to the *sam*. This *uṭhāv* is used at the end of the 12 *mātrā sār* text, both to fill the 'empty' *mātrās* remaining and to lead it back to the *ṭek*, or to the next line to be sung. This method of filling in empty *mātrās* in a text is common to *tāl* singing in general and may have been used by singers in the repertoires under study. However, no tradition of Nāmdev singing today can be linked to those repertoires.

The fillers we are talking about are different from those Snell refers to. They consist of *texts* added as *stobhas* or fillers. Not all songs have them nor do all singers use them, as is evident in the manuscripts we studied. But their use was common and they were a common source for a kind of variant which clearly fulfils a musical need. This need arises when a singer does not use the *uṭhāv* technique which requires some musical sophistication. Instead he starts each line on the *sam* and this leaves empty *mātrās* to be filled in. This is where the fillers come in. Their use suggests a simpler attitude to the singing on the part of many of our singers, as may be expected in the Santa tradition.

Many songs of Nāmdev, especially those in *rāg ṭoḍī*, are nearly straightforward lines of 16 *mātrās*[31]. They hardly have any empty space and pose little problems of adjustment to *tāl*. In most cases the text fits neatly into the *āvarta*. A *sār* song *does not* fit so simply, unless empty spaces in *tāl* are filled in. Many of our Santa singers appear not to have

---

(30) See 'Metrical Forms in Braja Bhāṣā verse: The *Caurāsī Pada* in Performance'. In: M. Thiel:1983, 353-383.

(31) In songs 1, 2, 5, 7, 10, 11-15, 17-18, 20-22, 24-27, 29-30, 32-33, 35-44. We should, however, note the following:

a) the lines of the *ṭek* are sometimes of a different length (see further);

b) *varṇa-prakarṣa* --turning a *guru* into a *laghu*, or reading a *guru* as a *pluta*-- is sometimes needed in order to get a 'good' 16 *mātrā* line. This is not uncommon in Hindī poetry either.

used the more complex *uṭhāv* approach and we suggest that, instead, the addition of fillers indicates a tendency towards simplifying the correspondence between the text and the *tāl.*

A filler can easily be discovered in the manuscripts because it stands out: it has different readings in some manuscripts while the remaining text is uniform, or it is found in some repertoires and missing in others. We examine the examples of fillers at length, because the matter is very enlightening for a text-critic. For more details about the variants, we refer the reader to Ch. 5.

Song 6 has the filler *re bhāī* in the *ṭek:*

rāma bolai rāma bolai
rāma binā ko bolai re bhāī.

Quite different from this reading in all the Rājasthānī manuscripts, we read in the *Guru Granth* the filler *sabhai ghaṭa:*

sabhai ghaṭa rāmu bolai rāmā bolai
rāma binā ko bolai.

Looking at the number of *mātrās,* both fillers serve the same purpose in the *āvarta.*

The *antarās* of song 6 are clearly in *sār,* with a 16-12 pattern of *mātrās.* No version adds a filler in the empty 4 *mātrās* of the 12 *mātrā* line. It may be that the last vowel *ā* at the end of these lines was stretched --while singing-- into an additional 4 *mātrās.* The singers of the repertoires preserved in the *Guru Granth* stretched the line on a different syllable: *re,* added to the 12 *mātrā* lines. Such 'incomplete' fillers were also very common.

All the *antarās* of song 43 have a regular 16 *mātrā* count. The first line of the *ṭek* has 15 *mātrās* and can in fact be uttered more smoothly if we read *se* in *kaise* short, the line thus giving only 14 *mātrās.* It would appear that most singers probably stretched the last syllable in order to arrive at 16 *mātrās.* But some added a filler. We find the filler *dev* in Ms. *a* and *nāth* in Mss. *c/j,* at the beginning of the line. Like many other fillers, these too are words of address *(sambodhan pad).* Here they add a shade of meaning, because God is addressed. Although the fillers are added at the beginning of the line, it probably did not affect the place of the *sam,* which was, apparently, on the *kai* of the other repertoires. Adding a filler at the beginning or at the end of an *āvarta* makes no difference, if the *sam* does not change; the *āvarta* goes in a circle, repeated again and again.

In song 50 0b

saṁsāra samande tāri gobinde
hūṁ tirahi na jānū bāpajī,

we have the filler *bāp jī* (in some Mss.) and *keśav* (in others); this filler adds 5 *mātrās,* which can be stretched to 6, by changing the first *guru* into a *pluta.* The second line of the first *antarā* has 8 *mātrās,* to which *keśav* is added. But there are no variants in this case and we cannot be certain that what we have is really a filler. Like the *keśav* in line 0b, we find in line 2b

(āni de (or *da) bhelā khei na jānau*
pāra de pāra de bīṭhalā).

mādhave/ai in Mss. *c/j,* instead of *bīṭhalā,* thus arriving at 8+5 *mātrās.* A *varṇa-prakarṣa* can be used, making the first *guru* a *pluta* and stretching the last *guru* to 4 *mātrās*. These fillers do not fill the entire empty space, but there was *one* attempt to do that: in line 3b Ms *m* has *bābla merā* giving the needed 8 *mātrās*. Or could these epithets used to address God be variants, rather than fillers? They are not detachable units, and they are part of the meaning of the song. All manuscripts have one or the other.

In song 63 we find several fillers. In line 1a the readings are generally uniform in all Mss., except for *prāṇī*, clearly a filler, which is missing in Mss. *m, c'j, GG* and the Fatehpur Ms. (and again in lines 2a, 3a and 4d). Another filler, *hari hari*, is missing in the *Guru Granth;* this is a fine example of a detachable filler; also in the Fatehpur Ms. we read only *hari*. At the beginning of line 4b, we find the filler *āpanau* in Mss. *c'j*. Unlike the other lines, where the *āvarta* is not clear, we can clearly see that *āpanau* is used to turn a 12 *mātrā* line into a 16 *mātrā* line.

Song 92 is found in nearly all the Rājasthānī manuscripts and is most probably old. Ignoring the minor scribal variants, we can see that the song is in *sār* (16-12), *because* the phrase *re nar* is missing in Mss. *c* and *j*. Otherwise, we would have seen in the song only straightforward 16 *mātrā* lines. Further in the song, the phrase *re nar* is dropped in a few more repertoires. It is curious to see how in the next *antarās*, there is no consistency in the occurrence of *re nar* in the different repertoires. Some have it sometimes, but not always; others at times drop only *nar*, but keep *re*. We also notice that line b in every *antarā* keeps a 12 *mātrā* line in every repertoire. No filler is added. This seems to suggest that the filler was not always used when it *seems* needed. About the reasons we can only speculate. Perhaps music was used to fill in the empty *mātrās*, where the phrase *re nar* was not used, or where only *re* was used. Or perhaps *re nar* was not written down in every case that it *was* used.

In song 94, line 0a was stretched to a 16 *mātrā* line, for we find the filler *tū* in several Mss.; in actual singing this certainly came at the end of the line, or just before the *sam* at the *ā* of *āv*. Other singers undoubtedly filled the empty space in the *āvarta* through *varṇa-prakarṣa*. In line 0b *bābā* looks like a filler; it is missing in Ms. *u*, which gives *vai*. In the *Guru Granth* the empty space is filled by stretching *bheṣ* to *bheṣavā*. In song 94, we would not be certain that *jī* was indeed brought in as a filler for a 11 *mātrā* line, if it was not missing in the *Guru Granth*. Instead, we read *samsārā*, not *samsāra;* see also lines *GG* lines 2d, 3b and 4b). In 4b *terā* might have been added as a filler, as it is missing in Ms. *m*.

Song 95 too has a *'sār'* pattern, where one might expect fillers. And we have the 'address' *nārad*, to render a 12 *mātrā* line into a 16 *mātrā* line, in several manuscripts. In line 2d *nārad* is added in several manuscripts, although the line is a good *caturasra* 16 *mātrā* line without the filler. Curiously, the filler is missing in line 6d, in all manuscripts.

In song 96, line 1d, the filler *jo* (or *je* in some Mss.) was added to reduce the *varṇa-prakarṣa* at the end. The expression *re avadhū* seems to be a filler, not found in all manuscripts, and a few times found only partly. *Re avadhū* is an address found in a Nāth context.

There is a number of *'sār'* songs where, apparently, no filler was added, or we find no traces of it in our manuscripts. In actual singing fillers may have been used, but we do not know. In songs 98 through 112, we find no evidence of a filler, except for line 112.2b (a 16-12 *sār* line), where *re* was added in several repertoires.

For song 138, we suggest that *bhaiyā* in 1a is a filler; in Ms. *v* it is added in the margin, while in the Fatehpur Ms. we have *hai kau* instead.

Many fillers are an 'address' *(sambodhan pad)*; they are meaningful, but also detachable. In other contexts these addresses are used without being fillers. Even *re man* or *ho* might be called 'addresses', to oneself or to another. *Re bhāi* or *re nar* is more clearly addressed to another. In *re nar* the 'other' is people in general, especially unredeemed persons. Fillers can also be addressed to a particular group, as in *re avadhū* used in Nāth songs.

Other fillers address the Lord. The choice can be made on a musical basis --and then the word has to fit--, or is suggestive of the singer's preference. Most names of God have a *sagun̩* connotation. The choice of *biṭhalā* seems to be based on the knowledge that Nāmdev was a devotee of Viṭṭhal.

Fillers like *jau lag* or *tau lag* are not meant to address anyone; they may help to clarify the meaning, but they do not interfere with it and can be detached. Fillers like *lā* seem to be meaningless, although the verbal ending in *lā* has a Nāth ring.

d) *'Varying the beat'*

Let us now consider another phenomenon, which we have named 'additions', because they cannot really be called fillers; they serve just the opposite purpose. These 'additions' are filler-like phrases or syllables *added* to lines, which are well-formed and have no empty *mātrās* in the *āvarta* that need to be 'filled'. The purpose of these 'additions' was not to fill a line, but to add flavour to its *mātrika* structure and to give it a dramatic twist. These additions result or have as aim the increase of *laghus* in a line.

Some of the songs in the present Nāmdev corpus do not make rhythmic or *mātrika* sense, unless we take every syllable in a line, whether *laghu* or *guru*, to be a *laghu*. For an example we refer to song 9, *antarā* 1 and 2. The *mātrika* measure of every line differs and seems to offer no clue as to the number of *mātrās* to which a line had to be sung, or what its *āvarta* may have been. However, if we take the *akṣar-mātrika* approach and count every syllable *(varṇa)*, *guru* or *laghu*, as one *mātrā*, we find good 16 *mātrā* lines.

The same phenomenon is noticed in song 28: almost every syllable (in the *antarās)* has to be read as a *laghu* (except for a few),if we want to make rhythmic sense of the song. We suggest that this *akṣar-mātrika* tendency was an extreme result of the introduction of *laghus*. An *akṣar-mātrika* trend has been part of the Indian metrics, during Vedic times. It came into prominence once again in Apabhramśa and in Hindī prosody[32].

(32) The *ghanākṣarī* or the *kabitta*, which has been called the distinctive metre of old Hindī poetry is an *akṣar-mātrika* metre. See B.S. Vyās, ed., *Prākrita Paiṅgalam*, part II

A fine example of an 'addition' is found in song 12, which is preserved in many manuscripts, with quite uniform readings. Line 2b

āgama nigama beda purānā

is 'heavy' with *guru* syllables. Singers of the repertoire preserved in Ms. *u* added *ara* after *nigama,* causing a flowing together of the syllables *ma+ar* in *nigama ara,* thus breaking the effect of the *gurus.* Later singers (see Miśra:1964) sang *saba* instead of *ara,* thus bringing in even more *laghus* in the first half of the line (changing *āgama* into *agama).*

Song 43 has quite uniform readings, with some variation in the *rāg.* In order to modulate the pattern of the *gurus* the singers of the repertoires *c/j* added, in line 1.1, the 'additions' *terī, tero* (or *mero).* In line 2.2 the singers of *c/j* and *u* broke the *guru* pattern of *cānā* by inserting *merī.* This addition also acts as a bridge between the two semantic units. Similarly, in song 44, *sab* is inserted in line 0b by the singer of repertoire *a* Besides varying the rhythmic flow, this has another effect: as the line stands, *ja* of *jagata* is part of the first 8 *mātrā* unit. By inserting *sab, ja* fits in the second unit.

e) *Ṭek*

The *ṭek* is the core text of a song, repeated again and again after every *antarā* or even after parts of an *antarā,* depending on the feeling of the singer or the demands of the song. The refrain or *dhruva* in musical texts and in older songs (e.g. the *aśṭapadīs* of the *Gītagovinda,* 12th century AD) is called *ṭek* in the Rājasthānī collections and *rahāv* in the *Guru Granth.* The refrain being a key-line for musicians, it is clear that the difference in name points to a distinct musical tradition. This is corroborated by the fact that in all the Rājasthānī manuscripts (read repertoires) the refrain or *ṭek* is given as the first stanza of each song. But in the *Guru Granth* the refrain or *rahāv* comes after the first verse in most songs (i.e., in 45 out of 61 songs; see below. Ch.5.3).

Both musically and semantically the *rahāv* or *ṭek* dominates a song. It is the central core which is repeated again and again after each *antarā.* The whole song, in fact the whole performance of a single song develops around it. Often also, the refrain gives the central idea or mood of the song. Today songs start with the refrain *(ṭek),* as seems to have been the practice in Rājasthān in the 16-17th centuries. However, in older *prabandha* practice the *dhruva* or refrain was preceded by an 'introductory' portion of the song. That was called the *udgrāha,* which literally means 'taking up'. The *antarā* preceding the *rahāv* in the *Guru Granth* seems to act as an *udgrāha,* although it is not quite the same as the ancient *udgrāha,* which had a structure that was distinct from the rest of the song, both in the music and the text. Also, the *udgrāha* in ancient practice was followed by a *melāpaka,* which joined it to the *dhruva.* The *Guru Granth udgrāha* is different from the *rahāv* or refrain,

---

(Prākrit Grantha Pariṣad, Vārāṇasī, 1962, 573-580). Interestingly, the *kabitta* had connexions with both the singing and the poetic traditions. As discussed earlier, there was also a musical form called *kabitta,* related to the *kabitta* metre; it was popular in the 17-18th centuries, but is out of use now.

but similar to the other *antarās*. There is also nothing like a *melāpaka* in the *Guru Granth*, although we should add here that even in the ancient *prabandhas* the *melāpaka* was not an essential part. The *udgrāha* and *dhruva* were indeed essential components in all *prabandhas*[33].

In two predecessors of the Santa songs, the Buddhist Siddha *Caryāgītis*[34] and the *Gītagovinda*, we find the refrain *(dhruva)* as the second *stanza*. No doubt the first *stanza* acted as an *udgrāha*. It is a characteristic still found in the *Guru Granth*, but not in the repertoires reflected in the Rājasthānī manuscripts[35]. This distinction confirms the early division between the repertoires in the two regions: in Panjāb an old tradition was preserved, in Rājasthān it was not.

In the songs of Nāmdev, as with other Sants, the musical structure of the *ṭek* is often different from the *antarās*. The *antarās* usually have a uniform melodic movement, except for the last *antarā*, which has the *bhaṇitā* and may introduce a slight modification. In ancient practice the *dhruva* or *ṭek* was distinguished by its *mātu* (text) and by its *dhātu* (musical movement).

In the first section of the corpus of Nāmdev's songs, however --those classified under *rāg ṭoḍī*-- the textual structure of the *ṭek* and of the *antarās* is often not very different. We might even not be able to distinguish one from the other, if the *ṭek* were not marked in the manuscripts. In other songs the distinction is clearer, when e.g. the *ṭek* is much shorter than the *antarās*. Traces of such structures in a song are found in the songs of Jaydev and in the *Caryāgītis* of the Siddhas. The link of the Sants with this Siddha literature --attested in the

---

(33) See, e.g., the *Saṅgīta Ratnākara* of Śāraṅgadeva (early 13th century), which is the standard text for these matters:

प्रबन्धावयवो धातुः स चतुर्धा निरूपितः ।
उद्ग्राह प्रथमस्तत्र ततो मेलापकध्रुवौ ।
आभोगश्चेति तेषां च क्रमाल्लक्ष्माभिदध्महे ।
उद्ग्राह प्रथमो भागस्ततो मेलापकः स्मृतः ।
ध्रुवत्वाच्च ध्रुवः पश्चादाभोगस्त्वंतिमो मतः ।
तत्र मेलापकाभोगौ न भवेतां क्वचित्क्वचित् ।

These lines (4.7-11) are quoted from the Adyar edition, vol. 11, 204-206 and may be rendered into English as follows:

'A limb of the musical structure of a *Prabandha* (as distinct from its textual structure) is known as *dhātu*. *Dhātus* are classified in four classes: *udgrāha* is the first, followed by *melāpaka* and *dhruva* and finally the *ābhoga*.
Now their characteristics. *Udgrāha* is the initial part of a *prabandha*. It is followed by the *melāpaka*. Then comes the *dhruva*, which is known by that name because of its constant presence. The final part of a *prabandha* is known as *ābhoga*. There are some *prabandhas* which have no *melāpaka* or *ābhoga*.

(34) See Per Kvaerne, *An Anthology of Buddhist Tantric Songs*, (1977), 2nd ed., Bangkok, 1986.

(35) We noted one exception and there may be more. In the Nāth manuscript *j* (see below, Ch. 2.8) a song by Kabīr in *rāg suho*, following the *bāvanī*, begins with an *antarā*, followed by the *tek* called *rahāv*. Striking here also is the use of *vār* (see below, Ch. 2.6).

imagery and esoteric language-- is also seen in the musical structure of the songs.

In its chapter on *prabandhas*, the *Saṅgītaratnākar* has a short section on the *Caryā prabandhas*[36]. Śārṅgadeva speaks of the *paddhaḍi* metre as typical of the *caryāgīti*, although other metres too are accepted[37]. The *paddhaḍi* in Śārṅgadeva's time, as attested by Hemacandra (d. 1173 AD, a few decades before the *Saṅgītaratnākar* was written), was a metre with a 16 *mātrā* line, divisible into 4+4+4+4 and carrying a rhyme at the end. It was, Hemacandra says, a great favourite with Apabhramsha poets. Unlike the similar *paddhati*, there was no rule in *paddhaṭikā* as to the *laghu-guru* structure of the final 4 *mātrā* cluster; it could have any pattern[38]. This agrees well with what we have in the *Caryāgītis* and in many of the 16 *mātrā* line songs of Nāmdev, especially in the *ṭoḍī* section, which seems to be the best established and the oldest collection of songs of Nāmdev. Further, we notice that the Caryā songs which have a '*paddhatī*' structure[39], are semantically divisible into two units of 8 *mātrās* each, in striking resemblance to songs of Nāmdev.

Śārṅgadeva makes an interesting observation about the *dhruva* or *ṭek* in a *caryāgīti*. It can be either a *sama* ('equal') or a *viṣama*. A *dhruva* is 'equal' when it 'fills the metre' *(chandasaḥ pūrtyā)* and *viṣama* when it does not. Kallinātha, the famous commentator on *Saṅgītaratnākar*, says that Śārṅgadeva speaks of the measure or the length of a *dhruva*. A *sama dhruva* is a refrain which is equal in metric measure to other *antarās*. A *viṣama dhruva* can be either shorter or longer in measure than the other *antarās*[40]. This seems to apply to the fact that the *ṭek* in Nāmdev is at times equal in length to the other *antarās*, at times unequal.

Most *caryā* songs in the edition mentioned have a *dhruva* which is equal to the other *antarās;* in several cases the *antarās* are distinctly larger or shorter in measure than the *dhruva*. As an example we quote from *gīti* 16, composed by Mahīdharapāda, in *rāg bhairavī*. The first *antarā* comes before the *dhruva* and has to be sung as an *udgrāha*.

(36) *Op.cit.*, 4, 292-294; Adyar ed., II, pp. 327-328.

(37) *Ibidem*, 4, 492: *paddhaḍīprabhṛti chandaḥ*.

(38) *Chando'nuśāsana*, 6, 31; Bhāratīya Vidyā Bhavan Series, Bombay, pp. 211-212. See also the discussion on *pajjhaṭikā* (another name for the *paddhaḍī*) in Vyās, *Prākrita Paiṅgalam*, part II, pp. 458-462.

(39) See Per Kvaerne, *op.cit.*

(40) Kallinātha explains the length of the *dhruva* in terms of the *udgrāha*, which is sung just before the *dhruva*. The *sama dhruva* is equal in measure to the *udgrāha*, the *viṣama* is shorter or longer: *samaśabdasya sāpekṣatvādatra pratyāsattyodgrāha evāpekṣyate; tena dhruvasyodgrāhasamatvatmevāvagamyate. Evaṁ viṣamadhruvetyatrāpi dhruvasyodgrāhāpekṣayā nyūnatvena vādhikatvena vā viṣamatvam draṣṭavyam.*
However, the *udgrāha* in a *caryāgīti* is distinguished from the other *antarās (antarā)*, by its position and not by its measure.

१ तिनिएँ पाटें लागेलि रे अणह् कसण घण गाजइ ।
१ ता सुनि मार भयङ्कर रे सअ मणडल सअएल भाजइ ।
• मातेल चीअ गएन्दा धाबइ ।
• निरन्तर गअण उएसें घोलइ ।
२ पाप पुण्य बेणि तिडिअ सिकल मोडिअ खम्भाठाणा ।
२ गअण टाकलि लागेलि रे चित्ता पइठ णिबाना ।
३ महारस पाने मातेल रे तिहुअन सएल उएखी ।
३ पञ्च बिसयेर नायक रे बिपख कोबी न देखी ।
४ खर रबि किरण सन्तापे रे गअण-गंगा गइ पइठा ।
४ भणन्ति महित्ता मइ एथु बुडन्ते किम्पि न दिठा ।

In each line of the first *antarā re* acts like a filler and seems to be followed by a pause. Thus the line can be divided into two sections; 15-12 *mātrās* in the first line and 14-14 in the second line. It has a good *caturasra* flow and the structure is similar to the *'sār'* songs of Nāmdev. Most lines in the next *antarās* of this song have a similar pattern, with in reality 4 lines for each *antarā* and 4 *āvartas* (if we are dealing with a 16 *mātrā tāl*, or more if the *āvarta* consisted of 8 *mātrās*)[41].

The *dhruva* of song 16 is clearly shorter: two lines forming two semantic units.

Or, with two 16 *mātrā āvartas* we have a *viṣama dhruva*, with shorter measure than the *udgrāha* and the other *antarās*. However, 'shorter or longer in measure' can also have another meaning, as is suggested by the Śārṅgadeva's phrase 'filling in the metre'.

In many songs of Nāmdev the *ṭek* has a different number of *mātrās* when compared to the *antarās*. In song 6, the *antarās* consist of a 16 *mātrā* and a 12 *mātrā sār* line. But the *ṭek* is different: 14 + 16.

• रांम बोलै रांम बोलै रांम बिनां को बोलै रे भाई ॥
१ एकल मींटी कुंजर चींटी भाजन रे बहु नांनां ॥
१ थावर जंगम कीट पतंगा सब घटि रांम समांनां ॥
२ एकल चिंता रहिले निता छूटीले सब आसा ॥
२ प्रणवत नांमां भये निहकांमां तुम ठाकुर मैं दासा ॥

Like the *antarās* the *ṭek* has two lines, but the first is shorter in measure than the corresponding *antarā* line and the second is longer in measure. This is a *viṣama ṭek*. Since the *ṭek* alternates with the *antarās*, this difference in structure can help to break monotony[42].

---

(41) The *tāl* prescribed by Śāraṅgadev for the *caryāgīti* is *'dvitīya'* and 'others'. Kallinātha understands 'others' as meaning 'other *tālas* with the same number of *mātrās*'. In his chapter on *tāla*, Śārṅgadeva describes *'dvitīya'* as consisting of two *laghus*. However, *laghu* in the *tāl* terminology of Śārṅgadeva's days did not consist of a fixed number of *mātrās*. Kallinātha says that the *mātrika* value of *laghu* could be equal to 4, 5 or even 6 short syllables *(laghvakṣara)*. Kallinātha on *Saṅgītaratnākara*, 5, 261-262. Considering the fact that the line in this song is divisible into 4 *mātrā gaṇas*, the *āvarta* intended here could be of 8 *mātrās*.

(42) A similar phenomenon is seen in *Caryāgīti* songs 13, 18, 28, 32, 43 *(ṭek* has a longer measure) and songs 27, 34, 35, 39, 49 *(ṭek* has a shorter measure).

In most cases, this phenomenon is not a *geyavikāra*, possibly also because tampering with the *ṭek* was less frequent. Because of its central position in the repetitive pattern of a song, the *ṭek* was like an identity tag and a change in the *ṭek* would have been more drastic than in an *antarā*. Nevertheless, we do find some interesting differences in the different repertoires. Variations in the manuscripts suggest that some singers did try to bring some variety in the *ṭek*. In some songs a *sama ṭek* (equal in length to the *antarās*) has become a *viṣama* in some repertoires, by adding or taking away words or lines.

Song 63 is found in all the repertoires (except for Ms. *u*), basically under the same *rāg*. In Mss. *d a v* we read 0a as:

apane rāma kū bhaji re mana ālasiyā.

In Ms. *m* we read a shorter line:

bhaji re mana ālasiyā.

An 8 *mātrā* phrase is dropped. Interestingly, this phrase was also missing from Mss. *v, p, h* in the original version. In Mss. *v h* the phrase was added in a different hand. In Ms. *p* the later addition is more obvious, since the phrase is added on top of the page, not only in a different hand, but also in a different, thinner pen. Apparently, a reader must have tried to correct the *ṭek*, conform to the current singing practice. For the same song we find in Ms. *m:*

bhaji re mana ālasiyā
rāma binā jamajāli siyā.

In Mss. *c/j* we read:

apane rāmajī kū bhaji re mana ālasiyā
ālasiyā janama jāli siyā

instead of

rāma binā jamajāli siya

in other manuscripts.

The first line of the *ṭek* clearly shows differences in metric length. In the Fatehpur manuscript we find that the line is repeated and has two different readings. First it has

ramai bhaju re mana ālasīyā,

which is a well-formed *caturasra* 16 *mātrā* line. Later in the song it has

ramai bhaju re ālasīyā,

which is 2 *mātrās* shorter. Here the final *ā* has to be lengthened to 4 *mātrās* in order to get 16 *mātrās.* This is a good musical strategy, for in this manner variation can be brought into a line which has to be sung repeatedly, without changing its meaning. Variation is possible in other ways as well, without changing the meaning, like

bhaji re mana ālasīyā,

in which *rām* is dropped. Others, on the other hand, added the 8 *mātrā apane rām ku.*

In song 13 --with a *viṣama ṭek*-- too we notice an addition of 6 *mātrās* in line 0a. In all the manuscripts it reads:

sabai caturatā baratai apani
aisā na koi nirapakha hvai khelai, tāthai miṭāi antara kī tapanī.

It is a *viṣama ṭek,* having one line more than the *antarās*. Ms. *u* adds 6 *mātrās* to it, in the first line:

sabai caturatā lai bartai apanī apanī

making it really more *viṣama* than the others. The added 6 *mātrās* would perhaps have to be sung to 8.

In song 84 the two *antarās* hardly have any variants, but the *ṭek* has as many as 7 versions, nearly as many as there are repertoires:

d;• कहि मन गोब्यंद गोब्यंद गोबिंदा
d;• हरि के चरन कमल छिन छिन जिनि बिसरै
;• कहि मन गोब्यंद गोब्यंद गोब्यंदा
v;• कहि मन गोब्यंद गोब्यंदा
v;• हरि के चरंन कंवल जिनि बिसरै
g;• कहि मन गोबिंद गोबिंद गोबिंदा
g;• चरन कवल चितवनि जिनि बिसरौ
गोबिंद गोबिंद गोबिंदा
c;• कहि मन गोबिद गोबिद
c;• चरन कवल चितवनि जिनि बिसरो
गोबिद गोब्यंद गोबिद

a;• कहि मन गोव्यंद गोब्यंद गोव्यंदा
a;• हरिजी के चरण कवल जिनि --
गोव्यंद गोव्यंद गोव्यंद
m;• कहि मन गोबिंद गोबिंद गोबिंद गोबिंदा
m;• चरण कंवल चितवंनिं जिंनिं बीसरै
गोबिंद गोबिंद गोबिंद गोबिदा
j;• कहि मन गोबिद गोबिद
j;• चरन कमल चितिवनि जिनि बिसरो
गोबिंद गोब्यंद गोब्यंद
u हरि चरन कवल चितवनि जिनि बिसरै

It is interesting to note how the singers made the *ṭek viṣama* in different ways. Most *ṭeks* are longer than the *antarās*, possibly due to the *nām-saṅkīrtan* effect brought about by the repetition of the Lord's Name *(gobinda)*. Only in Ms. *v* a lengthening of 2 *mātrās* seems to be needed in the final *ā* of *gobyandā* to arrive at 16 *mātrās* and this version also comes close to a *sama ṭek*. The version in Ms. *u* has 18 *mātrās*. In both lines the purpose seems to be to increase rather than decrease the length: the addition of *kahi man* to *gobyandu gobyanda gobyanda* --which others singers apparently sang in 16 *mātrās*-- does not point to a desire to achieve a 16 *mātrā* line; that needs 2 *mātrās*, not 4. No doubt, the purpose was to make the *ṭek* longer than the *antarās*.

In song 51 we find a similar phenomenon:

d;• तुझै बिन क्यों जीऊं रे तुझै बिन क्यूं जीऊं
d;• तूं मंझा प्राण अधार
a;• तुझ बिन क्यों जीऊं रे तुझ बिन क्यों जीऊ
a;• तूं मंझा प्रांण अधार नांउं बिन क्यों जीऊं
u नांउ बिन क्यूं जीउं रे
;• तू मंझा प्रांण अधार
v;• तुझै बिन क्यूं जीऊं रे तुझै बिन क्यूं जीवों
v;• तूं मंझा प्रांण अधार
m;•१ तुझ बिंन क्यों रहों -
m;• तू मझा प्रांन अधार

p;• तुझ बिन क्यों जीऊं रे तुझ बिन क्यों जीऊं
p;• तूं मंझा प्रांन अधार तुझ बिन क्यों जीऊं
g;• तुझ बिन क्यूं जीऊं रे तुझ बिन क्यूं जीऊं
g;• तूं मझा प्रांण अधार तुझै बिन क्यू जीऊं
c;• तुझ बिन क्यों जीऊं
c;• बाला तू मेरौ प्रांन अधार
j;• तुझ बिन क्यूं जीवुं
j;• बाला तू मेरे प्राण आधार
h;• तुझ बिन क्यों जीवै रे
h;• तूं मझा प्रान अधार

In the *ṭek* of Mss. *a p g* we notice an attempt to make it *sama*, while the others have shorter measures when compared with the *antarās*. The readings are almost identical; the variation lies in the repetition of *tujha bin kyūṅ jīūṅ*, which nearly all repertoires give. This is a musical change, a *geyavikāra*.

Of song 206, found in 3 repertoires, we find 3 versions (for the variants in the *antarās*, see above, and Ch. 5). Despite the difference in reading between the version of the *Guru Granth* and Ms. *a* (second line), we find the same metric length. In the Fatehpur manuscript, one line is added *(harai harai harai nama)*; this seems to have the effect of *nāma-saṅkīrtan*, as in song 84, or song 177 where *lai hari nāma* is repeated in Ms. *g*.

Again, in song 91, we notice that the *nām-saṅkīrtan* line *rāma rāma rāma sari taū na tulai* of the *antarās* is added to the *ṭek* in Mss. *a* and *m*[43].

If, in song 131, the readings of the *antarās* are rather uniform, we find an amazing variety in the readings of the *ṭek*, in the *Guru Granth*, the Fatehpur Ms. and the Rājasthānī Mss.; Ms. *u* has only the first two lines of the *ṭek*, turning the *sama dhruva* of the other repertoires into a *viṣama*. For the details, see below Ch. 5, where the different versions are printed.

2.4. Manuscripts with Nāmdev's *padas*

Since 1973 we have travelled all over North India to examine many manuscripts containing Nāmdev's Hindī songs and we have photographed quite a few of them[44]. For a fresh edition of the Hindī songs bearing the *chhāp* of Nāmdev (1280-1350?), we had 26 manuscripts at our disposal. Fourteen manuscript versions were collated and entered into the computer[45]. Although, with regard to variants and the order of *rāgas* and of songs, none of these versions is identical with any other, the versions do fall roughly into eight subdivisions. Each of these subdivisions starts with a different first song and arranges the songs in a very different order.

"Drinking tea for years takes you to the manuscripts and the manuscripts take you to the archetype": training and experience have taught us this simple rule (sometimes not so simple) and thus text-editions of Rājasthānī *nirguṇ* literature were produced. This approach did not work when we tackled Nāmdev, or the manuscripts in Rājasthān with Hindī songs bearing his *chhāp*.

Interaction in the oral tradition and corruption in the scribal tradition act like fog and pollution, creating a nebulous environment where it becomes very difficult to find the archetype, or the version of the songs as they were composed and sung originally by their author.

Rājasthān is a treasure-house for manuscript hunters. There have not been too many floods, rulers were patrons of art and literature and several *panths* protected their manuscripts jealously. Was that an imitation of the thoroughness of the Jain *bhaṇḍārs* or the result of a sect's *nirguṇ* devotion to the book? One such a sect is the Dādūpanth (Dādū: 1544-1603) in whose temples and private collections I have been working and making photographs for more than two decades. More than ten thousand negatives of precious manuscripts, containing mainly *nirguṇ* literature, are now in Leuven, Belgium (Callewaert:1978,1). Some of these manuscripts have in the meantime disappeared.

---

(43) The additional *rām* in Ms. *m* may be a scribal error.

(44) For the list of 27 Nāmdev *Vāṇīs* available on film in Leuven, see Callewaert:1980,1.

(45) For a description of these programmes, see Callewaert 1984:2 and below Ch. 3.

Three different *sampradāyas* began to record Santa songs independently: Nānak *sampradāy* (Panjāb), Dādūpanth and Nāth *sampradāy* (Rājasthān).

The *Guru Granth* was compiled in 1604 by Guru Arjandev, who most probably used (written) material available to his predecessors. The *Guru Granth* gives 61 songs attributed to Nāmdev.

Some of the earliest Rājasthānī collections belong to the Dādū *sampradāy*[46]. The disciples of Dādū (like the followers of Nānak) collected songs not only of their own guru, but also of earlier, renowned Sants. Nāmdev was one of them. The earliest manuscript in the Dādū collection (with siglum *d)* is dated 1636 AD or 33 years after Dādū's death. As we shall demonstrate below, this manuscript *d* is clearly a copy of an earlier manuscript. This may suggest that the process of collecting Santa songs in writing began early in the *sampradāy*, possibly even inspired by Dādū himself, although not a single reference to writing' is found in his Biography[47].

The Nāth *sampradāy* seems to be another group which collected Santa songs. This is illustrated by two early manuscripts, sigla *c* and *j* in our list, dated 1669 and 1681 AD. They are large compendiums, giving mainly the songs and other works of Nāth Siddhas. These collections are free of Dādūpanthī influence, as will be demonstrated later.

In the list below we give a description of the manuscripts selected, with the siglum, collection[48] and catalogue number, *lipikāl*, number of Hindī songs of Nāmdev and the folios where these songs are found.

Groups I-IV are 'musical recensions': the songs were grouped during the singing tradition. In the Mss. of groups I and II *Pañcavāṇī* collections are given and we find the complete works of the poets in a regular order: Dādū, Kabīr, Nāmdev, Raidās, Hardās. We noted two exceptions: Ms. *m* gives Dādū, Garībdās, Kabīr, Nāmdev, Raidās and Hardās. In Ms. *v* we find Dādū, Rajab, Kabīr, Nāmdev, Raidās and Hardās. Groups III and IV are non *Pañcavāṇī* and we find in them the complete *vāṇīs* of (only) Nāmdev, Kabīr and Raidās (Mss. *c* and *j)* or just Nāmdev and Kabīr (Ms. *u)*.

In subdivision VIII we find the most ancient manuscript in which songs of Nāmdev are quoted, viz. the 'Fatehpur Ms. of the City Palace, Jaipur.

I. *Rām nām khetī*
 d: DMVJ, No. 12; 1636 AD; 140 songs; fo. 191-208
 v: VBJ, No .34; 1658 AD; 120 songs; fo. 220-234
 a: Amritsar, GNDU No. 875; 1675 AD; 146 songs; fo.236-254

II. *Hari nām hīrā*

(46) We do not consider here the 'Fatehpur Manuscript', which does not belong to any *sampradāy*, but was made for private use only. See below, Ch. 2.4.VIII.

(47) See Callewaert:1988.

(48) The following abbreviations are used:
DMVJ: Dādū Mahāvidyālay, Jaipur;
GNDU: Guru Nānak Dev University, Amritsar
VBJ: Vidyā Bhūshan Saṅgrah, Jaipur;
CPJ: City Palace, Jaipur.

The order of songs in this group is generally followed by Bh. Miśra:1964 and by us.
h: Narainā, private copy; 1653 AD; 117 songs; fo.218-235; for the colophon, see Ill. 1 (App. 7).
n: Narainā, No. 36; 1664 AD; 122 songs; fo.258-272
m: DMVJ, No. 2; 1676 AD; 133 songs; fo.130-137; for the colophon, see Ill. 2 (App. 7).
p: Patiala, No. 2706; 1698 AD; 126 songs; fo.212-224

III. *Lādhau tau lādhau*
u: VBJ, No. 12; 1684 AD; 103 songs; fo.201-213; for the colophon, see Ill. 3 (App. 7).

IV. *Rām nām boli*
c: CPJ, No. 3322; 1660 and 1669 AD; 85 songs; 27 fo.; for the colophon see Ill. 5 (App. 7).
j: CPJ, No. 1853; 1681 AD; 85 songs; fo.152-172

V. *g:* Gopāldās *Sarvāṅgī;* (1627 AD; *lipikāl* 1724); 123 songs. The *Śrī Sarvāṅgī Sarah Cintāmaṇi* of Gopāldās is the only one of the three[49] vast anthologies of *nirguṇ* Hindī poetry made in the early Dādū *panth* which is dated with certainty: the colophon[50] at the end of the work states that Gopāldās completed this immense compilation of 364 folios in 1627 AD, at the age of 37. Clearly, its transmission was intended to be scribal and not oral. The material here is arranged thematically and not musically. There is also no desire to note down all of a poet's work.

If we accept that a copying tradition may in a work of compilation undergo fewer intentional changes than in a more musical record, it becomes evident that the *Sarvāṅgis* are important for a text-critic wishing to study Nāmdev and the other poets quoted in them.

In the list below we give the chapters in the Gopāldās *Sarvāṅgī, in* which the compiler has classified the songs of Nāmdev. The usual *'kau ang'* in each title has been omitted. here. The first figure refers to the song in our edition and in brackets we give the folio number in the Ms. of the *Sarvāṅgī.*

1. *Gurdev:* 29 (2b)
8. *Sumiraṇ:* 55 (13a); 79 (15a); 84 (13a); 86 (13a); 88 (16ab); 124 (14a); 177 (17b); 239 (15a)
9. *Nāv pratāp:* 1 (20a); 2 (20a); 28 (20b); 54 (20b); 81 (19a); 113 (20a)
10. *Nāv mahimā nāv bin akārya janma:* 10 (24b); 92 (26b); 93 (28); 125 (26b)

(49) The two other collections were made by two of Dādū's disciples: the *Sarvāṅgī* of Rajab (see further, VI) and the *Guṇgañjanāmā* of Jagannāth. The latter work supposedly has 5600 *dohe,* quoted from 162 poets. The earliest manuscript we saw, in the DMVJ, is dated 1676 AD, folios 521-536. For more Mss., see Callewaert:1973, p. 160.

(50) See Callewaert:1974,1, p. 187, n. 2.

11. *Nāv mahimā:* 63 (28b); 91 (28); 138 (29a); 196 (28b)
13. *Tap tīrtha taskār patibrat:* 35 (33b); 108 (36a); 129 (36b); 240 (36b)
14. *Bharma bidhāsan:* 20 (37a); 21 (37a); 56 (39a); 137 (39b)
15. *Bheṣ:* 25 (43a); 26 (42a); 142 (42a); 224 (43b)
16. *Sādh:* 82 (48a); 95 (47b); 102 (50a); 180 (49a); 241 (48b)
17. *Sādh mahimā:* 4 (57a); 17 (54b); 60 (57a); 114 (57a); 117 (55a); 131 (56b); 158 (57a); 234 (57a)
18. *Milāp maṅgal:* 31 (60a); 135 (59a)
20. *Ātam ārambha jog:* 18 (76b); 67 (77b); 98 (77b)
24. *Asādh bheś:* 23 (87a); 24 (87a); 43 (87a)
25. *Sādh saṅgati:* 32 (91b)
29. *Kusaṅgati kukarni tasakār:* 16 (97b)
45. *Mālīnatā cāṇak:* 121 (127b)
47. *Cāṇak:* 22 (134b); 64 (133b)
49. *Jhūṭhī anabhai karanī binā kathanī:* 103 (147b)
50. *Kāl bacnā jaranā updeś:* 89 (149a); 106 (150a); 119 (150a)
52. *Din garībī laghutā:* 242 (156a)
54. *Madhi:* 13 (161b)
57. *Sikār saṅgrām:* 97 (169b); 243 (170b)
59. *Javāb su milat aḍig upajaṇi:* 11 (176a); 53 (178a); 70 (175b)
62. *Sagun sādh su milat govindajī kā gunāh:* 163 (189b)
63. *Piv pichān:* 57 (197a); 99 (198a); 100 (197a)
64. *Sākhībhūt samrathāī:* 110 (205b)
65. *Hairān:* 238 (211a)
66. *Ān dev:* 30 (214b); 47 (215a); 126 (214b)
67. *Kasturiyā mrig:* 40 (221b); 72 (221b); 73 (222a); 74 (222b); 148 (222b)
71. *Prīti saneh surati syābati dhyān:* 19 (230a); 58 (230a); 59 (230b); 71 (230a); 115 (230b); 136 (231a)
73. *Paracā:* 107 (234b)
74. *Sevā pujā ārati:* 61 (238a); 144 (237b); 145 (236b)
75. *Nihikram bhagati:* 38 (243a); 48 (241b); 49 (241b); 52 (246a); 69 (243a)
78. *Karuṇā bīnatī:* 15 (253b); 50 (259b); 80 (254a)· 96 (251b); 194(259a)
79. *Man:* 62 (267a); 78 (267b)
85. *Māyā:* 39 (276a); 109 (275a); 181 (275b)
90. *Ātamā kau biśrām ādhār ādi ghar karubai man:* 34 (294a)
92. *Besās:* 123 (297a)
96. *Bharosā besās:* 3 (300a); 128 (301a)
103. *Garva gañjan cintāvanī kāl:* 105 (313b); 140 (313b)
107. *Kāl:* 44 (316a)
105. *Sañjīvanī:* 7 (318b); 8 (319a); 45 (319a)
109. *Citāvanī:* 75 (329b)
111. *Citāvanī:* 120 (334b); 122 (334b)
122. *Virah binati:* 51 (363a)

VI. *r:* Rajab *Sarvāṅgī;* (1620 AD?; *lipikāl* 1714); 44 songs[51].

(51) See Callewaert:1978, pp. 81f. (Ms. A).

In the list below we give the chapters in the Rajab *Sarvāṅgī*, in which the compiler has classified the songs of Nāmdev. The usual *'kau ang'* in each title has been omitted here. The first figure refers to the song in our edition and in brackets we give the folio number in the Ms. of the *Sarvāṅgī*.

9. *Virah:* 136
17. *Sumiraṇ:* 19; 71
19. *Ajapājāp:* 77
26. *Sādh saṅgati param lābh:* 225
30. *Māyā madhya mukati:* 82; 109
32. *Sādh milāp maṅgal uchāh:* 31; 135
39. *Karuṇā:* 96; 226
41. *Bhagati pasāv:* 49
43. *Pīv pichānan:* 134
49. *Paracā:* 7; 73
58. *Patibrat:* 30
62. *Beli:* 97
66. *Apārikha:* 148
69. *Updes citāvanī:* 78
70. *Kāl:* 44
71. *Sañjīvanī:* 147
72. *Anabhai:* 67; 100
74. *Pāraṅgat bamek:* 76; 101
76. *Nirpakhi madhi:* 11
96. *Bheṣ:* 25; 26; 43; 64; 142; 224
97. *Tīrath taskār:* 63; 91; 99; 108; 121; 138
100. *Jhūṭhanī:* 61
102. *Bharam vidhūsan:* 20
118. *Māyā:* 39
123. *Besās santoś:* 3
144. *Āratyūm:* 144; 145

A detailed comparison of the two *Sarvāṅgis* shows that both works are independent products of compilation, differing both in the amount and choice of the material and in the way it has been arranged. Gopāldās has titles for his 121 chapters which differ generally in wording and length from the 144 chapters in Rajab's work. He quotes from 182 poets, Rajab only from 88. Arranging his literature thematically, Gopāldās has much more variety within one chapter, quoting at times as many as 30 different poets and 100 *padas*. This feature makes one wonder what his sources were. If he did not know everything by heart (which is not impossible), he must have had many manuscripts at his disposal (which is unlikely, in 1627 AD). Like Rajab, Gopāldās gives plenty of space to the five important gurus of the tradition, quoting extensively from Dādū, Kabīr, Nāmdev, Raidās and Hardās. These are the poets of the *Pañcavāṇī*.

It is interesting to note that very few *padas* of Nāmdev appear under the same thematic heading in the two *Sarvāṅgis*.

	aṅga in Gopāldās	*aṅga* in Rajab
71	Prīti saneh surati..	Sumiraṇ
19	Prīti saneh surati..	Sumiraṇ
136	Prīti saneh surati	Virah
61	Sevā pūjā ārati	Jhūṭhanī
144	Sevā pūjā ārati	Ārati
145	Sevā pūjā ārati	Ārati
25	Bheṣ	Bheṣ
26	Bheṣ	Bheṣ
142	Bheṣ	Bheṣ
224	Bheṣ	Bheṣ
43	Asādh Bheṣ	Bheṣ
64	Cānak	Bheṣ
82	Sādh	Māyā madhya mukti
109	Māyā	Māyā madhya mukti
39	Māyā	Māyā
18	Milāp maṅgal	Sādh Milāp maṅgal uchāh
96	Karuṇā bintī	Karuṇā
73	Kasturiyā mrig	Parcā
148	Kasturiyā mrig	Apārikh
30	Ān dev	Patibrat
97	Sikār saṅgrām	Beli
78	Man	Updes citāvanī
44	Kāl	Kāl
67	Ātam ārambh jog	Anabhai
11	Javāb su milat..	Nirpakhi madhi
63	Nāv mahimā	Tīrath taskār
91	Nāv mahimā	Tīrath taskār
138	Nāv mahimā	Tīrath taskār
99	Pīv pichān	Tīrath taskār
100	Pīv pichān	Anabhai
108	Tap tīrath taskār patibrat	Tīrath taskār
121	Mālīntā cāṇak	Tīrath taskār
20	Bharam bidhāsan	Bharam bidhāsan
3	Bharosā besās	Besās santos

Further, both compilers arrange thematically --all in one chapter-- *sākhīs, savaiye, ślokas, kavittas* and *padas* of different poets, a feature not found in the manuscripts which give the complete *vāṇī* classified according to *rāg*. Interestingly, the *padas* of different poets are grouped according to their identical *rāg*[52].

VII. *GG: Guru Granth;* 1604 AD; 61 songs.

Below are given the page-references to the standard Devnāgarī edition of the *Guru Granth* where the Hindī songs of Nāmdev occur (see also below, 3.4 and 3.5). We give the *rāg* 'heading' of the Rājasthānī Mss.

(52) For a complete list of poets quoted in this anthology, see Callewaert:1974,1 and the forthcoming edition of the Gopāldās *Sarvāṅgī*.

and in brackets, we give the *rāg* under which the song is classified in the *Granth.*

Rāg toḍī

6 in II,988 *(mālī gauḍī)*
-10[53].
18 in I, 485 *(āsā)*
19 in II, 972 *(rāmkalī))*
23 in I, 485 *(āsā)*
28 in I, 718 *(ṭoḍī)*

Rāg gauḍ

50 in II, 1196 *(basanta)*
58 in II, 873 *(gauḍ)*
59 in II, 874 *(gauḍ)*
61 in I, 485 *(āsā)*
62 in II, 1252 *(sāraṅga)*
63 in II, 873(G)
-64[54].

Rāg gauḍī

76 in I, 718 *(ṭoḍī)*[55]

Rāg rāmkalī

91 in II, 973 *(rāmkalī)*
94 in II, 1167 *(bhairū)*
99 in II, 972 *(rāmkalī)*

Rāg bhairū

115 in II, 1164 *(bhairū)*
118 in II, 1165 *(bhairū)*
125 in II, 1163 *(bhairū)*
131 in II, 1292 *(malār)*[56]

Rāg dhanāśri

140 in I, 692 *(dhanāśrī)*
-141[57].
149 in I, 345 *(gauḍī)*
150 in I, 485 *(āsā)*
151 in I, 486 *(āsā)*
152 in I, 525 *(gūjarī)*
153 in I, 657 *(soraṭhī)*
154 in I, 657 *(soraṭhī)*
155 in I, 694 *(dhanāśrī)*
156 in I, 718 *(ṭoḍī)*
157 in II, 727 *(tilaṅga)*
158 in II, 727 *(tilaṅga)*
160 in II, 988 *(mālīgauḍī)*
161 in II, 1252 *(sāraṅga)*

(53) See next footnote.
(54) See next footnote.
(55) Song 17 in vol. I of the *Granth* (p. 718) has one line found in our song 76, one found in our song 10 and one found in our song 64.
(56) The *ṭek* in the *Granth* is found in our song 141.
(57) See previous footnote.

162 in II, 1351 *(prabhātī)*

Only in the *Granth*

199 in I, 525 *(gūjarī)*
200 in I, 656 *(soraṭhī)*
201 in I, 693 *(dhanāśrī)*
202 in I, 693 *(dhanāśrī)*
203 in I, 693 *(dhanāśrī)*
204 in II, 857 *(bilāval)*
205 in II, 873 *(gauḍ)*
206 in II, 874 *(gauḍ)*
207 in II, 874 *(gauḍ)*
208 in II, 874 *(gauḍ)*
209 in II, 973 *(rāmkalī)*
210 in II, 988 *(mālīgauḍī)*
211 in II, 1105 *(mārū)*
212 in II, 1163 *(bhairū)*
213 in II, 1163 *(bhairū)*
214 in II, 1164 *(bhairū)*
215 in II, 1164 *(bhairū)*
216 in II, 1164 *(bhairū)*
217 in II, 1165 *(bhairū)*
218 in II, 1165 *(bhairū)*
219 in II, 1166 *(bhairū)*
220 in II, 1195 *(basanta)*
221 in II, 1196 *(basanta)*
222 in II, 1252 *(sāraṅga)*
223 in II, 1351 *(prabhātī)*
238 in II, 1292 *(malār)*
248 in I, 1318 *(kānaḍa)*
249 in II, 1350 *(prabhātī)*

VIII. *f:* Fatehpur Ms.,CPJ; 1582 AD; 11 songs[58]

"Out of the 411 songs compiled in this manuscript, 262 bear the chāp of Sūrdās,..., and 149 songs are by other saints... The manuscript appears to have been written in three sections based on three separate examples" (Bahurā, *op.cit,* passim).

Of the 149 songs by other saints, at least 34 may be considered 'nirguṇ': Ravidās (or Raidās) 5, Kabīr 15 and Nāmdev 11. All eleven songs by Nāmdev appear in the third section of the manuscript, which was written by the scribe who is responsible for the colophon. (See also below, Ch. 3.4 and 3.5).

The following songs are found in this earliest manuscript:
21: fo. 134; song 72; *rāg ṭoḍī;* found in many Mss.

(58) Edited by G.N. Bahurā, *The Padas of Surdas,* (City Palace) Jaipur, 1982. For a fine description of this very valuable manuscript, see Bahurā, G.N., 'Sūrdās kā Pad: The Fatehpur Manuscript of 1639 V.S. (1582 AD)', in Monika Thiel-Horstmann (ed.), *Bhakti in Current Research, 1979-1982,* 1983, pp.19-23.

59: fo. 137; song 77; *rāg sorațhī;* found in many Mss.
62: fo. 129; song 66; *rāg sorațhī;* found in many Mss.
63: fo. 163; song 120; *rāg gauḍī* (different *țek);* found in many Mss.
115: fo. 162; song 118; *rāg bhairū;* found in many Mss.
131: fo. 163-164; song 121; *rāg gauḍ* (different *țek);* found in many Mss
138: fo. 151; song 98; *rāg sāraṅg;* found in many Mss.
206: fo. 130; song 67; *rāg bilāval;* found in Ms. *a* and the *Guru Granth.*
231: fo. 140; song 73; *rāg sorațhī;* found only in Ms. *a.*
257: fo. 133; song 71; *rāg gauḍī;* found in no other Ms.
258: fo. 164; song 122; *rāg mārū;* found in no other Ms.

IX. *GP: Gāthā Pāñcak* Marāțhī Collection

Āvațe T.H., edited the *Sakal Santa Gāthā* or *Gāthāpañcak,* Pune, 1908 AD; repr. in 5 vols, by R.C. Dhere, Pune, 1983. Vol. 2 (804p. and 32pp.) is about Nāmdev only, without any reference to a manuscript or to the sources from which the information was collected. On pp. 678-700 the author quotes 102 'Hindustāni' songs, again without referring to any manuscript. Until we see a more critical edition of the *abhaṅgas* of Nāmdev, we cannot accept *abhaṅgas* in these editions as early evidence'.

In all manuscripts of the 17th century the *rāgas* are carefully noted down, reflecting the singers' concern to keep a record of the *rāg* to which a song could or had to be performed. No trace, however, is found of any musical annotation and no information is given as to how a particular *rāg* had to be sung. This information was apparently handed down orally, as is still the practice today. Such a practice was common even for songs recorded within a musical context where the motivation of the record was mainly musical. Evidence of this is seen in three 'musical' records from the 17th century. The first is *Kitābe-nauras,*[59] in which are recorded the *dhrupads* composed by Ibrahām Ādil Shāh II (Bijapur, 1580-1627); the text of the *dhrupads* is given, not the music. The second work is a collection of 990 songs composed by the famous musician Nāyak Bakhshū, who started his career in the court of Mān Singh of Gwalior (r1486-1516) and moving later to the court of Sultān Bahādur of Gujarāt. Emperor Shāh Jahān (r1628-1658) was so impressed with these compositions that he commissioned the collection of 2000 songs and had 1000 of them published in a book[60]. There again, only the text is given --classified under 46 *rāgas* and *tālas*--, not the music.
The third collection is an anthology of *dhrupads* made by Bhāva Bhațța as part of a large treatise on music, *Anūpa Saṅgita Ratnākara.* written under the patronage of Anūp Singh (r1679-1698) of Bikaner[61].

(59) Edited, with an Introduction, by Nazir Ahmad, and published by the Bhārtīya Kalā Kendra, New Delhi, 1956.
(60) See the Persian Introduction to the *Sahas-ras,* in: Prem Latā Śarma, ed., *Sahas Ras* (Hindī), Saṅgīt Nāțak Akademy, New Delhi, 1972, pp. 10-11.
(61) The *Anūpa Saṅgita Ratnākara* was published by D.K. Joshī and B.S. Sukthankar, Pune, 1921, along with other works on music by Bhāva Bhațța. Interestingly, the *dhrupad* texts were not printed, not even mentioned. They may have been considered to be of no value; unlike the *dhrupads* of Bhaṭkhaṇḍe and his group, there is no

The *dhrupads* collected or sometimes composed by Bhāva Bhaṭṭa himself were meant to be illustrations of different *rāgas*. Only the text is recorded and for the music the reader was expected to refer to the oral tradition.

To conclude, it should not amaze us if in the Santa songs we find only the *rāgas*, and no musical annotation.

2.5 The Miśra and Maurya:1964 edition[62]

Pioneering work, in editing the Hindī songs of Nāmdev, has been done by Bhagīrath Miśra and Rāj Nārāyan Maurya in their Hindī publication *Santa Nāmdev kī Hindī Padāvalī*, Pune, 1964.

Of the Mss. described by Miśra in their *Introduction* (p. 43f.), only six are referred to in their critical edition: *p, r* (the only 2 Mss. we consulted for our edition), and *np* (1409), *gh, pan, pu*. Looking at the classification of the songs, manuscripts *np* and *pu* seem to belong to the *'hari nāv hīrā'* group, while manuscripts *gh* and *pan* seem to belong to the *'rām nām khetī'* group.

In their *Introduction*, Miśra and Maurya give the following description of the Mss. they found:

- *p:* Patiala: 2706:

This is the most ancient Ms. used in Miśra:1964 for the critical edition (siglum *p* in our list). In the list of Hindī songs of Nāmdev (see below, Ch. 3.4), we have marked with the sign '-' the songs referred to in Miśra:1964, i.e. a total of 120. However, we copied 126 songs from this Ms. In the *Introduction* of Miśra:1964 the authors say that in this Patiala Ms. *(p)*, there are "128 songs of Nāmdev: only 20 of these are found in the *Guru Granth* and 54 in the Marāṭhī *Gāthā collection*" (p.54).

Miśra missed songs 10, 64, 71, 73, 238, which we did find in the *Grantha*. It may be added here that we did not find song 163 in the *Guru Granth*, although Miśra marks it as such.

Miśra wrongly adds: "The only written source before this Ms. is the Guru Grantha. Nowhere else are the Hindī songs of Nāmdev found." (p.54).

In this Patiala Ms. we did not find song 84. On the other hand Miśra does not give songs 79, 82, 113, 141, 195, 234, 238 (resp. Nos. 76,114,101,123,117,84,54 in the Patiala Ms.).

Patiala 2446:

Rajab's *Sarvāṅgī*, dated 1796 AD. This Ms. was not consulted by Miśra for collation, but "there appears to be very little difference with the text of the Sarvāṅgī of the Pune Ms." (see below *pu:* Pune 394).

---

annotation of the songs of Bhāva Bhaṭṭa. Recently, we have seen two manuscripts of the *Anūpa Saṅgīta Ratnākara*, one in the Jaipur City Palace and one in the Palace Library, Bikaner. These have an abundance of *dhrupad* texts.

(62) Henceforth referred to as Miśra:1964 or Miśra.

Counting the 3 songs of Vishṇudās, we have a total of 53 songs in the Sarvāṅgī" (Miśra, p.55).
However, we identified only 43 songs of Nāmdev in Rajab's *Sarvāṅgī*[63] but failed to find songs 42, 45, 49, 95, 111, 142, 147, 148, 165, 226 referred to in Miśra. Song 70, on the other hand, is not identified in Miśra as occurring in the *Sarvāṅgī*.

- Banaras, NPS, 1407: 136 songs, 1815 AD
- Banaras, NPS, 1408: 123 songs, 1779 AD
- *np:* Banaras, NPS, 1409: 123 songs, 1714 AD[64]

This Ms. includes a *Pañcavāṇī* and a *Sarvāṅgī* of Rajab. "Only this Ms. was consulted for collation because there is little difference between the three Mss. in the NPS collection. Besides, this Ms. is the most ancient and there are very few errors" (Miśra, p. 57).
In our study of this Ms., it was our experience that "although this manuscript is the most ancient we found, it is not the one that has the least mistakes"[65].

- *gh:* Ghuman, ca. 1760 ("about 200 years old", Miśra p. 45): 157 songs (no date).

"Folios 1 and 14 are missing but are available on a copy". Songs 194, 196-198 are found only in this Ms.

- *pan:* Pandharpur.

This copy (date?) of a lost Ms. has 182 songs. Fourteen songs (180-181, 183-185, 187, 189, 191-193, 194, 196-198) are found only in this Ms., which has the greatest number of songs.

- *pu:* Pune 393 (1811 AD): 161 songs.

Eleven songs (166-170, 172-173, 175-176, 178-179) are found only in this Ms.

Pune, 394, 1808 AD, has the *Sarvāṅgī* of Rajab from which the "ca. 50 songs" were copied for Miśra:1964. "This Ms. was used for collation because the Patiala Ms. with the *Sarvāṅgī* was not available" (p. 55).

- Mss. *np, gh, pan, pu* were as such not consulted by us. We have copied the Miśra text for those songs which were not found in the Mss. we consulted.

It is noteworthy that songs 75 and 129 are found only in the Gopāldās *Sarvāṅgī* on the one hand and in Mss. *gh, pu, (pan)* on the other hand. Song 134 is found in the Rajab *Sarvāṅgī* and Mss. *gh* and *pun*.
From the fact that 12 songs (149-157, 159-160, 162) are found only in the *Granth* and in the Pandharpur Ms. (total 182; recent date?), we may

(63) See Callewaert, *The Sarvāṅgī of the Dādūpanthī Rajab*, 1978, pp. 402f.
(64) *Ibidem*, p. 93. The correct No. of this Ms. in the NPS collection is 2244/1408 (*samvat* 1771 or 1714 AD)
(65) *Ibidem*, p. 93.

perhaps conclude that from the Sikh tradition some songs have entered into the written tradition of Rājasthān.

2.6. The *Guru Granth*[66]

The *Guru Granth* is one of the earliest written collections we have of Santa literature. It was compiled by Guru Arjan Dev in 1604. Later, some *padas* of the 9th Guru, Tegh Bahādur (and a single verse by the tenth, Guru Govind Singh) were added, but without disturbing the earlier scheme into which the material had been organised by Arjan Dev.

It is a compilation mainly of songs. The principle followed in arranging and grouping the songs is musical, not thematic. The songs are classified under 31 *rāgas*, each *rāg* group forming a chapter in the collection. This musical grouping in a religious work distressed the famous *Granth* scholar Trumpp[67], who failed to see any logic in such a scheme of arrangement. Yet, in analysing the contents of the *Granth*, he had listed the 31 *rāgas* under which the songs have been neatly classified and remarked that these *rāgas* form 'the body of the contents'. This, to him, revealed no scheme in the arrangement:

> 'The verses of the different Gurus have been distributed into these forementioned Rags, apparently without any leading principle, as hardly any verse is internally connected with another. The name of the Rag is therefore a mere superscription, without any reference to its contents'[68].

Trumpp was looking for a thematic connection between songs, but he failed to find one. To him the *rāgas* were 'mere superscription'. But the distribution of songs into *rāgas* should have made him realize that a musical principle had been followed, not only in structuring the collection as a whole, but also in making sub-groups within each *rāg*. Before we look at this classification, it is useful first to note a few facts about the *Guru Granth*.

The *Guru Granth* is a collection of 5894 songs and poems mainly by the first five Sikh Gurus: Nānak, Aṅgad, Amardās, Rāmdās and Arjan Dev. All the Gurus sign their songs with the same name, Nānak. They have been distinguished in the *Guru Granth* by giving each of them a number, going from 1 (Nānak) to 5. These numbers are noted as *mahlā* 1, *mahlā* 2 and so forth. Thus a song ascribed to *mahlā* 1 is by Nānak. One ascribed to *mahlā* 2, by Aṅgad and so on. This numerical succession of *mahlās* follows the order in which the Gurus succeeded one another. *Mahlā* 5, that is Guru Arjan Dev has the largest number of compositions in the collection (2216). Nānak

(66) See also below, Ch. 3.6.
(67) His translation was published in 1877.
(68) Trumpp, Ernst: *The Ādi Granth or Holy Scriptures of the Sikhs*, (second ed. Delhi 1970), Introduction p. CXX.

has 976, Aṅgad 61, Amardās 907 and Ramdās 679. To these were added 118 songs by Tegh Bahādur, *mahlā* 9.
Besides these the *Granth* also has songs by famous non-Sikh saints: Kabīr, Raidās, Nāmdev, Trilochan, Shekh Farīd and others. This body of songs is generally termed *'bhagatanī kī vānī'*. If we add to this the compositions by different *bhāṭs* (bards) written in praise of the Gurus, we have a total of 937 songs and verses.

All this -with a few exceptions- is arranged into *rāgas*. Each *rāg* group has distinct sub-groups and the arrangement here generally follows a uniform pattern (with negligible exceptions). Three norms emerge as basis for assigning a song to a particular group within a *rāg*.

1. the number of *padas* or stanzas a song has,
2. its *gharu* and/or its *saṅkar rāg*,
3. its author.

The number of padas

By far the largest number of songs in the *Guru Granth* are what the *Granth* itself terms *caupade*. Then come *aṣṭapadīs* (*aśatpadīā* in the *Granth*) and *dupade*, and further *tipadas* and *pañcapadas*. The number of *padas* in a song is the number of *antarās* it has. Thus *caupade* are songs with four *antarās* (though a few have five or even six). The term seems to be very suggestive of the *catuśpadi* of ancient *prabandha* singing, equivalent to the *caupāī* of Nāmdev and the *caupadī* of Dāmodar Pandit. The *aṣṭapadīs*, or *aśatpadīā*, are (like the *Gītagovinda aṣṭapadīs*), songs with eight *antarās*, though as in the *Gītagovinda*, the number eight is a norm rather than a strict rule. Yet, it is an important norm in the *Granth*, because the number of *antarās* in a song is a major consideration in assigning it to a particular group within a *rāg*. Other structural 'poetic' characteristics, such as its metre or the number of lines within an *antarā* are not important, although in some instances *aṣṭapadīs* with *antarās* of three and of four lines have been allotted a separate section to themselves.

Gharu and saṅkar rāg divisions

Besides the division based on *pad*, there are --within *rāg* groups-- subgroups distinguished on the basis of what appear to be variant forms of the same *rāg*. These are recorded chiefly in two ways:

a. as different *gharus*, literally 'sets' of the same *rāg*;
b. as *saṅkar rāgas*.

Gharus seem to be variants *within* the same *rāg* pattern. Other subgroups seem to point to 'hybrid' or 'composite' patterns, where the main *rāg* is associated with another: *gauḍī-majh*, for example, *gauḍī* being the main *rāg*. Songs to be sung in these composite *rāgas* are carefully marked, if not assigned a separate section. We do not know how these *saṅkar rāgas* were constructed. The original musical tradition for the *Guru Granth* has not survived. In modern practise, there is no single 'method' of combining *rāgas* to form a hybrid; and this was perhaps true of older practise as well. We may presume that the *saṅkar* form was dominated by the *rāg* under which it is listed.

Other divisions within *rāgas* point to specific melodies associated with certain social groups, such as *gauḍī guwārerī* (the *gauḍī* as sung by milkmen) or *gauḍī bairāgani* (the *gauḍī* as sung by *bairāgīs*). Certain tunes are associated with specific composers or singers: the *vār* of *āsā, mahlā* 1, for example was to be sung in *rāg āsā,* to a tune composed by Asrāj, 'the one without an arm' (*ṭuṇḍe asrāj kī dhuni*). Some variations may be due to style: thus many *rāgas* have a '*kāfī*' which may have been a particular manner of singing[69].

Author or mahlā

Authorship is also made an important basis for distinguishing groups of songs within a *rāg*. One major division is between *mahlā* and *bhagat* songs. The *mahlā* songs always come first, beginning usually with the *caupade* of *mahlā* 1. If *mahlā* 1 has no *caupade* in that *rāg*, then the *caupade* of the second *mahlā* take precedence over those of the third or the fourth *mahlā,* as the case may be. The *dupade,* if any, are usually placed together with the *caupade,* after which come the *aṣṭapadīs*. Here, too, the same logic is followed as with the *caupade:* songs of *mahlā* 1 come first followed by those of his successors, in numerical order. These are followed by '*chant*' (Skt. *chanda*') songs and '*Vars*'. Then follow the compositions of the *bhagats* or saints other than the Gurus. An arrangement according to author is followed here too. The songs of Kabīr, if there are any in a given *rāg,* always come first, followed usually by Nāmdev who, in turn, precedes Raidās.

The Granth pattern illustrated

The pattern of arrangement within a *rāg* group that emerges may be illustrated from *rāg āsā,* one of the major *rāgas*.

* First the *caupade* are grouped; the first sub-group of *caupade* comprises the two famous prayers '*so daru*' and '*so purukhu*'. The second group is entitled *rāgu āsā mahlā caupade gharu* 2. The third group is: *āsā gharu* 3 *mahlā* 1 and the fourth *āsā gharu* 4 *mahlā* 1. Such a grouping continues till *gharu* 6. Some of these 6 groups have only one song each. This significantly illustrates the importance accorded to *gharu*, as a distinct category.

The *caupade* of *mahlā* 1 arranged in 6 separate *gharus,* are followed by the *caupade* of *mahlā* 3, with the following sub-groups:

- *āsā gharu* 2 *mahlā* 3 (the word *caupade* is not mentioned in the title but later, after song 49);
- *āsā gharu* 8 *kāfī mahlā* 3.

Then come the songs of *mahlā* 4, with the following groups:

- *rāgu āsā gharu* 2, *mahlā* 4;
- *mahlā* 4 *rāgu āsā gharu* 6 *ke* 3 (a group with 3 songs).

(69) In the Rājasthānī Mss. *rāg kāfī* occurs only once, for song 82 in Ms. *a;* see below, Ch. 2.9, *Variation in rāg*.

- *rāgu āsā gharu* 8 *ke kāfī, mahlā* 4 (2 songs);
- *rāgu āsāvarī* (another name for *āsā*) *gharu* 16 *ke* 2 *mahlā* 4 *sudhang* (2 songs, sung in the manner of *sudhang?).*

Then follow the *caupade* of *mahlā* 5 with separate groups for as many as 17 *gharus*[70].

* The *caupade* are followed by *aṣṭapadīs* and we first have the *aṣṭapadīs* of *mahlā* 1, distributed over 3 groups, each with a new *gharu*. These are followed by the *aṣṭapadīs* of *mahlā* 3 and *mahlā* 4, similarly distributed.

* The *aṣṭapadīs* are followed by *'chant'* and divided in groups on the basis of *mahlā* and *gharu*. the plan followed being the same as for *caupade*.

* This section is followed by the *'vār'*, entitled, *āsā mahlā* 1 *vār saloka nāli mahle pahile ke likhe, tuṇḍe asrājai kī dhuni āsā mahlā* 1. This may be translated as: "the *vār* along with *ślokas* of *mahlā* 1 have been written down to be sung to the tune composed by Asrāj, 'the one without an arm'.

* Then come the songs of the *'bhagats'*, introduced with: *rāgu āsā bāṇī bhagatā kī, kabīr jīu, nāmdevjīu, ravidās jīu, āsā srī kabīr jīu.* Kabīr has many songs in this *rāg* and as with the *mahlā* songs they are distributed into *gharus*. Kabīr is followed by Nāmdev and Raidās.

The Guru Granth and the Rājasthānī collections

Several factors distinguish the Rājasthānī collections from the *Guru Granth:*

1. The Rājasthānī collections, both Dādūpanthī and Nāth, aim at collecting all available songs and other sayings of the major Sants, including Nāmdev[71].
2. The *Guru Granth* was eventually given a canonical status, as an extreme development of the *nirguṇ* devotion to the Word of God in the Book. It was regarded as the only and correct version recognised by Sikh orthodoxy. 'Dissident' copies like the Banno Manuscript[72] were very soon ostracized and even at the present day orthodox Sikh scholars are anxious to avoid the question of variant readings and interpolations.

In the Dādūpanth and the Nāthpanth, on the other hand, no attempts were ever made to compile a canonical and final collection. As a result the text-critic meets with considerable diversity in these collections. It is important to note that in these *sampradāyas* different collectors made individual collections, each of them going back to his own oral tradition. These collections proliferated in different manuscript traditions which, in turn, underwent a certain degree of contamination in the scribal period.

(70) The word *āsāvarī* occurs a number of times in the *āsā* 'chapter'. *Āsāvarī* seems to have been another name for *āsā* or perhaps a melodic variant of *āsā*, for the title of one sub-group reads, *'rāgu āsā mahlā 5 gharu 17 āsāvarī'*.

(71) The *Sarvāngīs* (of Rajab and Gopāldās, see above, 2.4, V and VI) are thematically arranged, as in the *Guru Granth*.

(72) See Pritam Singh, *Bhāī Banno's Copy of the Sikh Scripture*, in Monika Thiel:1983, 325-341.

3. Finally, unlike the case for the Sikh tradition, the manuscript tradition in Rājasthān does not seem to have stopped the development of the oral tradition. The oral tradition in Rājasthān has remained dynamic and has continued to be a vital source for Santa songs and sayings, even after a rich manuscript tradition was established. The two traditions have run parallel, up to the present day. The oral tradition remained alive and active, till perhaps two generations ago, adding to and modifying earlier material. Proof of this lies in the fact that Mss. dated after 1750[73] give 'new' songs of early Sants, especially Kabīr and Nāmdev. Some songs also appear in larger editions.

A continuing oral tradition was in a sense inevitable. At all time. the transmission of the music of the songs was carried on orally. Even the Sikh tradition made no attempt to fix and freeze the *music* through writing, as was done for the *words* of the songs.

Every *sampradāy* organised *bhajan* singing. Some did it more thoroughly than others, creating and propagating a distinct style, if not an entirely fixed body of music. Among the Vaishṇavas of the North, the Vallabh *sampradāy* and the Gauḍīyas come immediately to mind. Among the *nirguṇ* groups he Sikhs stand out, with their institution of *rāgīs* to take care of the singing of the *Guru Granth*. As a result, the *Granth* is a meticulously arranged musical collection. Today the institution has been modernised and there are schools for training *rāgīs*. The Sikhs do not, however, seem to have devoted much attention to preserving a fixed form or character for their music, being open to the influence of what was popular or current at different times.

These are important distinctions *within* the oral tradition, which should not be thought of as monolithic. There was as much variety and creativity in it as in any institution which transmits knowledge, art or literature. Unlike the Sikhs and their *rāgis*, other *nirguṇ* groups relied on institutions outside the *sampradāy* for their more professional *bhajan* singing. This does not deny the presence within the *sampradāy* of skilful musicians and singers.

Summing up

We have in the *Granth* a very conscious and meticulous arrangement of songs, with a musical criterion in mind. The role music plays in the *Granth* is also reflected in the fact that the *Granth* ends with a *rāgmālā*[74]. Most of the *rāgas* named in the *rāgmālā* are not found in the *Guru Granth*. The *rāgmālā* has no relevance in the *Granth*, except as a kind of tribute to the importance of music for it. Another and more specific tribute is paid by the Gurus themselves, especially the third Guru, Amardās. He wrote verses in praise of various *rāgas*. Songs

(73) The Rājasthānī manuscripts dated after 1700 AD give excellent material to study the symbiotic relation between the scribal and oral traditions (as is still to be seen in Hindustānī music). For a complete list of the manuscripts with songs of Nāmdev, see Callewaert:1980,1; film 14.

(74) For the controversy about the origin of this *rāgmālā*, see S.S. Kohli, *A critical study of Ādi Granth*, Motilal, Delhi, (1961), 1976, pp. 101f.

praising *rāgas* were not uncommon in the literature of this period and the attempts of Amardās fall within an established genre. The difference is that in his praise of a *rāg, bhakti* takes precedence over music:

'A (major) *rāg* among *rāgas* is the *rāga siri,* (you can realise this) if you have love for the truth...'[75].

'*rāginī gauḍī* is a charming lady, (but only) if she keeps her mind on her Lord ...'[76].

'*malār* is a cooling *rāg*. Meditate on Hari and find peace'[77].

Until a detailed comparison can be made between the *rāg* pattern in the 'Kartārpur' version and the 'Banno' version of the *Guru Granth,* we can only speak of *one Guru Granth rāg* pattern. *Rāgas* are assigned to a song in the singing tradition (not in scribal collections) and from the analysis of the *Guru Granth* above, we may conclude that songs were already well defined under particular *rāgas* before the *Guru Granth* was written down. This suggests a strong 'Nānak' singing tradition from at least 1500 AD onwards. By then, the songs of Nāmdev had already acquired a very well defined *rāg* pattern, quite distinct from the Rājasthānī pattern. Of course, the question still remains *why* the arrangement according to *rāgas* seemed to be so sacrosanct. It could not have been just a mnemonic device.

The following 17 *rāgas* are found in the Nāmdev repertoire in the *Guru Granth* (61 songs):

mālīgauḍ	3	*gauḍī*	1
sāraṅg	3	*goṇḍa*	7
āsā	5	*gūjrī*	2
bhairū	12	*soraṭhī*	3
rāmkalī	4	*tilaṅg*	2
malār	2	*bibhāsprabhātī*	3
ṭoḍī	3	*bilāval*	1
dhanāśrī	5	*mārū*	1
basanta	3		

From this list and from the analysis in Ch.2.4.VII above it appears that the songs of Nāmdev must have been well established in a distinct *rāg* pattern early in the 16th century AD or maybe even before 1500 AD. It is striking that the *Guru Granth* does not have Bhagat songs or even songs of *mahlā* 1 to 3 in all the *rāgas*. This perhaps suggests that a conscious classification was made into the traditional *rāg* framework by later Gurus, especially Rāmdās and Arjandās, who added *rāgas* to those they inherited from their predecessors. Might they also have changed the *rāgas* suggested by their predecessors?

(75) *Guru Granth,* Vol. I, p. 83.
(76) *Ibidem,* p. 311.
(77) *Ibidem,* Vol. II, p. 1283; see also p. 1285.

2.7. The 'musical' collections

The Rājasthānī anthologies, as we have seen, can be grouped as 'musical' and 'thematic'. The thematic anthologies were made by Dādūpanthīs only. The musical collections have different origins, but most of them are Dādūpanthī. They are called *Pañcavāṇī* and are an outstanding product of the Dādūpanthī literary activity in the early 17th century AD. These are collections of the *Vāṇīs* of the five gurus revered in the *panth:* Dādū, Kabīr, Nāmdev, Raidās, Hardās (in that order). In each *Vāṇī* are given the *sākhīs* and the *padas* of one poet. The aim seems to have been to preserve the complete collection of a poet's work. The *padas* are arranged under particular *rāgas,* in a pattern reminiscent of the *Guru Granth* (see above, 2.6). *Pañcavāṇī* manuscripts served Pārasnāth Tivārī for his edition of Kabīr and Parshurām Caturvedī for his edition of the *Dādūvāṇī.* Bhagīrath Miśra consulted this 'recension' for his edition of the Hindī songs of Nāmdev.

In her paper *'Kabīr in the Guru Granth'* in the First Berkeley Conference on Sikh Studies, Karine Schomer states that the *Pañcavāṇī* "tradition is believed to go back to the last quarter of the 16th century, though at present no manuscript earlier than 1774 has been discovered"[78]. We now have on film in Leuven several important manuscripts of more than one hundred years before this date.

The *Pañcavāṇī* looks like a unique example of devotional compilation, illustrating the zeal of the Dādūpanth in preserving *bhakti* literature. However, the *Pañcavāṇī* manuscripts now at hand -and also the non *Pañcavāṇī* manuscripts, of Nāth origin- do not go back to one archetype, a single compiler or one repertoire. With the hypothesis that the *Pañcavāṇī* tradition in the Dādūpanth started around 1600 AD, we face the amazing fact that there must have been different *Pañcavāṇī* compilers, each one working separately either in direct contact with the oral tradition or from existing manuscripts. At the same time, it is evident that the variants, be they oral or scribal, in all manuscripts are *not* very significant. This would point to a well established oral (singing) tradition written down by several scribes at more or less the same time.

Let us briefly point out the factors which suggest that there must have been several 'musical' compilers (see also below, Ch. 3.3).

- No 'musical' manuscript gives the same *number* of *padas.*
- No manuscript --not even of the same group-- gives *identical padas.* Some *padas* are missing in one Ms. of one group, but are found in one or two of the other group.
- Even within one 'musical' group we find different *rāgas* for the same *pad.*
- Further, a detailed analysis of the variants in the 'musical' Mss. shows that there is no consistency at all in the variants. If we try to categorise that phenomenon as scribal contamination, adopting the archetype approach, we can easily send an entry to the Guinness Book of Records. Nowhere else can such a huge amount of scribal 'contamination' be found.

(78) M. Juergensmeyer and N. G. Barrier, eds., *Sikh Studies, Comparative Perspectives on a Changing Tradition,* Berkeley, 1979, p. 76, n.5; see also Ch. Vaudeville, *Kabīr I,* p. 56 and P.N. Tivārī, *Kabīr Granthāvalī,* p. 55f.

The musical collections aim at completeness: *all* the *padas* of Nāmdev, known at a particular place, are recorded, as a single corpus.

It is interesting to note the attempts to make the existing 'musical' corpus more complete, possibly by a scribe (or a reader) at a later date who knew some songs not registered. These songs are in a distinctly different hand and do not fit into the pattern of classification. One example may be given from Ms. *u*, song 15b (see Ill. 4; App. 7): a later reader or collector took advantage of the fact that the page was relatively empty and added a song. Not only is the hand in which the new song is written different, but the *rāg lalit* is given nowhere else in the entire Nāmdev corpus. The song must have been copied from another Ms. or may have been written from memory.

The *padas* in the musical collections are arranged according to *rāg:* all the *padas* which are meant to be sung to the same *rāg* are brought together into a single group. In this way the whole *pad* corpus of a poet is divided into a number of *rāg* groups, a pattern reminiscent of the *Guru Granth.* The difference is that in these collections, the *padas* of different saints are separately recorded: the corpus of one saint is recorded in full before the corpus of another saint is taken up for a similar treatment. Also, unlike the *Guru Granth,* these collections do not have, with a few exceptions, sub-groups within individual *rāg* groups.

Though most of our musical manuscripts *(h, a, n, v, m, d, p)*[79] can be classified as Dādūpanthī and *Pañcavāṇī,* manuscript *u* is Dādūpanthī, but not *Pañcavāṇī.* It shows clear Nāthpanthī influences. All the *Pañcavāṇī* Mss. record the *padas, sākhīs* and *ramainīs* of the *Pañcavāṇī* saints in the order noted earlier. The works of Kabīr, Nāmdev, Raidās and Hardās follow those of Dādū in an unbroken sequence except in the case of Mss. *m* and *v.*

Manuscript *m* inserts a small work called *Anabhay Prabodha* of Dādū's son[80] Garibdās and a *pad* of Rāmānand and Maskīn between the works of Dādū and Kabīr. The remaining classification is the same. Manuscript *v* also has the same order, but inserts a short work by Rajab called *Utpatinirṇay Granth,* between Dādū and Kabīr.

Summing up

All *Pañcavāṇī* Mss. are copied within the Dādūpanth, as is indicated not only by the prominence given in them to Dādū's writings, but also by the fact that they include many works of Dādū's followers.

One factor which sharply distinguishes them from the non *Pañcavāṇī* manuscripts is the inclusion of the songs and verses of Hardās, the fifth of the five *Pañcavāṇī* poets. Who this Hardās was, we do not know, but he is certainly not to be identified with Haridās *nirañjanī,* as is sometimes done[81]. His songs are written in a fresh and forceful style which is remarkably different in diction and imagery from the general

(79) See above, Ch. 2.4.

(80) See Callewaert:74,2.

(81) Swami Mangaldās gives convincing arguments against such an identification. See *Shrī mahārāj Haridās jī kī Vāṇī saṭipaṇī va apar Nirañjanī mahātmāoṅ kī racnā ke*

run of Santa songs. His is a very 'individual' oeuvre. But, curiously, it is not to be found outside the *Pañcavāṇī* sets --not even in *guṭkās* which otherwise appear quite Dādūpanthī in character. And for this reason, Mss. *m* and *v* are *Pañcavāṇī*, although works by other Sants are inserted between the works of Dādū and Kabīr.

The Nāmdev corpus in the *Hari nām hīrā* group is relatively homogeneous[82]. The smallest, Ms. *h*, has 117 songs; Mss. *n, p* and *m* have 122, 126 and 138 respectively. We find that there are 116 songs common to all of them. The sequence in which these songs are recorded is also, to a remarkable degree, parallel.

The *Rām nām khetī* group is not so homogeneous. The smallest corpus in this set is that of Ms. *v* which has 120 songs. This corpus is much smaller than those of either Ms. *d* (which has 140 songs) or Ms. *a* (which has 146). The three manuscripts in this group have only 107 songs in common. Their sequences, also, do not agree well, not as well, that is, as the sequences we notice in the *Hari nām hīrā* set.

It is to be noted, however, that there are clusters of songs which are common to this set only. Of the three songs 126 to 128 (not found in the *hari nām hīrā* group)[83] two are common to all three Mss. of this set, and all three to Mss. *v* and *d*. The three songs 146 to 148 are missing from the *Hari nām hīrā* group and other 'musical' Mss. Song 148 is found in all three of the *Rām nām khetī* set, 146 is found in *d* and *a*, while 147 is in *d* and *v*. Song 182 is found in all the Mss. of the *Rām nām khetī* set alone. Of songs 224 to 226, 224 and 225 are missing from the *Hari nām hīrā* set, 224 is found in *d* and *v*, 225 in a, whereas 226 is found in all three Mss. of *Rām nām khetī* and only in Ms. *m* of the *Hari nām hīrā* set. Of the four songs 234 to 237 which are almost[84] unknown to the *Hari nām hīrā* set, two --234 and 235-- are found in all three Mss. of the *Rām nām khetī* set; the other two are found in *d* and *a*.

There are also certain songs found in *Hari nām hīrā* but uniformly missing in *d, v* and *a* as a group: songs 72[85] 80, 84[86]. These uniformities, though not as great as those between the Mss. of the *Hari nām hīrā* set, are sufficient for us to consider Mss. *d, v* and *a* as forming a separate set.

2.8. The non *Pañcavāṇī* Mss. *u, c* and *j*

Besides the two *Pañcavāṇī* sets, there are three other manuscripts which fall distinctly into two sets: the *lādhau tau lādhau* set and the *rām nām boli* set.

---

anshānsh, Jaipur, 1962. See also L. De Brabandere, *The Haridāsa of the Dādūpanthī Pañcavāṇī*, in Monika Thiel:1983, p. 85-86.

(82) See also below, Ch. 3.3.

(83) These numbers refer to the numerical place which the songs occupy in our own 'exhaustive' corpus.

(84) We say 'almost' because song 234 is found in *m* and *p* of the *Hari nām hīrā* set.

(85) This is a song missing only from the three Mss. of the *Rām nām khetī* set.

(86) Found in only two Mss. of the *hari nām hīrā* set (*m* and *p*).

Ms. u.

Of the *lādhau tau lādhau* set, we discovered only one manuscript: *u*. Like the other Mss. we have examined, this is clearly a copy and presumably other Mss. of the set are or were in existence. For that reason the use of the word 'set' is not misplaced, though we have only one sample in this case. Ms. *u* is Dādūpanthī, but non *Pañcavāṇī*, though it includes the works of Dādū, his son Garibdās, his disciples Rajab, Sundardās and others of the Panth. In fact, Ms. *u* records works of all the *Pañcavāṇī* poets except Hardās[87]. Ms. *u* is also different from Mss. *c* and *j*, which also exclude Hardās, but which are distinctly non-Dādūpanthī: they do not record the work of Dādū, although Dādū was one of the most celebrated Sants in Rājasthān when these *guṭkās* were copied. Significantly, *c* and *j* include the works of Kabīr, Nāmdev and Raidās. These 3 poets are not given together in Ms. *u*, which gives as many Dādūpanthī as Nāth Siddha works, along even with Tulsīdās and Sūrdās[88].

Mss. c and j

Mss. *c* and *j*, which form the *Rām nām boli* set, are almost like twins. They show a similarity in their Nāmdev corpora which is much greater than between any two other Mss. in our collection[89]. This similarity is all the more remarkable since it is limited to the Nāmdev corpus alone; in other ways they are as dissimilar as two *guṭkās* can be.

Ms. *u*, -although it is a non *Pañcavāṇī* collection- records works of Dādū and his disciples. But *c* and *j* seem almost untouched by Dādūpanthī influence as the list of their contents illustrates[90]. The list also shows that the two *guṭkās* are, except for Nāmdev, very distinct entities. Some further details, besides the lists of their contents may help to appreciate the great difference between them. Both Mss. *c* and *j* give preference to Nāth works, which form the bulk of their contents. But Ms. *c* also has Vaiṣṇava leanings. It begins with some Sanskrit *stotras* and the Sanskrit -both the language and the orthography- of its first three works *(Viṣṇusahasranāma, Viṣṇupañjarastotra* and *Rāmarakṣāstotra)* is much better than the Sanskrit, wherever it occurs, of the Dādūpanthī Mss. The remaining Hindī works in this manuscript are written in the same hand, interspersed with a few pages clearly written by other scribes.

Ms. *c* has two colophons by the scribe Venīrām in whose hand the bulk of the collection is written. The first colophon occurs on folio 16 and reads 1717 VS (see Ill. 5; App. 7). The second, again by Venīrām was written seven years later in VS 1726, though in the same place, which in this colophon is written 'Lavāin' instead of the earlier 'Lavāṇi'.

---

(87) For a detailed list of the poets and their works found in Ms. *u*, see G.N. Bahurā, *Vidyā-Bhūshan-Sangrah-Sūci*, Jaipur,1961, p. 201-213.

(88) For the colophon of Ms. *u*, (1741 VS) see App. 7, III.3.

(89) See also below, Ch. 3.3.

(90) For the contents of Ms. *c* (1660 AD) and (1681 AD), see Callewaert:1980,1, pp. 37-38.

The colophon occurs at the end of the songs of Datta *(Dattajī kī sabadī;* see Ill. 6; App. 7).

The manuscript also has a third colophon' (dated Vikram 1742 or seven years after the second colophon noted above). It is not in Venīrām's hand and is rather odd because it is noted in the margin of a page which is clearly in Venīrām's hand. The 'colophon', if it can be called one, occurs on folio 17 (see Ill. 7; App. 7). There are also some *padas* and *sākhīs* written by different hands in different parts of the Ms., evidently on spaces which had been blank, but we are not able to decide which of these --if any-- are by the scribe who wrote this 'colophon'.

Of the five Sants quoted in the *Pañcavāṇī,* both Mss. *c* and *j*, as we have said earlier, record only Kabīr, Nāmdev and Rāidās. Both Mss. also record them in that order. While *c* has only a handful of *sākhīs* by Kabīr, *j* has 847. Ms. *c* records the *padas* of Kabīr in two separate instalments. At the end of the first instalment, the scribe Venīrām informs us that 80 more *padas* of Kabīr are recorded on pages to follow. The oeuvre of Kabīr in *j* is not only more exhaustive but also better organised. After the 847 *sākhīs* of Kabīr, *j* records his *Vār*, his *Bāvani,* his *Tithi,* his *Saptapadi* and his *Daśapadī* before it comes to the *pad* corpus, which is followed by the *Ramainīs.* Nāmdev follows Kabīr, but not directly, as in manuscript *c,* since the *śabdī* (verses) of Pātu come in between.

There are reasons to believe that Mss. *c* and *j* are not direct copies made from the same exemplar, although the charts (3.2. ff.) reveal a relatively 'close' resemblance. We list the reasons below:

1. There is one case of a difference in the sequence in which the songs are recorded in the two Mss. The song which is no. 5 in *c* is no. 6 in *j* (see Table II; below, 3.5, under *rāg gauḍ).*
2. Both Mss. group songs in *rāg* sets, as do the others, but we notice a curious case of misplacement which both Mss. share. In the *gauṇḍ* set (the same as the *gauḍ* of our Table II), Ms. *c* has two songs marked *rāg soraṭhī;* which should have been placed in the *soraṭh* set. The same two songs (nos. 49 and 50 in our collection) occur at the same place in Ms. *j* (they are 62 and 63 in both Mss.), but here --and this is a revealing fact-- only the *second* of them is marked *soraṭhī,* the first is marked *guṇḍ* (see Table II).
3. There are also differences in readings which cannot be mere scribal errors. We quote a few examples:

In song 13, *antarā* 3, line 1, Ms. *j* has *sādh* where all other Mss. (including *c)* have *sant.*

In song 21, *antarā* 3, line 1, Ms. *j* has *jāne* where all other Mss. (including *c)* have *rījhe.*

In song 51, *antarā* 1, line 2, Ms. *j* has *kesav* where all other Mss. (including Ms. c) have *keval.* In the same song *antarā* 4, line 2, *c* has *sāhib* where all other Mss. including j, have *svāmi.*

In song 61, *antarā* 4, line 1, *j* has *prīti* where Ms. *c* and one other Ms. has *dīpa* while no other Ms. has *prīti.* In the same song (61) *antarā* 6, line 1, Ms. *j* and one other Ms. have *khīr* where all other Mss. (including Ms. c) have *bhog*.

Like other Mss., *c* and *j* show signs of being copies. But they are not copies made from the same exemplar. Their differences are too great to allow such a conclusion. What we have seem to be copies of copies which go back to two separate though closely related ancestors, representing a distinct manuscript tradition.

This is an important conclusion, since both *c* and *j* were copied at a date much later than many of the *Pañcavāṇī* Mss. This could wrongly cause us to give more importance to the *Pañcavāṇī* Mss., especially because they are also greater in number. If, however, Mss. *c* and *j* belong to a manuscript tradition which could be as old as the *Pañcavāṇī* Mss. tradition, then they deserve equal weight in our consideration. It may seem strange that we have only two examples of this tradition. This is not, however, surprising since the Dādūpanth was clearly the most active sect in copying and preserving *nirguṇ* works. The tradition was less strong in other sects. Because of their independence from the Dādūpanth Mss. *c* and *j* have a unique value for text-critical research in *nirguṇ* material.

The absence of Dādūpanthī influence in the Nāmdev corpus of Ms. *c* is also revealed by another significant circumstance. At the end of Ms. *c* occurs a miscellaneous collection containing 15 *padas* by different Saṇts. Two of them (4 and 7) are by Nāmdev. These two songs do not occur in the 'complete' Nāmdev corpus recorded earlier in the manuscript. No. 7 is the same as our no. 170, a song found only in a Poona Ms. The *ṭek* of no. 4 has the same beginning as our no. 113 *(jab tab rām nām nistārai)*, but the rest of the song is entirely different. Interestingly, one of the 15 *padas* -- which include these two Nāmdev songs-- is a song by Hardās, who as we said is a poet so far not found outside the Dādūpanthī *Pañcavāṇī* collections. One might expect that the two extra Nāmdev *padas* which Ms. *c* records separately, along with Hardās, were collected from Dādūpanthī sources, since Hardās is recorded only in Dādūpanthī Mss. But none of these two Nāmdev songs occur in any Dādūpanthī manuscript.

The dissimilarity between *c* and *j* as *guṭkās* makes the striking similarity between their Nāmdev corpora all the more remarkable. How great this similarity is can perhaps best be seen in the two tables (see below Ch. 3.4 and 3.5), where we can see more graphically that no two other Mss. have the same degree of similarity. See also Ch. 3.3.

We have seen that many of our 'musical' manuscripts are copies. Indeed, most manuscripts we consulted show obvious signs of being copies of older manuscripts. Manuscript *d*, the oldest, reveals features clearly suggesting that it is copied from another manuscript; our examination is limited to the portion which records the songs of Nāmdev. The features are as follows:

a. On folio 194a we have an interesting omission: in copying the song (148 in our list), the scribe by mistake wrote *antarā* 4 after *antarā* 2. He immediately realised his mistake and deleted the line he had

written with a horizontal stroke. To make sure that there should be no mistake about the deletion, he added small vertical strokes above the letters. This was the usual sign for deletion in 17th century Rājasthānī Mss. He then wrote *antarā* 3 and rewrote *antarā* 4 again, this time in its proper place (see Ill. 8; App. 7).
A similar mistake is found in song 235 (115 in Ms. *d;* see Ill. 9; App. 7).

b. In Ms. *d,* song 67 (67 in our list) is followed by song 66. The scribe of manuscript *d* does not separate the second from the first, which has two *antarās,* the second containing the *bhaṇitā.* The *ṭek* of the second is made into the 3rd *antarā* of the first song, while the rest of the song is recorded as *antarā* 4. This is even more obviously a scribe's mistake, a conclusion further strengthened by another fact. The two songs merged into one in this manuscripts are both in *rāg rāmkalī.* The manuscript numbers every song in a *rāg* individually. The last song in *rāmkalī* bears the number 22, but the song before it is numbered 20. The preceding one, number 19, is the two-in-one song where the numbering went wrong. It is clear that number 22, the correct number of songs in that *rāg,* was copied by the scribe from another manuscript. For what reason, otherwise, would he have the correct number? In *his* count the songs number only 21.
Further, at the end of the Nāmdev corpus, this manuscript notes the total number of songs recorded as 140. We can get this figure only if song 19 is counted as two songs instead of one. Merging these two songs into one was obviously a mistake made by the scribe who wrote Ms. *d.* The manuscript from which he was copying did not have this mistake. In making a copy, the scribe of Ms. *d* boxed together the two songs by mistake, but carefully retained the correct numbering of the original from which he was copying.

If our manuscripts are copies, the question arises of *when* the manuscript tradition started. We may perhaps assume that the recording of oral repertoires started during Dādū's life (d.1603). However, we have so far not found any records *about* literary activity in the early Dādūpanth.

2.9 The puzzle of the variants

The puzzle of classification

Although we have spoken of the *Pañcavāṇī* Mss. as falling into two distinct groups, distinct also from the non *Pañcavāṇī* Mss., this does not preclude the curious and baffling fact that in many cases, the Mss. of one group show clear signs of relationship not only with each other, but also with Mss. of a different group altogether. This could point to some kind of contamination between, on the one hand, the repertoire a scribe knew by heart and, on the other hand, the manuscript he had before him.

As illustrations we note the following:

- Group I (Mss. *d,v,a*).

Ten songs (81; 107; 116; 161; 195; 247; 250; 251; 253; 254) are found in only Ms. *d* (1636 AD; 140 songs) and in no other Ms. of group I, but are found in Mss. of group II and in other recensions. This most ancient Ms. was clearly not copied from any of the Mss. of our selection.

Songs 104 and 158 are found only in Ms. *v* (1658 AD; 120 songs) and in no other Ms. of group I, but are found in Mss. of group II and in other recensions.

Nineteen songs (17; 32; 40; 45; 46; 47; 69; 85; 114; 137; 140; 141; 163; 186; 188; 190; 225; 231; 232) are found only in Ms. *a* (1675 AD; 146 songs) and in no other Ms. of group I, but are found in Mss. of group II and in other recensions.

- Group II (Mss. *h,n,m,p*).

Song 102 is found only in Ms. *n* (1664 AD;122 songs) and in no other Ms. of group II, but is found in Mss. of group I and in other recensions.

Thirteen songs (83; 84; 130; 143; 163; 171; 174; 227; 244; 245; 246; 255; 256) are found only in Ms. *m* (1676 AD;133 songs) and in no other Ms. of group II, but are found in Mss. of group I and in other recensions.

Songs 82 and 195 are found only in Ms. *p* (1698 AD; 126 songs) and in no other Ms. of group II, but are found in Mss. of group I and in other recensions.

It is equally puzzling that several songs found only in two Mss. of one *Pañcavāṇī* group, occur also in the Mss. of the other group and in other recensions. Some songs are found in only one of the selected Mss. They are not even found in the Mss. selected by Bh. Miśra:1964 (see above, 2.5; see also those found after song 230).

The following songs were found only in three later Mss. consulted by Bh. Miśra:1964 (Pune, 1811; Pandharpur, n.d.; Ghuman, ca. 1750): 166-170; 172-173; 175-176; 178-181; 183-185; 187; 189; 191-194; 196-198; 228-230, i.e. a total of 28.

From this analysis we draw the following conclusions. Except for Mss. *c* and *j* which are clearly related, no Ms. is directly derived from any other at our disposal. They all seem to depend on a separate oral source. Considering their rather direct dependence on the oral tradition, we may reasonably assert that all Mss., including those within one *Pañcavāṇī* group, are like distinct recensions. Moreover, as the charts reveal, the patterns of classification of the songs are so divergent that we must think of more than one *Pañcavāṇī* compiler, each most probably working independently. Further, the non *Pañcavāṇī* recensions seem to depend on quite a different singing tradition.

This must lead us to the conclusion that the variants we find in the Mss. are to a great extent due to dialectical and regional peculiarities of the oral tradition. For this reason we found it useful to give the variants in the Word-Index (Ch. 6).

It would be very interesting to study the works of another poet, perhaps Kabīr, in these *Pañcavāṇīs* in order to see if the same conclusion is reached that *several compilers have drawn from different singing traditions.* The *rāg* pattern in which the songs are classified in the 'musical' Mss. points to a nebulous oral tradition developing into separate writing traditions.

Variation in rāg

We call this tradition nebulous because it eludes our text-critical grasp. However, looking at manuscripts at our disposal, certain facts emerge. There was clearly a great diversity among the different 'versions', but there was also a remarkable degree of uniformity, as the *rāg* pattern reveals. This uniformity perhaps points to a single Rājasthānī tradition from which different *gharānās* branched off.

Let us now look at each set of songs classified under one *rāg.* It appears that those songs which show some irregularity as far as the *rāg* is concerned, are often also less 'authentic' from the point of view of occurrence in Mss., of order and of variants. Of the 27 songs listed below, only 3 with a different *rāg* are found in all the musical recensions. In other words: nearly all songs found in all the 'recensions' are also classified under the same *rāg.*

For an overall view of this interesting correlation that there is a greater variety of *rāg* for those songs which are found in fewer 'recensions', we give in Table A below those songs which have a different *rāg* in different manuscripts, with the following abbreviations: A for *āsāvari,* B for *bhairū,* G for *gauḍ,* Gi for *gauḍī,* Gu for *guṇḍa,* K for *kalyān,* Ka for *kāfī,* Kd for *kanaḍau,* L for *lalit,* M for *mārū,* P for *parjīyau,* R for *rāmkalī,* S for *soraṭh,* Sa for *sāraṅg,* Su for *sūhav,* T for *ṭoḍī.*

Table A

	h	n	m	p	d	v	a	u	c	j
rāg ṭoḍī										
43*	43	43	42	43-	28	30	94K	55	13K	13K
44*	44	44	43	44-G	31	31	40	56		
rāg gauḍ										
49*	46	46	45	46-	67	40	68	71	62So	62So
55*		52		52-	82	42T	84			
65*	62	63	61	63-	61R	54	62	78		
66*	63	64	62	64-	62R	55	63	79		
67*	64	65	63	65-	63R	56	67	80		
68*	66	67	65	67-	65R	58	77	82		
69						44T		61	61	

rāg sorath										
79*	75	76	80	76	90	6T	93	29T	1	1
82*				114	89	5T	41T	65bKa	4	40
Rāg māli gauḍī										
83*			67Gu		112		78Gu		8Gi	8Gi
84*			85		88G	68T	92Gi	98	9	9
85						79Gu		10	10	
86				110		80Gu		11	11	
87				113		81	6Gi	5Gi		
Rāg rāmkalī										
100*	89	91	100	92-	49	81	46T	13		
Rāg basant										
112*	97	100	108L	100-	103L	93L		94		
113*	98	101	109	101	104L		117R	15bL		
114*	99	102	111	102-			136P			
Rāg dhanāśrī										
143			110L							
146				38T		4T				
147				99A	90A					
148				29T	112	138Su				
163			124M			100Kd				
164*	88	90	99R	91-	44R	80	112R	12R		
165*	65	66	64	66-G	64R	57Gu	59G	81G		
	h	n	m	p	d	v	a	u	c	j

Rāg ṭoḍī (songs 1-47)

Although the order of the songs in this set varies considerably in the different recensions, nearly all the songs are classified under *ṭoḍī*, even

in Mss. *f* (Fatehpur) and *g* (Gopāldās *Sarvāṅgī*). The only exceptions are song 1 and song 31, which in Ms. *g* appear under *guṇḍa*.
Song 43 appears in Mss. *c, j* and *a* under *kalyān*. The next song appears in Ms. *m* under *guṇḍa*. On the whole the *ṭoḍī* set may be said to be very regular and uniform. It seems to rely on an ancient source. The pattern looks more erratic in the next sets. More songs are found under different *rāgas*.

- *Rāg gauḍ (songs* 48-69).
  Song 49 appears in Mss. *c* and *j* under *soraṭh*.
  Song 55 appears in Ms. *a* under *ṭoḍī*.
  Songs 65-68 appear in Ms. *d* under *rāmgari*.
  Song 69 --occurring in very few Mss.-- appears in Ms. *a* under *ṭoḍī*.
  Song 58 appears in Rajab's *Sarvāṅgī* under *ṭoḍī*.
- *Rāg soraṭh (songs* 70-75).
  The few songs in this set are all classified under *soraṭh*.
- *Rāg gauḍī (songs* 76-82).
  Song 79 appears in Mss. *u* and *v* under *ṭoḍī*.
  Song 82 appears in Ms. *u* (65b, added in a later hand) under *rāg kāfī --a rāg* not found in any other Ms.--, in Ms. *v* and *a* under *ṭoḍī* and in Rajab's Sarvāṅgī under *sāraṅg*.
- *Rāg māligauḍī (songs* 83-87).
  Song 83 appears in Mss. *c* and *j* under *gauḍī*, in Ms. *a* and *m* under *guṇḍa*.
  Song 84 appears in Ms. *u* under *gauḍī*, in Ms. *v* under *ṭoḍī* and in Ms. *d* under *gauḍa*.
  Songs 85 and 86 appear in Ms. *a* under *guṇḍa*.
  Song 87 appears in Mss. *c* and *j* under *gauḍī*.
  This set clearly shows more diversity than uniformity.
- *Rāg rāmgarī (songs* 88-105).
  Song 100 appears in Ms. *a* under *ṭoḍī*.
  Except for the fact that in several Mss. we find *rāmkalī* for *rāmgarī*, this set is fairly uniform.
- *Rāg āsāvarī (songs* 106-109).
  This set is remarkably uniform, but is missing in Mss. *c* and *j*.
- *Rāg vasant (songs* 110-114).
  Song 112 appears in Ms. *v, d* and *m* under *lalit*.
  Song 113 appears in Ms. *d* and *u* (15b, in a different hand), under *lalit*, and in Ms. *a* under *rāmgari*. Song 114 appears in Ms. *a* under *parajīyau*.
  In Mss. *c* and *j* no song is found in this *rāg*.
- *Rāg bhairū* (songs 115-130).
  All songs are classified under *bhairū*.
- *Rāg kanaḍau* (songs 131-134).
  Only one song (131) appears in Mss. *c* and *j* under *kānharau*, which is another name for *kānaḍau*.

Rāgas mārū, parjīyau, kalyān and *sāraṅg* (songs 135-139).
  All songs appear under the same *rāg*.
- *Rāg dhanāśrī* (songs 140-165).
  Song 143 appears in Ms. *m* (110) under *lalit*.
  Song 146 appears in Ms. *a* and Ms. *d* under *ṭoḍī*.

Song 147 appears in Rajab's *Sarvāṅgī*, in Ms. *v* and in Ms. *d* under *asāvarī*.
Song 148 appears in Ms. *a* under *sūhav* and in Ms. *d* and Rajab's *Sarvāṅgī* under *ṭoḍī*.
Song 158 appears in Ms. *v* under *bhairū*. Bh. Miśra:1964 classifies it under *dhanāśrī*.
Song 163 appears in Ms. *a* under *kanaḍau* and in Ms. *m* under *mārū*.
Song 164 appears in Ms. *u, a, m* and d under *rāmgarī*.
Song 165 appears in Mss. *u, p* and *a* under *gauḍ*, in Ms. *v* under *guṇḍa* and in Ms. *d* under *rāmgarī*.
'No *rāg*' in Miśra:1964 (166-230).
Song 171 appears in Ms. *m* (70) under *guṇḍa*.
Song 177 appears in Ms. *u* (15c, in a later hand) under *lalit*.
Song 182 appears under *bhairū*, song 186 under *guṇḍa*, song 188 under *bhairū*, song 190 under *ṭoḍī*, song 195 under *bhairū*, song 206, 224 and 225 under *guṇḍa*.
Song 226 appears in Ms. *a* (140) under *sūhav*, in Ms. *d* (30) under *ṭoḍī* and in Ms. *v* (112) under *parajīyau*.

Table B: sequence of rāgas in the 'musical' collections of Rājasthān

The numbers indicate the sequence of songs in each Ms. We have standardized the spelling of the *rāgas*. Note that Ms. *p* has *rāg gauḍī* twice. The first *gauḍī* seems to be a scribal error for *gauḍ*, as all the Mss. of the *'hari nāv hīrā'* group have *gauḍ*.

In Ms. *v* we find two songs under *'ārati'*, which is not a *rāg*. It suggests the liturgical use of these songs, which in other Mss. are in *dhanāśrī*. In Ms. *v* we notice another peculiarity: *rāg ṭoḍī* occurs twice; the second occurrence, however, is qualified by *'dakkhinī pad'* (southern song); indeed, these songs show a clear Marāṭhī influence.

Group I: Mss. *h n p m (hari nāv hīrā)*

h	n	p	m
ṭoḍī 1-44	ṭoḍī 1-44	ṭoḍī 1-44	ṭoḍī 1-43
gauḍ 45-66	gauḍ 45-67	gauḍi 45-67	gauḍ 44-70
sorath 67-71	soraṭh 68-72	soraṭh 68-72	soraṭh 71-76
gauḍi 72-76	gauḍi 73-77	gauḍi 73-77	gauḍi 77-84
--	--	--	māligauḍī 85-86
rāmkalī 77-90	rāmkalī 78-93	rāmkalī 78-93	rāmkalī 88-101
āsāvarī 91-94	āsāvarī 94-97	āsāvarī 94-97	āsāvarī 102-1
basant 95-99	basant 98-102	basant 98-99	basant 106-107
--	--	lalit 100-102	lalit 108-111
bhairū 100-108	bhairū 103-113	bhairū 103-114	bhairū 112-121
kanaḍau 109-110	kanaḍau 114-115	kanaḍau 115-117	kanaḍau 122-123
mārū 111	mārū 116	mārū 118	mārū 124-125
parajīyau 112	parajīyau 117	parajīyau 119	parajīyau 126
kalyān 113	kalyān 118	kalyān 120	kalyān 127
sāraṅg 114	sāraṅg 119	sāraṅg 121	sāraṅg 128
dhanāśrī 115-117	dhanāśrī 120-122	dhanāśrī 122-126	
dhanāśrī 129-138			

Group II: Mss. *v a d (rām nām khetī), c/j* and *u.*

v	a	d	c/j	u
ṭoḍī 1-38	ṭoḍī 1-53	ṭoḍī 1-43	gauḍi 1-8	rāmkalī 1-15
gauḍ 39-59	gauḍ 54-82	rāmkalī 44-65	mālīgauḍī 9-11	lalit 15b-15c
soraṭh 60-63	soraṭh 83-87	gauḍ 66-83	kalyān 12-13	bhairū 16-24
gauḍi 64-68	gauḍi 88-91	gauḍi 84-91	kānhaḍau 14	ṭoḍī 25-65
rāmkalī 69-86	mālīgauḍī 92-93	soraṭh 92-95	kedārau 15	kāfī 65b
āsāvarī 87-90	kalyān 94-95	āsāvarī 96-100	rāmkalī 16-23	āsāvarī 66-69
basant 91-92	kanaḍau 96-98	basant 101-102	parajīy 24	gauḍ 70-84
lalit 93	mārū kh. 99-100	lalit 103-104	sāraṅga 25	soraṭh 85-89
			ṭoḍī 26-55	
bhairū 94-106	rāmkalī 101-117	kanaḍau 106-108	soraṭh 56-59	parajīy 90
kanaḍau 107 -109	āsāvarī 118-121	mālīgauḍī 109-113	gauḍ 60-72	dhanāśrī 91
parajīy 110-111	basant 122-123	parajīy 114-115	bhairū 73-81	basant 92-94
ṭoḍī 112-114	bhairū124-134	bhairū 116-130	dhanāśrī 82-85	gauḍi 95-99
bilāval 115	parajīy 135	aibilā 131-135		kalyān 100
kanaḍau 116	parajīyau 136	bilāval 136		kanaḍau 101-103
sāraṅg 117	sūhav 137-141	mārū 137		
dhanāśrī 118	dhanāśrī 142-146	dhanāśrī 138-140		
ārati 119-120				

2.10. Orthography in the manuscripts

The following pages may be discouraging to all of us who hope one day to feed Devnāgarī manuscripts into the computer through optical scansion. Every scribe had his particular handwriting, often difficult to decipher even for the human eye. Anurādhā Pātnī, Jaipur, thought of both the human reader working with manuscripts and the designer for optical scansion, when she --very meticulously-- copied via a projection the peculiar letters scribes produced in the manuscripts we studied. The definition of several letters was possible only through induction, comparing the line with the parallel passage in other manuscripts. This list may be helpful for the reading of a difficult letter when parallel manuscripts are not available. We are obliged also to Bart Op de Beeck for the careful layout of this list.

इ इंद्र इव आइ जाइ
कांइ इक पाइ

ई होई जाई जाई काई
केई सुई कोई

उ उज्जल उतरे उतरे उपाइ
उतरे उतरे जीउं उदास

ऊ ऊठ ऊजल गाऊं तऊ
तऊ ऊधारा सीऊं

ए एक एक

ऐ एकल ऐसे ऐकल ऐकल
ऐक

कु ठाकुर

कु

क्त

क्ष

ष

घ

घ्र

छ

छू

छ्य

झ

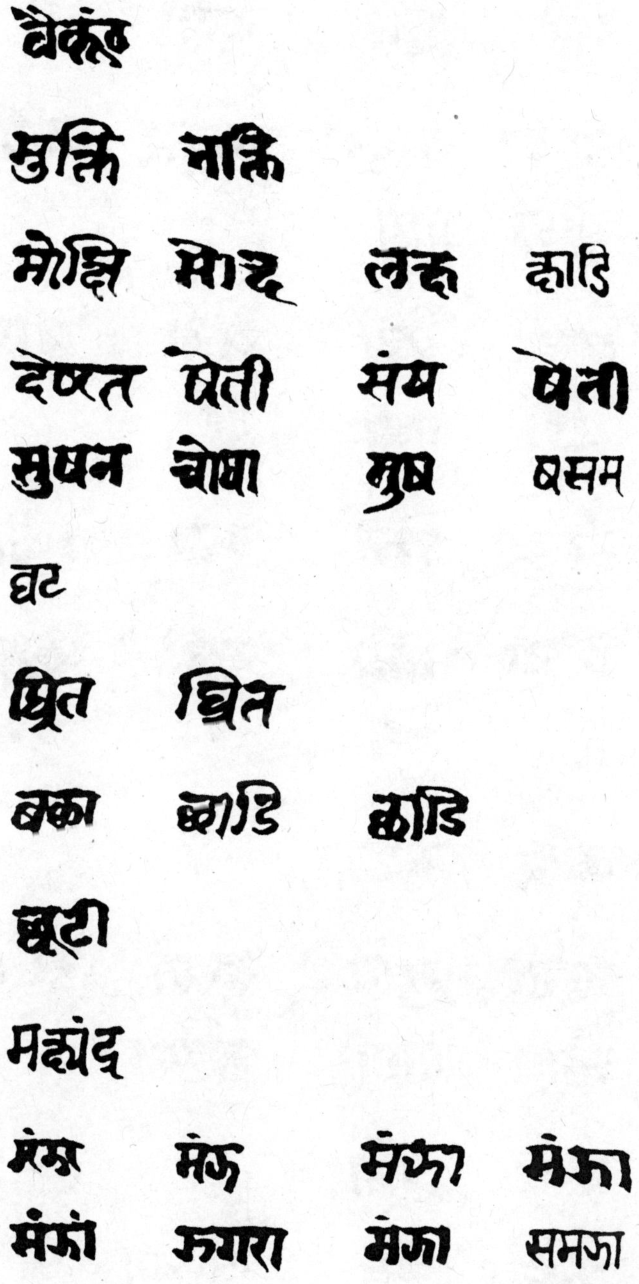

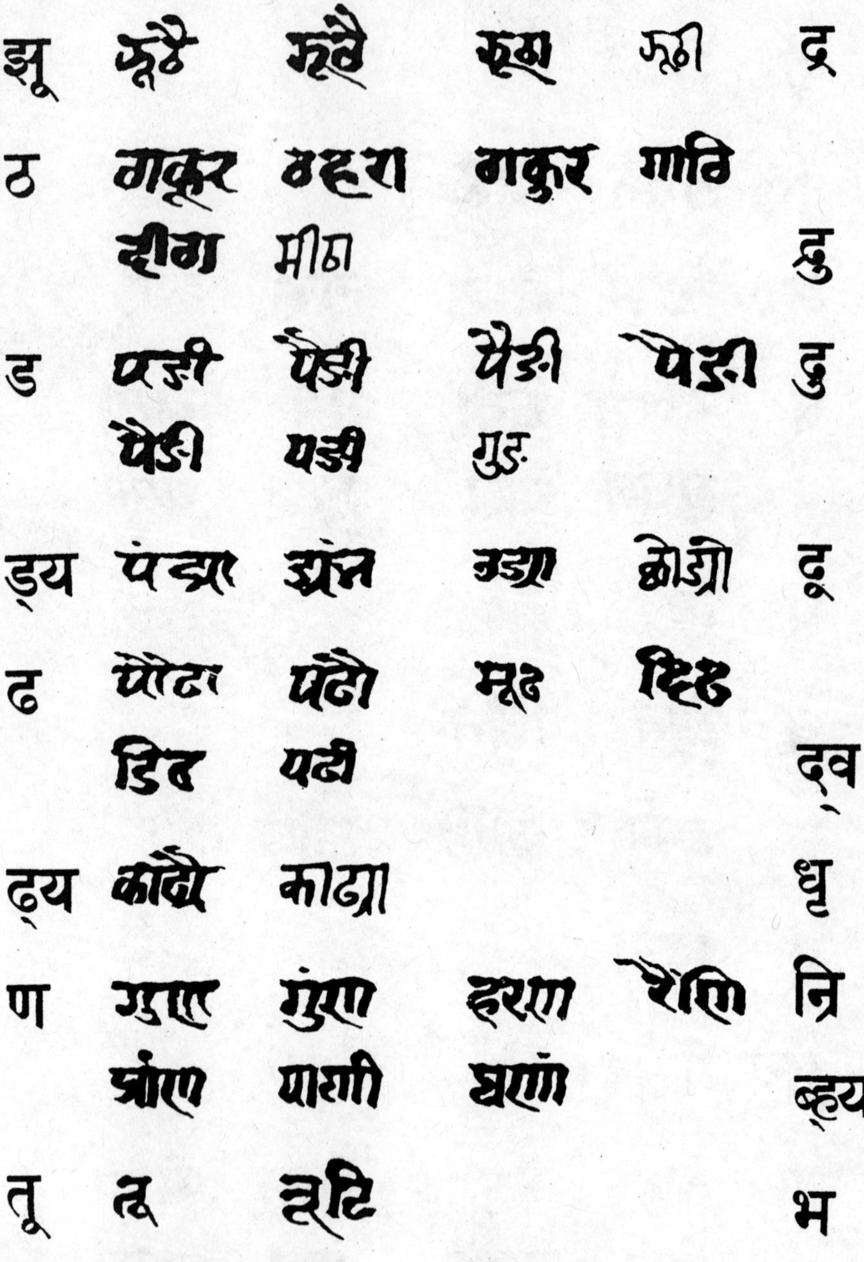
झू
ठ
ड
ड़्य
ढ
ढ़्य
ण
तु
त्र
द्र
द्व
त्रि
ह्‌य
भ

द्र यंद्र यंद्र द्रिढ द्रिष्टी
कालेंद्री

द्रु द्रुमति द्रुमति द्रुमति

दु दुवार दुष दुहेली दुवार
दुवार

दू दूध दूजा दूजा माहू
दूजा दूजा

द्व द्वाद द्वार द्वार द्वार

धृ धिग धृग

न्त्रि न्त्रिमल

ह्य जिह्वा जिह्वा

भ भवन भौरे भाव भये
भये भगति भाई

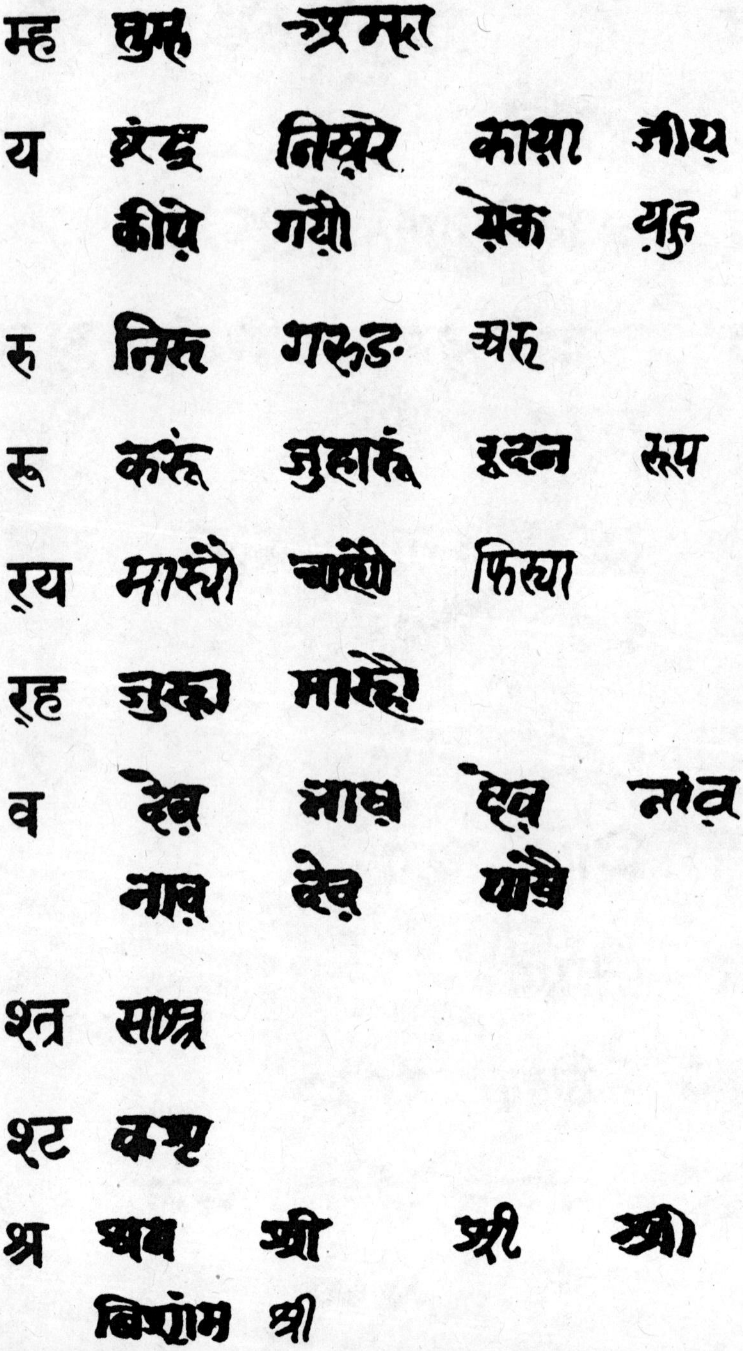
म्ह
य
रु
रू
ऱ्य
ऱ्ह
व
श्त्र
श्ट
श्र

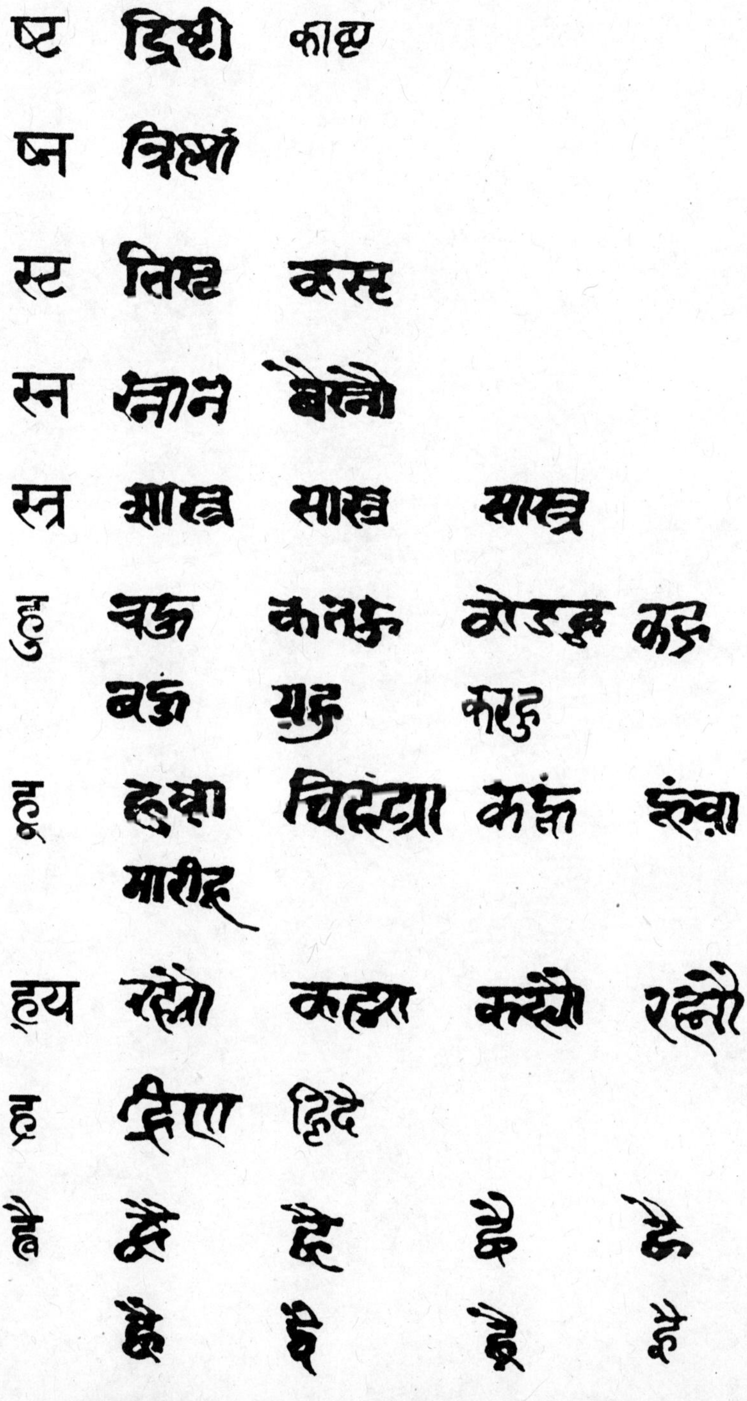
ष्ट
ष्न
स्ट
स्न
स्त्र
ह्य
है

CHAPTER 3

NĀMDEV COMPUTED

3.1. Computer programmes

In the next sections we should like to describe how the computer was useful in formulating a hypothesis about the relation between 'Early Hindī' manuscripts written around 1640 AD, and the original version of hymns of the poet-mystic Nāmdev, who lived around 1400 AD, in North-West India. The methodology may be helpful to others working on oral or on manuscript literature, especially in non-European alphabets.

We have described elsewhere[1] how we feed Hindī texts into the computer in the original Hindī alphabet, which appears both on the screen and on paper. The input of the manuscripts is highly facilitated because only the largest manuscript (or the most reliable) is typed in fully. Of the other manuscripts only the variants are typed, while identical forms are entered by simply pressing one key. Depending on the number of variants, only a small portion of each manuscript may actually have to be typed. Further, an alphabetical concordance --in the order of the Hindī alphabet-- is made by the computer, with reference to the line number. These aids are helpful for writing the 'critical text', that is the text which is most likely to represent the original version of the poet. Writing the critical text is, of course, the work of the scholar, not of the computer. Another programme produces a *glossary* in which is given all --or selected strings-- of the critical line (with the variants of the manuscripts in brackets), with references. Again, the computer produces the *'critical apparatus'* or footnotes with all variants of the manuscripts, together with the corresponding form in the 'critical text'.

The hymns of Nāmdev (1350-1430) under study here have passed through several centuries of oral transmission. Handled by guilds or families of musicians, they were subject to the creative genius of these musicians, who often changed them to suit their metrical or musical requirements, or to adapt them to a different audience and dialectical idiom. As a result, the songs were already divided into variant repertoires when scribes started to write them down, from 1600 AD onwards. And then the tampering of the scribes started.

---

(1) Callewaert:1984,1.

There is a difference between the variants which result from the oral transmission and those which are the result of the scribe's intervention. It is important to note this difference and computer programmes were written to handle this problem. Manuscripts give us 'variant readings' and, traditionally, on the basis of these variants scholars try to reconstruct the relation between the manuscripts, eventually arriving at a pedigree of manuscripts. This is called a stemma. A scholar studying manuscripts aims at climbing up the family tree of manuscripts to the highest point in order to reach the archetype or the version closest to the original.

In our text this does not work so simply. We do not have 'just variants' on the basis of which the stemma of manuscripts can be reconstructed. We have two kinds of variants, those resulting from the oral tradition and those from the scribal tradition. If we are able to separate the 'scribal variants' we can construct a scribal stemma, viz. a pedigree showing the relation between the manuscripts as written documents. For the text under study, however, this takes us to the confusing realization that at the beginning of the scribal period there were *several oral traditions which were written down simultaneously.*

A hypothesis about this phenomenon could be formulated only with the psychological help of mathematical certainty: this was given, with minute accuracy, through computer programmes developed to count and compare the variants.

In a general way we define the following as *'scribal' variants:* omissions or additions or synonyms which make no sense in the line or which may result from a sectarian bias, variant words which betray an effort to bring in a word as a substitute for a difficult or a controversial term in other versions. We distinguish between 'intentional' and 'unintentional' variants; the first are intended by the scribe, because he thinks he knows better or because of a sectarian bias. The second are the result of distraction or laziness. But all can be interpreted to point to a relation between manuscripts. In practice, the critic has to decide for each single case whether a particular form in a manuscript has to be considered as a scribal variant or not, intentional or not.

Again in a general way, *variants of the oral tradition* may be defined as minor changes brought about by the singer *(geyavikāras,* see Ch. 2.3), minor differences in nasalization or even spelling which may have been made in order to adapt to a particular audience and to a local idiom. We call these rather 'musical' variants, because they were generally introduced by singers and musicians. These musical variants often do not drastically change the meaning of the line. The decision which variant comes from the oral period and which variant is due to the scribal transmission is to be made by the scholar, not by the computer. Counting and comparing both types of variants in the different manuscripts is the task of the computer. But again, the interpretation is the work of the scholar.

Before we describe how the computer was useful in determining how the relation between the manuscripts on the one hand and between the musical recensions on the other is to be established, we should like to add three considerations:

1. The need for a statistical count of the variants in order to interpret the relations between manuscripts and recensions is by no means the only reason why the text was fed into the computer. This time-consuming and expensive task was justified by other very interesting results. For example, after a revision of the input the text is totally error free. Since the computer produces camera-ready copy, recopying, which in a traditional text edition often must be done as many as three times, can be avoided. Moreover, the concordance (including all variants) is produced by the computer, error free and as a camera-ready copy. Throughout the long period of study for a text of this size, we have continuous access to each line and each word through a search command for any string we want.
2. A text-edition usually takes several years. During this period the scholar not making use of a computer copies the text and slowly becomes familiar with it. As the work goes on he forms a picture, based on intuition and his manual statistics about variants. This eventually enables him to construct the stemma or family tree of the manuscripts: manuscripts which have identical variants or errors are grouped together, others are put on different branches. Thus he arrives at one or several common ancestors and on the basis of these ancestors the 'original' version is reconstructed.
Totally new in the text under study here is that in it we find variants introduced during the musical transmission along with those produced by scribes. To remember and clearly distinguish these two types of variant is a gigantic task for a human memory which has to collect its data over a span of several years.
3. Fortunately, consideration of 'musical' variants in the text does not provide the only clue pointing to an interaction and independent development during the oral period. Indian musicians used to sing clusters of songs according to particular melodies, called *rāg*, and songs were often classified under the names of these melodies. It appears that one song could be sung to different melodies and as a result we find some songs classified under a different *rāg* in different manuscripts. This variation in classification is not due to a scribe's intervention, but stems from the oral period. Thus, looking at the *rāg* pattern we are able to make a preliminary classification of the musical recensions. The statistical computer count corroborates this classification or adds nuances.

Let us now go back to our initial material, the twelve manuscripts dated 1640 AD and later. None of them seems to be a first-hand copy written straight from musical memory: they are copies of copies, and perhaps originate a musician's notebook. In each of these manuscripts we find roughly 125 songs.

If we classify the manuscripts at hand according to the arrangement of the songs, we have basically 6 recensions.

groups I-II or Mss. *dva hmp (Pañcavāṇī)*
group III or Ms. *u*
group IV or Mss. *c* and *j*
groups V-VI or Mss. *g* and *r (Sarvāṅgī)*.

Within this basic framework we have an enormous number of variant spellings, omissions and interpolations which have to be considered for the construction of the stemma. And these variants are the final, decisive clue because they are inherent in the text. It is here that the computer becomes useful, giving us an exact picture of the number of variants in each manuscript, with a distinction between the 'musical' variants and the 'scribal' variants. This distinction is entered at the moment of input.

Without the aid of a computer, when the statistical count and comparison must be based on manual count and intuition, the scholar becomes completely confused and discouraged in a dense jungle of intertwining vines and creepers.

In making a statistical analysis of the variants in the manuscripts now at hand, the musical variants were marked with an asterisk. This enabled us to visualize the interaction during the musical transmission, while scribal variants (without asterisk) allowed us to study with minute accuracy the relations in the scribal recensions and to construct a 'stemma' based on the 'scribal variants'.

As we became familiar with the manuscripts, we realized that there were two 'stemmas', one for the oral tradition and one for the written tradition. If the Nāmdev corpus had been passed on during the musical period' in one single collection (the 'One Archetype Theory'), one would expect that each song would be classified under the same musical tone *(rāg)*. But this is not the case.

3.2. The computer counts the variants

In order to illustrate the signs and conventions that were introduced during the input, we take LORD RĀM LIVES as the basic string in the 'critical text'.

LORD RĀM LIVED*: LIVETH is a *synonymous*, minor variant (in the input file marked with *)
JAGAT DĀS SINGS: three major or 'scribal' variants
LORD RĀM SINGS(NOW: NOW is an additional string
MASTERa KRISHNAa: MASTER KRISHNA is an additional line
LORD RĀM -: one string is omitted
--: a complete line is omitted
LO+ RĀM LIVES: the manuscript is broken and part of a string is missing
LORD RĀM +: the manuscript is broken and a string is missing
++: the manuscript is broken and a line is missing

On graphs (see App. 6) are shown the results of the computer count of variants in the complete Nāmdev file (nearly 2000 lines of 'critical text').

Programme I enables the scholar to distinguish between the major and the minor variants and to interpret the counts and statistics produced by the next programme by eliminating the omissions, the broken lines etc. For Graph I, see App. 6.

Programme I gives:
1. the total number of lines in the critical text and in each manuscript.
2. the total number of words in the critical text and in each manuscript.
3. the number of omitted words (represented by hyphens) in each manuscript when compared to the critical text.
4. the number of words that are broken due to the bad condition of the manuscript.
5. the number of 'dialectical' or 'minor' variants in each manuscript; in the input file an asterisk (*) is added to such a string.
6. the number of omitted lines.
7. the number of lines that are missing due to the bad condition of the manuscript.
8-9. additional words or lines (when compared to the critical text); one + represents one missing string; + attached to a word signifies that part of the word is missing.
10-11. the number of words that are half broken due to the bad condition of the manuscript.
12. the number of interpolated words in each manuscript when compared to the critical text.

Programme II gives the *absolute number of variants* when comparing *two* manuscripts or when comparing a manuscript to the critical text. For Graph II, see App. 6.

Programme III gives the *relative number of variants* in a manuscript when compared to the critical test. This relative number is obtained by multiplying the absolute number of variants in a manuscript by a factor which relates the total number of words in that manuscript to the total in the critical text. Thus we can compare the relative number of variants in a manuscript. The percentage count of these 'relative' figures is also given. For Graph III, see App. 6.

Programme IV compares only the lines that are common to two manuscripts and gives in graph IV the number of variants shared by two Mss. In brackets is given the total number of words that are identical in the two manuscripts compared. A high score of common variants suggests a close relation between two manuscripts. For each two manuscripts compared, the computer gives
- the number of identical variants
- the percentage of this number in the total amount of identical words in the two manuscripts
- the total number of identical words in two manuscripts.

Of these identical words, the words that are variant from the critical text may suggest a branching off of the two manuscripts. On the basis of these indications an attempt can be made at defining both the 'musical' and the 'scribal' traditions.

3.3. Analysis of the computer results

The bewilderment at the end of Ch. 2.9 was only a beginning. At first sight, one may be inclined to expect a close relation between manuscripts *d, v, a* (*Pañcavāṇi* group I) and between Mss. *h, m, p* (*Pañcavāṇī* group II), and a relative distance between *d, v, a* on the one hand and *h, m, p* and *u* and *c, j* on the other.

The computer count confirms just the opposite: there is no consistent relationship between two Mss. of the same 'recension'. It will also be seen that, when looking at variants from different angles, there does not even seem to be any consistent relation between manuscripts. This suggests a very nebulous interaction between singing traditions. As a result, we should not even think of looking for the 'original' Nāmdev songs.

1. Let us look at the results of analysis in Graph I (see App. 6):
   - as expected, Mss. *d,a,v* and *m,p,h* have more or less the same number of lines, followed by Ms. *g* (scribal recension), and *u, r, c* and *j*.
   - for omission of words, we note a high score in Ms. *j* (with fewer lines), and Mss. *m* and *h*.
   - Ms. *d* (the oldest Ms.) has a high score for omitted lines or, other repertoires have more additional lines.

2. Looking at the 'relative' number of 'musical' or 'dialectical' variants --those marked with an * in our input--, we classify the Mss. as follows, the highest score coming first (see Graph III, App. 6):
   j 3127; c 2227; m 2005; u 2000; v 1923; a 1569; d 1522; h 1463; p 1415; r 1245; g 1149.

and we note:
   - Mss. *c* and *j* have the top score, being quite distinct, in their musical origin, from the others.
   - Mss. *r* and *g* (scribal recensions within the Dādūpanth) have the lowest score. They possibly derive from a common (oral?) origin.
   - The *Pañcavāṇī* Mss. of both groups show no particular affinity within their own group; there is a slight pairing off of *v* and *m* (I-II), *a* and *d* (I), *h* and *p* (II).

3. Looking at the number of 'scribal' or 'major' variants (see Graph IV, App. 6), we get a list which may suggest a different origin in the musical tradition: h 38% of the total number of variants; d 33%; c 32%; j 28%; u 28%; a 27%; r 25%; p 24%; g 23%; m 22%; v 21%.

A high score suggests a more isolated position in the scribal tradition and may indicate that in the musical tradition a unique change took place in particular verses.

If this order does not correspond exactly to the list under 2, we may accept that the Mss. with a high score have undergone more scribal tampering. Ms. *h* is a clear example: it has indeed more scribal errors than the other Mss.
Mss. *c* and *j* have pretty high scores too; so does Ms. *d,* which is the oldest Ms. Again, the *Pañcavāṇī* Mss. of both groups show no particular affinity within their own group.

4. Comparing the number of variants shows plainly that the Mss. of each *Pañcavāṇī* group show *no clear affinity* within the group. Sometimes an even better affinity is seen with a Ms. of another *Pañcavāṇī* group.

- group I	d,a	2149	words differ
	d,v	2139	words differ
	a,v	2161	words differ
- group II	m,p	2227	words differ
	m,h	1965	words differ
	p,h	1915	words differ
- I-II	m,v	2154	(31% of total in m)
	p,d	2075	words differ
	p,v	2057	words differ
	m,a	2418	words differ

Although Mss. *m* and *p* are not close, Mss. *m* and *h* and Mss. *p* and *h* seem to be close. The *m-p* (II) affinity is weaker than *p-d* or *p-v* (I-II). In fact there are more variants when comparing the Mss. within group I than when comparing Mss. of group I with Mss. of group II.

5. If we find a confused pattern of interaction between the two *Pañcavāṇī* 'recensions', they seem relatively in agreement when we observe how distinct they are from the recension represented by Ms. *u* (see Ch. 2.8).

u,d 2553 (or 36% of total in d); u,a 2524; u,v 2440; u,m 2661; u,p 2605; u,h 2569.

6. Very clearly standing apart are Mss. *c* and *j* (see Ch. 2.8):

2668 c --d-- j 3262 (46% of total in d)
2755 c --a-- j 3284
2675 c --v-- j 3199
3630 c --m-- j 3192
2493 c --p-- j 3052
2289 c --h-- j 2868 (43% of total in h)

Comparison with Ms. *u:*

1902 c---u---j 2296 (39% of total in *u).*

Noteworthy is the closeness between *u,c* (and *j*). There are 1912 variants even between *c* and *j,* or 38% of the total.
The closest relation --or the lowest number of variants when compared to the critical text-- so far noticed is between the two Mss. of the scribal recension: 20% of the words in *g* (a total of 1278 words) are variant from *r.*

7. When we compare the *relative number of variants,* we note the following:

- Mss. *c* and especially *j*, stand out by their very high number of variants.
- a low count is noted for the scribal recensions *g and r,* i.e. the critical text appears to be close to that text, as well as to Ms. *p* (*Pañcavāṇī* II).
- there is no striking affinity between the Mss. of each *Pañcavāṇī* group:
  * Ms. *v* (25.6%) is quite apart from Ms. *a* (22.89%) and from Ms. *d* (23.95%).
  * Ms. *h* (group II) is closer to Ms. *d* (group I) than to Mss. *m* or *p* (II).
  * Ms. *p* is much closer to the critical text than Mss. *h* and *m*.
- Ms. *u* is pretty far from the critical text.

Looking at the *relative percentage of forms variant from the critical text,* we find the Mss. in the following order, which suggests once again that there is no consistent affinity between Mss. of the same 'recension':

g 15%; r 17%; p(II) 19%; a(I) 22%; d(I) 23%; h(II) 24%; v(I) 25%; m(II) 27%; u 29%; c 34%; j 45%.

8. For a more refined analysis of the affinity between Mss. we now turn to the next programme, where the identical variants in 2 Mss. are counted. A high percentage of common variants suggests a close relation:

Group I: d,a 4.5%; d,v 5.9%; v,a 4.5%.
Group II: m,p 4.9%; m,h 9.2%; p,h 5.8%.
I-II: h,d 3.7%; h,a 3.8%; m,v 5.7%; p,d 2.8%; p,v 3.7%; m,a 4.5%.

Looking at the identical variants, Ms. *u* seems to be close to the Mss. of the *Pañcavāṇī* groups: u,d 4.6%; u,a 4.7%; u,v 5.6%; u,m 5.5%; u,p 3.5%; u,h 5.1%.

A rather mediocre relation between *r* and *g* is noticed, if we consider the common variants: 4.2%. Quite striking is the affinity between h (*Pañcavāṇī* II) and Mss. *c* and *r* (not *g*).

9. Looking at the (Dādūpanthī) scribal recensions, we note that Ms. *g* (Gopāldās) is close to *Pañcavāṇī* group I, whereas Ms. *r* (Rajab) is clearly closer to group II.

g,d 4%; g,a 3.4%; g,v 4.7%; g,m 3.3%; g,p 3.9%; g,h 2.8%;
r,d 3%; r,a 2.8%; r,v 4.3%; r,m 4.8%; r,p 7,5%; r,h 6.5%.

10. Another computer count displays how many words in a Ms. are identical with the critical text: d 5381 76%; a 5606 77%; u 4117 70%; v 4916 74%; m 5057 72%; p 5706 80%; g 5284 84%; r 2086 82%; c 3223 65%; j 2681 54%; h 5004 75%.

11. We further note how two Mss. are related when looking at their identical forms:

Pañcavāṇī I:	d,a	4156	58%
	d,v	4166	63%
	v,a	4596	69%

Pañcavāṇī II:	m,p	4507	64%
	m,h	4612	69%
	p,h	4704	70%
Pañcavāṇī I-II:	h,d	3694	55%
	h,a	3989	60%
	m,v	3673	55%
	p,d	4102	58%
	p,v	3851	58%
	m,a	4078	58%

Ms. *u:*
u,d 3293 56%; u,a 3289 56%;
u,v 3116 53%; u,m 3305 56%;
u,p 3564 61%; u,h 3281 56%.

3.4. Hindī songs of Nāmdev (Table I)

In the Table below we give the complete list of Hindī songs of Nāmdev, with the corresponding numbers of songs in the following Mss.:

I. *Rām nām khetī*
d : DMVJ[2], 12; 1636 AD; 140 songs; fo. 191-208.
v : VBJ, 34; 1658 AD; 120 songs fo. 220-234.
a : Amritsar, 875; 1675 AD; 146 songs; fo. 236-254.

II. *Hari nām hīrā*
h : Naraina, private copy; 1653 AD; 117 songs; fo. 218-235.
n : Naraina, 36; 1664 AD; 122 songs; fo. 258-272.
m : DMVJ, 2; 1676 AD; 133 songs; fo. 130-137.
p: Patiala, 2706; 1698 AD; 126 songs; fo. 212-224.
The order of songs in this group is generally followed by Bh. Miśra and by us.

III. *Lādhau tau lādhau*
u : VBJ, 12; 1684 AD; 103 songs; fo. 201-213.

IV. *Rām nām boli*
c : CPJ, 3322; 1669 AD; 85 songs; 27 fo.
j : CPJ, 1853; 1681 AD; 85 songs; fo. 152-172.

V. *g* : Gopāldās *Sarvāṅgī;* (1627 AD; *lipikāl* 1724); 123 songs.

VI. *r* : Rajab *Sarvāṅgī;* (1620 AD?; *lipikāl* 1714); 44 songs[3].

(2) The following abbreviations are used:
DMVJ: Dādū Mahāvidyālay, Jaipur;
VBJ: Vidyā Bhūshan Sangrah, Jaipur;
CPJ: City Palace, Jaipur.
(3) See Callewaert:1978, pp. 81f. (Ms. *A*).

VII. GG: *Guru Granth;* 1604 AD; 61 songs.

VIII. f: Fatehpur Ms., CPJ; 1582 AD; 11 songs.

IX. GP: '102 Hindusthānī songs in Mahārāshtra' *(Sakal Santa Gāthā)*[4].

In Table I below we have marked with siglum GP those songs which are found in the *Sakal Santa Gāthā.* It is interesting to note that of the 102 songs given there, 45 are found in the *Guru Granth.* Of these 45, as many as 26 belong to the set of 36 songs which are *not* found in the Rājasthānī Mss., but *only* in the *Guru Granth.*

X. Manuscripts consulted by Bh. Miśra:1964 (see above, Ch. 2.5).

The numbers marked with * refer to the songs selected for translation. The numbers marked with '-' indicate that the song is referred to in the Miśra edition; if only '-' is given (and no number); this indicates that the song is referred to in Miśra but was not found by us in the particular manuscript, e.g. song 84 (not found in Ms. *p)* or song 226 (not found in the Rajab *Sarvāṅgī).* The numbers in brackets (159, 232) were cancelled when the list was nearly final. They were not removed from the list since this would have caused confusion. Poem 159 appeared to be identical with song 91, while 232 was identical with song 206.

Numbers between brackets refer to extra songs, added in a different hand: see under songs 170 and 177. For irregularities in the *rāg* pattern, see Ch. 2.9; for the inverted order of lines within songs, see *Geyavikāras,* Ch. 2.3.

	GP	h	n	m	p	d	v	a	u	c	j	g	r	GG	f	np	gh	pan	pu
Rāg ṭoḍī																			
1		1	1	1	1-		38	53				g				1	57	129	1
2*		2	2	2	2-	1	1	1	25	26	26	g				2	1	1	
3*		3	3	3	3-	2	2	2	26	27	27	g	r-			3	3	2	3
4*		4	4	4	4-	3	3	3	27	28	28	g				4	4	3	4
5*		5	5	5	5-	4	4	5	28	29	29					5	5		5
6*		6	6	6	6-	5	7	6	30	30	30			GG-		6	6	6	6
7*		7	7	7	7-	6	8	7	31	31	31	g	r			7	7	7	7
8*		8	8	8	8-	7	9	9	32	33	33	g				8	9	9	8
9*		9	9	9	9-	8	10	10	65	34	34					9	10	10	9
10*		10	10	10	10-	41		11	58	35	35	g		(GG)		10	11	11	10
11*		11	11	11	11-	10	12	12	39	36	36	g	r-			11	12	12	11
12*		12	12	12	12-	11	13	13	40	38	38					12	13	13	12
13*		13	13	13	13-	12	14	14	41	39	39	g.				13	14	14	13

(4) See R.C. Miśra, *Santa Nāmdev aur Hindī Pad Sāhitya,* 1969; pp. 127-192: 'songs in the Guru Granth' (with Hindī Commentary) and pp. 195-248: 'Hindusthānī songs' (with Hindī equivalents for certain words).
These songs are also found in the re-edition by Dhere:1983 of the *Sakal Santa Gāthā,* II, pp. 678-700. It is interesting to note that these 'Hindusthānī' songs are not given in the big volume of Nāmdev's Marāṭhī *abhangas: Śrī Nāmdev Gāthā:1970c.* Instead we find (pp. 807-872) a reprint of 229 'Hindī songs', as edited by Bh. Miśra:1964.

	GP	h	n	m	p	d	v	a	u	c	j	g	r	GG f	np	gh	pan	pu
14*		14	14	14	14-			48	61	37	37				14	15	125	15
15*		15	15	15	15-	13	15	15	42	40	40	g			15	16	15	15
16*		16	16	16	16-	14	16	16	43	41	41	g			16	17	16	16
17*		17	17	17	17-			47		42	42	g			17	18	123	17
18*	GP	18	18	18	18-	15	17	17	44	43	43	g		GG-	18	19	17	18
19*	GP	19	19	19	19-	16	18	18	45	44	44	g	r-	GG-	19	20	18	19
20*		20	20	20	20-	20	20	19	36	45	45	g	r-		20	22	19	20
21*		21	21	21	21-	9	11	20	33	46	46	g		f	21	23	20	21
22*		22	22	22	22-	39		21	60	47	47	g			22	24	21	22
23*	GP	23	23	23	23-	34	34	22	35	48	48	g		GG-	23	25	22	23
24*		24	24	24	24-	35	35	23	37			g			24	26	23	24
25*		25	25	25	25-	36	36	24	38	49	49	g	r-		25	27		25
26*		26	26	26	26-	37	37	25	59	50	50	g	r-		26	28		26
27*		27	27	27	27-	21	21	26	46	51	51				27	29	24	27
28*	GP	28	28	28	28-	22	22	27	47	52	52	g		GG-	28	30	25	28
29*		29	29	29	29-	23	23	28	48	53	53	g				31	26	29
30*		30	30	30	30-	25	25	29	50			g	r-		30	32	27	30
31*		31	31	31	31-	42		30	64			g	r-		31	33	28	31
32		32	32	32	32-			50				g			32	34	127	32
33*		33	33	33	33-	24	24	31	49						33	35	29	33
34*		34	34	34	34-	17	19	32	63			g			34	36	30	34
35*		35	35	35	35-	18	26	33	51			g			35	37	31	35
36*		36	36	36	36-	33	33	34	34						36	38	32	36
37*		37	37	37	37-	32	32	35	57						37	39	33	37
38		38	38		38-	40		36				g			39	40	34	38
39*		39	39	38	39-	26	27	37	52			g	r-		39	41	35	39
40*		40	40	39	40-			45	62			g			40	42	44	40
41*		41	41	40	41-	19	28	38	53						41	43	36	41
42*		42	42	41	42-	27	29	39	54	54	54				42	44	37	42
43*		43	43	42	43-	28	30	94	55	13	13	g	r-		43	47	38	43
44*		44	44	43	44-	31	31	40	56			g	r-		44	48	39	44
45								8		32	32	g				8	8	45
46								49								21	126	46
47								51		55	55	g				45	128	47

Rāg gauḍ

	GP	h	n	m	p	d	v	a	u	c	j	g	r	GG f	np	gh	pan	pu
48*		45	45	44	45-	66	39	54	70	60	60	g			44	49	46	48
49*		46	46	45	46-	67	40	68	71	62	62	g	r-		46	50	49	49
50*	GP	47	47	46	47-	68	41	71	72	63	63	g		GG-	47	52	63	50
51*		48	48	47	48-	80	59	75	83	64	64	g			48	53	131	51
52*		49	49	48	49-	69	42	61	73			g			49	54	53	52
53*		50	50	49	50-	70	43	55		65	65	g			50	55	47	53
54*		51	51	50	51-	83		76		66	66	g			51	56	132	54
55*			52		52-	82		42	84			g			52	52	41	55
56*		52	53	51	53-	71	44	70	74			g			53	59	60	56
57*		54	55	53	55-	72	46	69		67	67	g			55	61	61	57
58*	GP	55	56	54	56-	73	47	72	75	68	68	g	r-	GG-	56	62	63	58
59*	GP	56	57	55	57-	74	48	66	76	69	69	g		GG-f	57	63	57	59
60		57	58	56	58-	75	49	56				g			58	64	48	60
61*	GP	58	59	57	59-	76	50	58	77	70	70	g	r-	GG-	59	65	50	61
62*	GP	59	60	58	60-	77	51	57		71	71	g		GG-f	60	66	49	62
63*	GP	60	61	59	61-	78	52	65		72	72	g	r-	GG-f	61	67	56	63
64*		61	62	60	62-	79	53	60				g	r-	(GG)	62	69	53	64
65*		62	63	61	63-	61	54	62	78						63	70	54	65
66*		63	64	62	64-	62	55	63	79						64	71	55	66
67*		64	65	63	65-	63	56	67	80			g	r-			72	58	67
68*		66	67	65	67-	65	58	77	82						67	74		69
69								44		61	61	g				51	43	70

	GP	h	n	m	p	d	v	a	u	c	j	g	r	GGf	np	gh	pan	pu
Rāg soraṭh																		
70*		67	68	72	68-	92	60	83	85	56	56	g			67	76	66	78
71*		68	69	73	69-	93	61	87	86	57	57	g	r-		69	77		79
72*		69	70	74	70-				89	58	58	g			70	78		81
73*		70	71	75	71-	94	62	85	87			g	r-		71	79	68	82
74*		71	72	76	72-	95	63	86	88	59	59	g			72	80	69	83
75												g				81	168	85
Rāg gauḍī																		
76*	GP	72	73	77	73-	84	64	88	95	5	6		r-	GG-	73	83	71	86
77*		73	74	78	74-	85	65	89	96	7	7		r-		74	84		87
78*		74	75	79	75-	86	66	91	97	2	2	g	r-		75	85	71	88
79*		75	76	80	76	90	6	93	29	1	1	g			76	89		89
80		76	77	81	77-							g			77	92		90
81						91				3	3	g				90		91
82*					114	89	5	41	65b	4	4	g	r-			88	40	90
Rāg mālī gauḍī																		
83*				67		112		78		8	8					145	132	93
84*				85		88	68	92	98	9	9	g			79	87	73	94
85								79		10	10						133	95
86						110		80		11	11	g					134	96
87						113		81		6	5						135	97
Rāg rāmgiri																		
	GP	h	n	m	p	d	v	a	u	c	j	g	r	GGf	np	gh	pan	pu
88*		77	78	88	78-	52	69	103	1	16	16	g			78	93	77	98
89*		78	79	89	79-	50	70	105	2			g			90	94	79	99
90*		79	80	90	80-	53	71	109	3	17	17				81	95	83	100
91*	GP	80	81	91	81-	58	72	114		18	18	g	r-	GG-	82	97		101
92*		81	82	92	82-	54	73	108	5	20	20	g			83	99	82	102
93*		82	83	93	83-	55		112	7			g			84	100	86	103
94*		83	84	94	85-	51	83	110	15					GG-	86	102	84	104
95*		84	85	95	86-	56	75	104	4	21	21	g	-		87	103	78	105
96*			86		87-	57	76	101	8			g	r-		88	105	75	106
97*		85	87	96	88-	46	77	107	9			g	r-		89	106	81	107
98*		86	88	97	89-	48	78	115	10			g			90	107	90	108
99*	GP	87	89	98	90-	45	79	106	11	23	23	g	r-	GG-	91	109	80	109
100*		89	91	100	92-	49	81	46	13			g	r		93	111	89	111
101*		90	92	101	93-	47	82	116	14				r-		94	112	91	112
102			93									g			95	104		113
103						59	84			19	19	g				98		114
104							86									113		115
105						60	85			22	22	g				108		116
Rāg āsāvarī																		
106*		91	94	102	94-	96	87	118	66			g			93	114	93	117
107*		92	95	103	95-	100			69			g			97	115		118
108*		93	96	104	96-	97	88	119	67			g	r-		98	116	94	119
109*		94	97	105	97-	98	89	120	68			g	r-		99	117	95	120
Rāg basant																		
110*		95	98	106	98-	101	91	122	92			g			100	120	97	121

	GP	h	n	m	p	d	v	a	u	c	j	g	r	GG f	np	gh	pan	pu
111*		96	99	107	99-	102	92	123	93						101	121	22	122
112*		97	100	108	100-	103	93		94						102	122		123
113*		98	101	109	101	104		117	15b			g				92		124
114		99	102	111	102-			136				g			104	147	117	125
Rāg bhairu																		
115*	GP	100	103	112	103-	116	94	125	23	73	73	g		GG-f	105	123	101	126
116			104		104-	128			21						106	125	122	127
117*		101	105	113	105-	126	105	82	22	74	74	g			107	126	136	128
118*	GP	102	106	114	106-	117	95	128	24	75	75			GG-	108	127	103	129
119		103	107	115	107-							g			109	130		130
120*		104	108	116	108-	118	96	127	16			g			110	132	103	131
121*		105	109	117	109-	119	97	124	17	78	78	g	r-		111	133	99	132
122*		106	110	118	110-	120	98	126	20	77	77	g			112	135	101	133
123			111		111-							g			113	136		134
124*		107	112	119	112-	121	99		18			g			114	137		135
125*	GP	108	113	120	113-	122	100	130	19	80	80	g		GG-	115	138	105	136
126						127	106	133				g				124	108	137
127*						125	104	134		79	79					128	109	138
128*						123	102	132		76	76	g				129	106	139
129												g				131		140
130				121						81	81					134		141
Rāg kānaḍau																		
	GP	h	n	m	p	d	v	a	u	c	j	g	r	GG f	np	gh	pan	pu
131*	GP	109	114	122	115-	105	107	97	101	14	14	g		GG f	116	139	113	142
132*		110	115	123	116-	107	109	98	103						117	141	114	143
133*						106	108		102	15	15					140		144
134													r-			46		145
Rāg mārū																		
135*		111	116	125	118-	137		99				g	r-		118	143	120	146
rāg parajīy																		
136*		112	117	126	119-	114	110	135	90	24	24	g	r-		119	116		147
Rāg kalyān																		
137*		113	118	127	120-			95	100	12	12	g			120			148
Rāg sāraṅg																		
138*		114	119	128	121-		116	96		25	25	g	r-	f	121			149
139															128	150		150
Rāg dhanāśri																		
140*		115	120	129	122-			143				g		GG-	130	153	152	151
141*				131	123			144	91	83	83				131			154
142*				130	124-	138	117	142		82	82	g	r-		129	152		155
143				110													171	161
144*		116	121	132	125-	139	118	146		85	85	g	r		123		162	162
145*		117	122	133	126-	140	120	145		84	84	g	r		122	146		163
146						38		4								4	4	
147						99	90						r-			118		
148						29	112	138				g	r-				118	
149														GG-			144	
150	GP													GG-			142	

	GP	h	n	m	p	d	v	a	u	c	j	g	r	GG	f	np	gh	pan	pu
151	GP													GG-				145	
152	GP													GG-				149	
153	GP													GG-				150	
154	GP													GG-				151	
155														GG-				153	
156	GP													GG-				155	
157	GP													GG-				158	
158							101					g		GG-				-	
(159)																			
160														GG-				-	
161	GP													GG-				-	
162														GG-				-	
163				124				100				g						-	
164*		88	90	99	91-	44	80	112	12							92	110	87	11(
165*		65	66	64	66-	64	57	59	81							66	73	51	68

Pune Ms. (Mishra:1964)

	GP	h	n	m	p	d	v	a	u	c	j	g	r	GG	f	np	gh	pan	pu
166																			-
167																			-
168																			-
169																			-
170										(87)									-
171				70															-
172																			-
173																			-
174				82															-
175																			-
176																			-
177									15c			g							-
178																			-
179																			-

	GP	h	n	m	p	d	v	a	u	c	j	g	r	GG	f	np	gh	pan	pu
Pandharpur Ms. (Mishra:1964)																			
180												g						-	
181												g						-	
182						124	103	132										-	
183								102										-	
184																		-	
185																		-	
186								73										-	
187																		-	
188								129										-	
189																		-	
190								43										-	
191																		-	
192																		-	
193																		-	
Ghuman Ms. (Mishra:1964)																			
194												g					-		
195					117	129											-		
196												g					-		
197																	-		
198																	-		

Only in the *Guru Grantha*

	GP	h	n	m	p	d	v	a	u	c	j	g	r	GG	f	np	gh	pan	pu
199														GG-					
200	GP													GG-					
201	GP													GG-					
202	GP													GG-					
203														GG-					
204	GP													GG-					
205	GP													GG-					
206	GP							74						GG-f					
207	GP													GG-					
208	GP													GG-					
209	GP													GG-					
210														GG-					
211	GP													GG-					
212														GG-					
213	GP													GG-					
214														GG-					
215														GG-					
216														GG-					
217	GP													GG-					
218	GP													GG-					
219	GP													GG-					
220	GP													GG-					
221	GP													GG-					
222	GP													GG-					
223														GG-					

Only in the *Sarvāñgī* according to Mishra:1964

	GP	h	n	m	p	d	v	a	u	c	j	g	r	GG	f	np	gh	pan	pu
224						134	114					g	r-						
225								121					r-						
226*				66		30	113	140				g	r-						

Anya śrot in Mishra:1964

	GP	h	n	m	p	d	v	a	u	c	j	g	r	GG	f	np	gh	pan	pu
227				83															
228																			
229																			
230																			

Not found in Mishra:1964

	GP	h	n	m	p	d	v	a	u	c	j	g	r	GG	f	np	gh	pan	pu
231								84							f				
232								a											
233						87	67	90											
234*				86	84	109	74	111	6			g							
235						115	111	137											
236						132		139											
237						133		141											
238*	GP	53	54	52	54	81	45	64				g		GG					
239												g							
240						108	115					g							
241												g							
242												g							
243												g							

	GP	h	n	m	p	d	v	a	u	c	j	g	r	GG	f	np	gh	pan	pu
244				68															
245				69															
246				71															
247						43													
248	GP													GG					
249				68										GG					
250						111													
251						130													
252						131	119												
253						135													
254						136													
255				84															
256				87															
257															f				
258															f				
	102	117	122	133	126	140	120	146	103	85	85	123	44	61	11	123	157	182	161

3.5. Table II: sigla only

Table.II graphically demonstrates
- which songs (marked with *; see below, Ch. 3.6 and Ch. 5) have been selected for English translation.
- which songs appear in only the *Guru Granth* or in only one manuscript.

From the fact that 12 songs (149-157, 159-160, 162) are found *only* in the *Granth* but *also* in the Pandharpur Ms. (total 182; recent date?), we may perhaps conclude that from the Sikh tradition songs entered into the written tradition of Rājasthān.

Several songs --towards the end of the Table-- were found in only one of the 'Rājasthānī' manuscripts. For the sigla see above, Ch. 3.4. The Table neatly illustrates how the *rāg* groups occurring first in the manuscripts *(ṭoḍī, gauḍ* etc.) also give the *padas* found in most manuscripts. Towards the end of the collections we find the songs which are given in less repertoires.

rāg ṭoḍī

1 h m p v a g np gh pan pu
2* h m p d v a u c j g np gh pan
3* h m p d v a u c j g r np gh pan pu
4* h m p d v a u c j g np gh pan pu
5* h m p d v a u c j np gh pu
6* h m p d v a u c j GG np gh pan pu
7* h m p d v a u c j g r np gh pan pu
8* h m p d v a u c j g np gh pan pu
9* h m p d v a u c j np gh pan pu
10* h m p d a u c j g (GG) np gh pan pu
11* h m p d v a u c j g r np gh pan pu
12* h m p d v a u c j np gh pan pu

13* h m p d v a u c j g np gh pan pu
14* h m p a u c j np gh pan pu
15* h m p d v a u c j g np gh pan pu
16* h m p d v a u c j g np gh pan pu
17* h m p a c j g np gh pan pu
18* h m p d v a u c j g GG np gh pan pu GP
19* h m p d v a u c j g r GG np gh pan pu GP
20* h m p d v a u c j g r np gh pan pu
21* h m p d v a u c j g f np gh pan pu
22* h m p d a u c j g np gh pan pu
23* h m p d v a u c j g GG np gh pan pu GP
24* h m p d v a u g np gh pan pu
25* h m p d v a u c j g r np gh pu
26* h m p d v a u c j g r np gh pu
27* h m p d v a u c j np gh pan pu
28* h m p d v a u c j g GG np gh pan pu GP
29* h m p d v a u c j g gh pan pu
30* h m p d v a u g r np gh pan pu
31* h m p d a u g r np gh pan pu
32 h m p a g np gh pan pu
33* h m p d v a u np gh pan pu
34* h m p d v a u g np gh pan pu
35* h m p d v a u g np gh pan pu
36* h m p d v a u np gh pan pu
37* h m p d v a u np gh pan pu
38 h p d a g np gh pan pu
39* h m p d v a u g r np gh pan pu
40* h m p a u g np gh pan pu
41* h m p d v a u np gh pan pu
42* h m p d v a u c j r np gh pan pu
43* h m p d v a u c j g r np gh pan pu
44* h m p d v a u g r np gh pan pu
45 a c j g r gh pan pu
46 a gh pan pu
47 a c j g gh pan pu

rāg gauḍ

48* h m p d v a u c j g np gh pan pu
49* h m p d v a u c j g r np gh pan pu
50* h m p d v a u c j g GG np gh pan pu GP
51* h m p d v a u c j g np gh pan pu
52* h m p d v a u g np gh pan pu
53* h m p d v a c j g np gh pan pu
54* h m p d a c j g np gh pan pu
55* n p d a u g np gh pan pu
56* h m p d v a u g np gh pan pu
57* h m p d v a c j g np gh pan pu
58* h m p d v a u c j g r GG np gh pan pu GP
59* h m p d v a u c j g GG f np gh pan pu GP
60 h m p d v a g np gh pan pu
61* h m p d v a u c j g r GG np gh pan pu GP
62* h m p d v a c j g GG f np gh pan pu GP

63* h m p d v a c j g r GG f np gh pan pu GP
64* h m p d v a g r (GG) np gh pan pu
65* h m p d v a u np gh pan pu
66* h m p d v a u np gh pan pu
67* h m p d v a u g r gh pan pu
68* h m p d v a u np gh pu
69 a c j g gh pan pu
rāg soraṭh
70* h m p d v a u c j g np gh pan pu
71* h m p d v a u c j g r np gh pu
72* h m p u c j g np gh pu
73* h m p d v a u g r np gh pan pu
74* h m p d v a u c j g np gh pan pu
75 g gh pan pu
rāg gauḍī
76* h m p d v a u c j r GG np gh pan pu GP
77* h m p d v a u c j r np gh pu
78* h m p d v a u c j g r np gh pan pu
79* h m p d v a u c j g np gh pu
80 h m p g np gh pu
81 d c j g gh pu
82* p d v a u c j g r gh pan pu
mālī gauḍī
83* m d a c j gh pan pu
84* m p d v a u c j g np gh pan pu
85 a c j pan pu
86 d a c j g gh pan pu
87 d a c j gh pan pu
rāg rāmgiri
88* h m p d v a u c j g np gh pan pu
89* h m p d v a u g np gh pan pu
90* h m p d v a u c j np gh pan pu
91* h m p d v a c j g r GG np gh pu GP
92* h m p d v a u c j g np gh pan pu
93* h m p d a u g np gh pan pu
94* h m p d v a u GG np gh pan pu
95* h m p d v a u c j g r np gh pan pu
96* n p d v a u g r np gh pan pu
97* h m p d v a u g r np gh pan pu
98* h m p d v a u g np gh pan pu
99* h m p d v a u c j g r GG np gh pan pu GP
100* h m p d v a u g r np gh pan pu
101* h m p d v a u r np gh pan pu
102 n g np gh pu
103 d v c j g gh pu
104 v gh pu
105 d v c j g gh pu
rāg āsāvarī
106* h m p d v a u g np gh pan pu
107* h m p d u g np gh pu

108* h m p d v a u g r np gh pan pu
109* h m p d v a u g r np gh pan pu
rāg basant
110* h m p d v a u g np gh pan pu
111* h m p d v a u r np gh pan pu
112* h m p d v u np gh pu
113* h m p d a u g gh pu
114 h m p a g np gh pan pu
rāg bhairu
115* h m p d v a u c j g GG f np gh pan pu GP
116 n p d u np gh pan pu
117* h m p d v a u c j g np gh pan pu
118* h m p d v a u c j GG np gh pan pu GP
119 h m p g np gh pu
120* h m p d v a u g np gh pan pu
121* h m p d v a u c j g r np gh pan pu
122* h m p d v a u c j g np gh pan pu
123 n p g np gh pu
124* h m p d v u g np gh pu
125* h m p d v a u c j g GG np gh pan pu GP
126 d v a g gh pan pu
127* d v a c j gh pan pu
128* d v a c j g gh pan pu
129 g gh pu
130 m c j gh pu
rāg kanaḍau
131* h m p d v a u c j g GG f np gh pan pu
132* h m p d v a u np gh pan pu
133* d v u c j gh pu
134 r gh pu
rāg mārū
135* h m p d a g r np gh pan pu
rāg parajīy
136* h m p d v a u c j g r np gh pu
rāg kalyān
137* h m p a u c j g np pu
rāg sāraṅg
138* h m p v a c j g r f np pu
139 np gh pu
140* h m p a g GG np gh pan pu
141* m p a u c j np pu
142* m p d v a c j g r np gh pu
143 m pan pu
144* h m p d v a c j g r np pan pu
145* h m p d v a c j g r np gh pu
146 d a gh pan
147 d v r gh
148 d v a g r pan
149 G pan
150 G pan
151 G pan

152 G pan
153 G pan
154 G pan
155 G pan
156 G pan
157 G pan
158 v g GG pan
(159)
160 G pan
161 G pan
162 G pan
163 m a g pan
164* h m p d v a u np gh pan pu
165* h m p d v a u r np gh pan pu
Pune Ms. (Miśra:1964; see above, Ch. 2.5)
166 pu
167 pu
168 pu
169 pu
170 c pu
171 m pu
172 pu
173 pu
174 m pu
175 pu
176 pu
177 u g pu
178 pu
179 pu
Pandharpur Ms. (Miśra:1964)
180 g pan
181 g pan
182 d v a pan
183 a pu
184 pan
185 pan
186 a pan
187 pan
188 a pan
189 pan
190 a pan
191 pan
192 pan
193 pan
Ghuman Ms. (Miśra:1964)
194 g pu
195 p d gh
196 g gh
197 gh
198 gh

Only in the *Guru Granth*
199 G
200 G
201 G
202 G
203 G
204 G
205 G
206 a GG f
207 G
208 G
209 G
210 G
211 G
212 G
213 G
214 G
215 G
216 G
217 G
218 G
219 G
220 G
221 G
222 G
223 G
"Only *Sarvāṅgī*" in Miśra
224 d v g r
225 a r
226* m d v a g r
227 m
228
229
230
231 a f
232 a
233 d v a
234* m p d v a u g
235 d v a
236 d a
237 d a
238* h m p d v a g GG
239 g
240 d v g
241 g
242 g
243 g
244 m
245 m
246 m
247 d

248 G
249 G
250 d
251 d
252 d v
253 d
254 d
255 m
256 m
257 f
258 f

3.6. Selection of songs for translation

After a careful analysis of the conclusions arrived at above we distinguish 8 'recensions':

- four major 'recensions': *Pañcavāṇī* groups I and II, Ms. *u* and Mss. *c* and *j*:
- four minor 'recensions: the Gopāldās *Sarvāṅgī*, the Rajab *Sarvāṅgī*, the Fatehpur Ms. and the *Guru Granth*.

The major recensions are directly connected to the oral tradition and we presume that texts wich reflect a singing tradition take us closer to Nāmdev. It is also important to note that the major recensions were meant to be complete recensions: they give all the songs known as Nāmdev's songs in a particular repertoire. A comparison of these 'complete' repertoires helps the editor to draw certain conclusions, looking e.g. at the order of songs, the *rāg* etc.

Of the minor recensions, we consider the two *Sarvāṅgīs* and the Fatehpur Ms.[5] as written recensions, i.e. they are written anthologies and do not directly reflect a singing recension. The Gopāldās *Sarvāṅgī* has 123 songs and the Rajab *Sarvāṅgī* has 44. The Fatehpur Ms. has 11 songs of Nāmdev. Although it is the oldest written collection, it is classified as of minor importance: like the minor recensions it selective, and small. Its early date does not give it any particular importance, since we opted to rely on collections (rather than on selections) made during the singing tradition. The collections made by singers are earlier than the Fatehpur Ms. and are also more important because of their completeness.

The *Guru Granth* selection of Nāmdev's songs is peculiar for more than one reason. In the first place, 36 of its total of 61 songs by Nāmdev are not found in any other of our Mss. Furthermore, many of the *Guru Granth* songs are classified under a *rāg* differing from the *rāg* common to the songs in the Rājasthāni Mss.[6] Several *rāg* clusters

(5) "The manuscript seems to have been written in three sections, based on three exemplars", see G.N. Bahurā, *op.cit.*, p.22.

(6) Six songs classified under *ṭoḍī* in the Rājasthānī Mss. are also in the *Guru Granth*, but only two of them are found under *ṭoḍī* in the *Guru Granth*. Of the 6 songs classified under *gaur* in the Rājasthānī Mss., only 3 are under *gaur* in the *Guru Granth*. The only

found in the Rājasthānī Mss. are not found in the *Guru Granth* and vice versa (see above, Ch. 2.6). The *Guru Granth* can be called the result of a singing tradition, if one accepts that the handwritten material possibly underlying the compilation of the Granth served mainly for the *sabads* of the Gurus. This presupposes that within the Sikh tradition handwritten copies were made of the *sabads* of the Gurus, while the popular Santa lore, sung in the early Sikh Panth, was still passed on in an oral tradition. The high respect for the Guru's word makes the writing down of their *sabads* first quite plausible.

Of the Nāmdev songs in the *Guru Granth* only 25 are in other Mss. that we have consulted. If we presume that we have five 'singing' traditions reflected in our manuscripts *(d,v,a; h,n,m,p; u; c,j; GG)*, it is interesting to note the following for the 25 songs in the GG also found in Rājasthān:

- 17 of these songs are also found in the other four 'singing' traditions;
- 5 are found in only 3 'singing' traditions and 2 are found in only 2 traditions.

This points to a high degree of popularity (we do not use the term authenticity) of the 17 songs mentioned.

Considering all this, we propose the hypothesis that the *Guru Granth* selection of 61 songs of Nāmdev --from the oral repertoires like those in Rājasthān-- was made at some stage in the history of the Sikh Panth, most probably (long) before Arjandev. Guru Nānak lived from 1469 to 1539. This would confirm that a singing tradition of Nāmdev's songs existed in Panjāb after Nāmdev's death. On the hypothesis that songs of a particular poet travelled in specific repertoires, our evidence makes it unlikely that Nāmdev's songs travelled from Panjāb to Rājasthān. The traditional biographical description of Nāmdev's peregrinations supposes that from Mahārāshtra he travelled to Panjāb 'from where his songs came back to Rājasthān'. The high diversity in *rāg* structure between the *Guru Granth* and the Rājasthānī Mss. (see above, Ch.2.9) suggests that Nāmdev --or his repertoires-- developed independently in Rājasthān and in Panjāb. This explains why there is such a difference between the songs known in both regions, a difference both musical and linguistic.

Looking at the 3 minor 'scribal' recensions, we note that within the *ṭoḍī rāg* set of the Gopāldās *Sarvāṅgī*, 21 songs are found in four, 9 in three and 5 in two 'singing' recensions. For the remaining *rāg* sets, however, only 24 are found in four such recensions, 26 in three, 10 in two and 5 in one 'singing' recension. Thus again, the *ṭoḍī rāg* set *seems* to be most ancient. In the other *rāg* sets we find more songs under a different *rāg* in the different traditions (see above, Ch. 2.9). However, a difference in *rāg* should not necessarily suggest that a song must have

---

song classified under *gauṛī* in the Rājasthānī Mss. is classified under *ṭoḍī* in the *Guru Granth*.

Of the three songs classified under *rāmkalī* in the Rājasthānī Mss., two are classified under this *rāg* in the *Guru Granth*. Of the four songs classified under *bhairu* in the Rājasthānī Mss., three are under *bhairu* in the *Guru Granth*. Finally, of the 14 songs under *dhanāśrī* in the Rājasthānī Mss., only 2 are under the same *rāg* in the *Guru Granth*.

been less 'popular'. We suggest that a song *looks* more popular if it is given under a uniform *rāg*, and that such a song is more likely to have been part of the 'original' or 'early' Rājasthānī repertoire from which our recensions developed.

Out of a total of 258 songs in all our manuscripts, only 59 --of which 28 songs were under *rāg ṭoḍī*-- were found in four of the major recensions, 56 in three and 26 in two major recensions. This is not a low percentage, if we take into account that one of our major recensions (Mss. *c/j*) has only 85 songs and that Ms. *u* has only 103.

There are two major patterns (Group I, Group II) in the order of songs with, however, this remarkable feature that songs may be found in only one or two manuscripts of one Group, but also in manuscripts of another Group (see above, Ch. 2.9). Such an addition can hardly have occurred during the scribal tradition (see also above, Tables I and II, Ch. 3.4 and 3.5).

This phenomenon of 'contamination' can only be explained in an oral tradition which set the pattern of order of songs under a *rāg*, before the scribal tradition started. 'Contamination' of this kind cannot have occurred in a scribal tradition.

Summing up

The disheartening conclusion is that no valid hypothesis can be made as to the 'authenticity' of a particular song. With some certainty one may say that a song found in only one 'recension' -- or one manuscript for that matter-- was not commonly known/sung at the beginning of the scribal tradition. This might imply that such a song has little chance of belonging to the earliest core of Nāmdev's songs. Following this logic, we hypothetically state that those songs which are found in most manuscripts/recensions have the greatest chance of belonging to the earliest core.

Based on this hypothesis we define as 'core-songs' of Nāmdev, those which meet one or more of the following conditions:

- the song is found in 3 major recensions
- the song is found in 2 major and in 2 minor recensions

On this basis we selected the songs for translation. These norms are as good or as bad as any other norm. Additional norms may be

- uniformity in *rāg*,
- conformity to the general order in which a song is found in the repertoires,
- conformity to the general order of refrain and stanzas (*ṭek* and *antarā*).

As such, the 'variants' are clues of only minor importance and in this way our 'critical' edition is different from a traditional text edition based on 'scribal' collections.

We cannot claim to mark any song as having been composed, beyond any doubt, by Nāmdev. We can, at the most, point out that some songs, with the *bhaṇitā* of Nāmdev, were well established in several singing traditions, possibly around 1500 AD or even earlier. Moreover, in harmony with these norms, we must include song 226, even though it has a *bhaṇitā* of Vishnudās.

CHAPTER 4

'THE SONGS IN ENGLISH'

2

The Lord's name
is my farm.
The Lord's name
is my orchard.
Lord Banvārī[2]
is my treasure.

Look at the greatness
of my treasure.
No thief can steal it,
never will it rot[3].

Rām fills the whole world[4],
but he is close to the Sants
and far from the wicked[5].

He is the field I plough[6],
no one can measure
its extent[7],
says Nāmdev.

3

Rām is the master

(1) For the norms for selection of poems for translation, see above Ch. 3.6. More explanation is given in the glossary (App. 2) for those words in the translation which are marked with *.

(2) *Banvārī* (Skt. *vanamālī*, 'one who wears a garland') is an epithet for Krishna.

(3) *Na lāgai kāī*, lit.: 'moss won't adhere to it'.

(4) Lit.: 'the ten directions', i.e. the 4 cardinal and the 4 intermediate points of the compass, and the up and down directions of the spherical cosmos.
The variant lines 1-2 in Mss. *c* and *j* are also found in song 128, where they are more appropriate in view of the similarity of theme.

(5) *Sākat* or *sākhat* (Skt. *śākta**).

(6) *Karasan* (Skt. *karṣaṇ*) refers to the act of ploughing (see Rām Sinha, et alii, *Dholā Mārū rā Dūhā*, p. 264). We render it as 'the field I plough'.

(7) *Masāiti*, (from Ar. *misāhat*), meaning 'to measure', 'survey of land dimensions'. See *masāhat*, in J.T.Platts, *Dictionary of Urdū, Classical Hindī and English*, p.1029.

of the eight godly powers[8]
and the nine godly
treasures[9].
No wonder he was treasure enough
for Prahlād*.

Having slain Hiraṇyakaśipu
Rām offered kingship
to Prahlād,
who spurned even the
glory of Indra.

That which is wealth
for gods or demons
is a torment
for a servant of Govind.

A man will not crave
for *artha, dharma, kāma* or even *mokṣa*[10]
if love of Rām
takes hold of his heart
says Nāmdev.

4

You are my life
O Viṭṭhal.
My path is blocked
Father.

Wicked is Kali*
and this Kali age.
Untie my fetters
Lord Gopāl.

Undo the shackles
of *samsār*
O Nārāyaṇ.
Carry me securely
on your shoulders
Mighty One.

And Nārāyaṇ came to me

(8) *Aṣṭa siddhi**.
(9) *Nav nidhi**.
(10) We prefer the reading given in Mss. *u* and *m*. This gives a meaning which is closer to the often repeated *bhakti* ideal that a true *bhakta* does not desire the common goals of life *(artha, dharma, kāma)*, not even *mokṣa* or liberation. All he wants is to be able to worship God, seeking his presence.
This sentiment, indeed, comes out in the reading of the *Guru Granth* also: *mohi* there makes no sense unless the line is construed as uttered by God, thus meaning 'Me'.

and rescued me[11].
Sailing in his ship
I crossed to the other shore
says Nāmdev.

5

Rejoice
in Rām.
Fix your mind joyfully
on him[12].

I give myself to him
who never forgets Rām[13].

Rejoice
in Rām.
Clap your hands joyfully.
You will find the Lord of Paradise,
Lord Banvārī.

Rejoice
in Rām.
Sing his name joyfully.
Do not let these brutes[14]
make you feel ashamed.

I love such fortunate mortals
who sing the praises
of the Supreme Brahma[15].

Such is the glory
of being mortal:
never to forget Rām,
says Nāmdev.

---

(11) The *kī* after *Nāmdev* is a burden to the metre and is understandably missing in several Mss. It would appear, however, that it is present in other Mss. in order to make the meaning of the line clearer to the singers and to their audience. Without the *kī* the line retains an ambiguity and one could ask: whom did Nārāyaṇ save?
The word 'Nāmdev' (not qualified by *kī)* could be taken here as just a *bhaṇitā* ('Nāmdev says'), as in other songs, but *Nāmdev kī* gives quite another meaning: it is Nāmdev himself whom the Lord saved.

(12) *Rām rame rami* is a frequently used expression, here repeated in every stanza. It is found also in song 7, stanza 3.
The verb *ramnā* (Skt. root *ram)* has many connotations and may best be rendered as 'to lose oneself joyfully in', 'to immerse oneself'.

(13) The translation is supported by a variant in Ms. *u: bali tākī jo.*

(14) *Paśu.*

(15) *Pārabrahma,* lit.: 'the transcendental Brahma'.

6

Rām speaks
Rām alone speaks.
Who can speak without Rām,
brother?

The elephant
and the ant
are one, being both dust.
These are vessels[16]
many and varied.
The worm
or the moth[17]
whatever moves or is still
everything is filled[18]
with Rām.

All my cravings
have gone.
Only one thought remains.
Desireless,
Nāmdev bows.
You are my master
I am your servant
Lord.

7

Rām is
Nāmdev.
Nāmdev
is Rām[19].
You are my master
I am your servant
Lord.

Rām, they say
is a lake
where his devotee
is a ripple.
Tell me then
how can I, his servant,

---

(16) Nearly all Mss. have *bhañjan,* lit. 'to break', which hardly makes sense in the context. We have taken the modified form *bhājan,* as found in Ms. *u* and in the *Guru Granth,* the addition of the nasal being common enough.

(17) This line is a recurring expression often used in Sant literature to denote life in all its varied forms.

(18) *Samānā* (modern Hindī *samāyā huā)* means 'to be filled', 'to be permeated'.

(19) *Nāmā* and *nāmahī* clearly indicate Nāmdev.
The *sa* in this line is a short form of *so,* which would not have fitted the metre. In one singing tradition *so* was shortened to *su* (Ms. *r).*

get away from
Rām?

Rām is
a tree.
His devotee is a bird
in its shade.
Serving Rām
the devotee is not himself.

I have found
Narhari.
Rejoicing in Rām I am joyfully
merged in him,
says Nāmdev.

8

Nāmdev has found
the name *Hari.*
If death comes now,
what can it do
crazy one?
I am now free.

In countless ways
I worshipped with love.
What use have I
for pious merit?
My spark of love
has found the One Brahma.
Should I worry now
about mere liberation?

Though they could not fathom
its greatness,
yet Sanak* and his brothers
were freed
as they uttered
the name.
Listen to me, O Sants.
Now at last I have
understood
says Nāmdev.

9

Say[20] *Rām.*
Hear *Rām.*
Do not be swept away
by the waters of delusion.

That
which is beyond speech
cannot be spoken of.
Nor written down
on paper.

Effortlessly[21] I found
the master of
the universe.

Rām
is my father.
Rām
is my mother.
He gives life to all beings.

So says the tailor[22]
Nāmdev,
so proclaims
the Gītā.

10

Foolish are the speakers
and foolish the listeners
who do not cherish the name
of the Lord of Life.

Mere noise: the Vedas
putrid: the Purāṇas.
They do not know the secret
of the name *Rām.*

The learned expound the Vedas
but silly Nāmdev
knows only Rām.

---

(20) The forms *japibau, sunibau, jāibau* seem parallel to the *japibau, sunibau* and *jāibau* of Nāth* usage and would mean accordingly 'should utter', 'should hear' and 'should go'.

(21) *Sahaj**.

(22) In Hindī *chīpī* means 'a dyer', or a person who makes a living by dying and printing clothes or a man belonging to such a caste. Tradition has it that Nāmdev was a tailor, not a dyer. In Mārvāṛī, however, *śimpī* means 'a tailor'
In Rājasthān the two castes of Hindu tailors and dyers both consider themselves descendants of Nāmdev and worship him; see Ch.1.2.

11

My goal
is Rām.
He
is my goal.
Nāmdev is a fool
people are wise.

When my heart
thought of love
I gave up dominion[23]
and became a beggar.

When God showered grace
I knew
I had been a slave
but now I was king.

I sing Rām.
I was looking for status
but I found the truth
says Nāmdev.

12

You are unfathomable
Lord of Heaven[24].
I bow at your feet.

I see beings of all
kinds before me.
I see you
wherever I go:

In water, on land,
in earth, wood or stone.
And in Āgamas*, Nigamas*,
Vedas and Purāṇas.

I was born a man
for whom life

(23) *Raj bal* in this context suggests 'kingly power', because of the contrast with *bhikhārī* in the same line and the clearly intended equivalence with *rāṇā* in the next stanza. The term has also other meanings. *Raj* suggests *rajas*, 'passion, activity', etc. according to Sāmkhya. The line thus suggests the contrast between the life of worldly activity and pursuits and that of a mendicant who has given up the world.

(24) Mss. *c* and *j* have *tribhuvananāth*, which is another epithet for God, meaning 'Lord of the three worlds'. Substitution of epithets is a common phenomenon, in this case representing two different singing traditions.

is an unquenchable fire.
Nāmdev's Lord
is merciful
to the meek.

13

Everyone is busy
using his cunning.
None plays the game
with the detachment
that can cure
the fever within.

Men draw out their days
polishing their exteriors.
But crooked within
their hearts are like demons.

No one knows the All-knowing[25]
without whom all life is a dream
sleeping or waking.

A man who learns to
cherish[26] the flame
is a saint, a sage
a knower.

Only the man who sings the name
in his heart
unceasingly, has attained
true being[27]
says Nāmdev.

14

You alone
know your truth[28].
Short
is a mortal's reach
how can he know[29]?

---

(25) *Sarbang* (Skt. *sarvajña), 'the All-knowing'*, can here refer to the guru, or to God, as the next line seems to suggest, or to both, the equation of the guru and God being common in Sant literature.

(26) *Rasani* or *rasanī* (Skt. *rasan),* means 'to savour, to cherish, to enjoy'.

(27) *Thiti* (Skt. *sthiti)* is a Nāth* term for the final state of the liberated being. See Barathvāl, *Gorakha Bānī, sākhī* 80, p.28.

(28) *Gati* occurs in both lines of the refrain, each time with a different meaning. In the first line it means 'movement', 'mode of being'; in the second it means 'to arrive', the goal being 'understanding'.

(29) Lit.: 'explain'.

You are not
what you are said
to be.
You are what you are
O Lord.

Salt and water
cannot be sifted.
The Lord is my master
my life.

I met God
like a lover[30].
With Sants and holy men
Nāmdev bows.

15

I am guilty
  Father
I am guilty.
I was untrue
  to my love for you[31].

Full of ignorance
  I broke your commands.
I acted in ways
  that come of evil company.
Such is the path
  of ignorance
  and of degeneration.
Every gain withers[32]
  ending in ruin.

Our acts of murder
  Govind knows them all[33].
He can lay low
  a mountain like Meru*.

---

(30) *Saheṭā* (or *saheṭ* Skt. *saṅketa)* is the place of a secret meeting with a lover. The term seems to be used as a verbal noun, meaning 'to meet secretly like a lover'.

(31) *Sāncilī tumhacī* is a strange juxtaposition of Rājasthānī and Marāṭhī forms. This is not uncommon in these songs.

(32) *Niṣar* (Hindī *nikhar)* means 'pure, blameless', which seems to be contrary to what the context demands. In Marāṭhī, *nikharāi (nikharaṇai,* Skt. *nikṣarana*) means 'dry, nearly exhausted' and is applied to a well, a river etc.

(33) Like many verses of Nāmdev (and other Sants) these lines are like aphorisms, which could be --and probably were-- understood by the audience in both a personal and a general way. The reading *kiyā khūn* (not nasalized) in all Mss. seems, however, to support a more personal interpretation, already suggested by the refrain 'I am guilty'.

Blameless is the man
  who sings Rām[34]
All these others
  are crooked
  O Lord.

Rām is the antidote
  against hell.
I praise him
  till I am content[35]
  says Nāmdev.

16

The one
everlasting word
in the world
'God'[36]
is my life.

A *bhakta*
is not even tinged
by the hues that
colour the world.

He stays away
from the path
the world travels.

Rare is the man
who knows *nirvāṇ*.
Everyone is lost
in lies and delusion.

Nāmdev bows
to the supreme truth.
They say
the Sadguru is close
to you.

17

People speak of materialism
Nāmdev.

---

(34) Grammatically, *narāin nāmī* means 'he who has the name Nārāyaṇ', with little meaning in the context. We understand *nāmī* as *nām lenevālā,* rendering it as 'one who says Nārāyaṇ'.

(35) Lit. *kīle mek* means 'to hammer a stake'. We interpret *kāmā* here as *yathākām.*

(36) *Sāraṅgaprāṇī* (Skt. *śārṅga-pāṇi).* Lit.:– 'He who has the bow in his hand', an epithet of Viṣṇu.

Do not go
to the six philosophies.
Love will abandon[37] you
Nāmdev.

These punctilious Brahmans
performing their six duties.
I have nothing to do
with them.
But even the lowliest
servant of Rām
speaks of nothing
but Rām.

Vile, unclean, depraved or wanton
if he sings *Paṇḍarīnāth*[38]
he is my kin
my life.
With him I sing *Rām*.

Give a million cows
to a Brahman
and have your cherished
desires fulfilled.
Yet you will not equal
a *bhakta*.

For the sake of love
I sing His praises
says Nāmdev.

18

What have I to do
with caste
or status[39]?
I worship king Rām
day and night.

With my heart
as a yardstick
my tongue
the scissors

(37) *Jāigī jāi* is an odd expression. We should perhaps read *jāigī jāigī*, the verb being repeated for emphasis. The second *gī* is dropped for metre and for rhyme (with *lokāi)* in the first line.

(38) Paṇḍarīnāth is the name of the form of Viṣṇu worshipped at Paṇḍharpur.

(39) *Pāti* lit. means : 'a line', 'a row'. It appears that the phrase *jāti-pāti* has here been split into two for emphasis. Both terms of the phrase often have the same meaning, *pāti* being an echo-word. But *pāti* (Skt. *paṅkti*, 'row') also suggests a man's place in the social hierarchy. We here render it as 'status'.

I cut the noose
    of death
rejoicing in Rām.

Always at work
    at my sewing
how can I live
    without Rām?

Remembrance
    is my needle
and love
    my thread.
My heart is devoted
    to Rām
    says Nāmdev.

19

The name *Rām*
    has entered my heart
placing a golden scale
    within.

A man makes
    a paper kite
and flies it
    in the sky.
And though
    he keeps talking
    to his friends,
his mind
    is on the string[40].

The perfect[41] princess balances
    a pot full of water
    on her head.
Laughing[42] and joking

(40) All the metaphors in this song underline the need of concentration on God while one is engaged in daily activities.

(41) *Pulandari* (probably from Skt. *purandhrī)* means: 'a married woman able to bear children', 'a woman with sons and daughters', 'the mistress of a rich house'.

(42) Most Mss. have *hast*. The word intended seems to be *hasat*. *Hast* (hands) would be repetitious for *kar* in *karatālī*. The idea seems inspired by the Nāth* ideal expressed in verses attributed to Gorakhanāth:

> 'Laugh and play, live merrily. Don't be angry or lustful. Laugh and play, sing songs, but keep your mind firm. Laugh and play, but meditate. Spend your days talking of the knowledge of Brahma. Those who laugh and play, not letting the mind wander, are forever with the Nāth'.

See Barathvāl, *Gorakh-Bānī*, pp.3-4.
See also the verses of Sundardās, in P.H.Śarmā, *Sundar Granthāvalī*, I,p.99,34-36.

she claps her hands.
Her mind
is on the pitcher.

There is a house
with ten doors
from which the cows
go to pasture[43].
Wandering, a cow
grazes for ten miles,
her mind on the calf.

The child lies
in the cradle
and the mother
works in her room.
Her mind
is on the child.
Listen to me, Trilochan*,
says Nāmdev.

20

Why dance,
why sing?
Why make sandalwood paste
to anoint yourself
again and again[44]?

You cannot tell
the Self from the Other
your mind deluded
by what it sees[45].

People dance
before an idol
not knowing
the Self-born[46].

If you but knew
how to serve
the Self-born
your divine vision
could see all.

(43) The 'house with ten doors' stands for the human body and the 'cows' represent the five senses. 'Calf' then would be a metaphor for 'God'.

(44) Refers to the ritual anointment before worshipping the image of a god.

(45) *Citārai,* from *citārnā,* 'to see'. The word may also be construed as the locative of citār: 'a thing of many colours', referring metaphorically to the world of the senses.

(46) *Syambha-dev* (Skt. *svayambhū),* 'born of its own'.

I worship only
God-within
nothing else[47]
says Nāmdev.

21

Love of Rām
is hard, Father
till you see the self
pervading everything[48].

Your fine exterior
filthy within
cannot be washed
with water, idiot.

God is no idol
nor the proffered leaves.
Nāmdev does not worship
in this manner.

False worship
cannot please Rām.
It may fool
the shallow
and the blind.

My eyes have turned
inward.
My heart clings
to the feet
of Rām,
says Nāmdev.

22

We grab at things
saying 'mine' 'mine'
Wasting life without love
for Rām's name.

---

(47) Besides 'other', *avar* also suggests 'lower'.

(48) Lit. : 'Rām's *bhakti* is difficult, O Father, everywhere, continuously (Skt. *nirantaram* 'without space')know the Self.'
There is no connective between the two lines. The connection has to be supplied by the imagination of the listener, as is not unusual in these songs. The term *sakal nirantari* sounds odd. The singer may have meant *antari* (within), using *nirantari* because of the metre. We render *sakal nirantari* as 'pervading all'.

A filthy man
    washing in slime
squanders his life.
    Can he ever be clean?

A fine exterior
    filthy within.
Pouring water on it
    is just a sham.

If you abandon Surabhi*
    can you cross
the sea of *samsār*
    holding on
    to a sheep's tail
    Nāmdev?

23

    Why meditate
    Why mutter prayers
    When you are blind
        to your self[49]?

The serpent
    sloughs its skin
but not its poison.
The heron
    stands meditating
a *yogī* only in looks[50].

Can the prey hide
    from the lion?
This is all a worship
    of false gods.

Nāmdev's Lord has
    silenced all strife.
Drink the medicine *Rām*
    you hypocrite[51].

---

(49) Lit.: 'if the mind does not know (*sudh,* probably from Skt. *su+ dhī,* 'awareness, consciousness') itself'.

(50) The heron, standing still on one leg in the shallow waters of a pond, looks like a meditating ascetic but all he is seeking is fish. This was a common metaphor for those who were *yogis* or *bhaktas* only in appearance.

(51) *Bhagarā,* with the preceding *re,* is clearly a vocative, possibly connected with *bhagar,* delusion, magic show, mirage'. So, we render *bhagarā* as hypocrite', or 'one who is not what he pretends to be'.
Under *bhagarā* the HSS quotes a similar couplet of Nāmdev from S.R.Śarmā, *Dakhinī Hindī kā Gadya aur Padya,* with the following meaning for *bhagarā:* 'dry or coarse-

24

He is a good *bhakta*, Father,
the crow[52],
he understands nothing
and worships a stone[53].

Men wash and scrub themselves
they take ritual baths.
But their hearts have no eyes
their heads no ears.

They wear a garland
of *tulsī* beads[54]
around their necks
but they are black as coal
within.

The demands of the stomach
are powerful.
People are dull red within
but vermillion[55]
on the outside,
says Nāmdev.

25

People will kill me
if I tell the truth.
One always loses against
the many.

A word of truth
can scatter an assembly.
It can ridicule, hurt[56]

---

grained powder'. The line makes better sense if *bhagarā* is understood as 'the deluded one'.

(52) For *kāgilā* several Mss. have *kāḍalā*, which is not clear, but is possibly a variant form of the Marāṭhī *kāvalā*, 'crow'.

(53) Crows sharpen their beaks against stones. Is this seen here as an act of devotion of a stupid devotee, who rubs his forehead on the feet of the image of a deity? The metaphor is not fully clear.

(54) The *tulsī* plant (holy basil) is sacred to Vaiṣṇavas* who worship Tulsī as a goddess and celebrate her marriage with Viṣṇu. Its wood is cut into small beads and strung into ritual garlands.

(55) The intention of the last verse is clear: people practice religion as a business for material profit; they have a showy exterior while their hearts are impure. Puzzling, however, is the contrasting juxtaposition of *lākh* (Skt. *lākṣā*), red lac and *hīngalū* (Skt. *hīṅgula)*, vermillion. Ms. *v* gives exactly the opposite : *bāhari lākh bhītari hīngalū.*

(56) The use of *abhāvai* in this context is curious. With the meaning 'lack, absence' it makes little sense. It can perhaps be understood as an unusual construction of *a+bhāv*, meaning 'lack of pleasure or appreciation', hence 'that which displeases, hurts'.

break bones.

People do not know
the filth in their minds
putting their faith
in soap and water.

Arrayed in bright garments
they keep low company
shaming themselves[57]
the dressed-up hypocrites.

The ignorant fool
puts up a bright show
till the noose of death
tightens around his neck
and he dies.

Such are fools
cursed people
sinful, they do not remember
Paṇḍarīnāth
says Nāmdev.

26

Truth alone
can please my Lord
not guile or cunning.

Sing or dance
as much as you will
what you need
is a truthful heart.

With infinite care
the temptress
adorns herself.
But her coquetry[58]
cannot entice
her lord.

The faithful one
knows only
her husband.
Hari listens to her
says Nāmdev.

(57) *Pati* (Hindī *pat*, Skt. *pratiṣṭhā)* means 'honour'. *Pat jānā* means 'to lose face, honour or credibility'.

(58) This metaphor compares with song 56 of Bakhṇā; see *Bakhaṇā jī kī Vāṇī*, p.87.

27

He is close at hand
he who knows the gem.
The gem is lost
in glittering paste[59].

A jeweller knows a fake
at a glance,
a diamond from a diamond mine
cannot be false.

A man keeps poison[60]
hidden in his dress
he gives it to others
and takes it himself.

I took the poison
and it spreads through me.
Hari alone is the
antidote[61]
says Nāmdev.

28

Who can be tainted
once he says *Rām?*
Sinners become pure
when they cry *Rām*.

Those who live
in the truth of Rām
should they fast
or visit holy sites?

In remembrance
I found
the right thing to do
says Nāmdev.

They will surely
find *mokṣa*,
those who say

(59) *Mulamā* (from Ar. *mulammā)*, 'plating', as of gold or other metals. Hence the derivative meaning: something shiny on the outside but without lustre within.

(60) *Kālakūṭ* was the lethal poison produced when the gods and demons churned the ocean.

(61) *Garudadvār* is a 'kind of copper --said to come from peacocks-- that is used as an antidote to poison'. See V.L. Varmā, *Rajab Bāṇī*, Ch. 26.35 (p.60).

Rām.

29

Sing *Rām*,
Narhari, Srī Banvārī.
Constantly worship
the feet of Murārī.

The guru's word
is a stairway to heaven.
the heart is Prayāg*
where sweet love flows.

I wandered
through the cosmos
in search of the treasure
but found it within me.

Do not come or go
stay at home and
sing of your Rām
says Nāmdev.

30

I have pleaded with Rām
I shall not ask another.
My life grows shorter
I cannot waste another birth.

I will not implore
another god.
My tongue will taste only
the elixir of *Rām*.

Rām is with everyone,
whether a worm or a moth[62]
moving
or still.

Rām is my life
other gods are empty
and useless
says Nāmdev.

(62) See song 6 and 57.2.

31

The day the saints
came to me
I found
liberation[63].

All my doubts
about seeing God
disappeared.
A primal deed
of merit
bore fruit.

I saw him
before me
and knew
that my life
was fulfilled.

The Vaiṣṇav* truth
entered
my heart.
Nāmdev
the Lord's man
sings with joy.

33

Give up this
worldly business.
Rām will look after
you.

Nārāyaṇ is
my mother.
Nārāyaṇ is
my father.
The Vaiṣṇavas*
full of love
are my kin.

Keśav has
many sons.
You are
one
Nāmdev.

(63) Lit.: the four *mokṣas*. Bhakti doctrines speak of four 'states', sometimes considered as 'stages' of *mokṣa:* 1) *sālokya:* attaining to the same divine *loka* (world) as God, 2) *sāmīpya:* attaining a place near or close *(samīpa)* to God, 3) *sārūpya:* becoming identical in form with God, 4) *sāyujya:* merging in God.

34

You are
my mother
you are
my father.
You are
my family
O Viṭṭhal.

Hari is
my boat
he will
carry me
to the other
shore[64].

I row
across[65]
in the company
of the holy.
Keśav is
generous to
Nāmdev.

35

Govind is
my mother
Govind is
my father.
Govind is
my caste
my status[66]
my guru.

Govind is
my knowledge
Govind is
my prayer.
King Rām is
a constant

(64) The obscure *pailī tirī* (from *pailī*, 'other' and *tīr?*, 'shore') is rendered as 'the other shore'. The expression occurs also in the Marāṭhī *abhaṅga* 637 (*Nāmdev Gāthā*, p. 254).

(65) The meaning of stanza two is not clear. In several Mss. we read *kheicā*, which does not rhyme with *dātār* in the next line. Apparently the expression *khei cār* was not clear to many singers and their audience, and became *kheicā*. One may understand *cār* here as the four *mokṣas* of the *bhakti* doctrine (see fn., song 31). The line could then be translated as: 'In the company of saints I rowed to the four *mokṣas*'.

(66) See above, song 18, note on *pāti*.

source of bliss.

Govind sings
Govind dances.
Dressed as
Govind
I ceaselessly
dance.

Govind is
my offering[67].
Govind is
my worship.
I have no
other god
says Nāmdev.

36

The heart is
the garland
the heart is
Gopāl.
The heart is
the Gracious One
merciful
to the meek.

The heart is
the dye
and it is
the dyer[68].
The heart is
the earth
and also
water.

The heart is
the lamp
that lights
the house[69]
where the latch
and the lock
and the door

(67) *Pāti,* lit.: 'leaf'. Leaves of certain trees are placed before an image as offering. Here 'leaves' clearly stand for offering in general.

(68) See above, song 9.

(69) Several Mss. have *ghaṭi,* which gives the same metaphorical sense in the context. Both *ghari* and *ghaṭi* refer to the human body. We prefer *ghari* because with it the next line makes better sense.

are all open[70].

The heart has
no colour
no body
no caste.
Dye it
the colour
of Rām
Nāmdev.

37

I remember
Rām.
Never shall I
forget him.

Every moment
I dedicate
my body, my heart
to Rām.

Not for an hour
a minute
the fraction of a second,
is he out of my mind[71].

I inhale remembrance
with every breath
a poor man lives on raw sugar
I live on Rām.

Ceaselessly I cry
Rām Rām
loudly shouting[72] his
name.
Miserably I weep
when I forget him.

No desire
have I
but to die

(70) The image seems to convey the idea that, at a particular moment of mystical insight, the 'enclosed' house becomes one with the universe that is God.

(71) *Gharī* is equal to the 32nd part of a day (roughly 24 minutes); *muhūrt* could be either the 30th part of a day or equal to 2 *gharīs*. *Pal*, the smallest measure of time, is equal literally to the batting of an eye.

(72) The expression *ārau māṇḍi* is obscure. We translate *ārau* as derived from Skt. *ārava*, 'cry, clamour'. Thus *ārau māṇḍi*, means 'to make a clamour'. Elsewhere, (song 29, 2) Nāmdev speaks of 'shamelessly shouting the name of God'.

for my treasure
Rām,
says Nāmdev.

39

I dread
I dread your terrible
māyā.
So many has it led
astray.

Brahma is not to be seen
in *māyā.*
There is no *māyā* in
Brahma.

So says the creator himself
O Nāmdev.

Do not make me ride
two horses together
O Krishna.

40

You have put up a show,
Father,
a magic show.
I like the man
who is not taken in.

Life is a show
death is a show
to these the mind clings.

Thus I meditated:
You are both
the string
and the puppeteer.

I seek your shelter.
End our birth
and death,
says Nāmdev.

41

Do not forget me,
O do not forget me.

Cursed am I
that I forgot you.

Ruler of the world,
riding the Garuḍ bird[73].
Inner Witness
at life's end
O Hari.

In life and in death
am I dedicated to you
to your worship.
There is no god like you.

You are the Sustainer of the world
I am your devotee Nāmdev
O Fulfiller
of the desires of Sants.

42

I do not understand, Father
why truth is thrown away
and replaced
with falsehood.

A picture painted in water
a pillar of wind.
How can one even think
of making such things[74]?

What is born here
disappears.
Where is the speaker
concealed?

If Rām is not revealed
during life
What hope after death
says Nāmdev.

---

(73) *Garuḍāgāmī*, from Skt. *garuḍagāmin*, is an epithet of Viṣṇu who rides on a divine eagle named *garuḍ*.

(74) In Mss. *dav* and *cj*, an *antara added*:
'Says Nārāyaṇ: Listen, O devotee Nāmdev,
Where there is remembrance, desires are fulfilled'.
The lines were obviously added as an answer to the rhetorical question of the first *antarā*.

43

Being so crooked
how can I be redeemed?
I saw the signs
of the Kali* age
and was not alarmed.

My worship and prayer
are like the heron[75]
pure only in appearance.

The heart is a serpent
drinking milk[76]
prayer a falcon
and the mind
a wildcat[77].

Many are tethered
to this rope.
The witch's offspring[78]
feed on the whole world
says Nāmdev.

44

Unbearable,
this fear of death, O Father
this great consuming fire
that terrifies all.

Many sages
have struggled with it
gods and men have tried in vain
to overcome it.

Dervishes, God's messengers
and demons[79] tremble.
Even the *rishis* tremble
all eighty-four of them[80].

Everything trembles:
moon, sun, earth, air, space.

---

(75) See above, song 23.

(76) Even if you feed a serpent on milk, it remains poisonous and dangerous.

(77) We here translate *surati* as 'prayer. For synonyms of *surati* in *nirguṇ* literature, see Callewaert:1977, verse 57. In verse 34 the female cat is given as a synonym for *manasā*.

(78) In the *Anabhai Prabodh of Garībadās* (Callewaert:1977), verse 34, *māyā* is compared to a witch *(ḍaṅkinī)*.

(79) Considering the context, *dev* has to be understood in its Persian meaning of 'demon'.

(80) This seems to be a reference to the Nāth* Siddhas, traditionally 84 in number.

Water too trembles
  for fear of the bite of fire.

Every part, every region
  of the world trembles
as do all temporal things.

Lord Nārāyaṇ alone is constant
  in him there is no fear.
Nāmdev bows to him
  the Indefinable, the Formless.

48

I am incapable
  of devotion to you
  Lord
Unable to serve my master
  in ways that will
  please him.

I cannot declaim
  scripture
I would be vain
  if I could.
Whatever I say
  rebounds
  on me
and binds me.
Save me
  save me
  O Lord.

In him all life is born
  who is in all
  life.
Him the world
  forgets
deluded by false
  attachments.
Father
  you fill every
  creature.

Tell me
  I beg you
what is that heaven
where one goes
  at death?
I cannot believe

there is no liberation
in life.

I am a servant
a creature.
You Mādhav
are Brahma.
Not seeing you
I suffer.
Let me be with you
your servant Nāmdev
pleads.
I will sing your praises.

49

Grant me *bhakti*
Father
I do not ask for *mokṣa*
O Hari Viṭṭhal.

I will give up my life
if you do not
grant me *bhakti.*
Do what you will
I will still want
bhakti.

I have wandered
for endless lives
redeemed each time
as I sang
your name.

You are my life
the sea where I am
a fish
says Nāmdev.

50

Take me across
the sea of *samsār*
Govind.
I do not know
how to swim
Father.

Lashed by foaming[81] waves
  of greed
I am going under
    Keśav.

You brought me[82] a raft
  but I cannot row.
Take me across
  take me across
    O Viṭṭhal.

I am your servant
  give me your hand
    Viṭṭhal
  says Nāmdev.

51

How can I live
  without you?
You are the rock
  of my life.

Your name is
  the substance
the rest of the world
  is hollow.
Your name is
  the support
in thought word and deed
  in this Kali* age.

The world has many hells
  terrible sufferings
  without end
  O Creator.
Let me live in bliss
  at your lotus feet.

What is this veil
  that keeps me
  from you?
Greed
  ambition
  lust?
A rare devotee finds redemption
  his mind fixed on

(81) *Nijhar*, 'mountain stream', suggests the idea of foam.
(82) The phrase *āni de* seems to have confused the singers. See the variants in the critical apparatus.

Rām.

Men flow with the Vedas
in the swift waters
of delusion.
Viṭṭhal is the Lord
of his servant Nāmdev.
O take me
to the other shore.

52

Undo the bonds
of your servant
Banvārī.
I never called on you
Shelter of the shelterless.
I fell
into the flood
of death.

Some are chained
to yoga
and sacrifices
or gifts
or pilgrimages.
Some are bound
by rules or vows.
It's all in your hands
O Lord.

Your maid *Māyā*
that enchantress
has great skill
in deception.
She captures all
whatever moves
or is still
not knowing
what is hers
from what is not.

I will not part
from you
unless you abandon me
Gopāl.
I have no patron
other than you, O Merciful
Lord of the meek
says Nāmdev.

53

My caste is lowly
O Lord.
People have nothing but
scorn for me.

It's not me
not me, O Mādhav
It's you
it's not me.
You are one
spread out as many.
I am mere nothingness.

I am a river
that has flowed
through land
to be lost
in the sea.
Your mercy lifts up
the lowly
O Destroyer of death.

No gods, no goddesses
for me
no companion or ally
O Friend.
I've come running to you
for refuge.
Cast off my shackles
Father Viṭṭhal
says Nāmdev.

54

Hari's name resounds
Hari's name
shines.
Why be ashamed
of singing Hari's name?

Hari is my mother
father
guru.
Forever shall I serve
my Rām.

Hari's name

makes Lakṣmī[83]
your slave.
Hari's name
made Śiva a god[84].

Hari's name
made Dhruv* constant.
Hari's name
redeemed Prahlād*.

Hari is my companion
in life and death.
Hari, who rescued
the drowning creature.

Hari, the Giver of joy
is always with me.
I am immersed in
the name of Hari
says Nāmdev.

55

What can you lose
if you sing
Rām?
Sing that name
sleeping or waking.

The glory of that name
saved Dhruv*
and Prahlād*
who meditated on the *mantra*
Rām.

Sanak* and others
cherished the name
the name *Rām*
which grants freedom[85].

This is my message
says Nāmdev
What you receive
is what you desire.

---

(83) Kamvalā (Skt. *kamalā)* is another name of Lakṣmī, the goddess of wealth and fortune; she is the consort of Viṣṇu or Hari.
(84) In Vaiṣṇav* lore, Śiva is said to derive his power, even his godhood, from Viṣṇu, the supreme Lord.
(85) Lit.: 'the state of fearlessness'.

56

Sing the name
Rām,
the state of *nirvāṇ*.
Your tongue lies idle
what better can it do?

Service.
Worship.
Remembrance.
Meditation.
All are false
without God.

Fasts
pilgrimages
serve worldly goals
they are empty without faith.

These regular fasts
are worldly efforts
they are like a ladder
discarded
when the citadel is scaled.

My heart lies at your feet
you are my refuge
says Nāmdev.

57

Dwell on Rām
brother
like the caterpillar
meditating
in the cocoon[86].

The Lord has all
shapes.
He is the master of
everything.
Untarnished
by the three *guṇas*[87]
he lives within
all.

---

(86) The metaphor of the caterpillar turning into a butterfly was so well-known, that it is here barely sketched in a single line.

(87) For the *guṇas*, see *puruṣ**.

A worm or a moth
whatever moves or is still
Rām is with
everyone.

I have no kin
no brother.
In the name *Rām* I found
the nine treasures[88]
says Nāmdev.

58

Such is Rām
and such is the way
to behold him:
let not your mind wander
away from him.

Be like a lecher
eyeing another's wife
or a gambler
lost in gaming.

A cheat
playing with loaded[89] dice
or a goldsmith scheming
to steal the gold
with which he works[90].

I find you
Rām
wherever I go.
My heart with you
I bow
says Nāmdev.

59

Like a fish
out of water
floundering
such is Nāmdev
without the name,
Rām.

---

(88) *Nav nidhi**

(89) *Pasavārā* (possibly Skt. *pārśva,* 'side'). The meaning of the line is not entirely clear but the phrase 'throwing the dice on a side' suggests trickery.

(90) It is still a popular belief in India that a goldsmith always steals some gold, replacing it with base metal, as he works with it.

My whole body is anxious
like a cow
without her calf.
The milk in her udder
painfully churns
melting like butter
in hot sunshine.
Such is poor Nāmdev
without the name
Rām.
As the heart of a libertine
aches
for another's wife
Nāmdev craves
the love of
Banvārī.

61

Wherever I go
I see Viṭṭhal
Viṭṭhal, king Rām
my Lord.

Here is a jug
full of fresh water
to bathe the image
of Bālgovind
But the fish which it contained
have desecrated it[91].
What shall I do?

Here is saffron,
dry and smooth
to mark the forehead
of Bālgovind. But the serpents who have
smelled its fragrance
have desecrated it.
What shall I do?

Here are flowers
to be strung together
to make a garland
for Bālgovind.
But the bees who have
savoured them
have desecrated them.
What shall I do?

(91) Nāmdev suggests that ritual purity is impossible, since all objects used in ritual have been already touched by someone or something, and hence are impure.

Here is some *ghee*
and here is a wick
to light a flame
for Bālgovind.
But the eyes which have
looked at the flame
have desecrated it.
What shall I do?

Here is some aloe-wood
and here is fire
to make sweet incense
for Bālgovind.
But the nose which
smelled the fragrance
has desecrated it.
What shall I do?

Here is some rice
and here is boiled milk
for the food offering
to Bālgovind.
But the calf who sucked the teat
that gave the milk
has desecrated it.
What shall I do?

Wherever I come or go
I see Lord Viṭṭhal
and Viṭṭhal's all-covering
māyā.
Nāmdev's heart has found
the love of God.
He has reached
the final Goal.

62

O do not go
my heart
into the wilderness
of the senses.
You will be drugged
and robbed[92]
the minute you are
there.

(92) The *ṭhagamūlī* is a root which was used by robbers to drug their victims.

The bees make much honey
but only to lose it.
All they get is ash
in their mouths[93].

A cow has milk
for her calf.
But with a noose
around her neck
the cowherd takes it
all.

Deep in the water
lives the fish
unaware of the
net of death.

Full of greed
it swallows the hook.
Men too are snared
by women
and gold.

You toil and you sweat
for *māyā*
and she shoves you
into an abyss.

In his ignorance[94],
the fool does not see
his treasures
are sand
trickling out of his pouch[95].

Inflamed by lust
and greed
and anger
one never seeks
the company of saints.
With reverence
Nāmdev bows
before that man
who has given himself
to God
fearlessly.

---

(93) Bees were smoked out for their honey.
(94) Several manuscripts give just the opposite reading: [illegible], '[illegible], [illegible]', obviously meant as irony.
(95) In India money is tied up in a pouch formed from the hem of one's clothing.

63

Sing of your Rām
lazy heart.
All else is weaving
a web of death.

Performing a horse sacrifice,
fellows,
or giving away
your weight in gold
or bathing at holy Prayāg*
nothing can equal
singing *Hari*.

Offering rice-balls in Gayā*,
fellows,
or living in sacred Banāras
and chanting
the Vedas, Purāṇas
nothing can equal
singing *Hari*.

To observe the commandments
to have the wisdom
of a guru
controlling the senses
or strictly carrying out
the six duties*;
nothing can equal
singing *Hari*.

Give up all worship
all debates
all activity.
Give up all distinctions.
Keep your mind on Govind.
his name
will row you across
the ocean of *samsār*
says Nāmdev.

64

Though their minds are in turmoil
they put on a big show
can such rogues cross *samsār?*

(96) The six duties of a Brahman are: *yajana* (sacrifice) and *yājana* (conducting a sacrifice for others), *adhyayana* (study) and *adhyāpana* (teaching), *dāna* (giving gifts) and *pratigraha* (receiving gifts).

These clowns
 with their sacred beads
 and rosaries
know nothing about truth.
They see nothing
 but claim to give insight
 to others.
Can deception lead to liberation?

Carrying horns
 with matted hair
their bodies smeared
 with ash[97]
they are called accomplished sages[98].
Blind to the highest Nāth
 the secret essence
they make a frenzied display.

Acting like Brahmā[99]
 some study and chant the Vedas
 their hearts deluded
busy with ritual
 they do not know what they are doing.

Some keep the month-long fast
 of Ramadan
while the muezzin
 shouts the *kalimā*[100].
Carrying knives[101] in their souls
 they make a mockery
 of the name of Allah.

Those who really know
 the One Brahma
they meditate on the Real.
Nāmdev bows
 to the grace of the guru.
 He who finds it
 keeps it hidden.

(97) The horn, matted hair and ash-besmeared body are marks of a Nāth* yogī.

(98) *Sambar*, (from Skt. *saṁvara*,(lit.: 'to cover') is a term for 'one who has shut off the world'; *siddha* is 'a perfected one' in Nāth* terminology.

(99) According to Puranic thought Brahmā, the creator in the Hindu trinity, utters the Veda at the beginning of every cycle of the universe.

(100) The *kalimā* is the well-known Muslim expression: "There is no God but Allāh and Muhammad is his prophet".

(101) Lit.: 'scissors'.

65[102]

The sound of the flute
fills the sky
O Lord.
The silent sound
resounds.
Ignorant of his Self
the fool wanders
lost.

Moving the sun*
to the moon*
making firm the mind
the breath
the spinal column
effortlessly I rose
through the *suṣumnā**
to the star cluster[103]
thus slaying desire.

I do not sit
or move
or wander.
I never starve
I never eat.
I do not live
I never die.
I am ever joyful
neither coming
nor going.

Dwelling in the skies[104]
I have made my home
the self-born Void[105].
My heart is rapt
in the music within.
Rare is the yogī
who hears it.

I gather no leaves
for ritual offerings.
There is no god
in the shrine.

I have found shelter with Rām,

(102) See Glossary: 'Song 65'.
(103) *Tārā-maṇḍal* (lit.: 'star-cluster'), is an esoteric term for the *sahasrār-cakra**, the mystic opening at the top of the skull.
(104) *Gagan-maṇḍal* (lit.: 'the region of the sky') is another esoteric term for the *sahasrār-cakra**; see *KV*, p. 130.
(105) *Sahaj**.

never to be born
again
says Nāmdev.

66

My kite[106] hangs motionless
in the sky
O Lord.
I see it when I am not.

The heart is blind
with desire
and frustration.
When words and speech
are left behind
one knows.

I have left behind
all songs[107]
Why sing of what is
beyond?
I have no desires now
only effortless contemplation
says Nāmdev.

67

It is right
that the yogī should live
for ever.
He imprisons the sky[108]
and dragging it down
he fills his cup
and drinks.

His father[109] guided him
to the pool
of immortal waters.
His mother
died of grief.

(106) For the image of the kite in Kabīr, see *KG*, p. 137, song 91.

(107) The expression *gāye gaye gaye te gāye* is obscure, but it evidently emphasizes the idea that the mystical experience is difficult to express.

(108) *Ākāś* ('sky'), like *gagan maṇḍal,* is another term for the *sahasrār cakra**, which contains the waters of immortality that are dragged down or rain down when the sun* is united with the moon*.

(109) Father, mother and kin have in this song an esoteric meaning. Father stands for the Sadguru (or God), mother for *māyā* and kin for the senses or passions.

The hopes of his kin
were shattered
everyone fled.

Shut the outward eye
begin the search.
Quench the inner thirst
of your senses.
Offer yourself to
the Pure[110]
in effortless contemplation
says Nāmdev.

68

It is your music
I hear
O Lord.
The rhythm of drums
jantar
and *viṇā*.
The supreme moment
has come.

I had my faith
in iron
and copper.
I had chains around
my feet.
But now I have no fear
of this ocean
of *samsār*.
Liberation awaits
like a serving girl.

The lion[111] has turned its back
and runs
the goats return
to pasture.
I was going out
I looked within
and perfected devotion
says Nāmdev.

70

Right here.

(110) For *nirañjan* (lit.: 'without impurity'), see *KV*, p. 138.
(111) The lion symbolises death.

Govind is right
here.
My heart dwells
at his feet.
Never will I give up
my love for him
let people laugh
all they wish.

Govind's name
will take you across
the ocean of *samsār*.
Why work yourself
to death
for the falsehood
of *māyā*?

If the master
gets him into trouble[112]
should a servant
run away,
disgracing himself
and his master?
No one can live
for ever.

A man will stake his life
for his money.
Should a *bhakta* not cherish
his love?

Gangā, Gayā*, Godāvarī*.
These are worldly
journeys.
All that I want
is to please Rām
says Nāmdev.

71

Pervading her body
and her mind
the dancer's spouse
lives with her
within her.
Countless princes wait
in a row.
But her heart

(112) *Sānkarai* (possibly Skt. *saṅkīrṇa*), 'in a bad spot', 'in trouble'.

is not with them.

The dancer gazes
at His body
the body adorned
with wisdom.
The echoing drum
of Rām's name
is struck
and truth is ushered in.

Thus should you play the game
with one mind
and one heart:
Let go,
let go of
that thing
that you hold
in your fist
like a monkey[113]
and you will be free.

I danced
like a dancer
with my mind on him
Upholder of the World
the Inner witness,
and my Lord was pleased
says Nāmdev.

72

My delusion
has vanished
brother.
I am free
of rebirth.
The Lord's devotee
has come

(113) The phrase also occurs in Kabīr *(KV,* song 97):
"Greedily you stretched out your hand like a monkey,
O foolish heart,
Holding the food-grains in your fist.
But now running frantically from house to house,
O foolish heart,
you find no way to free yourself".
A passage from Bakhaṇā *(Bakhaṇā jī kī vāṇī,* song 8, p.51) makes the meaning clearer. The poet speaks of the monkey putting his hand in a jar. Apparently, food-grains were stored in jars with a small opening; a monkey could squeeze his hand into the jar but could not take it out while holding a fistful of grains. He could free himself only if he let go of what he held.

where he belongs.

The magician
beat his drum
and the whole world came
for the show.
The magician stopped
his show
and lo
there was nothing
but he.

When king Rām
spread out his *māyā*
the whole world
came out shopping[114].
They were so engrossed
in buying
that no one saw
the Lord-within.

A deer caught sight
of a scarecrow
he was startled
his eyes full of fear.
But when he came close
he saw
it was nothing
but a dummy
nothing at all to fear.

The scarecrow
is only to scare you.
Rid your heart of fear
and you will see.
I assure you
like a guru.
What more can I say
says Nāmdev.

73

He can be found
here
He can also be found
there.
No wonder people
argue.

(114) *Saudā* (Ar.), 'goods for sale', but also 'madness'.

Those who call him
    indivisible
find him
    indivisible.
Yet those who call him
    divisible
find him so.
Those who speak of
    *sahaj**
find him as
    sahaj.
And those who talk of
    play
find him playful.

Those who sing of
    pain
discover him in
    suffering.
Yet those who harp on
    joy
discover him there.
Those who hold to
    knowledge
find him as
    knowledge.
And those who speak of
    meditation
find him there.

If I speak of what I see
    I lie.
If I speak of what I hear
    I lie again.
If I speak of something
    beyond my grasp
to ask is
    not to ask
    says Nāmdev.

74

The bee[115] cannot find
    the lotus.
Life after life
    she is misled.

---

(115) The bee is a symbol for the seeking soul. See R.C. Miśra, *Hindī Santon kā ulaṭbānsī Sāhitya*, p. 119.

A frog[116] lives
under that lotus
dead to all
sensibility.
While the bee flies
for miles
longing for that
fragrant flower.

The sun* and the moon*
whirl the churning stick[117].
Not reaching her goal
the bee weeps
age after age.

When devotion grows
attachment[118] disappears.
Never again a return
to the ocean of *samsār*.
Nāmdev sings
living in endless space
beyond form.

76

It's weird.
It leaves one speechless.
How can an elephant[119] find room
in an ant's eye?

Some say: it is near
others say: it is far.
Can a fish who live
in the water
climb up a palm[120] tree?

Some say: bind your senses.

---

(116) *Dādur* (frog) is a symbol for the outgoing mind; see *Ibidem*, p. 126.

(117) *Net* (or the rope by which a churning stick is moved) may be an esoteric word for the *kuṇḍaliṇī?* Churning is the process of extracting butter, i.e. the essence, from milk. In mythology, the churning of the ocean by the gods and demons produced *amṛta* or the elixir of immortality.

(118) *Pacīsau*, (lit.: 'twenty-five'), refers to the Sāmkhya *Prakṛti*, which contains 25 elements. *Prakṛti causes Puruṣ*, pure consciousness, to be attached to objects. Hence *pacīsau* here suggests 'attachment'; see below, song 97. The names of the twenty-five elements are enumerated in Callewaert:1978, p. 174.

(119) In the esoteric terminology of the Sants the elephant and the ant stand respectively for 'the sensual mind' and 'discriminative knowledge'. See Miśra, *op.cit.*, p. 180. See also below, song 101.

(120) The allusion is to the *kuṇḍalinī* moving up to the *sahasrār**. This ascension is not a natural movement, but something a seeker has to attain through yoga. See Miśra, *op.cit.*, p. 117.

Others say: free them.
The ignorant do not know
effortless contemplation.

Some say: go to the Vedas, Smrtis*, Purāṇas.
But the Sadguru
has taught me *nirvāṇ*.

Such is the real:
it has no form, no contour.
How can I tell its colour?
Nāmdev.

77

Effortlessly,
my kite[121] flies up
O Lord
and merges into the sky.
The speaker has entered
the string[122].
He neither comes
nor goes.

Three colours
has the string
white, yellow and black.
Gods, men and sages
all want it for themselves.
But the wind is a horse[123]
that takes it away
beyond the sky.

The kite was born of twelve[124].
Few really know it.
The mind alone can touch it
and see it
if the guru shows the way.

It is not a kite
made of paper.
It gives effortless joy.
Like the sea

(121) The kite symbolizes the soul, entering the highest level of contemplation.

(122) The string here represents *Prakrti* as is evident from its three colours: white for *sattva*, yellow for *rajas* and black for *tamas*. The natural movement of *Prakriti* is towards *Puruṣ**, as that of the kite towards the heavens.

(123) For the symbol of horse and wind, see Barathvāl, *Gorakh-bānī*, songs 174, 316, 365 and P.H. Śarmā, *Sundar-Granthāvalī*, song 4 (p. 916).

(124) For *dvādas dal* in *KG* 2 (song 130, p. 261) we read in the *Kabīr-Koś,* (p. 201): *bārah dal vālā anāhat cakra*.

and a drop of rain
from the clouds
joined into one
says Nāmdev.

78

Why wander deluded
my heart?
Meditate at the feet of Rām
All-awareness.

Sing Narhari
my heart;
the end of your days
is near.

You have pinned your faith on sons
on wife and wealth.
Give up false hopes.
What do you know of house
or household?
Your body will wither
in no time at all.

The body is false
says Nāmdev.
And yet it is real
if Rām is your lover.

79

Utter
the name *Rām*
the very sound
of *nirvāṇ*.
All else is false
my tongue.

The Lord of Paradise
is my Master.
Who has he not
redeemed?
Who has he not
rowed across?

A golden wedge[125]
has split the stone

(125) *Bhāli* lit. means 'the sharp, pointed end of a weapon'.

And out of the cleft
grows a tree[126].
Look
there is no one here
but king Rām.

In all the seven worlds
and all the nine continents
was anyone ever freed
without Rām?

Though you are made of dust
you must not mingle
with dust.
Take my advice
says *bhakta* Nāmdev.

82

The *bhakta*
stands apart
from the world.
Read the Vedas
or the Purāṇas
pore over them
to your heart's content
But remember this,
O Paṇḍit:

The milk
churned into butter
will never be milk
again.
Wood, producing
fire
will never be wood
again[127].

A touch
of the *pāras* stone
and copper
turns to gold
never to be copper
again.

(126) The translation of this line is not certain. *Jhīnjh* is not found in dictionaries, nor in the vocabulary of other Sants. The RSK has *jhinjhau,* 'a kind of tree that grows on hills or mountains'. The *Gujarātī-English Dictionary* (M.B. Belsare) has *jhinjhī* (Skt. *jhinṭikā),* 'a kind of tree'.

(127) This metaphor is based on the belief that fire is contained in the wood and is extracted from it by rubbing dry sticks together.

Grow them
  near a sandalwood tree
and the *āk*
  and the *palās*
will be fragrant
  forever.

Worship Rām
  let your mind
dwell on him alone.
  Give up
all desire for *karma*.
  For he
who sings *Rām*
  becomes Rām.
  Bhakta Nāmdev
  bows to him.

83

  Gopāl is my king
  I have no use
    for other gods.

Some have Smrtis*
    Vedas and Purāṇas,
but my heart has found
    his lotus feet.

Some have wealth
    in millions and millions
my only support
    is the name of Rām.

Some have armies
    of footmen and elephants
my only companion
    is the name of Rām.

His praise resounds
    in all the worlds.
Nāmdev's heart
    goes out to him.

84

  Sing my heart
    sing *Govind*
    Govind.
  Do not forget

his lotus feet.

In agony I lived
in the womb
returning to the womb
again and again.

So I sing
the praises of Hari.
Never shall I
come back.
Nāmdev.

88

Yes, I have found it.
I have found the name of
Rām.
I have strung it
on the silken cord of
love
and wear it around
my neck.

The name of Rām
is the truth.
Singing *Rām* his devotees
cross to the other
shore.

My mother is
Krishna
My father is
Krishna.
He is the kinsman
who saves me from *samsār*.

I sing his praises
never to return to the
womb
Nāmdev.

89

Why argue
bhaktas?
You have found the treasure
Rām.
I will never leave Rām
for other things.

I have strung him on a rosary
  and placed him within me.
The man who argues
  wastes his life
turning away from
  Rām.

  Sing
  Sing
the name of Rām.
Rām is the truth
  filling the three worlds.
There is no
  other.

Rām is the fountain
  of life[128].
Sing of him
  and dance.
There is no way out,
  but the name *Rām*.

Nāmdev has crossed
  to the other shore.
Wake up, take heed,
  those who will.
Without love for Rām
  you will be born
again and again.

90

O take it Hari
  please take it.
Take all my love
  and make it pure.

With a Lord like you
  should I lack in faith[129]?
I will give my life

(128) *Sañjīvaṇī* (Skt. *sañjīvanī*) is a magic plant which brings the dead back to life; some great yogīs claim to have its secret; here the *sañjīvanī* is the *sahaj**-*samādhi*, which confers immortality. According to Vaisnav *bhakti*, the *sañjīvanī* represents true devotion to Rām or Viṣṇu-Hari; see *KV*, p. 253.
As the major Sants have much to say about the *sañjīvanī*, we find the *Sañjīvanī kau aṅg* in the *Kabīr Granthāvalī*, the *Sākhibhāg* of the *Dādū-Vāṇī*, the *Rajab-Vāṇī* etc.

(129) *Pratīti* (lit.: 'going towards, approaching') is rich with meanings: 'clear apprehension, realisation, insight, conviction, confidence, faith, trust'. We render it as 'faith', although for devotees all the suggested meanings may be present at the same time.

for my inheritance.

With trust in you
I have no evil thoughts.
Can a mother poison
her son?

She will give her life
for a son who cries in pain.
My father, the Supreme Brahma,
loves me
says Nāmdev.

91

Brother
you are lost in delusion.
Better give up your
deceit.
Let your tongue sing
the name of Govind Nārāyaṇ.

Pilgrimages
a hermit's death
in the Himalayas
nothing equals
singing *Rām*.

Be an ascetic
in Vārāṇasī
or die
a wandering pilgrim
mortify your body
with fire.
give away
presents of gold,
or perform
Vedic sacrifices
nothing equals
singing *Rām*.

Travel to Mānasarovar
bathe at Gayā*
or Kurukṣetra.
immerse yourself
in the Gomatī.
give away
a million cows.
journey to Kedārnāth
or to Prayāg*

during Kumbha,
bathe in the Godâvarī
with Jupiter
in Leo
nothing equals
singing *Rām*.

Give away horses
elephants
land
or the dowry that gets
a young girl
married
give away houses
or couches
or the equal of
your weight
in gold
nothing equals
singing *Rām*.

Do not blame death
do not revile
your heart
concentrate on *nirvāṇ*
sing the name of
Rām.
Embrace the Self
worship it
effortlessly
drink the nectar of
immortality
says the tailor
Nāmdev.

92

Try a million
ways if you will
my friend.
But only with
Rām's love can you
swim across.
For no matter
how much
you water it
a *babūl*[130] tree
can never bear

(130) The *babūl* (Skt. *babbūla)* is the thorny, desert tree *Acacia Arabica*.

mangoes.

Full of conceit
and egotism, you brag
about yourself
reviling other people.
That is foolish
you will regret it.
Borrowed jewels
can never be yours
my friend.

You think they are
yours, but
they are not:
wealth, youth, children, wife
these are castles
made of sand.
Soon to be nothing.
All your grasping
is in vain
my friend.

Pleasure or penance
clinging or illusion
all are equally false.
There is no point, really
in being a hermit
in a forest.
For if there is no love
for his lotus feet
in your heart
then everything will be
a vain hope
my friend.

Born human, you have
no awareness.
You are blind
a beast, a clod.
There stands death
aiming an arrow
at your head.
I cry out to
warn you, my friend
says Nāmdev.

93

Why do you forget

stupid people
this bag[131] of leather
it's not yours.

It's nothing but a bag
full of blood
this body
it's not yours.

Nāmdev sings the glory
of Nārāyaṇ.
Shame on him who does not
sing *Rām*.

94

Come Keshav
my ecstatic fakir[132].
Come in the guise
of an Abdāl[133]
O Father.

The world
is your crown
the seven nether-regions
your feet.
The earth[134]
is your leather apron.
Such is
your guise
Gopāl.

The green
of the earth
is your mace
the whole world
your bowl.
And you have
fifty-six million sixteen thousand[135]
drawstrings
in your apparel.

The body

(131) *Karavā*, lit.: 'a small pot with a spout'. See R.C. Miśra, *op.cit.*, p. 130.

(132) The Kalandars are fakirs known for their free ways and their love of mystic ecstasy.

(133) The Abdāl were a special group in the hierarchy of saints among the Sufis. They are said to have had special powers: bringing down rain, ensuring victory etc. See *Encyclopédie de l'Islam*, Leyde, Paris, 1960, p. 97.

(134) *Aṭhārah bhār**.

(135) For *chappan koṭi*, see *KG2*, song 42/2.

is the mosque
the heart
the *maulvī*
quietly praying.
Sometimes he has
a form, but sometimes
none[136].

You roamed
over cities
and jungles.
No one could fathom
your secret.
Nāmdev's heart
is drawn to him.
Come sit near me
Lord Rām.

95

I am a *vaiṣṇav**
I am a *vaiṣṇav*
that is the truth,
O Nārad.
I dance in the heart
of *bhaktas* who sing
my praises
O Nārad.

Nārad said: "Lord Nārāyaṇ,
do you live in Vaikuṇṭh or
Kailāś?"
I live where men sing
of my deeds[137]. I live
in the homes of
*vaiṣṇavas**
O Nārad.

"A man may go to the Gangā
and to all the holy sites
visiting 490 million of them.
He may fast and abstain
but he will never find
me, not even in his
dreams
O Nārad.

(136) The meaning of the first part of this line is obscure.
(137) *Kathās* or *harikathās* are the accounts of the Lord's deeds as they are narrated in the Purāṇas and other scriptures.

"Ascetics, yogīs, *yatis,*
tapasvīs and *sanyāsis:* the *muni*
who sits meditating; men
who sacrifice or chant
the Vedas: they never
    see me
    O Nārad.

"Sacrifice, yoga, mortification
observing commandments, rituals
no one who pins his hope on
these, or on gifts of land
and other things, can find a place
    at my feet
    O Nārad.

"*Bhaktas* who sing my praises
are my being. I live as they
live. I drink as they drink.
The *vaiṣṇavas** are my
    people
    O Nārad.

I hold back nothing
from *bhaktas* who love my name.
I give them *bhakti* and *mokṣa."*
Nāmdev's Lord
grants the ultimate.

96

  Hard to bear
    these wounds within
    O Mādhav.
  I am weak
    I cannot bear them
    O Lord.

I am alone, Gosvāmī,
  they are many.
  How can I cope?
Can a field be saved
  from encroachments,
  if the owner does not
patrol it?

There is no doctor
  no medicine
  like you.
And I do not know

any other
mantra.
My disease is fatal
it is incurable
Lord of mercy.

Many clever men
have tried
in vain.
But cured by you
no one
can suffer again.

I am helpless
be gracious to me
Remover of sorrow
says Nāmdev.

97

Up goes the vine[138]
O yogī
It reaches the Pure
without attributes.
Nothing will kill it
now.

The Sadguru tends the vine
O yogī
in the garden of
effortless meditation
watering it with the sweet waters
of immortality.
And up goes the vine
climbing up the tree
of truth.

The deathless vine[139]
enters mystic vision.
No one can move it

---

(138) *Belī* (Skt. *veli)* symbolizes the seeking soul or the *kuṇḍalinī;* see *KV*, p. 218. This song has a close parallel in a song by Dādū's disciple Bakhaṇā; see *Bakhaṇā jī kī Vāṇī*, ed. Svāmī Maṅgaladās, song 41, p. 76.

(139) The *amar beli* (Skt. *amṛtavallī)* is a yellow creeper that has no roots in the earth and lives as a parasite on the tree on which it grows. By Rajab, the *amaraveli* is compared to a holy man:

'Without roots, the *amar beli* blossoms
and spreads all over the branches and leaves of a tree;
So is a holy man free of *māyā*,
he remains always distinct from it'.
(Callewaert:1978, p. 228, *sākhī* 30.25).

now.
It has no form
no contour
it fruits in a
million moons[140].

A whiff of it can kill
the five stags
the twenty-five does[141].
Its fruit is deathless.
eternal.
O Nāmdev
you have a formless vine.

98

Many will die
as they must
O yogī.
The one truth will remain
the name of
Rām.

My desire
is dead.
My greed
is dead.
My mother
the mind
is dead.
My sister
temptation
is dead.
I mourn
them not.
O yogī.

My mothers' people.
pride and envy
are dead.
My father's kinsman,
egotism
is dead.
My cousins.

(140) In Sant esoteric language the 'moon' is the source of *amṛt*, the waters of life and immortality. See sun* and moon.

(141) The '25 does' represent Prakṛti, which, according to Sāmkhya, has 25 elements (see above, song 74). The five stags are the five senses, which flow towards their objects and become attached to them. The yogī must control his senses and become free of his desire for sense-objects before he can attain mystic knowledge and bliss.

lust and anger
are dead.
I mourn
them not
O yogī.

To his house shall I go
by whose deeds
the lord of yogīs died.
The Sadguru has
taught me.
I will melt into
the feet of Govind
O Nāmdev.

99

I will be a recluse
I will sing *Rām*.
I love the sound
that cannot be heard.
I will go to the home
of the Homeless.

I will not go
to holy places.
I will not bathe
in sacred waters.
I will not hurt
any living thing.
My guru has shown me
sixty-eight holy places
and they are all
within me.
There will I bathe.

I will not chant
the Vedas, Purāṇas, the Gītā.
I will not be a poet
declaiming verse.
I will sit playing
my silent flute
in the limitless land
without form.

Controlling my breath,
I will enter
the yogic[142] veins.

(142) *Iḍā, piṅgalā, suṣumnā**.

Moving the sun*
to the moon*
I will merge
into the light supreme.

The beauty of the mind
has five faces.
I will not be called good
or bad.
I meditate
on Krishna.
I will live
in effortless contemplation
says Nāmdev.

100

The Puruṣ* is here
but he has no form
he speaks in us
yet stands aloof.

Without knowledge
or meditation
he sports, seeing
what cannot be seen.

Before or behind.
he is the same
but he wears a disguise
when in company.

His home has no
smell or form.
Rām's *bhakta* Nāmdev
bows to him.

101

It's a strange
mind-boggling sight.
Let the learned Paṇḍit
expound it.
The drum is dancing
and the dancing girl
resounds like a
drum.
Fire has plunged into

the waters[143].

The ant gives birth
to an elephant[144].
A marvel, indeed.
As it stood[145], it fell
and now it comes swaying
like an elephant in rut.

It has no feet
no wings
but it flies and sits
on the branch of a tree[146].
Perennially, the *nīm* tree
yields plentiful fruit
sweet to my tongue.

The hare grows horns
the fish grow hoofs
the sheep wear earrings,
the fly has collyrium in its eyes.
Such is the vision
of truth[147].

The cow gives birth
to a calf
and look
she pursues the calf.
I bow to the guru.
By his grace the seeker
shall find
says Nāmdev.

106

Don't spend these coins[148]
rashly, O yogī
Meet your Rām

(143) For the commentary of Sundardās on the marvel of 'a fire burning in water', see P.H. Sarmā, *Sundar-Granthāvalī*, II, pp. 521-522.

(144) See above, song 76.

(145) *Ubhā*, 'standing (along the road)' has also the suggested meaning of 'people waiting for death'; see *KV*, *sākhīs* 15.53 and 16.30.

(146) In Kabīr the *kevarā* tree (Skt. *kevikā; Pandamus odoratissimus)* is a kind of jasmine, symbolizing the human body; see *KV*, *sākhī* 16.33, (p.251,n.33).

(147) For the meaning of these paradoxes, see *KV*, pp.133-34. On p. 218, n.6, Vaudeville refers also to S.B. Dāsgupta, *Obscure Religious Cults*, 2nd ed., Calcutta, pp.41-42.

(148) *Dāmā* (Pers. *dām)* was the fortieth part of a rupee (in Mughal currency). Here, there may be a pun on *dāmā* which also stands for *dam* (breath). A yogī should control his breath, this being an essential step in the yogic process of the Nāthas*.

like a miser.

The Lady abhors
losing money.
You will learn this
when you have it.

Keep an eye
on what you have.
There was no lamp
nor a wick
yet there was
light
says Nāmdev.

107

Ceaselessly
the star shimmers
dear to the three worlds.

There it is,
in the sky
beyond vision.
You cannot
catch it
or touch it.

A lamp without oil
or wick
it's made of light
shining day and night.

I have found
immortality.
I had a body
now I am free.
I have seen
the truth
says Nāmdev.

108

Bathe, my heart
bathe at Prayāg*
where the three rivers
meet.
Serve King Rām

the Pure[149].

Near the city of Dvārakā
flows the river Gomatī[150].
Between Gangā and Yamunā
flows Sarasvatī.

The sixty-eight holy sites
are all within.
There is a lake
where an ascetic
has his home.

Listen, Trilochan*
these holy sites
dispel all sin
says Nāmdev.

109

She keeps me
from you
this *māyā*
O Mādhav
Do something
so your devotee
may live
my Love.

Māyā is the sea
where I am a fish
thirsty for *māyā*
I cannot live without it.

But if you leave me
I lose everything.
I bear a burden
I cannot breathe.

You are the support
for those who have none
O Gracious One
says Nāmdev.

(149) Both *alakh* and *nirañjan* are epithets for the Supreme Being in the *Gorakh-bāṇī;* see *KV*, p. 138.

(150) Dvārakā was the ancient city built by Krishna and his clan, in North Gujarat. It sank into the sea after Krishna's death. To say that the Gomatī flows near it is a geographical error. Was it deliberate, suggesting an esoteric meaning?

110

A clever gardener[151]
lives hidden within
O Mādhav.

This gardener
is also the flower
blooming with
every new bud.
But he plucks
what he wants
heedless of whether
the flower blooms.

He is the wind
and the water.
He pours down
as rain.
He is man
and also woman.
He is affection
and love.

He is the moon
and the sun
the earth
and the sky.
Thus the creator
made his creation.
To him I bow,
his servant,

Nāmdev.

111

Tomorrow I will think
of what is right
of the Brahman, the Kāyastha[152]
and the *tilak* mark
on the forehead.

To hell now with
right behaviour

(151) In Kabīr *(KV,* 16.34) the Gardener is Kāl (death). But here it is the Creator himself, the *antaryāmī*.

(152) The Kāyasthas are one of the higher castes. They were often accountants, managers and administrators, and therefore belonged to the 'educated class'. This is perhaps the reason why they are here listed with the Brahmans, which is rather unusual. The idea seems to be that like Brahmans, they were also educated in 'right behaviour'.

and the four Vedas
bossy as the wife[153]
of a village headman.

Why are you puzzled,
brewer's wife?
I have tied the sun*
and the moon
to my heart.

The Brahman fills his cup
with wine.
The more he drinks
the more he wants
to drink.

I know nothing
but the name of Rām
says Hari's servant
Nāmdev.

112

Does it matter
that you know
the Vedas
the Purāṇas?
Give up your books
your scriptures.
Look, there are pearls[154]
everywhere.
There is no cloud
in the sky
but it is raining
pearls.

The strings make music
without being played
their music fills
the sky.
A drum sounds
but there is no drum
no drummer.

There is light without flame
the wakeful are awake

(153) *Caudharanī*, lit.: 'headwoman, mistress of the house'.
(154) The pearls *(muktāphal)* are a symbol of 'knowledge, realization'; see R.C. Miśra, *op.cit.*, p.121. In the present context, the pearls stand for 'raindrops' and seem to symbolise *amṛt;* see *ibidem*, p.114.

in the Void[155]
as they sleep
So I have heard
and I do not fear the dark.
Whatever I want
appears before me.

With folded hands
I declare:
I am ignorant
I understand little.
Humbly I shall touch
the feet of the man
who knows the secret
of my song
says Nāmdev.

113

The name *Rām* redeems
whenever you think of it.
A day has countless minutes
think of Rām for a few of them
all your sins will turn to ashes.

Day and night Śiva sings *Rām*
in holy Banāras. Even bugs and moths
are redeemed as they hear it.
And they spread the glory of
Govind.

The sinner Ajāmil*, the prostitute*
and the parrot; the elephant* and
the hunter*, they uttered *Rām*
and were saved. The sage Vyās
contemplates the glory of the name.

Sing this holy name, day and night.
Rām will befriend you. He will fulfill
his promise[156]. The man who never for a moment
forgets Rām, he alone is a *bhakta*
says Nāmdev.

115

I fell in love
with Nārāyaṇ

(155) For *suni (śūnya),* see Callewaert:1978, p. 337.
(156) It is said in the Purānas that the Lord has decided to redeem any creature uttering his Name.

and renounced the world
without effort.

I need Nārāyaṇ
as the hungry need food
or the thirsty need water
or these men need a family.

A married woman
pines for her lover.
A greedy man
pines for money.

A lustful man
pines for a lusty woman.
I pine for Murārī
Nāmdev.

Like a mother's love
for her child
is my love for
him.

I am in love,
says Nāmdev.
Govind lives
in my heart.

117

The two are one
God and his *bhakta*.
Only foolish brutes think
they are two.

He who forsakes love
for Vedic rules
is tortured by fire
and birth and death.

It is easy to talk
and make an assertion
but few can live
the truth.

A man free of 'me'
and 'mine'
seeks godly company
says Nāmdev.

118

All he says is
Rām, Rām, Rām.
He thinks of nothing
but Hari.

He never studies
we have tried and failed,
Saṇḍa and Marka[157]
complained.
He claps his hands
in rhythm and sings
just *Rām, Rām, Rām.*
He also corrupts
the others.

The queen then said:
"You have the world
in your hands, O king,
but not Prahlād*, your son.
He does as he pleases."

His childishness
had gone too far.
The ministers counselled
action.
But nothing ever
harmed Prahlād
in fire, water, land
or mountain
for God saved him
with His power.

At last the king
unsheathed his sword
and grim as death
he said:
"O tell me who will
save you now."
The pillar split
into two. Almighty God
who is everywhere
came out and kept his word.

He slew the king
Hiraṇyakaśipu
protecting gods and men.

---

(157) See Prahlād*.

I too now seek his shelter
may he dispel my fear
O Nāmdev.

120

Chant *Rām*
  the great *mantra*.
These are the days
  of Kali*
and Death is
  in a hurry.

You waste the day
  in worldly things
and dark comes
  the night.

The goal is far
  and the path is wild.
How can you cross it
  alone?

Yes, the Lord is the path
  in the wilderness.
Call out his name
  or even half of it.
  He will come to your help
  says Nāmdev.

121

The whole world
  is dirty and defiled.
Only Hari, the eternal
  is pure.

The field is defiled
  and also the seed[158].
The mind is defiled
  it desires the body.

The pearl is defiled
  and the diamond.
Air and fire and water
  are all defiled.

---

(158) *Bīraj* (Skt. *vīrya)* means seed and semen; *khet* (Skt. *kṣetra)* means field and wife.

The cosmos is defiled
  with its twenty-one regions[159].
The day is defiled
  and the night and the month.

Indra and Brahmā, the two gods
  are defiled.
The moon is defiled
  and the sun, with its thousand phases[160].

Everything here
  is equally defiled.
But a *bhakta* is pure
  when he sings Hari's glory.

Sin and virtue
  are both defiled.
And defiled is the worship
  of another god.

Defiled is pilgrimage
  and ritual giving
And fasting and bathing
  and the liturgy.

The gods are defiled
  and the Gangā.
But Lord Hari is pure
  says Nāmdev.

122

Get up my soul
  do not be forgetful.
You know you must
  leave this place
now
  or a little later.

A few days more
  and you must
leave this company[161].
  How can you laugh?

(159) The 21 *brahmāṇḍas* refer to an obscure cosmology perhaps popular in *nirguṇ* circles.

(160) *Sahas kalā*. The word *kalā* refers to the moon's phases. The moon has sixteen phases since it becomes full on the sixteenth day after the moonless night. Perhaps on this analogy the sun is said to have a thousand phases. See also song 137

(161) *Govali* (Skt. *gokul?)*, 'cattle-shed, group, crowd'.

How can you sleep
deluded
or waste your life
in vain dispute?

Why hesitate
again and again.
Sing the name *Rām*
stupid fellow.

Wake up, you clod
you have far to go
and there is no path[162]
in the wilderness
says Nāmdev.

124

Sing *Hari*
O sing *Hari*.
Hari is the source.
The man
who does not sing *Hari*
let his mouth be full
of dust.

Time and again
you were born a brute.
You wandered through
eighty-four million lives.

Never could you
find peace. Never did you
seek refuge with the Sadguru,
singing *Rām*.

Kingdoms
wealth and sons will go.
Let the Indestructible
be your love.

If truly
you are firm in your love
you will be freed from old age,
death and *samsār*.

Govind
is a sea of virtue.

(162) *Aughaṭ ghāṭ*, lit.: 'broken bank'.

Sing his praises. He will not
  forget you[163].

  The Sants
never lose heart.
  O Hari
keep me close to you
in the shelter of your feet.
  Nāmdev bows.

125

  I never even look
    at people
  who do not worship
    Nārāyaṇ.

They go out in the morning
  and return at dusk.
Such men should be listed
  with cattle[164].

Men whose heart
  is not with Hari,
they are cattle
  not men.

Listen to me
  good people
another man's wife
  is a lump of poison.

Give up another's wife
  another's money.
Narhari will be
  with you.

If you have no nose
  all other marks of beauty[165]
look ugly
  says Nāmdev.

---

(163) Lit.: the Lord will not forget his *birad*. *Birad* (Skt. *viruda)* is 'an epithet of praise or merit'. The *viruda* meant here is the unfailing quality of God as a protector of those who have faith in him. See also song 131, where one sees a demonstration of this quality.

(164) *Paśu*, is here rendered as 'cattle'. On the Indian countryside, the cattle go out every morning for grazing and return in the evening.

(165) *Batīs lakhanā* are the 32 physical signs and characteristics with which great men (Buddha, Rām etc.) are said to be endowed. We should remember also that having the nose cut off is a traditional punishment for adultery; e.g. Śūrpaṇakhā in the Rāmāyaṇ.

127

Teach me *Hari*
O Paṇḍit.
Keep your learning
to yourself.

Every letter of the alphabet
has twelve forms[166].
They are all like a pit[167]
without Hari.

Just two letters
Ra and *Ma*
can row you across
samsār.

What's the point
in arguing, Paṇḍit?
Rām is all
I will study[168].

Give up your books
your scriptures.
Sing *Rām* and cross
the difficult sea.

From a pillar
emerged Hari
the Lord
of Nāmdev.

128

The name *Rām*
is my capital, my wealth.
It is a capital
dear to my heart.

It is a capital
that will never end.
No trader
has a capital like it.

A trader's money

(166) Every consonant sign of the Nāgarī alphabet can be combined with a vowel sign to give a total of twelve syllable signs for each consonant.

(167) *Ākhari*, Rājasthānī for 'pit'.

(168) Although Prahlād* is not clearly the speaker here, the statements are his, as is clear from the final stanza.

comes and goes.
Sometimes
there is nothing left.

My capital can
never catch fire.
It can never
rot.
No king can
seize it.
And no thief can
ever steal it.

Śrīgopāl is
my wealth
Unstained, Indefinable,
Gracious to the meek,
says Nāmdev.

131

You are my Lord
my King
I have come to you.
But as I sang
your praises, O Govind
some people drove me away.

They saw the whole world
flock around me
and the great Brahmans
seethed with rage.
They called me a Śūdra
they beat me and chased me away.
What should I do
my Father?

If *mokṣa* is nothing but death
no one has *mokṣa*.
These Brahmans call me a Śūdra
will they score a victory over you[169]?

But suddenly the world
was filled with wonder
a miracle happened
unsurpassed.

The temple doors swung open

(169) See song 124, fn.

for Nāmdev, the *bhakta*.
And slammed shut
in front of the Paṇḍits.

132

I am Rām's poor
weakling.
I am your servant
your slave, O Hari.

Proper conduct
and behaviour
the right method of worship:
these I do not know.
Such am I
a devotee, seeking shelter.

I sing *Rām*
life after life
I am your servant
Nāmdev.

133

I can never get
that fruit.
Never, without your
help.

Bhakti, the creeper
bears that fruit
as it climbs up
the tree of love.
Who will give me
that sweet fruit, Lord?

From you alone
can I get it.
How should I plead,
says Namdev?

135

Blessed[170] is the day
the hour[171].

---

(170) This song is like a *badhāvarā*, a joyful and auspicious song, sung when a welcome guest arrives or on other happy occasions.
(171) The filler *sādhau bhāi* ('o brother saint') in each stanza is not translated.

Govind has come
to my house.

Let my courtyard
be fragrant
with sandal-paste[172].
Let these five[173] women
sing
songs of joy.

I have now a seat
in the Void
above the sky
where silent
trumpets
play.

Hari is here
as my guest.
My cup of blessings
overflows.

Clouds of joy
gather in the sky
raining gentle
showers.

Nāmdev, his servant,
worships Hari.
Let people mock
if they will.

136

My love for him
cannot die.
Life after life
He shall be
in my heart.

A glimpse of his face
brings me joy.
Will you go
and tell him
this?

---

(172) This refers to the practice of making various auspicious designs in the courtyard of a home on festive occasions.

(173) Ideally, seven married women whose husbands are alive, should together sing a *badhāvarā*. The number five here is significant: it refers to the five sense-organs, which are 'singing' with joy at having found fulfilment.

Boundless love
  binds me to him.
But why is he
  displeased?

The lake is full
  the waves dance
  over it.
But the *chātak* bird
  will not drink
  from it

The cloud alone
  can quench
her thirst.
Ah, such is love.

The moon lives
  two hundred thousand
  miles away.
But a glimpse of it
  makes the lily
  bloom.

My lord is kind.
He knows my pain

  says Nāmdev.

137

Learn this
  my heart.
Learn to dance
  before Rām.
For this is yoga
  and knowledge
  and renunciation.

Brahmā dances
  Indra dances.
The sun and the moon
  both dance
  in a thousand phases[174].

And Śiva dances
  before Rām

(174) See also song 121, where only the sun is said to have a thousand *kalās*.

scanning Time
  Non-time
  Beyond-time[175].

And Narad dances
  with folded hands.
The gods dance
  in all their
  thirty-three forms.

I will let my heart
  dance, O Nāmdev.
Dancing, it finds
  the final goal.

138

Can anything at all
  equal the name *Rām*
    brother?
Why then this yoga,
  sacrifice,
  commandments, penance,
    mortification?

Put them on the scale:
  the Vedas and Purāṇas.
Only half of the name *Rām*
  will equal their weight.
Visit every holy place
  if you will
never will you find one
  as holy as
  the name *Rām*.

Reflect, Sants,
  on the Inner Witness
the Great Saviour
  the Slayer of Mur[176]

  says Nāmdev.

140

Loving Rām
  is our maker.
Be not

---

(175) *Akāl* suggests the final state which is outside time. *Vikāl* is an obscure term. In Mss. *a* and *m* we read: *kāl akāl.*

(176) Mur is the name of a demon slain by Viṣṇu.

proud, man,
your body will
soon be dust.

You dug a
deep foundation
and built a
lofty house.
But who was mightier
than Mārkaṇḍey*?
On him the sky
showered woes.

'This is ours
and this too'.
The Kauravas
never relented
proud of their brother
Duryodhan.
Their heads held
a kingly parasol
full twelve miles
in length.
But their bodies
were food
for vultures.

Ten heads
had Rāvaṇ
and twenty arms.
His word
was command
for gods and men.
But soon he was slain
reduced to dust
that great egoist

The Yādavas perished
every one of them,
for they had ridiculed
the sage Durvāsā[177].

My lord destroys pride.
Nāmdev sings his praises.

(177) The sage Durvāsā is famous in Puranic and epic lore for his great spiritual power and his volatile temper. Towards the end of Krishna's life, the Yādav clan became very arrogant and power-drunk. Once, in a state of intoxication, young Yādavas dared to ridicule Durvāsā who cursed them saying that all Yādavas would perish fighting each other.

141

You have been my lover
since childhood
O Govind.
Do not leave me
now.
My heart lies
with you.
There is no one for me
but you.

You are pure
I am defiled[178].
We live
in the same house
we share
the same bed.
Why are you so cold
to me?

My husband's older wife
is dead now
and my power is quite
unchallenged.
I am now my husband's
favourite,
I can never come
to harm.

My husband's older brother
bows to me
but I renounce him, I renounce
my loving father-in-law.
I have married the primal Puruṣ*
never can I come to harm.

I have renounced
my father-in-law's family.
Nothing can hold me
to my father's home.
I have found
my husband
and washed away the sin

(178) *Nirguṇ* and *guṇabharā*, lit: 'without *guṇas* and full of *guṇas*'. *Guṇ* has here the Sāmkhya meaning: 'something that taints the pure consciousness of the Puruṣ*'. In theistic Sāmkhya God is Puruṣ in its highest form, the primal Puruṣ as he is called later in the song.

of my whole brotherhood[179].
O Nāmdev.

142

There is no room
for guile.
Govind Gopāl
is the sea
of virtue.
Why then this mark
of sandalwood paste
on your forehead?
This garland
around
your neck?

You have no feeling
for the divine
in your heart,
fellow,
yet you preach it
to others.
You tell others
the road
to heaven
as you travel
down the path
to hell.

You are taking poison
from a
blind man
and you know it.
You are jumping into a pit
with a
blind man
your eyes wide open.

With your mind on things like
yoga and sacrifice,
jap, tap, pilgrimage
and religious vows,
you are blind to charity
and compassion,
to good deeds, *dharma,*
humility and
devotion to Hari.

(179) The idea that a *bhakta* redeems not only himself but also his kin. is often expressed in *bhakti* literature.

Sing of the Lord
and his *bhaktas*,
fellow.
Never put your faith
in anything
else.
Sing of him
who has form
and is formless
who is both
good
and evil.
And you will
never be a slave
to your ego.

Your devotees are
gentle, pure
and brave.
They put their faith
in you
O Keśav.
Be merciful to them.
Nāmdev, your slave
bows before you.

144 *Āratī*

With what flame
should I light the lamp
to worship you?
Yours is the light
that lights
the three worlds.

The seven seas
lie at your feet.
What good is this
pot of water
I bring to you?

Your nails shine
like a million suns.
What good is the lamp
I hold before you?

All the earth's vegetation[180]

(180) *Aṭhār bhār**.

is your garland.
What good
my little flower offering?

The eight million
four hundred thousand species
of living things
are pervaded by Rām.
All that I can do
is sing his glory
says Nāmdev.

145 *Ārati*

Lamp in hand
I worship you
Murārī
my husband

whisk-bearers
wait upon you.
I offer you
myself.

The four ages
revolve like a lamp
worshipping you.
The four ages
are Rām.
There is no other.

Worship with joy
like Dhruv*,
like Prahlād*.

Joy is the lamp
and the *ātman*
the worship.
No other god
for me,
says Nāmdev.

164

You will find
him
You will find
Murārī
effortlessly.
The bell rings

with the
soundless sound.
Reflect
and meditate
on Viṭṭhal.

I will bathe
at the meeting
of the three rivers.
I know what to do:
with my eyes
as flowers
and my heart
as the
sandalwood paste

with love
as the leaves
to be offered
and meditation
as the
incense
I will worship him
who is
beyond worship.
I will say
the unsaid
rosary
at the place
where there is
no death.

I saw something
where there was
nothing
and it
captured
my heart.

In the light
of my soul
blazed forth
another light.
In that brilliance
of a million suns
risen together
the Pure
lives
the Lord of Paradise
bringing forth
all forms.

He takes
    the form
    of action
and that of
    every
    thing.
With the wind
    as the whisk
    and the
    whole world[181]
as the food offering
    I come,
    O Lord.

I hear the Vedas chanted
    but there is
    no priest
and the sound is
    all the
    sweeter.
The sage Nārad dances
    he makes
    music
but no instrument
    is played
    and no drum.

I plunged within
    and discovered
    the spark
in the Void
    beyond form
    and attribute.

I have met him
    and embraced him.
With joy I will sing *Hari*,
    ever and ever.
    Viṣṇudās Nāmdev.

165

I am not telling a lie[182].

---

(181) *Guṇ* here refers to the *guṇas* of Sāmkhya philosophy. All forms of being are formed by the three *guṇas* in different combinations.

(182) For the Marāṭhī version of this song, see below in Ch. 5, song 165. *Laṭaki* (Hindī *laṭaka)*, 'a stylish manner of gesture suggestive of a dishonest, false or artificial feeling or sentiment'. Moleworth gives a similar meaning for the word in Marāṭhī.

Father
but the present is
inscrutable[183].
I saw pearls as large as
pumpkins[184]
with my own eyes[185].

A goat gave birth[186] to a
tiger,
and cats[187] are growing
snouts[188].
The *lavarū* bird[189] I saw
flying,
and men becoming
bullocks[190].

The madman[191] stumbled[192] into
a block of butter.
The frogs frolic at the
the place
where a boar[193] killed a
dog[194].

When we went to the land of
Virāṭ[195]
we got milk from a
mare[196]
and it filled fourteen
pots[197]

Proudly, I walked to the
fortress
and I laid it
low.
I saw a pod of beans[198] on
wings.

---

(183) *Gāṭhau*, lit.: 'dense, deep, profound'.
(184) *Kolhā* (Rāj. *kolau*, Hindī *kohḍā)*, 'a pumpkin'.
(185) *Ḍalau* (Rāj. *ḍolau)*, 'the white of the eye'.
(186) *Chelī bailī* or 'a goat was born'? *Bailī* from *byāhlī*, 'gave birth'?
(187) *Mānjariyā* (Skt. *mārjāra)*, 'a cat'; see also RSK.
(188) *Tūṇḍai* (Skt. *tuṇḍa)*, 'a snout'; see also RSK.
(189) *Lavarū*, 'a kind of bird'; see RSK.
(190) *Ṭāṇḍai* (Hindī *ṭāṇḍā)*, 'a group of bullocks'.
(191) *Bāvaliyā* (Skt. *vātula)* 'a crazy person'.
(192) *Ṣoṭai* (Hindī *khoṭai)*, 'fault, error'.
(193) *Śamsā* or 'the tusk of a boar'.
(194) *Suṇahā* (Skt. *śvāna)*, 'a dog'.
(195) *Brāṭ* (Skt. *vrātya* or *virāṭa?)*.
(196) *Gājhī* (Rāj. *gāj* or 'a horse'?). We are unable to translate the first part of the line.
(197) Rañja (Marāṭhī *rāñjan)*, 'a pot'.
(198) *Mūngī* or *mūnga*, a vegetable common in Rājasthān.

It was as large as a
ball[199].

These are words of a man,
unredeemed,
proudly putting on a
show[200].
But this is no way to
nirvāṇ
says Viṣṇudās Nāmā.

226[201]

When will your mercy
enfold me
and make disease, disaster,
death,
powerless?

A turbulent city
burns within.
The soul holds it
in its hands
like a Tartar.

There is a place
on this earth
where I saw a lamp
giving riches
to the poor.

Hari did not wait
for Dīpāvalī.
He was true
to his promise.

I heard the serpent
move stealthily.
and it
bit the hunter.

The tiger jumped on a cow
for a kill.

(199) *Bāṭī* is a favourite Rājasthānī bread, in the shape of a ball, made by roasting wheat on a slow fire.

(200) *Sāngīlā,* meaning 'to put up a *svāng* or act?'

(201) This song poses problems similar to those of song 165. The language has Marāṭhī-looking elements, distorted by Rājasthānī singers who did not understand it. One wonders what sense the singers or their audiences made of this song. Our translation too is tentative.

but the soul, a lion,
  tore him to pieces.

Such is that restless
  woman *Māyā*.
But you have nothing
  to do with her, Lord.
  Viṣṇudās Nāmā
  bows to Keśav.

234

You are my Lord
  O Hari
You are my Lord
You are my kin[202]
  my brother.

O how mighty is the Lord
  of the world
whose devotee am I
  Nāmdev.
I have found the love
  of my childhood
he is here, my guest,
  in my house.

People jeer at me
  and say:
there goes that Nāmā.
  Point a finger
at a pumpkin
  and it withers[203].
How can I live
  O Lord?

Sweetly you saunter
  on the banks of the Yamunā.
No sight could be lovelier.
  I saw you
and this tailor Nāmdev
  became one with you.
Nothing remained
  of my caste.

I have come to see you
  at your palace, Krishna
a poor man carrying

(202) *Sajan* (Skt. *svajana)*.
(203) This is a popular saying in Hindī and Rājasthānī.

a coarse blanket,
a tattered bag[204].
These wretched Brahmans
call me defiled.
Shall I uproot
the pillars of your temple[205].

He appeared then
a living god
the Mighty One.
Fortune smiled on Nāmdev
the tailor
He found his Lord.

238

Pay homage
to King Gopāl
the Pure
the Infinite.
His devotees
implore him
to grant them
the gift of
bhakti.

The ten quarters
are his royal camps.
Vaikuṇṭha
his picture gallery.
With his consort
Lakṣmī
He rules over
the seven worlds.
The sun and
the moon act
as his lamps.
Love and Time
look upon him
as their Father.
The great Śukra[206]
is his
chief of police.

---

(204) This is obviously a reference to Sudāmā, a Brahman boy who studied with Krishna. Poor all his life, he came to Krishna's palace and was given all riches.

(205) Here is a reference to the temple incident (see above, Ch. 1.1; E5). The line is also suggestive of the Prahlād* story, where God appeared from a pillar; the suggestion is strengthened by the next line which speaks of the Lord appearing in a 'powerful form'.

(206) Śukra is a well-known ancient teacher of political science. Making use of his shrewd tactics the Asuras became victorious over the gods.

Such is King
  Narhari.

Brahmā, the four-faced god,
  the controller,
who created the
  world, bestowing
gifts upon it,
  is his household
  potter.
His counsellor is
  Śiva, full of frenzy,
who speaks of
  Tantra Mantra and
  immortality.
Sin and virtue
  are his painters
decorating his door
  with checkered
  designs.
Death stands guard
  at his gate.
Such is the great King,
  Śrī Gopāl.

The four Vedas
  attend on him
as his court singers.
  The Gandharva gods
are his musicians.
His courtiers are
  the eighteen Purāṇas.
The Śāstras,
  his court jesters.
Tantras and Mantras[207]
  stand liveried
in his city of Tretā[208]
  uttering sweet words.
The wind god whisks
  his chowrie.
The Goddess Devī,
  Vanquisher of the three worlds,
serves as his
  maid.
The earth is only

---

(207) Tantras and Mantras are here referred to as a body of texts. Earlier in the song *Tantra Mantra* referred to magic chants and esoteric practices, not to texts.

(208) Tretā is the name of third age in the Hindu four-age cycle of time. It is not clear how a word standing for a duration of time can be used to denote a city which lies in space.

a fragment
of his cosmic egg.
Such is the great King
the husband of Lakṣmī.

The tortoise
who upholds the world
is his palanquin.
The great serpent Śeṣa
his bed.
The greenery[209] of the world
is the woman
who tends his garden.
These clouds of fifty six kinds
are his water bearers.
The great Ganges
is the sweat that flows
from his toenails.
The seven seas
are his mattresses.
Every living thing
is his vessel.
Such is the king
of the three worlds.

These *bhaktas* live
in his house:
Sanak*, Sanandan, Sanatkumār,
Ambarīṣ, Śuk, Prahlād,
Vibhīṣaṇ, Hanumān, Nārad
Dhruv*, Uddhav and Akrūr[210].
Innumerable *siddhas*[211]
and saints are his watchmen.
Such are the people
who work for him.
Nāmdev bows
before his glory.
The all-pervasive
indwelling Lord
has the *bhaktas*
for his standard.

---

(209) *Athārah bhār**.
(210) All these persons are devotees famous in Vaiṣṇav lore.
(211) This may be a reference to the Nāth Siddhas.

CHAPTER 5

THE SONGS IN HINDI

5.1. First line index

२१ रांम ची भगति दुहेली रे बापा
२२ जौ लग रांम नामैं हित न भयौ
२३ काहे कौं कीजै ध्यांन जपनां
२४ भगत भला बाबा कागिला
२५ साच कहूं तौ जीव जग मारै
२६ सांई मेरौ रीझैं साचि
२७ रतन पारषू नीरा रे
२८ कौनैं कै कलंक रह्यौ रांम नांम लेत हीं
२९ रांम नांम नरहरि श्री बनवारी
३० रांम जुहारि न और जुहारूं
३१ जा दिन भगता आईला
३२ संत सौं लेणां संत सौं देणां
३३ परहरि धंधाकार सबैला
३४ माई तूं मेरे बाप तूं
३५ माइ गोब्यंदा बाप गोब्यंदा
३६ हिरदै माला हिरदै गोपाला
३७ अब न बिसारूं रांम संभारूं
३८ रांम राइ उलगूं और न जाचूं
३९ बोहूं बीहूं तेरी सबल माया
४० बाजी रची बाप बाजी रची
४१ तूं न बिसारी तूं न बिसारी
४२ बाप मंझा समझि न परई
४३ कैसें तिरौं बहु कुटिल भरयौ
४४ काल भै बापा सह्या न जाई
४५ सहजैं सहजैं सब गुंन जइला
४६ कैसैं न मिलै रांम रूटा मोटां
४७ कहा करूं जग देषत अंधा
४८ देवा तेरी भगति न मोपैं होइ जी
४९ भगति आपि मोरे बाबुला
५० संसार समदि तारि गोबिंदे
५१ तुझ बिन क्यौं जीऊं रे
५२ बंदे की बंदि छोडि बनवारी
५३ देवा मेरी हीन जाती हो
५४ हरि नांव गाजै हरि नांव राजै
५५ इतना कहत तोहि कहा लागत

५६ बोलि धौं त्रिबांणपद रांम नांम
५७ अैसैं रांमहि जांनौं रे भाई
५८ अैसैं रांम अैसैं हेरौ
५९ पांनियां बिन मीन तलफै
६० अनबोलतां चरन नहीं छाडौं
६१ जत्र जांउं तत्र बीठल भैला
६२ कांइ रे मन बिषिया बन जाइ
६३ अपने रांम कूं भजि रे मन आलसिया
६४ मन थिर होइ रे बा न होइ
६५ देवा बेन बाजै गगन गाजै
६६ देवा गगन गूडी बैठी मैं नांहीं तब दीठी
६७ जोगी जन न्याइ जुगे जुगि जीवै
६८ देवा तेरा नीसांण बाज्या हो
६९ संत प्रवांणीं भगति आपिला
७० याही गोब्यंदा चरन मेरौ जीयरौ बसै रे
७१ देवा नटणीं कौ तन मन बांसां बर तां मांहि रे
७२ भाई रे भरम गया भौ भागा
७३ जहां तहां मिल्यौ सोई
७४ बीठल भौंरौ कंवल न पावै
७५ रे मन न पडि भोला प्यंजरै
७६ अदबुद अचंभौ कथ्यौ न जाई
७७ देवा आज गुडी सहजि उडी
७८ काहे रे मन भूला फिरई
७९ रांम नांम बोलि त्रिबांन बांनी
८० मेरी कौंन गति गुंसांई तुम जगत भरन देवा
८१ ऐवडी सी मूंनैं बुधि आवडी
८२ अैसैं जग थैं दास नियारा
८३ हमारै गोपाल राजा गोपाल राजा
८४ कहि मन गोबिंद गोबिंद गोबिंदा
८५ रांम गोब्यंदा कमोदनि चंदा
८६ जपि रांम महामंत्र रांम महा
८७ गुड मीठा रांम गुड मीठा
८८ लाधौ तौ लाधौ रे मैं रांम नांम लाधौ
८९ बाद छाडि रे भगता भाई
९० हरि लै हरि लै हरि लै हरी

९१ छाडि छाडि रे मुगध नर कपट न कीजै
९२ रांम भगति बिन गति न तिरन की
९३ कांइ रे भूले मूढ जनां
९४ आव कलदर केसवा
९५ बैस्नौं ते मैं मैं ते बैस्नौं
९६ माधौ भीतरिमार दुहेली
९७ अवधू बेली बिरधि करैली
९८ अनेक मरि मरि जांहिगि रे अवधू
९९ बैरागी रांमहि गाऊंगा
१०० पुरिष हाजिर बरन नांहीं
१०१ देवा पातुरि बाजै मांदल नाचै
१०२ आज कोई मूनैं मिलिसी रे रांम सनेही
१०३ नारांइंण सूं मन न रंजै
१०४ पांडे देह् अरथि लगाइ
१०५ मन मंझा तूं गोबिंद चरन चित लाइ रे
१०६ जोगिया जिनि षरचसि दांमां
१०७ झिलिमिलि झिलिमिलि झिलिमिलि तारा
१०८ त्रिबेणी प्राग करौ मन मंजन
१०९ माधौ जी माया मिलन न देई
११० माधौ माली एक सयांनां
१११ काल न्याइ बिचरिहूं
११२ जांणौं नैं जांणौं बेद पुरांनां
११३ जब तब रांम नांम निस्तारै
११४ बाप जी एतलौं अंतरौं कीधौं
११५ नांमदेव प्रीति नरांइंण लागी
११६ नांइं तिरूं तेरे नांइ तिरूं
११७ भगत भगवंत नहीं अंता
११८ रांम रांम रांम रांम जपिबौ करै
११९ जौ बोलै तौ रांमहिं बोलि
१२० जपि रांम नांम मंत्रावला
१२१ मैला मलिता सब संसार
१२२ जागि रे जीव कहा भुलांनां
१२३ छाडि रे मन हमिता ममिता
१२४ हरि भजि हरि भजि हरि भजि मूल
१२५ जे न भजैं नर नारांइंणा

१२६ आंन न जांणूं देवी न देवा
१२७ पाडि मोहि पढावहु हरी
१२८ रांम नांम मेरे पूंजी धनां
१२९ रांम नांमैं प्यंड पषाल
१३० हरि दरजी का मरम न पाया
१३१ तूं मेरौ ठाकुर तूं मेरौ राजा
१३२ द्रुबल गरीबौ रांम कौ
१३३ तुम्हारी क्रिपा बिना न पाइये हो
१३४ चूक भजीला चूक भजीला
१३५ धनि दिहाडौ धनि घडी ए
१३६ लागी जनम जनम नी प्रीति
१३७ नाचि रे मन रांम कै आगैं
१३८ भया कोई तूलै रे रांम नांम
१३९ गोबिंद राषउ चरणन तीर
१४० हमारै करता रांम सनेही
१४१ मेरे बाल सनेही गोब्यंदा
१४२ कपटैं नां मिलै रे गोबिंदौ गुणसागर गोपाल
१४३ तत कहन कौं रांम है सुंनिं लीज्यौ लोई
१४४ कहा ले आरती दास करै
१४५ आरती पतिदेव मुरारी
१४६ गरुड मंडल आव
१४७ धीरैं धीरैं षैबौ कथन न जैबौ रे
१४८ तैसी चूकली रे जगजीवनां
१४९ देवा पाहन तारीअले
१५० एक अनेक बिआपक पूरक जत देखउ तत सोई
१५१ पारब्रहमु जि चीनसी आसा ते न भावसी
१५२ जौ राजु देहि त कवन बडाई
१५३ पाड पडोसणि पूछिले नांमां
१५४ अणमडिआ मंदलु बाजै
१५५ पतित पावन माधउ बिरदु तेरा
१५६ तीनि छंदे खेलु आछे रहाउ
१५७ मै अंधुले की टेक तेरा नामु खुदंकारा
१५८ हाल बाबा हाल बाबा षुसषबरी
१५९ बानारसी तपु करै उलटि तीरथ मरै
१६० मेरो बापु माधउ तू धनु केसौ सांवलीओ बीठुलाइ

१६१ बदहु कीन होड माधउ मो सिउ
१६२ आदि जुगादि जुगादि जुगो जुगु
१६३ रे अभिमांन लीयें नर आयौ
१६४ पावघे पावघे सहजैं मुरारी
१६५ लटकि न बोलूं बाप ब्रतमांन गाढा
१६६ नहीं ऐसो जन्म बारंबार
१६७ उठि रे नांमदेव बाहरि जाइ
१६८ आ भडै रे नौआ आ भणै रे
१६९ गाइ मन गोबिंद गाइ रे गाइ
१७० झिलिमिलि झिलिमिलि नूरा रे
१७१ गाइ रे भावै जिंनिं गावै रांम
१७२ ऐसे ही मना रे मेरे ऐसे ही मनां
१७३ तू सुष सागर नागर दाता
१७४ इन औसर गोबिंद भजि रे
१७५ माधो जी कहा करूं या मन कौ
१७६ रुंडा रांम जीसूं रंग लगाया रे
१७७ रसना रंगी लै हरि नांम
१७८ हरि बिन कौन सहाइ करैगो
१७९ जागौ न बैरागी जोगी
१८० सहज बोलणैं बोल बोलीजै
१८१ नको नको रे संसार महाजड
१८२ जपि रांम नांम त्रिभै पुरी
१८३ रांम नांमैं नींसांण बागा
१८४ हीन दीन जात मोरी पंढरी के राया
१८५ हम तो भूले ठाकुर जानें
१८६ रांम बीठला देव वीठला
१८७ भले बिराजे लंबकनाथ
१८८ रांम नाम विन और न दूजा
१८९ पंढरीनाथ विठाई बतावो मुजे
१९० मैं को माधौ मलमूत्र धारी
१९१ तुम बिन घरि येक रहूं नहि न्यारा
१९२ सावध सावध भज ले रे राजा
१९३ नांमां तुं हि तूं झूठा रे
१९४ ए माधौ कैसैं कीजै जोग
१९५ ताहि गावै दास नांमां रे

१९६ सुणि भाई महिमां नाम तणीं
१९७ जाबा न देख्यूं हो नर हरी
१९८ पायौ मैं रांम संजीवनि मूरी
१९९ मलै न लाछै पारमलो परमलीओ बैठो री आई
२०० जब देखा तब गावा
२०१ दस बैरागनि मोहि बसि कीन्ही पंचहु का मिट नावउ
२०२ मारवाडि जैसे नीरु बालहा बेलि बालहा करहला
२०३ पहिल पुरीए पुंडरक वना
२०४ सफल जनमु मो कउ गुर कीना
२०५ मोकउ तारि ले रांमां तारि ले
२०६ हरि हरि करत मिटे सभि भरमा
२०७ भैरउ भूत सीतला धावै
२०८ आजु नामे बीठलु देखिआ मूरख को समझाऊ रे रहाउ
२०९ माइ न होती बापु न होता करमु न होती काइआ
२१० धनि धंनि ओ रांम बेनु बाजै
२११ चारि मुकति चारै सिधि मिलि कै दूलह प्रभ की सरनि परिओ
२१२ रे जिहबा करऊ सत खंड
२१३ दूधु कटोरै गडवै पानी
२१४ मै बउरी मेरा रांमु भतारु
२१५ कबहू खीरि खाड घीउ न भावै
२१६ हसत खेलत तेरे देहुरे आइआ
२१७ घर की नारि तिआगै अंधा
२१८ सुलतानु पूछे सुनु बे नांमां
२१९ जउ गुरदेउ त मिलै मरारि
२२० साहिबु संकटवै सेवकु भजै
२२१ सहज अवलि धूडि मणी गाडी चालती
२२२ दास अनिंन मेरो निज रूप
२२३ अकुल पुरख इकु चलितु उपाइआ
२२४ एकै बीठुला सरणैं जा रे
२२५ पद निरषत कि न जाइ रे दिनां
२२६ कुनूं क्रिपा तूंझी होइ ज्यूं आवरी
२२७ भाई रे इन नयननि हरि पेषो
२२८ रुखडी न खाइयो स्वामी रुखडी न खाइयो
२२९ अस मन लाव राम रसना
२३० मोर पिया बिलम्यो परदेस होरी मैं का सौं खेलौं

२३१ तू मति बरजै माइ हे
२३२ हरे नमस्ते हरे नमां
२३३ डोला चै डोल कान्हां
२३४ तुम्ह देवा हरि तुम्ह देवा
२३५ न होइ ज्यौ तीरथ ब्रत अस्नांन करीता
२३६ हरि हरी दून्यूं अष्यर ऊचारी
२३७ पाया पडूं देव पाया पडूं देवा रांमां
२३८ सेइये गोपाल राइ अकल निरंजन
२३९ रांम नांम सुमिरी रे मनां भव बंधन छूटै यातनां
२४० हरि नांव अंम्रित पषालि मुषां थैं
२४१ ऐसे कैसैं न मिलंत ते साधू रे
२४२ बस्त गरीबनि गांम
२४३ सुणौ रे अवधू अनभै बांणीं
२४४ सिरजंनहार सुंमरि मंन मेरा
२४५ नांमदे नांमदे साहिब मोरा
२४६ म्हारै मंदिर आव हो नरहरी
२४७ तू मूझा तूंगा तूं मुझा तूंगा
२४८ ऐसो राम राइ अंतरजामी
२४९ मन की बिरथा मनु ही जानै कै बूझल आगै कहीऐ
२५० तू मेरे तीरथ तू मेरे कासी
२५१ अकिवला तैं को को न लूटे
२५२ सजल जल नीर न दीसै डोला
२५३ मनां सेविया रे हरी नाम ओषदी
२५४ टाली बाजै टाली बाजै वा
२५५ जै जै जै जगदीस हरे
२५६ कीजै रे जन मन बैरागी
२५७ जीवरा भेरौं गुनहगार
२५८ बीठुला देन न जाई माई

5.2. Alphabetical first line index

5.3. Hindī 'edition'

The critical apparatus has been produced by the computer. After all the manuscripts were entered into the computer and revised, the 'critical' line was written by us. Then the programmes were run to pick out all the forms variant from the 'critical' form and print them in a separate file. In the apparatus we give first the form in the 'critical line', followed by the variant forms in the different manuscripts. As a rule we have not given in the apparatus the variations due to inversion of lines (see Ch. 2.3, *Geyavikāra)*. The following figures are used for the manuscripts referred to in the apparatus, with the following abbreviations:

DMVJ: Dādū Mahāvidyālay, Jaipur;
VBJ: Vidyā Bhūshan Sangrah, Jaipur;
CPJ: City Palace, Jaipur.

1 : *a* Amritsar, 875; 1675 AD; 146 songs; fo. 236-254.
3 : *c* CPJ, 3322; 1669 AD; 85 songs; 27 fo.
4 : *d* DMVJ, 12; 1636 AD; 140 songs; fo. 191-208.
7 : *g* Gopāldās *Sarvāṅgī;* (1627 AD; *lipikāl* 1724); 123 songs.
8 : *h* Naraina, private copy; 1653 AD; 117 songs; fo. 218-235.
10: *j* CPJ, 1853; 1681 AD; 85 songs; fo. 152-172.
13: *m* DMVJ, 2; 1676 AD; 133 songs; fo. 130-137.
14: *n* Naraina, 36; 1664 AD; 122 songs; fo. 258-272.
16: *p* Patiala, 2706; 1698 AD; 126 songs; fo. 212-224.
18: *r* Rajab *Sarvāṅgī;* (1620 AD?; *lipikāl* 1714); 44 songs
21: *u* VBJ, 12; 1684 AD; 103 songs; fo. 201-213.
22: *v* VBJ, 34; 1658 AD; 120 songs fo. 220-234.

For the signs used in the apparatus, see Ch. 3.2. Considering the great variety in words and word-order, we have not included in the apparatus the variants in the versions of the *Guru Granth* and in the Fatehpur manuscript. These have been printed separately, along with the song. The indented printed text gives the version of the Standard edition of the *Guru Granth,* the copy is of the Fatehpur manuscript. For the poems which were found only in one of our manuscripts (17 in all) or only in one of the additional versions of Miśra:1964, we reproduce the text as it appears in that manuscript or in the Miśra edition.

१

• हरि नांव हीरा हरि नांव हीरा । हरि नांव लेत मिटै सब पीरा ॥
१ हरि नांव जाती हरि नांव पांती । हरि नांव सकल जीवन मैं क्रांती ॥
२ हरि नांव सकल सुषन की रासी । हरि नांव काटै जम की पासी ॥
३ हरि नांव सकल भुवन ततसार । हरि नांव नांमदेव उतरे पार ॥

२

• रांम नांम षेती रांम नांम बारी । हंमारै धन बाबा बनवारी ॥
१ या धन की देषौ अधिकाई । तसकर हरै न लागै काई ॥
२ दह दिसि रांम रह्यौ भरपूरि । संतनि नेरै साकत दूरि ॥
३ नांमदेव कहै मेरै करसन सोई । कूंत मसाइति करै न कोई ॥

३

• रांम सौ धंन ताकै कहा ब थोरौ । अठ सिधि नौ निधि करत निहोरौ ॥

१;• नांव। नाउं १; मिटै। मिटैं १६

१;१ नांव। नांऊं २१; नांव। नांऊं २१; पांती। पाती ७ ८ १२ १६ २१; नाव। नांउं २१; जीवन। जीवनि १२ २१; मैं। मै १२; में ७

१;२ सुषन। शुषन १; नांव। नाउं २१; जम। जंम २१

१;३ नांव। नांइ ८; नांइं १६; नाइं ७; उतरे। उतरया २१

२;• बारी। बाडीं २० २१; वारी १ १२; हंमारै। हमारै १ ३ ७ १६; हमारे १०; धन। धंनि २०; धंन १२; बाबा। बाबौ ३; बाबो १०; वावौ १; बनवारी। बंनवारी २१; बनमारी २०; वनवारी १

२;१ या। साह ३ १०; धन। धंन १२ २०; की ३ १०; की। पुंजी १०; पूंजी ३; देषौ। आवै ३ १०; देषहु १ ४ ७; अधिकाई। जाइ ३ १०; तसकर। कबहू ३ १०; हरै। बैठैगी ३; बेठेगी १०; न। मूल ३ १०; लागै। गमाइ १०; गवाय ३; काई। - ३ १०

२;२ दह। जारी ३ १०; दिसि। जरै ३; जरे १०; रांम। नई ३; नइ १०; रह्यौ। रहे ८; रह्या १२ १६ २१; लीषाई ३ १०; भरपूरि। - ३ १०; भरिपूरी २०; भरपूर २१; संतनि। संतन १२ १६; राजा ३ १०; नेरै। डंढै ३; डंडे १०; नियरे २१; नैरै ८; नीयरै १ ७ १६; साकत। न ३ १०; साखत १६; साषित ८ १२ २१; साषत २०; दूरि। चोर ले जाइ ३ १०; दूर २१

२;३ मेरै। मेरे १ १० १२ २१; करसन। करसंण ४; करसंन १२ २१; करसण १; सोई। सोइ ३ १०; कूंत। कुंत १०; कूत ७ १६; मसाइति। मुसाइति १; मसाहित ३; मसाईति ४; मसाहति १६; मसादती १०; मसाइत २०; करै। करे १०; कोई। कोइ ३ १०

३;• सौ। सो १ ३ १०; धंन। धन १ ३ ७ ८ १० १६ १७ २०; ताकै। जाकै ३; जाके १०; तार्कें ७; ब। अब ४ ८ १६ २०; व १; थोरौ। थोरो ३ १०; अठ। अठ सठ २०; अष्ट ३ १०; सिधि। सेधि २०; नौ। नव १ ४ ७ २१; निहोरौ। निहौरौ ३; निहोरो १०; निहारौ २०

१ हरणकसिब बध करि अधपति देही । यंद्र कौ बिभौ प्रहिलाद न लेही ॥
२ देव दांनव जाहि संपदा करि मांनैं । गोबिंद सेवग ताहि आपदा करि जांनैं ॥
३ अरथ धरम काम मोषि न मांगै । दास नांमदेव प्रेम भगति अंतरि जौ जागै ॥

४

० मंझा प्रांण तू बीठला । पैडी अटकी हो बाबुला ॥
१ कलि षोटी कुसमल कलि काल । मेरे बंधन मोचौ श्री गोपाल ॥
२ काटि नरांइण भवचे फंध । संम्रथ द्रिढ करि वोडौ कंध ॥
३ नांमदेव की नरांइण कीन्हीं सार । चले परोहन उतरे पार ॥

५

० रांम रमे रमि रांम संभारै । मैं बलि ताकी छिन न बिसारै ॥

३;१ हरणकसिब। हिरणांकुसब २०; हिरनकस्यप १०; हरंणकसिब ४; हरंनकसिब २१; हरणकसिव १; हरणांकसिब ७; हरनकसिब ३ ८ १३ १६ १७; बध। बधि २०; वध १; अधपति। अधिपति १०; देही। देई ७ ८ १३ १६ १७ २०; यंद्र। ईद्र ८; इंदू १० २०; इंद्र ३ ७ २१; कौ। कौं १६; को १० २०; बिभौ। विभौ १ ४ १३ १६; प्रहिलाद। प्रहलाद ३ १० २०; लेही। लेई ३ ७ ८ १३ १६ १७ २०; लोई २१

३;२ देव। देवता १३; दांनव। दांणव १ ४ ७ २० २१; दांनां १० १३; दाना ३; जाहि। नाहि ११; जांहिं १३; जांहि ८; ताहि ३ १०; संपदा। सति ३ १०; करि। - ४; करि १०; मांनैं। जांनै ३; जाने १०; गोबिंद। गोब्यंद ८ १७ २० २१; गोव्यंद १ १६; ताहि। जाहि १३; आपदा। आपद ८; करि। - ८; जांनैं। मांनैं ३; मानै १०

३;३ अरथ। अर्थ १ ४ ७ ८ १३ १६; धरम। घरम १०; धर्म्म ४; ध्रम १७ २१; र्धम ८; धर्म १ ७ १३; धरंम २०; काम। - १; कांम ८ १३ २०; कांम की कहा ३ ४ ७ १७; काम को कहा १०; काम की कहा १६ २१; मोषि। मुक्ति ४; मुकति ३ १०; मोछि हूं २०; मोक्षि १३; मोहि ७; मोक्ष ८; मोष २१; की कहा मोक्षि १; न। - १ ३ ४ ७ १० १६ १७ २१; मांगै। मागि १०; मागै १७; भगति। भक्ति १३; भगति जो ३ १०; अंतरि। अंतरगति १ ३ १० २० २१; जौ। - ३ १०; जो १६ २०; जागै। जागे १०

४;० मंझा। मंझ २१; मंझां १३; मझा १६; प्रांण। प्रांन १६; प्राण २१; तू। तु २०; तूं ७ ८ १३ १६ २१; बीठला। बिठला १०; मीठुला २१; सांवला ४; पैडी। पैरी ३ १०; बाबुला। बाबला ३; बावला १ १०

४;१ कलि। कली २०; मेरे। - ३ ८ १० १३ १६ २१; बंधन। वंधन १; मोचौ। श्री १०; छोड्यो ३; मोचउ १६; मोचहु १ ४ ७; श्री। छोड्यो १०

४;२ नरांइण। नरांईण २०; नरांईण ८ १३; नरांयण १०; नरांइंन ७; नारांईण ४; नाराइण ३; भवचे। भौचे ८ १३ १६; भवके ३; भवच १; जमके १०; फंध। बंध ४ ८ १३ १६ २०; वंध १; फंद ३ १०; संम्रथ। संम्रंथ ह्वै १०; संम्रथ ह्वै १३ २०; संम्रथ होइ २१; संमरथ ह्वै ८; सम्रथ १६; सम्रथ ह्वै ३; द्रिढ। डिढ १३ २० २१; किन १०; किनी ३; दिढ १ ८ १६; करि। - ३ ८ १० १३ २० २१; वोडौ। ओडौ ७; ओडौ १६; वोटो ३; वोडो ८; वोडहु ४; वोढो १०

४;३ नांमदेव। नांमें २० २१; की। - ८ १३ १६ २० २१; नरांइण। नरहरि ३ १०; नरांइंण १ २१; नारांईण ४; कीन्हीं। कींन्ही ८; कींनी ३; कीनी १०; चले। चढे १; चलि १०; चल ३; परोहन। पिरोहित १०; प्रोहन ७; परोहंण ४ २१; परोहंन १३ २०; परोहण १; उतरे। उतरै ४

५;० रमे। रमि ८ २०; रमें २१; रमें १३; रमि। रंमि ४ ८ २० २१; संभारै। संभारो ३; संभालै ४ २० २१;

१ रांम रमे रमि दीजै तारी । वैकुंठनाथ मिलै बनवारी ॥
२ रांम रमे रमि दीजै हेरी । लाज न कीजै पसुवां केरी ॥
३ सरीर सभागा सो मोहि भावै । पारब्रह्म का जो गुन गावै ॥
४ सरीर धरे की इहै बडाई । नांमदेव रांम न बीसरि जाई ॥

० रांम बोलै रांम बोलै रांम बिनां को बोलै रे भाई ॥
१ एकल मींटी कुंजर चींटी भाजन रे बहु नांनां ॥
थावर जंगम कीट पतंगा सब घटि रांम समांनां ॥
२ एकल चिंता रहिले निता छूटीले सब आसा ॥
प्रणवत नांमां भये निहकांमां तुम ठाकुर मैं दासा ॥

० सभै घट रामु बोलै रामा बोलै । राम बिना को बोलै रे ॥ रहाउ ॥
१ एकल माटी कुंजर चीटी भाजन हैं बहु नान्हा रे ॥
असथावर जंगम कीट पतंगम घटि घटि रामु समाना रे ॥
२ एकल चिंता राखु अनंता अउर तजहु सभ आसा रे ॥
प्रणवै नामा भए निहकामा को ठाकुरु को दासा रे ॥

सभारो १०; मैं। मे २०; मे १०; बलि। वलि १; ताकी। ताकी जो २०; छिन। छिंन १२ २१; बिसारै। बिसारे १०; बिसारो ३; बिसारै १

५;१ रमे। रंमि ८ २०; रमें २१; रमि। रंमिं १३; रंमि ८ २०; रमिं ३; दीजै। दीजे ३ १०; तारी। ताली २१; वैकुंठनाथ। त्रिभुवननाथ ३ १०; बैकुंठनाथ ४ ८ २१; बैकूंठनांथ २०; बैकूंठनाथ १३; मिलै। मिले १० १३; बनवारी। वनवारी १

५;२ रमे। रंमि ८ २०; रमें १३; रमें २१; रमि। रंमिं १३; रंमि २०; रमिं २१; दीजै। दीजे ३ १०; हेरी। होरी ३; कीजै। कीजे ३ १०; पसुवां। पसुवा ३ ८ १० २० २१; पसवा १ १६; पसवां ४

५;३ सरीर। सरिर १०; सो। जो ८ १३; भावै। भावे १०; का। के ८; को १०; जो। जे १ ८ १६ २० २१; गुन। गुंन १३; गुण १ ४ २० २१; गावै। गावे १०

५;४ सरीर। देहि ३; देही १०; इहै। ईहै ४; यहै ३; इहा १६; बडाई। वडाई १; नांमदेव। मांमदेव २०; नांमदेवां ८; जन नांमदेव ३ १०; रांम। - ८; नां १०; नांम ३; न। - १०; बीसरि। बिसरि २०; बिसरी १०; वीसरि १; जाई। जाइ १०

६;० बोलै। बोले १० १६; वोलै १; बोलै। बोले १० १६; वोलै १; बिनां। बिना १६ २०; विनां १; बोलै। बोले १० १६; वोलै १; भाई। भाइ १०

६;१ एकल। ऐकल १ ३ ४ १२ १६; येकल ८ १० २०; मींटी। मिंटी १३; मींटीं २१; कुंजर। कुजर ४ ८; कूंजर ३; चींटी। चीटी ८ १६; भाजन। भंजंन ४; भंजन १ ३ १० १२ १६ २१; भजन ८; भाजंन २०; रे। - ४; बहु। वहु १ २१; नांनां। नांना १३; नाना ४ १६ २०; जंगम। जंगमां ३; पतंगा। पंतंगा ४; सब। सव १; घटि। घट १ १०; रांम। ब्रह्म २१; समांनां। संमांनां २० २१; समाना १६; समानां ४ १२

६;२ एकल। ऐक ३; ऐकल १ ४ ८ १२ १६; येक १०; येकल २०; चिंता। चिता १ ३ ४ १० १३ १६ २१; चंता २०; रहिले। हरिले १०; राहिले १६; निता। निंता १२ २० २१; छूटीले। छूटे १६; छूटी ४; छूटीलै २०; छूटिले २१;

७

• रांम स नांमां नांमही रांमां । तू साहिब मैं सेवग स्वांमां ॥
१ हरि सरवर जन तरंग कहावै । सेवग हरि तजि कहु कत जावै ॥
२ हरि तरवर जन पंषी छाया । सेवग हरि भजि आप गंवाया ॥
३ नांमौं कहै मैं नरहरि पाया । रांम रमे रमि रांम समाया ॥

८

• जन नांमदेव पायौ नांव हरी ॥
जंम आइ कहा करिहै बौरे अब्र मोरी छूटि परी ॥
१ भाव भगति नांनां बिधि कीन्हीं फल का कोन करी ॥
केवल ब्रह्म निकट ल्यौ लागी मुकति कहा बपुरी ॥
२ नांव लेत सनकादिक तारे पार न पायौ ता स हरी ॥
नांमदेव कहै सुनौं रे संतौ अब मोहि समझि परी ॥

सब। सव १; प्रणवत। प्रगत २१; प्रणवंत १३ २०; प्रनवत ३ १०; नांमां। नांम २१; निहकांमां। निंहिंकांमां २१; निहिकांमा ४; निहंकांमां १३ २०; निहकामा १० १९; तुम। तुंम १३; तू ३ १०; ठाकुर। ठाकूर १० २१: मैं। मै ३; में १०

७;० स। सं २१; सु १७: नांमां। नाम १३; नामहो। नांमहि ३ २१; नांमहीं ७ २०; नांम स ४; नांम सु १; नामहो सो १९; रांमही १३; रांमां। नांमां १३; तू। मैं २१; तुंम १३; तुम्ह ७ १७; तुम ८ १९ २०; तूं १; साहिब। सेवग २१; साहिव १; मैं। मै ३ २०; में १०; तूं २१; सेवग। साहिब २१; स्वांमां। स्यांमां २१; स्यामा २०; स्यामां १३; स्वांमा ४; स्यामां १९

७;१ जन। जंन १३ २१; तरंग। तरग १०; कहावै। कहांवै ३; कहावो १०; सेवग। हरि १९; हरि। तजि १९; तजि। सेवग १९; कहु। कहुं १ ७ १३ १९; कहीं २०; कतहु ८; कत। न ८ २०; जावै। जांवै ३; जावे १० १९

७;२ जन। जंन ४ २१; पंषी। पषी ८; छाया। छामया १३; माया २०; सेवग। हरि २०; सेवगि १७; हरि। भजि २०; भजि। सेवग २०; गंवाया। गंमाया २०; गमाया १०; गवाया १९ १७ २१

७;३ नांमौं। नांमौ ३; नांमो २०; नांमदेव १ ८ १३ १९ १७; नामों १०; कहै। भणै २०; कहे १०; मैं। मै १३ २०; में १०; पाया। राषा ४; रमे। रंमे ८; रमि। रंमि ८; समाया। संमाया ८

८;० जन। - ७ ८ १३ २१; पायौ। पायो ३ १०; पाया १९; नांव। नांम ४ ७ १० २०; नांउ १; नाव २१; हरी। हरि ३ ४ १०; जंम। जम ८; आइ। आई ४ २०; आय १९; कहा। का १ ३ ४ ८ १० १३ २१: करिहै। करिहै रे ८; करिहे १०; करिहौं ४; करैहै २०; बौरे। बौरा ३; बोरे २०; बोरा १०; वौरे १; अब। ईब ४; अव ८; इब ७ १० २०; इव १; मोरी। मेरी ३ १०; मोहि ८ २०; छूटि। छूट २०; छूटी ३; परी। परि १०

८;१ भगति। भक्ति १३; नांनां। ना २०; नाना ३ ८ १९; बिधि। विधि १; कीन्हीं। पूजा ३ १०; कींन्हीं ४ १३ २०; कीन्ही ८ १९; कीर्नी ७; का। + ४; कोन। + ४; कौन ७ १९; कोंन १०; करी। + ४; केवल। +ल ४; निकट। निकटी ८; निकटि ३ १३ १९ २० २१; ल्यौ। + ४; लिव १; ल्यो ३ १०; लागी। + ४; लागे ८; मुकति। मुक्ति १ ७ १९; मुकित २०; बपुरी। बपुरि ४; बपूरि २०; बपरी १०; वपुरी १

८;२ नांव। नांम ४ १३ २० २१; नाव ३; सनकादिक। संनकादिक ८ १३ २१: सनकादीक २०; पायौ। पायो १ ३ १० १९ २०; हरी। हरि ३ १० २०; सुनौं। सुंनौ १३; सुंनहु २१; सुणौ ७ १९; सुणौं १ ४; सुनौ २०;

९

• रांम नांम जपिबौ श्रवननि सुनिबौ ॥
  सलिल मोह मैं बहि नहि जाइबौ ॥
१ अकथ कथ्यौ न जाइ कागद लिष्यौ न माइ ॥
  सकल भुवनपति मिल्यौ है सहज भाइ ॥
२ रांम माता रांम पिता रांम सब जीव दाता ॥
  भणत नांमइयौ छीपौ कहै रे पुकारि गीता ॥

१०

• धिग ते बकता धिग ते सुरता । प्रांननाथ कौ नांव न लेता ॥
१ नाद बेद सब गलित पुरांनां । रांम नांम कौ मरम न जांनां ॥
२ पंडित होइ सु बेद बषानैं । मूरिष नांमदेव रांम ही जांनैं ॥

११

• अपनां पयांनां रांम अपनां पयांनां । नांमदेव मूरिष लोग सयांनां ॥

सुनो १०; सुनहु ३; संतौ। संतो ४ १०; अब। ईब्र ४ २१; इब ७; इव १; मोहिं। मोहिं ७ १६ २०; समझि। संमझि ८ २१; संमझ १३; संमझी २०; समझ १६; परी। पडी ४

९;० जपिबौ। जपिबो ३ १०; जपिवौ १; श्रवननि। श्रवनौं ८; सुनिबौ। सुनिंबौ १३; सुणिबौ ८; सुनिबो १०; मैं। मै २०; में १०; महि ३; बहि। बैहि ८ २०; वहि १; नहि। नहिं १३; नही ३ ८ १०; नहीं ४ १६ २१; जाइबौ। जइबो २०; जाईबौ ४; जाइबो १०; जाइवौ १

९;१ कथ्यौ। कथ्यो ३; कथ्यों १०; जाइ। जाई ४ १६ २१; कागद। कागदि ४ ८; लिष्यौ। लिष्यो ३ १०; माइ। भाई १६; माई १ ४ ८ २१; सकल। अषिल ३ २१; भुवनपति। भूवनरपति ३; भवनपति ८ २१; मिल्यौ। मिल्यो ३ १०; है। - १; रे ३ १० २१; भाइ। भाई ४ १० १६ २१

९;२ सब। श्रब २०; सबै १६; सर्ब ८ १३; सव १; भणत। भनत ३ १०; नांमइयौ। नमईयौ ८; नमइयौ १६; नांमईयौ ४; नांमदेव ३ १०; नांमयौ १३; नांमइयौं २०; छीपौ। - ३ १०; छींपौ १ २१; छीपौं १३; कहै। कहे १०; कहत १६; रे। - १६; पुकारि। पूकारि २०; पूकार ४

१०;० धिग। + ४; धग १० १३; धृग १ ८; धिर्ग १६; ते। + ४; तै १०; बकता। +कता ४; - २०; वकता १; धिग। धग १०; धृग १ ७ ८ १६; ते। त ३; सुरता। श्रुता ३; श्रोता १०; प्रांननाथ। प्राणनाथ ४; प्रांनंनांथ २०; कौ। को २०; का ३ १०; नांव। नांवं २०; नाव ७; न। - ८; लेता। नाव ८

१०;१ नाद। ना+ ४; नांद १०; बेद। +द ४; वेद १ १६; सब। सव १; गलित। गनिक १ ४; गलिक ३ १०; गालि ७ ८ १३ १६; पुरांनां। पुरानां १०; पूरांणां २०; कौ। को १ १० १६; का २०; न। - १०; जांनां। जांणां २०

१०;२ होइ। होई ४; सु। स ३ १३; सो १६; बेद। वेद १; बषानैं। बखानै १६; बषांणैं २०; बषांनै ३ १३; बषांनैं ७; ब्रषाने १०; वषानै १; मूरिष। मूरष ७; नांमदेव। नांमौ ८; ही। हि १ ३ ४ ७ १०; हीं २०; जांनैं। जांणैं २०; जानि १०

११;० अपनां। अपणां ४ ७ २०; अपने १०; अपनौ ३; आंपण। २१; आपणां १; पयांनां। पयांणां १ ४ ७ २०

१ जब हंम हिरदै प्रीति बिचारी । रज बल छाडि र भये भिषारी ॥
२ जब हरि क्रिपा करी हंम जांनां । तब था चेरा अब भया रांनां ॥
३ नांमदेव कहै मैं नरहरि गावा । पद षोजत परमारथ पावा ॥

१२

• तूं अगाध बैकुंठनाथा । तेरे चरनौं मेरा माथा ॥
१ सर्बे भूत नांनां पेषूं । जत्र जाउं तत्र तूं ही देषूं ॥
२ जल थल महियल कष्ट पषांनां । आगम निगम बेद पुरांनां ॥
३ मैं मनिषा जनम निरबंध ज्वाला । नांमां का ठाकुर दीनदयाला ॥

१३

• सबै चतुरता बरतै अपनीं ।
ऐसा न कोई निरपष ह्वै षेलै ताथैं मिटै अंतर की तपनीं ॥

२१; पयानौं ३; पयानो १०; पयानां ८; अपनां। अपणां ४ ७ २० २१; अपनौं ३; अपनो १०; आपणां १; पयांनां। - १३; पयांणां १ ४ ७ २०; पयाणां २१; पयानौं ३; पयानो १०; पयानां ८; नांमदेव। मूरष २०; मूरिष। मुरिष १०; नांमदेव २०; लोग। लोक ७ २० २१; सयांनां। संयांणां २१; सयांणां १ ४ ७ २०; सयांनौं ३; सयांनो १०

११;१ जब। हरि १०; जव १; हंम। हम ७ १७; जब १०; हिरदै। ह्रिदै ३; ह्रदे १०; प्रीति। प्रिति २०; बिचारी। विचारी १; बल। वल १; र। - ४ ८ १३ १६; भये। भऐ १३; भिषारी। भिष्यारी ४ ७ २० २१; बिषारी १०

११;२ जब। जव १; क्रिपा। कृपा १६ १७; करी। कही २१; हंम। मै ३; हम १७; हमें १०; तब। तव १; था। थे ८; अब। अव १; भया। भये ८ १३ १६; भयौ १७

११;३ कहै। कहे १०; मैं। मै ३ ४ २०; में १०; नरहरि। नरहर १६; गावा। गाया ३ ८ १० १६ १७; परमारथ। परमार्थ ८ १३; परमारंथ ४; पावा। पाया ३ ८ १० १६ १७

१२;० तूं। तुं ३ १०; तू ८; बैकुंठनाथा। त्रिभुवननाथा ३ १०; बैकुठनाथा २१; बैकूंठनाथा ४ २०; वैकुंठनाथा १; तेरे। तेरा १०; चरनौं। चरणूं १ ४ २१; चरन ३ १०; माथा। मांथा ३

१२;१ सर्बे। श्रबे ४ ८ १३ २० २१; स्रबे १६; सर्वे १; भूत। भूतं ८ १३ २०; भूतैं ४; भूते ३ १० २१; नांनां। नाना १ ३ १६; पेषूं। पेषू ४ २१; पेषौं १६; पर्षौं ८; देषूं १; जाउं। जाऊं २१; जांउ ४; जांउं ८ १३; जाऊं १६; जाउ ३; तूं। तुं ४ १०; तू ३ ८; ही। ही जु ४; देषूं। पेषूं १; देषौं ८ १६; देषो १०

१२;२ महियल। महिला ८; महीथल १६; महीयल १ ३ १०; कष्ट। कस्ट ४; पषांनां। पषांण ४; पषांणा २१; पषांणां २०; आगम। अगम ३; आगंम २१; निगम। निगंम २१; निगम अर २०; निगम सब १६; नीगम १३; बेद। वेद १; पुरांनां। पुरांण ४; पुरांणां २०; पुरानां ३ १० १६; परांनां १

१२;३ मैं। नामैं १०; मनिषा। मंनिषा १३ २१; मनिष ३ १०; जनम। जन्म १३; जनंम २०; निरबंध। न्रिबंध २०; न्रिबंधन २१; निर्बंध ३; निर्बंध १०; निरवंध १; न्रबंधन १३; नृबंध ८; ज्वाला। जवाला १६; नांमां। नांमा ४; का। को १० २०; ठाकुर। ठाकूर ४ २०; दीनदयाला। दींनदयाला १३

१३;० सबै। सबे १०; सवै १; चतुरता। चतूरता लै २०; बरतै। बरतैं १३; बरते १०; अपनीं। अपणी २१; अपणीं ४; अपनी १ ८ १३ १६; अपनी अपनी २०; ऐसा। अैसा १ ८ २०; औसा ४; आसा ३ १०; निरपष।

१ अंतर कुटिल रहत षेचर मति । ऊपरि मंजन करत दिन षपनी ॥
२ ऐसा न कोई सरबंग पहिचांनैं । प्रभु बिनां और रैंनि दिन सुपनी ॥
३ सोई साध सोई मुनि ग्यांनीं । जाकी लागि रही ल्यौ रसनीं ॥
४ भणंत नांमदेव तिनि थिति पाई । जाकै रांम नांम निज रटनीं ॥

१४

० तेरी तेरी गति तूं ही जांनैं । अलप जीव गति कहा बषांनैं ॥
१ जैसा तूं कहिये तैसा तूं नाहीं । जैसा तूं है तैसा आछि गुसांई ॥
२ लूंण नीर थैं ना ह्वै न्यारा । ठाकुर साहिब प्रांण हमारा ॥
३ साध की संगति संत सूं भेटा । प्रणवंत नांमां रांम सहेटा ॥

१५

० मैं अपराधी बाप मैं अपराधी । सांचिली तुम्हची भगति न साधी ॥

त्रिपष ३ ७ ८ १२ २०; नृपष १०; षेलै। षैलै ८; तार्थैं। जाथै २०; ताथै १६; तार्तैं ८ १३; तातें १०; मिटै। मिटैं ३; मिटे १०; मिठै ७; अंतर। अंतरगति २०; तपनीं। तपर्णीं ४; तपनी ३ ८ १३ २०

१३;१ अंतर। अंतरि ७ १६ २०; षेचर। षचर १०; मति। म+ ८; ऊपरि। उपरि ३ ८ १० १३ २०; मंजन। मंजंन ४ २१; मजन ८; षपनी। षपनि १०; षपनीं ३ ७

१३;२ ऐसा। ऐसो ७; अैसा ३ ८ १३ २१; न। - २०; कोई। कोइ १०; सरबंग। श्रबंगि २०; श्रबंग १३; निरपष ह्वै १; सबंगि ८; पहिचांनैं। पिछांनै १३; हिचांनै ३; हिचनि १०; मछानैं ८; पछानै १६; पहिछांनै ४; षेलै १; प्रभु। प्रभू १ ३ ७ ८ १० १३ २०; बिनां। बिंनां १३; बिना १ २०; और। ओर १०; सबै २०; रैंनि। रैंणि ८ १३ २० २१; रैणि ४; रैनि ३; रैन १६; रेंनि १०; सुपनी। सुपिनी ८ २०; सुपिनीं १३; सुपनीं ७; सपनी २१

१३;३ सोई। सोइ १०; साध। साध १०; सोई। सोइ १०; मुनि। सुणि ४ १६ २० २१; सुनि १ ७; ग्यांनीं। ग्यानी ८; लागि। लागी ३ १६; रही। रहि २०; रहें १०; ल्यौ। ल्यो ३ १०; सो ८; रसनीं। रसंनी १३ २१; रसनी ४ ८ १० १६ २०

१३;४ भणंत। भंणत ८; भनंत ३; भनत १०; तिनि। तिनिं १३; थिति। थिती ४; पाई। पाइ ८ १०; जाकै। जाके १० १६; नांम। नाम २०; निज। निंज १३; रटनीं। + ४; रंटंनी २१; रटनी ८ १० १६; रटनी पाई २०

१४;० तेरी। तेरि २०; तेरी। तेरि २०; तूं। तू ३ ८ १० २०; जांनैं। जांणैं २०; जानि १०; अलप। अल्प १६; गति। मति १

१४;१ तूं। तू १०; कहियेे। कहिऐ ३; तैसा। तेसा १०; तूं। तू ३ १०; नाहीं। नांही ३ १०; नांहीं १ ८ १३; नाही २०; जैसा। जेसा १०; तूं। - २०; तू ३ ८ १० १३; है। हे १०; तैसा। तेसा १०; आछि। आथि १०; गुसांई। गुंसांई १३; गुसांई ३ ८ २०; गुसांइ १०; गुसाई १६

१४;२ लूंण। लूण ८; थैं। तै ३; तैं ८ १३; ते १०; ना। नां ३ ८; ह्वै। होइ ३ १०; ठाकुर। ठाकूर २०; साहिब। सहिब २०; साहिव १३; प्रांण। प्रांन १ १३; प्राण १०; हमारा। हंमारा १ ८ १३ २०

१४;३ साध। सध २०; संत। - १६; साध १०; वह्या २०; सूं। स्यूं ३ २०; सु १०; सौं ८ १३; भेटा। भेंटा १६; भेठा ८; प्रणवंत। प्रनवंत १०; प्रनवत ३; नांमां। नांमदेव ३ १० २०; रांम। चित ३ १०; सहेटा। चिहूटया ३; चहुंट्यां १०

१ घर्णों अग्यांन आगिना भंगी । कीया काम कुसंगा संगी ॥
२ यह् अग्यांन इहीं परि घाठौ । निषर कमाई न छूटै नाठौ ॥
३ कीया षूंन गोबिंद सब जांनैं । पौढा परबत मेर प्रंवानै ॥
४ नर निरदोष नरांइण नांमीं । ए सब बंक अम्हंचा स्वांमीं ॥
५ नरक निवारन नरहरि नांमां । कीले मेक सराहूं कांमां ॥

१६

• लोक एक अनंत बांनीं । मंझा जीवनि सारंगप्रांणीं ॥
१ जिहिं जिहिं रंगै लोक राता । ता रंगि जन न राचिला ॥
२ जिहिं जिहिं मारगि संसार जाइला । सो पंथ दूरै बांचिला ॥

१५;• मैं। मै २•; अपराधी। + ४; अपरांधी १•; बाप। + ४; रांम २•; वाप १; मैं। + ४; में १•; साचिली। सांचली २•; साचिली २ ४ ७ ८ १२; साचली १• २१; तुम्हची। भगति १•; तुंम्हचीं १२; तुमची १ २•; भगति। भक्ति १; तुम्हाची १•

१५;१ घर्णों। घ+ ४; घणे ३; घर्णे १२; धने १•; अपर्णों २१; आगिना। अगिनां ८; अवग्या ४; आगिनां ७ १२ २१; आग्या १•; आग्यां १६; कीया। कीयै १• १६; कीये १ १२; कीयो २•; कीरो ८; काम। कांम २ ७ ८ १• १२ २• २१; कुसंगा। कुसंग १; कुसंगां ४; संगी। कुसंगी १

१५;२ यह। यहु १ २ ४ ७ ८ १• १२ २• २१; इहीं। ईही ४; इंही १२; इंहीं ३; इहि ८; इही १• २१; इहां ७; घाठौ। घाठौं ७; घाठो १•; घाठा ८ १२; पाठा १६; कमाई। कंमांई १२; कंमाई २१, कमाइ १ १•; छूटै। छुटै २१; छूटे १•; नाठौ। नांठौ ३; नांठां १२; नाठो १•; नाठा ८ १६

१५;३ षूंन। षून ३; गोबिंद। गोबिद १•; गोव्यंद २• २१; गोव्यंद १ १६; सब ८ १२; सब। गोबिंद १२; गोबिद ८; सव १; जांनैं। जांणै २•; जांर्णै ४; जांनै १६ २१; जानि १•; जानैं १, पौढा। पोढा १•; परबत। प्रबत ४ ७ ८ १२ २१; प्रवत १; बरपत १•; प्रंवानै। प्रंबाने १६; प्रंवानैं १२ २•; प्रमांनै ३; प्रबाणै १•; प्रवांणै २१: प्रवांनैं ४ ८; प्रावांनैं ७

१५;४ नर। -- ४; नर नर २१; निरदोष। न्रदोष १२; नरदोष २•; नादोष २१; नरांइण। नंराइण ७; नराईण २•; नरांइंन १; नरांइन १२; नराड्णि ८; नराईण २१; नराइन १६; नारायण १•; नांमीं। नांमी ८ १•; ए। -- ४; ऐ ३ १२; ये १ ८ १६ २•; सब। सव १; बंक। वंक १; अम्हंचा। अमंचा १२; अह्मचा १•; स्वांमीं। स्वांमी ८

१५;५ नरक। न्रक ८ १२ २१; निवारन। निवारंण ४; निवारण १ ७ ८ १२ २• २१; सराहूं। सरांहूं २ ७ २१; सरांहौं ८; सराहौ १२

१६;• एक। ऐंक १२; ऐक ३ ४; अनेक १ २•; येक ८; अनंत। अनेक २•; अनत ८; बांनीं। बांणीं १ ४ ७ २• २१; बांनी ८; बानी ३; वांर्णी १२; मंझा। मंझी १•; जीवनि। जीवन ४ १६ २• २१; सारंगप्रांर्णीं। सारंगप्रांणी ८; सारंगप्राणी ४; सारंगपांनी ३ १•; सारंगपानी १६

१६;१ जिहिं। जिंहिं ४ १२; जिंहि १; जिहि ३ ७ ८; जिहिं। जिंहिं ४; जिंहि १; जिहि ३ ७ ८ १६; रंगै। रंगैं ४ ७ ८ १२; रगै १•; लोक। लोग १६; ता। तिहि ३ १•; रंगि। रंग ७ १२; जन। संत १; न। नं २१; नहीं २•; राचिला। रांचीला २१; राचीला १२ २•

१६;२ जिहिं। जिहि ३ ८ १६ २•; जिहिं। - ८; जिहि ३ १६ २•; मारगि। मारग १ ७ २१: जाइला। जाई ३; जाईला ४ २•; जाइ १•; दूरै। दूरैं ४ ७ ८ २• २१; दूरे १ ३ १•; बांचिला। बंचिला ७ २१; बंचीला ३ २•; बचीला १•; वंचीला १; बांचीला १२

३ निरबानै पद कोई एक चीन्हैं । झूठै भ्रंमि भुलाइला ॥
४ प्रणवंत नार्मौ परम तत रे । सतगुरि निकटि बताइला ॥

१७

• लोग कहैं लोकाइ रे नांमां । षट दरसन कै निकटि न जाइबौ ॥
भगति जाइगी जाइ रे नांमां ।।
षट क्रम सहित बिप्र आचारी तिन सौं नाहिंन मेरौ कांमां ॥
१ जौ हरिदास सबनि थैं नीचे तेउ कहैंगे केवल रांमां ॥
अधम असोच भिष्ट बिभचारी पंडरीनाथ कौ लैंहि जु नांमां ॥
२ वै सब बंध बरग मेरी जीवनि तिनकै संगि कह्यौ मैं रांमां ॥
गउ सत लछि बिप्र कौं दीजै मन बंछित सब पुरवै कांमां ॥
३ दास पटंतरि तऊ न तूलै भगति हेत जस गावै नांमां ॥

१६;३ निरबानै। त्रिबांण २०; त्रिबांणैं ४ ८ २१; त्रिवांणे १; निर्बाणैं १६; निरबांणैं ७; निरबांनैं ३; निरबाने १०; त्रबाणैं १३; पद। पदै १३; एक। - ८ १६; ऐक १ ३ ४; न १३; क २०; येक १०; चीन्हैं। चिन्हेंला १०; चींन्हैंला ३; चींन्हींला २०; चीन्है १६; चीन्हैं ८; झूठै। झूठैं ७ २१; झूठे १०; भ्रंमि। भर्मि १६; भ्रमि १०; भ्रम ३ ८ २०; र्भमि ४; भरमि १; भुलाइला। भुलाईला १; भूलाईला ३ ४ २०; भूलाइला १० २१

१६;४ प्रणवंत। भनत ३ १०; प्रंणवंति २१; प्रंणवंत १३; प्रणंवंत २०; प्रणंवत ४ ७; प्रणवत १ ८; नार्मौ। नांमौ २०; नांर्मौ १ ४ ७ २१; नांमदेव ३ १०; नांमां ८ १३ १६; परम। प्रम ८ १३; परंम २१; रे। पाईला २०; है ३ २१; हे १०; सो १३; सतगुरि। सतगुर १ ३ १० २०; सतगुरी २१; निकटि। निंकटि १३; निकट ३ १० २०; बताइला। बताईला ३ ४ २०; वताईला १

१७;० लोग। लोक ७; कहैं। कहै १ १६; कहे १०; लोकाइ। लौकांई ३; लौकांइ ७; लौकाई १; लोकांइ १० १६; लाकांइ ८ १३; दरसन। दर्शन ७; दसन १०; दरसंन १३; दरसण १; कै। के ७ १०; निकटि। निंकटि १३; नेडै ७; संगि १ १०; संगिन ३; न। - ७; जाइबौ। जाइबा ३; जाइवा १ १०; भगति। भक्ति १३; जाइगी। भाइगी १०; जाइ। जाई ८; जाइगी १०; रे। - १

१७;१ क्रम। क्रंम १ १३; कर्म ७; सहित। सहत ८' १३; तिन। तिनि ३; सौं। स्यौं १; स्यो ३; सूं ७; सों १०; नाहिंन। नांहिंन १३ १६; नांहिन ३ ८ १०; नाहिन १ ७; मेरौ। - ८ १३ १६; मेरे १; मेरो ३ १०; कांमां। कांम १०; कांमा ३; जौ। जो ३ १०; हरिदास। हरीदास १०; थैं। ते ३ ८ १०; तें १३; नीचे। निचे १०; नीचा १; तेउ। तुउ ८; तेऊ १; तेऊं १६; तऊ ७; तउ ३ १०; कहैंगे। कहेंगे १ १०; रांमां। रांम १०

१७;२ भिष्ट। भिस्ट १६; बिष्ट ७; भ्रष्ट ३ १०; बिभचारी। कुलहींनां ३; कुलहीना १०; पंडरीनाथ। पंढुरीनाथ १; पुंडरीनांथ १०; पुडरीनाथ ३; कौ। कूं १; को १०; लैंहि। लिहि ८; लेंहि १०; लेहि ७ १६; जु। ज ३ १३; नांमां। नांम ३ १०; वै। - १; बै ३; बे १०; सब। सव १ १०; जीवनि। जीवंनि १; जीवनिं १३; तिनकै। तिनके १०; कह्यौ। कह्यो ३ १०; मैं। मे १०; रांमां। रांम ३ १०

१७;३ गउ। गऊ १ ७; गौ १०; गो ८ १३ १६; सत। - ७ १०; स्ति १६; सति १; लछि। ल+ ८; लछ १०; लक्षि १; लक्ष १३; कौं। कूं १ ७; कों १०; दीजै। दींजै ८; दीजे १०; दीजें ३; बंछित। बछित ८; सब। पुरवै ८ १३; फल १; पुरवै। पुरवैं ७; पुरवे १०; पूरै १६; सब ८ १३; कांमां। कांम ३ १०; दास। रांम १; पटंतरि। पटंत ३ १०; पटंतर ७ ८; तऊ। उ ३; उन १०; तुवु ८; तउ १३; न। भ ३; तु १०; तूलै। - ३ १०; तुलै ८ १३ १६; हेत। हेति १३; गावै। गावैं १३; नांमां। नांम ३

१८

० का करूं जाती का करूं पांती । राजा रांम सेऊं दिन राती ॥
१ मन मेरौ गजा जिह्वा मेरी काती । रांम रंमें काटूं जंम की पासी ॥
२ सींवनां सींऊं हूं सींऊं हूं सींऊं । रांम बिनां हूं कैसैं जीऊं ॥
३ सुरति की सुई प्रेम का धागा । नांमां का मन हरि सौं लागा ॥

१ मनु मेरो गजु जिहबा मेरी काती । मपि मपि काटउ जम की फासी ॥
० कहा करउ जाती कह करउ पाती । राम को नामु जपउ दिन राती ॥ रहाउ ॥
२ रांगनि रांगउ सीवनि सीवउ । राम नाम बिनु घरीअ न जीवउ ॥
३ भगति करउ हरि के गुन गावउ । आठ पहर अपना खसमु धिआवउ ॥
४ सुइने की सूई रुपे का धागा । नामे का चितु हरि सउ लागा ॥

१९

० ऐसैं मन रांम नांमैं बेधिला । जैसैं कनक तुला चित राषिला ॥
१ आंनिलै कागद साजिलै गूडी आकास मंडल छोडिला ॥

१८;० का। क ४; कां २१; करूं। करौ १५; करौं ३ ८ १३; करों १०; जाती। जांति १०; जांती २१, जाति ३ ४ २०; करूं। करौं ३ ८ १३ १५; करों १०; पांती। पांतीं २०; पाती ४ १० १३; राजा। रांजा १५; रांम। सम १०; राग ३, सेऊं। सेउ १०; सेउं १३; दिन। दिंन १३; दीन २०

१८;१ मन। मंन २१; मेरौ। मेरो ३ १०; गजा। गेजा ३ १०; जिह्वा। जिभ्या ८ १३ १५ २०; जिह्बा २१; जिब्ह्या ३ १०; जिव्ह्या ४; रंमें। रंगें ७, रंमें रंमि २०; रमे ३ ८ १५; रमें १३; रमे रमि ४; काटूं। काटौं ३ ८ १३ १५; काटों १०; जंम। - २०; जम ३ ८ १५; जन १०; की। - ३ १० २० २१; पासी। पासीसी १०

१८;२ सींवनां। सींवणां ७; सीवण २०; सीनणां १ ४ २१; सीवन १०; सीवनां १३; सींऊं। सींउं २०; सीऊं १५; सीउ १० १३; सीउं ८; सीवूं ४; हूं। - ४ २१; हुं १०; हू ३; हौं १५; सींऊं। सींउं २०; सीऊं ३ १५ २१; सीउं ८ १० १३; सीवूं ४; हूं। - ३ १०; ईब १५; ही ८ १३ २०; सींऊं। - ३ १०; सींहूं २०; सीऊं १ १३ १५; सीउं ८; सीवूं ४; बिनां। बिंनां १३; बिना २०; हूं। हौं ८ १५; जीऊं। जीऊं अनंत नांम का सींऊं बागा जा सींवत जंम का डर भागा ७; जीऊं अनंत नांम का सीऊं बागा जा सीवत जंम का डर भागा १; जीऊं अनंत नांव का सीऊं बागा जा सीवत जंम का डर भागा ३ १०; जीऊं सहंश्र नांम का सीऊं बागा जा सीवत जंम का डर भागा २१; जीउं ८ १३; जीवूं सहंसु नांम का सीवूं बागा जा सींवंत जंम का डर भागा ४

१८;३ सुरति। श्रुरति १; सुरती १०; सुई। श्रुई १; सुइ १०; सुइी ८; सूई ३ १३ १५ २०; धागा। तागा २०; नांमां। नांमा २१; नामां ३; मन। चित ३ १० २०; मंन २१; सौं। स्यूं ४; स्यौं १ ३ २०; सूं ७ २१; सो १०

१९;० ऐसैं। ऐसै २०; अैसै १३; अैसैं १ ३ ८ १५ १७; अैसें २१; अेसे १०; मन। मंन ४ १३; नांमैं। नांमै १३; नांमहि ३; बेधिला। बेधीला ३ १० २०; वेधिला १; जैसैं। जैसै ३; जेसे १०; कनक। कनंक २१; राषिला। राषीला ३ २०

१९;१ आंनिलै। आंणिंलै ४ १३; आंणिलै १ ७ ८ २१; आंनिले १०; आनिलै ३ १५; आणीलै २०; साजिलै। साजीलै २०; साजीले १०; गूडी। गुडी ४ ७ ८ १३ १७ २१; गूढी २०; आकास। अकास १७; आकासि ३ १०; मंडल। मंडलि ३ १३; मंडली १०; मडल २१; छोडिला। छोडीला ३; पंच। पांच १ १७ २१; जनां। जणां २१;

पंच जनां सौं बात बतउवा चित सौं डोरी राषिला ॥
२ आंनिलै कुंभ भराइलै ऊदिक राजकुंवारि पुलंदरि ए ॥
हस्त बिनोद देत करताली चित सौं गागरि राषिला ॥
३ मंदिर एक द्वार दस जाकै गऊ चरावन चालिला ॥
पांच कोस थैं चरि फिरि आवै चित सौं बाछा राषिला ॥
४ भणत नांमदेव सुनौं त्रिलोचन बालिक पालणि पौढिला ॥
अपनैं मंदिर काज करंती चित सौं बालिक राषिला ॥

१ आनीले कागदु काटीले गूडी आकास मधे भरमीअले ॥
पंच जना सिउ बात बतऊआ चीतु सु डोरी राखीअले ॥
मनु राम नामा बेधीअले । जैसे कनिक कला चितु मांडीअले ॥ रहाउ ॥
२ आनीले कुंभु भराईले ऊदक राजकुआरि पुरंदरीए ॥
हसत बिनोद बीचार करती है चीतु सु गागरि राखीअले ॥
३ मंदरु एकु दुआर दस जा के गऊ चरावन छाडीअले ॥
पांच कोस पर गऊ चरावत । चीतु सु बछरा राखीअले ॥
४ कहत नामदेउ सुनहु तिलोचन बालकु पालन पउढीअले ॥
अंतरि बाहरि काज बिरूधी चीतु सु बारिक राखीअले ॥

जनन ४; जना ३ ७ २०; सौं। स्यूं ३ ४ २०; स्यौं १; सूं ७ २१; सों १०; बात। बत ३ १०; बा+ ४; वात १; बतउवा। करनां ८; करता १३; बतऊवा १६; बतवा ७ २१; बतांउवा २०; वतउवा १ ३; सौं। स्यु ३; स्यूं २०; स्यौं १; स २१; सु ४ १३; सुं १०; सूं ७; डोरी। डोरि २०; राषिला। राषीला ३ ८ १० १३ २०

१६;२ आंनिलै। आंणिंलै ४; आंणिले १ ७ २१; आंनिले १०; आनिलै १६; आणीलै २०; कुंभ। कुभ ८ १६; कूभ ३; भराइलै। भरइलै ३; भरइले १०; भराईलै ४ २०; ऊदिक। उदिक १ ३ ७ ८ १३ १६ १७ २० २१; उदक १०; राजकुंवारि। राजिकंवारि २१; राजकुंवार १ १३; राजकुवारि ७; राजकूंवारि २०; राजकवारि १०; पुलंदरि। पुलिदरि २१; पुलंदरिला ३ १०; पुलदरि ८; ए। - ३ १०; ऐ ४ २१; यै १३; ये १ ८ १६ १७ २०; बिनोद। विनोद १; देत। दुंहुं १०; दहुं ३; करताली। करतली १०; करता+ी ८; करतारी १३; सौं। स्यूं २०; स्यौं १; स २१; सु १३; सुं १०; सूं ३ ४ ७; गागरि। गांगरि १०; गागरी २०; राषिला। राषिले ८ २१; राषीला १३ २०

१६;३ एक। ऐक १ ३ ४ १३; येक ८ १० २०; द्वार। दूार ८; जाकै। जाके १०; गऊ। गउ ३ ८ १३ २०; गवु १०; चरावन। चरांवंण ४; चरांवण ७ २१; चरांवन १७; चरावण १ २०; चलीबन ८ १३; चालिला। चलिला १०; चालेला २०; चाली+ ४; चालीला ३; षंडीला १३; षंडिला ८; पांच। पंच ८ १३; चारि ३ १०; थैं। तैं ३ ८ १३ २०; तें १०; चरि। फिरि १; फिरि। चरि १; आवै। आर्वै १ १६; आवे १०; सौं। स्यूं २०; स्यौं १; सु १३ २१; सुं १०; सू ४; सूं ३ ७; बाछा। बछा ८ १३ १६; बाछै ३; वाछे १०; वाछा १; राषिला। राषीला ३ १० २०

१६;४ भणत। भणंत ७ ८; नांमो २०; नांमौं २१; नांमदेव ३ १०; नांमदेव। कहै ३ १० २० २१; सुनौं। श्रुणौं १; सुंणैं २१; सुंनौं १३; सुणो ४; सुणौं ७ १७; सुनो ८; सुनहु ३ १०; सूणौं २०; त्रिलोचन। तिलोचन ३; तिलोचन ८ १० १३ १६ १७; बालिक। बालक ८ १० १३; बालीक ४; वालक १; पालणि। पालनै ३; पालने १०; पालाणि ४; पौढिला। पौढीला ३ २०; अपनैं। अपणे २०; अपणैं १ ७ १६ १७; अपनै ३; अपने १०; आपणै २१; मंदिर। मंदिरि ४ ८; मंदरि १७ २०; मंदीर ३; मदिर १३ २१; काज। कांम ३; काम १०; करंती। करता

२०

० का नाचीला का गाईला । का घसि घसि चंदन लाईला ॥
१ जो आपा पर नहीं चीन्हीला । तौ चित चितारै डहकीला ॥
२ क्रितम आगै नाचै लोई । स्यंभदेव चीन्हैं नहीं कोई ॥
३ स्यंभदेव की सेवा जांनैं । तौ दिवद्रिस्टी ह्वै सकल पिछांनैं ॥
४ नांमदेव भणै मेरे एही पूजा । आतमरांम अवर नहीं दूजा ॥

२१

० रांम ची भगति दुहेली रे बापा । सकल निरंतरि चीन्हि लै आपा ॥
१ बाहरि उजला भीतरि मैला । पांणीं प्यंड पषालि न गहिला ॥
२ पुतली देव कि पाती देवा । इहिं बिधि नांम न जांनैं सेवा ॥

१२; सौं। स्यूं २०; स्यौं १; सु १२ २१; सुं ३ १०; सू ४; सूं ७; बालिक। बालक ८ २०; वालक १; राषिला। राषीला ३ १० १२ २०

२०;० का। क्या ८ १३; कां १०; नाचीला। नांचीला ३ १३ २०; नाचिला १०; का। क्या ८ १३; क १०; गाईला। गईला ३; गाइला १०; का। क्या १३; घसि। घसिं ४; लाईला। लावीला २१; लाइला १०

२०;१ जो। - १ ८ १२ १६ १७ २० २१; -- ४; जेतैं ७; नहीं। नहि १; नही ३ ८ २१; चीन्हीला। चींन्हींला १; चींन्हीला १३ १६ २१; चीन्हींला ३ ७ ८ १७ २०; तौ। -- ४; तो १०: चितारै। चितारे १०

२०;२ क्रितम। क्रित्म १ ४; क्रितंम २१; क्रतम १३; कृत १०: कृतम ८ १७; आगै। आंगै २१; आगैं १२; आगे १०; नाचै। नांचै ३ ४; नांचैं १३; नाचे १०; लोई। लोइ १०; स्यंभदेव। सिंभूदेव १७; सिंभदेव ८ १३; स्यंभूदेत १६; सिभदेव १०; चीन्हैं। - ८; न १३ १६ १७ २०; पूजै ३; पूजे १०: चींन्है ४, नहीं। न ८; नहि १ ३; नही १० २१; चींन्हे १३ २०; चीन्है १६ १७; कोई। कोइ ४ १०

२०;३ स्यंभदेव। सिंभूदेव १७; सिंभदेव ८ १३; स्यंभूदेव १६; स्यभदेव ४; सिभदेव १०; जे तूं स्यंभदेव ७; सेवा। पूजा ३ १०; जांनैं। जांणैं १७: जानैं १ ३ ४ ७ ८ १३ १६ २० २१; जाने १०; तौ। - ३ १०; दिवद्रिस्टी। दिबिद्रिष्टि ३; दिबिद्रिष्टी १३; दिविदिस्टी १; दिबद्रिस्टी १६; दिबद्रिष्टि २०; दिबद्रिष्टी ७ ८ १७; दिवदिस्टि ४; दिवद्रिष्टी २१; दिव्यद्रष्टी १०; ह्वै। होइ ३ १०; पिछांनैं। पिछांणैं १ ८ १७ २१; पिछानै ३; पिछाने १०

२०;४ नांमदेव। भनत ३ १०; भणै। भणैं १ ७ ८ १२ १६ १७ २०; नांमदेव ३ १०; मेरे। मेरै ४ १७ २०; यह १०; यहु ३; एही। ऐही ८ १३; एकै १६; एहीं ७; मेरे ३ १०; येही १ २०; याही ४; आतमरांम। आंतमरांम १२ २१; आत्मरांम १: आतमराम ३; अवर। और ३ १०; औवर १६; नहीं। नहिं १३; नहि १; नही ३ ८ १० १६ २०; दूजा। दुजा १०

२१;० रांम। राम ३; भगति। भक्ति १ १३; दुहेली। दुहैली ३; रे। - १३; बापा। वापा १; सकल। सर्ब ३ १०; निरंतरि। निरंतर ८ १० २० २१; चीन्हि। चिन्हि १०; चीन्हि ४; चींन्हीं २०; चींन्हि १ ३; चीन्ही २१; चीन्हि ८ १३ १६; लै। ले ४ ७ १० १६

२१;१ बाहरि। वाहरि १; उजला। ऊजल १ २१; उजल ४ ७ ८ १३ २०; भीतरि। भींतरि १ ३ ४ १३ २०; मैला। मैंला १३ १६; मेला १०; पांणीं। पांणी ८ २१; पांनी ३ १०; प्यंड। प्यंड न ३; पिंड न १०; पषालि। पषारि १०; पषाली २०; न। स २१; रे ३; गहिला। गहला ३ १० २०

२१;२ पुतली। पुतलि ४; पूतरी २०; पूतली १ ७ २१; पाती ३ १०; तुलसी १६; कि। क १ ३ १०; पाती। पूतरी ३

३ पाषंड भगति रांम नहीं रीझै । बाहरि अंधा लोक पतीजै ॥
४ नांमदेव भणैं मेरा नेत्र पलटचा । रांम चरनां चित चिहूंटचा ॥

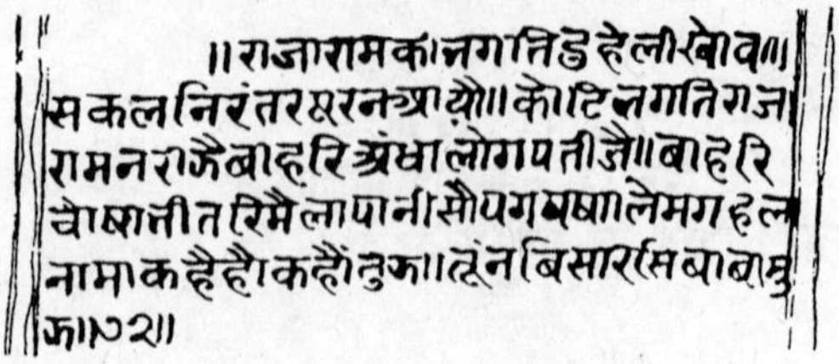
॥राजारामकीजगतिडेहेलीखेव॥
सकलनिरंतरसरनच्याये॥कोटिजगतिराज
रामनरीझैबाहरिअंधालोगपतीजै॥बाहरि
चोषातीतरिमैलापानीसौपगमषालेमगहल
नामाकहैहोकहैतुफ॥तूंनबिसारंसबाबामु
फा॥२१॥

२२

• जौ लग रांम नांमैं हित न भयौ । तौ लग मेरी मेरी करतां जनम गयौ ॥
१ लागी पंक पंक ले धोवै । न्रिमल न होवै जनम बिगोवै ॥
२ भीतरि मैला बाहरि चोषा । पांणीं प्यंड पषालि न धोषा ॥
३ नांमदेव कहै सुरही परहरिये । भेंड पूंछ कैसैं भौजल तिरिये ॥

१०; पाति २०; इहिं। ईहिं १३; ईहि ४; इंहिं २१; इंहि १; इहि ८ १९; इस ३ १०; नांम। नांमदेव ४ ७ १९ २० २१; जांनैं। जांणे २० २१; जांणैं ७; जानि १०

२१;३ पाषंड। पषड ८; कूरि ३; कूरी १०; भगति। भक्ति १; भगती २०; रांम। राम ३; नहीं। नहि १; नही ८ १०; रीझै। जनि १०; बाहरि। बाहर १०; वाहरि १; अंधा। अंधला ३ १०; आंधा १९; लोक। लौक २०; लोग १ ३ ८ १० १९; पतीजै। पतिजै ४; पतीजे १० २१

२१;४ नांमदेव। -- २०; भणैं। कहै १ ३ ८; कहैं १३; कहे १०; मेरा। मोरा २१; नेत्र। नेत ३ १०; रांम। -- २०; चरण ३; चरन १०; चरनां। कमल मे १०; कवल मैं ३; चरणां ४ ७ २१; चरनौं १३; चिहूंटचा। चिऊटचा १९; चिहुंटचा ७ १० १३; चहूंटचा ४

२२;० जौ। - ७ ८ १३ २०; जो १०; लग। - ७ ८ १३ २०; नांमैं। नांम २०; नांमें १०; हित। चित ३ १० १९; न। - १०; भयौ। चिहुंयो १०; भयो ३; तौ। - ७ ८ १३ २०; तो १०; लग। - ७ ८ १३ २०; करतां। करत १ ४; जनम। जंन्म १३; जंनम २०; गयौ। गयो ३ १०;

२२;१ लागी। लागै ७; पंक। कंप ८; पंक। पंक पंक ४; कंप ८; ले। लै ८ १३; धोवै। धौवै २०; धोवे १०; न्रिमल। न्रिंमल २०; निर्मल ७ १९; न्रमल १० १३; नृमल १ ८; होवै। होवे १०; जनम। जन्म १ १३; बिगोवै। बिगोवे १०; विगोवै १; बीगोवै २०

२२;२ भीतरि। भींतरि १; माहैं २०; मैला। मैंला १९; मैलौ ४; पांणीं। पांणी ८; पांनी ३; प्यंड। पिंड १० १३; पिंड ८; पषालि। न ३ १०; पषलैं ८; पषाले १ ४ १९; न। - १ ४ ८ १९; पषाले ३; पषाले १०; धोषा। धौषा २०

२२;३ कहै। कहे १०; सुरही। शुरही १; परहरिये। परहरियै १९; पूंछ। पूछ ३ १९; कैसैं। केसें १०; भौजल। +जल ४; भौजलि ७; भोजल १०; भवजल १९; तिरिये। तिरि+ ४; तिरियै १९

२३

० काहे कौं कीजै ध्यांन जपनां । जौ मन नांहीं सुध अपनां ॥
१ सांप कांचली छाडै बिष नहीं छाडै । उदिक मैं बग ध्यान मांडै ॥
२ स्यंघ के भोजन कहा लुकांनां । ए सब झूठे देव पुजांनां ॥
३ नांमदेव का स्वांमीं भांनिलै झगरा । रांम रसांइन पीव रे भगरा ॥

१ सापु कुंच छोडै बिखु नही छाडै । उदक माहि जैसे बगु धिआनु माडै ॥
० काहे कउ कीजै धिआनु जपंना । जब ते सुधु नाही मनु अपना ॥ रहाउ ॥
२ सिघच भोजनु जो नरु जानै । ऐसे ही ठगदेउ बखानै ॥
३ नामे के सुआमी लाहि ले झगरा । राम रसाइन पीउरे दगरा ॥

२४

० भगत भला बाबा कागिला । बिनहीं परचै पूजैं सिला ॥
१ न्हावैं धोवैं करैं अस्नांन । हिरदै आंषि न माथै कांन ॥
२ गलि पहरैं तुलसी की माला । अंतरगति कोइला सा काला ॥
३ नांमदेव कहै ये पेटा बलू । भीतरि लाष ऊपरि हींगलू ॥

२३;० काहे। काहें १०; कौं। कूं १ ४; को १९; कों १०; कीजै। कीजे ३ ४ १०; ध्यांन। ध्यान ३; जौ। जो ३ १० २०; मन। मंन २१; नांहीं। माहीं २०; नहीं १९; नांहि १०; नांही ३ ८; सुध। सूध १; अपनां। अप+ ४; अपंनां १ २१

२३;१ सांप। साप १ ८ १३ २१; कांचली। कंचली ४; कचुली ८; कांचुली १३; कांचरी ३ १०; काचली १९; छाडै। - २० २१; छाडे १०; बिष। बिष हि ४; बिष ही १ ३ १०; नहीं। न १ ३ ४ १०; नही ८; छाडै। छांडै १; छाडि १०; उदिक। ज्यूं उदिक ४; उदक ८ १० १३; मैं। में १०; मांहीं २०; बग। + ४; बुग २० बगु ३ १०; ध्यान। +न ४; ध्यांन १ ८; ध्यांन जैसैं २१; मांडै। मांडैं १३ २१; माडि १०

२३;२ स्यंघ। सिंघ ७ १९; स्यग्ध ३; सिघ १०; सिध ८; कहा। कहां २०; लुकांनां। लुकां+ ४; ए। + ४; ऐ १ ८ १० १३; ये ३ २०; सब। सव १; झूठे। + ४; देव। + ४; पुजांनां। +नां ४; पूजांनां २१

२३,३ नांमदेव। नां+ ४; का। को १०; स्वांमीं। स्यांमी २०; स्वांमी ३ ८; स्वामीं १९; भांनिलै। भांनिंलै १३; भांनि ३ १०; भांनिदे १९; भांनिले ७; भांनीलै २०; झगरा। झगडा २०; रांम। ++ ४; रसांइन। रसांईन २०; रसांइंण २१; रसांइंन १ ८ १९; पीव। पी १ ३ ७ १० २०; भगरा। भंगरा २०

२४;० भगत। ++ ४; कागिला। कांगिला १३; काडला ८ १९ २० २१; बिनहीं। बिंनंहीं २१; बिण ४; बिणही २०; बिणहीं १; बिन १३ १९; बिनही ८; परचै। प्रतीतैं ८ १३; परतीतैं ४ १९; पूजैं। पूजे १९ २०

२४;१ न्हावैं। + ४; न्हांवैं १ ८ १३; धोवैं। +वैं ४; अस्नांन। स्नांन ७; अस्ना+ ४; असनांन २०; सनांन ८ १३ १९; हिरदै। हिर्दै ७; आंषि। अंषि ४; माथै। मांथै ७ १३ १९; मांथैं ४

२४;२ गलि। ग+ ४; गल २१; पहरैं। पहिरै १९; पहरै ७; तुलसी। तुलछी १; तूलसी २०; अंतरगति। अंतरिगति ४; कोइला। ह्वै ला १; कोईला ४ २०; काईला ८

२४;३ नांमदेव। भणत ७; कहै। भणैं ८ १३; नांमदेव ७; ये। - ७; ए १९ २१; ऐ ४ ८ १३; बलू। बल्यू २०; बलु २१; भीतरि। भीत+ ८; मांहि ७; मांही २०; बाहरि २१; ऊपरि। भीतरि २१; उपरि ४ ८ १३; बाहरि

२५

० साच कहूं तौ जीव जग मारै ।एक अनेक आगैं नित हारै ॥
१ साचै आषरि गोठि बिनासै ।भाजै हाड अभावै हासै ॥
२ मन मैले की सुधि नहीं जांनीं ।साबण सिला सराहै पांणीं ॥
३ उजल बांनां नीच सगाई ।पाषंड भेष कीयें पति जाई ॥
४ अपस अग्यांनीं उजल हूवा ।संसै गांठि पडी गलि मूवा ॥
५ नांमदेव कहै ए संष सरापी ।पुडरीनाथ न सुमिरैं पापी ॥

२६

० सांई मेरौ रीझै साचि ।कूडै कपटि न जाई राचि ॥
१ कोई बहु गावौ कोई बहु नाचौ ।जब लग नांहीं हिरदै साचौ ॥

२०; वाहरि १; हींगलू। हींगुंलू १६; हींगलूं २१; हीगलू ८ १३

२५;० साच। सांच १० २०; कहूं। कौं ८; कहौं ३ १३ १६ १७; कहो १०; तौ। तो १०; जीव। जी ७ १६; जीय १ ८ १३; जग। जंग २०; जुग ८; जक १३; मारै। मारे १०; एक। ऐक १ ३ ४ ८ १३; येक १० २०; अनेक। अनिक १३ २१; आगैं। आ+ ४; आगै ३ २१; आगे १०; नित। नित १३; निति ३; हारै। हारे ४ १०

२५;१ साचै। सांचै ३ ७; सांचे १०; सांचौ २०; आषरि। अषिर २०; आषिरि ३; आषिर ४ २१; बिनासै। बिणांसै २१; बिणासै ४ ७; बिनांसै ३; बिनांसें १०; विणासै १; भाजै। भाजे १०; अभावै। अभावें १०; हासै। हासे १०

२५;२ मैले। मैलै १ ४ ७ २१; मेले १०; मलीन १६; सुधि। शुधि १; नहीं। न ३ ७ ८ १० २०; नहि १; नही १६ २१; जांनीं। जांणी २१; जांणीं १ ४ ७ १६ १७; जांनी ८ २०; जानी १०; साबण। सांबण २१; सांबण १३; साबंण ३; साबुण ८; सावण १; सिला। मिला २१; सीला १०; सराहै। +राहै ४; सरांहै ७; सरांहैं १६; सराहैं १७; सराहे १०; पांणीं। पांनी ८ १०; पांनीं १३ २०

२५;३ उजल। ऊजल १ ७ २१; बांनां। बांनौं ७; नीच। नींच १ ३ १० २०; सगाई। सगाइ १०; कीयें। धरयां २०; कीऐ ४; कीयैं १६ १७, कीये २१; जाई। जाइ १०

२५;४ अग्यांनीं। अग्यांनि ३; अग्यांन १०; अग्यांनी ८ २१; उजल। ऊंजल १; हूवा। हुवा १०; संसै। संसैं १६; सांसै ३ ४ २०; सांसें १०; सासै १; गांठि। गांठि ३ १० १७; पडी। +डी ४; परी ३ १०; मूवा। मुवा १०; मूंवा २१; मूंवा। ग्यांन का ऊरा स्वाग का पूरा पेट का टूटा डचंभ का सूरा २०; मूवा। स्वांग का पूरा ग्यांन का ऊरा पेट का टूटा डचंभ का सूरा १

२५;५ नांमदेव। नांमदे २०; कहै। कहैं २१; कहे १०; ए। ऐ ४ ८ १३ १६ २१; ये १ ३ १० २०; सरापी। सराफी २०; सारापी ८; पुंडरीनाथ। निरगुननांथ १०; निरगुननाथ ३; पंडरीनाथ २१; पुंडरीनाथ १६; पुडरीनाथ ८; प्रांणनाथ ७; प्राणनांथ २०; न। नहीं ७ २०; सुमिरैं। शुमिरैं १; सुंमिरैं १३ २१; सुमिरै ३; सुमिरे १०; जाणैं २०

२६;० सांई। सांई ४ ८; सांइ १०; मेरौ। मेरो ३ १०; साचि। सांचि ३; कूडै। कूडैं ८ २१; कूरै ३ १०; कपटि २०; कपटि। न २०; न। संतौ २०; जाई। जाइ ३ १०

२६;१ कोई। भावै ८ १३ १६ १७ २०; कोइ ३ १०; बहु। गावै २०; गावौ १६; गावो ८ १३ १७; वहु १; गावौ। भावै ८ १३ १६ १७ २०; गावै ३; गावो १ १० २१; कोई। नांचौ १३; नाचै २०; नाचौ ८ १७; नाचौं १६; कोइ १०; बहु। - ८ १३ १६ १७ २०; वहु १; नाचौ। - ८ १३ १६ १७ २०; नांचौ ३; नाचो १०; नांहीं। हिरदै १; नांही

२ अनेक सिंगार करै बहु कांमनि । नांहिन पीव मनि भावै भांमनि ॥
३ पतिब्रता पति ही कौं जांनैं । नांमदेव कहै हरि ताही की मांनैं ॥

२७

• रतन पारषू नीरा रे । मुलमां मंझे हीरा रे ॥
१ संष पारषू निरषि र जोई । बैरागर क्यौं षोटा होई ॥
२ कालकुष्ट बिष बांध्यौ गांठि । कहा भयौ जे न षायौ बांटि ॥
३ षायौ बिष कीन्हौं बिस्तार । नांमदेव भणैं हरि गरडदुवार ॥

२८

• कौंनैं कै कलंक रह्यौ रांम नांम लेत हीं ॥
पतित पांवन भये रांम कहत हीं ॥
१ रांम संगि नांमदेव जिनहु प्रतीति आई ॥

३ ८; नाहीं १०; हिरदै। नांही १; हिरदो १०; साचौ। सांचौ ३; साचो १०

२६;२ अनेक। अनिक १३ २१; सिंगार। स्यंग्यार १०; सिगार ३ ८; सींगार २०; करै। करे १०; बहु। जैसैं ३; जे ८ १३ २०; जेसे १०; कांमनि। कांमंणिं २१; कांमनिं १३ १६; कांमणीं ४; कांमीनी १०; नांहिन। नांहींन २१; नांहीं न ३; नाही न १०; पीय १६; पीय के १७; पीव ८; पीव कै १३ २०; पीव। पिंव १०; मनिं १३; मनि १७ २०; के ८ १६, मणि। भावे ८; नही २०; नहीं १३ १७; भावै। भावे १०; नही ८; नहीं १६

२६;३ पतिब्रता। पतिभरता ३ १०; पतिर्बा १६; पतिबरता २१; पतिवरता १; ही। हीं ४ ७ १७ २०; कौं। कूं १ ७ १७; को १०; जांनैं। जांणैं ४ २० २१; जांनै १३, जानि १०; कहै। कहे १०; ताही। हित २१; ताकी ४ १० १३ १६ १०; ताका २०; की। - ४ १३ १६ १७ २०; मांनैं। मांनै ३; मानि १०

२७;० रतन। रतंन २१; पारषू। पारिषू १६; नीरा। नियरा १०; नीयरा ३; रे। रै २०; मुलमां। मुलमा १३; मूलमा २०; मूलमां १०; मंझे। मंझै ४ १६ २०; मंझें १ ८; मझे २१; मांही ३ १०

२७;१ पारषू। पारिषू ४ १६; निरषि। निरिषि १०; त्रिषी १३; निरषी ८; र्नषि ४; र। - ८ १३ १६; म ३; मी १०; न १; जोई। जोइ १ १३ १६ २० २१; बैरागर। बेरागर १०; वैरागर १३; क्यौं। क्यूं ४ २० २१; क्यौ ३; क्यों १०; होई। होय १०; होइ १ ३ १३ २० २१

२७;२ कालकुष्ट। कालकुस्ट ४; कालकुश्ट २१; कालकस्ट १६; बिष। विष १ ४; बांध्यौ। बंध्यौ ८ १३; बांधौं २०; बांध्यो ३ १०; गांठि। गांठी २०; गाठि ३; भयौ। भयो ३ १०; जे। - ८ १३ १६; ज १; जै ३; न। - १०; नही ८; नहीं १६ २०; षायौ १३; षायौ। नहिं १३; षायो ३; बांटि। बाटि १३

२७;३ षायौ। षायो ३; षाया ८; कीन्हौं। कींन्हौं ४; कीन्हां ८; कीनौ २०; कीयो ३ १०; कार्नौ २१; बिस्तार। बिसतार १६ २०; विस्तार १; नांमदेव। नांमदे ८; भणैं। प्रनवे १०; प्रनवौं ३; कहै ८ १३ २०; गरडदुवार। गडददवार १०; गरडडुवार २१; गरडदवार ३; गरुडदुवार १

२८;० कौंनैं। कौंणैं ४; कौंन ३ ८; कौन २०; कोंन १०; कै। कैं १; के १०; रह्यौ। रह्यो ३ १०; रांम। राम ३; नांम। रांम १६; हीं। ही ८ १३; पतित। पतीत २०; पांवन। पावन २१; भये। भए ७ १६ २१; भऐ ४; कहत। कहंत १०; कहतं ४; हीं। ही ८ १३ २१

२८;१ रांम। राम ३; जिनहु। जिंनहुं १३; जिनहूं ८; जंनकौं २० २१; जनकौं ३; जनको १०; प्रतीति। प्रतीती

एकादसी ब्रत करै काहे कौं तीरथ जाई ॥
२ भणत नांमदेव सुम्रित सुक्रित पाई ॥
रांम कहत जन को को न मुकति जाई ॥

• कउन को कलंकु रहिओ राम नामु लेत ही ।
पतित पवित भए रामु कहत ही ॥ रहाउ ॥
१ राम संगि नामदेव जनकउ प्रतगिआ आई ।
एकादसी ब्रतु रहै काहे कउ तीरथ जांई ॥
२ भनति नामदेउ सुकृत सुमति भए ।
गुरमति राम कहि को को न बैकुंठि गए ॥

२६

• रांम नांम नरहरि श्री बनवारी । सेइये निरंतर चरन मुरारी ॥
१ गुर कौ सबद बैकुंठ निसरनी । हिरदै प्रियाग प्रेम रस बहनी ॥
२ जा कारनि त्रिभुवन फिरि आये । सो निधांन घट भीतरि पाये ॥
३ नांमदेव कहै कहूं आइये न जाइये । अपनौं रांम घरि बैठैं हीं गाइये ॥

२०; परतीति ७; आई। आइ १० २० २१; पाई ८; एकादसी। ऐकादशी ३; ऐकाद्सी १ ४ ८ १३; येकादशी १०; येकादसी २०; ब्रत। बर्त १६; करै। कहरे ३; करें १०; काहे। काहें १०; कौं। कूं १ ४ ७ २० २१; कों १०; तीरथ। तिरथ १०; तीरथि ८ १३; जाई। जाहीं ३; जाइ १०

२८;२ भणत। भ+त ४; भणंत २१; भनत ३ १०; सुम्रित। शुमति १; सुम्रिति ४; सुमिर्त १६; सुमृत ३ ७ ८; सम्रंत १०; सुक्रित। शुक्रित १; सुक्रिति ४; सुक्रत ३ १०; सुकृत ७ ८; पाई। पाइ १०; रांम। राम ३; कहत। कहेत २१; जन। - ३ ८ १० १३ २०; जंन ४ २१; मुकति। मुक्ति ७ २१; मुकित ८: मूकति २०; बेकुंठ १; बेकूं+ ४; बैकूंठि १३; रामं १०; राम मैं ३; जाई। समाई ३; समाइ १०; जाई ४

२६;• बनवारी। बंनवारी २१; बनबारी १६; बनवारि ३; सेइये। सेविऐ ८; सेवियै १६; सेविये १३; सेईऐ ४; सेईये २०; सेइए २१; निरतर। निरंजंन १०; निरंजन ३ ७; निरंतरि २०; निरंर्त ८; चरन। चरंण ४ २१; चरण २०; मुरारी। मुरारि ३

२६;१ गुर। गुरु १ १३; कौ। को १० २०; का ८; सबद। ग्यांन ८ २०; सबद सबद २१: बैकुंठ। बैकुंठि १३; बैकुठ ८ १६; बैकूठ ३ २१; बेकु १०; निसरनी। निसरंणी २१; निसरणीं १ ४ २०; निसरनी १३; नीसरणी ८; हिरदै। ह्रिदे ७; हृदे ३ १०; प्रियाग। पिराग ८ १६; प्रीयाग ४ ७ २०; प्रयाग १०; प्राग १३ २१; रस। - ८; बहनी। बेंणी २०; बहंणी २१; बहनीं ७; बरणीं ४; बांणी ८; बांणीं १३ १६; वहणीं १

२६;२ कारनि। कार्नि ७; कारंणिं १३; कारंणि ४ २१; कारणि २०; त्रिभुवन। त्रिभुवंन १ १३; त्रिभुवण २१; त्रिभवन ८ २०; फिरि। भ्रमि ३ १०; आये। आए ७ १६ २१; आऐ ४; आयो ३ १०; सो। सोई ३; सोइ १०; निधांन। निध+ ४; रांम १०; राम ३; भीतरि। भींतरि १ ३ ४ २१; भीतरी १०; पाये। पाए ७ १६; पाऐ ४; पायो ३ १०

२६;३ नांमदेव। नामदेव ३; कहै। कहे १०; कहूं। कहु १०; कहुं २१; कहौं ३; आइये। अईए ४; आईये २०; आइए ७ २१; आइऐ २ १३; आइयै १६; जाइये। जाईऐ ४; जाईये २०; जाइए ७ २१; जाइऐ ३; जाइयै १६;

३०

• रांम जुहारि न और जुहारूं । जीवनि जाइ जनम कत हारूं ॥
१ आंन देव सौं दीन न भाषूं । रांम रसांइन रसनां चाषूं ॥
२ थावर जंगम कीट पतंगा । सति रांम सबहिन कै संगा ॥
३ भणत नांमदेव जीवनि रांमां । आंन देव फोकट बेकांमां ॥

३१

• जा दिन भगता आईला । चारचौं मुकती पाईला ॥
१ दरसन धोषा भागीला । कोई आदू सुक्रित जागीला ॥
२ सनमुष दरसन देषीला । तब जनम सुफल करि लेषीला ॥
३ बैस्नौं हिरदै समाईला । जन नांमदेव आंनंद गाईला ॥

३२

• संत सौं लेणां संत सौं देणां । संत संगति मिलि दूतर तिरणां ॥

अपनौं। अ+नूं ४; अपने ३; अपनैं १३; अपने १०; आपनौं २०: घरि। घट ३ १०; बैठें। भीतरि ३ १०; बैठे ४: बैठा ८ २०; बैठां ७ २१; हीं। - ३ ७ ८ १० १३ १६; गाइये। पाईये २०; गाईऐ ४; गाईये ८; गाइए ७ २१; गाइऐ ३; गाइयै १६

३०;० जुहारूं। जुहारौ ७; जुहारौं ८ १६ १७; जीवनि। जीवन १३ २०; जाइ। जाई ४ २०; जनम। जंनम २१: जन्म १६; हारूं। हारौं ८ १३ १६ १७

३०;१ आंन। आन २१; सौं। स्यूं ४ २० २१: स्यौं १; सूं ७; न। नहीं २०; भाषूं। भाषौं ८ १३ १६ १७; रसांइन। + ४; रसांईन २०; रसांइंण १३; रसांइंन १; रसांइण ८; रसनां। +ना ४; रसना १६; चाषूं। चाषौं ८ १३ १६

३०;२ जंगम। जंगंम २०; पतंगा। पंतंगा २१; सति। सत्य १ ४; सबहिन। सबहि+ ४; सबहि हिन ८; सबहीन १३; कै। कैं २०; के ७ ८ १७; संगा। + ४

३०;३ भणत। भंणत २१; भणंत १३; नांमदेव २०; नांमदेव। कहै मेरे २०; जीवनि। जीवनिं १३; रांमां। रांमा २१

३१;० दिन। दिनि १६; चारचौं। चारचूं ७ १३ १७; चारचों २०; चारी ८; च्यारचौं ४; मुकती। मुक्ती १३ १७; मुक्ति १; मुकति २०

३१;१ दरसन। दर्सन ७; दरसंन १३; धोषा। धौषा २०; भागीला। भागेला २०; कोई। कोइ २०; सुक्रित। शुक्रित १; सुकृत ४ ७ १७; सूक्रि २०; जागीला। जागेला २०

३१;२ सनमुष। संनमुंष १३; संनमुष ४ ७; सनमूष २०; दरसन। दर्शन ७; दरसंन ४; दरसण २०; देषीला। देषिला ४; तब। तौ ४; जनम। जन्म १३; जन्मं १; सुफल। शुफल १; लेषीला। लेषील+ ४

३१;३ बैस्नौं। बैस्नौ ४; बैश्नैं ८; बैश्नौं ७ १७; बैसनौं १३ १६; वैस्नौं १; हिरदै। रिदै १ ७; समाईला। संमांईला १३; समाइला २०; आंनंद। आंनद ८; मंगल १; गाईला। गाईल २०; गाईल+ ४

३२;० संत। सत ७; सौं। सूं १ ७; लेणां। लीणां १६; सौं। सूं १ ७; सौ ८; देणां। दीणां १६

१ संत की छाया संत की माया । संत संगति मिलि गोबिंद पाया ॥
२ असंत संगति नांमां कबहूं न जाई । संत संगति मैं रह्या समाई ॥

३३

० परहरि धंधाकार सबैला । तेरी च्यंता रांम करैला ॥
१ नाराइण माता नाराइण पिता । बैस्नौं जन परिवार सहेता ॥
२ केसौ कै बहु पूत भयेला । तामैं नांमदेव एक तू दैला ॥

३४

० माई तूं मेरे बाप तूं । कटूंबी मंझा बीठला ॥
१ हरि है हंमची नांव री । हरी उतारै पैली तिरी ॥
२ साध संगति मिलि षेईचा र । केसौ नांमदेव चा दातार ॥

३५

० माइ गोब्यंदा बाप गोब्यंदा । जाति पांति गुरदेव गोब्यंदा ॥
१ गोब्यंद ग्यांन गोब्यंद ध्यांन । सदा अनंदी राजा रांम ॥

३२;१ गोबिंद। मंगल १९; गोबिद ८; वैकुंठ १; पाया। गाया ८ १९

३२;२ नांमां। नांमौं १; नांमदेव १२; कबहूं। नेडै ७; रह्या। रह्यौ १; समाई। संमाइ १२

३३;० धंधाकार। धंधकार ४ १२; सबैला। सबै+ ४. तेरी। मेरी १; तेरि ४; च्यंता। चिंता १२ २०; चिता ८

३३;१ नाराइण। नारांईण ४; नांरायण १२; नारांयन १; नाराईण २०; नाराइंण २१; नाराइण। नांरांय्यण १२; नांरांइंण २१; नांरांइंन १९; नारांयण ४; नारांयन १; नाराईण २०; बैस्नौं। +स्नौं ४; बै+ २१; बैश्नौं ८ १२; बैसनौं १९ २०; जन। जंन १२ २१; परिवार। परिबार १९

३३;२ केसौ। केंसो २०; बहु। बहू २०; भयेला। भऐला ४ १२; भएला १९ २१; तामैं। तामै ४ २०; एक। ऐक १ ४ ८ १२; येक २०; तू। तु ८ १२ २१; तुं ४; तूं १९; दैला। दैंला २१

३४;० माई। मा+ ४; माइ १ ७ १२ १९; तूं। तुं २०; तू १; मेरे। - २१; मंझा २०; मेरै ४; तूं। तुं २०; तू १; कटूंबी। कडूंबी ७; कडूवी १; कुटंबी ८ १९ २१; बीठला। बीठुला ४ २१

३४;१ है। - ८ २०; हंमची। अम्हंची १२; मची २१; हंमाची १; हमची १९; नांव। नाव ८; री। + ४; हरी। हरि ८ २० २१; उतारै। ऊतारै २०; तिरी। तीरी २०; तरी ४ २१

३४;२ षेई। षेलिचा २०; षेइ ८; चार। - २०; चा ४ २१; केसौ। केसौं २१; नांमदेव। +मा ४; चा। चौ १ ८ २१; दातार। दार १९

३५;० माइ। माई ४ ८ २०; गोब्यंदा। गोबिंदि ७; गोबिंदा १२; गोब्यंदा। गोबिंदा ७ १२; जाति। जांति १९; पांति। पां+ ४; गोब्यंदा। गोबिंदा ७ १२; गोब्यादा ८

३५;१ गोब्यंद। गोबिंद ७ १२; गोबिद ८; गोब्यंद। गोबिंद ७ १२; गोबिद ८; अनंदी। अंनंदी २१; अनदी ८; आनंदी ७; राजा। रा+ ४; रांम। + ४

२ गोब्यंद गावै गोब्यंद नाचै । गोब्यंद भेष सदा न्रिति काछै ॥
३ गोब्यंद पाती गोब्यंद पूजा । नामौं भणैं मेरे देव न दूजा ॥

३६

• हिरदै माला हिरदै गोपाला । हिरदै सिष्टि कौ दीनदयाला ॥
१ हिरदै मांहीं रंग हिरदै छीपा । हिरदै रैंणीं पांणीं नींका ॥
२ हिरदै दीपक घरि उजियाला । षूटि किवार तूटि गयौ ताला ॥
३ हिरदै रंग रोम नहीं जाति । रंगि रे नांमां हरि की भांति ॥

३७

• अब न बिसारूं रांम संभारूं । जौ र बिसारूं तौ सब हारूं ॥
१ तन मन हरि परि छिन छिन वारूं । घडी महूरत पल नहीं टारूं ॥
२ सुमिरन स्वासा भरि भरि पीऊं । रंक रांम गुड षाइ र जीऊं ॥
३ आरौ मांडि रांम रटि लैहूं । जौ र बिसारूं तौ रोइ दैहूं ॥

३५;२ गोब्यंद। + ४; गोबिंद ७ १३; गोबिद ८; गावै। +बै ४; गोब्यंद। गोबिंद ७ १३; गोबिद ८; नाचै। नांचै ४ ७ १३; गोब्यंद। गोबिंद ४ ७ १३; गोबिद ८; भेष। भष २०; न्रिति। नित ८ २१; निती ४; निरति ७; नृति १६

३५;३ गोब्यंद। गौबिंद ७ १३; गोबिद ८; पाती। + ४; गोब्यंद। गोबिंद ७ १३; गोबिद ४ ८; पूजा। देवा २०; नामौं। नांम ८; नांमौं १ ४; नांमदेव १३ २० २१; नांमां १६; मेरे। मेरै ७ २०

३६;० हिरदै। हृदै २१; हिरदै। हृदै २१; गोपाला। गोपा। ४; सिष्टि। सिस्टि ४ १६; ष्टि २०

३६;१ हिरदै। हृदै २१; मांहीं। मंही १; मैं ८ १३; महीं २१; मांहि १६; माही २०; रंग। रंगि १३; रग ८; हिरदै। हिरदै महीं १; हृदै २१; छीपा। छींपा १; छीपां १३; हिरदै। हृदै २१; रैंणीं। पांणीं २०; रैंणी ८; पांणीं। पांणी ८; रैंणीं २०; नींका। नीका ८ २१

३६;२ हिरदै। +दै ४; ह्रिदै १३; हृदै २१; घरि। घटि ८ १३ १६ २०; षूटि। पूटि २०; फूटि १३; किवार। कीवाड २०; तूटि। तूंटि १६; तूटी २०; गयौ। गए २१; गये १ ४; गया २०; ताला। ता+ ४

३६;३ हिरदै। हृदै २१; रोम। रोमि ४; नहीं। नंही ४; नहिं १३; नहि १; नही ८ २१; जाति। जति ८; जांति २१; भांति। भांती ८

३७;० बिसारूं। बिसारौं ८ १३ १६; रांम। + ४; संभारूं। संभारौं ८ १३; सभारौं १६; जौ। जे १३; रांम ८; र। - ८; बिसारूं। बिसारौ ८ १६; बिसारौं १३; बिसारं २१; सब। अब १६; हारूं। हारौ १६; हारौं ८; हारं २१

३७;१ तन। तंन २१; मन। मंन २१; परि। प+ ४; छिन। छिंन १३ २१; छिन। छिंन १३ २१; वारूं। वारौ १६; वारौं ८ १३; घडी। घरी ८ १३; महूरत। महूर्त १६; महरत ८; नहीं। नहिं १३; नहि १; नही ८; टारूं। टारौं ८ १३ १६

३७;२ सुमिरन। शुमिरंन १; सुंमिंरन १३; सुंमिरंण २१; सुमिरंन ४; सुमिरण २०; स्वासा। सांसा २०; पीऊं। पीउं ४ १३ २०; पीवौं ८; रंक। रांक २०; षाइ। षाई ४; जीऊं। जीउं ८ १३ २०

३७;३ आरौ। + ४; रंक रांम-२१; मांडि। माडि ४; गुड २१; लैहूं। लैहौं ८ १३ १६; जौ। जे ८ १३; र। रे २०;

४ नांमदेव कहै और आस न करिहूं । रांम नांम धन लाग्यौ मरिहूं ॥

३८

० रांम राइ उलगूं और न जाचूं । सरीर अनंत जाउ भलैं जाउ ॥
१ जोग जुगति कछू मुकति न भाषूं । हरि नांव हरि नांव हिरदै राषूं ॥
२ रांम नांम नांमदेव अनहद आछै । भगति प्रेम रस गावै नाचै ॥

३९

० बीहूं बीहूं तेरी सबल माया । आगैं इणैं अनेक भरमाया ॥
१ माया कै अंतरि ब्रह्म न दीसै । ब्रह्म कै अंतरि माया न दीसै ॥
२ भणत नांमदेव आप बिधांनां । दहुं घोडां न चढाइ हो कांन्हां ॥

४०

० बाजी रची बाप बाजी रची । मैं बलि ताकी जिनि र बची ॥
१ बाजी जांमण बाजी मरनां । बाजी लागि रह्यौ रे मनां ॥

बिसारुं। बिसारै १२; बिसारौ १९; बिसारौं ८; रोइ। रोई ४; देहूं। देहौं ८ १२ १९

३७;४ नांमदेव। नांमो २०; आस। आंस २१; करिहूं। करिहौं ८ १९; धन। धंन २१; धुंनिं १२; लाग्यौ। लाग्यौ ही १ २० २१; लाग्यौ ही ४; मरिहूं। मरिहौं ८ १२ १९

३८;० राइ। राई ४; उलगूं। ओलगौं १९; उल+ ४; उलगौ ८; और। औंर ८; जाचूं। जा+ ४; जाचौं ८; जाच्यौं १९; सरीर। ++ ४; अनंत। अनत ७ ८ १९; भलैं। भले १; जाउ। जाउ जाउ १९

३८;१ जोग। ++ ४; कछू। कछु ७; कति ८; मुकति। - ८; भाषूं। भाषौं ८ १९; नांव। नांऊं ४; नांम १; नांव। नांऊं ४; नांम १; राषूं। रा+ ४; राषौं ८ १९

३८;२ रांम। ++ ४; नांम। नाम ८; आछै। छाजै ८; नाचै। + ४

३९;० बीहूं। बींहूं ७; बीहौं ८ १९; बीहूं। बींहूं ७; बीहुं ४; बीहौं ८ १९; आगैं। आगै १ ८ २०; इणैं। - ८; एणैं २१; ईणैं २०; ईणीं ४; इंनिं १२; इंणि १; इनि १९ १७; अनेक। अनिक १२; भरमाया। भ्रमांया १२; भ्रमांया २०; भ्रमाया ८ १७

३९;१ कै। कैं २०; के ४ १९ १७; ब्रह्म। प्रेम ८; ब्रहंम २०; न। प्रकासै ८; ब्रह्म। ब्रहंम २०; ब्रह्मं १२; कै। के १ १९ १७

३९;२ भणत। भंणत २१; भणंत १२; आप। आपा २१; बिधांनां। बंधांणां २०; दहुं। दुं+ ४; दुंहुं १; दहु १९ १७; दहूं २०; दहौं ८; घोडां। घोडे १७; घोडें ८ १९; घोडा २१; चढाइ। चढाई ४ १२ २०; हो। - २१; हौ २०

४०;० बाजी। दहौं ८; रची। घोडें ८; जिनि। जिंनि १२; र। रू ७; रु १९ २०; बची। बंची ७ १२ २०

४०;१ बाजी। बाजी १२; मरनां। मरण १; मरणां ८ २०; रह्यौ। रहै १; रहे १२; रह्यो ७; रह्या ८; मनां। मंन १

२ बाजी मन मैं सोचि बिचारी । आपैं सूत आपैं सुत्रधारी ॥
३ नांमदेव कहै मैं तेरी सरनां । मेटि हंमारै जांमण मरनां ॥

४१

• तूं न बिसारी तूं न बिसारी । मैं तूं बिसारयौ सु मोर अभागा ॥
१ अषिल भवनपति गरुडागांमीं । अंतकालि हरि अंतरजांमीं ॥
२ जांमण मरण बिसरजन पूजा । तुम सा देव अवर नहीं दूजा ॥
३ तूं जु बिसंभर मैं जन नांमां । संत जनन के पुरवन कांमां ॥

४२

• बाप मंझा समझि न परई । सांचौ ढारि अवर कछू भरई ॥
१ पांनी का चित्र पवन का थंभा । कौंन उपाइ रच्यौ आरंभा ॥
२ इहां का उपज्या इहां बिलांनां । बोलनहारा कहां समांनां ॥
३ कहै नरांइण सुनि जन नांमां । जहां सुरति तहां पुरवनकांमां ॥

४०;२ मैं। मे २०; बिचारी। बिचारि २०; सूत। सुरति ७ ८ १२ १९ २०; आपैं। आपे ८ १३; सुत्रधारी। सुधारी १२

४०;३ कहै। कहे ८; मैं। मे १९; तेरी। तेरे १; सरनां। मरनां १३; सरणां ७; मेटि। मेटी २०; हंमारै। षालि १; हंमारे २०; हमारे ७ १९; जांमण। जांमन अरु १; मरनां। मंरणा २०; मरणां ७ १३

४१;० बिसारी। बिसारि १९; बिसारी। बिसारि १९; बिसारयौ। बिसारयौं १३; सु। - १ ८ १२ २०; अभागा। अभाग १ १९

४१;१ भवनपति। भुवंनपति १३; भुवनपति ४ १९ २१; भवनपती २०; गरुडागांमीं। गरडाग्रांमी ४; गरडागांमीं १९ २१; गरूडागांमी १३; गरुडग्रांमीं १; गंरुडागांमी ८; सब घटि स्यांमी २०; अंतकालि। अंतिकालि १ २१; अंतकाल ८ १२ २०; अंतरजांमीं। अंतरजांमी ८

४१;२ तुम। तुंम १२ २०; तुम्ह ४ १९ २१; अवर। और १३; नहीं। नहि १; नही ८ २०

४१;३ तूं। तुम ४; जु। ज ८ १२ २०; जन। जंन १३; संत। सकल १ ४ २१; जनन। संत २१; संतनि १ ४; पुरवन। पुरवंन १; पुरवहु २१; पुरवान ८; पूरवंण ४; पूरवन २०

४२;० बाप। बाप र १; मंझा। मइया १; समझि। संमझि ८ २१; संमझ २०; न। - २१; परई। परहीं २०; परइ १०; सांचौ। संचौ २०; संचा १२ २१; सचा ८; सांचों १०; कछू। कुछ ४; कछु १ १९; कछूक २०; भरई। भरहीं २०; भरइ ८ १०

४२;१ पांनी। पांणी १९; पांणीं १ ४ १२ २० २१; पांनीं ३; पवन। पवंन २१; कौंन। कंवन १३; कूंण १ २०; कौंण २१; कोंन १०; कवन ८; उपाइ। उपाई ४ २१; उपाय २०; रच्यौ। रच्या १०

४२;२ इहां। ईहां ४ २१; उपज्या। उपज्य २०; उपना १०; उपनां ३; इहां। ईहां ४; यहां १३; इहा ३; इहां ही २१; बिलांनां। बिलांणां २१; बोलनहारा। बोंलनहारा १३; बोलणहारा २१; कहां। काहां २०; समांनां। संमांणां २१; संमांना २०; संमांनां १२

४२;३ कहै। -- ८ १२ १९ २०; कहे १०; नरांइण। नरायण १०; नांरांयण ४; नांरांइंण २१; नाराइण १; सुनि। शुणि १; सुणि २ ४ २१; जन। जंन २१; जहां। -- ८ १२ १९ २०; जहा ३; सुरति। शुरति १; तहां। तहा

४ जीवत रांम न भये प्रकासा । भणत नांमदेव मूवां कैसी आसा ॥

४३

• कैसैं तिरौं बहु कुटिल भरयौ । कलि के चिहन देषि नांहिन डरयौ ॥
१ कैसी सेवा कैसौ ध्यांन । जैसैं उजल बग उनमांन ॥
२ भाव भुजंग भये प्यौहारी । सुरति सिंचांणौं मति मंजारी ॥
३ नांमदेव भणैं बहु इहि गुणि बांधा । डांइंणि डयंभ सकल जग षाधा ॥

४४

• काल भै बापा सह्या न जाई । महा भै भीत जगत्र कौं षाई ॥
१ अनेक मुनेस्वर झूझैं जाइ । सुर नर थाके करत उपाइ ॥
२ कंपै पीर पैकंबर देव । रिषि कंपै चौरासी जेव ॥

३; पुरवनकांमां। पुरवंनंकांमां २१; पुरवंनकांमां १; पूरवनकांमां ३

४२;४ रांम। राम ३; न। - १०; भये। भ+ ४; भए १६ २१; भएं १३; भयौ १; भयो ३ १०; प्रकासा। परकासा १६; भणत। भंणत २१; भणंत १२ २०; भनत ३; मूवां। मूंवा १३; मूंवां १ ८; कैसी। केसी १०

४३;० कैसैं। नांथ केंसे १०; नाथ कैसैं कैं ३; देव कैसैं १; तिरौं। +त ४; तिरों १०; तिरत १ ७ १२ १७ २०; तिरूं २१; बहु। बहू २०; कुटिल। कूटिल २०; भरयौ। भरयां १०; चिहन। चिहंन ४ १२ २१; चहंन २०; देषि। देषें ३ २०; दषें १०; नांहिन। नांहिंन १३; नांहिनैं २१; नांही २०; डरयौ। डरयो ३; डरों १०

४३;१ कैसी। कैसी तेरी ३; केसी तेरी १०; कैसौ। कैसौ तेरो ३; कैसो मेरो १०; कैसा १ ४ ७ १६ २१; जैसैं। - १३; जेसों १०; उजल। ऊजल १ ४; बग। बुग ३; बग जैसौ १३; उनमांन। उंनमांन २१

४३;२ भये। भए १६; भयौ २१; प्यौहारी। पैहारी १७; पौहारी १६ २०; व्योहारी ३ १०; सुरति। सुर्ति ७; सुराति ८; सिंचांणौं। सिंचांणां ४; सिंचांनां ७; सिंचाणौं १३; सिंचाणौ मेरी २०; सिंचानौं मेरी ३; सिचांणौं ८ २१; सिचांणां १६ १७; सिचानो मेरी १०; मति। मंति ४; मुति ३; मत ८; मंजारी। मंजारि ४; मंझारी २१; मजारी १६

४३;३ नांमदेव। भनत ३ १०; भणैं। नांमदेव ३ १०; कहै ८; बहु। - ३ १०; इहि। ईहि ४ २१; इंहिं १३; इहिं १७; इन ३ १०; गुणि। गुंणिं १६ २१; गुनि ३; गुणी ४; गुन १०; बांधा। बंध्यौ ३; बांधां २१; बाधा १ ४ ७ ८ १७; बाध्यों १०; डांइंणि। डांईण २०; डांईणि ४; डांइंण १३; डांइणि ८; डांइनि ३ १६ १७; डांइण ७; डाइन १०; डयंभ। डिंभ ७ १० १३; डिंभ्य ३; डिभ १६; जग। ज+ ४; जुग ३ ८ १० २०; षाधा। +धा ४; षाधौ ३; षाधो १०

४४;० काल। +ल ४; बापा। बाप १२ १६ २०; सह्या। सह्ला १ २१; सह्यौ १६ २०; न। नहीं १६; जाई। जाइ ७ १७ २१; भीत। भीत सव १; जगत्र। जंत्र २१; जगत १ २०; कौं। कूं १ ४ ७ ८ २१; षाई। षाइ ७

४४;१ अनेक। अनिक १२ २१; मुनेस्वर। मुनींस्वर १३; मुनेसुर २० २१; मुनीसुर १७; झूझैं। उरझे २०; जुझैं २१; झूझै १ ४; जाइ। आइ २०; जाई ४ १३; सुर। स्वर १३; शुर १; सूर २०; उपाइ। +पाइ ८; उपाई ४ १३ २१

४४;२ कंपै। कंपैं १ १३; पैकंबर। पैंकंबर १६; पैंकबर २१; देव। देवा २०; रिषि। रिष २१; ऋषि १७; कंपै। कंपैं १३ १६ १७; कंपैं र १ २१; कंपं र ४; जेव। देव २१; देवा २०

३ चंद सूर धर पवन अकास । पांणीं कंपै अगनि गरास ॥
४ कंपै लोक लोकंतर षंड । ते भी कंपैं अस्थिर प्यंड ॥
५ अबिचल अभै नरांइण देव । नांमदेव प्रणवैं अलष अभेव ॥

४५

• सहजैं सहजैं सब गुंन जइला । भगवंत भगता ए थिर रहिला ॥
१ मुकति भयेला जाप धायेला । यूं सेवग स्वांमीं संगि रहेला ॥
२ अंम्रित सुधानिधि अनत न जाइला । पीवत प्रांन कदे न अघाइला ॥
३ रांम नांमां मिलि संगि रहेला । जब लग रस तब लग पीवैला ॥

४६

• कैसैं न मिलै रांम रूटा मोटां । चित न चलै कुचित मेरा षोटा ॥
१ बाइर मांटी बार लगीला । अैसै जै मन लागै बीठला ॥
२ नांमौ भणै मन मारगि लगीला । जैसै निसगत सूर ऊगीला ॥

४७

• कहा करूं जग देषत अंधा । तजि आनंद बिचारै धंधा ॥
१ पांहन आगैं देव कटीला । वाकौ प्रांण नहीं वाकी पूज रचीला ॥

४४;३ पवन। +न ४; पउन ७; पवंन १२; अकास। अकासा १६; आकास ४ २०; पांणीं। पांणी ८; पांनीं २१; कंपै। कं+ ८; कंपैं २१; अगनि। अग्नि ४ २१; अगनिं १२; गरास। ग्रास ४; गरासा १६

४४;४ कंपै। कंपैं १ ७ १७ २१; लोक। - १७; लौक २०; लोकंतर। लोकतर ८; षंड। +ड ४; कंपैं। कम्पैं २१; अस्थिर। मस्थीर २०; असथिर १६; प्यंड। पिंड १२; पिड ८

४४;५ नरांइण। नरांइंण १२ २१; नरांइन ७; नारांयणं ४; नारांइंन १; नारांइण १६ १७; देव। + ४; प्रणवैं। प्रनवैं १

४५;० सहजैं। सहजें १०; सहजैं। सहजें १०; गुंन। गुन २; जइला। जाईला २; जाइला १०; ए। - १०; ऐ २; ये १; थिर। थिरि २; रहिला। रह्वायला १०

४५;१ भयेला। भएला ७; धायेला। छायेला १०; यूं। ये १०; यौं ७; सेवग। सेवक ७; संगि। संग १; रहेला। रहैला २ ७

४५;२ अंम्रित। अमृत २; अम्रंत १०; सुधानिधि। श्रुधानिधि १; सुधातजि ७; अनत। अनंत १०; जाइला। जइला ७; पीवत। पींवत ७; प्रांन। प्रांण १; प्रांण रस ७; अघाइला। अंघाइला १०; उघइला ७

४५;३ नांमां। नांम १०; नामां २; रहेला। रहैला ७; पीवैला। पीवेला १०

४७;० करूं। करौं २; करों १०; जग। जुग १०; जुगु २; देषत। - १०; बिचारै। बिचारैं ७; बिचारे १०

४७;१ पांहन। पांहण १ ७; आगैं। आगै २; आगे १०; देव। जीव ७; कटीला। काटीला ७; वाकौ। वाकौं १

२ नरजीव आगैं सरजीव मारैं । देषत जनम आपनौ हारैं ॥
३ आंगणि देव पिछोकडि पूजा । पाहन पूजि भये नर दूजा ॥
४ नांमदेव कहै सुनौं रे धगडा । आतमदेव न पूजौ दगडा ॥

४८

० देवा तेरी भगति न मोपैं होइ जी ॥
जिहि सेवा साहिब भल मांनैं करि नहि आवै मोहि जी ॥
१ सुम्रित कथा होत नहीं मोपैं कथौं त होइ अभिमांन जी ॥
जोइ जोइ कथौं उलटि मोहि बांधै त्राहि त्राहि भगवांन जी ॥
२ जामैं सकल जीव की उतपति सकल जीव मैं आप जी ॥
माया मोह करि जगत भुलाया घटि घटि व्यापक बाप जी ॥
३ सो बैकुंठ कहौ धौं कैसा प्यंड परे जहां जाइये ॥
यहु परतीति मोहि नहीं आवै जीवत मुकति न पाइये ॥

५; बाको १०; प्रांण। पांण १ ७; पांन ५; कौंन १०; बाकी। बाकी १; पूज। पुजा १०; पूजा २
४७;२ नरजीव। -- ७; आगैं। अगैं ५; आगें १०; मारैं। मारै ५; मारे १०; देषत। -- ७; आपनौ। आपणौं १; आपने १०; हारैं। हारै ५; हारे १०
४७;३ आंगणि। अगनि १०; पाहन। पांहण १ ७; पूजि। पूजी १०; भये। भया ७
४७;४ नांमदेव। नामदेव ५; कहै। कहे १०; सुनौं। शुणौं १; सुणौं ७; सुणहुं ५; सुनहु १०; आतमदेव। आत्मदेव १ ५; पूजौ। पूज्यो ५; पूजो १०
४८;० भगति। भगंति ५; मोपैं। मोपै ८ १९; मोपें १०; होइ। होई २ ४ ७ २०; जिहि। जिंहिं १२; साहिब। साहीब २०; करि। करिहूं ४ ७ १९; करत २१; सो करि १; सो करिहूं २०; सो करत २ १०; नहि। न २ ४ ७ १० १९ २० २१; नहिं १२; नही ८; आवै। आवे १०; जांणैं ८; जांनैं १ ४ ७ १९ २०; जांनौं १२; मोहि। कोई ४ ७ १९; कोइ १ ८ १२ २०
४८;१ सुम्रित। सुमृति १; सुम्रिति १२; सुम्रिन ८; सुमृत १९; सुमृति ४; देवा सुमिरन २ १०; कथा। भजन २ १०; नहीं। नहिं १; नही २ ८ १०; मोपैं। मोपें १०; कथौं। कथु २०; कथूं १ ४ ७ २१; कथी १९; त। तौ २ ७ २०; तो १०; होइ। होई ४; अभिमांन। अभिमांनीं ५; अभीमांन ४; जोइ। जोई २ ४ ७ १२ १९; जोइ। जोई २ ७ १२ १९; जोई ४; कथौं। कथूं ४ ७ २० २१; कथों १०; करौं १; उलटि। सोई १; मोहि। मोही ४; बांधै। बंधै ८; बांधे १०; बांधौं १२
४८;२ जामैं। - २ १०; जामै २०; जीव। जीवनि २०; जीव जंत २ १०; की। तेरी २ १०; जीव। + ४; मैं। + ४; मै २०; मे १०; आप। ढीठला १०; दीठला ५; जी। - २ १०; भुलाया। भुलांनौं ५; भुलांना १२; भुलांनां १; भुलानों १०; भुलाये ४; भुलायौ ७ २१; भूलानौ २०; घटि। घट ४ ७ २१; अंतरजांमीं २ १०; तूं घटि १; घटि। घट ४ ७ २१; बिठला १०; बीठला ५; व्यापक। - २ १०; बाप। - २ १०; जी। - २ १०
४८;३ सो। देवा सो २ १०; बैकुंठ। बैकंठ ४; बैकूंठ २ १२ २०; बैकूठ २१; बेकुंठ १०; कहौ। कहौं १ ७ १२; कहो १०; काहौ २०; धौं। धू २१; धूं १ ४ ७; धौ १९; कैसा। केसा १०; प्यंड। पिंड २ १० १२; पिड ८; परे। परै १९; परें ४ ८ १२; परयां १; जहां। तहां २ ४ १०; जाइये। जाईये ४ २०; जाइए २१; जाइऐ १२; जाइवौ ८; यहु। यह १०; परतीति। प्रतीति १२; परतिति १०; परातीति २०; मोहि। मोही ४; होत १; नहीं। नहिं १२ २१; नहि १ १०; नही ८ २०; आवै। आवत २ १०; मोपै १; जीवत। जौ जीवत ४; मुकति। मुंकति १२; मुक्ति १;

४ मैं जन जीव ब्रह्म तूं माधौ बिन देषें दुष पाइये ॥
राषि समीप कहै जंन नांमौं संगि मिले गुन गाइये ॥

४९

० भगति आपि मोरे बाबुला । तेरी मुकति न मांगौं हरि बीठला ॥
१ भगति न आपै तौ तन आर्डौं । कोटि करै तौ भगति न छाडौं ॥
२ अनेक जनम भ्रमतौ फिरचौ । तुम्हारौ नांव ले ले उधरचौ ॥
३ नांमदेब कहै तू जीवनि मोरा । तूं सायर मैं मंछा तोरा ॥

५०

० संसार समदे तारि गोबिंदे । हूं तिरिही न जांनौं बापजी ॥
१ लोभ लहरि अति नीझर बरिषै । काया बूडै केसवा ॥

पाइये। पाईयि ४; पाइए २१; पाइ जी २०

४८;४ मैं। में १०; तूं। तुम ३ १०; तू १ ४; माधौ। माधो १०; देषें। देषैं ४ २१; देषे १६; देष्यां १; दरसन ३ १०; दुष। जीव १२; पाइये। पाईयि ४ ८; पाइऐ २१; पाइयै १६; पाइला १०; जाइऐ १२; समीप। संमींप २१; संमीप १२; समींप ३ ७; कहै। कहे १०; जंन। जन ३ ७ ८ १६; नांमौं। नांमो २०; नांमां ३ १० १६; नामां ८; संगि। संगी ४; मिले। मिल्या १; मिल्यां ८ १२ १६; मिलैं ४; मिलें ७ २०; गुन। गुंण ७ १६ २१; गुंन १ १० १२; गुण ४ ८ २०; गाइये। गाईयि ४ २०; गाइए २१; गाइऐ १२; गाइयै १६; गाइला १०

४९;० भगति। भक्ति १ १२; आपि। आप ८; मोरे। मेरे ३; मोरै ८; बाबुला। बाबला ३ १० २०; बावला १; तेरी। - २१; मुकति। मुंकति १२; मुक्ति १ १७ २०; मांगौं। मांगू २१; मांगूं १ ७; मांगो ३; मांगौं ४ १०; मागूं २०; हरि। हो १; बीठला। बिठुला १० १७; बीठुला ४ ७ २१; बीठूला २०

४९;१ भगति। तूं ३; तू १०; न। ही ३; व ही १०; आपै। आपे ८ १०; आपूं २१; तौ। मैं ३; मे १०; तन। - १०; तंन १२ २१; आर्डौं। आडूं १ ४ ७ २१; आडो १०; वाडूं २०; करै। करे १०; तौ। तो १०; भगति। भक्ति १ १२; छाडौं। छांडूं १; छाडूं ४ ७ २० २१; छाडों १०

४९;२ अनेक। अनिक १२; जनम। जंनम २० २१; भ्रमतौ। भ्रंमतौ १; भ्रमतो १०; भर्मतौ ४ ७ १६; फिरचौ। फिरचो १२; फिरूं १०; तुम्हारौ। तुंम्हारौ १२; तुम्हारो ३ १०; तेरौ १६ १७ २१; तूम्हारौ २०; नांव। नांम ४ १२ २०; ले। लै १ ८; ले। कै ३; के १०; लै १ ८; उधरचौ। उधरों १०; उधरयौ ४

४९;३ कहै। प्रनवै ३; प्रनवे १०; तू। - ३ १०; मैं १२; तूं १ ४ ७ ८ १६ १७ २० २१; जीवनि। जीवनिं १२; जीवला ३ १०; मोरा। तोरा ३ १०; तूं। तुम ३; तूंम १०; सायर। सांइर १; साय ७; साइर ३ १० १७ २१; मैं। में १०; मंछा। मंछला ३; मांछला १०; तोरा। - ३ १०

५०;० संसार। संसारि १०; समदे। समुदे २१; संमदि ४; संमदे ८ १२; समुदे २०; गोबिंदे। गोबिंदे ८ १०; गोव्यंदे ३ ४ २१; गोव्यदे २०; गोव्यंदे १ १६; हूं। मैं ३; मे १०; हौं ८ १६; तिरिही। - १०; तिरि १ ८ २०; तिरिहि १२; तिरिहीं ४ ७ १६; न। नहि १; नहीं १० २०; नांही ८; जांनौं। जांणौं २०; जांनूं ७ २१; जांनो १०; बापजी। केसवे ३ १०; केसवा १ २० २१

५०;१ लहरि। लैहरि २०; नीझर। निझर १०; बरिषै। बरिषैं ४ १२; बरषैं ३; बरषे १०; बूडै। डूबै ७; बूडै ८; बूडी २१; केसवा। केसवे ३ १०

२ आनि दे भेला षेइ न जांनौं । पार दे पार दे बीठला ॥
३ नांमौं कहै मैं सेवग तेरा । बांह दे बांह दे बीठला ॥

१ लोभ लहरि अति नीझर बाजै । काइणा डूबै केसवा ॥
२संसारु समुदे तारि गोबिंदे । तारि लै बाप बीठला ॥ रहाउ ॥
१ अनिल बेडा हउ खेवि न साकउ । तेरा पारु न पाइआ बीठुला ॥
३ होहु दइआलु सतिगुरु मेलि तू । मोकउ पारि उतारे केसवा ॥
४ नामा कहै हउ तरि भी न जानउ । मोकउ बाह देहि बाह देहि बीठुला ॥

५१

• तुझ बिन क्यौं जीऊं रे तूं मंझा प्रांण अधार ॥
१ सार तुम्हारा नांव है फूटा सब संसार ॥
मनसा बाचा क्रमनां कलि केवल नांव अधार ॥
२ दुनियां मैं दोजग घणां दारण दुष अधिक अपार ॥
चरण कंवल की मौज मैं मोहि राषौ सिरजनहार ॥

५०;२ आनि। आनं १२; आंनि १ ७ १९; आंन ४; आंनं ३ २१; आनं १० २०; दे। द ३ ४ १० १२ २० २१; ले १९; भेला। भेरा १९ २०; षेइ। षेवि ८ १९; षेई ४; जांनौं। जांनैं जानौं ८; जांनूं १ ७; जानों १०; दे। दै ३; दे। दै ३; बीठला। माधवै ३; माधवे १०; बीठुला १ २१; बीठूला २०

५०;३ नांमौं। म्नांमौं ४; नांमदेव ३ १० १२; नांमां १९; नामदेव ८; कहै। कहैं १२; कहे १०; मैं। मै २१; मे १०; सेवग। तिरिहि न ३ १०; तेरा। जांनौं ३; जांनो १०; तौरा २०; तोरा ४ ७; बांह। बाह ३; दे। दै ३; बांह। बाह ३ २१; दे। दै ३; बीठला। बिठले १०; केसवा ४; बीठुला १; बीठले ३; बाबुला ७ १९ २१; बाबूला २०; बाबला ८; बाबल मेरा १२

५१;० तुझ। नांउ २०; तुझै ४ २१; बिन। बिंन १२; क्यौं। क्युं १०; क्यूं ७ २० २१; क्यों ३ ४; जीऊं। जीउं २०; जीवुं १०; जीवै ८; रहौं १२; रे। - ३ १० १२; रे तुझै बिन क्यूं जीऊं ४; रे तुझै बिन क्यूं जीवौं २१; रे तुझ बिन क्यूं जीऊं ७; रे तुझ बिन क्यौं जीऊं १ १९; तूं। बाला तू ३ १०; मंझा। मेरे १०; मेरौ ३; मझा ७ ८; प्रांण। प्रांन ३ १२ १९; प्राण ४ १०; प्रान ८; अधार। अधार नांउं बिन क्यौं जीऊं १; अधार तुझै बिन क्यूं जीऊं ७; अधार तुझ बिन क्यौं जीऊं १९; आधार १०

५१;१ सार। सरे १०; सारै ३; सारा १ ४ ७ २१; तुम्हारा। तुंम्हारा १२; तेरा ४ ७ २१; तूंम्हांरा २०; नांव। नांम १ ७ २१; है। ह्वो १०; फूटा। फूटचा २०; फूटौ ३; फूटो १०; सब। हुं १०; हू ३; मनसा। मंनसा २१; क्रमनां। क्रंमना २०; क्रंमनां १ १२; कर्मणां २१; कर्मना १०; करामणां ४; केवल। केसव १०; नांव। नांम ४ १९; नांउं १; नांवं २०

५१;२ दुनियां। दुनिया १०; दुनीयां १९; मैं। मै ३ २१; में १०; दोजग। +जग ४; दोजिग १२; घणां। घंणां १२ २१; घनां ७; दारण। दुष ३ १०; दारूण ८; दारुंण २१; दारुण १२; दुष। दारन ३ १०; चरण। चरंण ४ २१; चरन ३ १० १२ १९; कंवल। कमल १०; कव+ ४; कवल ३ ७ १९; की। - ४; मौज। मोज १०; मैं। में १०; मोहि। महि २०; राषौ। राषिलै ३; राषिले १०; राषहु १ ७; सिरजनहार। सिरजंनहार १२ २१

३ मो तो बिचि पडदा किसा लोभ बडाई कांम ॥
कोइ एक हरिजन ऊबरै जिनि सुमिरचौ निहचल रांम ॥
४ लोक बेद कै संगि बह्यग सलिल मोह की धार ॥
जन नांमदेव कौ स्वांमीं बीठला मोहि षेइ उतारौ पार ॥

५२

• बंदे की बंदि छोडि बनवारी ॥
असरनसरन रांम कहे बिन आइ परै जमधारी ॥
१ केई बांधे जोग जगि करि केई तीरथ दांनां ॥
केई बांधे नेमां बरतां तेरे हाथि नाथ भगवांनां ॥
२ रांम देव तेरी दासी माया नाटी कापट कींन्हां ॥
थावर जंगम जीति लीया है आपा पर नहीं चींन्हां ॥
३ नांमदेव भणैं मैं तुम्ह थैं छूटूं जे तुम्ह छुडावो गोपाल जी ॥
तुम्ह बिनां मेरे गाहक नांहीं दीनांनाथ दयाल जी ॥

५१;३ मो। हम ३ १०; तो १ ४; तो। मो १ ४; तुम ३ १०; तौ २१; पडदा। पडदौ २०; परदौ ३; परदो १०; किसा। येहो १०; इहै ३ २०; लोभ। बाला लोभ ३ १०; बडाई। बडाइ १० २०; कोइ। को ७ १६; कोई १ ४ ८ १३ २१; एक। - ८; ऐक १ ४ २१; येक ३ १० १३ २०; हरिजन। + ४; हंरिजंन १३ २० २१; ऊबरै। ऊबरे १ ४; उबरै २० २१; उबरे ८ १३; उबरया ३ १०; जिनि। जिंनिं १३; जिनिं २१, जिहि १०; सुमिरचौ। शुमिरचौ १; सुमिरचौ १३; सुंमरचौ २१; सुमिरचा १०; सुमरचा ३ ८ १६; निहचल। निहिचल ४ १०; निहंचल १३ २० २१; केवल ८; रांम। रांमां २०

५१;४ कै। के १०; बह्यग। बह्यौ १; बह्यो ३; बहो १०; सलिल। बाला सलिल ३ १०; धार। धारा २०; जन। ३ ८ १० १३ २०; जंन ४ २१; नांमदेव। नांमदे २१; नांमां ७; कौ। नौ १६; ना १ ७; को १०; का ८; स्वांमीं। स्यांमी २०; स्वांमी १ ४ ८; स्वामी ७; साहिब ३; बीठला। बिठलो १०; बीठुला ४; बीठलौ ३ २१; षेइ। षेवि १६; षेई ४ २१; उतारौ। उतारै २१; उतारो १०; पार। पार हो ८

५२;• बनवारी। बंनवारी २०; असरनसरन। असरंणसरंण २१; असरंणसरण ४; असरणसरण १ ७; असरनसरना ८; कहे। कहें १३; बिन। बिंन १३; आइ। आय ४; परै। पडै ७ १६; पडे २१; परे २०; परी १; जमधारी। जंमधारि ४; जंमधारी १३ २१

५२;१ केई। केइ २०; कोई ७; बांधे। बंधे ८ १३; बाधे २१; जगि। जिगि १; जपि १३; जप ४ ७ ८ २१; जग १६; केई। केई तप १; तीरथ। तीर्थ ७ १३; बांधे। बंधे ८ १३; नेमां। नेम १ ४ ८ १३; बरतां। ब्रता २०; ब्रत करि ८ १३; बरता ७; हाथि। हाथ ४; नाथ। नांथ २१; भगवांनां। भगवांन जी ८

५२;२ दासी। माया १ २०; माया। दासी १ २०; नाटी। नटी १; नाटि २०; नाटिक ४; कापट। कपट ४ ८ १६; कींन्हां। कीन्हां ८ १३; जीति। भूलि १३; वाधि १; लीया। लिया ७; पडे १३; लीये ८; है। हैं १ ४ ८ १३; आपा। आप १; पर। आप १; नहीं। नहि १; नही ८ २१; चींन्हां। चीन्हां ८ १६

५२;३ नांमदेव। नांमौं १; नांमदेव देव २१; भणैं। भणै १६; कहे २०; कहैं १; मैं। मै २०; हूं १; तुम्ह। तुंम १३; तुम ८ २०; थैं। तैं ८ १३ २०; छूटूं। छूंतूं २१; छूटौं ७ ८ १३ १६; छूमटूं २०; जे। जै १; तुम्ह। तुंम १३; तुम ८; तू २०; छुडावो। छुडावौ १६; छुडावहु १; छूडावौ २०; छूडावो २१; गोपाल। गुपाल १; तुम्ह। तुंम्ह ४ १३; तुम ८ २०; मेरे। मेरैं २०; नांहीं। नांही ८; दीनांनाथ। दींनानाथ १३; दीनांनांथ २१

५३

• देवा मेरी हीन जाती हो । काहू पैं सही न जाती हो ॥
१ मैं नहीं मैं नहीं मैं नहीं माधौ तूं है मैं नहीं हो ॥
तूं एक अनेक ह्वै बिस्तरयौ मेरी चरम नसाई हो ॥
२ जैसें नदियां समदि समांनीं धरनी बहंती हो ॥
तुम्हारी क्रिपा थैं नीच ऊंच भये तूं काल की काती हो ॥
३ नांमौं कहै मेरे देवी न देवा संग न साथी मीतुला ॥
तुम्हारी सरनि मैं भाजि दुरयौ हूं बंदि छोडि बाबा बीठुला ॥

५४

• हरि नांव गाजै हरि नांव राजै । हरि कौ नांव लेतां काई लाजै ॥
१ हरि मेरे मात पिता गुरदेवा । अपनें रांम की करिहौं सेवा ॥

५३;० मेरी। मेरि ४; हीन। हींन ३ ७ १२ १६ २१; जाती। जाति ३ १०; हो। हौ ३; काहू। काहु १०; काहूं १६; पैं। पें १०; जाती। जाति १०

५३;१ मैं। मे १०; नहीं। नहि १; नही ३ ८; मैं। में १०; नहीं। नहि १; नही ४ ८ १२; मैं। - ८ १२; तू १०; तूं १ ३; नहीं। - ८ १२; हे १ ३; हे १०; माधौ। मांधौ २१; तूं। तु १०; तू ३ ४ ८ १२; है। हे १०; ही ८; मैं। में १०; नहीं। नहिं ३; नही ७; नांही ८ १२; नांहीं १; हो। रे ८; तूं। येक ३ १०; तू ८; एक। स्यौं ३; ऐक ४ ८ १२; सु १०; अनेक। अनिक १२ २१; येक ३ १०; ह्वै। अनेक ३ १०; बिस्तरयौ। बिस्तरया ८ १६; बिसतरयौ ४; विस्तरयौ १; माधौ ३; माधो १०; मेरी। चरन ३ १०; चरम। मन ३ १०; चर्म १२; चरंम २१; नसाई। नसांई :३; नसांई १; नसाइ ८; जाती ३ १०

५३;२ जैसें। ज्यूं १०; ज्यूौं ३; जैसे १; नदियां। नंदिया १२; दरिया मैं ३; दरिया में १०; समदि। नदी ३ १०; संमदि ८ १२; समंदि ४ ७ १६; समंद २१; समांनीं। संमांनीं १२ २१; समांणी ४; समांनी ८ १०; धरनी। धरंणी ४; धरनिं १२; धरणि ७; धरनि १ ३ १६ २१; बहंती। बहति १०; बहती ८ १६; तुम्हारी। तुंम्हारी १२; क्रिपा। क्रपा १२; कृपा ४ १०; थैं। करि ३; थें १ १०; तैं ८ १२; नीच। उंच १२; नींच ७ १० १६; ऊंच। ऊच १०; उंच ३ ४ ८; नींच १२; भये। भए २१; भऐ १६; भई १२; भयो ३ १०; तूं। - ३ १०; तू ८; काल। कर्मनि ३ १०; का+ ४; की। + ४; - ३ १०; काती। + ४; कांती १ १० २१; काति ३; हो। + ४

५३;३ नांमौं। +मौं ४; नांमदेव ३ १० १२; नांमां ८ १६; कहै। कहे १०; मेरे। मेरै ३; देवी। देई ३; देइ १०; संग। सगो ३; सगो १०; साथी। सोई ३; सोइ १०; मीतुला। +तुला ४; म्यंतुला १; मितला १०; मींतुला २१; मींतला ३ १२; तुम्हारी।

सरनि ३ १०; तुंम्हारी १२ २१; सरनि। सरंणिं ४; सरनिं १२; सरणि ७; तुम्हारै ३; तुम्हारे १०; मैं। - ३ १० २१; हूं १; हौं १२; भाजि। भाई ४ २१; दुरयौ। डरयो १०; परयौ ४; दुरे २१; दुरयौं १; हूं। हुं १०; हैं २१; हौं ३ ८ १६; बंदि। बंदी १०; छोडि। छोडी १०; बीठुला। मींठुला २१; बीठला ३ ८ १० १२

५४;० नांव। नांम १; नाव १०; गाजै। गाजे १०; नांव। नांम १; राजै। गाजै ३; गाजे १०; कौ। - ८; को १०; नांव। नांम १ ४; लेतां। लेता ३ ८ १०; काई। कोइ १०; कांई ४ १२; कांई नर १६; कांइ ७ ८; कांइं १ ३; लाजै। लाजे रे १ ४ ७; लाजे १०

५४;१ मेरे। मेरै ४; मेरो ३ १०; मात। माता ७; अपनें। अपनैं ३ ४; अपने १० १२ १६; रांम। राम ३; करिहौं।

२ हरि नांमैं निज कंवला दासी । हरि नांमैं संकर अबिनासी ॥
३ हरि नांमैं ध्रू निहचल करिया । हरि नांमैं प्रहिलाद उधरिया ॥
४ हरि मेरे जीवन मरन का साथी । हरि जलमगन उधरचौ हाथी ॥
५ हरि मेरे संगि सदा सुष दाता । हरि नांमैं नांमदेव रंगि राता ॥

५५

० इतना कहत तोहि कहा लागत । रांम नांम लै सोवत जागत ॥
१ ध्रू प्रहिलाद इहीं गुनि तारे । रांम नांम अषिर हिरदै बिचारे ॥
२ रांम नांम सनकादिक राता । रांम नांम त्रिभैपद दाता ॥
३ भणत नांमदेव भाव ऐसा । जैसी मनसा लाभ तैसा ॥

५६

० बोलि ध्रौं त्रिबांणपद रांम नांम । ठाली जिभ्या कौंणैं कांम ॥
१ सेवा पूजा सुमिरण ध्यांन । झूठा कीजै बिन भगवांन ॥

करिहु १०; करिहूं १ ४ ७

५४;२ हरि। -- ३ १०; नांमैं। नांव मैं १ ८ १३; निज। निंज १३; कंवला। कमला ४; कवला ७ १६; हरि। -- ३ १०; नांमैं। नांउं मैं १; नांव मैं ८ १३

५४;३ नांमैं। नांव मैं ३ ८ १३; नांव मे १०; नामैं १; ध्रू। धु ३; ध्रू ४ ७ १६; निहचल १०; निहचल। निंहंचल १३; ध्रू १०; करिया। करीया १०; नांमैं। नांव मैं ८ १३; नांव लेत ३ १०; नामैं ७; प्रहिलाद। प्रहलाद १ ३ १०; उधरिया। उधिरिया १०

५४;४ मेरे। नांव ३ १०; जीवन। जीवत ३ १०; मरन। मरत ३ १०; का। के ७ १६; जलमगन। नांव लेत ३ १०; जलमंगन १३; उधरचौ। उधरचो १०; उधारचो ३

५४;५ मेरे। मेरो ३; संगि। मोछ १०; मोछि ३; सदा। मुकति ३ १०; सुष। शुष १; कौ ३; को १०; सो ८; हरि। हरि कै ३; हरि के १०; नांमैं। नांई ३; नांव मै १३; नांव मैं ८; नांइ १०

५५;० इतना। ईतनां ४; इतनौं १; इतनां ७; लागत। लागत है २०; लै। रटि १

५५;१ ध्रू। ध्रूं ७; प्रहिलाद। प्रहलाद २०; इहीं। ईही ४; इहि २०; गुनि। गुणिं १; गुणि २०; गुन ४; अषिर। अंषिर ४; अक्षिर १; हिरदै। हिदै ४; रिदै १; बिचारे। बिचारै २०

५५;२ त्रिभैपद। निरभैपद ७

५५;३ भाव। वीसौं १; ऐसा। विसा १; अैसा ४ १६; लाभ। तैसी १ २०; तैसा। दसा १ २०

५६;० ध्रौं। ध्रूं ४ २१; त्रिबांणपद। त्रिबांणैंपद २१; त्रिवांणैंपद १; निर्बांणपद ७; निर्बांणैंपद १६; नृबांणपद ८; र्नबांणैपद ४; रांम। रांमैं १; नांम। नांमां ८; जिभ्या। रसनां १; कौंणैं। कूंणैं १ ४; कौंण ७; कांम। कांमां ८

५६;१ सुमिरण। शुमिरन १; सुंमिरंन १३; सुमिरंण ४ २१; सुमिरन ८; बिन। बिंन १३ २१; बिनबि ४; बिना २०; विण १

२ तीरथ ब्रत जगत की आस । फोकट कीजै बिन बिसवास ॥
३ ऐकादसी जगत की करनीं । पाया महल तब तजी निसरनीं ॥
४ भणंत नांमदेव तुम्हारै सरणां । मुझा मनवां तुझा चरणां ॥

५७

० अैसैं रांमहि जांनौं रे भाई । जैसैं भ्रिंगी कीट रहै ल्यौ लाई ॥
१ श्रब रूप श्रबेस्वर स्वांमीं । त्रिगुण रहित देव अंतरजांमीं ॥
२ थावर जंगम कीट पतंगा । सति रांम सबहिन कै संगा ॥
३ नांमौं कहै मेरै बंध न भाई । रांम नांम मैं नौ निधि पाई ॥

५८

० अैसैं रांम अैसैं हेरौ । रांम छाडि चित अनत न फेरौ ॥
१ ज्यूं बिषई हेरै परनारी । कौडा डारत हिरै जुवारी ॥
२ ज्यूं पासा डारै पसवारा । सोनां घडतां हरै सुनारा ॥

५६:२ तीरथ। तीर्थ ७ १३; ब्रत। बरत १ १६; आस। आसा २० २१; करंणी ४; फोकट। -- ४; बिन। बिंन १३; बिसवास। बिसवासा २०; विश्वास १; बेसास ७

५६:३ ऐकादसी। -- ४; एकादसी ७ १६; येकादसी २०; जगत। संत ८ १२ १६; करनीं। करंनी १३; करंनीं २१; करणी १ २०; करणीं ७; करनी ८; पाया। नांव ७; पायौ १ ४ २० २१; महल। बिनां ७; तब। सब ७; तजी। झूठी ७; निसरनीं। निसरंनी १२ २१; निसरणी २०; निसरणीं १ ४; नीसरनी ८; बरणीं ७

५६:४ भणंत। भणत ७ ८ १६; तुम्हारै। तुंम्हारे १३; तुम्हरैं ७; तुम्हारे १ ८; सरणां। सरनां ८ १२ १६; मुझा। मुंझा ७; मनवां। मंनवां २१; तुझा। तूझा २०; चरणां। चरंणां ४ २१; चरनां १२ १६

५७;० अैसैं। ऐसैं ७; अेसे १०; रांमहि। रांमहिं १२ २१; रामही ८; जांनौं। जांनो १०; जानूं ७; रे। रि १३; जैसैं। - १; जैसै २१; जेसें १०; भ्रिंगी। +गी ४; भ्रंगी १० १३; भ्रीगी २१; भ्ररगी ३; भृगी ८ १६; ल्यौ। ल्यो २ १०

५७;१ श्रब। सर्ब २ १०; सर्व १; रूप। रुप १०; श्रबेस्वर। श्रबेसुर ८ २१; सर्बेसुर १०; सरबेस्वुर ३; सरबेस्वर ४; सरबेसुर ७; सर्वेस्वर १; स्वांमीं। स्वांमी २ ८; त्रिगुण। त्रिगुंण १६ २१; त्रिगुंन १३; त्रिगुन २ ८ १०; रहित। रहत ८; अंतरजांमीं। अंतरजांमी ८

५७;२ जंगम। जगम ८; सति। सत्य २ ४ ८; कै। के २ ७ ८ १० १६

५७;३ नांमौं। नांम १३; नांमां ८ १६; नामो १०; कहै। कहे १०; मेरै। मेरे १ २ ८ १० १२ २१; भाई। भाइ १०; मैं। विन १; मै २१; में १०; नौ। नौं १६; नो १०; रह्यौ १; निधि। निंध्रि १३; न १; पाई। पाइ १०; जाई १

५८;० अैसैं। ऐसैं १७ २०; ऐसें ७; अेसे १०; अैसैं। ऐसैं १७ २०; ऐसें ७; अैसै ३; अेसे रांम १०; हेरौ। हेरौं ७ १६ १७; हेरो १०; हेरु २०; छाडि। छाडी २०; अनत। अंनंत २१; अनंत १ १३; आनत १६; फेरौ। टरौं १६; फेर+ ४; फेरौं ८ २०; फेरो २ १०

५८;१ ज्यूं। ज्यौं १ ८ १२ १६; बिषई। बिषिया २१; विषिया १; विषइ २०; हेरै। हेरैं २०; हेरे १०; कौडा। कोडा १०; हिरै। हिरे १०; फिरै ४ ८ १२ १६ १७; हारे २०; जुवारी। जुंवारी २०

५८;२ ज्यूं। ज्यौं १ ३ ८ १२ १६; पासा। पासो १०; डारै। ढोरै ३; ढारे १०; पसवारा। पसिहारा २०;

३ जत्र जांउं तत्र तूं ही रांमां । चित चिहूंटचौ प्रणवै नांमां ॥

१ नाद भ्रमे जैसे मिरगाए । प्रान तजे वाको धिआनु न जाए ॥
० ऐसे रामा ऐसे हेरउ । राम छोडि चितु अनत न फेरउ ॥ रहाउ ॥
२ जिउ मीना हेरै पसूआरा । सोना गढते हिरै सुनारा ॥
३ जिउ बिखई हेरै पर नारी । कउडा डारत हिरै जुआरी ॥
४ जह जह देखउ तह तह रामा । हरि के चरन नित धिआवै नामा ॥

५९

० पांनियां बिन मीन तलफै । अैसैं रांम नांम बिन बापुरौ नांमां ॥
१ तन लाइलै तालाबेली । बछा बिन गाइ अकेली ॥
२ जैसैं गाइ का बछा छूटिला । थन लागिलै मांषन घूंटिला ॥
३ मांषन मेल्हिलै ताती घांमां । अैसै रांम नांम बिन बापुरौ नांमां ॥
४ जैसैं बिषई चित परनारी । अैसैं नांमदेव हेत बनवारी ॥

१ मोहि लागती ताला बेली । बछरे बिनु गाइ अकेली ॥
० पानीआ बिनु मीनु तलफै । ऐसे राम नामा बिनु बापरो नामा ॥ रहाउ ॥
२ जैसे गाइ का बाछा छूटला । थन चोखता माखनु घूटला ॥

पसुहारा १३; पासावारा १०; सोनां। सोनौं १ ३ ४ २१; सोनों १०; घडतां। घरता २ १०; घरतां १; गढतां ७; हरै। हिरै १ ४ ७ १६ २१; हैरै ८; हरे १०; सुनारा। शुनारा १; सुंनारा २१; सोनारा १७

५८;३ जत्र। जहां ७; जांउं। देषूं ७; देषौ ३; देषो १०; जांऊं १७ २१; जांउ ८; तत्र। तहां ७; तूं। तू १०; ही। हीं जु ४; ही नां ८; ही जू २१; रांमां। रांम १०; चिहूंटचौ। चिहुंटया ७; चिहुटयौ ३; चिहुटयो १०; चिहूंटया ८ १३; चिहूटया १६; चहुटया ४; प्रणवै। प्रंनवे १०; प्रणवैं १ ४ ७ ८ २०; प्रनवै ३

५९;० पांनियां। पांनिंया १३; पांणियां ४; पांनिया १०; पानिंयां २१; बिन। बिंनिं १३; बिण ४; बीन २०; मीन। मींन १ ३ ७ १३ २०; तलफै। तरफै ३; तरफे १०; तलपै ७ ८ १६; अैसैं। अेसे १०; जैसै २०; बिन। बिंन १३; बापुरौ। - २०; बापुरो ८ १०

५९;१ तन। तंन २१; तनि ३ १०; लाइलै। लागिले १ ४; लाइले १० १६; तालाबेली। तालावेली २१; बछा। ज्यूं बाछा २०; बछरा १०; बछरां ३; गाइ। गाई ४ ८ २१

५९;२ जैसैं। - १; जेसें १०; गाइ। गाई ४ २१; बछा। बाछ ३ १०; बाछा ४ ७; थन। थंण १३; थंन २१; थुन ३ १०; तन ८; लागिलै। लागिले ७ १६; लागीले ८; लाइलै ३; लाइले १०; मांषन। मांषण १३ २०; माषण ८; माषन ३ १० २१; घूंटिला। घूटिला ३ ८ १६

५९;३ मांषन। -- ३ १०; मांषण ४ १३; माषण १६; माषण ८; मेल्हिलै। मेल्हिले ४ ७; राषिलै २०; राषिले ८ १६; अैसै। -- ३ १०; अैसैं १ ४ १३ १६ २१; बापुरौ। बापूरौ २०; बाबुरौ २१

५९;४ जैसैं। -- २०; जेसे १०; बिषई। बिषै ३ २१; बिषे १०; बिषौ ४; विषै १; चित। हेत ३ १० २१; अैसैं। -- २०; ऐसे ७; अेसें १०; नांमदेव। नामदेव ३; हेत। भनैं ३; न १०; बनवारी। मुरारी १ १०; बंनबारी २१

३ नामदेउ नाराइनु पाइआ । गुरु भेटत अलखु लखाइआ ॥
४ जैसे बिखै हेत पर नारी । ऐसे नामे प्रीति मुरारी ॥
५ जैसे ताप ते निरमल घामा । तैसे राम नामा बिनु बापुरो नामा ॥

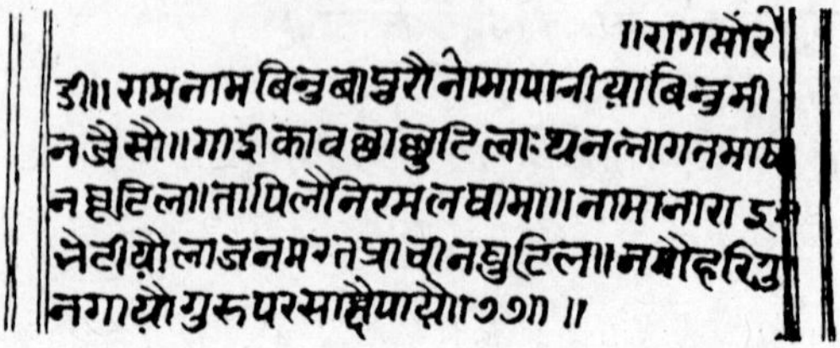
॥रागसोर
ठी॥ रामनाम बिनु बापुरौ नामा पानीया बिनु मी
न जैसैं॥ गाइ का वछा छूटिला॥ थन लागन मा
न छूटिला॥ तापिलै निरमल घामा॥ नामा नारा इ
नै टीयौ लाजन मगत पाचा न छुटिला॥ नबो हरि गु
नगायौ गुरु परसादै पायौ॥७७॥ ॥

९०

० अनबोलतां चरन नहीं छाडौं । मोहि तुम्हारी आंन बाबा बीठुला ॥
१ टगमग टगमग क्या चोघता । एक बोल बोलौ बोलता ॥
२ कहिधौं कूंतल कहिधौं बली । प्रणवत नांमदेव पुरवौ रली ॥

९१

० जत्र जांउं तत्र बीठल भैला । बीठलियौ राजा रांम देवा ॥
१ आनिलै कुंभ भराइलै उदिक बालगोब्यंदहि न्हांण रचूं ॥
पहली नीर जु मंछ बिटाल्यौ जूठणि भैला कांइ करूं ॥

९०;० अनबोलतां। अंणबोलतां १२ २१; अंनबोलतां १६; अणबोलता १; अनबोलतैं ८; चरन। चर्ण १२; चरंण ४ २१; चरण १; नहीं। नहिं १२; नहि १; नही ८; छाडौं। छांडूं १ ७; छाडूं २१; छाडों ४; मोहि। - ८ १२ १६; माहि ४; तुम्हारी। तुंम्हारी १२; मांन। आंण १ ८ १२ १६; बाबा। बाप १६; बीठुला। बीठला ७ ८ १२ १६

९०;१ एक। ऐक १ ४ ८ १२; एकल १६; बोल। - १६; बोलौ। बोलो ८; वोलौ १६

९०;२ कहिधौं। कैधूं १; कहिंधौं १२; कहिधूं ४ ७ २१; कूंतल। कूंतिल १; कूतिल १६; कूतल ८ २१; कहिधौं। कैधूं १; कहिधूं ४ ७ २१; प्रणवत। प्रंणव्रंत ७ १२; प्रणवंत १६ २१; प्रनवैं १; पुरवौ। पुरवो ८ १२ २१; पुरवहु १ ४

९१;० जांउं। जांऊं १७ २१; जाऊं ४; जाउं २०; बीठल। बिठल १०; भैला। भैलो १०; बीठलियौ। बिठलि १०; मींठलियौ २१; बीठुलियौ ४; बीठल १२; बीठलीयौ २०; बीठलीयो ३; रांम। + ४; देवा। + ४

९१;१ आनिलै। +लै ४; आंणिलै १ २१; आंनिलै १२; आणिंले १६; आणिलै ७ २०; आनिले १०; कुंभ। कुभ ८; कूंभ ४ १२ २०; कूभ ३; भराइलै। भराईलै ४; भराईले २०; भराइले १० १६; उदिक। उदिका २०; बालगोब्यंदहि। बालकुवारि ४; बालगोबिंदहिं १६; बालगोबिंदही १२; बालगोबिन्दहि ७ १०; बालगोबिदही ८; न्हांण। न्हांइ १०; न्हान ३; पुल+ ४; रचूं। दरिये ४; रचू १७; रचौ २०; रचौं ८ १२;

२ आंणिलै केसरि सूकडि समसरि बालगोब्यंदहि षौलि रचूं ॥
पहली बास भुवंगम लींन्हीं जूठणि भैला कांइ करूं ॥
३ आणिलै पहुप गूंथिले माला बालगोब्यंदहि हार रचूं ॥
पहली बास जु भंवरा लींन्हीं जूठणि भैला कांइ करूं ॥
४ आंणिलै घ्रित जोइलै बाती बालगोब्यंदहि जोति रचूं ॥
पहली जोति जु नैंनौं देषी जूठणि भैला कांइ करूं ॥
५ आंणिलै अग्र षेइलै धूपं बालगोब्यंदहि धूप रचूं ॥
पहली बास नासिका आई जूठणि भैला कांइ करुं ॥
६ आंणिलै तंदूल रांधिलै षीरो बालगोब्यंदहि भोग रचूं ॥
पहली दूध जु बछ बिटाल्यौ जूठणि भैला कांइ करुं ॥

रच्यौं १६; पहली। पहिली १० १६ १७; पहल ३; मंछा। मंछि ८ १७; मछि १६ २१; बिटाल्यौ। बिटास्यौ ८; बिटाल्यो ३; बिटारचौ १ २०; जूठणि। जूठणिं १२; जूठनि ३ ८ १६; झूठणि ७ १७; झूठनि २१; झूठणी २०; भैला। ह्वैला २०; भेला ८ २१; कांइ। कांई ३ ४ २० २१; कांइं १६; करूं। करुं २१; करी १६; करौं ८ १२ १७

६१;२ आंणिलै। आंणिंलै १२; आंनिले १०; सूकडि। संकडि २१; सुकडी २०; सुकडि ३ १०; सूकड ४; समसरि। संमसरि २० २१; समिसरि १; समसर ४ ७ १० १६ १७; समसार ३; 'बालगोब्यंदहि। बालगोबिंदहि ४ ७ १०; बालगोबिंदही १२; बालगोब्यंदही ८ २०; षौलि। षोलि १०; रचूं। रचौं ४ ८ १२ १६ १७ २०; भुवंगम। भुयंगम १ ३ १०; भवंगम १७ २०; लींन्हीं। लींन्ही ३; लींनीं १; लीन्ही ८ १६; जूठणि। जुठनि २१; जूठणिं १२; जूठिनि ३ १६; झूठणि २०; भैला। भेला ८ १० २१; कांइ। कांई ३ ४ ८ २०; कांइं १६ २१; करूं। करो १६; करौं ८ १२ १७; करुं १० २१

६१;३ आणिलै। आंणिंले १२ १६; आंणिले १ २० २१; आंणिले ३ ७, आंणिलै ८; आनिले १०; पहुप। पुहप १६; पहूप २०; गूंथिले। गुंथाइलै १; गुथाइले २१; गूंथिलै २०; गूथिलै १६; गूथिले ४ ८; बालगोब्यंदहि। बालगोबिंदहिं ७ १०; बालगोबिंदहि ३; बालगोबिंदही ४ १३; बालगोबिहि ८; बालगोब्यंदहिं १ २१; बालगोब्यंदहीं २०; हार। माल १ २१; रचूं। रचौं ८ १२ १६ २० २१; जु। भौंवर २०; भंवरा। भंवरै ८; भंवरैं १३; भंवरहि १६; भंवरां २१; भौंरा १; भौरा १०; भमरा ४; भवरै १७; भवरा ७; कौं २०; लींन्हीं। आई २०; लीन्ही ८ २१; लीन्हीं ३ १६; लीनी १०; लीनीं १; जूठणि। जूंठणि २१; जूंठिनि ३; जूठणिं १३; जूठनि १६ १७; झूठणि २०; भैला। भेला ८ १० २१; कांइ। कांई १ ३ २० २१; करूं। करौं ८ १२ १६ १७; करुं १०

६१;४ आंणिलै। आंणिले ४ ८ १६; आंनिले ३ १०; घ्रित। घ्रत १०; घृत ७ ८ १७; घिर्त १६; जोइलै। जोइिले ८; जोईले ४; जोइले ३ ७; बालगोब्यंदहि। बालगोबिंदहि ४ ७ १०; बालगोबिंदही १२; बालगोबिदहि ८; बालगोब्यंदहिं १७ २१; बालगोब्यंदहीं २०; जोति। प्रीति १०; दीप १ ३; रचूं। रचू ३; रचौं ४ ८ १२ १६ १७ २०; जोति। बास ४; जु। - १ २०; नासिका ४; जू २१; नैंनौं। आई ४; नैंनूं १७; नैंनौ २१; नैंनहुं १६; नैंना ३; नैनौ १२; नैनौं ७; नैना १०; नांमदेव १ २०; देषी। - ४; जूठणि। जूंठंणि २१; जूटनि ८; जूठनि ३ १६ १७; झूठणि २०; भैला। भेला ८; कांइ। कांई ४ २१; कांईं २०; काई ३; करूं। करौं ८ १२ १६ १७; करुं २१

६१;५ आंणिलै। आंणिंलै १२ १६; आंणिले ४ ७; आंनिले ३; अग्र। अगर ८ १२ १६ १७; षेइलै। षेविलै १७; षेविले १६; षेईलै ३; षेईले ४; षेइले ७ १०; जोइलै १; धूपं। धूप १६; धूपा १ ४ ७ २०; बालगोब्यंदहि। बालगोबिंदहिं ४ ७ १०; बालगोबिंदहि ३; बालगोबिंदही १२; बालगोब्यंदहिं १; बालगोब्यंदही २०; रचूं। रचौं ८ १२ १६ २०; नासिका। नासीका ४; आई। लीन्हीं १२; लीनी २०; जूठणि। जूठंनि २१; जूठणिं १२; जूठनि ३ १० १६ १७; झूठणि २०; भैला। भेला ८ १० २१; कांइ। कांई ४; कांईं २०; कांइं १६ २१; करूं। करौं ८ १२ १६ १७; करुं १० २१

७ आंऊं तौ बीठल जांऊं तौ बीठल व्यापक माया ॥
नांमां का चित हरि सौं लागा तार्थें परम पद पाया ॥

१ आनीले कुंभ भराइले ऊदक ठाकुर कउ इसनानु करउ ॥
बइआलीस लख जी जल महि होते बीठलु भैला काइ करउ ॥
० जत्र जाउ तत बीठलु भैला । महा अनंद करे सद केला ॥ रहाउ ॥
२ आनीले फूल परोई ले माला ठाकुर की हउ पूज करउ ॥
पहिले बासु लई है भवरह बीठल भैला काइ करउ ॥
३ आनीले दूधु रीधाईले खीरं ठाकुर कउ नैवेदु करउ ॥
पहिले दूधु बिटारिओ बछरै बीठलु भैला काइ करउ ॥
४ ईभै बीठलु ऊभै बीठलु बीठल बिनु संसारु नही ॥
थान थनंतरि नामा प्रणवै पूरि रहिओ तूं सरब मही ॥

६२

० कांइ रे मन बिषिया बन जाइ । देषत ही ठगमूली षाइ ॥
१ मधुमाषी संचियौ अपार । मधु लीन्हीं मुषि दीन्हीं छार ॥
२ गऊ बछ कूं संचै षीर । गलै बांधि दुहि लेइ अहीर ॥

६१;६ आंणिले। आंणिंले १२ १६; आंणिले ४ ७ १०; आंनिलै १७; आंनिले ६; तंदुल। तंदूल २०; तुंदल २१; तदूल ३; रांधिलै। रांधिले ३; रांधिले ४ ७ १७; राधिले १० १६; षीरो। षीरं २ १०; षीरी ८ २०; बालगोब्यंदहि। बालगोबिंदहिं १६; बालगोबिंदहि ४ ७ १०; बालगोबिंदही १२; बालगोबिंदहि ८; बालगोब्यंदही २०; भोग। षीर १ १०; रचूं। रचौं ८ १२ १६ १७ २० २१; दूध। दुध २०; जु। जू १०; बछा। बछु २०; बछै १; बछां १२; बछि १७; बछे १६; बिटाल्यौ। बिटास्यौ ८; बिटाल्यो २ १०; बिठाल्यौ १७; बोटयौ १; जूठणि। जूठंनि २१; जूठणिं १२; जूठनि २ ८ १० १६ १७; झूठणि २०; भैला। भेला ८ १० २१; कांइ। कांई ४ ८; कांई २ २०; कांइं १६ २१; करूं। करौं ८ १२ १६ १७; करुं १० २१

६१;७ आंऊं। आंउ १०; आंउं २ ८ १२ २०; तौ। त १; तो १०; बीठल। बिठला १०; मीठुल २१; बीठा ३; जाऊं। जांउं २ ८ १२; जाउं १० २०; तौ। त १; तौ तौ १७; तो १०; बीठल। बिठला १०; मीठुला २१; बीठला २ १२; बीठल। बिठल १०; मीठुल २१; बीठुल २०; नांमां। नांमा २ २१; का। क ६; सौं। स्यूं २०; स्यौं १; स्यों ३; सु १०; सूं ४ ७ १७ २१; तार्थें। तहां १२; तातैं १ ८; ताते १०; परम। पर्म १२

६२;० कांइ। कांई ४; कांइं २ १६; मन। मंन १२; बिषिया। बिषया १०; बन। बंनिं १२; बंनि २१; बनि ८ १६; बीन ३; जाइ। जही १०; जाहि ३; जाई ४ ८; ही। हीं २१; ठगमूली। ठगमूरी २ ७ १०; षाइ। पाई २१; षही १०; षाहि ३; षाई ४ ८

६२;१ मधुमाषी। ज्यूं मधुमांषी ३; ज्यु मधूमांषी १०; मधुमांषी ४ ७ १२; मधमाषी १; संचियौ। संन संच्या १२; संचिया १६; संचै ३; संच्या ८; सचे १०; मधु। मध १; लीन्हीं। लींन्हीं १२; लीन्हां ८; लीनी ६; लीनो १०; लीयी ४; मुषि। मुष २ ७ १० १२; दीन्हीं। दींन्हीं १२; दीन्हीं १ २१; दीनीं ३; दीनो १०; दीनीं ७

६२;२ गऊ। गऊं १६; गउ २ ८ १२; गवु १०; गाइ १; बछ। बछा ३ १०; कूं। की १६; कौं २ ८ १२; को १०; संचै। संचो १०; सांचैं १६; गलै। गले १०; बांधि। बंधि ८; बाधि ३; लेइ। लेई ४

३ जैसें मीन पांणी मैं रहै । काल जाल की सुधि न लहै ॥
४ जिभ्या स्वारथ निगल्यौ लोह । कनक कांमिनीं बांध्यौ मोह ॥
५ माया काजि बहुत कर्म करै । सो माया ले औंडै धरै ॥
६ अति अयांन जांनैं नहीं मूढ । धन धरती अंचला भयौ भूड ॥
७ कांम क्रोध त्रिस्ना अति जरै । साध संगति कबहूं नहीं करै ॥
८ प्रणवत नांमदेव ताकी आंण । त्रिभै होइ भजौ भगवांन ॥

• काएं रे मन बिखिआ बन जाइ । भूलौ रे ठग मूरी खाइ ॥ रहाउ ॥
१ जैसे मीनु पानी महि रहै । काल जाल की सुधि नही लहै ॥
जिहबा सुआदी लीलित लोह । ऐसे कनिक कामनी बाधिओ मोह ॥
२ जिउ मधु माखी संचै अपार । मधु लीनो मुखि दीनी छारु ॥
गऊ बाछ कउ संचै खीरु । गला बांधि दुहि लेइ अहीरु ॥
३ माइआ कारन स्रमु अति करै । सो माइआ लै गाडै धरै ॥
अति संचै समझै नही मूढ । धनु धरती तनु होइ गइओ धूडि ॥
४ काम क्रोध तृसना अति जरै । साध संगति कबहू नही करै ॥
कहत नामदेउ ताची आणि । निरभै होइ भजीऐ भगवान ॥

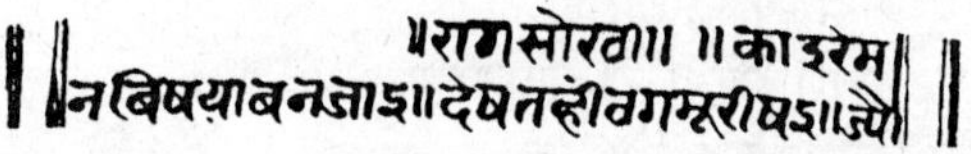

६२;३ मीन। मींन २ ७ १० १३; पांणी। पांणीं १२ २१, पांनी ३; मैं। मै २ १३; मे १०; रहै। रहें १०; सुधि। शुधि १; न। नहिं १३; नहि १; लहै। लहे १०

६२;४ जिभ्या। ज्यभ्या १; जिव्ह्या ३; जिव्हा १०; स्वारथ। स्वादै १; स्वारंथि ४; स्वारथि २ ८ १० १३; निगल्यौ। निगिल्यौ १६; निगल्यो २ १०; कनक। कंनक २१; कनिक २ १०; कनंक १३; कांमिनीं। कांमिनि १०; कांमिणीं ४; कांमनी २ २१; कांमनीं १ १३; कामनिं ८; बांध्यौ। बंध्यौ ८; बध्यौ २१; बाध्यौ ३; बाध्यो १०

६२;५ माया। विषिया १; काजि। स्वादि १; काज ७ १६ २१; बहुत। जतन २ १०; कर्म। श्रम १ १३; श्रमु ८; क्रम ७; सुरंम २१; बहु २ १०; करै। करे १०; माया। विषिया १; औंडै। ऊंडै ७; ऊडै २१; औडै ३; ओंडि १०; उंडै १३; उडै ८; कुंडै १६; धरै। धरे १०

६२;६ अयांन। सयांन २ ४ १०; सयान १; जांनैं। जांनै १ १३; जानि १०; जानैं २ १६; नहीं। नहिं १३; नहि १ १०; नही २ ८; मूढ। मूंढ ७ १३; मूठ २१; मूलि १; धन। धंन २१; धरन १६; अंचला। अचरा ४; अचला ८ १३; भयौ। मैं २ ७; में १०; परि ८; पर १६; भूड। धूंल २१; धूलि १; धूल ७ ८ १६; भुंडं १०

६२;७ त्रिस्ना। त्रिश्नां १३; त्रिश्ना ३; त्रिश्नां ८; त्रिसनां १६; त्रिष्णां २१; त्रस्ना १०; तृष्णां ७; जरै। जरे १०; कबहूं। कबहू २ ८; नहीं। न ३; नहिं १ १३; नही ८ २१; करै। करे १०

६२;८ प्रणवत। प्रंणवंत २१; प्रणवंत ७ १३ १६; प्रनवे १०; प्रांनवंत ३; आंण। आंन २ १०; त्रिभै। निर्भै १६; निरभैं ८; त्रभै १०; होइ। ह्वै १; होई ४ २१; होइ पद ३; भजौ। भजि १ २ १० १३; भजे ८; भगवांन। त्रिबांण २१; किन रांम ८ १६; बिणं ४; भगवान्न ७; सारंगप्रांण १; सारंगपांण १३

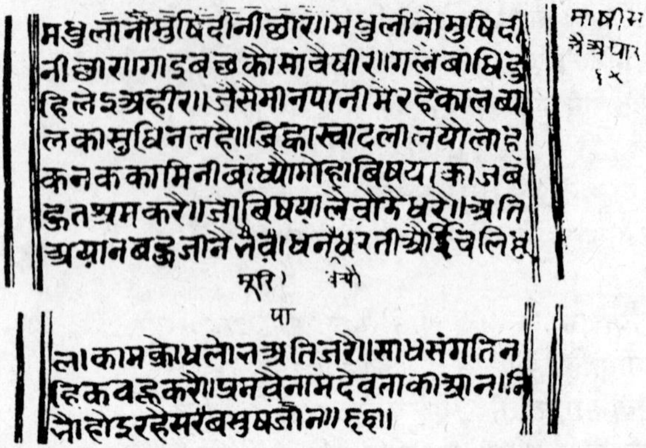

६३

• अपने रांम कूं भजि रे मन आलसिया । रांम बिनां जमजाल सिया ॥

१ प्रांणीं अस्वमेद जगने तुलापुरिष दानें हरि हरि प्राग अस्नानें ॥

तऊ न तुलै हरि कीरति नांमां ॥

२ प्रांणीं गया प्यंड भरता बानारसियै बसता ॥

मुषि बेद पुरांण पढता तऊ न तुलै हरि कीरति नांमां ॥

३ प्रांणीं सकल धरम अछता गुर ग्यांन इंद्री द्रिढता ॥

६३:० अपने। + ४; - १३: अपणे ८; अपने ३; अपनें १ ७ १७; रांम। - १३. रांम जी ३ १०; राम २१: कूं। + ४; - १३. कुं १०; कौं ३ ८ १७; भजि। भजियें ७; भजी १०; आलसिया। आलिसिया २१: आलसीया ३ १०: रांम। - ३ १०; बिनां। - ३; बिंनां १३: आलसिया १०; जमजाल। जंमजाल १ २१; जमंजाल ८; जमजालि १३ १६; जनभजालि १०

६३:१ प्रांणीं। - ३ ८ १० १३; प्रांनीं ७: अस्वमेद। अस्वमेध ८ १३; असुमेद १६ १७; अस्मेद १ ३ २१; जगनें। जिग्यनें १; जगिनें १३ २१: जग्यनें ४ ७ १०. दानें। दानें १ १३ १७; दानें १६: हरि। हरिं ७: हर ३; हरि। हर ३ १०; प्राग। प्रिराग १६ १७: प्रायाग ३. अस्नानें। स्नानें ७ १३: श्नानें १७; अस्नानें ४: अश्नानें २१ असनानें ३; सनानें ८ १६; तऊ। तुवु १०; तउ ३ ८ १३: तुलै। तुले १०: कीरति। कीर्ति १३: नांमां। नांमदेव ३ १०

६३:२ प्राणां। - ३ १०; प्रांणी ८ २१; प्यंड। पिंड १३; पिड ८, भरता। भरत १०; भरते ३ २१ बानारसियै। बांणांरसियैं ४; बांणांरसियां २१: बांणारसीयें १३. बांनारसिया ३: बांनारसीये १७. बाणांरसियैं ७: बाणारस्यये ८: बाणारसी १; बसता। बस्ते २१; बस्ता ४ ७: बस्ते ३ १०: वस्ता १; बेद। देव २१; पुरांण। पुरांन १६; पुरांन १० १७; प्रुांन ३; प्रोण १३ पढता। पढते ३ २१; पढतां १३: पढिते १०; पढिता १७; तऊ। तउ ३ ४ ८ १० १३: तुलै। तुलें ७ १०: कीरति। कीर्ति १३: कीरती ३

६३:३ प्रांणीं। - ३ १०; प्रांणो ८: धरम। धंम १: धर्म १७: धर्म ४ १३: धरंम २१: अछता। अछते ३ २१; अछिता १; पालते १०; इंछता १३. गुर। गुण २१; गुंन १०; गुन ३; इंद्री। ईंद्री १३: यद्री १ ४ ८ १० १६: दिढता।

षट क्रम सहित रहिता तऊ न तुलै हरि कीरति नांमां ॥
४ प्रांणीं सकल सेवा श्रम बादं छाडि छाडि बहु भेदं ॥
सुमरि सुमरि गोबिंदं नांमदेव नांइं तिरै भौसिंधं ॥

१ असुमेध जगने । तुला पुरख दाने । प्राग इसनाने ॥
तउ न पुजहि हरि कीरति नामा ॥
अपुने रामहि भजु रे मन आलसीआ ॥ रहाउ ॥
२ गइआ पिंडु भरता । बनारसि असि बसता । मुखि बेद चतुर पडता ॥
३ सगल धरम अछिता । गुर गिआन इंद्री दृ । खटु करम सहित रहता ॥
४ सिवा सकति संबादं । मन छोडि छोडि सगल भेदं ॥
सिमरि सिमरि गोबिंदं । भजु नामा तरसि भव सिंधं ॥

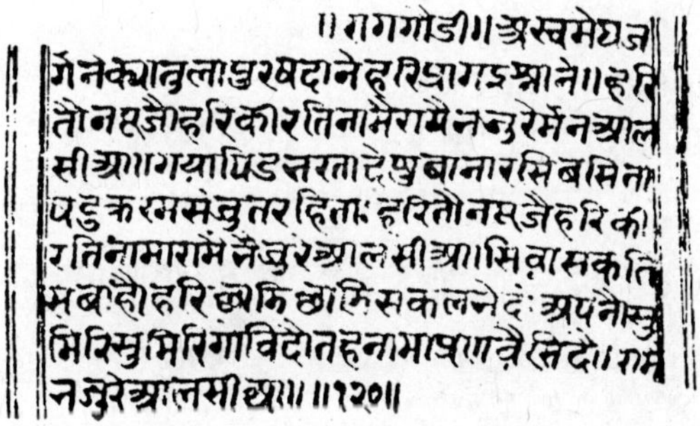

६४

० मन थिर होइ रे बा न होइ अैसा चिहन करै संसार ॥
भीतरि मैला धूतिग फिरै क्यौं उतरै भौ पार ॥

डिढता ४; दिढते २१; द्रिढते ३ द्रिढता १; द्रढते १०; क्रम। क्रंम १३; कर्म १०; करंम २१; सहित। सहत ८ १३; रहिता। राहते ३ १०; रहते २१. रहता १३; तऊ। तउ ३ ४ ८ १० १३; तुलै। तुले १०; कीरति। कीर्ति १३

६३:४ प्रांणीं। - १ ३ १०; प्रांणी ८ १६ २१; प्रांनीं १७; श्रम। श्रुम २१; श्रब ८ १६; स्यूं ३; सु १०; बादं। बांदं २१; बहु। सकल १; सुमरि। अपनौं शुनरि १; अपनौं सुमरि ३; अपनो सुमिरि १०; सुंमरि १३ २१; सुमिरि ४ ८ १६; सुमरि। शुमरि १; सुंमरि १३; सुमिरि ४ ८ १० १६; गोबिंदं। गोबिदं ८; गोब्यंदं ३ १६ १७; गोव्यंद १ २१; नांमदेव। नां १०; नांमदे २१; नांइं ३; नामदेव ८; नांइं। तिरै ३; तिरे १०; नांई ४; नांइ ८ १७; तिरै। तिरे ८ १३ २१; नांमदेव ३ १०; भौसिंधं। सिंध १०; भौंसिध ४; भौस्यंध ३ ८; भौस्यंधं ७ १३ २१; भवस्यंध १

६४:० मन। मंन २१; थिर। थिर न ४ २१; होइ। होई ४; रे। बा १६ १७; वा १; बा। रे १ १६ १७; न। नं २१; होइ। होई ४; अैसा। ऐसा ७; चिहन। चिहिंन २१; चिहंन ८; कपट १ १३; भीतरि। भींतरि १३; मंन

१ रुद्राष सषा जपमाला भंडे ताको मरम न जांनैं कोई रे ॥
आप न देषै और दिषावै कपट मुकति क्यौं होई रे ॥
२ सीगी जटा बिभूति लगावैं संबर सिध कहावैं रे ॥
नाथ न वोलषैं मरम न जांनैं भाव चिंडाली ल्यावैं रे ॥
३ ब्रह्मा पढि गुंनि बेद सुनावैं मन की भ्रांति न जाई रे ॥
करम करैं सो सूझै नांहीं बहुतक करम कराई रे ॥
४ मास दिवस लग रोजा साधै कलमां बंग पुकारैं रे ॥
मन मैं काती जीव बधारैं नांव अलह का सारैं रे ॥
५ केवल ब्रह्म सति करि जांनैं सहज सुंनि मैं ध्याया रे ॥
प्रणवंत नांमदेव गुर परसादैं पाया तिनिहीं लुकाया रे ॥

९५

० देवा बेन बाजै गगन गाजै सबद अनाहद बोलै ॥
अंतरगति की जांनैं नांहीं मूरिष भ्रमत डोलै ॥

मैं २१; मैला। मैंला २१; धूतिग। धूतग १३; धूतत ८; क्यौं। क्यूं ४ ७ ८ १७ २१; उतरै। उतरि ४; उतरैं १; भौ। बौ ४; पार। पारं ८

९४;१ रुद्राष। रुद्राष ४ ८ १३; सषा। सिषा १९; भंडे। भंडैं १७; भांडैं ८ १३; मंडे १९; ताको। ताका १; मरम। म्रंम २१; जांनैं। जांणैं ४; रे। - ८ १३ १९ १७; आप। आपं २१; न। ण १; णं २१; देषै। देषैं १९; दषैं ८; दिषावै। दिंषावैं ८; कपट। कपटि ४ १९ १७; मुकति। मुंकति १३; मुक्ति १ २१; क्यौं। क्यूं ४ १७ २१; होई। होइ १ २१; रे। - ४ ८ १३ १९ १७

९४;२ सीगी। सींगी १ ४ १७; लगावैं। लगावैं १३; संबर। सांबर ४; सिध। सिंध १ ४; कहावैं। कहांव ७; कहावैं १७; रे। - ८ १३ १९ १७; वोलषैं। उलषै १३ २१; उलषैं ८; बोलषैं १; मरम। मरंम १३; जांनैं। जांणैं ७ १९; जांने ४; जानैं १; चिंडाली। चिडाली ८ १७; ल्यावैं। आंणैं २१; लांवे १३; लावै १; रे। - ४ ८ १३ १९ १७

९४;३ ब्रह्मा। ब्रह्मां ४ १३ २१; गुंनि। - ४; गुंनिं १३; गुंणि २१; गुणि १; गुनि ७ ८; सुनावैं। शुणावैं १; उच्चारैं ८ १३; सुंणांवैं २१; सुणावौं ४; सुणावे ७; सुनावैं १९ १७; मन। मंन २१; की। + १९; भ्रांति। + १९; भ्रांति ४; न। + १९; जाई। + १९; जाइ २१; रे। + १९; - ८ १३ १७; करम। ++ १९; क्रंम २१; कर्म ४; करंम १३; करैं। करैं १३; सो। जुग ८; जग १३; नांहीं। मांहीं २१; नांही ८; बहुतक। ++ १९; बहुतकिं १३; बहुतकि ७ ८; करम। क्रंम २१; कर्म ४ १३; रे। - १ ४ ८ १३ १७

९४;४ मास। ++ १९; दिवस। दिंवस १३; साधै। साधैं ७ ८ १७; कलमां। ++ १९; कलंमां १३; बंग। बंगी ४; बंगि १; पुकारैं। पुकारे १ ४ २१; रे। - ८ १३ १७; मन। मंन १३ २१; बधारैं। संघारे १९; संघारैं १७; सधारैं ८; बंधांवैं १३; बंधारैं ७; बधारे २१; वधावे १; का। कौ ७; सारैं। सारे १ ४ ७ १९ २१; रे। - ८ १३ १९ १७

९४;५ सति। सत्य १ ४; जांनैं। जांणे ४; जांणौं ७; जांनौं १९ १७; सुंनि। शुंनि १; सुंन्यं ४; सुंनिं १३ १९ २१; सुनि ८ १७; ध्याया। धाया १; ध्यांया १९; ध्याये ८; रे। - १९ १७; परसादैं। प्रसदैं ७; प्रसादैं ८ १३ १७ २१; तिनिहीं। तिन्हैं १; तिनिंहिं २१; तिनिहि ७; तिनिही ४; तिनैं ८ १३; रे। - १३ १९ १७

९५;० बेन। बैंनन १; सबद। सब्द २१; बोलै। बोलै हो २१; बोलै रे १; अंतरगति। अंतरिगति २०; जांनैं। जांणैं ४ २० २१; नांहीं। नांही ८ २०; भ्रमत। भ्रंमत २१; भ्रंमतौ १; भ्रंमत ४; भरमत १९

१ चंद सूर दोउ समि करि राषौं मन पवन दिढ डांडी ॥
सहजैं सुषमन तारामंडल इहि बिधि त्रिस्नां षांडी ॥
२ बैठा रहूं न फिरूं न डोलूं भूषां रहूं न षाऊं ॥
मरूं न जीऊं अहि निसि भुगतौं नहीं आऊं नहीं जांऊं ॥
३ गगन मंडल मैं रहनि हमारी सहज सुंनि ग्रिह मेला ॥
अंतरधुनि मैं मन बिलमाऊं कोई जोगी गंमि लहैला ॥
४ पाती तोडि न पूजौं देवा देवलि देव न होई ॥
नांमां कहै मैं हरि की सरना पुनरपि जनम न होई ॥

९६

० देवा गगन गूडी बैठी मैं नांहीं तब दीठी ॥
१ जब लग आस निरास बिचारै । तब लग ताहि न पावै ॥
२ कहिबौ सुनिबौ जब गत होइबौ । तब ताहि परचौ आवै ॥

९५:१ सूर। सुर २० २१; दोउ। दोऊ १ २१; दोइ ८ १२ १६; राषौं। राषे २०; राषूं १; मन। मंन २१; पवन। पवंनां १२; दिढ। द्रिढ ४ १२; द्रिढ १; डांडी। डांडी हो ४ २१; सहजैं। संजम ४ २१; तारामंडल १; सुषमन। शुषमन १; सुषमंन २१; सूंषमन ४; सूषमन २०; तारामंडल। मंजम १; तारामडल १२; इहि। ईहिं ४; इंहिं १२; त्रिस्नां। त्रिश्नां ८ १३; त्रिस्ना २०; त्रिष्णां २१; त्रिसनां १६; षांडी। षांडी हो २१

९५:२ बैठा। बैठौं १० रहूं। रहौं ८ १२ १६; फिरूं। फिरौ १६; फिरौं ८ १२; फीरूं २०; डोलूं। डोलौं १ ८ १२ १६; भूषां। भूषा ८ २०; रहूं। रहौं ८ १२ १६; षाऊं। षांऊं १२ १६; षांउं ८; षाऊं हो १ २१; मरूं। मरौं ८ १२ १६; मरं २१, जीऊं। जीउं ८ १२; अहि। ईहिं ४; अह ८ १२ २०; इंहिं २१; निसि। निंसि १२; निहि ८; भुगतौं। भुग्तौं ४; भुगतूं १ २०; भुगतौ १२; नहीं। नहि १; नही ८ २१; आऊं। आंऊं १ १२ १६; आंउं ८; नहीं। नहि १; नही ८ २१; जांऊं। ज्यांऊं २०; जांऊं हो २१; जांउं ८ १२

९५:३ रहनि। रहंनि २१; रहणी २०; हमारी। हंमारी ८ २०; सहज। शुनि १; सुंनि। सुंनिं १२; सुन्यि २१; सुनि ८; सहज १; ग्रिह। गिर्ह १६; ग्रह १ १२; गृह ८; अंतरधुनि। अंतरिधुंनिं १२; अंतरिधुनि ८; अंतरिजोति २०; अंतरजोति १ २१; बिलमाऊं। बिलमांऊं २०; बिलमांउ ८; बिलमांउं १२; बिलबांऊं १६ २१; बैलांऊं ४; कोई। कोको ४; जोगी। जोगि या १६ २१; जोगीं १२; गंमि। गंमिं १२; गंम १ २०; गमि ४; लहैला। व्हैला ४

९५:४ तोडि। तौडी २०; पूजौं। पूजू २०; पूजूं १; देवलि। देवल १; देवली २०; होई। होई हो १; होइ हो ४ २१; नांमां। नांमौं ४ २१; कहै १; कहै। नांमदेव १; मैं। - १; हरि। अहनिसि २०; हरी ४; की। - २०; का १ ४ २१; सरना। ध्यांउं २०; चरणां १ ४ २१; पुनरपि। पुनरप २१; पुन्रप ४; पुनरपी २०; जनम। जंनम २१; होई। होई हो १ ४; थाई २०

९६:० गगन। गगंन २१; गूडी। गुडी २०; गूंडी ८ १२; बैठी। बीठी १; नांहीं। नांही ४ ८ २१

९६:१ ताहि। ताही ४ २०

९६:२ कहिबौ। कहिबा ८ १२; कहिवौ १; सुनिबौ। शुंणिवौ १; सुंनिंबा १२; सुनिंबौ २१; सुनिबा ८; जब। तब १२; गत। लग १२; होइबौ। होई २०; होईगौ ४; होइब। ८ १२; ताहि। ताह १; ता ४; ताही २०; परचौ। परचा ८ १२

३ गाये गये गये ते गाये । अगई कौं का गाऊं ॥
४ प्रणवंत नांमां भये निहकांमां । सहज समाधि लगाऊं ॥

६७

• जोगी जन न्याइ जुगे जुगि जीवै ॥
आकास बांधि पाताल चलावै आप भरे भरि पीवै ॥
१ अंम्रित षात पिता परमोध्यौ माइ मुई करि सोग रे ॥
भाई बंध की आस न जुगी भाजि गये सब लोग रे ॥
२ बाहिली मूंदिलै मांहिली चोघिलै पंच की आस मिटाइ रे ॥
भणत नांमदेव सेइ निरंजन सहजि समाधि लगाइ रे ॥

६८

• देंवा तेरा नीसांण बाज्या हो ॥
ताल पषावज जंत्र बेनां औसर साज्या हो ॥
१ लोहा तांबा बंदन कीन्हां पाइ परी है बेरियां ॥
भौसागर की संक्या छूटी मुकति भई है चेरियां ॥

६६;३ गाये। पंच २०; गाए १६ २१; गाऐ ४ ८ १३; गये। गए १६ २१; गऐ ४ १३; सुभाइ २०; गये। - ८; मन २०; गए १६ २१; गऐ ४ १३; ते। की २०; गाये। गाए १६ २१; गाऐ ४ ८ १३; सोभा २०; अगई। भला २०; अंगइ २१; कौं। कै १; कौ ८; बूरा २०; का। क्या २१; अंब १६; अब ८ १३; न २०; गाऊं। कहाऊंगा २०; गांऊं १ १६; गांउंगा ८ १३; गाऊंगा २१

६६;४ प्रणवंत। भणंति १; भणत २०; प्रंणवंत २१; प्रणवति ४; प्रणवत ८; नांमां। + ४; भये। + ४; भए १६ २१; निहकांमां। +कांमां ४; निहिकांमां १६ २१; निहंकांमां १३ २०; सहज। सहजि १ ४; समाधि। संमांधि १३; संमाधि २० २१; लगाऊं। लगाऊंगा २० २१; लगांउंगा ८ १३

६७;० जन। जंन २१; न्याइ। न्यांई २०; न्याई ४; जुगि। जुग २०; जुगे ७; आकास। आकासि १; बांधि। बंधि ८; चलावै। चलावैं २०

६७;१ अंम्रित। अँम्रत १३; अंमृत ८ १६ १७; अमृत ७; परमोध्यौ। प्रमोध्या ८; प्रमोध्यो ४; परमोधौ २०; माइ। माई ४ १३ २०; मुई। मूई १६ २०; रे। - ८ १६ १७; भाजि। भागि १; गये। गए १६ २१; गऐ ४; गयौ ७; रे। - ४ ७ ८ १६ १७

६७;२ बाहिली। बाहरिली २०; मूंदिलै। मूंदिले २१; मूदिले ८ १६; मांहिली। मांहिंली २१; मांहलि २०; चोघिलै। चोघिले २१; आस। प्यास १ १३ २०; मिटाइ। मिटाई १ ४ ८; भणत। भणंत १३; नांमौं १; प्रणवंत २१; नांमदेव। कहैं तव १; सेइ। सेवि ८ १३ १६ १७; सेई ४; सहजि। सहज १ ७ ८ १६ २०; समाधि। संमांधि १३; संमाधि २१; लगाइ। लगाई १ ४ २०

६८;० नीसांण। निंसांण १३; बेनां। बेणां १ ४ २१; औसर। अैसर १; साज्या। साजया १६

६८;१ तांबा। कांचन २०; तंबा १ ४ २१; बंदन। बंधंन २०; बंधन २१; कीन्हां। कींन्हां १३; पाइ। पाई ४; बेरियां। बेरीयां २०; बरियां ८; मुकति। मुक्ति १ २१; भई। भइ २० २१

२ स्यंघ भागा पूठी फेरी षांण लागी छेरिग्य ।
 बाहरि जाता भीतरि पेष्या नांमैं भगति [illegible]ग्यां ॥

६९

० संत प्रवांणीं भगति आपिला । नहीं आपिला तौ प्रांण त्यागिला ॥
१ हमची थाती तुम बसि भईला । अम्हचा जीवला किमचि लागिला ॥
२ चारि मुकति आठौं सिधि आपूं । भगति न आपूं दास नमइया ॥
३ नांमदेव बीठल सनमुष बोलिला । भगति आपिला मुकति त्यागिला ॥

७०

० याही गोब्यंदा चरन मेरौ जीयरौ बसै रे ॥
 भगति न छाडौं हरि की भावै लोग हसौ रे ॥
१ गोब्यंदा कौ नांव लीयैं भौजल तिरियै रे ॥
 झूठी माया लागि लागि काहे कौं मरियै रे ॥
२ सांई कैं सांकडै छाडै सेवग भाजै रे ॥

६८;२ स्यंघ। सिंघ १३; सिंघ ८; पूठी। पूठि १ १९ २०; पीठि ८ १३; फेरी। फेरि २०; षांण। षांन १३; षाण २०; जाता। जात २०; भीतरि। भींतरि १ १३; पेष्या। आंण्यां २०; नांमैं। नांमौं ४; नबेरियां। निबेरियां १९; नबेरिया ४

६९;० संत। सत ३ १०; प्रवांणीं। प्रबेनी १०; प्रवेणीं ७; प्रवेनीं ३; नहीं। नहिं १; आपिला। आपीला १; तौ। - १; तो १०; प्रांण। प्रांन ३ १०; प्राण १; त्यागिला। त्यागीला ३

६९;१ हमची। हंमची १; तुम। तुम्ह ७; भईला। भइला १ ७ १०; अम्हचा। हमचा १; जीवला। जिवला १०; किमचि। किमचित १

६९;२ आठौं। आठूं ७; आठो १०; आगैं १; सिधि। सिधी १०; आपूं। आंपूं ३; आपौं १; आपूं। आपू ३; [illegible]पौं १; नमइया। नमईया ७

६९;३ बीठल। बिठल १०; भगति। भक्ति १; मुकति। मुक्ति १

७०;० याही। यांही ४; गोब्यंदा। गोबिंदा ७ १३; गोबिदा ८; चरन। चरंण ४; चरंणा २१; चरनि १९; चरण २०; मेरौ। मेरे १०; मेरो ३; जीयरौ। जीयरो १०; जीयरा ३; जीवरौ २१; बसै। बसे १०; भगति। हरि भगति ३ १०; छाडौं। छाडूं ७ २१; छाडों १०; हरि। - ३ १० १३; की। - ३ १० १३; भावै। - ७ ८ १० १९ २१; भलैं ४; लोग। लोक ७; हसौ। हसै ८; हसै ४ १९ २०; हसौं १; हसो १०

७०;१ गोब्यंदा। गोबिंदा ४ ७ १३; गोबिदा ८; कौ। कै ८ १९; के ४; को १०; नांव। नांई ४; नांवं १; नांइ ८; नाव ७; नाइ १९; लीयैं। लींयिं १३; लीये १०; लीयें १ ३ ८; लीयौ २०; लयें ७; लागि ४; भौजल। भौसागर २०; भोजल १०; भवजल ४ २१; तिरियै। तिरिए २१; रे। - ८ १३ १९; कौं। कुं १०; कूं १ ७ २१; मरियै। मरिऐ ४; मरियै १९; मरीये १० २०; रे। - ३ ७ ८ १३ १९

७०;२ सांई। सांईं ७ २०; सांइ १०; साइं १; कैं। नैं ३; ने १०; कै ४; कूं १ ७ २१; को १९; कौं ८ १३; सांकडै। सांकरे १०; साकडै ८; साकरै ३; छाडै। छाडि १०; दीयैं १९; दीयें ८ २०; दीया १ ४; दीयां ७;

चिंरकालि नां को जीवै दोउ पष लाजै रे ॥
३ आपणां धन कारणि प्रांणीं मरण मांडै रे ॥
भगति भगता जन काहे कौं छाडै रे ॥
४ गंगा गया गोदावरी संसारी धरमा रे ॥
सपरसन नारांइण सेवग नांमां रे ॥

७१

• देवा नटणीं कौ तन मन बांसां बर तां मांहि रे ॥
अनेक राजिंद्र बैठे तिनहूं सौं चित नांहि रे ॥
१ सुमति सरीर संवारै नटणीं निहारै ॥
रांम नांम नींसांण बाजै इहिं तति पाव धारै रे ॥
२ एक मन एक चित षेलीलै षेला रे ॥
मरकट मूंठी छाडि दे ज्यूं मुकति भैला रे ॥

भाजै। भागै ३; भागें १०; भाजे १ ४; चिंरकालि। चिंरकाल ७ ८ १६ २०; चिंरकाली १ ४ १३; चिरकाली १०; चीरांकाली ३; नां। ना ४ १६; को १ २०; को। नहि १; ना २०; कोई १३; कोउ ३ १०; जीवै। जीवे १०; दोउ। दोऊ १ ४ १६; दोऊं २१; लाजै। लाजे १०

७०:३ आपणां। आपणडा १३; आपनडा ३ १० २०; धन। धंन १३ २० २१; कारणि। कारंणि १३; कारंणि २१; कारंणि ७; कारनि ३ १६; कारण २०; प्रांणीं। प्रांणी ८ २१; प्रांनी १०; प्रांनीं ३; मरण। मरणां २१; मरन ३ १०; मांडै। माडै ३; रे। रै ४; भगति। तौ भगति ३; तो भगति १०; जन। जंन २० २१; जन तेरौ ३; जन तेरो १०; कौं। कुं १०; कूं १ ७ २१; छाडै। छांडै १ ७; रे। - २१

७०:४ गोदावरी। गुदावरी १६; गायत्री १०; गाइत्री ३; संसारी। संसारि २०: सेवग ८: धरमा। धर्मा १३; धरमां ३; धामां १; जंमा २१; जांमा २०; जांमां ४ ७ ८ १६; सपरसन। श्रुप्रसन १; नरांइन ३: नरायण १०; नारांयण १३; सुप्रसंण २१; सुपरसण २०; सप्रसन १६; सपरसंण ७; सपरसंन ४; नारां[illegible]ण। मुष १०; नारांयण ४; नारांइणा २०; नाराइण ८ १६; सनमुष ३; सपरसंन १३; नांमां। नांमा २०

७१:० नटणीं। नटंनी २१; नटणी ८ १३; नटनी १०; नटनीं ३; कौ। कौं १६; [illegible]ो १०; तन। तं[illegible] ४ २० २१; मन। मंन २१; मना १३; बांसां। बंसा ४; बंसां ७ ८; बांसा १२ १७; [illegible] १: वर। ब १२ १७; तां। ता १२ १७; राजिंद्र। राज्यंद्र ३ ४ १७ २० २१; राज्यंद्रा १०; राजिद्र ८; बैठे। बैंठा २१; बेठे १०; तिनहूं। तिनंहीं २१; तिनंहीं ४; तिनहु १०; तिनहीं ७ १६ १७; ताहू २०; सौं। स्यूं ३ २० २१; स्यौं १; सु १०; सूं ४ ७; नांहि। [illegible] नांहिं २१

७१:१ सुमति। श्रुमति १; सुंमति १३ २१; सुरति १६; संवारै। संवारे १०; संवारी १३; नटणीं। नटणी ८ १७; नटनी १० २१; नांटनी ३; निहारै। निंहारौ रे १३; निहारै रे ३ ७ २०; निहारे १०; नांम। नांव ३; नींसांण। निंसांण १३; निसांन ३; निसाण २०; नीसांण ८ २१; नीसांन १०; बाजै। बार्जे १३; बाजे १०; इहिं। तिहि ३ १०; ईहिं ४; इंहिं १३ २१; इहि ७ ८ १७; तति। तटि ३ १०; पाव। न ३ १०; धारै। धारे १०; रे। - १ ४ ८ १६ १७ २१

७१:२ एक। ऐक १ ४ ८ १३; येक २०; येकै ३; मन। मंन २१; मनि ३ १० २०; एक। ऐक १ ४ १३; येक ८ २०; येकै ३; चित। चिति ३ १०; षेलीलै। षेलिलै २०; षेलिले १०; षेलीले १ १६; मरकट। म्रकट ८ १३ १७ २१; मर्कट १६; मूंठी। मुंठी १० २०; मूठी ४ ८ १६ १७; दे। दै ३ १३; रे १६; ज्यूं। ज्यौं १ ३ ८ १६; मुकति। मुंकति १३; भैला। भेला १०; भईला १६; रे। - ८ १३ २१

३ धरणींधर सौं ध्यांन लागौ अंतरजांमीं रे ॥
नांमदेव नटवा ह्वै नाच्यौ तब रीझ्यौ स्वांमीं रे ॥

७२

• भाई रे भरम गया भौ भागा ॥
तेरा जन जहां का तहां जाइ लागा ॥
१ बाजीगर डांक बजाई सब दुनी तमासै आई ॥
बाजीगर षेल सकेला तब आपैं रह्या अकेला ॥
२ रांम राइ माया लाई सब दुनियां सौदै आई ॥
सब दुनियां सौदा कींन्हां काहू आतमरांम न चींन्हां ॥
३ म्रिग षेत बिझूका देषै भैचकि भैचकि पेषै ॥
निकटि गयां सुधि पाई अडवा थैं कहा डराई ॥
४ यहु म्रिगनि षेत बिझूका गई संक्या मन ढूका ॥
नांमदेव सतगुर ह्वै समझावै याही थैं कहा बतावै ॥

७३

• जहां तहां मिल्यौ सोई ताथैं कहै सुनैं कोई ॥

७१;३ धरणींधर। धरंणीधर २१; धरनधीर ८; धरनींधर ३ १३; सौं। स्यूं ४ २० २१; स्यौं १; स्यो ३; सूं ७; ध्यांन। ध्यान १०; लागौ। लागो १०; अंतरजांमीं। अंतरजांमी १ ७ ८ १७; मनहीं धांमीं ३; मनही धामी १०; नटवा। नवा २०; ह्वै। होई ४; होइ ८; नाच्यौ। न्याच्यौ ८; नांचो १०; नांच्यो ३ २१; तब। तौ ७ ८ १७ २० २१; रीझ्यौ। रीझे ३; रीझो १०; स्वांमीं। स्वांमी ८ १७; स्वामी ३; स्वामीं १९

७२;० भरम। भर्म १९; भौ। भो १०; तेरा। - ३ १०

७२;१ डांक। डंक १९; डाक ८ २०; ढाक १०; बजाई। बजाइ १०; दुनी। दुनीं ३ ७ १९; तमासै। तमांसैं १३; तमांसे ३; तमासे १०; आई। आइ १०; सकेला। सकेल्या २०; सककेला ८; सषेला १९; तब। - ८; अैसैं २०; आपैं। आपै १३; आपन ३ १०; रह्या। रहै ७ ८ १३ १९

७२;२ राइ। राई ३; माया। माइ १०; लाई। लाइ १०; दुनियां। दुंनिंयां १३; दुनीसं ३; दुनीया १०; दुनीयां २०; सौदै। सोदे १०; आई। आइ १०; दुनियां। दुंनिंयां १९; दुनिया ३ ७ १०; दुनीयां २०; सौदा। सोदा १०; कींन्हां। कीन्हां ३ ८ १९; काहू। काहूं १९; आतमरांम। आतमराम ३; आतमरांम १३; चींन्हां। चीन्हां ३ ७ ८

७२;३ म्रिग। म्रिघ ३ ७; म्रग १० १३; मृग ८ १९; षेत। षेती २०; बिझूका। विझूका १०; देषै। देषे १०; भैचकि। भैचषि २०; भौंचकि १३; भैचकि। भैंचकि १३; पेषै। पैषै २०; पेषे १०; निकटि। निंकटि १३; निकट ३ १० २०; गयां। गया ३ १९; सुधि। सुध्यि २०; पाई। पाइ १०; अडवा। अडबा १०; थैं। तैं ३ ८ १३ २०; ते १०; डराई। डराइ १०

७२;४ यहु। न २०; यह १३; इंनि ३; इन १०; इहां ७; म्रिगनि। म्रिघन्य ३; म्रिघन ७; मिगनिं १३; म्रगन १०; मृघनि १९; बिझूका। विझूका १०; गई। गइ १०; संक्या २०; संक्या। गई २०; ढूका। ढुका १०;

१ अभेदैं अभेद मिल्यौ भेदैं मिल्यौ भेदू ॥
सहज सोई सहजैं मिल्यौ षेलैं मिल्यौ षेलू ॥
२ दुष सोई दुषैं मिल्यौ सुषैं सुष समांनां ॥
ग्यांन सोई ग्यानैं मिल्यौ ध्यांनैं मिल्यौ ध्यांनां ॥
३ देष्यौ कहूं तौ निपट झूठा सुणीं कहूं तौ झूठा रे ॥
नांमदेव कहै जे अगम भणौं तौ पूछ्या ही अणपूछ्या रे ॥

७४

• बीठल भौंरौ कंवल न पावै ताथैं जनमि जनमि डहकावै ॥
१ दादुर एक बसै पडवणि तलि स्वाद कुस्वाद न पावै ॥
पहुप बास कौ लुबधी भौंरौ सौ जोजन फिरि आवै ॥
२ महणारंभ होत घट भीतरि रवि ससि नेत बिलोवै ॥
वो हालै वो ठौर न पावै ताथैं भौंरौ जुगि जुगि रोवै ॥

टूका ३ १३ १६; नांमदेव। जन ३ १०; सतगुर। नांमदेव कहि ३ १०; ह्वै। - ३ १०; होइ १३; समझावै। समझांवै १३; समझावे १०, थैं। थें और २०; तें ३; तैं ८ १३; तें १०; बतावै। बतावे १०

७३;० मिल्यौ। मिल्यौ है २०; ताथैं। तातिं ८; तातैं १३; सुनैं। श्रुणैं १; सुंनैं १३; सुंणे २१; सुणैं ४ १७; सुनैं सब १६

७३;१ अभेदैं। अभेद १६; अभेदें ८; अभेद। भेद ८ १३ १७; मिल्यौ। मिल्या ८ १३; भेदैं। भेदें ८; अभेदैं १६; मिल्यौ। मिल्या ८ १३; भेदू। भेद २१; सहज। सहजे २०; सहजैं। सहजे १६ २०; मिल्यौ। मिल्या ८ १३; षेलैं। षेलौं ४; मिल्यौ। मिल्या ८ १३; षेलू। षेल २१; षेलूं १६

७३;२ दुष। दूष ४; दुषैं। दुष २०; दुषै १६; मिल्यौ। मिल्या ८ १३; सुषैं। शुषैं १; सुषै १३ १७; सुष। शुष १; सुख १६; समांनां। संमांनां १३ २० २१; ग्यांन। मन १; ग्यानैं १३; ग्यानैं। मनैं १; ग्यांन ८ १३; ग्यांनैं १६ २१; मिल्यौ। मिल्या १३; ध्यांनैं। ध्यांन १६; ध्यांनै २०; ध्यांनय ४; ग्यानैं १; मिल्यौ। मिल्या १३; मील्यौ २०, ध्यांनां। ध्यांना २०; ग्यांनां १

७३;३ देष्यौ। देष्यौं १६; देष्या ८ १३; कहूं। कहो १६; कहौं ८; तौ। त १; झूठा। झूठ १७; सुणीं। शुण्यां १; सुंणीं १३ २१; सुणें ४; सुणी ८; कहूं। कहे १६; कहौं ८ १३; तौ। त १; रे। - ८ १३; र १; नांमदेव। नांम ८ १३ २१; नांमौं १ २०; जे। मैं १३; अगम। अगंम १ १३; आगंम २१; भणौं। भणैं ८ १६ १७ २०; भणूं १; पूछ्या। पूछ्यां ४ १७; ही। हीं १६ १७; अणपूछ्या। अंणपूछ्या २० २१; रे। - १ ८ १३ २१

७४;० बीठल। बींठल २१; बीठूला २०; बीठला ८ १६; राम राइ ७; भौंरौ। भंवरो ४ २०; भंवरा १६; भोरों १०; भवरौ ७; कंवल। कमल १०; पावै। पावै रे २०; पावे १०; ताथैं। तातैं १ ८; ताते १०; जनमि। जनंम २१; जनमिं १३; जनम ७; जनमि। जनंमिं १३; जनंम २१; जनम ७; डहकावै। डहकावे १०

७४;१ दादुर। +दुर ४; दादूर २०; दादर ३ १०; एक। ऐक १ ३ ४ १३; येक ८ १० २०; बसै। बस्त १६; बसे १०; पडवणि। पडवंणि १ २१; पडवांणि ८; परवनि ३ १०; तलि। +ली ४; कुस्वाद। कुसाद १३; पावै। पावे १०; पहुप। पुहप १६; पहूप ४ २०; कौ। को १०; का १६; लुबधी। लूबधी २०; लोवधी १०; भौंरौ। भौंरो १०; भौरा १६; सौ। - २१; सो १० २०; जोजन। जोजंन २१; आवै। आवे १०

७४;२ महणारंभ। महिणारंभ १; महिरणरंभ १०; महंणारंभ १३ २० २१; मांहिंणरंभ ३; होत। तास ३ १०; भीतरि। भींतरि १ ४ १३ २०; भीतर १६; रवि। रबि ३ २१; रव ७; नेत। नेत्र १ ४ १३ २१; बिलोवै।

३ उपजी भगति पचीसौं परहरि बहुरि न भौजलि आवै ॥
अषंड मंडल निराकार मैं दास नांमदेव गावै ॥

७५

• रे मन न पडि भोला प्यंजरै संसार माया जाल ॥
एक दिन मैं तीनि फेरा तोकूं सदा झपै काल ॥
१ धन रूप जोबन देषि करि रे गरब्यौ कहा गंवार ॥
कुंभ काचौ नीर भरियौ बिनसतां नहीं बार ॥
२ कपूर भोजन सब किये नित नवां सिंणगार ॥
हंस कावडि छाडि चाल्यौ देह ह्वैली छार ॥
३ तें पिता जननी आथि लिछिमीं पूत सोह परिवार ॥
इता ऊभा मेल्हि करि एकलौ जाहि गवार ॥
४ भणत नांमदेव सुणौं त्रिलोचन घटि दया धर्म पालि ॥
अम्हे पांहुणां दिन चारि का सुक्रित रांम संभालि ॥

७६

• अदबुद अचंभौ कथ्यौ न जाई । चींटी कै नेत्र कैसैं गज्यंद्र समाई ॥
१ कोई बोलै नीयरै कोई बोलै दूरि । जल की मछली कैसैं चढै षिजूरि ॥

बिलोवै १०; वो। ओ ७ १६; यह १०; यहु ३; हालै। हाले १०; वो। ओ ४ ७ १६; वहु १०; वहुं ३; ठौर। ठोर १०; पावै। पावे १०; तार्थैं। तातैं ८ १३ २०; ताते १०; भौंरौ। भौंरौं १३; भौंरो ३; भौंरा ८; भौरी २१; भोंरो १०; भवरौ ४ ७; भवरा १६; रोवै। रौवै २०; रोवे १०

७४;३ भगति। भगती १०; भागति २०; पचीसौं। पचिंसो १०; पचीसूं ७ २१; परहरि। परहारि ४; बहुरि। बहूरि २०; वहुरि १; न। जंनमि ४ २१; जनमि १६; जनम १; भौजलि। भौजल २०; भोजलि १०; नहि १; नही २१; नहीं ४ १६; संकुटि १३; संकटि ८; आवै। आवे १०; अषंड। निराकार २०; अंषंड ८; मंडल। अषंड २०; निराकार। मंडल २०; मैं। मे १०; दास। नांमदेव हरि २०; नांमदेव। गुण २०; गावै। गावें १०

७६.० अदबुद। अदबूद २०; अचंभौ। अचंभौ भारी २०; अचंभो १०; अचंभा ८ १३ १६ १७; कथ्यौ। कथियो ४; कह्यो १०; कथ्यो ३; कथ्या ८ १३ १६ १७; न। नहीं २०; जाई। जाइ १० १६ १७ २१; चींटी। चीटी ८ २० २१; कै। के २० २१; नेत्र। निकासि १०; निकालि ३; नेत्रि ४ १६ १७ २१; नेत्र मैं २०; कैसैं। मै १३; केसें १०; गज्यंद्र २०; गज्यंद्र। कैसैं २०; गजिंद्र १३ १६; हस्ती ३ १०; समाई। संमांई १३; संमाई २०; समाइ १० १६ १७

७६;१ कोई। कोउ ३ १०; बोलै। बोले १०; नीयरै। नियरै २०; नियरे ४ २१; नीरा ३ १०; कोई। कोउ ३ १०; बोलै। बोले १०; दूरि। दूरी ८; मछली। मंछी ३ २१; मछी १०; कैसैं। - २०; केसे १०; चढै। चढी २०; षिजूरि। षजूरि ३ १६ १७ २०; षीजूरी १०

२ कोई बोलै इंद्री बांध्यां कोई बोलै मुकता । सहज समाधि न चीन्हैं मुगधा ॥
३ कोई बोलै बेद सुम्रित पुरांनां । सतगुरि कथिया पद न्रिबांनां ॥
४ कहत नांमदेव परम तत अैसा । जाकै रूप न रेष बरन कहूं कैसा ॥

१ कोई बोलै निरवा कोई बोलै दूरि । जल की माछुली चरै खजूरि ॥
० कांइ रे बकबादु लाइओ । जिनि हरि पाइओ तिनहि छपाइओ ॥ रहाउ ॥
२ पंडितु होइकै बेदु बखानै । मूरखु नामदेउ रामहि जानै ॥

७७

० देवा आज गुडी सहजि उडी गगन मांहि समाई ॥
बोलनहारा डोरि समांनां नहीं आवै नहीं जाई ॥
१ तीनि रंग डोरि जाकै सेत पीत स्याही ॥
छाडि गगन बाजि पवन सुर नर मुनि चाही ॥
२ द्वादस थैं उपजि गडी जांनैं जन कोई ॥
मनसा कौं दरस परस गुर थैं गमि होई ॥

७६;२ कोई। कोउ २ १०; कोइ २१; बोलै। बोले १०; इंद्री। ईंद्री ४; ईंद्री १३; यंद्री १ १० १६ १७; इद्री ८; बांध्यां। बंध्या ८ १३; बांधै १; बांधें ३; बांध्यें १०; कोई। कोउ २ १०; मुकता। मुक्ता १ १७ २१; सहज। सहजि ३; समाधि। संमांधि १३; संमाधि २० २१; चीन्हैं। चींन्हैं १३ २१; चींन्हैं रे ३; चीन्हैं यं ४; चीन्हे रे १०; जांनैं १; मुगधा। मुग्ध्या २१

७६;३ कोई। कोउ २ १०; बोलै। बोलें १०; सुम्रित। शुम्रिति १; सुम्रत १३; सुमृत्य ४; सुमृत ८ १६; सास्त्र १०; साश्त्र ३; पुरांनां। पुरांणां ४ २०; परवांन ३; परवान १०; सतगुरि। सतगुर २ ४ १० १३; न्रिबांनां। न्रिबांणां २०; न्रिबांना २१; न्रिबाण ३; निंबांणां ४; निर्बांनां १६; निरबान १०; निरवांनां १; त्रबांनां १३; नृबांणां ८

७६;४ कहत। भणंत २०; भनत २ १०; परम। पर्म १३; परंम २० २१; हरि १; यह १०; यहु ३; तत। तत है १६ १७; अैसा। अेसा १०; जाकै। - १ २ १०; ताकै २१; न। - २१; बरन। बरं ४; बरंण २१; बरण १ २०; कहूं। कहु १; कहू १३; कहौं १६; बपु २ १०; कैसा। केसा १०

७७;० आज। आजि १ ३ १० २१; गुडी। गूडी १ १२ १६ २१; सहजि। सहज ८ १३; सहजी ४ १०; उडी। ऊंडी १३; ऊडी १ ४ १६; गगन। गगंन २१; सुनि २०; मांहि। मांहिं १२ १६; माहि ३ ८; समाई। संमांई १३; संमाई २१; समाइ १०; बोलनहारा। बोलंनहारा २१; बोलणहारा १; बोलहारा १०; समांनां। समाया १ ४; लागी १०; लागा ३ २१; नहीं। नहि १; नही ८ १०; आवै। आवे १०; नहीं। नहि १; नही ८; जाई। जावै २०

७७;१ तीनि। तीनिं १३; तीन ३; तोनी १०; जाकै। जाके १०; स्याही। स्यांही १३; गगन। गंगंन २१; बाजि। बाजी २ १०; पवन। पवंन १२ २१; बाव २ १०; सुर। शुर १; सुरनि ३; सुरन १०; नर। - २ १०; मुनि। मुंनि १३; मुनिं १६

७७;२ द्वादस। द्वादश १०; थैं। तैं २ ८ १२ २०; तें १०; उपजि। उपजी २ ८; रहित ४; रहत २०; गडी। गुडी २ ८ १० १६ १७ २१; गूंडी १३; गूडी १ ४ २०; जांनैं। -- ४ २०; जांणैंगा १; जांनै ३; जन। जंन २१; कोई। कोइ १०; मनसा। -- ४ २०; मंनसा २१; कौं। कूं १ २१; को १०; गुर। -- ४ २०; थैं। तैं ८ १३; ते ३ १०; गमि। गंम्य १३; गंमि १ १७ २१; होई। होइ १०

३ कागद थैं रहित गूडी सहजि आनंद होई ॥
नांमदेव जल मेघ बूंद मिलि रह्या ज्यौं सोई ॥

७८

० काहे रे मन भूला फिरई । चेतनि रांम चरन चित धरई ॥
१ नरहरि नरहरि जपि रे जीयरा । अवधि काल दिन आवै नीयरा ॥
२ पुत्र कलित्र धन चित बिसासा । छाडि मनां सब झूठी आसा ॥
३ तूं जिनि जांनैं ग्रेही ग्रेहा । बिनसत बार नहीं कछू देहा ॥
४ कहत नांमदेव झूठी देही । तौ साची जे रांम सनेही ॥

७९

० रांम नांम बोलि त्रिबांन बांनी । जिभ्या आंन मिथ्या करि जांनीं ॥
१ को को न तारे को को न उधारे । बैकुंठनाथा षसम हमारे ॥
२ सोना की भालि पाषांण बेधीला । झींझ फूटी राजा रांम अकेला ॥

७७;३ कागद। -- ४ २०; थैं। तैं २ ८ १३; ते १०; रहित। रहत ८ १३; गूडी। गुडी २ ८ १० १७ २१; सहजि। बिरले ३; बिरले १०; सहज ४; आनंद। आंनंद १३ १७ २१; आंनद ८; जनि ३; जन १०; होई। जांणीं २ १०; जल। प्रभू ३ १०; मेघ। यूं १०; यों ३; बूंद। मिले २ १०; बुंद २१; मिलि। जैसैं ३; जेसें १०; रह्या। मेघ २ १०; ज्यौं। - २१; ज्यूं ४ १९ १७; त्यौं १३; बुंद १०; बूंद ३; सोई। पांनी १०; पांनीं ३

७८;० मन। मंन २१; भूला। भूल्यौ १ २०; भूल्गो ३ १०; भूलौ ७ १३; फिरई। फिरही १; चेतनि। चेतंनि २१; चेतनिं १३; चरन। चरंण २१; चरण ४ २०; धरई। धरही १

७८;१ नरहरि। न्रहरि ८; जपि। जपिऐ १९; जीयरा। जियरा २ १०; जीइरा १९; अवधि। अंति २०; दिन। दिंन १३; आवै। आवे १०; नीयरा। न्यिरा १०; नियरा ४ १९ २० २१

७८;२ कलित्र। कलित ४ १७; धन। धंन १३ २० २१; बिसासा। बेसास १; बेसासा ३ ७; सब। रे १ ४ ८ १९ १७ २१; आसा। आस १

७८;३ तूं। तू ३; जिनि। जिंनिं १३ २१; जिन्य ३; जांनैं। जानि १०; जांगै २०; ग्रेही। - २ १०; ग्रेंही १९; ग्रेहा ७; ग्रेहा। ग्रेही २०; बिनसत। बिंनसत १३; नहीं। नही २ ८ १० २१; कछू १ ७ १९ १७; कछू। छिंन १३; नहि १; नहीं ७ १९ १७; कछु १०; तंन २१; वह २०

७८;४ कहत। भणंत १३ २०; भणत ७; देही। आसा ८; देहा २०; तौ। तो १०; साची। सांची ३; जे। जौ १ १३; जो २ १०; रांम। राम ३; सनेही। पियासा ८; सनेंही १३; सनेहा २०

७९;० रांम। रांमैं १; नांम। नांमैं ८ १३; नामैं १ १९; रामै २०; बोलि। बोली ४; त्रिबांन। त्रिंबांन १३; त्रिबाण ४ २१; निर्बांण १९; निरबांण ७ ८; निरबांन ३ १०; बांनी। बांणी ४ ७ ८ २१; बांणीं १३ १९; जिभ्या। ज्यभ्या १; जिभ्यां ३; जीभ्या १०; जांनीं। जांणी ८; जांणीं ४ ७ १३ १९ २१; जांनी ३ १०

७९;१ को। - १ ७ ८ १९; बैकुंठनाथा। त्रिभुवननाथ ३; त्रिभुवननाथा १०; बैकुंठनाथ ७ २१; बैकुठनाथा १९; बैकूंठनाथ १३; बैकूंठनाथा २०; षसम। षसंम २१; हमारे। हंमारे ८ १३ २१

७९;२ सोना। सोनैं ४ २१; सोनें ७; सोनां ३ ८ १३ १९; भालि। भांलि १९; भाली ४; पाषांण। +षाण ४;

३ सपत पुरी नौ ऊषर भाई । रांम बिनां कौनैं गति पाई ॥
४ माटी देषि माटी कहा भुलांनां । कहि समझावै दास नांमां ॥

८०

• मेरी कौंन गति गुंसांई तुम जगत भरन देवा ॥
जनम हीन करम छीन भूलि गयौ सेवा ॥
१ बडौ पतित पतितन मैं गज गनिका गांमीं ॥
और पतित जगत प्रगट तिनमैं हूं नांमीं ॥
२ तुम दयाल मैं गरीब टेरि कह्यौ रांमां ॥
दींन जांनिं बीनती मांनिं गावै दास नांमां ॥

८१

• ऐवडी सी मूंनैं बुधि आवडी । रांम न बिसरौं एकौ घडी ॥
१ हरि हरि कहतां जे नर लाजै । जम की डांग तिनैं सिरि बाजै ॥
२ हरि हरि कहतां न कीजै बूता । गयें पाप जे पोतै हुता ॥
३ नांमदेव कहै मैं हरि हरि भनौं । कटै पाप अरु लाभ होइ घनौं ॥

पषांण ८ १६; पषांन ३ पाषांन २१; पाषांन २०; पाषाण १०: बेधीला। भेदिला १०; बेधिला २०; झींझि। झिझि १०: झींझि ३; झीझ ८; फूटी। फूटि ३ २०; राजा। रांम ७ १६ २० २१: रांम। नांम ७ १६ २० २१

७६:३ सपत। सप्त १ ३ ७ १८ २१; पुरी। पूरी २०; नौ। नो १०; नव १ २१. ऊषर। उषर ३ ८ १० १३ २० २१; भाई। भाइ १०: रांम। रांम ३ १०; बिनां। बिना ३ १०; बिना १३. बिन २१. कौनैं। कौनैं ३: कोने १०; कूवनैं ४; कौंणैं १ ७ २१; कौंनैं १३; गति। गति ३ १०; पाई। पाई ३; पाइ १०

७६:४ माटी। मांटी १ ३ ४ ८ १० १३: देषि। +षि ४; माटी। मांटी १ १३; माटी नर ३ १०; कहा। कहा रे १ ४ २१; काहे रे २०; भुलांनां। भुलानां २१; भूलांणां ४; समझावै। संमझावै २१; समझावै वै ३; समझावे १०; नांमां। नांमा ८ २०

८०:० गुंसांई। गुंसाई १३; गुसांई ८; सांई ७; जनम। जन्म १६: हीन। हींन ७ १३ १६; करम। कर्म १३

८०:१ बडौ। बडा ८ १३: पतितन। पतितन १३; मैं। मै १६: गनिका। गनिंका १३; गनिकां १६; गांमीं। कांमीं १३; गांमी ८; हूं। हौं १६. नांमीं। नांमी ८

८०:२ तुम। तुंम १३; दींन। दीन ८ १६; जांनिं। जांनि ८ १६; बीनती। बिनती ७: बींनती १३: मांनिं। मांनि ८ १६

८१:० ऐवडी। येकबडी १०: येवडी ३; मूंनैं। मूनैं ३, मोने १०; रांम। नांम ३; नाम १०: न। - १०; बिसरौं। बिसारौं ३: बिसारो १०: एकौ। ऐकै ४; येकौ ३: येको १०

८१:१ लाजै। लाजे १०; जम। जंम ७; तिनैं। तिनै ४; तिनौं ३; तिनों १०

८१:२ कहतां। कहता १०; न। - ४ ७; कीजै। कीजे ३; बुता। वुता ३; गये। गए ४; गयौ ७; पोतै। पोते १०

८१:३ नांमदेव। नामदेव ३; मैं। में १०; भनौं। भणूं ७; भणों ४; भनों १०; कटै। कटैं ७; कटे १०; काटै ४; अरु। और ४ ७; अरू ३; होइ। है ४; घनौं। घणूं ७: घणों ४: घनों १०

८२

• अैसैं जग थैं दास नियारा ॥
बेद पुरांन पढीं कि न सोचौ पंडित करौ बिचारा ॥
१ दधि बिलोइ जैसैं घ्रित लीजै बहुरि न एकठ थाई ॥
पावक दार जतन करि काढ्यौ बहुरि न कष्ट समाई ॥
२ पारस परसि होत जैसैं कंचन बहुरि न त्रंबक होई ॥
आक पलास बेधिया चंदन कष्ट कहै नहीं कोई ॥
३ रांमहि जपै रांमहीं जांनैं छाडि करम की आसा ॥
रांमहि जपै रांमही होई प्रणवंत नांमदेव दासा ॥

८३

• हमारै गोपाल राजा गोपाल राजा । और देव सूं नांहीं काजा ॥
१ काहू कै सुम्रित बेद पुरानां । चरन कंवल मेरे मन मांनां ॥

८२;० अैसैं। भाई रे १७ २०, ऐसो १०; अैसें ७, अैसे ३ २१; संतो १६; जग। जुग १०; जगु ३; थैं। मैं १; थे ७; ते २०; तैं ३; तें १०; पुरांन। पुरांण ४ २०; पढौ। सुम्रत १०; सुमृत ३; सोधि १७ २०; समझि १६; कि। क्यों १६; नि ३; सब १७ २०; न। १७ २०; नि १ २१. सोचौ। देषौ १६; देषौं १७, देषो १० २०; करौ। करऊ १६; करहु ३ १०

८२;१ दधि। जैसें १६; बिलोइ। बिलोई ४ २१; मथि २०, मथि ३ १० १७; दधि १६; जैसैं। मथि १६; तक्र काढि ३ १०; घ्रित। घ्रत १०, घृत करि १७ २०; घंत ४; घ्रित करि १६; लीजै। लींनां १०; लीन्हा १६; लीन्हां १७; लीना २०; लीनां ३; एकठ। ऐकठ ४; एकठ १; तक्र १६, तक्र ३ १०; थाई। मिलाई ३, मिलाइ १०, समाई १६; दार। जारि १६; जतन। जतंन २१; काढ्यौ। काढ्या १६; काढै १७, काढे २०; काढया ३ १०; काढै १; कष्ट। कस्ट ४; कास्टि १६; दासी १०; दार ३; समाई। माइं १०; संमाई २१

८२;२ पारस। पावक ४; परसि। परसें १६; होत। कंचन १६; होई २१; होइ ७; लोह ३; लोहा १०; जैसैं। भैला १६; भया ३ १०; कंचन। - १६; त्रंबक। तंबक १६ १७; त्रंबक १; लोहा ३ १०; होई। होइ २० २१; थाई १६; आक। ढाक १७; अक १०, सैंबल २०; पलास। ढाक २०; बेधिया। बेढिये २०; बेढियो १७; चंदन। चंदनि २१; कष्ट। कस्ट ४; कास्ट १६; काष्ट १ ३; कहै। कहे १०; कह्या १६; नहीं। न १ ३ १० १६; नही २१; कोई। कोइ १०; जाई १६

८२;३ रांमहि। जे जन ३ १० १७ २०; रांमै २१; रांम नांम १६; जपै। भजै ७; करौं १६; रांम नांम ३ १० १७ २०; रांमहीं। ही २०; हीं १७; सति करि १६; रंगि ३ १०; रांमही २१; जांनैं। जानै २०; जानैं ७ १७; राता ३ १०; छाडि। काटि ३; करम। भरम १६; क्रम १७; कर्म ७; करंम २१; की। कुल १६; आसा। पास १०, पासा ३; रांमहि। रांम कहै १६; ते जन १७ २०; रांमहीं २१; रांम कहत ३ १०; जपै। ते १६; भजै १; रांमैं १७; रांमहिं २०; रांमही ३ १०; रांमही। रांमैं १६; ह्वै ३; ह्वै १०; रांम १७ २०; रांमहीं ४ ७; होई। भाला १६; समानें १७; समानें २०; रहिये ३ १०; प्रणवंत। प्रणवै ४; प्रणवैं ७; प्रनवै २१; प्रनवैं १; पनवत ३ १०; दासा। दास १०

८३;० हमारै। - १३; हमारे १०; और। ओर १०; आंन १३; आंवर ४; सूं। स्यू ३; सु १०; सौं १३; नांहीं। नांही ४ १३; नाहिन १०

२ काहू कै लक्षिन कोटि भंडारा । मेरे रांम का नांम अधारा ॥
३ काहू कै ह्वैंगि पाइक हाथी । मेरे रांम का नांव संगाती ॥
४ श्रब लोक जाका जस गाजा । नांमां का चित हरि सूं लागा ॥

८४

• कहि मन गोबिंद गोबिंद गोबिंदा । हरि के चरन कवल जिनि बिसरै ॥
१ अंतरि ग्रभ सहे दुष भारी । आवत जात परचौ मैं हारी ॥
२ ताथैं नांमौं हरि गुण गावै । बहुरि न भौजलि नियरे आवै ॥

८५

• रांम गोब्यंदा कमोदनि चंदा । छिन छिन पांन करै मकरंदा ॥
१ जैसैं कमल मैं कुसमलताई । मधि गोपाल परसि फिरि आई ॥

८३;१ काहू। काहु १०; कै। के १०; सुम्रित। सुम्रिति १; सुमृत ३; सम्रत १०; पुरांनां। पुरांणां १३; चरन। चरण १३; कंवल। कमल १०; कवल १ ४; मेरे। मेरै ३; मेरा १३; मांनां। मांनां काहू के तीरथ ब्रत बेसासा मेरे हरि बिन और न आसा १३

८३;२ कै। के १०; लक्षिन। कोडी १३; लछिमीं ३; लछिन ४; लक्ष्मी १०; कोटि। धज ग्रंथ १३; भंडारा। भंडार १०; मेरे। मेरै ३ ४; नांमां १३; रांम। कै १३; राम ३; का। केवल १३; कौ ३; को १०; नांम। नांव ३; रांम १३; अधारा। अधार ३; आधार १०

८३;३ काहू। -- १३; कै। के १०; ह्वैंगि। ह्वैगा ४; हैगे १; हेगे १०; पाइक। पईगा ४; पाइगा १; मेरे। -- १३; मेरै ३ ४; रांम। रांमैं ४; का। - ४; को १०; नांव। नांम १ ४

८३;४ श्रब। -- १३; सर्ब १०; जाका। जाकौ ३; जाको १०; नांमां। -- १३; सूं। स्यूं ३; सुं १०

८४;० गोबिंद। गोबिद ३ १०; गोब्यंद ४ २० २१; गोव्यंद १; गोबिंदा। - २१; गोबिंद गोबिंद १३; गोबिद ३ १०; गोब्यंद १ ४ २०; गोबिंदा। - ३ १०; गोब्यंदा २० २१; गोव्यंदा १; हरि। - ३ ७ १० १३; हरिजी १; के। - ३ ७ १० १३ २०; चरन। चरंन २१; चरण १ १३; कवल। कंवल २१; कंवल चितवंनिं १३; कमल छिन छिन ४; कमल चितिवनि १०; कवल चितवनि ३ ७ २०; जिनि। जिंनिं १३; बिसरै। बिसरौ गोबिंद गोबिंद गोबिंदा ७; बिसरो गोबिंद गोब्यंद गोब्यंद १०; बिसरो गोबिद गोब्यंद गोबिद ३; गोव्यंद गोव्यंद गोव्यंद १; बीसरै गोबिंद गोबिंद गोबिंद गोबिदा १३

८४;१ अंतरि। अंतर ४ २१; ग्रभ। गर्भ १०; सहे। सह्यौ १३; सह्यो ३ १०; परचौ। फिरि फिरयो ३; फिरयो १०; पढ्यौ १३; मैं। में १०; हारी। हारि २०; हारी ध्रू प्रहिलाद बिभीषन तारे जन किरपा करि पार उतारे ३; हारी ध्रू प्रह्लाद बिभीषन तारे जन किरपा करि पार उतारे १०

८४;२ ताथैं। भणंत १; भनत ३ १०; दास १३ २०; नांमौं। नांमू ४; नांमदेव १ ३ १० १३ २०; नामौं ७; गुण। गुंण १३; गुंन २१; गुन ३ १०; गावै। गांउं १०; गांवुं ३; गावैं १३; बहुरि। ताथैं बहुरि १; तातैं १३; तातैं बहूरि २०; न। भौजलि १३; भौजलि। भौजिल २०; भौजल ४; भोजलि १०; बहुरि १३; नियरे। - १ २०; नियरै २१; न १३; नेरो १०; नीरौं ३; आवै। आंउं ३ १०

८५;० गोब्यंदा। गोव्यंदा १; कमोदनि। कमोदनीं ३

८५;१ जैसैं। जैंसैं ३; जेसे १०; कमल। कवल ३; मैं। मे १०; कुसमलताई। कुसमलताइ १०; मधि। मध्य १०

२ अष्ट कमल दल नांमदेव गावै । चरन कमल रज काहे न पावै ॥

८६

० जपि रांम महामंत्र रांम महा । रांम रमैं रमि रांम महा ॥
१ महादेव उपदेसी गौरी । रांम महामंत्र लेसनि बौरी ॥
२ जिहि मंत्र नारद धूवहि पढावा । संत संगति मिलि दासनि गावा ॥
३ आदिगुरू रघुनाथ उधरनां । रांवण कुंभकरण बंधनां ॥
४ नांमौं भणैं रांम नांम पबित्रा । रांम बिनां नहीं मुकति अनंता ॥

८७

० गुड मीठा रांम गुड मीठा । जिनि लाहा तिनि गुंन दीठा ॥
१ नैंननि पाया श्रवननि षाया । त्रिपति भई त्रिस्नां मधि माया ॥
२ पांचौं उष हनि ग्यांन गडासी । कोल्हू ध्यांन धरौ तिहि पासी ॥
३ घट कूंडा जब होइ निदोषी । सहज अनल गुड सोना होसी ॥
४ गरवा सो गरवाई साजा । सो गुर हुवा तिहूं परि राजा ॥
५ नांमदेव प्रणवैं कसन मिठाई । जहां जतन सुमिरन बनि आई ॥

८५;२ कमल। कवल ३; गावै। गावे १०; कमल। कवल ३; पावै। पावे १०

८६;० रांम। राम ३; रमैं। रमे ३ १०

८६;१ उपदेसी। उपदेशी ७; गौरी। गोरी १०; महामंत्र। महांमंत्र १०

८६;२ जिहि। जिंहिं ४; जिहिं १; धूवहि। ध्रूवहि ३ ४ १०; संत। सत ७

८६;३ आदिगुरू। -- ३ १०; रघुनाथ। रघुनांथ १; रघूनाथ ४; उधरनां। उधरणां ४; रांवण। -- ३ १०; सकल अघ द्रुमति ७; कुंभकरण। कुभकरन १; दल ७; बंधनां। हरनां ७; बधनां १

८६;४ नांमौं। नांम ४; नांमां ३ १०; भणैं। भनैं ३; भने १०; पबित्रा। पवित्र ३; पवित्रा १ ७; बिनां। बिणां ४; विनां १; नहीं। नहि १ ३; नही १०; नांहीं ७; मुकति। मुक्ति १; मुति ४

८७;० तिनि। तिन १०

८७;१ नैंननि। नेंननि १०; पाया। जाया ४; श्रवननि। श्रवनेन्य ३; श्रवनेनि १०; त्रिपति। त्रपति १०; भई। भइ १०; त्रिस्नां। त्रिश्नां १; तिसनां ३; त्रस्ना १०; माया। पाया ३ १०

८७;२ पांचौं। पांच ४; पांचं १; पांचौ ३; पांचों १०; उष। ऊष ४; हनि। हनी १०; गडासी। गंडासी १ ३ १०; कोल्हू। कोलूं १०; धरौ। करौ ३; करों १०; पासी। पासें ४

८७;३ कूंडा। कुंडा १०; होइ। होई ४

८७;४ गरवाई। गरवाइ १०; सो। स १०; सु ३; गुर। गुड ३ १०; हुवा। हूवा १ ४; तिहूं। तिहु १०: तिहुं ३; परि। पुरि १

८७;५ प्रणवैं। प्रनवैं ३; प्रनवे १०; कसन। किसन ३; क्रस्न १०; सुमिरन। सुमिरिन १०; सुमिरंण ४; सुमिरण १; बनि। बंणि ४; बणि १; आई। आइ १०

८८

• लाधौ तौ लाधौ रे मैं रांम नांम लाधौ ।
प्रेमैं पाटैं सुत्रैं पोयौ कंठ लै बांधौ ॥
१ रांम नांम ततसार । सुमरि सुमरि जन उतरे पार ॥
२ क्रिस्न जननी क्रिस्न पिता । क्रिस्न बंधू भौतारिता ॥
३ भणत नांमदेव हरि गुंण गाऊं । बहुरि न जोनी संकुटि आंऊं ॥

८६

• बाद छाडि रे भगता भाई हरि सी तैं निधि पाई ॥
रांम तजि मेरौ मन अनत न जाई ॥
१ जपमाला तागै पोई सरीर अंतरि है सोई ॥
बादि बिमुष हरि बिन दिन षोई रांम नांम जपि लोई ॥
परम तत है सोई तीन्यूं रे त्रिलोक ब्याप्यौ दूजौ नहीं कोई ॥
२ सजीवनि मूली साई नटारंभ संगि गाई ॥
रांम नांम बिन नाहीं आंन उपाई ॥

८८:० तौ। - १३: तो १०; लाधौ। लाधो १०; रे। - १ २०; मैं। में १०; नांम। रसाइन ७; लाधौ। लाधौ रे २१: लाधो १०; प्रेमैं। प्रेंमें १०; पाटैं। पाटै १६; पाटे १०: सुत्रैं। शुत्रैं १; सुत्रे १६; सूते २०: पोयौ। पोयो ३ १०; कंठ। कांठु १; लै। लैं १; ले १०; बांधौ। बांधो १०; बाधौ १ ४ १२ १६ २१

८८:१ नांम। नांम सकल १; ततसार। सतिसार १ २१; सुमरि। शुमरि १
सुंमरि १२ २१; सुमिरि १० १६; सुमरि। सुंमरि १३; सुमिरि १० १६; जन। जंन १२ २१

८८:२ क्रिस्न। क्रिशनं २१; क्रिसन १६ २०; क्रस्न १३; कृस्न ४; कृस्नो १; कृशन ८; कृष्न ७; रांम ३ १०; जननी। जंननीं २१; जननो १०; जननीं ३ ७ १३; क्रिस्न। क्रिशन २१; क्रिसन १६ २०; कृस्न ४; कृस्नो १; कृशन ८; कृष्न ७; रांमहि ३ १०; क्रिस्न। क्रिशन ८ २१; क्रिसन १६ २०; क्रस्म १३; कृस्न ४ ७; कृस्नो १; रांम हि १०; रांम ही ३; बंधू। बंधव १: बधू १६; वंधू ४; भौतारिता। भोतारिता १०; भवतारिता १; हौतारिता २०

८८:३ भणत। भणंत १३: भनंत ३; भनत १०; कहत १; गुंण। गुंन १ १०; गुण ८; गुन ३; हरि ७; गाऊं। गांउ १३; गांउं ३ ८; गाऊं २१; गाउं १०; बहुरि। बहूरि २०; जोनी। भौजलि २० २१; भवजलि १; जौनी ३; जोनीं ७ १३; संकुटि। निंयरैं २१; नीयरै १; नीरैं २०; संकट १०; संकुट ७; संकटि ३ ४; आंऊं। आंउं ३ ८ १३; आउं १०; जांऊं १ २०

८६:० बाद। वाद १ २०; सी। सि २०; तैं। निधि २०; निधि। तैं २०; तजि। छाडि १; मेरौ। मेरा ८ १३; अनत। अनंत १३

८६:१ जपमाला। जपभा २०; तागै। धागै १३; बादि। बादि ही २१; बाद १६; वादि ही १; बिमुष। बिमुंष १३; विमुष १; बिन। बिंन १३: विन १; दिन। दिनन ४ ७ २१; दिन दिन १३; षोई। +ई ४; जपि। जपी ४; परम। परंम २१; तीन्यूं। तीन्यौ १ ८; तीन्यौं १६; रे। + ४; त्रिलोक। +क ४; तृलोक ७; ब्याप्यौ। ब्याप्या ८ १३; दूजौ। दूजा ८ १२ १६ २०; नहीं। न २०; नहि १; नही ४; नांही ८; नांहीं १३

३ नांमदेव उतारचौ पार चेतौ रे चेतनहार ॥
हरि की भगति बिना औतरौगे बारंबार ॥

६०

० हरि लै हरि लै हरि लै हरी ।अपनी भगति बाप करि लै षरी ॥
१ तुम्ह सौ ठाकुर कीजै काहे न प्रतीति लीजै ।अपणी बापौती कारणि प्रांण दीजै ॥
२ तुम्हची प्रतीति आई द्रुमति तजि लै भाई ।सुत कौं जननी कैसैं बिष पाई ॥
३ बालिक रुदन करै मइया जैसैं प्रांण धरै ।पारब्रह्म पिता नांमदेव लाड लडै ॥

६१

० छाडि छाडि रे मुगध नर कपट न कीजै ॥
गोबिंदा नारांइण नांम मुषां लीजै ॥

८६;२ सजीवनि। सजीवंनिं १३; मूली। + ४; साई। + ४, सहाइ २०; नटारंभ। +रंभ ४; नाटारंभ १ १३; संगि। - २०; संगी ४; गाई। गांई २१; लाई ७; नांम। + ४; बिन। + ४; बिंन १३; बिना २०; बिनां २१; विना १; नाहीं। + ४; नहीं २० २१; नांही ८; नांहीं १३ १६; आंन। + ४; उपाई। + ४

८६;३ नांमदेव। ++ ४; उतारचौ। उतरचा ८ १३; चेतौ। ++ ४; चेतहु ७ १६ २१; चेतनहार। चेतंनहार २१; की। + ४; भगति। + ४; भक्ति १३; बिना। बिंनां १३; बिन ४ ८ १६; बिनां ७ २१; विनां १; औतरौगे। +तरौगे ४; बारंबार। बारबार ४ ७ २०; वारंबार १६; वारवार १

६०;० हरि। हेरि २१; लै। ले १०; हरि। हेरि २१; लै। ले १०: हरि। - २०; हेरी २१: लै। - २० २१; ले १०; हरी। - २१; हरि ३ १०; हरि लै हरी १३; अपनी। अपणी २१; अपनीं १ २ १२ १६, आपणीं ४; बाप। बाबा २ २०; राम १ ८ १३ १६; करि। वारि १०; लै। ले १०; षरी। षरि ३ १०

६०;१ तुम्ह। षसम १; तुंम १३; तुम्हा ३; तुम्हां १०; तुम ८ १६; तूम २०; सौ। चौ ३; चो १०; सो २०; तुम्हसा १; ठाकुर। - १; ठाकूर ४ २०; कीजै। कीजे ३ १० २०; काहे। काहै २०; प्रतीति। प्रतिती ४; परतीति १६; लीजै। लीजे ३ १०; अपणी। अपणीं १३ २१; अपनी ८ १६; आपणी १; आपणीं ४; आपनी १०; आपनीं ३; बापौतो। बापोंती ३; बापोती १० २०; कारणि। कारंणिं १३; कारंणी ४; कारनि ३ ८; कारणी २०; कारनीं १०; प्रांण। प्रांन ३ ८; प्रान १०; दीजै। दीजे ३ १०

६०;२ तुम्हची। तुंम्हची १३; तुमची १० २०; प्रतीति। प्रतीती ४; परतीति १६; आई। आइ १०; द्रुमति। दुर्मति १० १६; दुरमति २०; द्रुंमति २१; द्रुमती १; तजि। मंजि १ २० २१; मूंदि १३; तजी १६; लै। ले १० १६ २१; भाई। भाइ १० १३; सुत। शुत १; सूत २०; कौं। कूं २१; कों १०; जननी। जंननी २०; कैसैं। केसें १०; बिष। विष १ ४ १०; पाई। पाइ ८ १०; षवाई १

६०;३ बालिक। बालक १ ८ १० १३ २०; रुदन। रूदन ३ ४ ८ २०; रुंदंन २१; करै। मांडैं १३; मइया। मईया ८; जैसैं। जैसै ८; जेसें १०; प्रांण। प्रांन २१; प्राण २०; प्रान ३ १०; धरै। छाडै १३; धरें १०; हरै २१; पारब्रह्म। प्रमोत्मं १; प्रसो+ १३; प्रसोतंम २१; परब्रह्म ८; ब्रह्म २०; नांमदेव। नांमां ८ १६; नार्मों २०; लाड। लाडि २०; लडै। लाडै ४ १३

६१;० रे। रै ३; कीजै। कीजे ३ १०; गोबिंदा। गोबिद ३; गोबिदा ८; गोब्यंद २१; गोब्यंदा ४ १७; गोव्यंद १०; गोव्यंदा १; नारांइण। नारांयंण ४ १३; नाराईन ३; नारायण १०; नाराइण ८ १७; नांम।

१ कोटि जौ तीरथ करै तन जौ हिवालै गलै ॥
रांम रांम रांम सरि तऊ न तुलै ॥
२ बानारसी तप करै पलटि तीरथ मरै ॥
काया जे अगनि मुषि कलेस कीजै ॥
हिरणग्रभ दांन दीजै अस्वमेद जगि कीजै ॥
रांम रांम रांम सरि तऊ न तुलै ॥
३ मांन जौ सरोवर जइये गया जौ कुरषेत न्हइये ॥
गोमती अस्नांन गऊ कोटि दीजै कुंभ जौ केदार जइये ॥
स्यंघहस्त गोदावरी न्हइये रांम रांम रांम सरि तऊ न तुलै ॥
४ अस्वदांन गजदांन भोमिदांन कन्यांदांन ग्रिहदांन सिज्यादांन दांन दीजै ॥
तन तुला तोलि दीजै मन जौ त्रिमल कीजै । रांम रांम रांम सरि तऊ न तुलै ॥

नांव ३ २१; मुषां। मुषांह ३ १०; लीजै। लीजे ३ १०

६१;१ तीरथ। तीर्थ ७; करै। फिरै २१; तन। तंन ४ १३ २१; जौ। जौं १६: जो ३ १०; हिवालै। हिंवालै ४ १३; हिवारैं ८; हिवालें १०; गलै। गरै ८; गलै प्रिथी सकल प्रदछन दीजै करवत कासी मैं लीजै स्यौं कूं जे सीस दीजै ७; गलै प्रिथी जे सकल परदक्षत दीजै करवत कासी मैं लीजै सिव कौं जो सीस दीजै १६, गलै पृथी सकल प्रदछिन दीजै करवत कासी मैं लीजै सिव कूं जो सीस दीजै १७; गलें १०; रांम। -- ३ १०; रांम। - १६; रांम रांम १३; सरि। संमिं १३; समि ४ ८; तऊ। तौ ८; तउ ४ १३ २१; न। उन ८; नं २१: तुलै। तूलै १

६१;२ बानारसी। बांर्णासी ८; बांणीरसी १३; ब्रांणारसी ४ २१; बांनारसी ३; वाणारसी १; करै। करे १०; मरै। फिरै ७ ८ १३ १६ १७ २१; मरि ४; जे। - ८ १३ २१; साधि ३ १०, जौ १६; अगनि। अंगनि २१; अग्नि ३ १० १७; मुषि। - ३ १० २१; मुंषि १३; मुष ७; कीजै। कीजे ८; करै ३ १० २१; हिरंणग्रभ। ह्रिणग्रभ ४; हिरण्यगरभ १; हिरन्यगर्भ १०; हिरनगर्भ १६; हंरंणंग्रभ २१; हर्नगर्भ ३; हरणग्रभ ८ १३; दांन। दान १०; दीजै। दीजे ३ १०; अस्वमेद। अस्वमेध ८; अस्वमेधा १३; असुमेद ४ १६ १७; असमेद १; असमेदे ३; जगि। जिग्य १; जग्य ७ १०;कीजै। कीजे ३ १०; सरि। स्मि ३; संमिं १३; समि १ ४ ८ १०; तऊ। तउ ३ ४ ८ १० १३ २१; तुलै। तुलै रे १; तूलै ३

६१;३ मांन। -- ३ १०; मांनसरोवरि १; जौ। - १ २१; सरोवर। - १; सरोवरि ८; सरोवरच १७; जइये। जईये ४ १३ १६ १७; जयीये ८; जाइए २१; जाइये १; जौ। जो ३ १० १७; कुरषेत। कुरषेति ३; कुरषेत्र ७ २१; कुरषेती ४; न्हइये। न्हईऐ ४; न्हईये १३ १७; न्हइयै १६; न्हाईये ८; न्हाइए २१; न्हाइये १; अस्नांन। अश्नांन २१; अष्नांनगऊ १; संगम ३ १०; सनांन ८ १३ १६; गऊ। कोटि १; गौ १०; गउ ३ ४ ८ १३; कोटि। कोटि दांन १७; सहंश्र १३; सहश्र ३; सहस्र १०; दीजे १; दीजै। दीजे ३ १०; कुंभ। -- ३ १०; कुभ ८; कूंभ ४; केदार। केदारि १ ४ ८ १३; जइये। जईये ४ १७; जये ८; जइए ७; जइयै १६; जाइए २१; स्यंघहस्त। सिंघहस्त १३ १७; सिंघसत ४; सिंगहसत १६; स्यंघ जो ३; सिघस्त ८; सिघ जो १०; गोदावरी। गोदावरि ४; गादावरि ८; न्हइये। न्हई ८; न्हईये ४ १७; न्हइए २१; न्हइयै १६; जइये ३ १०; रांम। रांम रांम १३; सरि। संमिं १३; समि १ ३ ८ १०; तऊ। तौ १०; तउ ३ ४ ८ १३ २१; न। नं २१; तुलै। तुलै रे १

६१;४ अस्वदांन। असुदांन ३; असदांन ७ १६ १७ २१; भोमिदांन। कंन्यांदांन ३; कन्यादान १०, कन्यांदांन। भौमिदान १०; भोमिदांन ३; कन्यांदांन दीजै १३; ग्रिहदांन। - १; गिर्हदांन १६; नारी ३ १०; ग्रहदांन ८ १३; गृहदांन ७; सिज्यादांन। सेज्यादांन १; सज्यांदांन ४; सहित ३; सहज १०; दांन। - ४ १३ १६; ग्रिहदांन ३; ग्रहदांन १०; दीजै। दीजे ३ १०; तुला। तोला १ ३ ७ १० २१; दीजै। दिजे १०; दीजे ३; जौ। जो

५ जमहि न दीजै दोस मनहि न कीजैय ॥
रोस निरषि न्रिबांणपद रांम नांम लीजै ॥
आतमां अंगि लगाइ सेइ लै सहज भाइ ॥
भणत नांमइयौ छीपौ अंम्रित पीजै ॥

१ बानारसी तपु करै उलटि तीरथ मरै अगनि दहै काइआ कलपु कीजै ॥
असुमेध जगु कीजै सोना गरभ दानु दीजै ॥
० राम नाम सरि तऊ न पूजै छोडि छोडि रे पाखंडी मन कपटु न कीजै ॥
हरि का नामु नित नितहि लीजै ॥ रहाउ ॥
२ गंगा जउ गोदावरी जाईऐ कुंभि जउ केदार
नहाईऐ गोमती सहस गऊ दानु कीजै ॥
कोटि जउ तीरथ करै तनु जउ हिवाले गारै राम नाम सरि तऊ न पूजै ॥
३ असुदान गजदान सिहजा नारी भूमि दान ऐसो दानु नित नितहि कीजै ॥
आतम जउ निरमाइलु कीजै आप बराबरि कंचनु दीजै ॥
राम नाम सरि तऊ न पूजै ॥
४ मनहि न कीजै रोसु जमहि न दीजै दोसु । निरमल निरबाण पदु चीन्हि लीजै ॥
जसरथ राइ नंदु राजा मेरा रामचंदु प्रणवै नामा ततु रसु अंमृतु पीजै ॥

६२

० रांम भगति बिन गति न तिरन की कोटि उपाव ज करहीं रे नर ॥
जल सींचै करि जतन प्रवालै आंब बंबूल न फल ही रे नर ॥

३ १०; न्रिमल। नृमल ३, निर्मल ७ १६; निरमल १०; नृमल ८; कीजै। कीजे ३ १०; रांम। रांम रांम १३; सरि। संमिं १३; समि ३ ८; समे १०; तऊ। तुउ ८; तौ १०; तउ ३ ४ १३; तउं २१; न। नं २१; तुलै। तुलै रे १

६१;५ जमहि। जंमहिं २१; जमहिं ४ १३ १६; जमहुं १०; जमहूं ३; जमहीं १; दीजै। दीजे ३ १०; मनहि। मंनहिं २१; मनहिं १७; मनहुं १०; मनहूं ३; मनहीं १३; कीजै। कीजे ३ १०; निरषि। निर्षि ७; न्रिषि १३ १६ २१; न्रिष्य ८; निरषि निरषि ३; नृषि ४; न्रिबांणपद। न्रि+पद १६; न्रिवांणपद १; निर्बांणपद ७; निरबांनपद १७; निरबाणपद १०; निरबानपद ३; रांम। मुषा १०; मुषां ३; नांम। - १ ३ ४ ८ १० १३ २१; लीजै। लीजे ३ १०; आतमां। आत्मां १; आतंमां २१; आतम १७; रांम नांम ३ १०; अंगि। निज ३ १०; अंतरि २१; लगाइ। सार ३ १०; देवा २१; लगाई ४; सेइ। सेवि १६ १७; सेबिऐ ८; सेई ४; सेइये १३; जन ३ १०; ताही २१; लै। - ८ १३; भजि ३; नजि १०; की २१; सहज। पावै ३; पावे १०; करिले २१; भाइ। भई ८; भाई ४; पार ३ १०, सेवा २१; भणत। भणंत १३ २१; भनंत ३; भनत १०; नांमइयौ। नमईयौ ८ १७; नांमईयौ १३; नांमदेव ३ १०; नामईयौ ४; छीपौ। - ३ १०; छींपौ १; अंम्रित। अंमिृत ३; अंम्रत १३; अंमृत ७ ८ १६ १७; अमृंत १०; पीजै। पीजे ३ १०

६२;० भगति। भगत २०; तिरन। तिरंण २१; उपाव। उपाइ ७; ज। जु ८ १० २१; जौ ४ ७ १६; करहीं। करई ३ ८; करही ७ १३; करइ १०; नर। - ३ ८ १०; सींचै। सींचत २०; सीचै ८; जतन। जंतन २१; प्रवालै।

१ आपौ थापि अवर कौं नींदैं ग्रब मांन के मारे ॥
फिरि पीछैं पछितावोगे बौरे रतन न मिलहि उधारे रे नर ॥
२ यहु ममिता अपनीं जिनि जांनौं धन ज़ोबन सुत दारा ॥
बालू के मंदिर बिनसि जांहिगे झूठा करत पसारा रे नर ॥
३ जोग न भोग मोह नहीं माया का भयौ बन मैं बासा ॥
चरन कंवल अनराग न उपज्यौ तब लग झूठी आसा रे नर ॥
४ मनिषा जनम आइ नहीं चेते अंधे पसू गंवारा ॥
तेरे सिरि काल सदा सर सांधै नांमदेव करत पुकारा रे नर ॥

६३

० कांइ रे भूले मूढ जनां । चांमद करवा नहीं आपनां ॥
१ लोही रकता मंझा घणां । तुम जिनि जांनौं तन आपणां ॥

+लै ४; प्रवांलौ ७; बंबूल। बंबूर ३ २०; बबुर १०; फल। फलई ३; फलइ ८ १०; ही। - ३ ८ १०; नर। - १ ८

६२;१ आपौ। ++ ४; आपो १०; आपा ७ ८ १६ २१; अवर। और ३ २०; ओर १०; कौं। कूं १ ७ २१; कों १०; नींदैं। निंदवै ३; निदवें १०; नींदै १३; नीदै ७ ८; ग्रब। ++ ४; ग्रभ १ २० २१; गर्ब १६; गरभ ३; गरब १०; मांन। अभिमांन २०; वांन ३ २१; वान १०; के। कें १०; फिरि। ++ ४; पीछैं। पिछे १०; पीछै ३ १६; पछितावोगे। पछिताऊगे १६; पछिताहिगौ रे ३; पछिताकुगे १३; पछिताहुगे १; पछितावेगो रे १०; पछितावहुगे ८ २१; बौरे। बोरे २०; बावरे ३ १०; रतन। + ४; रतंन २१; रतना ३; मिलहि। मिलै १; मिलैं ८ १३; मिलहिं २१; मिलही २०; मीलहि १०; उधारे। ऊधारा २०; उधारा ३; रे। - १ ४ ८ १० १३; नर। - १ ३ ४ ८ १० १३

६२;२ यहु। यह १३; या ३ १०; ममिता। मंमिता २१; ममता ७; अपनीं। + ४; अपणीं ७; अपनी ८ २०; जिनि। + ४; जिंनिं १३; जांनौं। + ४: जांणौं ७; जांनौ २०; जांनों १०; धन। धंन १६ २० २१; जोबन। जोबंन २१; सुत। शुत १; दारा। द्वारा १; बालू। बालु १०; के। के से ३ १०; जांहिगे। जाइगें १३; झूठा। झूठे १ ४; करत। करौ १; करहु ३ ७ १६; रे। - १ ८; ने १६; नर। - १ ३ ८ १० १३

६२;३ न। र १०; भोग। जुगति ३ १०; नहीं। नही ३ ८ २१; का। कहा १ २०; भयौ। भयो ३ १०; बन। बंन २१; वनषंड १; मैं। - १; चरन। चरंण ४; चरंन २१; चरण ७; कंवल। कमल १०; कवल ४ ७ १६; अनराग। अंनराग २१; अनुराग ३ १० १३: उपज्यौ। ऊपज्यौ ४; उपज्यै २१; उपजे १ ३ ८ १६; उपजे १०; रे। - १ ८ १३; नर। - १ ३ ८ १० १३

६२;४ मनिषा। मंनिंषा १३; मंनिषा २१; जनम। जनमि ३ ८ १६; आइ। आई ४; आय १०; नहीं। नही १ २१; कहा ३ १० १३; कहां ८; काहा २०; चेते। कींन्हां १३; कींनौ ३; कीन्हौं २०; कीनो १०; चेत्यौ २१; चेत्या १६; चेतै १; पसू। पसु १०; पसूं ३; गंवारा। गवारा ३ ४ ७ १६; तेरे। तेरै १६ २१; सिरि। सिर १०; सांधै। सांध १०; सांधे ८ २०; सांधें १३; सांध्यें ४; साधै ७; सार्धे १६; नांमदेव। जंन नांमदेव २०; जन नांमदेव ३; जन नामदेव १०; करत। करै १; रे। - १३; नर। - १ ३ १० १३

६३;० कांइ। कांई ४ २०; कांइं १३; काई ८; काहे ७; रे। - ७; मूढ। मूंढ १३ २०; मूढे ७; मूटे ८; मूढे १; जनां। जंनां २०; नहीं। नहि १; नही ८; नांहीं १३; आपनां। अपनां १६; आपणां ४

६३;१ रकता। रक्त १६; रगत २०; रगता १; मंझा। मेझा १६; मूंता १३; मूत ८; घणां। घंणां १३; घणीं ४; घनां १६; तुम। तुम्ह ४ ७; जिनि। जिंनिं १३; आपणां। अपनां १६; आपणीं ४

२ भणत नांमदेव नारांइणां । रांम नांम बिन धिग आत्मां ॥

६४

• आव कलंदर केसवा । धरि अबदालंम भेष बाबा ॥
१ ताज कुलह ब्रह्मंडै कीन्हां पाव सपत पतांल जी ॥
  चमर पोस म्रित मंडल कीन्हां इहि बिधि बने गोपाल जी ॥
२ अठारह भार का मुदिगर कीन्हां सहनक सब संसार जी ॥
  छपन कोडि का पहरण कीन्हां सोलह सहंस इजारं जी ॥
३ काया मसीति मन मुलांनां सहजि निमाज गुजारं जी ॥
  कंवला सेती कांइं ण पढिया निराकार आकारं जी ॥
४ सहर बिसहर सबै तुम्ह फिरिया तेरा किनहूं मरम न पाया जी ॥
  नांमदेव का चित हरि सौं लागा आसण करौ रांम राया जी ॥

• आउ कलंदर केसवा । करि अबदाली भेसवा ॥ रहाउ ॥
१ जिनि आकास कुलह सिरि कीनी कउसै सपत पयाला ॥
* चमरपोस का मंदरु तेरा इह बिधि बने गुपाला ॥*

६३;२ भणत। भंणत २०; नारांइणां। नांरांइंणां १३; नारांयणां ४; नाराईणां २०; नाराइणां ८; बिन। बिनां ८; विन १; धिग। धृग ८; धिर्ग १६; आत्मां। आतमां ४; जीवंनां १३; जीवणां ८ २०

६४;• आव। तूं आव २१; तू आव ४; कलंदर। कलंदर ८; कलंद्र २०; केसवा। केसवै २०; केसवे १; अबदालंम। अबदालंव १६; अबदालंब ४; अबदालम ८; भेष। भेस १ २१; बाबा। वै २०

६४;१ ताज। ताल २१; कुलह। कुल १३; ब्रह्मंडै। ब्रंह्मंडैं ४; ब्रह्मंड १३; ब्रह्मंडैं १६ २१; ब्रह्मडैं ८ २०; कीन्हां। कीन्हीं १; कीनां ४; पाव। पाए २१; पाये ४; पाया १; सपत। सप्त १; पतांल। पयांल १ ८, पताल १३ १६; पतालं २१; पातालं २०; चमर। चम+ ८; चमड ४ २० २१; पोस। +ोस ८; मोस १; म्रित। +त ८; म्रिति २०; म्रत १३; मृति १; मृत १६; मंडल। मडल ८; मल २०; कीन्हां। कींन्हां ४ १३; कीया १; इहि। -- १; इंहिं १३; इहिं २१; बने। बनें ८ १३; बनें १६; वने १; गोपाल। गुपालं २१; गोपालं ८ २०

६४;२ अठारह। -- ४; अ+ ८; अठाहर १६; अठार १३; का। - १३; मुदिगर। मूदिगर २०; कीन्हां। कींन्हां १३ २०; कीया १; सहनक। -- ४; सहजनक ८; सहजक २१; संसार। संसारं २१; छपन। -- ४; छपंन २१; कोडि। कोट २०; पहरण। पहिरण १६; पहरंणं २१; पहरन १; कीन्हां। कीन्हां १३; कीया १ २०; सोलह। सोल २०; सोलहं २१; सोला १३; सहंस। स २१; संहस ८; इजारं। ईजारं ४ २०; इजार १३

६४;३ मसीति। मंसीति करि १३; मसींती ४; मसीति करि १; मसीत २०; मन। मंन २१; मुलांनां। मुलंनां १३; मुलांणां २१; मुलांना ४; मुलानां ८; मूलहांनां २०; सहजि। सहज १; सहजे २०; निमाज। निंमाज ८; निवाज १ १३ १६; गुजारं। गुजार १; कंवला। कंवंला २१; कांइं। कांण्य २१; कांइ १ ८; काई ४ २०; ण। - २१; पढिया। पढीया १; कीया १६; निराकार। निराका ४; आकारं। अकारं १६; आकार १ २०

६४;४ सहर। सार ४ २१; बिसहर। बिसार ४ २१; तुम्ह। तुंम्हा १३; तुम ८ २०; फिरिया। फिरि आये १३; तेरा। - १; किनहूं। - ८; मरंम १३; मरम। मरंम १६ २१; न १३; ना। किंनहूं १३; न किनहूं ८; जी। - १; नांमदेव। नांमां १; चित। चीत २०; हरि। तुहरि ४; सौं। स्यूं २०; सूं १ २१; आसण। आसंण ४ १६ २१; आसन ८ १३; तातैं १; करौ। परम १; कंरो १३; रांम। पद १; राया। पाया १; राई २०; जी। - १

२ छपन कोटि का पेहनु तेरा सोलह सहस इजारा ॥
भार अठारह मुदगरु तेरा सहनक सभ संसारा ॥
३ देही महजिदि मनु मउलाना सहज निवाज गुजारै ॥
बीबी कउला सउ काइनु तेरा निरंकार आकारै ॥
४ भगति करत मेरे ताल छिनाए किह पहि करउ पुकारा ॥
नामे का सुआमी अंतरजामी फिरे सगल बेदेसवा ॥

६५

• बैस्नौं ते मैं मैं ते बैस्नौं सुनि नारद रिषि साचं ॥
जे भगता मेरे गुंण गावैं ताकै अंतरिथ कौ मैं नाचौं नारद ॥
१ नारद कहै सुनौं नारांइण बैकुंठ बसौ कि कबिलासं ॥
जहां मम कथा तहां मैं निहचल बैस्नौ मंदिर बासं नारद ॥
२ गंगा आदि सकल तीरथ करै गुणचास कोटि फिरि आवै ॥
ऐकादसी सहित सजम करै ते मोहि सुपिनैं कदे न पावै नारद ॥
३ जोगी जती तपी सिन्यासी इक मुनि ध्यांन बईठा ॥
जजै जगि बेद धुनि उचरैं तिनिहूं कदे न दीठा नारद ॥

६५;० बैस्नौं। बैस्नों १०; बैश्नौं ८ १३ २१; बैश्नव ७; बैसनौं १६; ते। मैं १३; तें १०; मैं। में १०; ते १३; मैं। मै १३ २१; में १०; ते। तै २०; तौ १०; तो १३; बैस्नौं। बैस्नों १०; बैश्नौ ८; बैश्नौं ७ १३ २१: बैसनौं १६; बेस्नौ ४; वैस्नव १; सुनि। शुणि १; सुंनिं १३; सुंणि २१: सुंनि ३; सुणि ४ ८ १६ २०; रिषि। रषि २१; साचं। सांच ७ १० २०; जे। मम ४; जो मम १; भगता। भगति १; मेरे। करै १; गीता ४ १३; गुंण। मम १; गुण ४ ८; गुन ३ १०; गावैं। भगता १; गांवै २०; गावै ४ ७; गावैं २१; गावे १०; ताकै। तिनकै १३; मैं ताकै १; मैं ताके २१; तीकों १०; अंतरिथ! अंतरि १ २१; कौ। - १ २१; को १०; का १६; मैं। - १ २१; में १०; नाचौं। नांच १; नांचूं २१; नाचं ८ १३ २०; नाचूं ४; नाचों १०; नारद। - १ ३ ४ १० २१; जी ८ १३

६५;१ कहै। कहे १०; सुनौं। शुणौं १; सुंणौं १३ २१; सुणौं ४ ७ १६; सुनों १०; नारांइण। नारांईण २०; नारांयंण ४; नारांइंन ३; नारांइन ७; नारायण १०; नाराइण ८; बैकुंठ। बैकुंठि ४ १६; बैकुठ १०; बैकुठि ८; बैकूंठ ३; बैकूठ २०; बैकूठि १३; कि। - ८; क २०; कबिलासं। कबिलास १०; कविलास १; कविलासं ४ ७ १३ १६; कलिासं ८; जहां। जहा ३; जांहां २०; मैं। मे १०: निहचल। निहिंचल २१; निश्चल १०; निहंचल १३; निहश्चल ३; निसचल २०; बैस्नौ। बैस्नौं ३; बैस्नो १०; बैश्नौं ७ ८ १३ २१; बैसनौं १६ २०; वैस्नौं १; मंदिर। मंदिरि ४; मंदरि १६; मदिर २१: बासं। बास ४ २०; वासं १; नारद। - १ ३ ४ ८ १० १३ २१

६५;२ आदि। आदि दे २०; तीरथ। तिरथ १०; करै। करैं १ ४ ८ २१; गुणचास। गुंणचास १ १३ २१; गुंनचास १०; गुनचास ३; आवै। आवैं ४ ८ १३; आवे १०; ऐकादसी। एकादसी ७; येकादसी ३ ८ १०; सहित। सहत ८ २०; संजम। संजंम ४; साधन १३; करै। करैं ४ ८ १३; रहै ३ १०; ते। - १; मोहि। शुपिनैं १; मौहि ८; सुपिनैं। मोहि १; सुपिनै २०; सुपिने १०; कदे। - १; कधे २०; पावै। पांवैं १३; पावैं ८ २१; पावे १०; नारद। - १ ३ ४ ८ १० १३ २१

६५;३ सिन्यासी। संन्यासी ३; सन्यासी ७ १० २०; इक। एक २१; ईक ४; मुनि। टग ८ १३; मुंनिं २१;

४ जगि जोग ब्रत धर्म नेम करैं जब लग इनकी आसा ॥
बसुधा आदि दींहि दांनादिक नहीं मम चरन निवासा नारद ॥
५ जे भगता निरमल जस गावैं ते भगता मम सारं ॥
बैस्नौं जीयां जीऊं पीयां पीऊं बैस्नौं मम परिवारं नारद ॥
६ बिसवाबीस आगैं बरतांऊं निज जन नांव सौं राता ॥
नांमां नौ स्वांमीं परमपद आपै भगति मुकति दोऊ दाता ॥

६६

• माधौ भीतरिमार दुहेली ॥
अबला कौ बल कहा गुसांई परतषि जाइ न पेली ॥
१ ये अनेक मैं एक गुसांई कहौ कहा बसु मेरा ॥

मुंनि १ १०; मूंनीं ३; ध्यांन। ध्यांनि ४ २१; बईठा। बइठा ८ १० २०; जजै। जैजै ३ १६ २०; जेंजें १०; जजैं ४ १३; जगि। जोग १ २१; जग्य ३ ७ १०; बेद। वेद १; धुनि। धुंनिं १३; धुंनि १० २०; धूंनि ४; उचरैं। उचरै १६ २०; उचरे १०; तिनिहूं। तिनिहौं १६; तिनहुं १०; तिनहू ३ ८; तिनहूं १ १३ २०; कदे। किनहूं १; कब ४; कबहुं १०; कबहू ३ २१; न। - १; नहीं ३; नारद। - १ ३ ४ ८ १० १३ २१

६५;४ जगि। -- १ ८ १३ २१; जग्य ३ ७ १०; ब्रत। बृत ३; तप १६; धर्म। ध्रम २०; धरम १६; नेम। नेंम १६; करैं। करै ७ १०; बर्त १६; जब। -- १ ८ १३ २१; इनकी। ईनकी ४ २०; बसुधा। -- १ ८ १३ २१; बसूधा २०; दींहि। दैहि १० २०; देहि ३ १६; दींहिं ४; दांनादिक। दहिंणांदिक १६; दांनांदिक २०; दांनादीक ४; दानादिक १०; नहीं। -- १ ८ १३ २१; चरन। चरंण ४; चरण ७; निवासा। निवासा हो ४; नारद। - ३ १० २०

६५;५ निरमल। न्रिमल ४ ८ १३ २० २१; निर्मल ७ १६; गावैं। गावै ३; गावैं ४; गावे १०; बैस्नौं। - ८ १६ २१; बैस्नों ४ १०; बैश्नौं ७ १३; वैस्नौ १; वैस्नौं २०; जीयां। जिंत्यां ८; ज्यांयां १३; ज्याई २०; ज्यायैं २१; जींया ३; जीय। १०; जीऊं। जींउं १३; जीऊं बैस्नौं २०; जीउं ३ ८; पीयां। प्यांयैं २१; पीया १०; पायां १३; पाइ २०; पीऊं। पीउ १३; पीउं ३ ८; पीवुं १०; बैस्नौं। नारद १; बैस्नैव ४; बैस्नो १०; बैस्ना २०; बैश्नौं ३ ७ ८ २१; बैसनौं १३ १६: परिवारं। परिवार १ १० १३; नारद। - १ ३ ८ १० २१; - बैस्नौ मैं दोई नही नारद प्रीत्य कीया + आंऊ बैस्नोव के कारंणि अवतार लीया बैस्नव पैं हा+ + ४; - बैसनौं मैं द्वै नांहीं नारद प्रीति कीयां ह्रिदै आंउं बैसनौं काजि अवतार कीयौ है बैसनौं हाथि बंधांउं १३; नांरद २०; नारद बैसनौं मैं दोइ नांहीं नारद प्रीति कीयां तैं पांऊं भगत हेत यहु बर्त धरयौ है बैसनौं हाथि बधांऊं नारद १६

६५;६ बिसवाबीस। बिस्वाबीस ३; विसवाबीस २०; आगैं। आगै ३ ८; आगे १०; बरतंणिं १३ २१; वरतणि १; बरतांऊं। आगे १३; आगैं १ २१; बरतांउं ८; निज। निंज १३; जन। +न ४; जंन १३ २० २१; नांव। नांमं १०; नांउं १; नाम ३; सौं। स्यूं ३ ४; स्यौं १ २०; सु १०; सूं ७ २१; नांमां। + ४; नांमदेव ७; नामां २०; नौ। नौं १३ २१; कौ ३ २०; को १०; स्वांमीं। स्यांमी २०; स्वांमी ८; परमपद। पर्मपद ७ १३; परंमपद २० २१; आपै। आपैं २०; पावे १०; भगति। मुकति १; मुकति। मुंकति १३; मुक्ति २१; मूकति २०; परम १; दोऊ। पद १ २१; दोउ ३ ८ १० १३

६६;० भीतरिमार। भीतरिमर ७; दुहेली। दुहेली माधौ २१; अबला। अबुला २०; परतषि। प्रतषि १ १७ २०; जाइ। जाई ४

६६;१ ये। ए ७ १७ २१; ऐ १; एक। ऐक ४; येक २०; गुसांई। गुसांई २१; कहा। कहां २१; बसु। बसि २०;

षेत की पहुंचि कहां लौं राषै षसम न करई फेरा ॥
२ तुम से बैद न ओषदि औरै मंत्र और नहीं जांनां ॥
ब्याधि असाधि अगाध दयानिधि पचि पचि गये सयांनां ॥
३ जिनकौं तुम हरि कारी कीन्हीं बिथा और नहीं ब्यापी ॥
नांमदेव कहै नहीं बस मेरा क्रिपा करौ दुष कापी ॥

९७

• अवधू बेली बिरधि करैली ॥
त्रिगुण जाइ निरंजन लागी मारी हूं न मरैली ॥
१ सहज समाधे बाडी रे अवधू सतगुरि बाही बेली ॥
अमी महारस सींचण लागा तत तरवर जाइ चढैली ॥
२ अमरबेलि अनभै जाइ लागी टाली हू न टलैली ॥
रूप रेष ताकै कछु नांहीं चंद्रहि कोटि फलैली ॥
३ पांचूं मृघ पचीसूं म्रिगी सूंघत देषि मरैली ॥
निराकार नांमां तेरी बेली अनंत अमर फल देली ॥

बस १ १७; की। का २०; पहुंचि। पहुंची १९; पहुचि १७; पहूंचे २०; लौं। लूं ७ २० २१; लों ४; राषै। राषौं १; षसम। षसंम २१; जे षसम २०; जौ षसम १ ४; करई। करही १; करहीं २०

९६;२ तुम। तुम्ह ४ ७ १७ २१; से। शे ७; सौ १; ओषदि। बौषदि २०; वोषदि १ ७; वोषद २१; औरै। औरैं २० २१; और। आंन २१; वोर २०; नहीं। नहि १; नही २१; ब्याधि। ब्याध्य १९; अगाध। अगाधि १९ २० २१; दयानिधि। दयालनिधि २०; पचि। -- १७; गये। गए १९ २१; सयांनां। संयानां २०

९६;३ जिनकौं। जिनिकौं १९; जिनकूं १ ७; जिनकों ४; तुम। हरि २० २१; तुम्ह १ ४ ७; हरि। तुम २० २१; कीन्हीं। कींन्हीं ४; कींनीं २१; नहीं। नहि १; नही २१; ब्यापी। ब्यापै २०; व्यापी १; बस। बसु ७ १९; क्रिपा। कृपा १७; करौ। करहु ४ २१; दुष। दुख १९

९७;० बिरधि। बिधि २०; ब्रिधि ८; विरधि १; वृधि १७; त्रिगुण। निर्गुण १९; निरगुंण २१; निरगुण ४; त्रिगुण ८; अंमीं १२; नृगुणि १; जाइ। महारस १२; जाई ४; निरंजन। निरंजनि १; रंजन १२; हूं। हू ८ २०

९७;१ सहज। सहजैं २१; समाधे। संमाधें १२; समाधैं २१; समाध्यें ७; समाधि ४; समाधि तेरी २०; बाडी। बाडा ४; सतगुरि। सतगुर ७ २१; बाही। बाहि २०; बेली। + ८; अमी। अंमी ४ १२; अंमीं ७; अमीं १७ २० २१; सींचण। सींचन १७ २०; सीचण ८ १९; लागा। लागी १२; तरवर। तरवरि १ ८; जाइ। जाई ४ ८

९७;२ अमरबेलि। अंमरबेलि ७ १२; अंमरबेली २१; अमरबेली २०; अनभै। अभै ४; जाइ। जाई ४; टाली। टारी १ ८ १२ २०; काटी १७; हू। हूं ४ ७ १२ १७ २१; टलैली। टरैली १ ८ २०; टरैलीं १२; कटैली १७; रूप। रूप न १७; कछु। कुछ ४ ७ १७; कछू ८ १२ २० २१; नांहीं। नांही ८ १७; चंद्रहि। चंदहि १; चद्रही ८; फलैली। फरैली ८ १२

९७;३ पांचूं। पंचौं ८ १२; पांचौं १ १९ २१; मृघ। म्रिग ७ १२; मिरघ ४; मिरघा २१; म्रघ २०; मृग १ ८ १९; पचीसूं। पचीसौं १ ८ १२ १९ १७; म्रिगी। म्रिघी २०; मिरघी ४ २१; मृघी १७; मृगी- ८; सूंघत। सूघत ८; मरैली। मरेली ८; अनंत। अंनंत २१; अंनत ४; अमर २०; अनत ८ १७; अमर। अंमर ७ २१; अनंत २०

९८

• अनेक मरि मरि जांहिगे रे अवधू ॥
इक रांम नांम तत रहिला ॥
१ मुई जु आसा मुई जु त्रिश्नां मुई जु मनसा माई ॥
लोभ हमारी बहनी मुई तिनका सोच हम नांहीं रे अवधू ॥
२ माइ का गोत मद मंछर मूवा बाप का गोत अहंकारं ॥
कांम क्रोध भाई भतीजा मरि गया तिनका सोच हम नांहीं रे अवधू ॥
३ जा स करणीं जोगेस्वर मूवा ता स घरनि मैं जांऊंगा ॥
नांमदेव सतगुर साहीला गोब्यंद चरन समांऊंगा रे अवधू ॥

९९

• बैरागी रांमहि गाऊंगा ॥
सबद अतीत अनाहद राता आकुल कै घरि जांऊंगा ॥
१ तीरथि जांउं न जल मैं पैसूं जीव जंत न सतांऊंगा ॥

९८;० अनेक। अनेक १३; जांहिगे। जांहिगे १६ २१; जाहगे ८; जाइला १; इक। ऐक १; ईक ४; येक २०; रहिला। रहैला १६

९८;१ मुई। मूंई २०; मूई १६; मई २१; मुई। मूई २०; जु। ज १३; त्रिश्नां। त्रिस्ना ४; त्रिसना २०; त्रिसनां १६; मुई। मूई २०; जु। ज १३; मनसा। मंनसा २१; हमारी। हंमारी ४ ८ १३ २० २१; बहनी। बंहनी ८; बहंनी २० २१; बहनीं १२; बहनीं १; मुई। मूंई २०; तिनका। तिनहूंका २०; तिनहींका ४ २१; सोच। सोग २०; हम। मोही २०; हंम ८ २१; हंमारै १३; नांहीं। नांही ८ १३ १६ २१; अवधू। - ८ १३

९८;२ माइ। -- ४; माई १ ८ २०; मद। मदं २१; मत ७; मंछर। मछर ८; बाप। -- ४; का। - १३; कांम। -- ४; क्रोध। क्रोध दोऊ १; गया। गया रहि गया तत सारं १३; तिनका। -- ४ १३; तिनको १६; तिनहूंका २०; तिनहींका ७; रहि ८; सोच। गया ८; सोक २०; हम। हंम २१; तत ८; नांहीं। नांही २१; सारं ८; रे। - ८; अवधू। - ८

९८;३ स। - १३ १६; करनी ८; करणीं। करंनी २१; करनी ४; कारंनि १३; जोगेस्तर ८; जोगेस्वर। मुये ८; जोगेसूर २०; मूवा। - ८; मूऐ १३; घरनि। घर २०; घरंनिं २१; घरनिं १३; धरणि १; जांऊंगा। जांउंगा ८; जांउंगां १३; जाउंगा २०; सतगुर। सतगुरि १ ८ १६; सतगूर २०; साहीला। सहाईला २०; साहिला १; गोब्यंद। गोबिंद ७ १३; गोबिद ८; गोब्यंद। २० २१; गोब्यंद १; चरन। चरंण ४; चरंन २१; चरण ७ २०; समांऊंगा। निवासा ४ ७ १६ २१; संमांउंगा १३; संमाईला २०; समांउंगा ८; समाऊंगा १; रे। - १ ८ १३ २० २१; अवधू। - १ ८ १३ २१

९९;० बैरागी। बेरागी १०; रांमहि। रांमहिं १० १७; रांमहीं २०; गाऊंगा। गांऊंगा ७ १६; गांउंगा ८ १३ १७ २०; गांउगा २१; गांवंगा ४; गाउंगा १०; सबद। सब्द ३; अतीत। अतीथ ३ १०; अनाहद। अंनाहद २१; राता। लागा १; कै। के १०; जांऊंगा। जांउंगा ८ १३ २०; जाउंगा १०

९९;१ तीरथि। तीर्थ ७ १३; तीरथ १ ४ १० २१; जांउं। जांऊं ३ १७ २१; जांउ १ ७ १३ १६ २०; जाउ १०; मैं। मे १६; में १०; पैसूं। पैसौं ८, पैसौं ३ १३ १६ १७; पेसों १०; जंत। न ८; जत १०; न। जंत ८; सतांऊंगा।

अठसठि तीरथ गुरू लषाये घट ही भीतरि न्हांऊंगा ॥
२ बेद पुरांन सास्त्र गीता कवित कबी न सुनांऊंगा ॥
अषंड मंडल निराकार मैं अनहद बेंन बजाऊंगा ॥
३ इला प्यंगुला सुषमन नारी पवनां मंझि समांऊंगा ॥
चंद सूर दोउ समि करि राषूं ब्रह्म जोति मिलि जांऊंगा ॥
४ पंच सुहाई मन की सोभा भला बुरा न कहांऊंगा ॥
नांमदेव कहै मैं केसौ ध्यांऊं सहजि समाधि लगांऊंगा ॥

१ बेद पुरान सासत्र आनंता गीत कबित न गावउगो ॥
अखंड मंडल निरंकार महि अनहद बेनु बजावउगो ॥
० बैरागी रामहि गावउगो । सबदि अतीत अनाहदि राता ॥
आकुल कै घरि जाउगो ॥ रहाउ ॥

संतांऊंगा १७ २१; संतांउंगा ८ १३ २०; सताउंगा १०; अठसठि। अठमठ २०; तीरथ। तीर्थ ७ १३; गुरू। गुरु १० २१; लषाये। बताए ७ २१; बताये २०; लषाए १६; लषाऐ ४; लषायो १०; लषाया ३ ८ १३; ही। हीं ४ ७ १७; भीतरि। भींतरि ४ ७ १३; न्हांऊंगा। न्हांऊंगा पाती तोरि न पूजूं देवा देवल दीप न जोऊंगा पांनि पांनि परसोतम राता ताकौं मै न संतांऊंगा ३; न्हांऊंगा तारूं न पाती पूजूं न देवा देवल दीप न जाऊंगा पांन पांन परसोत्म राता ताकूं मैं न सताऊंगा १; न्हांऊगा ७; न्हांउंगा ४ ८ १३; न्हाउगा पाती तोरि न पुजो देवा देवल दिप न जोउगा पांनि पांनि परसोतम राजा ताकों में न सताउंगा १०; नांहूंगा २०

६६;२ बेद। वेद १ ४; पुरांन। पुरांण ६ ७ २१; पुरांन न १७; पूरांण २०; सास्त्र। शास्त्र १३; अनंत ३ १०; सासत्र १६; सासत्री ८; गीता। अनंता १; सास्त्र १०; साश्त्र ३; कवित। कविता २०; गोत १ ३ ७ १०; कबी। कबित १ ३; कवित ७ २०; कबीत १०; कवी ८ १३ १७; कावी १६; न। - २०; सुनांऊंगा। गाऊंगा १ ३ ७; गाउंगा १०; सुणांऊंगा २१; सुणांउंगा १३; सुणांवूंगा ४; सुनांउगा ८; सूणांउंगा २०; अषंड। निराकार ७; अंषंड २१; अषढ ८; मंडल। अषड ७; मडल ८ २१; निराकार। मंडल ७; मैं। मे १०; अनहद। अंनहद १३ २१; बेंन। बैंन २०; बेन ३ ७ ८ १६ १७ २१; बजाऊंगा। बजांऊंगा ३ ७ १७ २१; बजांउंगा ८ १३ २०; बजांवूंगा ४; बजाऊंगां १६

६६;३ इला। ईला ४ २०; अला २१; प्यंगुला। पिंगुला १३ १७; पिगुला ८ १०; पीगुला २१; सुषमन। सुषनि १०; सुषमनि ३; सुषमना २०; सुषमनां १ ४; पवनां। पवंनां २१; पवना २०; मंझि। मझि ८; मांझि १०; माझि ३; समांऊंगा। संमांऊंगा २१; संमांउंगा १३ २०; समांउगा ८; समांवूंगा ४; लुकांऊंगा १ ७; लुकाऊंगा ३; लुकाउंगा १०; दोउ। दोऊ १ ७ १६ २१; दोइ १७; समि। संमि २१; राषूं। राषौं ३ ८ १३ १६ १७ २१; राषों १०; मिलि। मिल ३; जांऊंगा। जांउंगा ८ १३ २०; जांवूंगा ४; जाऊंगा ३

६६;४ पंच। पंपंच ३; गाए ७; गाये २०; सुहाई। गए ७; गये २०; सुभाई ८ १३ १६ १७; सुहाइ १०; मन। गए ७; गये २०; की। ते ७ २०; सोभा। गाए ७; गाये २०; भला। अगई ७ २०; बुरा ३ १०; बुरा। भला ३ १०; कूं ७ २०; न। अब ७; बगाउंगा २०; कहांऊंगा। - २०; कहांउंगा ८ १३; कहांवूंगा ४; कहाऊंगा १; कहाउगा १०; गांऊंगा ७; नांमदेव। भणंत ७; प्रणवंत २०; कहै। नांमां ७ २०; मैं। भए ७; भये २०; मै ८; में १०; केसौ। निहंकांमा २०; निहकांमां ७; केंसे १०; ध्यांऊं। - ७ २०; धांऊं १; ध्यांउं ८ १३; पाया ३ १०; सहजि। सुंनि ७; सुनि २०; सहज ८ १० १३ १६ १७ २१; समाधि। + ८; संमांधि २०; संमाधि १३ २१; लगांऊंगा। +गा ८; लगांउंगा १० १३; लगांवूंगा ४; लगाऊंगा १; लगाउंगा २०

२ इडा पिंगुला अउरु सुखमना पउनै बंधि रहाउगो ॥
चंदु सूरजु दुइ समकरि राखउ ब्रहम जोति मिलि जाउगो ॥
३ तीरथ देखि न जल महि पैसउ जीअ जंत न सतावउगो ॥
अठसठि तीरथ गुरू दिखाए घट ही भीतरि न्हाउगो ॥
४ पंच सहाई जन की सोभा भलो भलो न कहावउगो ॥
नामा कहै चितु हरि सिउ राता सुंन समाधि समाउगो ॥

१००

० पुरिष हाजिर बरन नांहीं । दूरि ठाढा बोलै मांहीं ॥
१ ग्यांन ध्यांन रहित षेलै । आद्रिष्टि मांहैं द्रिष्टि मेलै ॥
२ संगि लागा भेष काछै । सारीषा आगैं रु पाछै ॥
३ निगंध रूप बिबर्जित बास । प्रणवंत नांमदेव हरि का दास ॥

१०१

० देवा पातुरि बाजै मांदल नाचै येहडा अचंभा दीठा ॥
पूछौ पढिया पंडिता जलि बैसंदर बूठा ॥
१ चींटी ब्याई हस्ती जाया ऐहडा अचंभा थाया ॥
ऊभी ऊभी नाषीला मैंमंत घूमंत आया ॥

१००;० पुरिष। - ८; हाजिर। हाजरि १ ४ ८ १२ २१; बरन। बरंण ४; बरण १ २०; बारन २१; नांहीं। नांही ८; बोलै। देषै ७; बौलै १६ २१; मांहीं। मांही ८

१००;१ रहित। रहत ८; रतनौं १३; षेलै। षुरी १३; आद्रिष्टि। अद्रिस्टि १६; अद्रिष्टि १ २०; अदृष्टि १३; आदिष्टि २१; आद्रिम्टि ४; मांहैं। माहे २१; द्रिष्टि। दिष्टि २१; द्रिस्टि ४ १६

१००;२ संगि। सांगी २०; लागा। लागौ २०; सारीषा। सारीषौ २०; आगैं। आगे ४ ८ १७ २१; रु। अर २०; अरू ४; अरु १; र ८ १३; पाछै। पाछैं २१; पाछैयूं जे जांणि रमैं जे कोई तौ हरि समींप चीन्हैं जंन सोई १

१००;३ निगंध। त्रिगंध १२ २०; निगध २१; निगम १६; नृगध ८; रूप। + ८; रुप २१; बिबर्जित। बिबर्जिति ४; बिबजित २० २१; बिबरजित १२ १६; विवर्जित १; बास। बासा १; प्रणवंत। प्रणवत ४; नांमदेव। नांमदे ४; नांमां २१; दास। दासा १

१०१;० देवा। + ४ ८; पातुरि। + ८; +रि ४; बाजै। +जै ८; बाजे १; मांदल। मंदला १३; मेदल ८; नाचै। नांचै ४ २०; नांचैं १३; येहडा। ++ ४; ऐहडा ८ १२ २१; एहडा १६ १७; येहुडा २०; अचंभा। अचंभ २०; अच्यंभा २१; पूछौ। + ४; पूछो २० २१; पढिया। + ८; +ढिया ४; पढीया २०; पंडिता। + ८; पंडि+ ४; पंडित २१; जलि। जल्य १७; जल १ २०; बैसंदर। वैसांदर १; बूठा। बू÷ ४; बूठा १

१०१;१ चींटी। + ४; चीटी ८; ब्याई। + ४; ब्याई १; हस्ती। हसती २०; जाया। जा+ ८; ऐहडा। + ८; एहडा १६ १७ २१; येहुडा २०; अचंभा। +चंभा ८; अचभा ४; थाया। + ४; ऊभी। + ४; उभी ८ १२ २०; ऊभी। + ४; उभी ८ १२ २०; नाषीला। +षीला ४; नांषीला ८ १६ २१; नाषिला २०; मैंमंत। मैमत ८; घूमंत।

२ पांइ न पंष बिना हीं उडिया कैरूं डाली बैठा ॥
नींब सदाफल सूफल फलिया सो मोहि लागै मीठा ॥
३ ससै सींग मंछै षुरी भेड तडका कांनां ॥
मांषी काजल सारण लागी अैसा ब्रह्म गियांनां ॥
४ गाइ ब्याई बछी जाई गाइ बछी कौं धावै ॥
प्रणवंत नांमदेव गुर प्रसादैं जो षोजै सो पावै ॥

१०२

० आज कोई मूनैं मिलिसी रे रांम सनेही । तब सुष पावै हमारी देही ॥
१ भाव भगति मन मैं उपजावै । प्रेम प्रीति हरि अंतरि आवै ॥
आपा पर दुबिध्या सब नासै । सहजैं आतम ग्यांन प्रकासै ॥
२ जन नांमां मन षरा उदास । तब सुष पावै मिलै हरिदास ॥

१०३

० नारांइंण सूं मन न रंजै । संजम चूकै अरु ब्रत षंडै ॥
१ येकादसी ब्रत जुगति न जाणैं । चंचल चित मन थिर न धरै ॥
२ पंच आतमां राषि न सकई । रांम दोष दे भूष मरै ॥

घूंमंत १२ २१; घूंमत ४; घूमत ८ १६

१०१;२ पांइ। पव १; पांई ४ २०; पांयं १६; पांइं १२ २१; पाइ ८; पंष। + ४; बिना। + ४; बिंनां १२; बिनां ८ १७ २१; विनां १; हीं। + ४; ही ८; उडिया। +डिया ४; ऊडे १; उडया २० २१; कैरूं। कैरौं ८ १२ १६; कैरू २१; डाली। डारी ८ १३; बैठा। वैठा १; नींब। नींव १; नीब ४ ८ १२; सूफल। + ४; फलिया। +या ४; फलीया २०; मीठा। मींठा १२ २० २१

१०१;३ ससै। सूसै २०; सींग। सीग ८ १६; मंछै। मं+ ८; मछै १६ १७ २१; मांछै १; षुरी। षुरि २०; षू+ ४; भेड। + ४; तडका। +डका ४; तडकै १३; कांनां। कांन १७; कांनं १६; कांनूं ४ २१; मांषी। माषी १ ८ १७ २१; सारण। सारंण १३; सारंन २१; अैसा। ऐसा १ ४; येहुडा २०; ब्रह्म। ब्रंह्म २०; व्रंह्म १; गियांनां। गियांन ८ १६ १७; गियांनूं ४ २१

१०१;४ गाइ। गाई ४ २०; ब्याई। बियाई १६ १७; ब्याइ २१; व्याई १ १२; बछी। वछी १; गाइ। गाई ४ २०; बछी। वछी १; कौं। कूं ४ २० २१; प्रणवंत। प्रणवत ८; गुर १; नांमदेव। परसादैं १; गुर। नांमदेव १; प्रसादैं। प्रनवै १; प्रसादै १७; परसादैं ४; जो। जे १ ४ २० २१; षोजै। षौजै २० २१; सो। सां ८

१०३;० नारांइंण। नांरांइंण २१; नारांयण ४; नारांइन ३; नारायन १०; सूं। स्यूं ३ ४; मन। मंन २१; न। - ४ १०; रंजै। रंजे १०; चूकै। चूके १०

अरु। - ४ ७ २१; अरू ३; षंडै। भंजै ७; षंजै ४

१०३;१ येकादसी। एकादसी ७ २१; येका+ ४; ब्रत। + ४; जुगति। +ति ४; जाणैं। जांनैं ३; जाने १०; चित। + ४; मन। मंन २१; थिर। ठौर ४ ७ २१; धरै। धरों १०; रहै ४ ७ २१

१०३;२ पंच। पांच ३ १०; आतमां। आतंमा २१; राषि। रांषि २१; राषी १०; सकई। सकई ४; सकइ १०;

३ परनिंद्या जु आप परगासै । झूठी साषि सहजि टारै ॥
४ परत्रिया सूं रंमैं रैंणि दिन । नेम धरम दुवै हारै ॥
५ जलहर पैसि पषालै काया । अंतरि मैल न तउ छूटै ॥
६ भणत नांमदेव कछू न सूझै । पूजा कौन देव की करै ॥

१०४

• पांडे देह अरथि लगाइ ॥
सात बरस कौ मांहि थौ तब पांच बरस की माइ ॥
१ अगंम अषेल बिचारि देषौ सुसै स्वांन छिपाइ ॥
मींन जल कौ गगन चढियौ बाध षेदै गाई ॥
२ संमद भीतरि बूंद संमद संमाइ ॥
नांमदेव कै एक तूं हीं अलष लष्यौ न जाइ ॥

१०५

• मन मंझा तूं गोबिंद चरन चित लाइ रे ।
हरि तजि आंन न ध्याइ रे ॥
१ बलि राजा धुंधमार न जीवै को जुग च्यारि ।
मेरी मेरी करते ते भी गये रे मन मंझा ॥
२ रे मन मछिंद्रनाथ सहंस चौरंगी होते ।

रांम। किस्न २१; कृस्न ४; कृष्न ७; दोष। दोस ४ २१; मरै। मरे १०

१०३;३ परनिंद्या। परन्यंद्या ४ २१; परनिद्या ३; परनिद्यां १०; परगासै। प्रगासै ७; परकासै ३; परकासे १०; सहजि। सहिजि २१; टारै। टारें १०

१०३;४ परत्रिया। प्रत्त्या ४; परक्रिया २१; परतृया ७; सूं। स्युं १०; स्यूं ३; रंमैं। रंमै ७; रमै ३; रमें १०; रैंणि। रैंणिं ४; रैंनि ३; रेंनि १०; नेम। नेंम १०; धरम। धम २१; धर्म ७; धरंम ४; दुवै। दुवे १०; दूोवै ३; हारै। हे १०; हरै ३

१०३;५ जलहर। जलहरि ३; पषालै। पषाले १०; मैल। मेल १०; तउ। - ४; तऊ ७; तौउ २१; छूटै। उतरै ३; उतारे १०

१०३;६ भणत। भणंत २१; भनत ३ १०; कछू। कछु १०; सूझै। सूझे १०; पूजा। पुजा १०; कौन। कौंण ४ ७ २१; कौंन ३; कोन १०

१०५;० मन। मंन ४ २१; तूं। तु ३ १०; गोबिंद। गोबिद ३ १०; गोब्यंदा २१; चरन। चरंन ४ २१; चरनां ३ १०; लाइ। लाई ४; लाइं २१; न। - ३; ध्याइ। ध्याई ३; ध्याय ४

१०५;१ धुंधमार। धंधमार २१; धूंधमार ३ १०; जीवै। जीवे १०; च्यारि। चारि १०; च्यार ७; मेरी। मेरि ४; मेरी। मेरि ४; करते। कंरत १०; गये। गए ७ २१; गऐ ४; मन। मंन २१

१०५;२ मछिंद्रनाथ। मछंद्रनाथ १०; मछ्यंद्रनांथ २१; मछ्यंद्रनाथ ३; सहंस। सहस ३ १०; चौरंगी।

ते भी देषत कालि लीये रे मन मंझा ॥
३ रवि ससि दोऊ भाई फिरते गगन लाई ।
ऐसैं भूला भ्रम सब जाई रे मन मंझा ॥
४ अहंकार दिन दसा राषि लै दिन चारि ।
पसूडा नैं मुकति न होई रे मन मंझा ॥
५ नांमदेव छीपै चौपई गाई जाकौं जैसा भाव ।
तिनि तैसी सिधि पाई रे मन मंझा ॥

१०६

• जोगिया जिनि षरचसि दांमां । सूंम की नांई भेटि लै रांमां ॥
१ बाई कौ दांम न षरच्यौ भावै । गांठि परै तब परचौ आवै ॥
२ भणंत नांमदेव राषि लै थाती । प्रगटी जोति तहां दीवा न बाती ॥

१०७

• झिलिमिलि झिलिमिलि झिलिमिलि तारा । सो तारा तिहूं लोक पियारा ॥
१ रहै अकास पडै नहीं द्रिष्टी । पकडया जाइ न आवै मुष्टी ॥

चोरंगी १०; लीये। लिये ७; लीऐ ४; रे। - ३; मन। मंन २१

१०५;३ रवि। रबि ३ २१; दोऊ। दोउ ३ १०; भाई। भाइ १०; लाई। लाइ १०; अैसैं। ऐसैं ७; अेसे १०; भ्रम। भर्म ४; सब। राब १०; जाई। जाइ ३ १०

१०५;४ दिन। दिंन २१; दसा। दस ३ १०; चारि। च्यारि ३ ४; पसूडा। पसूडां ३; नैं। नै ३ ४; ने १०; होई। ह्योइ ३ १०; मन। मंन २१

१०५;५ छीपै। छींपै ७ २१; छीपे १०; छीपौ ४; चौपई। चोपदी २१. चोपइ १०; गाई। गाइ १०; जाकौं। जिनकूं २१; जाकूं ७; जाका १०; जैसा। जेसा १०; तैसी। तेसि ४, तेसी १०; सिधि। सीधि ४; पाई। पाइ १० २१; रे। - ३ १०; मन। मंन २१

१०६;० जिनि। जिंनिं १३; जिन २१; षरचसि। षरचिसि ७ १६; षरचिसी १३; षरचै ८; षरचहि १; सूंम। सूम १६; नांई। नांई २१; लै। ले ७ १६

१०६;१ बाई। वाई १ २१; कौ। कौं ४; का ८ १३; दांम। दाम १६; षरच्यौ। षरच्या ८ १३; परै। + ८; पडै १ १३ २०; तब। तौ १

१०६;२ भणंत। भंणत १६ २१; भणत ८; लै। ले ४ १६; प्रगटी। प्रगट १३ २०; जोति। जाति ८; दीवा। दिवा ७

१०७;० झिलिमिलि। - ४; तारा। झिलिमिलि १३ १६ २०; तिहूं। तिहि २०; त्रिहुं ७; तिहुं १३; तिहौं ८; बैकुंठ ४; लोक। - ४; पियारा। पीयारा २०

१०७;१ रहै। रिदै १३; अकास। अकासि ४; आकास १६; पडै। परै ४ ७; नहीं। नही ४ ८; द्रिष्टी। द्रिस्टी ४ १६; द्रिष्टि २०; दिष्टी १३; दृष्टी ७; पकडया। पडया २०; जाइ। जाई ४ ८ २०; मुष्टी। मुस्टी ४

२ दीपक पषै तेल बिन बाती । जोति सरूप बलै दिन राती ॥
३ भणत नांमदेव अमरपद परस्या । प्यंड भया मुकति तया तत दरस्या ॥

१०८

० त्रिबेणी प्राग करौ मन मंजन । सेंवो राजा रांम निरंजन ॥
१ पुरी द्वारिका निकटि गोमती । गंग जमुन बिचि बहै सुरसती ॥
२ अठसठि तीरथ मधि सरोवर । एक तपौ तांमैं ताकौ घर ॥
३ भणत नांमदेव सुणहु त्रिलोचन । ए तीरथ सब अघ के मोचन ॥

१०९

० माधौ जी माया मिलन न देई । जन जीवै त्यौं करौ सनेही ॥
१ माया जलध मोर मन माछी । नीर बिना क्यूं जीवै पियासी ॥
२ जे तोर्डौं तौ मूल बिनासा । बोझ पड्यां नहीं आवै सासा ॥
३ भणंत नांमदेव दीनदयाला । निरधारनि कै तुम्ह आधारा ॥

१०७;२ पषै। पंषै २०; पषैं ७; बिन। बिंन १३; सरूप। सरूपी ७ २०; दिन। दिंन १३

१०७;३ भणत। भणंत १३; नामो २०; कहत ४; नांमदेव। कहैप्रम २०; अमरपद। अंमरपद १३; पद २०; परस्या। परस्यां २०; प्यंड। पिंड १३; पिड ८; मुकति। मुकत ८ १३; तगा। वया १३

१०८;० त्रिबेणी। त्रिबेणीं १३ २१; तृबेणीं ७ १७; प्राग। प्रियाग २१; पिराग ७ ८ १९ १७; प्रीयाग २०; करौ। करहु ४ १९ २१; मन। मंन १३ २१; मंजन। मजन ८; सेवो। सेवौ १७; सेवौं १३; सेइये १; रांम। अलष १ ४ ७ ८ २१

१०८;१ पुरी। पुरिं १ २०; द्वारिका। द्वारका २०; निकटि। निकट ४; निकटी २१; निकी २०; मंझि ८ १३; गोमती। गोमति ४; जमुन। जंमुंन १३; जंमुन २१; जंमन २०; जमन ७ ८; बहै। बैहै २०; सुरसती। सुरसुती १९ २० २१; सरस्वती ४ ७

१०८;२ अठसठि। अठसठ २०; तीरथ। तीर्थ ७ १३; मधि। मंझि ८ १३ २०; मझि २१; सरोवर। सरौवर २०; एक। ऐक १ ४ ८ १३; येक २०; तपौ। तपा ८ १७; तया १३ १९; तांमैं। तामैं ८ २१

१०८;३ भणत। भंणत २०; कहै १; कहत २१; सुणहु। सुंणौं १३; सुणऊं १; सुणौ ८; सुणौं २०; सुणहुं ७; सुनहु १७; सुनहुं १९; त्रिलोचन। त्रिलोचंन २१; तिलोचन ८ १९ १७; ए। ऐ ४ ८ १३; ये १ २०; तीरथ। तीर्थ ७ १३; के। का २१; मोचन। भोचन १९

१०९;० मिलन। मिलण ७ ८ १३ १९; देई। देही १; जीवै। जीवैं ४ ८; जीवहिं २१; त्यौं। त्यूं ७ १७ २१; तूं २०; करौ। करौ हो ४ ७ २१; करहू २०; सनेही। सनिही १३ २१; सनेहीं १९

१०९;१ जलध। जलधर १९; मन। मंनिं १३; माछी। मंछी १ १३ २०; मछी १९; बिना। बिंनां १३; बिनां ४ ८ १९ १७ २१; क्यूं। क्यौ १९; क्यौं १ ८ १३; जीवै। जीवै हो ७ १९; रहै १७; पियासी। पीयासी २०

१०९;२ तोर्डौं। मोड़ूं ७; मोडौ १९; तोड़ूं ४ १३; तोडौ १७ २०; तोरौं १; तौ। - ७; मूल। मुल २१; मूंल २०; पड्यां। पडै १७; नहीं। आवै १७; नहिं १३; नहि १; नही ८; आवै। आवे १९; नहीं १७; सासा। सांसा २०

१०९;३ भणंत। भंणत २१; भणत ७ ८ १९; नांमदेव। नांमदेव सुणि १; दीनदयाला। दीनदयाल १; निरधारनि। त्रिधंन २०; त्रिधारंन २१; त्रिधारैं ४; निरधारां १; निरआधारनि ८; कै। के ७ ८ १९ २१;

११०

० माधौ माली एक सयांनां । अंतरगति रहै लुकांनां ॥
१ आपै बाडी आपै फूला कली कली करि जोडै ॥
पाका काचा काचा पाका मनि भावै सो तोडै ॥
२ आपै पवन आप ही पांणीं आपैं बरिषै मेहा ॥
आपैं पुरिष नारि पुनि आपैं आपैं नेह सनेहा ॥
३ आपैं चंद सूर पुनि आपैं आपैं धरणि अकासा ॥
रचनहार बिधि ऐसी रची है प्रणवैं नांमदेव दासा ॥

१११

० काल न्याइ बिचरिहूं । काइथ बांभण तिलक सुमिरिहूं ॥
१ चारि बेद चौधरनी । नरकि पडौ धरमादिक करनी ॥
२ सूंडणि नां परि धांधै । चंद सूर मैं उर धरि बांधै ॥

तुम्ह। तुंम्ह् १३; तुम्हही ४; तुम्हहीं ७; तुम ८ १६; तुमहीं २१; तूंहीं १; तूमहीं २०; आधारा। अधार १; आधार १३

११०;० एक। ऐक १ ४ ८ १३; येक २०; लुकांनां। लूंकांनां २०

११०;१ आपै। आपैं ४ १६ २० २१; आपै। आपैं ४ १६ २० २१; फूला। माली १३ १६; साली ८; फूल २१; कली। कलीक २०; जोडै। जौडै २१; पाका। पाके ८ १६ २१; काचे १३; काचा १; काचा। पाके १३; पाका १; काचे ८ १६ २१; काचा। पाके १३; पाका १; काचे ८ १६ २१; पाका। पाके ८ १६ २१; काचे १३; काचा १; मनि। मंनिं १३; जे १; भावै। मांने ८; मांनैं १३ १६; मःनैं २०; सो। ते ४ ७ १६; तोडै। तोरे १

११०;२ आपै। आपैं ४ ७; पवन। पवंन २१; आप। पांणीं १ १३; ही। परि १; पांणों १३; हीं ७ १६ २० २१. पांणीं। आपै १ १३; पांणी ८ २१; पांनीं १६; आपैं। आपै १ ४ ८ १३; आपैं। आपै १ ७ ८ १३; पुरिष। सत रज ७; नारि। आप २०; तम ७; पुनि। पंणिं १३; पुंनि १ २०; पणि ४; पनि १६; तीन्यूं ७; आपैं। आपै १ ८ १३; नारी २०; गुण ७; आपैं। धरै न ७; आपै ८ १३; नेह। करै १ ७

११०;३ आपैं। आपै १ ४ ७ ८ १३ २०; चंद। सूर २१; सूर। चंद २१; पुनि। पुंनिं १३; पुंनि २१; पुनिं १६; पणि ४ ७; आपैं। आपै १ ८ १३; आपैं। आपै १ ८ १३; धरणि। धरंणि २१; धरनिं १३; धरनि ८ १६; रचनहार। रचंनहार २१; रचणहार १; रचनहारि ४ ७; बिधि। विधि १; ऐसी। अैसी ४ ८ १३ १६ २१; रची। रचि २०; प्रणवैं। प्रणवंत १३ २० २१; प्रणवैंत ४; पणवैं ८

१११;० न्याइ। न्याई ४ ८ २१; न्याइ बिधि १३; बिचरिहूं। बिचरिहौं ८ १३; बिचारिहौं १६; विचरिहूं १; काइथ। काईथ २१; काईथा ४; कायथ ८; काइस्त १; बांभण। बांभंण १३; बांमून १६; बाभण १; तिलक। तिल+ १६; सुमिरिहूं। सुंमरिहौं १३; सुमिरिहौं ८ १६; सुमरिहूं १ २०

१११;१ चारि। च्यारि ४ १३; चौधरनी। चौधरंनी २१; चौधरणी १ १३; नरकि। नरकि ८ १३; पडौ। पडै १६; परौ १ ४ २१; धरमादिक। घमाधिक १; धर्मादिक ८ १३; धरमांदिक ४ २०; करनी। करंनी २१; करणी १; करनीं ८ १६

१११;२ सूंडणि। मूंडंणिं २१; सूंडणिं १३; सूडणि १; नां। ना १; परि। पर १; षरि १६; धांधै। धंधै २०; धंधे ८ १३; धांधै २१; धांधे ४; मैं। - २१; दोऊ २०; दोउ १३; ते ८; उर। धुर १३; मेर २१; धरि। धर ८; हर

३ बांभण मद भरि सरवा। जत न पीवै तत मातल बरवा ॥
४ हरि को दास भणैं नांमां। रांम नांम बिन और न जांनां ॥

११२

• जांणौं नैं जांणौं बेद पुरांनां छाडौ पांनां पोथी ॥
बिन मेघां मुकताहल बरिषैं श्रब निरंतर मोती ॥
१ बिनै बजाया बाजा बाजैं नादैं अंबर गाजै ॥
बिन भेरै होत झणकारा न दीसै बजांवणहारा ॥
२ बिन पावक जोति ही दीसै सुनि मैं सूता जागै ॥
अंधियारा नौ भौ भागौ रे भाई जे जोईये तें आगै ॥
३ कर जोडी नै नांमौ बिनवैं मैं मूरिष मति थोडी ॥
ए पद नौं हेतारथ जांणैं तेन्हैं पगि लागूं कर जोडी ॥

११३

• जब तब रांम नांम निस्तारै ॥
साठि घडी मैं ऐक घडी रे सोई सकल अघ जारै ॥

१३; बांधी। बंधे २०; बंधे ८ १३; बांधे १९

१११;३ बांभण। -- १; बांभंण २१; बांभन ८; बामून १९; वांभण ४; जत। -- १; जतं २१; तत २०; पीवै। पीवो ८ १२; मातल। मा+ २१; मांतल ४; बरवा। बंरंवा २१; बरवां १३

१११;४ भणैं। गंणैं २१, भणै जंन २०; गावे १२; बिन। विंन १२; बिणा ४; और। अवर ४

११२;० जांणौं। जांनौं ८ १२; नैं। - २०; जांणौं। जां+ौं १२; जांणैं नैं १९; जानौं ८; बेद। बैंद २१; पुरांनां। पुरांणां ४ २१; पूराणां २०; छाडौ। छोडो ४; छाड्यौं १९; पांनां। पांना २०; पोथी। पोथी रे ४ २१: मेघां। मेघा १९ मुकताहल। मुंक्ताफल २०; मुक्ताहल ४; मुकताफल २१; बरिषैं। बरिषै ४ २०; बरषैं १२; श्रब। साव ४ २१; निरंतर। निरंतरि २०; मोती। मोती रे ४ २१

११२;१ बिनै। बिण ४ २० २१; बिनैं १९; बजाया। बजांयां २०; बाजैं। बाजै २०; नादैं। नादै १२ २०; अबर। अबर ८; गाजै। गाजैं रे ४; गाजै रे २१; बिन। बिण ४ २० २१; बिनैं १२; भेरै। भेरैं ४ ८ १९; भेरे २१; होत। हेत ४; झणकारा। झुणकारा १२; झूणकारा २०; झणकार १९; झणकारे ४; झकारा २१; दीसै। दीसैं ४; बजांवणहारा। बजांबणहारा १२; बजांवणहार ४; बजांवनहार १९

११२;२ बिन। बिण ४ २० २१; पावक। पावकैं ४ २० २१; ही। हिं ४; हीं १९; दीसै। दीसैं ४; दरसै १२; सुनि। सुंनि १२ २१; सुपि २०; मैं। नै २०; सूता। सुता २०; नौ। नौं १२ १९; जे। ज २१; जो २०; जोईये। जोई ८ १२; जोईऐ ४; जोइए २१; जोइये १९; आगै। आगैं २०; आगैं रे २१; आगै रे ४

११२;३ नै। नैं ४ ८ २१; नांमौ। नांमौं १९ २१; नांमो २०; नांमां ८ १२; बिनवैं। बिंनवैं १२; बीनवै १९; बीनवैं २१; थोडी। थोरी ८; ए। ऐ ४ ८ १२; ये २०; नौं। नो ४ ८ २१; जांणैं। जांनैं १२; जाणैं २०; तेन्हैं। जेन्हैं २०; पगि। पग १२ २०; लागूं। लागौं ८ १२ १९; जोडी। जोडी रे ४; जोरी ८

११३;० जब। जाब २०; निस्तारै। निसतारै ७ २०; घडी। घरी ४ २०; मैं। में २०; ऐक। एक १ ७ १९ २०;

१ कासीपुरी मंझि गौरापति अहिनिसि सदा पुकारै ॥
कीट पतंग सुनत गति पावै गोबिंद जस बिस्तारै ॥
२ अजामेल गनिका सुक पंषी रसनां रांम उचारै ॥
गज पसु ब्याधि तिरे हरि सुमिरत महिमां ब्यास बिचारै ॥
३ परम पुनीत नांव निसि बासुर निज जन ह्वै ब्रत धारै ॥
नांमदेव कहै सोई दास कहावै जीव तैं छिन न बिसारै ॥

११४

• बाप जी एतलौं अंतरौं कीधौं । जनम नांव दरजी नौ दीधौं ॥
१ बांम्हण उचरैं बेद नै बांणीं । जेतलौं अंतरौं दूध नैं पांणीं ॥
२ जाग्र नैं आव्या ब्यास नैं भांटा । ऊठौं नांमदेव नांषियै छांटा ॥
३ अम्हारी भगति न जांणीं हो रांमां । हसि करि क्रिष्न बुलाये नांमां ॥

घडी। घरी ४ २०; रे। - ४; ले २०

११३;१ मंझि। मंझ २०; गौरापति। गिरजापति १ १३ २०; गोरापति ८; अहिनिसि। अहनिसि ८ १३ २०; रसना ४; सदा। नाम ४; पुकारै। उचारै ४; संभारै १३; सुनत। सुंनंत १३; पावै। पांवै १; पांवैं ४ १६; गोबिंद। गोबिद ८; गोब्यंद १; रघुपति ४; जस। जसु ४; बिस्तारै। बिसतारै ४ ७ १६

११३;२ गनिका। गंनिंका १३; सुक। सुष ४ ७; पंषी। पंछी १; रसनां। रसना २०; रांम। नांम ७ १६; नाम २०; उचारै। संभारै १ १३; गज। ग्रस १; पसु। पस ८; गज १; ब्याधि। ब्याध १; सुमिरत। सुंमिंरत १३; सुमिरन १६ २०; सुमरत ७; महिमां। महिमा ४; ब्यास। व्यास १; बिचारै। विचारै १ ४

११३;३ परम। पर्म १३; पुनीत। पुंनींत ७; पुन्यंत ४; पुनींति १३; पुनीति १ ८; नांव। नाव २०; सुल ८; सुलप १ ४ १६; निसि। निंस १३; निस १ ७ २०; पहरि ८; हरि ४ १६; बासुर। बासुरि ४ १३; जन। जंन ४; ह्वै। हरि ७ ८ १६; ब्रत। बर्त १६; सोई। सो २०; सोइ ८; दास। साध २०; कहावै। सिरोमनि २०; जीव। चित २०; जीय १ ४; तैं। थैं ४; छिन। छिंन १३

११४;० बाप। - १३; जी। - १३; एतलौं। ऐतली १३; ऐतलौं १ ८; अंतरौं। - १३; अंतरो १६; आंतरो १; आतरो ८; कीधौं। कीधू १; कीधूं ७; कीधो १३; जनम। - १३; नांव। नांम ८ १३; नांउं १; दरजी। छींपी १ १३; नौ। नौं १३ १६; दीधौं। दीधूं १ ७; दीधो १३; दीनौं ८

११४;१ बांम्हण। - ७; बांभण ८ १३; उचरैं। औचरे १६; बेद। - ७ १३; नै। नैं ७ ८ १३ १६; बांणीं। - ७ १३; बांणीं १; जेतलौं। एतलो १; जैतलो ८; जेतलो १३; अंतरौं। अंतरो १ १३; आंतरो ८; दूध। - १३; नैं। नै ७; नौं १६; पांणीं। - १३; पांणी ८

११४;२ जाग्र। जागि ८ १३; जाग्रि १; नैं। - १३; आव्या। - १३; अव्या १६; आव्या ७; ब्यास। - १३; ब्यास १; नैं। - १३; नै १; भांटा। भटा १३; भाटा ७ १६; ऊठौं। उठो ८ १३; नांमदेव। - १३; नांषियै। नांषिऐ १३; नांषियैं ७; नांषिये १ ८; छांटा। - १३

११४;३ भगति। - १३; न। - १३; जांणीं। जांणौं १३; जांणी ८; हो। - ८; हसि। - १३; हंसि १; करि। - १३; क्रिष्न। क्रिसन १६; क्रिष्न न ८; कृष्न १; बुलाये। बुलाए १६; बुलाइये १; बुलायो १३; नांमां। - १३

११५

• नांमदेव प्रीति नरांइंण लागी । सहज सुभाइ भये बैरागी ॥
१ जैसी भूषैं प्रीति अनाज त्रिषावंत जल सेती काज ॥
मूरिष नर जैसैं कुटंब परांइंण अैसी नांमदेव प्रीति नरांइंण ॥
२ जैसैं पर पुरिषा रत नारी लोभी नर धन कौ हितकारी ॥
कांमीं पुरिष कांम रत नारी अैसी नांमदेव प्रीति मुरारी ॥
३ जैसी प्रीति बालिक अरु माता अैसैं यहु मन हरि सूं राता ॥
नांमदेव कहै मेरी लागी प्रीति गोबिंद बसै हमारै चीति ॥

१ *जैसी भूखे प्रीति अनाज । तृखावंत जल सेती काज ॥*
जैसी मूड कुटंब पराइण । ऐसी नामे प्रीति नाराइण ॥
० *नामे प्रीति नाराइण लागी । सहज सुभाइ भइओ बैरागी ॥ रहाउ ॥*
२ *जैसी पर पुरखा रत नारी । लोभी नरु धन का हितकारी ॥*
कामी पुरख कामनी पिआरी । ऐसी नामे प्रीति मुरारी ॥
३ *साई प्रीति जि आपे लाए । गुर परसादी दुबिधा जाए ॥*
कबहू न तूटसि रहिआ समाइ । नामे चितु लाइआ सचि नाइ ॥
४ *जैसी प्रीति बारिक अरु माता । ऐसा हरि सेती मनु राता ॥*
प्रणवै नामदेउ लागी प्रीति । गोबिदु बसै हमारै चीति ॥

११५;० प्रीति। प्रीत्य ४; नरांइंण। नरांयण १०; नरांइण ७ ८ १६; नांराइन ३; नारायन ४: सहज। सहजि २ २०; सुभाइ। सुभाई ४; सुभाय १०; भये। भए १६ २१; भऐ ८ १३; भयै ७; बैरागी। बेरागी १०

११५;१ जैसी। जैसै २०; जैसैं ७ २१; जेसी १०; भूषैं। भूषै ७ १६ २०; प्रीति ३ १०; प्रीति। भुष अरु १०; भूष अरू ३; अनाज। नाज ३ १०; त्रिषावंत। -- ३; त्रिषांवंत २१; जेसेंही त्रिषावंत १०; मूरिष। जैसैं ३; जेसे १०; नर। मूढ ३ १०; लोग र २०; जैसैं। - ३ १०; जैसे १; कुटंब। कटूंब ३ १० १३ २०; परांइंण। परांईण २०; परांयण ४ १६; परांइंन १ ३; पराईण ८; अैसी। ऐसी १ ७; प्रीति। प्रीत्य ४; नरांइंण। नरांयण १०; नरांइंन १; नरांइण ८; नरायंण १६; नारांयण ४; नारांइन ३

११५;२ जैसैं। जैसे १; जेसें १०; रत। रति २०; नर। पर ३ १०; धन। धंन १३ २१; कौ। को १० २०; हितकारी। अधिकारी ३; कांमीं। कांमी २ ८; पुरिष। पुरिस २१; पूरष २०; रत। बसि ३ १०; नारी। नारि १ ७ २१; अैसी। ऐसी १ ७; अेसी १०; प्रीति। प्रीत्य ४; मुरारी। मुरारि १ ३ ७ २१

११५;३ जैसी। अैसी ८; जेसी १०; प्रीति। प्रीत्य ४; बालिक। बालक ८ १३; अरु। अर २०; अरू ३ ८ १०; रु १६; अैसैं। ऐसैं १; ऐसैं ७; अैसी ३; अेसे १०; यहु। ले ३; मन। मंन २१; सूं। स्यूं ३ ४ २०; स्यौं १; सुं १०; सौं ८ १३ १६; कहै। कहे १०; मेरी। मेरि ४; मेरे १; प्रीति। प्रीत्य ४; गोबिंद। गोबिद ४ ८; गोब्यंद २० २१; गोव्यंद १; साध संगति ३ १०; बसै। मेरे ३ १०; बसैं १६; बसैहि ७; बसहिं ४; हंमारै। हंमारे ४; हमारैं १६; हमारे १ ७; हम हमारे २०; रहि गई ३; रहि गइ १०; चीति। चिति ३; चित १०; चींति २०; चीत्य ४

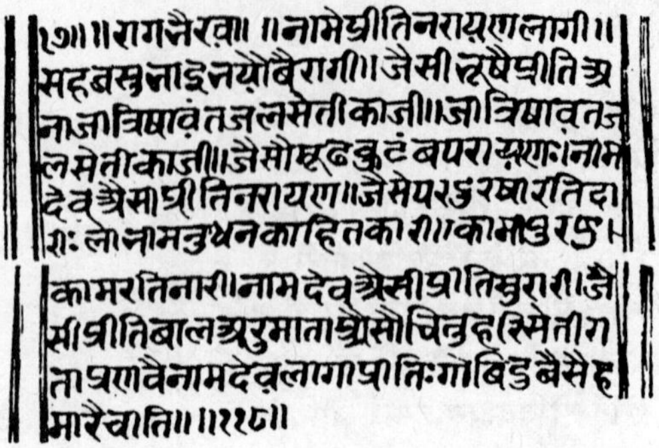

११६

• नांइं तिरूं तेरे नांइं तिरूं ॥
नांइं तिरूं हो बाप रांम देवा ॥
१ नित अमावस नितै पूंन्यूं नितै ही रवि चंदा ॥
गंगा जमुना संगमि देषूं आनंद लहरि तरंगा ॥
२ घट ही बेणीं तीरथ आछै मरम न जांणैं कोई ॥
चित बिहंगम चेति न देषै लिपति न काहू होई ॥
३ ग्यांन सरोवर मंजन मंज्या सहजैं छूटिलै भरमां ॥
नांमां संगै रांम बोलै रांम नांम निहकरमां ॥

११७

• भगत भगवंत नहीं अंता । द्वै करि जांणैं पसुवा नरा ॥
१ छाडि प्रतीति बेद बिधि करै । दाझै भूजै जांमैं मरै ॥

११६;• नांइं। नांई ४; नांइ २०; तिरूं। तिरौं १६; नांइं। नांई ४; तिरूं। तिरौं १६; नांइं। नांई ४; नांइ १६; तिरूं। तिरौं १६; हो। - ४; बाप। बाबा ४; रांम। रंमईया २०; देवा। - २०

११६;१ नितै। नितैं १६; पूंन्यूं। पूंन्यौं १६; नितै। नित २०; नितैं ४ १६; ही। हीं चलै २०; जमुना। जमूना २०; जमनां १६; संगमि। संगही २०; देषूं। आछैं २०; देषौं १६; आनंद। आंनद ४

११६;२ ही। हीं ४ १६; बेणीं। बेणी २०; लिपति। काहू १६; न। लिपत १६; काहू। न १६

११६;३ मंज्या। मंज्य ४; भरमां। भ्रमां २०; भ्रमा ४; संगै। संगैं १६; निहकरमां। निहिकरमां ४; निहक्रमां २०

११७;• भगत। भगवंत ८ १३ १६ २०; भगवंत। भगति २०; भगत १३ १६; भगता ८; नहीं। नही ३ ८ १० २१; अंता। अंतरा ८; द्वै। दोइ २०; जांणैं। जांणैं ते २०; जांनैं २१; जाने १०; जानैं ३; पसुवा। पसूवा २०; पसवा १ ८ १० १३; नरा। नराटेक १६

२ कथणीं बदणीं सब को कहै । सो साचा जे रहणी रहै ॥
३ कहत नांमदेव ममिता जाइ । तौ साध संगति मैं रहै समाइ ॥

११८

• रांम रांम रांम रांम जपिबौ करै ॥
हिरदै हरि जी कौ सुमिरन धरै ॥
१ सांडा मुरका जाइ पुकारे पढै नहीं हम पचि हारे ॥
रांम रांम कहै अरु ताल बजावै चटरा सबै बिगारे ॥
२ सब बसुधा बसि कीन्हीं हो राजा बिनती करै पटरांनी ॥
पुत्र प्रहिलाद कह्यौ नहीं मांनैं इहिं कछू औरै ठांनी ॥
३ राज सभा मिलि मंत्र उपायौ बालक बुधि घणेरी ॥
जल थल गिर ज्वाला थैं राष्यौ रांम राइ माया फेरी ॥

११७;१ छाडि। तजि २०; प्रतीति। भगवंत ८ १३ १६ २०; प्रतीत्य ४; परतीति ७; दाझै। दीझै १; दाघै २०; दाधै २१; दाझे १०; भूजै। भूगैं २०: भूझे १०; जांमैं। जांमै ३ १३; जामे १०; मरै। मरै छाडि भगवंत आंन कूं ध्यावै त्यूं बूडै ज्यूं थाह न पावै २०: मरे १०; रै ३

११७;२ कथणीं। कथणी ८ १६; कथनी ३ १०; बदणीं। बदणी ८ २१; बदनी ३ १०; को। का २१; सो। करणी २०: करणीं १६; करनी ८; करनीं १३; साचा। जंन १३; जन ८ १६ २०; जे। को १३ २०; कोई ८ १६; जो १ ३ १०; रहणी। बिरला ८ १३ १६ २०; रहनी १०; रहनीं ३; रहै। लहै २०

११७;३ कहत। भणत २०; नांमदेव। नांमदेव जो २०; ममिता। मंमिंता १३; मम्यता ३; ममता ७; जाइ। जाई १ ३ ४ ८ २०; तौ। - ८; तो १०; मैं। मे १०; रहै। रहे १०; रह्या १३; समाइ। संमाई २१; संमाइ १३; सभाई १ ३ ४

११८;• रांम। राम ३; रांम। राम ३; जपिबौ। जपिबो ३ १० २१; करै। करे १०; हिरदै। ह्रिदै १३; हिरदे १०; हृदै २१; हरि। हर १०; जी। - १ ८ १३ २०; कौ। के १०; को २०; सुमिरन। सुंमिंरन १३; सुंमिरंण २१; सुमिरण ४ ८; सूमिरण २०; धरै। करै ८

११८;१ सांडा। संडा १६; साडा ८; मुरका। मुरगा १०; जाइ। जाई ४; पुकारे। पुकारै २०; पढै। पढैं २१; पढत ३ १०; नहीं। नही ३ ८; हम। - १३; हंम ८ २१; पचि। पची २०; रांम। हरि ८ १३ १६ २०; रांम। हरि ८ १३ १६ २०; कहै। कहे १०; करै १ ८ १३ १६; अरु। अर १० १६ २०; अरू ८; र ३; रु ४; रु २१; बजावै। बजावे १०; चटरा। चटूरा ३; चतडा १ १३ २०; सबै। संबहिं १६; सबैंहि ४; सबे १०; सबहि २१

११८;२ सब। - ३ १०; बसुधा। बसधा ८; कीन्हीं। कींन्हीं १३; कीन्ही ८; कोर्नीं २१; हो। - ८ १३ १६; बिनती। बिंनती १३; बीनती १ १६ २०; करै। कहारै १०; पटरांनी। पटरांणी १; पटरांणीं २०; पटरांनीं १६ २१; पुत्र। पूत १ ३ १०; प्रहिलाद। पहिलाद १६; प्रह्लाद १०; पहलाद २०; कह्यौ। कह्यो ३ १०; नहीं। नहि १; नही ३ ८; मांनैं। मांनै १३; मांनत ३ १०; इहिं। ईही २०; ईहिं ४ १३; इंहि ३ २१; इनि १६; इहि ८ १०; कछू। कुछ ३ ४ १०; कछु १६; औरै। औरे ८; औंरै ४ २१; औरे १०; ठांनी। ठांणी १; ठांणीं २०; ठानी १६

११८;३ राज। असूर २०; सकल ३ १०; मंत्र। मत्र ८; उपायौ। उपायो ३ १०; उपाया २०; बालक। बलक २०; बालिक ३ ४; बुधि। बूधि २०; घणेरी। घंणेंरी १३; घंणेरी २१; घंणरीं २०; घनेरी ३ १०; गिर। गिरि १६; गीर २०; ज्वाला। ज्याल २०; थैं। मैं १ २१; थै २०; तैं ३ ८ १३; ते १०; राष्यौ। राष्यो ३ १०; राइ। राई २०; राय ४ १३

४ काढि षडग काल ह्वै कोप्यौ मोहि बताइ तोहि को राषै ॥
षंभा मैं प्रगट्यौ परमेस्वर सकल बियापी सति भाषै ॥
५ हरनाकुस कौ उद्र बिदार्‍यौ सुर नर कीये सनाथा ॥
भणत नांमदेव तुम्ह सरणागति रांम अभै पद दाता ॥

१ संडा मरका जाइ पुकारे । पडै नही हम ही पचि हारे ॥
राम कहै कर ताल बजावै चटीआ सभै बिगारे ॥
० राम नामा जपिबो करै । हिरदै हरि जी को सिमरनु धरै ॥ रहाउ ॥
२ बसुधा बसि कीनी सभ राजे । बिनती करै पटरानी ॥
पूतु प्रहिलादु कहिआ नही मानै तिनि तउ अउरै ठानी ॥
३ दुसट सभा मिलि मंतर उपाइआ करसह अउध घनेरी ॥
गिरि तर जल जुआला भै राखिओ राजा रामि माइआ फेरी ॥
४ काढि खडगु कालु भै कोपिओ मोहि बताउ जु तुहि राखै ॥
पीत पीतांबर त्रिभवण धणी थंभ माहि हरि भाखै ॥
५ हरनाखसु जिनि नखह बिदारिओ सुरि नर कीए सनाथा ॥
कहि नामदेव हम नरहरि धिआवहि रामु अभै पद दाता ॥

११९

• जौ बोलै तौ रांमहिं बोलि । नहीं तर बदन कपाट न षोलि ॥
१ जे बोलिये तौ कहिये रांम । आंन बकन सौं नांहीं कांम ॥
२ रांम नांम मेरे हिरदै लेष । रांम बिनां सब फोकट देष ॥
३ नांमदेव कहै मेरे एकै नांउं । रांम नांम की मैं बलि जांउं ॥

११८;४ षडग। षरग २ १०; ह्वै। है ८; होय १०; होइ ३; कोप्यौ। कौप्यौ २०; कोप्यो २ १०; बताइ। बताई ४; तोहि। ताहि १३; राषै। राषे १०; षंभा। षंभ १०; षंभां १६; षभ ३; थंभा २० २१; मैं। मै ४; महिं २१; मांहि ३; माहिं १६; फाडि १०; प्रगट्यौ। प्रगटे २ १०; ब्यापक २०; परमेस्वर। परमेसूर २०; परमानंद २ १०; बियापी। बीयापी २०; सति। स्ति ३; भाषै। भाषे १०

११८;५ हरनाकुस। हिंनाकुसि ३; हिरणाकुस २०; हरिनांकुसि १०; हरिनाकस १६; हरणांकुस ४; हरनांकुस १३; कौ। को १०; उद्र। उदर ४ ८ १० १३; इतद्र २०; बिदार्‍यौ। बिदार्‍यो २ १०; बिदार्‍यौ १; कीये। कीए १६ २१; सनाथा। सुनांथा २१; सुनाथा ३ १६ २०; भणत। भणंत २१; भनत २ १०; प्रणवंत २०; तुम्ह। तुंम १२ २०; तुम ३ ८ १०; सरणागति। सरंणागति २१; सरनांगति २ १३; सरनागति ८ १० १६ २०; अभै। अभे १०

११९;० जौ। जिभ्या ७; जो ८ १३; रांमहिं। रांमहि ७ १६; रांमही र ८; बोलि। बोला १३; नहीं। नहिं १३; नही ८; कपाट। कापाट १२

११९;१ कहिये। कहियै १६; बकन। बकण ८ १६; सौं। सूं ७; नांहीं। नांही ८

११९;२ लेष। लेषि ७; बिनां। बिंनां १३; देष। देषि ७

१२०

० जपि रांम नांम मंत्रावला । कलि जुग मरणां उतावला ॥
१ दिवस गंवायौ ग्रिह ब्यौहार । राति आई अंधाकार ॥
२ दूरि पयांनां औघट घाट । क्यौं निस्तरिबौ संग न साथ ॥
३ भणंत नांमदेव औघट तिरी । अरधै नांइ उबारै हरी ॥

१२१

० मैला मलिता सब संसार । हरि न्रिमल जाकौ अंत न पार ॥
१ मैला बीरज मैला षेत । मन मैला काया रस हेत ॥
२ मैला मोती मैला हीर । मैला पवन पावक अरु नीर ॥
३ मैला तीनि लोक ब्रह्मंड इकवीस । निस बासुरि मैला दिन तीस ॥
४ मैला ब्रह्मा मैला इंद्र । सहंस कला मैला रवि चंद ॥

११६;३ कहै। भणैं ७ ८ १६; एकै। ऐको १३; येको ८; नांउं। नांउ ८; जांउं। जां ८

१२०;० मंत्रावला। म्यंतावला १; मत्रावला ८; जुग। जुगि १६; मरणां। मरंणां २१; मरनां १६; उतावला। उतांवला २०

१२०;१ दिवस। दिंवस १३; गंवायौ। गंमा १३; गंमायौ १ २०; गवायौ ४ ७; गवाया १६; ग्रिह। ग्रहे ८; गृह १६; ब्यौहार। ब्यौहार १; राति। राति ज ७; राति जु ८ १३ १६; आई। आई रे २०; अंधाकार। अंधकार १६ २०

१२०;२ पयांनां। पयांणां १; पयांना ४ २०; क्यौं। क्यूं ४ ७ २० २१; निस्तरिबौ। निसतिरिबौ २०; निसतरिबौ ७ २१; निसातरिबौ ८; साथ। साध २०

१२०;३ भणंत। भणत ८ १६; तिरी। तिरि २१; अरधै। अरधै २०; अरधैं ७ १३; नांइ। नांद्रि ८; नांई ४; नांउं २०; नांइं १ १३; नाइ १६; हरी। हरि २०

१२१;० मैला। मैंला १६; मेला १०; सब। यहु १; न्रिमल। निर्मल ७ १६; निरमल १ ३ १०; जाकौ। जाको १० २०; ताकौ ८ १३

१२१;१ मैला। मैंलां १६; मेला १०; बीरज। बिरज १०; वीरज १; मैला। मेला १०; मन। मंन २१; तन ३ १०; मैला। मैंला ८; मन ३ १०; काया। मैला ३; मेला १०; रस। काया ३ १०; जस १६; रहै २०; हेत। सेत २०; सहेत ३ १०

१२१;२ मैला। मेला १०; मैला। मैली २१; मेला १०; हीर। हीरा २०; मैला। मेला १०; पवन। पवंन २१; अरु। अर २०; अरू ३ ४ ८ १३

१२१;३ मैला। मेला १०; तीनि। तीनिं १३; तीन १ ३ १०; ब्रह्मंड। - ८; बहमंड १७; तुम्हारा १०; इकवीस। ईकबीस ४; इकईस ८; इकीस १; इकबीस ७ १३ १६, इकवईस ३; इकइस १०; निस। निंस १३; निसु २०; बासुरि। बासुर १; बासूर २०; बासरि १७; बासर ३ १०; मैला। मैंले १३; मेला १०; दिन। दिंन १३; तीस। तीन ७

१२१;४ मैला। मेला १०; ब्रह्मा। ब्रह्म ३; ब्रह्मां १३ २१; मैला। मेला १०; इंद्र। ईद्रं २०; यंद १ ८ १३ १७; यंद्र ४ १०; इंद ३; सहंस। सहस ३; मैला। मैंला १६; मैले ८; मैला मैला ३; मेला १०; रवि। रबि ३; चंद। चंद्र ४ ७ २१; चंद मैला सुम्रित बेद पुरांनां मैला संझ्य सहित समांनां २०

५ सब जग मैला एकैं भाइ । जंन न्रिमल जब हरि गुण गाइ ॥
६ मैला पुंनि अरु मैला पाप । मैला आंन देव का जाप ॥
७ मैला तीरथ मैला दांन । ब्रत मैला पूजा र सनांन ॥
८ मैला सुर मैली सुरसुरी । नांमदेव कौ ठाकुर न्रिमल हरी ॥

१२२

० जागि रे जीव कहा भुलांनां । आगैं पीछैं जांनां ही जांनां ॥
१ दिवस चारि का गोवलि बासा । तामैं तोहि क्यौं आवै हासा ॥
२ इहि भ्रमि लागि कहा तूं सोवै । काहे कूं जनम बादि ही षोवै ॥
३ कहा तूं सोचै बारंबारा । रांम नांम जपि लेहु गंवारा ॥
४ भणत नांमदेव चेति अयांनां । औघट घाट रु दूरि पयांनां ॥

१२१;५ जग। जुग १ ३ १० २० २१; मैला। मैंला १३; मेला १०; एकैं। ऐणैं ८ १३; ऐके ४; एके ७; आंनहि १६ १७; येकैं २०; येकहि ३ १०; भाइ। भांई ३; भाई ४ १७; नांई १०; जंन। -- ३ १०; जन ८ १६ १७; न्रिमल। न्रिंमल १३; निर्मल ७ १६; नृमल ८; जब। जे ८ १३; तब १; गुण। गुन १ ७ ८ २१; गाइ। गाई ४ २०

१२१;६ मैला। मेंला १०; पुंनि। पुंनि १३; पुंन्य १०; पुंन्यि २१; पुन्य ४; पुनि १ ३ ८ १६; पूनि २०; अरु। अरु ४ ८; यर १; र ३ १० २०; रु १३ २१; मैला। मेला १०; मैला। मेला ७ १०; आंन। आन ३

१२१;७ मैला। -- १ ३ ८ १० १३ १६ १७ २०; तीरथ। तीर्थ ७; ब्रत। -- १ ३ ८ १० १३ १६ १७; र। अर २०; सनांन। स्नांन ७; समांन ४ २१

१२१;८ मैला। मेला १०; सुर। श्रु ३; सुं १०; मैली। मेला १०; सुरसुरी। श्रुसुरिजां ३; सुसरि १०; सुरसती ७; सुरसरी १; कौ। को ३ १० २०; का ८; ठाकुर। ठाकूर ४ २०; साहिब ३ १०; न्रिमल। निर्मल ७ १६; निरमल ३ १०; नृमल ८; हरी। हरि ३ २०

१२२;० जीव। जीय ८ १३; कहा। कहां १६; भुलांनां। भुलांनौं ४ ७ २१; भूलाना २०; आगैं। तोहि आगै ३; तोहि आगें १०; पीछैं। पिछे १०; पीछै ३; जांनां। जांनौं ४ ७ २१; जांना ८; ही। हीं २०; जांनां। जांनौं ४ ७ २१

१२२;१ दिवस। दिंवस १३; दिन ३ १०; चारि। च्यारि ४; दस ३ १०; का। कौ १ ४ ७ २१; गोवलि। गोवल ३ ४ १०; बासा। बासौ ४ ७ २१; तामैं। तामै २० २१; तातें १०; तोहि। तौहि ३; तोहिं ७; क्यौं। क्युं १०; क्यूं ७ १३ २० २१; आवै। आवे १०; हासा। हांसा २०; हासौ ४ ७ २१

१२२;२ इहि। ईहि ४; या १; इंहिं १३; इंहि ३ २१; भ्रमि। भूंमिं १३; भर्मि १६; भ्रंम १; भ्रमि ४; कहा। कहां २०; तूं। तु २०; तू १ ३ १०; सोवै। सोवे १०; काहे। - २०; हरि ३ १०; कूं। - १ २०; बिन ३ १०; कौं ८ १३ १६; जनम। जंनंम २१; जन्म १३; जनम अमोलिक २०; बादि। अबिरथा ३ १०; ही। - ३ १०; हीं ७ १६; षोवै। षोवे १०

१२२;३ कहा। -- ३ १०; क्या १ २० २१; तूं। तू १; सोचै। सोवै २० २१; रांम। -- ३ १०; लेहु। लेहुं १३; गंवारा। गवारा ४ १६

१२२;४ भणत। भणंत १ ४ १३ २० २१; नांमदेव ३ १०; नांमदेव। कहै ३; कहे १०; चेति। चिति चेत १०; चित चेति ३; अयांनां। अयांणां १ १३ २१; अयाना ३; अयानां १०; औघट। ओघट ३ १०; घाट। घांटा २०; घाटी १ ३ १०; घाटा ८ १३; रु। - १ ३ ८ १० १३ २०; अरु ७ १६; रू ४; दूरि। दुरि १०; पयांनां। पयांणां १ १३

१२३

• छाडि रे मन हमिता ममिता । सब घटि रांम रह्यौ रमि रमिता ॥
१ आसा करि मन जाइये जहियां । रांम बिनां सुष नांहीं तहियां ॥
२ जन की प्रीति अगम पियारी । ज्यौं जल निरषि भरै पनिहारी ॥
३ भणत नांमदेव सब गुण आगर । भजि हरि चरन क्रिपा सुष सागर ॥

१२४

• हरि भजि हरि भजि हरि भजि मूल । बिन हरि भजन परै मुष धूल ॥
१ अनेक बार पसू ह्वै अवतरयौ । लष चौरासी भ्रमत फिरयौ ॥
२ पायौ नहीं कहीं बिश्रांम । सतगुर सरनि कह्यौ नहीं रांम ॥
३ राज काज सुत बित सब जाइ । अबिनासी सौं प्रीति लगाइ ॥
४ इहिं उनमांन भगति ब्रत धरै । जुरा मरन भौ संकुट टरै ॥
५ गुणसागर गोबिंद गुण गाइ । अपनौं बिडद बिसरि जिनि जाइ ॥
६ प्रणवंत नांमदेव संत सधीर । चरन सरन राषौ हरि नीर ॥

१२३;० छाडि। छांडि १६; छाडि दे ७; हमिता। हमता ७; रमिता। रमता १६

१२३;१ मन। - ७; जाइये। जाइयै १६

१२३;२ ज्यौं। ज्यूं ७; निरषि। न्रिषि ७; पनिहारी। पनिंहारी १६

१२३;३ भणत। भणैं ७; चरन। चरण ७

१२४;० बिन। बिंन १३; परै। पडै ८ १३ १६; मुष। मुंषि १३; मुषि ८ १६; मूष २०; धूल। धुल २१; धूरि २०

१२४;१ पसू। पसु ४ २१; ह्वै। है २०; अवतरयौ। औतरयौ ८ १३ १६ २०; भ्रमत। भ्रंमत १३ २१; भ्रमतौ २०; भर्मत १६

१२४;२ नहीं। नही ८; कहीं। कही ८; बिश्रांम। बिश्राम २०; बिसरांम १३, सतगुर। सतगुरि ७ ८ १३ १६; सरनि। संगि १६; सरंण २१; सरनिं १३; सरणि ४ ७; नहीं। मैं ८ १३

१२४;३ जाइ। जाई ४ २०; जाइं ७; अबिनासी। अबिनासा २०; सौं। स्यूं ४; सूं २० २१; प्रीति। चित ४; प्रीती २०; पीर्ति १६; लगाइ। लगाई ४ २० २१

१२४;४ इहिं। ईहि ४; इंहिं १३; इंहि २१; इहि ७ ८ २०; उनमांन। उंनमांनि २१; उंनमांन १३; ब्रत। चित २०; बर्त १६; धरै। धरौ २०; जुरा। जुर्हा २१; मरन। मरंण ४; मरंन २१; मरण ७ २०; भौ। - २०; संकुट। संकट ८; संकूट बहु २०

१२४;५ गुणसागर। गुंणसागर १३ २१; गोबिंद। गोबिद ८; गोब्यंद १६ २० २१; गुण। गुंण १३ २१; गाइ। गाई ४ २०; अपनौं। अपणौं ७ २० २१; अपनौ ८; बिडद। बिरद ८ १३; बिसरि। जिनि २०; जिनि। जिंनिं १३; जिंनि २१; बीसरि २०; जाइ। जाई ४ ८

१२४;६ प्रणवंत। प्रणवत ४ ८; सधीर। सधिर २१; चरन। चरंण ४ २१; चरण ७ २०; सरन। सरंण ४ २१; सरण ७; सरणं २०; हरि। रघु ४; नीर। बीर ४

१२५

० जे न भजैं नर नारांइंणा । ताका मैं न करूं दरसनां ॥
१ जांहिं सवारा आंवैं सांझ । ते नर गिणियैं पसुवा मांझ ॥
२ जिनकै हरि नहीं अभिअंतरा । जैसे पसुवा तैसे नरा ॥
३ जैसी संतौ बिष की डरी । तैसी पर घर की सुंदरी ॥
४ परधन परदारा परहरी । तिनके निकटि बसै नरहरी ॥
५ प्रणवंत नांमदेव नांकी बिनां । ना सोहै बतीस लषनां ॥

१ परधन परदारा परहरी । ता कै निकटि बसै नरहरी ॥
० जो न भजते नाराइणा । तिन का मै न करउ दरसना ॥ रहाउ ॥
२ जिन कै भीतरि है अंतरा । जैसे पसु तैसे ओइ नरा ॥
३ प्रणवति नामदेउ नाकहि बिना । ना सोहै बतीस लखना ॥

१२६

० आंन न जांणूं देवी न देवा । जत जत प्रांण ततहि तेरी सेवा ॥

१२५;० भजैं। भजे १०; नर। - १३; नारांइंणा। नांरांईणा २०; नांरांइंणां १३; नारांयंणां ४; नारांयणां १६; नारांइंणां २१; नारायनां १०; नाराइणां ८; नाराइना ३; ताका। तिनका १ ४; मैं। मै २०; में १०; करूं। करौ ३ १६; करौं ८ १३; करो १०; करु २१; दरसनां। दरसंनां २१; दरसंरणां १३; दरसणां १ ४ २०; दरसना ३

१२५;१ जांहिं। जांहि १ ४ ७ ८ २०; जाहि ३; सवारा। संवार १३; संवारे ८; संवारा १ ४ २१; सवारे १६; सवारां १०; आंवैं। आंवहिं ११; आंवहि ७; आवै ३ २०; आवैं २१; आवे १०; सांझ। साझ २१; नर। नरा ३; गिणियैं। गिंगियैं २१; गिणिये १ २०; गिंगियें ४ ८ १३; गिनिये ३ १०; पसुवा। पसुवन ४; पसुवां ८; पसूवा ७ २०; पसवा १० २१; मांझ। मझा १०; माझ ३ २०

१२५;२ जिनकै। जिंनकै १३; जिनिकै १६; जीनकै २०; जीनके १०; जाकै १; नहीं। नहिं १ १३; नहो ८; नांही ३; नाहीं १०; अभिअंतरा। अभीअंतरा ४; जैसे। तेसें १०; पसुवा। पसुवां ८; पसूवा २०; पसवा १ ४ १० १३; तैसे। तेसे १०

१२५;३ जैसी। जेसी १०; संतौ। संतै ३; संतो ४ १०; बिष। विष १; तैसी। तेसी १०; घर। घरि १६; सुंदरी। सुदरी ८; सूदरी ३ १०

१२५;४ परधन। अपनी ३ १०; परधंन २०; परदारा। परद्वारा १; पराई सब ३; पराइ सब १०; तिनके। तिंनकै १३; तिंनके २१; तिनिके ४; तिनकै १ ३; तिनकैं २०; निकटि। निंकटि १३; निकट ३ ८; बसै। बसैं ३; बसे १०; नरहरी। नरहरि ३; नरहारी २०

१२५;५ प्रणवंत। प्रंणवंत २१; प्रणवत १ ८; प्रनवत ३ १०; नांकी। नांका ४; नांकां १; नाकी ७ ८ १६ २० २१; बिनां। बिंनां १३; बिना २०; ना। नहिं २१; नहीं १; नां ३ ४ ८ १३ १६; सोहै। सोभै ८ १३ २०; सोहे १०; लषनां। लषिणां १६; लषिनां ८; लष्रणां ४ ७ २०; लषना ३

१२६;० आंन। आन २१; जांणूं। जांणै ४; जांणैं न २१; जाणूं ७; न। - २१; जत। जित १; जत। जित १; ततहि। तितहि १; ततहिं ४

१ तूं सुष सागर आगर दाता । तूं ही मेरे प्रांण पिता गुर माता ॥
२ नांमौं भणैं मेरे सब कुछ सांई । मनसा बाचा दूसर नांहीं ॥

१२७

० पाडि मोहि पढावहु हरी । बिद्या अपनी राषहु धरी ॥
१ बारह अषिर की बारह षडी । हरि बिन पढिबे की आषडी ॥
२ ररौ ममौ दोउ अषिरा । पारि उतारौ भौसागरा ॥
३ हंम तुम पाडि कैसा बाद । रांम नांम पढिहै प्रहिलाद ॥
४ पतरा पोथी परहा करौ । रांम नांम जपि दूतर तिरौ ॥
५ थंभा मांहैं प्रगट्यौ हरी । नांमदेव कौ स्वांमीं नरहरी ॥

१२८

० रांम नांम मेरे पूंजी धनां । ता पूंजी मेरौ लागौ मनां ॥
१ यहु पूंजी है अगम अपार । अैसा कोई न साहूकार ॥
२ साह की पूंजी आवै जाइ । कबहूं आवै मूल गवाइ ॥

१२६;१ तूं। तू ४; आगर। - ४; अगर २१; ही। हीं ७; प्रांण। प्रांन ७, पिता। पति ४ २१

१२६;२ भणैं। भणै ४; मेरे। मेरै ४; कुछ। कछु १; कछू २१; सांई। सांई २१

१२७;० पढावहु। पढा+ ४; पढाइहो २ १०; हरी। हरि ३; बिद्या। विद्या १; अपनी। अपणीं १ २१; धरी। घरी १०; धरि ३

१२७;१ अषिर। अष्यर १; आषर १०; की। कौ ३; बारह। बार २ ४; षडी। षरी ३ १०; पढिबे। पढिबा १; आषडी। आषरी २ १०

१२७;२ ररौ। ररो २ १०; ममौ। ममौं १ २१; ममो १०; दोउ। दौउ ३; दोऊ १; दोई ४; दोइ २१; अषिरा। अक्षरा १; पारि। पार २ १०; उतारौ। अतारै ३; उतारे १०; भौसागरा। भोसागरा १०

१२७;३ हंम। हम २ १०; तुम। तुंम १ १०; पाडि। पाडे ३ २१; कैसा। केसा १०; पढिहै। पढिहे १०; प्रहिलाद। प्रह्लाद १०; प्रहलाद १ ३

१२७;४ पतरा। पतडा १ ४ २१; परहा। परहा २१; करौ। करों १०; रांम। राम ३; दूतर। दुस्तर १०; तिरौ। तिरो २ १०

१२७;५ थंभा। तब १०; तबैं आइ ३; मांहैं। आइ १०; मांही २१; है ३; प्रगट्यौ। प्रगटै ३; प्रगटेहें १०; हरी। हरि ३; कौ। को १०; स्वांमीं। स्वांमी ३; स्वांमीं है २१; स्वामी ४; नरहरी। नरहरि ३

१२८;० नांम। नांव ३; पूंजी। पुजी १०; पूजी २१; धनां। धंनां ४; पूंजी। पुजीं १०; पूजी ३; मेरौ। मेरो २ १०; लागौ। लागो १०

१२८;१ यहु। यह २ १०; पूंजी। पुंजी १०; है। हे १०; अगम। अगंम २१; अैसा। ऐसा १ ७; अैसां २१; अेसा १०; कोई। कोउ २ १०; साहूकार। साहूंकार २१

१२८;२ पूंजी। पुंजी १०; पूजी ३; आवै। आवे १०; जाइ। जाई ४; कबहूं। कबहू २ १०; आवै। बैसै ३; बेसे १०; गवाइ। गंवाई २१; गंवाइ १; गमाइ १०; गवाई ४

३ जाली जलै न काई षाइ । राजा डंडै न चोर ले जाइ ॥
४ अलष निरंजन दीनदयाल । नांमदेव कै धन श्रीगोपाल ॥

१२९

० रांम नांमैं प्यंड पषाल । मल नहीं लागै जपत गोपाल ॥
१ रांम नांम डूंगर सी सिला । धुबिया धोवै अंतरि मला ॥
२ बर्णा आश्रंम नांनां मती । नांमदेव कौ स्वांमीं कवलापती ॥

१३०

० हरि दरजी का मरम न पाया । जिनि यहु बागा षूब बनाया ॥
१ पानी का चित्र पवन का धागा । ताकूं सींवत मास दस लागा ॥
२ सो सूरवाल मुकट बनि आया । ये दोइ हीरा लाल लगाया ॥
३ भगति मुकति का पटा लिषाया । पूरण पारब्रह्म पहराया ॥
४ आपै सीवै आप पहरावै । निरत नांमदेव नांव धरावै ॥

१३१

० तूं मेरौ ठाकुर तूं मेरौ राजा हूं तेरे सरणैं आयौ हो ॥
जस तुम्हारौ गावत गोबिंद इन लोगनि मारि उठायौ हो ॥

१२८;३ जाली। जारी २ १०; जलै। जरै ३; जरे १०; काई। काइ १०; षाइ। षाई ४ २१; डंडै। डडे १०; डडै ३; न। - २१; जाइ। जाई ३ ४ २१

१२८;४ दीनदयाल। दींनदयाल २१; कै। के १०; कौ १; धन। धंन २१; श्रीगोपाल। श्रीगोपाला १०

१३०;० मरम। मरंम १३; जिनि। जिंनिं १३; यहु। यह १०; बनाया। बनांया १३

१३०;१ पानी। पांणीं १३; पांनी ३; ताकूं। ताकु १०; ताकू ३; ताकौ १३; सींवत। सीवत १०; मास। मांस १० १३

१३०;२ सो। स्यूं ३; सूं १०; सूरवाल। सरवाल १३; मुकट। बटवा १३; बनि। बंणिं १३; ये। ऐ १३; य १०; दोइ। दोइ ही ३

१३०;३ मुकति। मुंकति १३; का। - १३; लिषाया। लिषिया १३; पूरण। पुरन ३; पूरन १०; पहराया। पहिगया १३

१३०;४ आपै। आपे १०; सीवै। सींवै ३; सींवि १०; सीवैं १३; आप। आपै १३; पहरावै। पहिरावै १३; पहरावे १०; निरत। निरंतर १०; निरति १३; धरावै। धरावे १०

१३१;० तूं। तु १०; तू १ ३ १८; मेरौ। मेरो ३ १०; ठाकुर। ठाकूर ४; तूं। तू ३ ४ १०; मेरौ। मे+ ४; मेरो १०; राजा। + ४; हूं। हू १ १०; हौ १८; तेरे। तेरै १३ १८ २० २१; सरणैं। सरनै ३; सरनैं १३ १८; सरने १०; आयौ।

१ आलम दुनी आवती मैं देषी साइर पांडे कोपिला हो ॥
सुद्र सुद्र करि मारि उठायौ कहा करूं मेरे बाबुला हो ॥
२ प्रांण गयैं जे मुकति होत है सो तौ मुकति न जांनै कोई जी ॥
ये बांभण मोहि सुद्र कहत हैं तेरी पैज पिछौंडी होई जी ॥
३ भई चहूं दिसि अचिरज भारी अदबुद बात अपारा हो ॥
दास नांमां कूं भयौ दुवारौ पंडित कूं पछिवारा हो ॥

• मो कउ तूं न बिसारि तू न बिसारि ईआ । तू न बिसारे रामईआ ॥ रहाउ ॥
१ आलावंती इहु भ्रमु जो है मुझ ऊपर सभ कोपिला ॥
सूदु सूदु करि मारि उठाइओ कहा करउ बाप बीठुला ॥
२ मूए हूए जउ मुकति देहुगे मुकति न जानै कोइला ॥
ए पंडीआ मो कउ ढेढ कहत तेरी पैज पिछंउडी होइला ॥
३ तू जु दइआलु कृपालु कहीअतु हैं अति भुज भइओ अपारला ॥
फेरि दीआ देहुरा नामे कउ पंडीअन कउ पिछवारला ॥

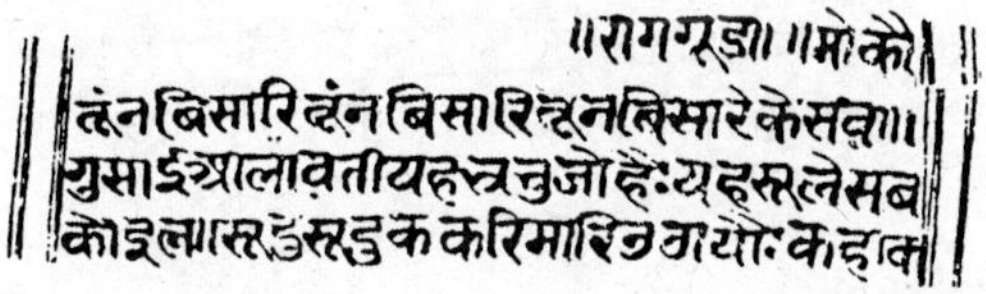
॥रागगूडी॥ ॥मो कौ॥
तूं न बिसारि तूं न बिसारि तूं न बिसारे केसवा॥
गुसाईं आलावंती यह भ्रम जो है यह हम ले सब
कोइला सूड सूड क करि मारि उठायो कहा क

आयो ३ १०; आया ४; हो। हौ २१; जस। -- २०; तुम्हारौ। तुंम्ह्रारौ १३; तुम्ह्रारो ३ १०; गोबिंद। गोबिद ८; गोब्यंद १० १६; गोब्यंदा २१; गोव्यंदा १; इन। - १; -- २०; यनि ३, इंन २१; इनि ७ ८ १०; इहि १६; लोगनि। लोकंनि १३ २१; लोकनि ८; उठायौ। उठायो ३ १०; उठाया ४; हो। - १०

१३१;१ आलम। आलंम १ १३ २० २१; दुनी। - १; दुनी १३, दुनीं ७ १६; आवती। आवत १ ४ ८ १३ १६; मैं। - ३ ७ १० २० २१; मै १३; साइर। पांवा १; सायर ३ ४ १० १६; कोपिला। कोप्योला ३; हो। - १ ८ १३ २१; जी २०; उठायौ। उठायो ३ १०; करूं। करौ १६; करौं ३ ७ ८ १३; करों १०; मेरे। मेरै १३; मोरै २१; बाबुला। बाबूला ४; बाबला ३ ७ १० १६; हो। - १ ८ १३; जी २०

१३१;२ प्रांण। प्रांन १ ३ २०; प्रान १०; गयैं। गये १० १३; गयें १ ३ ४ ८ २०; जे। जौ १ १३; ये ३ १०; मुकति। - ३ १०; मुक्ति १; होत। - ३ १०; कहत ७; है। - ३ १०; हैं ४; सो। -- ३ १०; तौ। - १ २०; मुकति। मुक्ति १; जांनै। - २१; दीसै १ ८ १६; दीसैं ४; जांणौं १३; जांनैं २०; कोई। कोइ १ ८ २०; होइ २१; जी। - ८; हो ७ १६; ये। - ३ १०; ए ७ १६ २१; ऐ ४ १३; बांभण। - ३ १०; पाडि १; बांम्हण ७ १६; बांभन ८ १३; मोहि। मोकौं ३; मोकों १०; हैं। है ४ १०; पैज। पैंज १३ २१; पेज १०; पिछौंडी। पिछौडी ८ १३ १६; पिछोडी ३ १०; पछौंडी २०; होई। होइ १ १० २० २१; जी। - ८ १३; हो ३ ७ १० १६

१३१;३ भई। भयो १०; भयोई ३; भया १३; चहूं। चहु १०; अचिरज। भई चहूं १ २०; भारी। दिसि १ २०; अदबुद। अदभुत ३ १०; अदबूद २०; अपारा। अपार १ ८ १० २० २१; हो। जी १ २०; नांमां। नांमदेव २०; नांमा ८; कूं। दिसि ३ १० २०; कौं ८ १३ १६; भयौ। भयो ३ १०; दुवारौ। दवारो १०; कूं। दिसि ३ १० १३ २०; दिस ८; कौ १६; पछिवारा। पिछ्वारा १६; पछिवार १ २०; पछिवारौ ४ २१; पछिवारो १०; हो। हौ ७; जी १ २०

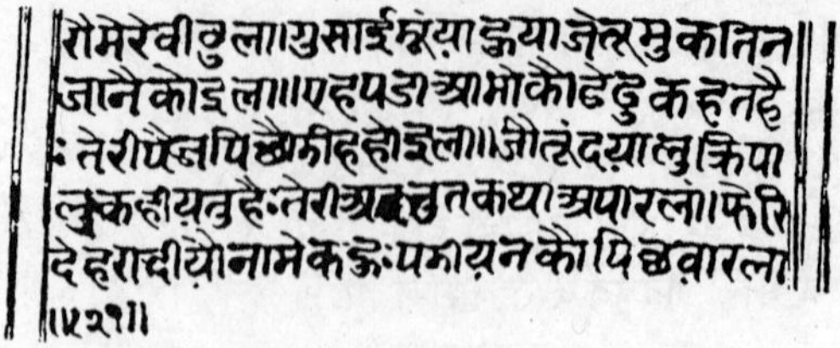

१३२

• द्रुबल गरीबौ रांम कौ ।हरि कौ दास मैं जन सेवग तेरा ॥
१ आचार ब्यौहार जाप नहीं पूजा ।अैसौ भगत आयौ सरणिला ॥
२ नांमौं भणैं मैं सेवग तेरा ।जनमि जनमि हरि उरगिला ॥

१३३

• तुम्हारी क्रिपा बिना न पाइये हो ।कांन्हां न पाइये हो ॥
१ भाव कलपतर भगति लता फल ।सो फल रसाल कै देसि देवा ॥
२ नांमौं भणैं केसवे तूं देसी तर लाहा ।येणैं उपाये तुझ भणीजे ॥

१३४

• चूक भजीला चूक भजीला ।चूकै चिति औतार धरीला ॥
१ द्रिगहीणौं दस रूप बषाणैं ।अकल अगोचर एक न जाणैं ॥
२ भोलैं जल पाषांण पूजीला ।अंतरजांमीं उरि न सूझीला ॥
३ नांमदेव न्रिषि निरंजन गावै ।अंजन आवै जाइ न भावै: ॥

१३२;• द्रुबल। दुर्बल १६; दुंबल २०; गरीबौ। गरीबा १६; कौ। कौं १; हरि। - १; कौ। - १; जन। जंन १२

१३२;१ ब्यौहार। ब्यौहार १३ २१; नहीं। नहि १; नही ८ २१; अैसौ। ऐसै २०; ऐसौ १; भगत। भगता १६; आयौ। सरणि २०; सरणिला। आयैला २०; सरंणिंला २१; सरंणिला ४; सरनिला १६; सरणला ८; सरला १३

१३२;२ नांमौं। नांमो २०; नांमां ८ १३ १६; भणैं। भणै २०; मैं। मै १६ २०; जनमि। जंनमि ४ २१; जनमिं १३; जनमि। जंनमि ४ २१; जनमिं १३; जानमि ८; उरगिला। ऊरगिला २०; उरिगिला ८

१३३;• तुम्हारी। तुंम्हांरी २१; क्रिपा। क्रपा १०; बिना। बिनां ३ २० २१; पाइये। पाईऐ ४; पाइ १०; पाइए २१; कांन्हां। कांन्ह ४; कान्हांजिय २०; रांम ३ १०; पाइये। पाईऐ ४; पाइए २१; हो। - ४ २० २१

१३३;१ कलपतर। कलपत्र २१; कै। कैं ४ २०; के १०; देसि। देस ४ २१

१३३;२ नांमौं। नांमूं ३; नांमों १०; भणैं। भणै २०; केसवे। केसवै ३; तूं। तू ३ १०; देसी। दैसी ४; येणैं। ऐणैं ४; एणैं २१; येणे १०; उपाये। उपायिं ४; तुझ। तूंझ २०; भणीजे। भणींजे ४ २०; भणींजे ३; भणीजे १०; णीजे २१

१३५

• धनि दिहाडौ धनि घडी ए । साधौ भाई गोबिंद जी घरि आव्या ए ॥
१ चंदनि चौक पुराविज्यौ ए । साधौ भाई पांच सषी ले र बधावो ए ॥
२ गगन मंडल म्हारौ बैसणौं ए । साधौ भाई बाजैं अनहद तूरो ए ॥
३ हरि जी आव्या म्हारै पाहुंणां ए । साधौ भाई आज बधावो पूरो ए ॥
४ आंबरि लागी बादली ए । साधौ भाई झिरिमिरि बरिषै मेहो ए ॥
५ दास नांमदेव हरि भज्या ए । साधौ भाई लोग हसेबा दीज्यौ ए ॥

१३६

• लागी जनम जनम नी प्रीति । चिति नहीं बीसरूं रे ॥
१ जेन्हौं मुषडौ दीठैं सुष थाइ । तेन्हैं कोई जई कहौ रे ॥
२ जा स्यूं मन बांधी प्रीति अपार । अपरछन थई रह्यौ रे ॥

१३५;० धनि। धंनि ४; धनि स १ १३; दिहाडौ। +डौ ४; दिहाडौं ७; धनि। धंनि ४ १३; ए। ऐ ४ १३; हे १; ये ८; गोबिंद। गोविंद ४; गोबिद ८; गोब्यंद ११ १७; गोब्यंद १; जी। जीयरि ८; घरि। घरि १६; आव्या। आविया १; आव्या ७; ए। ऐ ८ १३; ये १ ४

१३५;१ चंदनि। -- १३; चौक। चौंक १६; पुराविज्यौ। पुरावज्यौ ८; ए। ऐ ४ ८; ये १; साधौ। -- १३; पांच। पंच १ ४ ८; ले। - १ ४ ७; मिलि ८ १७; र। - ४ ७; बधावो। बधाव+ ४; बधाना ११ १७; ए। + ४; - ८; ये १

१३५;२ मंडल। मडल ८; म्हारौ। म्हांरौ १; मांहरौ १३; मार्ह्रौ ८; बैसणौं। बैसणौ ७; ए। - ८; ऐ ४ १३; ये १; बाजैं। बाजै १ अनहद। अंनहद १३; तूरो। तूरौं १ ४ ८ १७; ए। ऐ ४ ७ ८ १३; ये १

१३५;३ हरि। - ४ ७ ८; गोबिंद १३; आव्या। आया १; पाहुंणां। पाऊणां १६; पाहुणां १७; ए। ऐ १३; ये १; साधौ। - ४ ७ ८; आज। आजि १ १३; बधावो। बंधावो १३; बधावौ १७; पूरो। पूरौ १ १७; ए। ऐ १ १३; ये ११

१३५;४ आंबरि। अंबरि १; बादली। वादली ४; ए। + १६; - १३; ऐ ४ ८; ये १; बरिषै। बरिषैं ७ ८; मेहो। मेहौ ८ १७; ए। ऐ ४ १३; ये १ ८

१३५;५ दास। गरीब ७ ११ १७; भज्या। भज्यौ ८ १३ १६; ए। ऐ ४ ८ १३; ये १; लोग। लोक १ ७; हसेबा। हसीबा १ ४; ए। ऐ ५ ८ १३; ये १

१३६;० जनम। जंनम २१; जन्मं १; जनम। जंनम २१; जन्मं १; नी। नीं १ २ ४ ७ १० ११ १७; प्रीति। प्रीत्य ४; चिति। चिंतां १३; चितै ३; चिते १ १०; चिता २१; चितां २०; चीति ११ १७; नहीं। नहिं १३; नहि १; नही ८; बीसरूं। बिसरों १०; बिसारौं ३; बीसरौ १३ १६; बीसरौं ८; बीसरु २१, रे। - १ ३ १०; रे चिति नहीं बीसरूं ७

१३६;१ जेन्हौं। जिहिनौ ३; जिहनो १०; जेन्हैं १३; जेन्हें ८; जेन्हूं २१; जेन्हौ १; जन्हौ ४; मुषडौ। मुंषडौ १३; मुष ३ १०; दीठैं। देषि २०; देषें ८ १३; देष्यां ३ १०; दीठैं १ ७; दीठां २१; थाइ। होइ ३ ७ १०; थाई २०; थाय ४; तेन्हैं। तिन्हैं ३; तिहूं १०; कोई। कोउ ३ १०; जई। जै १ ३; जे ८ १० १३; जाई १६ २० २१; कहौ। कहै ३ ४ १० २० २१; कह्यौ १; रे। - १ ३ ८ १० १३

१३६;२ जा। - ३ १०; जां ८; स्यूं। - ३ १०; स्यौं १; सूं ७ १७ २१; सौं ८ १३ १६; मन। मंनिं १३; मंन १; मनि

३ भर्‍यौ सरोवर लहर्‍यां जाइ । धाइ नहीं पपीह्यौ रे ॥
४ तेन्हैं घण बिन त्रिपति न थाइ । जोवौ तेन्हौं नेहडौ रे ॥
५ दोइ लष चंदल दूरि कमोदनि बीगसै रे ।
जन नांमदेव नौं स्वांमीं दयाल ते बेदन लहै रे ॥

१३७

० नाचि रे मन रांम कै आगैं । ग्यांन बिचार जोग बैरागैं ॥
१ नाचै ब्रह्मा नाचै इंद । सहंस कला नाचै रवि चंद ॥
२ रांम कै आगै संकर नाचै । काल अकाल बिकाल हि बांचै ॥
३ नारद नाचै दोइ कर जोडि । सुर नांचै तैतीसौं कोडि ॥
४ भणत नांमदेव मन हि नचावै । मन के नचायें परमपद पावै ॥

२ ८ १० १६ २०; बांधी। बाधी २ ४ १६; प्रीति। प्रीत्य ४; थई। ह्वै १०; द्वै ३; थइ ७ ८; रह्यौ। रह्योगै ४; रह्यो ३ १०; रे। - ३ ८ १० १३; र ४

१३६;३ भर्‍यौ। भर्‍यो २ १०; सरोवर। सरवर १ ७ ८ १६ २० २१; लहर्‍यां। लहर्‍या १ ३ १० २० २१; लर्‍या ४; जाइ। जाई ४; लेई ३; लेइ १० २०; धाइ। धाइ १; धाई ४, धाय ८ १३; धाये १६; धायौ ७ १७; पपीह्यो ३ १०; नहीं। न १; नहिं १३; नही ८ २१; नां ३ १०; पपीह्यौ। पपीहरौ १३ २०; पीवै ३; पीवे १०; पापिह्यौ १७; पापिहौ ८; बापिह्यौ ७; बापिहो २१; बबीहडौ १; बापिह्यौ ४; रे। - १ १३; रे पपीहे ना पीवें १०; रे पपीह्यो ना पीवै ३

१३६;४ तेन्हैं। जेन्हैं १; तेन्है २०; वाकौं ३; वाको १०; घण। घंण १३; घंणं २१; घन ३ २०; प्रांन १०; बिन। बिंन १३; बिनि ३ १०; बिण १ २१; त्रिपति। त्रितति १३; तृपति १७; थाइ। होइ ३ १०; थाई ४ २१; जोवौ। जुदो ३ १०; जोवौं १३; जोवो ८ २०; जोवों १ २१; तेन्हौं। तेन्हौ २१; वाकौ ३; वाको १०; नेहडौ। नेहरौ २ ८ २० २१; नेहरो १०; रे। - १ ३ १०

१३६;५ दोइ। द्वै १; दोई ४ २०; चंदल। चंद ३ १०; चदल ८; दूरि। अकासि ३ १०; कमोदनि। कंमोदंनिं १३; कमोदंनी २१; कमोदेनि ३; कमोदनी २०; बीगसै। बिगसै २ ४ १६ २०; बिगसे १०; बीगसै १; रे। - १ २ ८ १० १३; जन। - ८ १३; जंन २० २१; नांमदेव। नांमदे २१; नांमां १ ८ १३; नौं। नौ ४ ८; को १०; कौं ३; स्वांमीं। स्यांमीं २०; स्वांमी ८; स्वामी १०; दयाल। दयाला २०; ते। म्हारी ३; हमारी १०; तेई १; बेदन। बेदंन १३ २१; लहै। लषै २०; रे। - ३ ८ १० १३

१३७;० नाचि। नांचि ३ १३; नाच ८ १६; रे। - १; मन। मनां १; कै। कैं १ २०; के १०; आगैं। आगै ७; आगे १०; बिचार। बिचारि ३ २०; बैरागैं। बैरागै ७; बैरागे १०

१३७;१ नाचै। नांचै ३; नांचैं १३; नाचे १०; ब्रह्मा। ब्रह्मां १३; नाचै। नांचै ३; नांचैं १३; नांचे १०; इंद। यंद ८ १३; यंद्र १ १६; यंद्रा १०; इंद्र २०; सहंस। सहस १; नाचै। नांचै ३; नांचैं १३; नाचे १०; रवि। रबि ३

१३७;२ कै। के १०; आगै। आगैं १ १३ १६; आगे १०; नाचै। नांचैं १३; नांचैं ३; नाचे १०; अकाल। किाल ८; बिकाल १६ २०; बिकाल। बिकल ७; अकाल ८ १६ २०; दहूं १ १३; हि। हीं २०; तैं १३; ते १; बांचै। बांचैं १३; बांचे १०

१३७;३ नाचै। नांचै ३ २०; नांचैं १३; नाचे १०; दोइ। गूंठा १०; गूठा ३; द्वै १ ८; दोई २०; कर। - ३ १०; जोडि। मोरि ३ १०; जोरि १ ८; सुर। सुर नर १०; नांचै। नांचैं ७; नांचे १०; नाचै १३; नाचैं ८ १६; तैतीसौं। तैतीस्यौं १; तेतीसौं ३ ७ ८ १३; तेतीसों १०; कोडि। कोरि १ ३ १०

१३७;४ भणत। भणंत २०; भनत १; नांमदेब ३ १०; नांमदेव। कहै जो ३ १०; हि। ही १३; हीं [illegible]; नचावै।

१३८

• भया कोई तूलै रे रांम नांम ॥
जोग जग्य तप होम नेम ब्रत ए सब कौनैं कांम ॥
१ एक पलै सब बेद पुरांनां एक पलै अर्ध नांम ॥
तीरथ सकल अंहडै दीन्हां तऊ न होत समांन ॥
२ भणत नांमदेव अंतरजांमीं संतौ लेहु बिचारी ॥
रांम नांम समि कोई न तूलै तारण तिरण मुरारी ॥

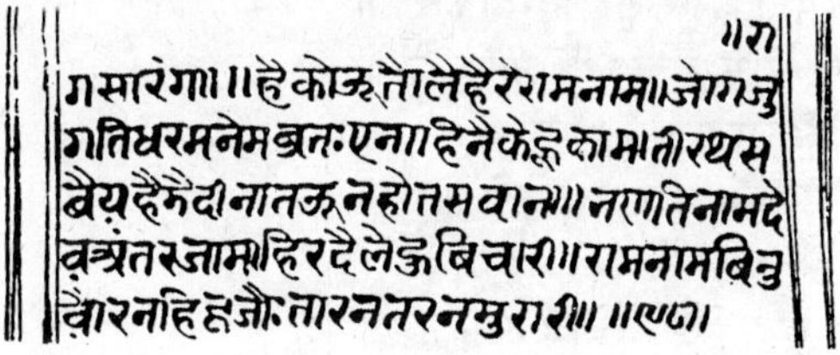

१३९

• गोबिंद राषउ चरणन तीर ॥
जैसें तरवर पात परै झरि बिनसै सकल सरीर ॥
१ जब त्रिया उद्र कीयौ प्रतिपाल ग्रभ संकट दुष भीर ॥
नरसहै यूं बिनसि जावे चलत मिटै नहीं पीर ॥
२ जैसें भुयंगम पंष बिहूनौं नलनी बिनि झरै नीर ॥
नामदेन जन जम की त्रास तैं प्राण धरत नहीं धीर ॥

नचंउं ८; नचांऊं ७ १६; नचावैं १३; नचावे १०; के। कै २ ८; नचायिं। नचांयैं १६; परमपद। पर्मपद १३; पावै। पांऊं ७ १६; पांउं ८; पावे १०

१३८;० भया। भिया १ १३; भईया ८ १७; कोई। को १ २१; कोउ २ १०; तूलै। तूंले १६; तोलै १ २; तोले १०; नांम। नाम २ ८; जग्य। ज्यग्य १; जिग १३; जगि ८ १६ २१; तप। जप २१; होम। बरत २ १०; नेम। धरम २ १०; ब्रत। नेम २ १०; बर्त १६; बरत ७; व्रत १३; ए। ऐ ८ १३; ये १ २ १०; कौनैं। कूंणें १; कौंनैं ७ १३ २१; कौनहि १०

१३८;१ एक। ऐक १ ८ १३; येक २ १०; पलै। पले १०; पुरांनां। पुरांणां १ २१; पुरांना १६; पुराना ३; एक। ऐक १ १३; येक २ ८ १०; पलै। पले १०; अर्ध। अरध २ १० १६ १७ २१; तीरथ। तीर्थ १३; अंहडै। अंहदे ८; अंहींडै १; अंहीडै १३; अहुंडै १६ १७ २१; दीन्हां। दींन्हां १३; दीन्हैं १०; दीन्हें १६ १७; दीया ३; तऊ। तौ १०; तउ २ ८ १३ २१; होत। नांम २ १०; समांन। संमांन १३ २१

१३८;२ भणत। भणंत १; भनंत १० २१; भनत ३; अंतरजांमीं। अंतरजांमी ८; संतौ। हिरदै २ ८ १३; हिरदे १०; बिचारी। बिचारि १ ७ ८ १० १३; समि। संमिं १३; संमि १७; कोई। और १; कोउ २ १० १३; कोइ २१; तूलै। दूजा १; तुलै २ १० १३ २१; तूंलै १६; तूलैं १७; तारण। तारन २ ८ १० १३ २१; तिरण। तिरन ८ १० १३ २१; तरन ३; मुरारी। मुरारि १ २ ७ १३ २१

१४०

• हमारै करता रांम सनेही ॥
काहे रे नर गरब करत हौ बिनसि जाइगी देही ॥
१ ऊंडी षणि षणि नींव दिवाई ऊंचे मंदिर छाये ॥
मारकंडे थैं कौंन बडौ है तिण सिरि द्यौस बलाए ॥
२ मेरी मेरी कैरौं करते जरजोधन से भाई ॥
बारह जोजन छत्र चलत सिरि देही गिरझनि षाई ॥
३ बीस भुजा दस मस्तक होते असुर सुर आग्याकारी ॥
सोई मारि कीयौ धरती समि रावण थौ अहंकारी ॥
४ दुर्बासा सौं करत ठगौरी जादौं सबै षपाये ॥
गर्ब प्रहारी हैं प्रभू मेरौ नांमदेव हरि जस गाये ॥

१ गहरी करि कै नीव खुदाई ऊपरि मंड छाए ॥
मारकंडे ते को अधिआई जिनि तृण धरि मूंड बलाए ॥
• हमरो करता रामु सनेही । काहे रे नर गरबु करत हहु ॥
बिनसि जाइ झूठी देही ॥ रहाउ ॥
२ मेरी मेरी कैरउ करते दुरजोधन से भाई ॥
बारह जोजन छत्रु चलै था देही गिरझन खाई ॥
३ सरब सुोइन की लंका होती रावन से अधिकाई ॥
कहा भइओ दरि बांधे हाथी खिन महि भई पराई ॥

१४०;० हमारै। हंमारे ८ १२; सनेही। सनेंही १२; गरब। ग्रब ८; बिनसि। बिंनसि १२

१४०;१ ऊंडी। औंडी १२; गहरी ८; षणि। षंणिं १२; षणि। षंणिं १२; नींव। नीव ८ १६; दिवाई। दिवावत ८; ऊंचे। उंचे १२; उचे ८; मंदिर। मदिर ८; छाये। छाए ८; छाए १६; छाई १२; मारकंडे। मारकंड १ ८; मारकुंड १२; थैं। तैं ८ १२; कौंन। कौंण ७; को १२; बडौ। अधिकाई १२; है। - १२; सिरि। धरि १२; दे ७ ८ १६; द्यौस। दिवस १६; द्यंस १२; द्यूंस ८; द्यौंस ७; बलाए। बलाऐ ८; बलाई १२; बलायै १

१४०;२ कैरौं। कैंरौं १२; कैरूं १ ७; करते। करिते १६; बारह। बारा ७; जोजन। जोजन जाकौ १२; सिरि। है १२; गिरझनि। गिरझन १२; ग्रीधनि ८; गीधनि १६

१४०;३ बीस। श्रब ८; -- १२; स्रर्द १६; भुजा। सोवंनी १६; सोवनी ८; दस। लंका ८ १६; मस्तक। - ८; मसतक ७; होती १६; होते। - १६; होती ८; असुर। -- १२; अस्वर ७; रांवण ८ १६; सुर। स्वर ७; से ८ १६; आग्याकारी। अहंकारी १६; अहकारी ८; सोई। -- १२; छाडि ८ १६; मारि। गए १६; गये ८; कीयौ। देरि ८; दरि १६; धरती। धरनीं ७; बंधे ८; बांधे १६; समि। होथी ८; हाथी १६; रावण। -- १२; छिन मैं ८ १६; थौ। भए १६; भये ८; अहंकारी। भिषारी ८ १६

१४०;४ दुर्बासा। दुरबासा १२; द्रुबासा १ ८; सौं। कौं ८; सूं ७; करत। करि १; करी ८ १६; ठगौरी। ठगोरी १६; षिटकौरी १; षपाये। षपाए १६; षपाऐ १२; गर्ब। ग्रब १ ८; गरब १२; हैं। है ८ १२; गाये। गाए ७ १६; गाऐ ८

४ दुरबासा सिउ करत ठगउरी जादव ए फल पाए ॥
कृपा करी जन अपुने ऊपर नामदेउ हरि गुन गाए ॥

१४१

• मेरे बाल सनेही गोब्यंदा अब जिनि छाडै मोहि ॥
मैं तोसौं चित लाइयौ मेरे और न दूजा कोइ ॥
१ तू त्रिगुण हूं गुंणभरी एकैं मंदिर बास ॥
एकैं पालिक पौढते अब क्यौं भये उदास ॥
२ बडी सौकि मेरी मरि गई भयौ निकंटौ राज ॥
अब हूं पीव कै लाडिली मेरौ कबहूं न होइ अकाज ॥
३ जेठ निमांणौं परहरचौ छाडि सुसर कौ हेत ॥
पुरिष पुरातंन ब्याहियौ कबहूं न होइ कुहेत ॥
४ सासरवाडौ परहरचौ पीहर लीयौ न्हालि ॥
नांमदेव कौ साहिब मिल्यौ भागी कुल की गालि ॥

१४१;• मेरे। - ११ २०; म्हांरा १०; म्हारा ३; सनेही। सनेही १३; सनेंही २०; गोब्यंदा। गोबिंदौं १३; गोबिंदा ३; अब। तु १०; तू ३; तूं १३; जिनि। जिंनिं १३; जिन २०; छाडै। छाडे १०, छाडौ २०; मोहि। मोहि हो १३; मैं। मैं १०; तोसौं। तोस्यूं ३ २०; तोसुं १०; चित। मन २०; लाइयौ। लाईयौं २०; लाइयो ३ १०; लाइया १३; मेरे। - २०; मेरै ३; मेरैं १६; और। अवर १६; दूजा। दुजा १०; कोइ। कोई हो १३; कोई रे २०

१४१;१ तू। तु १०; तू १ ३; त्रिगुण। निर्गुण १६; निरगुन २ १०; त्रगुंण १३; हूं। मैं १; हू ३; हौं १६; गुंणभरी। गुनभरी १०; गुनिभरी ३; गुणभरी ११ २०; एकैं। ऐकै १३, ऐकैं १; एकहि १६; येकैं २०; येकैंहि ३; ऐकहि १०; बास। बासो रे १; एकैं। ऐकैं १; येकैं १३ २०; येकहिं ३; येकहि १०; पालिक। पांलिक १६; पौढते। पौढता १ ३; पोढतां १३; पोढता १०; क्यौं। क्यूं १०; क्यों ३; कांई २०; भये। भए १६; भयो ३ १०; उदास। उदासो रे १; उदास रे २०

१४१;२ सौकि। सौति १६; सोकि १०; मेरी। म्हारी १३; गई। गइ १०; भयौ। हुवो १०; हूवो ३; निकंटौ। निकटो १६; निकाटौ ३; राज। राजो १६; राज हो १३; हूं। हुं १०; हौं १६; पीव। पीय ११ २०; कै। के १०; लाडिली। लाडली १०; मेरौ। - २०; मेरो १०; कबहूं। कबहु १०; कबहू ३ २०; अकाज। अकाजो १६; अकाज रे २०; दुहाग ३ १०

१४१;३ जेठ। चाचौ ३; चाचों १०; निमांणौं। निमांनौ १६; देवर ३ १०; परहरचौ। परहरया ३ १०; छाडि। छांडि १; तज्यौ १३; तज्यो ३ १०; कौ। को १०; पुरिष। अब मैं ३; अब में १०; पुरिषु १६; पुरष २०; पुरातंन। पुरातन १ १६; बुढो १०; बूढौ ३; ब्याहियौ। ब्याह्यिौ २०; ब्याहियो ३; ब्याहियो १०; कबहूं। मेरो कबहुं १०; मेरो कबहू ३; कबहुं १

१४१;४ सासरवाडौ। सासुरवाडौ १६; सासरबाडौ १३; सासरवाडो ३ १०; परहरचौ। परहरचो ३ १०; पीहर। लीयो ३ १०; लीयौ। पीहर ३ १०; लीयौं २०; न्हालि। न्हांलि २०; नाल्हि १३; नांमदेव। जन नांमदेव ३ १०; कौ। कौं १३; का ३ १०; साहिब। स्वामी साहिब १०; मिल्यौ। मिल्या ३ १०; भागी। मंटी १३; सबै ३; सबे १०; कुल। उतारी ३ १०; की। - ३ १०

१४२

• कपटैं नां मिलै रे गोबिंदौ गुणसागर गोपाल ॥
गोपीचंदन तिलक बनांवैं कंठि रुलावैं माल ॥
१ मन परतीति नहीं रे प्राणीं औरनि कौं समझाइ ॥
लोगनि कौं बैकुंठ बतावै आपण जमपुरि जाइ ॥
२ जानत ही बिष षाइयौ अंधे अंधा हाथि ॥
देषत ही कूवै पडै अंधौ अंधा साथि ॥
३ जोग जगि जप तप तीरथ ब्रत मन राषै इन पास ॥
दांन पुंन्य धंम दया दीनता हरि की भगति उदास ॥
४ भजि भगवंत भगत भजि प्राणीं छाडि अनेरी आस ॥
बरणांबरण सुभासुभ भजि करि कौंण भयौ निज दास ॥

१४२;० कपटैं। कपटै १२; कपटे १० १९; कपटें १७; नां। नहीं ७ २१; ना १७; मिलै। मिले १० १९ गोबिंदौ। - १०; गोबिंदौं १२; गोब्यंदौ २ १६ १७ २१; गोव्यंदो १; गुणसागर। गुंणसागर १२; गुंनसागर १०; गुनसागर २; गोपीचंदन। गोपीचंदण २१; गोपीचंदन का ४; बनांवैं। बणांवै ७; बणांवैं १ ४; बणावैं २१; बनावै २ १९; बनावैं १७; बनावे १०; कंठि। कंठ २ १०; रुलावैं। रलावै २; रलावे १०; रुलावै ४; रुलांवैं १ ७ २१; रुलावै १२ १९; माल। मांल २; माला १०

१४२;१ मन। मंन २१; मनि १ १९; परतीति। प्रतिति १०; प्रतीत १७; परतीत्य ४; नहीं। नही २ १० १२; प्राणीं। प्रांनीं २ १०; औरनि। औरौ १९; औरन ७ १२ २१; ओरनि १०; अरुरन ४; कौं। कूं १ ४ ७; को १०; समझाइ। संमझाइ १२ २१; समझाई २ ४; लोगनि। औरौं १९; लोकंनि २१; लोकनि २ ७ १०; लोगंनिं १२; कौं। - १०; कूं १ ४ ७ १७; कौ २१; बैकुंठ। + १२; बैकुठ १० २१; बैकुठि १९; बैकूंठ १ ४; बैकूठ २; बतावै। पठावै १९; बतांवैं १; बतावैं २१; बतावे १०; आपण। आपुण ७; आपुन १७ २१; आपैं १९; आपन १; जमपुरि। जंमपुरि १ ४ २१; जाइ। जाई २ ४

१४२;२ जानत। अंणजांणौं ४; अंणजांणत २१; अणजांणत १ ७; अनजंनि २; अनजानि १०; जांणि १७; जांनत १२ १९; ही। - १ २ ४ ७ १० २१; बूझि १७; बिष। विष १; षाइयौ। षाईया रे ४; षायौ प्रांणीं १७; षाइये रे २ १०; षाइयौ रे ७ २१; षाइया १९; अंधे। अंधै १९; अंधा १; अधे २; अंधा। अधा २; हाथि। हथि २ १०; साथि १२ १६ १७; देषत। कर १२; ही। हीं १६ १७; दीपक १२; कूवै। कुवै २१; कुवे १०; कूंवै १; पडै। पडै रे ४ २१; परै २ १९; परे १०; अंधौ। अधे १२; अंधो २ १०; दीपक १६ १७; अंधा। लीयै १९; लीयां १७; साथि। हाथि १२ १६ १७; सथि २ १०

१४२;३ जोग। जगि १९; जगि। जिग १ १२; जिग्य २; जोग १९; जग्य ४ ७ १०; जप। तप १० १६ १७; तप। धरम १९; ब्रत १७; तीरथ। तिरथ १०; संसारी १७; बर्त १९; तीर्थ ७ १२; ब्रत। - १६ १७; बरत २ १०; ब्रत १; मन। मंन १२ २१; करै १९; राषै। जु १९; बांध्यौ १७; राषैं ७; राषे १०; इन। ईहिं ४; अहिं १७; इंन १ १२; इनि ७; इहि २१; इनकी १९; पास। आस १९; पासी १७; दांन। धरम १७; ग्यांन १९; पुंन्य। - १७; ध्यांन १९; पुंन्यि २१; पुंनिं १२; पुंनि १ ७; पुन्य ४; धंम। धम ४ २१; धर्म २ ७ १०; नेम १७; तजि १९; दीनता। दींनता ४ १२; की। कै १९; भगति। भक्ति १२; नांइ १९; उदास। उदासी १७

१४२;४ भजि। भजी १०; प्राणीं। प्रांणि ४; प्रांनी २; प्रांनीं १०; छाडि। छांडि १०; आडि २१; अनेरी। अनिरी १२ २१; बरणांबरण। बरंणबरंण ४; बरणांबरणं १; बरनअबरन १९; बरनांबरन २ १०; सुभासुभ। रहित १९; भजि। जि १०; मन सो १९; करि। भजि १९; कौंण। कूंण १ २१; कौंन २; कौण १२; कोंण ४; कोंन १०; कोन १९; भयौ। भजौ १९; भय २; भये १२; भयो १०; निज। निंज १२

५ कोमल बिमल संत जन सूरा करैं तुम्हारी आस ॥
तिन परि क्रिपा करौ तुम केसौ प्रणवंत नांमदेव दास ॥

१४३

• तत कहन कौं रांम है सुंनिं लीज्यौ लोई ॥
लीला सिंघ अपार की गति लषै न कोई ॥
१ कंचन मेर सुमेर है दीजै दिज दांनां ॥
कोटि गउ जौ दांन दे नहिं नांव संमांनां ॥
२ जोग जिग तैं कहा भयौ तीर्थ स्नांनां ॥
वो सांप्या सन भाजई भजिये भगवांनां ॥
३ पूजंन कौं भगता जनां हरि के ब्रत धारी ॥
उन तैं गोबिंद पाइये ये पर उपगारी ॥
४ ऐकै मंनिऐ कै दसा हरि कौ ब्रत धरिये ॥
नांमदेव नांव जिहाज है भौ सागर तिरिये ॥

१४४

• कहा ले आरती दास करै । तीनि लोक जाकी जोति फिरै ॥
१ सात समंद जाकै चरन निवासा । कहा भयौ जल कुंभ भरै ॥
२ कोटि भांन जाकै नष की सोभा । कहा भयौ कर दीप फिरै ॥
३ अठार भार जाकै बनमाला । कहा भयौ कर पहुप धरै ॥
४ अनंत कोटि जाकै बाजा बाजैं । कहा घंटा झणकार करै ॥

१४२;५ बिमल। विमल १ ४ १३; जन। अर १६; करैं। करै ३ २१; करैं जु १६; करे १०; तुम्हारी। हरि की १६; तु+ ४; आस। आसा १७; तिन। तिंन २ २८; जा १६; क्रिपा। कृपा ४ १७; करौ। + ४; करै १६; करहु ३ १०; तुम। नित १६; तुंम १० १३; तुम्ह ७ १७ २१; केसौ। केसव १ ४ १०; केसवै ३; प्रणवंत। -- १०; प्रणवैं १ ४ ७ २१; प्रनवत ३; दास। दासा १७

१४४;० कहा। + ४; का २ १०; ले। + ४; आरती। +रती ४; आरति २ १०; करै। करे १०; तीनि। तीनिं ८ १३; तीन २ १०; जोति। + ४; जो १३; फिरै। + ४; फिरैं ७; फिरे १०

१४४;१ सात। ++ ४; समंद। समंद्र ३; समुंद्र १०; जाकै। जाके २ १०; चरन। चरण १ ७; निवासा। निंवासा १३; भयौ। भयो २ १०; कुंभ। कुभ १० १६ २१; कूंभ ४ १३; कूभ ३; भरै। भरैं ७ १७; भरे १ २ १०

१४४;२ कोटि। -- ४; भांन। भांण १ ८ १३ १६; भान १७; जाकै। जाके ३; जाकी १०; कहा। -- ४; भयौ। भयो २ १०; दीप। दीपक ३; फिरै। फिरैं ७; फिरे १०; फेरे ३

१४४;३ अठार। -- १ ३ ८ १० १६ २१; अठारह ७; अठारा ४; बनमाला। बंनमाला १३; बानावली ४; कहा। -- १ ३ ८ १० १६ २१; कर। करि १७; धरै। धरैं ४ ७

१४४;४ अनंत। अनत ४ १६; नंत २१; सबद २ १०; कोटि। अनाहद २ १०; जाकै। - २ १०; बाजा। बाजे १७;

५ चौरासी लष ब्यापक रांमां । केवल हरि जस गावै नांमां ॥

१४५

• आरती पतिदेव मुरारी । चंवर ढुलैं बलि जांउं तुम्हारी ॥
१ चहुं जुगि आरती चहुं जुगि पूजा । चहुं जुगि रांम अवर नहीं दूजा ॥
२ आरती कीजै ऐसैं जैसैं । ध्रू प्रहिलाद करी सुष तैसैं ॥
३ आंनंद आरती आतम पूजा । नांमदेव भणैं मेरै देव न दूजा ॥

१४६

• गरुड मंडल आव । प्रथीपति गरुड मंडल आव ॥
१ तूं प्रथीपति जाग्रित केला । मैं गाऊं गुण नागर चेला ॥
२ नांमदेव कहै मैं बालिक तेरा । भगति दांन दे साहिब मेरा ॥

१४७

• धीरैं धीरैं षैबौ कथन न जैबौ रे । आपन षैबौ तब निरमल ह्वैबौ ॥

बाजैं। बांजैं १६; बाजे २ १० १२ २१; कहा। कहां १६; का २ १०; घंटा। घटा १३; झालरि २ १०; झणकार। झंणकार ४ २१; झुंणकार ८; झुणकार १ १३; झनकार ३ १०; करै। करैं ४ ७

१४४;५ चौरासी। लष ३ १०; लष। चौरासी ३; चोरासी १०; ब्यापक। व्यापक १; रांमां। रांम १०; राम ३; केवल। निरगुन २ १०; हरि। का ३ १०; जस। गुन २ १०; गावै। गावै जन २ १०; नांमां। नांम ३ ८

१४५;० आरती। आरति १०; पतिदेव। प्रतिदेव १ ४; चंवर। +वर ४; चौंर ३; चोंर १०; चवर ७ १६ १७; ढुलैं। ढुरे १३; ढुले ७; ढरे ३; ढरें १०; जांउं। जांऊं २१; जांव ४; जाउ ३; जावुं १०; तुम्हारी। तुंम्हारी १३; तुम्हांरी ३; तुम्हारि ४

१४५;१ चहुं। चंहुं ४; चहु १६ १७; चहू ३; चहूं १०; जुगि। दिसि १; जूगि १०; आरती। आरति ३; चहुं। चहु १६; चहू ३; चहूं १०; जुगि। दिसि १; चहुं। चहु १६; चहूं २ १०; जुगि। दिसि १; जूगि १०; रांम। राम ३; अवर। और ३; ओर १०; नहीं। नंही ८; नहि १; नही २ १०; हीं ४; दूजा। दुजा १०

१४५;२ आरती। -- २ ४ १०; आरति २१; ऐसैं। ऐसे ७; अैसे ८; अेसैं १२ १६ १७; अैसे २१; जैसैं। जैसे २१; तैसैं १ १६ १७; ध्रू। -- २ ४ १०; ध्रु १२ १६ २१; तैसैं। जैसे २१; जेसैं १ १६ १७; तैसे ८

१४५;३ आंनंद। आंनद ४; आनंद ३ ७ १० १७ २१; आतम। आतंम १२; आत्म १ ८ १७; रांम की २१; रांम ची ४; नांमदेव। नांम ४; नांमौं १; भणैं। भनै ३; भने १०; मेरै। मेरे १ ४ ८ १० २१; देव। दैव ७

१४६;० मंडल। मंडलि ४; प्रथीपति। पृथीपति १; मंडल। मंडलि ४

१४६;१ तूं। तूंम ४; प्रथीपति। प्रिथीपति १; केला। कैला १; गाऊं। गांऊं १; गुण। गुन १

१४६;२ नांमदेव। नांम ४; बालिक। वालिक १

१४७;० षैबौ। षैबौं ४; षइबौ १७; कथन। कथंनं २१; न। नं २१; रे। - १७; निरमल। न्रिमल १७; ह्वैबौ। ह्वैबौ रे ४

१ पहली मैं षैहूं आई माई । पीछै मैं षैहूं घर कौ जवाई ॥
२ उगलिबा चंदा बिगलिबा सूर । फुनि मैं षैहूं घर कौ सुसूर ॥
३ फुनि मैं षैहूं पांचूं लोग । भणत नांमदेव ए सिध जोग ॥

१४८

• तैसी चूकली रे जगजीवनां । अणभवल्या बिनां लषी न ऐसी क्रुसनां ॥
१ पारब्रहमां ची गोडी नैंणती बापडी पडली ते संकडै बिषिया संगै ॥
२ सिलेस घातिले बैसाचे बैरणे । ते च बिध्यने नेतया रसाचे ॥
३ कमलनीं दुर्दुरा एकै जु बिढा । परमल मधुकर घिवन गैला ॥
४ थांनां चया दूधा नहोसी वरपडा । असूध सेवतां गूचडा जनम गैला ॥
५ नांमौं भणैं तैसी चूकली तूंझी तूंझ देषतां । अम्रित सेवतां चवि नैंणती ॥

१४९

• देवा पाहन तारीअले । राम कहत जन कस न तरे ॥ रहाउ ॥

१४७;१ षैहूं। षैहौं १७; माई। मा+ ४; पीछै। पीछैं १७ २१; मैं। - १७; षैहूं। षैहौं १७; घर। सगा १७; कौ। - १७; जवाई। जंवाई २१

१४७;२ उगलिबा। उगलिबां २१; बिगलिबा। गिलिबा १७, फुनि। फुंनि १७; मैं। मे २१; षैहूं। षैहौं १७

१४७;३ फुनि। फुंनि १७ २१; षैहूं। षैहौं १७; पांचूं। पंचौं १७; भणत। भंणत २१; ए। ऐ ४; सिध। सिधि ४

१४८;० तैसी। तैंसीं १; चूकली। चूंकली १; चूकिला ४; जगजीवनां। जगजीवना १; अणभवल्या। अनभवल्या ७ १७; बिनां। बिना ४; विण १; ऐसी। अैसी १७ २१; क्रुसनां। क्रिश्नां २१; क्रुश्नां १; क्रुष्णा ७; क्रृस्नां ४

१४८;१ पारब्रहमां। परब्रह्मां २१; पारब्रह्म १७; पारब्रह्मां ४; पारब्रहमा ७; नैंणती। नैंणंती ७; नेणती २१; बापडी। +डी ४; बापुडी १ ७ २१; पडली। पडी ७ १७, पडलंती १; ते। - १; संकडै। संकडौ ४; सांकडे १; बिषिया। विषिया १; संगै। संगैं १ ४

१४८;२ सिलेस। सिलेसं १७; घातिले। घाति+ ४; घातले १ ७; बैसाचे। +साचे ४; बैसाचें २१; बैरणे। बैरंणे २१; बैरणें ७; बिध्यने। बिघने १ १७; बिध्यनि ४; बिध्याने २१; बिधिने ७, नेतया। नेतिया १; रसाचे। रसाची १; रसाले ७

१४८;३ कमलनीं। +नी ४; कंवलनी २१; कवलनीं १; दुर्दुरा। ड्डुरा २१; दुरदुरा १; द्रुदुरा ४; द्रुद्रा १७; एकै। ऐक १; ऐकै ४; जु। ज १; बिढा। बिटा ४; बिठा २१; वढरा १; घिवन। घिंबन २१; घिवणि १; गैला। + ४

१४८;४ थांनां। थांन ४; थांना १; नहोसी। - ४; नहोइसी १ १७; वरपडा। बरपडा ७ १७ २१; असूध। असूद १; सेवतां। सेवता ४; जनम। जंनम ४ २१; गैला। + ४; मैला १

१४८;५ तैसी। तैसि ४; तैसी ज १; तेसी २१; चूकली। चूकिली १७; चूकीली ४; तूंझी। तुझी १; तूझी १७ २१; तूंझ। तुझ १; तूझ १७; देषतां। देषंतां ४; अम्रित। ++ ४; अंम्रित २१; अंम्रित १; अंब्रुत ७; मबुत १७; सेवतां। सेवता १७; चवि। चबि १७; नैंणती। नैंणंती १ २१; नैणंती १७

१ तारी ले गनिका बिनु रूप कुबिजा बिआधि अजामलु तारीअले ॥
चरन बधिक जन तेऊ मुकति भए । हउ बलि बलि जिन राम कहे ॥
२ दासी सुत जन बिदरु सुदामा उग्रसैन कउ राज दीए ॥
जपहीन तपहीन कुलहीन क्रमहीन नामे के सुआमी तेऊ तरे ॥

१५०

१ एक अनेक बिआपक पूरक जत देखउ तत सोई ॥
माइआ चित्र बचित्र बिमोहित बिरला बूझै कोई ॥
० सभु गोबिंद है सभु गोबिंदु है गोबिंद बिनु नही कोई ॥
सूतु एकु मणि सत सहंस जैसे ओति पोति प्रभु सोई ॥ रहाउ ॥
२ जल तरंग अरु फेन बुदबुदा जल ते भिंन न होई ॥
इहु परपंचु पारब्रहम की लीला बिचरत आन न होई ॥
३ मिथिआ भरमु अरु सुपन मनोरथ ॥
सति पदारथु जानिआ । सुकृत मनसा गुर उपदेसी जागत ही मनु मानिआ ॥
४ कहत नामदेउ हरि की रचना देखहु रिदै बीचारी ॥
घट घट अंतरि सरब निरंतरि केवल एक मुरारी ॥

१५१

१ पारब्रहमु जि चीनसी आसा ते न भावसी ॥
रामा भगतह चेतीअले अचिंत मनु राखसी ॥
० कैसे मन तरहिगा रे संसारु सागरु बिखै को बना ॥
झूठी माइआ देखि कै भूला रे मना ॥ रहाउ ॥
२ छीपे के घरि जनमु दैला गुर उपदेसु भैला ॥
संतह कै परसादि नामा हरि भेटुला ॥

१५२

१ जौ राजु देहि त कवन ब । जौ भीख मंगावहि त किआ घटि जाई ॥
० तूं हरि भजु मन मेरे पदु निरबानु । बहुरि न होइ तेरा आवन जानु ॥ रहाउ ॥
२ सभ तै उपाई भरम भुलाई । जिस तूं देवहि तिसहि बुझाई ॥
३ सतिगुरु मिलै त सहसा जाई । किसु हउ पुजउ दूजा नदरि न आई ॥
४ एकै पाथर कीजै भाउ । दूजै पाथर धरीऐ पाउ ॥
जे ओहु देउ त ओहु भी देवा । कहि नामदेउ हम हरि की सेवा ॥

१५३

१ पाड पडोसणि पूछिले नामा कापहि छानि छवाई हो ॥
तो पहि दुगणी मजूरी दैहउ मोकउ बेढी देहु बताई हो ॥
° री बाई बेढी देनु न जाई । देखु बेढी रहिओ समाई ॥
हमारै बेढी प्राण अधारा ॥ रहाउ ॥
२ बेढी प्रीति मजूरी मांगै जउ कोऊ छानि छवावै हो ॥
लोग कुटंब सभहु ते तोरै तउ आपन बेढी आवै हो ॥
३ ऐसो बेढी बरनि न साकउ सभ अंतर सभ ठाईं हो ॥
गुगै महा अंमृत रसु चाखिआ पूछे कहनु न जाई हो ॥
४ बेढी के गुण सुनि री बाई जलधि बांधि ध्रू थापिओ हो ॥
नामे के सुआमी सीअ बहोरी लंक भभीखण आपिओ हो ॥

१५४

१ अणमर्य मंदलु बाजै । बिनु सावण घनहरु गाजै ॥
बादल बिनु बरखा होई । जउ ततु बिचारै कोई ॥
° मोकउ मिलिओ रामु सनेही । जिह मिलिऐ देह सुदेही ॥ रहाउ ॥
२ मिलि पारस कंचनु होइआ । मुख मनसा रतनु परोइआ ॥
निज भाउ भइआ भ्रमु भागा । गुर पूछे मनु पतीआगा ॥
३ जल भीतरि कुंभ समानिआ । सभ रामु एकु करि जानिआ ॥
गुर चेले है मनु मानिआ । जन नामै ततु पछानिआ ॥

१५५

१ पतित पावन माधउ बिरदु तेरा ॥
धंनि ते वै मुनि जन जिन धिआइओ हरि प्रभु मेरा ॥
° मेरै माथै लागीले धूरि गोबिंद चरनन की ॥
सुरि नर मुनि जन तिनहू ते दूरि ॥ रहाउ ॥
२ दीन का दइआलु माधौ गरब परहारी ॥
चरन सरन नामा बलि तिहारी ॥

१५६

° तीनि छंदे खेलु आछै ॥ रहाउ ॥

१ कुंभार के घर हांडो आछै राजा के घर सांडी गो ॥
बामन के घर रांडी आछै रांडी सांडी हांडीगो ॥
२ बाणीए के घर हींगु आछै भैसर माथै सींगु गो ॥
देवल मधे लीगु आछै लीगु सीगु हीगु गो ॥
३ तेली कै घर तेलु आछै जंगल मधे बेल गो ॥
माली के घर केल आछै केल बेल तेल गो ॥
४ संतां मधे गोबिंदु आछै गोकल मधे सिआम गो ॥
नामे मधे रामु आछै राम सिआम गोबिंद गो ॥

१५७

• मै अंधुले की टेक तेरा नामु खुंदकारा ॥
मै गरीब मै मसकीन तेरा नामु है अधारा ॥ रहाउ ॥
१ करीमां रहीमां अलाह तू गनीं ॥
हाजरा हजूरि दरि पेसि तू मनी ॥
२ दरीआउ तू दिहंद तूं बिसीआर तू धनीं ॥
देहि लेहि एकु तूं दिगर को नही ॥
३ तूं दानां तूं बीनां मै बीचारु किआ करी ॥
नामे चे सुआमी बखसंद तूं हरी ॥

१५८

• हाल बाबा हाल बाबा खुसखबरी ॥
१ नहीं तौ पकरि मारूं करूं बिगरी । कुजा आमदी कुजा रफती कुजा माहरबी ॥
२ द्वारकें नगर बाबा रास मे गोई । लाल तेरा तरकस खूब तेरा बोल ॥
३ द्वारके नगर बाबा कहां के मंगोल । असपती गजपती नर नंदूं ॥
४ नांमदेव कौ स्वांमीं मीर मुकंदू ॥

• *हले यारां हले यारां खुसिखबरी बलि बलिजांउ हउ बलि बलिजांउ ॥*

१५८:१ पकरि। पकडि ७; आमदी। अंमदी २१; अमदी ७; माहरबी। महरबी ७
१५८:२ रास। रासमे २१; मे। - २१; तरकस। तकस ७; तेरा। तेरे ७
१५८:३ नगर। नगर २१; मंगोल। मुगोल ७
१५८:४ नंदूं। नंदू ७
१५८:५ स्वांमीं। स्वांभी ७

नीकी तेरी बिगारी आले तेरा नाउ ॥ रहाउ ॥
१ कुजा आमद कुजा रफती कुजा मेरवी । द्वारिका नगरी रासि बुगोई ॥
२ खूबु तेरी पगरी मीठे तेरे बोल । द्वारिका नगरी काहे के मगोल ॥
३ चंदीं हज़ार आलम एकल खानां । हम चिनी पातिसाह सांवले बरनां ॥
४ असपति गजपति नरह नरिंद । नामे के स्वामी मीर मुकंद ॥

१५९

१ बानारसी तपु करै उलटि तीरथ मरै अगनि दहै काइआ कलपु कीजै ॥
असुमेध जगु कीजै सोना गरभ दानु दीजै राम नाम सरि तऊ न पूजै ॥
छोडि छोडि रे पाखंडी मन कपटु न कीजै ।
हरि का नामु नित नितहि लीजै ॥ रहाउ ॥
२ गंगा जउ गोदावरि जाईऐ कुंभि जउ केदार न्हाईऐ ॥
गोमती सहस गऊ दानु कीजै । कोटि जउ तीरथ करै तनु जउ हिवाले गारै ॥
राम नाम सरि तऊ न पूजै ॥
३ असुदान गजदान सिहजा नारी भूमि दान ऐसो दानु नित नितहि कीजै ॥
आतम जउ निरमाइलु कीजै आप बराबरि कंचनु दीजै
राम नाम सरि तऊ न पूजै ॥
४ मनहि न कीजै रोसु जमहि न दीजै दोसु निरमल निरबाण पदु चीन्हि लीजै ॥
जसरथ राइ नंदु राजा मेरा रामचंदु प्रणवै नामा ततु रसु अंम्रितु पीजै ॥

१६०

० मेरो बापु माधउ तू धनु केसौ सांवलीओ बीठुलाइ ॥ रहाउ ॥
१ कर धरे चक्र बैकुंठ ते आए गज हसती के प्रान उधारीअले ॥
दुहसासन की सभा द्रोपती अंबर लेत उबारीअले ॥
२ गोतम नारि अहलिआ तारी पावन केतक तारीअले ॥
ऐसा अधमु अजाति नामदेउ तउ सरनागति आईअले ॥

१६१

० बदहु की न होड माधउ मो सिउ ॥
ठाकुर ते जनु जन ते ठाकुरु खेलु परिओ है तो सिउ ॥ रहाउ ॥
१ आपन देउ देहरा आपन आप लगावै पूजा ॥
जल ते तरंग तरंग ते है जलु कहन सुनन कउ दूजा ॥

२ आपहि गावै आपहि नाचै आप बजावै तूरा ॥
कहत नाम देउ तूं मेरो ठाकुरु जनु ऊरा तू पूरा ॥

१६२

१ आदि जुगादि जुगादि जुगो जुगु ताका अंतु न जानिआ ॥
सरब निरंतरि रामु रहिआ रवि ऐसा रूपु बखानिआ ॥
० गोबिदु गाजै सबदु बाजै । आनद रूपी मेरो रामईआ ॥ रहाउ ॥
२ बावन बीखू बानै बीखे बासु ते सुख लागिला ॥
सरबे आदि परमलादि कासट चंदनु भैइला ॥
३ तुम्ह चे पारसु हम चे लोहा संगे कंचनु भैइला ॥
तू दइआलु रतनु लालु नामा साचि समाइला ॥

१६३

० रे अभिमांन लीयैं नर आयौ ॥
परआतंम आत्मं नहिं चीन्हीं । नर बप नांव धरायौ ॥
१ ग्रभवास बहु त्रास दीनता । त्राहि त्राहि लिव लायौ ॥
हा हा करत बिसंभर आगैं । गहि आपदा छिडायौ ॥
२ माया सेती रातौ मातौ । संगि त्रिश्नां कै धायौ ॥
गुनहगार गोबिंद राइ कौ । कबहूं न हरि जस गायौ ॥
३ हैं हरि नांव अधार धार कौ । साधनि सरनि बतायौ ॥
नांमदेव कहै सुर्णौं मन मूरिष । जै समझै समझायौ ॥

१६४

० पावघे पावघे सहजैं मुरारी ॥
सबद अनाहद घंटा बाजै बमेक बिचारी बीठुला ॥

१६३;० लीयैं। लीये १; लीयें १२; परआतंम। आतम ७; परमात्मं १; आत्मं। आत्म १२; परआतम ७; नहिं। नहि १; नहीं ७; चीन्हीं। चींन्हीं १२; चीन्हीं ७; बप। बपु १; नांव। नांउं १; नांवं ७

१६३;१ बहु। मैं १; त्रास। हुतौ १; दीनता। दींनतां १२; लिव। ल्यौ ७; आपदा। आतमां ७

१६३;२ मातौ। मांतौ १२; त्रिश्नां। त्रिस्नां ७; कै। कैं ७; कौ १२; गुनहगार। गुंनहगार १२; गोबिंद। गोब्यंद १

१६३;३ नांव। नांम १; साधनि। संतनि ७; साधा १२; सरनि। सरंनिं १२; सरन ७; सुर्णौं। सुंर्णौं १२; मन। मंन १२; मूरिष। मूरिषां १; समझै। संमझै १२; समझायौ। संमझायौ १२

१ बेणीं संजम मंजन करिहूं मनैं बुझाया ॥
नैंन कुसम करि चरचूं चितैं चंदन लाया ॥
२ पाती प्रीति ध्यांन ले धूपं दीपक ग्यांनां ॥
अजपा जपूं अपूज्या पूजूं अजरांवर थांनां ॥
३ जहां कछू नाहीं तहां कछू देष्या जीयरा लोभांनां ॥
आतम केरे तेज मधे तेज दीपांनां ॥
४ अनेक सूर मिलि उदै कीये हैं ऐसी जोति प्रकासी ॥
तहां निरंजन अंजन षोलै बैकुंठ बासी ॥
५ करम सकल कौ भेष धरचौ है बिषई बिकारा ॥
चंवर पवन गुंन अष्यत करिहूं सारंगधारा ॥
६ बिना बिप्र बेद धुनि उचरै अधिक रसाला ॥
बिना तूंबर नारद नाचै गांवहि बाजहि ताला ॥

१६४;० पावघे। पवघे १३; पावधे ४; पावघे। पवघे १३; पावधे ४; मुरारी। मुसरी २१; सबद। सवद १; अनाहद। अंनांहद १३; अंनाहद २१; अनाहंद १; घंटा। घटा २१; बाजै। वाजै १; बमेरू। बिमेक २०; विमेक १; बंमेक १३ २१; बिचारी। विचारी १; बीठुला। - १ ८ १३ २० २१; बीठला १६

१६४;१ बेणीं। त्रिबेणीं १३ १६ २०; बेणी ८; वेणीं १; संजम। संगम ८ १३; संजंम २१; मंजन। मंजंन ४; मजन ८; करिहूं। करिहौं १३ १६; करिहो ८; मनैं। मंनैं २१; मैंनैं २०; बुझाया। वुझाया १; नैंन। नैन १६ २०; कुसम। कुसंम २० २१; कूसम ४; चरचूं। चरचौं १ ८ १६; चरच्यूं ४; चितैं। +ह २०; +तैं ४; चित ८ १३; चितै २१; लाया। लाया बीठुला ४; लाया ब|ठला १६

१६४;२ पाती। पातो १६; प्रीति। प्रीत्य ४; ध्यांन। +ांन ८; ध्यान २०; ले। लै १३; धूपं। धूप १६; दीपक। +पक ४; - १; ग्यांनां। - १; ग्यांन २०; ग्यांनौं २१; अजपा। अ+पा ८; जपूं। जपौं ८ १३ १६; जापूं ४; अपूज्या। अपूजा २०; पूजूं। पूजौं ८ १३ १६; अजराबर। अजरावर १ १३ १६ २०; थांनां। धांनां ८; थांनां बीठुला ४; धांनां बीठला १६

१६४;३ जहां। जांहां २०; कछू। कुछ ४; कछु १ १६; नाहीं। नही २१; नहीं १३; नांही ८; नांहीं १; कछू। कुछ ४ २१; कछु १६; देष्या। नांहीं १; देषा १६; लोभांनां। लुभांनां ८ १३; लूभांना २०; लोभानां १; आतम। आत्म १; आतंम १३; आतमा ४; आतमां २०; केरे। के २०; केर २१; केरी १; मधे। - २१; मंधे १३; मघे ४; मध्ये ८; तेज। दीपांनां २१; दीपांनां। - २१; दिपांनां १३ २०; दीपांनां बीठुला ४; दीपांनां बीठला १६

१६४;४ अनेक। अंनेक १३ २१; सूर। सूरि ८; सूरिज १३ १६; सूरज ४; उदै। उदौ १३; कीये। कीए २१; हैं। है २१; ऐसी। अैसी ८ १३ १६ २० २१; प्रकासी। प्रकीसी २०; तहां। जहां १; तहा ८; निरंजन। निरंज २१; निरंजंन १३; अंजन। + १६; अजन २०; षोलै। षोलि ८; षोले १ १६ २१; बैकुंठ। बैकुठ ८; बैकूंट २०; बैकूंठ १३; वैकुंठ १; बासी। बासी बीठुला ४; बासी बीठला १६; वासी १

१६४;५ करम। करंम १३ २१; कौ। को २०; भेष। भोष २०; धरचौ। धरयौ १६; बिषई। बिषइ २०; विषै १; बिकारा। विकारा १; चंवर। चवर १६; पवन। पवंन २१; गुंन। गुन १ ८ १६ २०; अष्यत। अषित १ ८ १३ १६ २०; करिहूं। करिहौं ८ १३ १६; सारंगधारा। सारंगधरी ८; सारंगधारा बीठ+ ४; सारंगधारा बीठला १६

१६४;६ बिना। + ४; बिनां ८ २१; विण १; बिप्र। + ४; विप्र १; बेद। + ४; वेद १ १३; धुनि। धंनि २१; धुंनिं १३; धू+ ४; धूनि २०; उचरै। + ४; उचरैं २०; अधिक। ++ ४; बिना। ++ ४; बिंनां १३; बिनहीं २०; बिनां ८ २१; विण १; तूंबर। तुंबर ८ १३ २१; तूंबरि १६; तूंवर १; नारद। नांरद २०; नाचै। नांचै १३ २१;

७ रूप अतीत सकल गुंन रहिता गगन समांनां ॥
तहां थैं अधिक लै लाई अंतरि ध्यांनां ॥
८ बिश्नदास नांमइया संगै भेटीला सोई ॥
हरि हरि हरि हरि कीरतंन करतां इहि बिधि आंनंद होई ॥

१६५

० लटकि न बोलूं बाप ब्रतमांन गाढा ॥
कोहला ऐवडा मोतीडा मैं मंझैं डोलैं देषीला ॥
१ छेली बैली बाघ जैला मांजरिया भै टूंडै ॥
उडत पंषि मैं लवरू पेष्या नर लीजे ह्वै टांडै ॥
२ बावलिया चै षोटं मांषणियां चै पोटै ॥
संषै सुणहां मारीला तहां मीडक अभिला लोटै ॥
३ अम्हे जु गैला ब्राट देस तहां गांझीं दूध कैला ॥

गावै २०; गांवहि। गावै १३; गावैं ८ १६; गावैहि १; गावहीं २०; बाजहि। ++ ४; बाजैं ८ १३; बाजहीं २०; बाजैहि १; ताला। ताला बीठला १३

१६४:७ अतीत। - ४; सकल। + ४; गुंन। + ४; गुण १ २०; गुन ८; रहिता। -हिता ४; रहित १; रहता ८; गगन। गगन मैं २०; गगंन २१; गगनैं १ ४ ८ १६; गगन मैं १३; समांनां। समांना १; संमानां २०; थैं। तैं ८ १३; अधिक। अ+ ४; अधीरक २०; लै। + ४; ल्यै १; लाई। + ४; लागी ८ १३ १६; अंतरि। अंतर १; ध्यांनां। ध्यांनां बीठुला ४; ध्यांनां बीठला १६

१६४:८ बिश्नदास। बिस्नदास ४; बिसनदास १६ २०; बिश्नदास १; नांमइया। नांम+ ४; [illegible] १३; नाम्हईया २०; नामइया १६; संगै। + ४; संगैं १ ८ २०; [illegible] २१; भेटीला। [illegible] ४; सोई। सोइ १६; हरि। [illegible] २०; हरि। - ४ १३ २०; कीरतंन। कीरतंन १३; कीरतंत २०; कीरतन १ ८ १६; करतां। करंतां ४ ८; इहि। + ४; इहि १३; बिधि। बिधि १; आंनंद। अनंद १६; आनंद ८; आनंद २०; होई। होई बीठुला ४; होई बीठला १६

१६५:० लटकि। लटके १३; बोलूं। बोलौं ८ १३ १६ २१; ब्रतमांन। बतमांन २१; बतमान २०; बर्तमांन १६; बरतमांन ४; ब्रतमान १ १३; कोहला। कोल्हा ४ १६ २१; कोहा ८; ऐवडा। एवडा १६; इंवडा ४; येवडा २०; मैं। मै २०; मंझैं। मंझैं १६ २०; मंझे २१; मंझें ४; मुझै १३; मांझें १; डोलैं। डालौं ८; देषीला। देषिला १ ४

१६५:१ छेली। छैली २०; बैली। बेली १३ २१; बेली १ ४; जैला। जैली २०; आइला १; मांजरिया। मंजरिया १ ४; मंजरियां २१; माजरीयां २०; भै। भैं २०; टूंडै। टूंडै रे ४ २१; टूंडे १६; पंषि। पंष १ ४; लवरू। लउरू १; लवरूं २०; पेष्या। पेषी २१; पेष्या ताकै ४; लीजे। लूजे १६; ह्वै। है ८ २०; टांडै। टोडै १; टांडै रे ४ २१; टांगैं १३; टाडे ८

१६५:२ बावलिया। बांवलि २१; बावलीया ४ २०; चै। चे आजै ४; षोटं। पोटं १ १६; षोंटै ८; मांषणियां। मांषणियां १३; मांषणिया १; मांषणियां ८ १६ २१; संषै। संषैं ४ २१; सषै ८; सुणहां। श्रुणहां १; सुणहा २१; सुंनहां १३; सुनहां ८ १६ २०; मारीला। मांरिला २१; मारिला १; तहां। - २१; मीडक। मैंडक १; मींडक २० २१; अभिला। अभियाला ४

१६५:३ अम्हे। अंम्हे २१; अंम्हे १३; अम्हैं २०; जु। + १६; गैला। + १६; गैल १; गेला ८ १३; भईला ४ २१;

श्रबै आटै गांझीला तहां चौदह रंजन भरिला ॥
४ लटक्यौ गइयौ गढिया जोलै गढिया एवडै रोलै ॥
उडत पंषि मैं मूंगी पेषी बाटी जेहै डोलै ॥
५ बिश्नदास नांमदेव इंम प्रणवैं ए छै जीव ची उकती ॥
लटकै आछै सांगीला ताछैं मोष न मुकती ॥

१६६

• नहीं ऐसो जन्म बारंबार ॥
कहीं पूरब लै पुनि पाईयौ मनिषा औतार ॥
१ ग्रभ बास मैं प्रतिपाल कीन्हीं ताहि सुमरि गंवार ॥
कहा उतर देहगौ राजारांम के दरबार ॥
२ बधत पल पल घटत छिन छिन जात न लागै बार ॥
तरवर सूं फल झडि पडै बहौरि न लागे डार ॥
३ संसार सागर मंडी बाजी सुरति कीन्हीं सारि ॥
मनिष जन्म का हाथि पासा जीति भावै हारि ॥
४ संसार सागर विषम तिरणां निपट उंडी धार ॥
सुरति निरति का बांधे भेरा उतरिंये लै पार ॥
५ काम क्रोध मद लोभ लालच ताहि बंध्यौ संसार ॥
दास नामैं जग जीति लीया कैंवल नांव अधार ॥
दास नामैं जग जीति लीया कैंवल नांव अधार ॥

१६७

• उठि रे नांमदेव बाहरि जाइ । जहां लोग महाजन बैंठे आइ ॥

बाट। + १६; बिराट ८; विराट १; बराट १३; देस। + १६; दास ८; तहां। + १६; - १; गांझी। + १६; गाझी १३; दूध। + १६; कैला। + १६; कैंला २०; श्रबै। ++ १६; श्रबैं ८ १३ २१; सरषैं ४; सरवै १; आटै। आटैं ८ १३ २१; तहां। जहां ८ १३; तहा २१; चौदह। चउदह १; चवदह २०; रंजन। रंजंन ४; भरिला। भरीला १३

१६५;४ लटक्यौ। + १६; लटक्यौं २०; लटिक्यौ १३; गइयौ। + १६; गईयौ ४; गयौ ८; गयौ १३; गाइयौ १; गढिया। + १६; जोलै। + १६; जौलौ ४; गढिया। + १६; गढियौ १; एवडै। +वडै १६; ऐवडै ४ ८ १३; एकडै २१; येवडा २०; इवडै १; रोलै। रौलौ ४ १६; उडत। उंडित १; पंषि। पंष ४ ८ २१; मूंगी। सूंगी ८; बाटी। बांटी १६; बाढी ४; वांटी १; जेहै। इवडै १; डोलै। कोलै १

१६५;५ बिश्नदास। बिसनदास ४ १६ २०; विस्नदास १; नांमदेव। नांमां ८ १३; इंम। - २०; ईम ४; इम ८ १६; इक १३; प्रणवैं। प्रंणवैं २०; ए। ऐ १ ४ १३; ये २०; छै। छैं ८ १३; जीव। जी २०; ची। जी १ १६; उकती। उक्ती १; लटकै। लटक्यौ १३ १६ २०; लटके १; लटकौ ८; आछै। आछैं २० २१; सांगीला। सागीलां २१; ताछैं। ताछे १ ८ १६; तार्थें १३ २०; मोष। मोषि २०; मुकती। मुक्ती १

१ बांभण बणीयां उत्तिम लोग । नहीं रे नांमदेव तेरा जोग ॥
२ बार बार सीधा कुण लेह । को छिपीया ढिग बैसण देह ॥
३ हम तौ पढीया बेद पुरानां । तू कहा ल्यायौ ब्रह्म गियाना ॥
४ नांमदेव मनि उपरति धरी । हीन जाति प्रभु काहे मोरी करी ॥
५ झाडि कब लीया चल्यौ रिसाइ । मठ कै पछिं बैठो जाइ ॥
६ पगां घूंघरा हाथां तारी । नांमदेव भगति करै पछिं वारी ॥
७ धज कांपी देवल धरहरया । नांमदेव सनमुषि दूबारा फिरया ॥
८ नांमदेव नरहरि दरसन भया । बांह पकडि मंदिर मै लीया ॥
९ जैसी मनसा तैसी दसा । नांमदेव प्रणवै बीसोबिसा ॥

१६८

• आ भडै रे नौआ आ भणै रे ॥
होति छोति कहीं नहीं छीपा सूं देवल मांही ना बडै रे ॥
१ उत्तिम लोग देहरे आया । च्यारुं वरण चा भडै रे ॥
२ उंठिभाई नांमदेव बाहरि आव । ज्यौं पंडित वेद भणैं रे ॥
३ नांमदेव उठि जब बाहरि आयौ । केसौ नै कल न परै रे ॥
४ देवल फिरि नांमां दिसि भईया । पंडित सब पांवा पडै रे ॥
५ दास नांमदेव कौ ऐसा ठाकुर । पण राषै हरि सांकडै परे ॥

१६९

• गाइ मन गोबिंद गाइ रे गाइ । तेरो हरि बिन जनम अकारथ जाइ ॥
१ मनिषा जनम न बारंबार । तातैं भजि लै रांमपियार ॥
२ रे मन गोबिंद काहे न गावै । मनिषा जनम बुरि नहिं पावै ॥
३ छाडि कुटिलाइ हरि भजि मनां । या जीवडा का लागू धना ॥
४ अब कै नांमदेव भया निहाल । मिले निरंजन दीनदयाल ॥

१७०

• झिलिमिलि झिलिमिलि नूरा रे । जहं बाजै अनहद तूरा रे ॥
१ ढोल दमामां बाजै रे । तहां सबद अनाहद माजै रे ॥
२ फिर रायां जोति प्रकासी रे । जहां आपै आप अविनासी रे ॥
३ जहां सूरिज कोटि प्रकासा रे । तहां निहचल नांमदेव दासा रे ॥

१७१

• गाइ रे भावै जिंनिं गावै रांम । मिथ्या बाद बकै बेकांम ॥
१ पढै गुनैं मन भवैं अनेक । बस्त भली परि भांडै छेक ॥
२ जब लग ह्रिदै नांहीं हेत । बीज बिंनां क्यौं निंपजैं षेत ॥
३ जब लग ह्रिदै नांहीं सूध । बांझ थणां क्यौं निकसै दूध ॥
४ भणंत नांमदेव सोचि बिचारि । बिण परचै मति मरै पुकारि ॥

१७२

• ऐसे ही मना रे मेरे ऐसे ही मनां । चलौ रे जहां साहिब अपनां ॥
१ ज्यू सापों सर लेने जाइ । जल को डर तो विलमग जाइ ॥
२ ज्यूं पंथी पंथ माहीं डरै । घर है दूरि रैनि जानि परै ॥
३ बाल बुधि जैसे कोडी देह । रिधना डर तो सांस न लेह ॥
४ ऐसे जारिम पऊ चरण करै । नांमदेव कहै ताको कारिज सरै ॥

१७३

• तू सुष सागर नागर दाता । तू मेरे प्रारभ पिता अरु माता ॥
१ और न जानूं देवी देवा । अपना रांम की करि हूं सेवा ॥
२ नांमदेव कहै मोहि तारि गोसाई । ब्याध बनचर भील की नांई ॥

१७४

• इन औसर गोबिंद भजि रे ॥
यह परपंच सकल बिनसैगे माया का फंदन तजि रे ॥
१ नांव प्रताप तिरे जठ जल मैं मांगत नांव कीयों हठ रे ॥
बिन सेवा बिन दान पुनि बिन चाढि विमांन सकल सझ रे ॥
२ तन सरवर एक हंस बसेत हैं ताहूं काल करत फंद रे ॥
नांमदेव भनै निरंजन का गुन रांम सुमिरि पिंजरा सझिरे ॥

१७५

• माधो जी कहा करूं या मन कौ ॥
मन मैमत नहीं बस मेरौ बरजत हार्‌यौ दिन कौ ॥

१ स्वांति प्रमोधि लै घरि आंऊं धीर पकरि बैठाऊं ॥
पीछै हीतै मतौ उपावै बहुरि न इहि घरि आऊं ॥
२ अम्रत झांडि बिषै क्यूं ध्यावै करत आप मनि मार्यौ ॥
कहै सुनै की कछू न मानै अनेक बार समझइयो ॥
३ कब लग तंत रहूं या मनकै जतन कीया नहीं जाई ॥
या अरदास करै जन नामौं सुनि लीज्यौं रांम राई ॥

१७६

• रुंडा रांम जीसूं रंग लगाया रे । सहजि रंग रंग आया रे ॥
१ ररै ममै की भांति लिषाई । हरि रंग में रैंणी रचि आई ॥
२ प्रेम प्रीति का बेगर दीया । हरि रंग मैं मेरा मन रंगि लीया ॥
३ नांमदेव कहै मैं हरि गुण गाऊं । भौ जल मांहि बहौरि नहीं आऊं ॥

१७७

• रसना रंगी लै हरि नांम । और झषन स्यूं कौंन कांम ॥
१ रसना है तूं बकबादनी । रांम न सुमिरै है पापनी ॥
२ रसना तो पैं मांगूं दांन । रांम छाडि जिनि उचरै आंन ॥
३ रसना मारि करूं नव षंड । रांम न सुमिरै श्री ब्रह्मंड ॥
४ जप तप तीरथ भये सकांम । नांमदेव कहै मोंहि तारिहै रांम ॥

१७८

• हरि बिन कौन सहाइ करैगो ॥
जौ ऐसौ औसर बिसरैगो तौ मरकट कौ औतार धरैगौ ॥
१ करम डोरि बाजीगर कै बसि नाचत घरि घरि बार फिरैगौ ॥

१७७;० रसना। लै ७; रंगी। हरि ७; लै। नांम ७; हरि। लै ७; नांम। नाम २०; हरि नांम रसनां रंगि ल्यौ ७; और। - ७; झषन। - ७; स्यूं। सरे ७; कौंन। सब ७; कांम। काम २०

१७७;१ रसना। जिभ्या ७; है। है ७; तूं। या ७; बकबादनी। अभष भाषणीं ७; है। है ७; पापनी। पापणीं ७

१७७;२ रसना। जिभ्या ७; रांम। गाइले ७; छाडि। गोबिंद ७; जिनि। छाडि ७; उचरै। दे ७

१७७;३ रसना। जिभ्या ७, मारि। काटि ७; नव। नौ ७; रांम। जपि ७; न। ले ७; सुमिरै। अनंत ७; श्री। कोटि ७

१७७;४ सकांम। सकाम २०; कहै भणै २०; मोंहि। मोहि २०

ले लुकटी तौहि त्रास दिषावै जन जन कै तूं पाइ परैगौ ॥
२ जूं हमाल सिरि बोझ बहत है लालच कै संगि लागि मरैगौ ॥
ज्यूं कुलाल चक्री कूं फेरै ऐसे तूं कई बार फिरैगौ ॥
३ भजि भगवंत मुक्ति कै दाता रांम कह्या कछु ना बिगरैगौ ॥
नांव पीताप राषि उर अंतर नांमदेव सरणै उबरैगौ ॥

१७९

• जागौ न बैरागी जोगी यही अनोपमि बाणी जी ॥
झिलिमिलि झिलिमिलि होइ निरंतर सो गति बिरलौ जाणी जी ॥
१ राग बैराग म्हारै मंडल चूवै कारण क्या भीजै जी ॥
निस अधियारा भौ सब भागा सुनि मैं सूता जागूं जी ॥
२ नारि न सारि तांत्य नहीं तूंबा पत्र पवन न पाणी जी ॥
एकै आसन दोइ जन बैठा रावल नैरौ हिताणी जी ॥
३ मनकरि हीरा तन करि कंथा जम मनी परि जागूं जी ॥
भणत नांमदेव अनहद जाचू बैकूंठा भिष्या मांगू जी ॥

१८०

• सहज बोलणैं बोल बोलीजै । पै अनुभै बिनां न नीपजै ॥
१ राजहंस चालिबो कौंणैं सीकवीला । सांगि मोरुला कौंणैं नांचवीला ॥
२ चंदण सीतल कौंणैं कैला । पैल सियांना दिढ कौंणैं कैला ॥
३ पहुपास कौंणैं दीधली प्रमला । सांगि मांगि कास कौंणैं दीधला क्रीला ॥
४ सुरैं आथी कोकिला पै बसंत बिनां नईं ब्रे रसाला ॥
५ अंम्रितास कौंणैं दीधली गौडी । जिभ्या नी बडी वलवतो स बोबडी ॥
६ नांमदेव भणैं सत संगति फली । मज केसौ चरणां नी बडी ॥

१८१

• नको नको रे संसार महाजड । छाडि परपंच कलपनां महा कड ॥
१ मल मुत्रा चैया भांडै । तामैं पाच बसैया भांडै ॥
२ पांच मद भूत गुण त्रिबिधा । तामैं भ्यंन्न परकूरति अष्टधा ॥
३ नांमदेव भणैं एणीं माया । चौरासी लष भरमाया ॥

१८२

• जपि रांम नांम त्रिभै पुरी । तिनि चरणैं अहल्या उधरी ॥
१ रांम नांम मेरे हिरदै लेषि । रांम बिनां सब फोकट देषि ॥
२ जे बोलिये तौ कहिये रांम । आंन बकन सूं नांहीं कांम ॥
३ नांमौं भणैं मेरै एकै नांउं । रांम नांम की मैं बलि जाऊं ॥

१८३

• रांम नांमैं नींसांण बागा ॥
ताका मरम कोई जांणैं सभागा ॥
१ बेद बिवर्जित भेद बिवर्जित ग्यांन बिवर्जित सुंन्यं ॥
बिवर्जित जुगति बिवर्जित तहां नहीं पाप न पुंन्यं ॥
२ स्वांग बिवर्जित भीष बिवर्जित ड्यंभ बिवर्जित लीलं ॥
कहै नांमदेव आपहि आपै ब्याप्या सकल सरीरं ॥

१८४

• हीन दीन जात मोरी पंढरी के राया ॥
ऐसा तुमने नांमां दरजी कायक बनाया ॥
१ टाल बिना लेकर नांमां राऊल में गाया ॥
पूजा करते बह्मन उनैन बाहेर ढकाया ॥
२ देवल के पिछे नांमां अल्लक पुकारे ॥
जिदर जिदर नांमां उदर देऊलहिं फिरे ॥
३ नाना बर्ण गवा उनका एक बर्ण दूध ॥
तुम कहां के बह्मन हम कहां के सूद ॥
४ मन मेरी सुई तनो मेरा धागा ॥
खेचरजी कें चरण पर नांमां सिंपी लागा ॥

१८२;० नांम। नाम ४; त्रिभै। त्रृभै ४; पुरी। पूरी २१; तिनि। तिन १; चरणैं। चरणौं १
१८२;१ मेरे। मेरो ४; रांम। रांम नांम २१; बिनां। विनां १
१८२;२ बोलिये। बोलिऐ २१; कहिये। कहि २१; कहिऐ ४; बकन। बकंण २१; सूं। स्यौं १
१८२;३ मेरै। मेरे १ ४; एकै। ऐकै ४; येही रांम १; नांउं। नांऊं ४· नाउं १; मैं। मै ४; जांऊं। जाउं १

१८५

• हम तो भूले ठाकुर जानें । तुम कौ गाई झूट दिवाने ॥
१ नाला अप आप सागर हुवा । काहे के कारण रोता है कुवा ॥
२ चंदन के साती लिंब हुवा चंदन । क्यौ कर रोवे देखो ए हिंगन ॥
३ गुरु की मेहेर से नांमां भये साधु । देखत रोने लगे जन हे भोदुं ॥

१८६

• रांम बीठला देव वीठला । हमं तेरे सेवग बालिक चेला ॥
१ माइ वीठला बाप वीठला । जाती पांती गुरगोत वीठला ॥
२ ग्यांन वीठला ध्यांन वीठला । नांमां के स्वांमीं प्रांण वीठला ॥

१८७

• भले बिराजे लंबकनाथ ॥
१ धरणी पाय स्वर्ग लोक माथ । योजन भर के हाथ ॥
२ सिव सनकादीक पार न पावे । अनगन सखा विराजत साथ ॥
३ नांमदेव के आप ही स्वामी । कीजे मोहि सनाथ ॥

१८८

• रांम नाम विन और न दूजा । कूंण देव की करिहूं पूजा ॥
१ रांम हि माई रांम हि बाप । रांम बिनां कूंण काटै पाप ॥
२ संपति विपति रांम हीं होइ । रांम बिनां कूंण तारै मोहि ॥
३ भणंत नांमदेव अंम्रित सार । सुमरि सुमरि जन उतरे पार ॥

१८९

• पंढरीनाथ विठाई बतावो मुजे ॥
पंढरीनाथ विठाई ॥
१ माय बाप के सेवा करीये पुंडलीक भक्त सवाई ॥
वैकुंठ से विष्णु लाये खडे करकर बतलाई ॥
२ चन्द्रभागा बालबंट पर कबिरा धूम चलाई ॥
साधु संत की हो गई गर्दी भजन कुटाई खूब खाई ॥

३ त्रिगुणा में रेनु बेनु बजावे सागर का जबाई ॥
दही दूध की हंडी फुट गई मर मर दुध्या पाई ॥
४ नांमदेव देके गुरु शिखावें खेचरी मुद्रा गाई ॥
कृष्ण जी की बार बार गावै हरि नाम बढाई ॥

१६०

० मैं को माधौ मलमूत्र धारी । मैं कहा जांनौं सेवा तुम्हारी ॥
१ तुम्हारे घर कौं भांडवि द्यावंत । तुम्हारे घर कौ आदि कलावंत ॥
२ नांमदेव कहै देवनि के देवा । शुर नर फुंनिग तुम्हारी सेवा ॥

१६१

० तुम बिन घरि येक रहूं नहि न्यारा । सुन यह केसव नियम हमारा ॥
१ जहां तुम मीरीवर ताहां हम मोरा । जहां तुम चंदा तहां मैं चकोरा ॥
२ जहां तुम तरुवर तहां मैं पंछी । जहां तुम सरोवर तहां मैं मच्छी ॥
३ जहां तुम दिवा तहां मैं बत्ती । जहां तुम पंथी तहां मैं साथी ॥
४ जहां तुम शिव तहां मैं बेल पूजा । नांमदेव कहे भाव नहीं दूजा ॥

१६२

० सावध सावध भज ले रे राजा । नहीं आवें ऐसी घडी जू ॥
१ उत्तम नरतनु पाया रे भाई । गाफल क्यों हुवा दिवाने जू ॥
२ जिन्ने जन्म डारा है तुज कूं । विसर गया उनका ग्यान जू ॥
३ फिर पस्तायेगा दगा पायेगा । निकल जायेगा आवसान जू ॥
४ क्या करना सो आजि कर ले । फिर नहीं ऐसी जोडी जू ॥
५ हंस जायगा पिंजरा पडेगा । तुज कैसा भुल पडी जू ॥
६ सुन्ने का मन्दिर मेहेल बनाया । धन संपत नहिं तेरी जू ॥
७ यामे न और जोरु लडके । सुख के खातर सोर जू ॥
८ अकेले आना अकेले जाना । सब झुटी माया पसरी जू ॥
९ लख चौरयासी का फेरा आवेगा । तब चुपी बैंठे बंदे जू ॥
१० फिरतां फिरतां जीव रमता है बाबा । कोन रखे तेरे तन कूं जू ॥
११ जिस माया उदरी जन्म लियेगा । तेरे संगत दुख उनकू जू ॥
१२ गरमी की यातना सुनले रे भाई । नवमास बंधन डारे जू ॥
१३ नहीं जगा हलने चलने कू बाबा । छडनिकु कोई नहीं आवे जू ॥

१४ आग लगी क्या देख न आंधे । काय के खातर सोया जू ॥
१५ ऐसी बात सुनके नांमां सावध हुवा । गुरु के पाव मिठी डारी ॥
१६ मैं आनाथ दुबले शरण सये तुज कू । आब जो मेरी लाज राखी जू ॥

१६३

• नांमां तुं हि तूं झूठा रे तेरा पंथ झूठा रे ॥
अल्लाहि अलम का साई सोहि गुप्त चहरा रै ॥
१ गुसलमीन तो हंबी जाणी नहीं रांम कु तोली ॥
पांच बखत निमाजु गुजारी मस्जित क्यूं नहीं बोली ॥
२ वाच्छाव तू ही तू दीवाना रे तेरा तू हिं दीवाना रे ॥
गाई की तो हंबी जाणी खेती वीराणा खाती ॥
एक पाव तो छीन लिया है तीन पाव पर चल जाती ॥
३ नांमां तू हि बकरी काटी मृगी काटी हलाल कीया कहता है ॥
मुरगी में सो अंडा निकला हलाल कैसा होता है ॥
४ वाच्छाव बाबा आदम हंबा जाणें ढबला नंदी आवे ॥
सीरा लसेट का बेटा मारे हरांम खाना खावे ॥
५ नांमां तू हि झूठा रे ॥
उन ने मारा उन ने तारा उनने किया उत्धारा ॥
६ मुवा पोगंडा आब जीवावै ऐसा रांम हमारा पाच्छा ॥
७ दशरथ को दोनो बेटे रांम लछीमन भाई डेरा छांड कर जंगल जावे ॥
जोरु अपनी गमाई ॥
८ नांमां तू हि जल ऊपर फत्तर तारी आहिल्या नारि उत्धारी ॥
रावण मारा बिभिषण थापा लंका बक्से झौरी । पात्छा तूं ॥
९ गोऊ बछरा दोनऊं काटे नांमां आगे डारे ॥
नांमदेव ने हाथ लगाया बछरा पीवन लागे ॥
१० अब तो भली बनी है जी सबका धनी रांमधनी है जी ॥
नांमां वाच्छाव सहज मिलै सांचा झगडा उनका ॥
११ ऊंचा नीचा कर कर देख्यो सोही ऊंचा नीचा ॥

१६४

• ए माधौ कैसैं कीजै जोग ॥
करत जोग बहुत कठिनाई तजि न सकूं या भोग ॥
१ नहीं मेरे रहणीं नहीं मेरे करणीं ॥

बंध्यौ पांच बसि पोष ॥
२ नहीं मेरे ग्यांनां नहीं मेरे ध्यांनां ॥
ब्यापै हरिष रु सोक ॥
३ मैं अनाथ सुकृत हीनौं तुम थैं परचौ बिजोग ॥
४ नांमदेव कहै हरि सरणि राषियौ ॥
नहीं तौ हसिबा लोग ॥

१६५

• ताहि गावै दास नांमां रे ॥
संत जननि के पुरवन कांमां ॥
१ असपति नांमदेव तमकि बुलाया पंल्यंग बेग दे ल्याव बे ॥
गिलसूरी गींदवो निहाली दर हालैं पहुंचाव बे ॥
२ अंबरीक प्रहिलाद परीछत जस गावैं प्रभू तेरा ॥
सुंदर स्वामि कवल दल लोचन प्रांण जीवन धन मेरा ॥
३ अपनें जन कौं दीनर दांनर दोऊ मनक जनावै ॥
भगत जनन कौं जयौ दमोदर पुनरपि जनमि न आवै ॥
४ त्रिभुवन धणीं पज प्रतिपालणा ताकौ जस नांमदेव गावै ॥
सूकी सेज जलांह तैं हाजरि दर हालैं पहुचावै ॥

१६६

• सुणि भाई महिमां नाम तणीं ॥
माह्रा सतगुर पासैं जो मैं सुणीं ॥
१ कोटि कोटि बार जौ पढिये बेद सब सास्त्र कौ लीजै भेद ॥
पुरांण अठारह कौ मत जोइ रांम नाम समि तुलै न कोइ ॥

१६५;० दास। - ४; रे। - १६; जननि। जनन ४; पुरवन। पुरवै १६

१६५;१ असपति। असपनिं १६; बुलाया। बुलाइया १६; पंल्यंग। बेगि १६; बेग। पल्यंग १६; दे। ले १६; ल्याव। आव १६; बे। रे १६; गिलसूरी। सवरि सपेती १६; गींदवो। गलौ १६; निहाली। गीदवा १६; पहुंचाव। लै आव १६; बे। रे १६

१६५;२ अंबरीक। -- ४; जस। -- ४; सुंदर। -- ४; प्रांण। -- ४

१६५;३ अपनें। -- ४; दोऊ। -- ४; भगत। -- ४; पुनरपि। -- ४

१६५;४ पज। सकल १६; प्रतिपालणा। प्रतिपालण ४; परपूरण १६; ताकौ। जस १६; जस। भरि १६; जलांह। जलहि १६; तैं। थैं १६; हाजरि। निकसी १६; दर। ले १६; हालैं। दीबांनि १६

२ कोटि कोटि कूप षणावै बाइ कोटि कोटि कन्यां दे परणाइ ॥
कोटि कोटि बार जौ कीजै जगि तुलै न नांम सहंश्र मैं भगि ॥
३ बिस्व सगली जौ दीजै दांन कोटि कोटि तीर्थ कीजै अस्नांन ॥
कोटि जप तप साधै पांन तऊ न आवै नांव समांन ॥
४ गज गनिका गोतमबधु तरी निर्मल नांम एह्नौं छै हरी ॥
पतित अजामिल सरणैं गयौ भाव कुभाव जिनि हरि नाम लयौ ॥
५ सुष नारद प्रहिलाद अभ्यास सुमिरचौ धू सति करि बिसवास ॥
तिनका हरि काटे भौफंद ते न चलैं चलैं रवि चंद ॥
६ हिरदै सति करि सुमिरचौ रांम आंन धरम सब तजि बेकांम ॥
भणत नांमदेव हरि सरणां आवा गवन मेटि मरणां ॥

१९७

• जाबा न देख्यूं हो नर हरी । मो नृधन कौ धन नरहरी ॥
१ आगल थयौ अगोचर थाइसि । मारहारि दयाथकौं मंजाइसि हो नरहरी ॥
२ तीन लोक मैं कहीं न समाणौं । संतनि हिरदै समौं हो नरहरी ॥
३ नांमदेव कहै मैं सेवग तेरा । आवा गवण निवारि हो नर हरी ॥

१९८

• पायौ मैं रांम संजीवनि मूरी । गुर मिल्यौ बैद बिथा गई दूरी ॥
१ पढि पुरांन पंडित बौराना । भ्रम क्रम संसार भुलानां ॥
२ आन देव सब भ्रमकी पूजा । देह घरे कौ धरम न दूजा ॥
३ फुनि मुनि वरनि धर्म मति चोषी । पीवत नांमदेव भये संतोषी ॥

१९९

• मलै न लाछै पारमलो परमलीओ बैठो री आई ॥
आवत किनै न पेखिओ कवनै जाणै री बाई ॥
कउणु कहै किणि बूझीऐ रमईआ आकुलु री बाई ॥ रहाउ ॥
१ जिउ आकासै पंखीअलो खोजु निरखिओ न जाई ॥
जिउ जल माझै माछलो मारगु पेखणो न जाई ॥
२ जिउ आकासै घड़अलो मृग तृसना भरिआ ॥
नामे चे सुआमी बीठलो जिनि तीनै जरिआ ॥

२००

• जब देखा तब गावा । तउ जन धीरजु पावा ॥
नादि समाइलो रे सतिगुरु भेटिले देवा ॥ रहाउ ॥
१ जह झिलि मिलि कारु दिसंता । तह अनहद सबद बजंता ॥
जोती जोति समानी । मै गुरपरसादी जानी ॥
२ रतन कमल कोठरी । चमकार बीजुल तही ॥
नेरै नाही दूरि । निज आतमै रहिआ भरपूरि ॥
३ जह अनहत सूर उज्यारा । तह दीपक जलै छंछारा ॥
गुरपरसादी जानिआ । जनु नामां सहज समानिआ ॥

२०१

• दस बैरागनि मोहि बसि कीन्ही पंचहु का मिट नावउ ॥
सतरि दोइ भरे अंमृतसरि बिखु कउ मारि कढावउ ॥
पाछै बहुरि न आवनु पावउ ॥
अंमृत बाणी घट ते उचरउ आतम कउ समझावउ ॥ रहाउ ॥
१ बजर कुठारु मोहि है छीनां करि मिंनति लगि पावउ ॥
संतन के हम उलटे सेवक भगतन ते डर पावउ ॥
२ इह संसार ते तब ही छूटउ जउ माइआ नह लपटावउ ॥
माइआ नामु गरभ जोनि का तिह तजि दरसनु पावउ ॥
३ इतु करि भगति करहि जो जन तिन भउ सगल चुकाईऐ ॥
कहत नामदेउ बाहरि किआ भरमहु इह संजम हरि पाईऐ ॥

२०२

• मारवाडि जैसे नीरु बालहा बेलि बालहा करहला ॥
जिउ कुरंक निसि नादु बालहा तिउ मेरै मनि रामईआ ॥
तेरा नामु रूडो रूपु रूडो अति रंग रूडो मेरो रमईआ ॥ रहाउ ॥
१ जिउ धरणी कउ इंद्रु बालहा कुसम बासु जैसे भवरला ॥
जिउ कोकिल कउ अंबु बालहा तिउ मेरै मनि रामईआ ॥
२ चकवी कउ जैसे सूरु बालहा मानसरोवर हंसुला ॥
जिउ तरुणी कउ कंतु बालहा तिउ मेरै मनि रामईआ ॥
३ बारिक कउ जैसे खीरु बालहा चातृक मुख जैसे जलधरा ॥
मछुली कउ जैसे नीरु बालहा तिउ मेरै मनि रामईआ ॥

४ साधिक सिध सगल मुनि चाहहि बिरले काहु डीठुला ॥
सगल भवण तेरो नामु बालहा तिउ नामे मनि बीठुला ॥

२०३

• पहिल पुरीए पुं वना । ताचे हंसा सगले जना ॥
कृस्ना ते जानऊ हरि हरि नाचंती नाचना ॥
पहिल पुरसाबिरा अथोन पुरसादमरा । असगा अस उसगा ॥
हरि का बागरा नाचै पिंधी महि सागरा ॥ रहाउ ॥
१ नाचंती गोपी जंना । नईआ ते बैरे कंना ॥
तरकु न चा । भ्रमीआ चा ॥
केसवा बचउनी अईए मईए एक आन जीउ ॥
२ पिंधी उभ कले संसारा । भ्रमि भ्रमि आए तुमचे दुआरा ॥
तू कुनु रे । मै जी । नामा । हो जी ॥
आला ते निवारणा जम कारणा ॥

२०४

• सफल जनमु मो कउ गुर कीना । दुख बिसारि सुख अंतरि लीना ॥
गिआन अंजनु मो कउ गुरि दीना । राम नाम बिनु जीवनु मन हीना ॥ रहाउ ॥
१ नामदेइ सिमरनु करि जानां । जगजीवन सिउ जीउ समानां ॥

२०५

• मोकउ तारि ले रामा तारि ले ॥
मै अजानु जनु तरिबे न जानउ बाप बीठुला बाह दे ॥ रहाउ ॥
१ नर ते सुर होइ जात निमख मै सतिगुर बुधि सिखलाई ॥
नर ते उपजि सुरग कउ जीतिओ सो अवखध मै पाई ॥
२ जहा जहा धूअ नारदु टेके नैकु टिकावहु मोहि ॥
तेरे नाम अविलंबि बहुतु जन उधरे नामे की निज मति एह ॥

२०६

• हरे नमस्ते हरे नमां ॥
हरि हरि हरि हरि उचरसि मनां ॥

१ हरि हरि कहत कटे सब क्रमां हरि कौ नांम लीयें उतिम धरमां ॥
हरि हरि करत जाति कुल हरी सो हरि नैंननि की पूतरी ॥
२ बालघातनीं कपटां भरी हरि हरि करत पूतना तिरि ॥
सो हरि अंधे की लकरी ॥
३ हरि हरि कहत गजा उधरी सूवा पढावत गनिका तिरी ॥
केसी कंस मथन जिन कीयौ जीवदांन काले कूं दीयौ ॥
४ हरि हरणांकुस हरे परांन अजामेल बैकुंठां ठांन ॥
हरि हरि कहत दुवै उधरी प्रणवत नांमदेव हरि सूं रली ॥

१ हरि हरि करत मिटे सभि भरमा । हरि को नामु लै ऊतम धरमा ॥
हरि हरि करत जाति कुल हरी । सो हरि अंधुले की लाकरी ॥
॰ हरए नमसते हरए नमह । हरि हरि करत नही दुखु जमह ॥ रहाउ ॥
२ हरि हरनाखस हरे परान । अजैमल कीओ बैकुंठहि थान ॥
सूआ पढावत गनिका तरी । सो हरि नैनहु की पूतरी ॥
३ हरि हरि करत पूतना तरी । बाल घातनी कपटहि भरी ॥
सिमरन द्रोपद सुत उधरी । गऊतम सती सिला निसतरी ॥
४ केसी कंस मथनु जिनि कीआ । जीअ दानु काली कउ दीआ ॥
प्रणवै नामा ऐसो हरी । जासु जपत भै अपदा टरी ॥

॥रागबिलाव
ल॥हरेनमस्तेहरेनमः॥हरएहरएहरएनमः॥
हरिहरिकरतनहीफरजमा॥हरिहरिकहतक
टेसबकरमा॥हरिकौनावलीयेउतिमधरम
॥हरिहरिकहतजातकुलहरी॥सोहरिअंध
कीलाकरी॥हरिहरि[illegible]नाकुसहरेप्रान॥अ
जामिलगयौबैकुंठथान॥सूवापढावतगनि
कातिरी॥सोहरिनैननिकीपूतरी॥हरिह
रिकरतपूतनातिरी॥बालघातिनीकपटाभरी
कंसकेसिमथनजिनिकीनै॥जीवदानकाली
कौदीनै॥हरिगजग्राहगहनउधरीगौतमस
तीसिलाउधरी॥हरिहरिकहतद्रोपदीउबरी॥प्र
णवतनामदेवसुमिरौहरी॥हरेनमस्तेहरेन
मः॥छ॥

२०७

• भैरउ भूत सीतला धावै । खर बाहन उहु छार उडावै ॥
हउ तउ एक रमईआ लैहउ । आन देव बदलावनि दैहउ ॥ रहाउ ॥

१ सिव सिव करते जो नरु धिआवै । बरद चढे ढमकावै ॥
२ महा माई की पूजा करै । नर सै नारि होइ अउतरै ॥
३ तू कहीअत ही आदि भवानी । मुकति की बरीआ कहा छपानी ॥
४ गुरमति राम नाम गहु मीता । प्रणवै नामा इउ कहै गीता ॥

२०८

• आजु नामे बीठलु देखिआ मूरख को समझाऊ रे ॥ रहाउ ॥
१ पांडे तुमरी गाइत्री लोधे का खेतु खाती थी ॥
लै करि ठेगा टगरी तोरी लांगत लांगत जाती थी ॥
२ पांडे तुमरा महादेउ धउले बलद चढिआ आवतु देखिआ था ॥
मोदी के घर खाणा पाका वाका लड़का मारिआ था ॥
३ पांडे तुमरा रामचंदु सो भी आवतु देखिआ था ॥
रावन सेती सरबर होई घर की जोइ गवाई थी ॥
४ हिंदू अंन्हा तुरकू काणा । दुहां ते गिआनी सिआणा ॥
हिंदू पूजै देहुरा मुसलमाणु मसीत ॥
नामे सोई सेविआ जह देहुरा न मसीति ॥

२०९

१ माइ न होती बापु न होता करमु न होती काइआ ॥
हम नही होते तुम नही होते कवनु कहां ते आइआ ॥
राम कोइ न किसही केरा । जैसे तरवर पंखि बसेरा ॥ रहाउ ॥
२ चंदु न होता सूरु न होता पानी पवनु मिलाइआ ॥
सासतु न होता बेदु न होता करमु कहां ते आइआ ॥
३ खेचर भूचर तुलसी माला गुर परसादी पाइआ ॥
नामा प्रणवै परम ततु है सतिगुर होइ लखाइआ ॥

२१०

• धनि धंनि ओ राम बेनु बाजै । मधुर मधुर धुनि अनहत गाजै ॥ रहाउ ॥
१ धनि धनि मेघा रोमावली । धनि धनि क्रिसन ओढै कांबली ॥
२ धनि धनि तू माता देवकी । जिह गृह रमईआ कवलापती ॥
३ धनि धनि बनखंड बिंद्राबना । जह खेलै स्री नाराइना ॥
४ बेनु बजावै गोधनु चरै । नामे का सुआमी आनद करै ॥

२११

१ चारि मुकति चारै सिधि मिलि कै दूलह प्रभ की सरनि परिओ ॥
मुकति भइओ चउहूं जुग जानिओ जसु कीरति माथै छत्रु धरिओ ॥
॰ राजा राम जपत को को न तरिओ ॥
गुर उपदेसि साध की संगति भगतु भगतु ता को नामु परिओ ॥ रहाउ ॥
२ संख चक्र माला तिलकु बिराजित देखि प्रतापु जमु डरिओ ॥
निरभउ भए राम बल गरजित जनम मरन संताप हिरिओ ॥
३ अंबरीक कउ दीओ अभै पदु राजु भभीखन अधिक करिओ ॥
नउनिधि ठाकुरि दई सुदामै ध्रूअ अटलु अजहू न टरिओ ॥
४ भगत हेति मारिओ हरनाखसु नरसिंघ रूप होइ देह धरिओ ॥
नामा कहै भगति बसि केसव अजहूं बलि के दुआर खरो ॥

२१२

१ रे जिहबा करउ सत खंड । जामि न उचरसि स्री गोबिंद ॥
॰ रंगीले जिहबा हरि कै नाइ । सुरंग रंगीले हरि हरि धिआइ ॥ रहाउ ॥
२ मिथिआ जिहबा अवरें काम । निरबाण पदु इकु हरि को नामु ॥
३ असंख कोटि अनपूजा करी । एक न पूजसि नामै हरी ॥
४ प्रणवै नामदेउ इहु करणा । अनंत रूप तेरे नाराइणा ॥

२१३

१ दूधु कटोरै गडवै पानी । कपल गाइ नामे दुहि आनी ॥
॰ दूधु पीउ गोबिंदे राइ । दूधु पीउ मेरो मनु पतीआइ ॥
नाही त घर को बापु रिसाइ ॥ रहाउ ॥
१ सोइन कटोरी अंमृत भरी । लै नामै हरि आगै धरी ॥
२ एकु भगतु मेरे हिरदे बसै । नामे देखि नराइनु हसै ॥
४ दूधु पीआइ भगतु घरि गइआ । नामे हरि का दरसनु भइआ ॥

२१४

१ मै बउरी मेरा रामु भतारु । रचि रचि ता कउ करउ सिंगारु ॥
॰ भले निंदउ भले निंदउ भले निंदउ लोगु । तनु मनु राम पिआरे जोगु ॥ रहाउ ॥
२ बादु बिबादु काहू सिउ न कीजै । रसना राम रसाइनु पीजै ॥

३ अब जीअ जानि ऐसी बनि आई । मिलउ गुपाल नीसानु बजाई ॥
४ उसतति निंदा करै नरु कोई । नामे स्त्रीरंगु भेटल सोई ॥

२१५

१ कबहू खीरि खाड घीउ न भावै । कबहू घर घर टूक मगावै ॥
० कबहू कूरनु चने बिनावै । जिउ रामु राखै तिउ रहीऐ रे भाई ॥
हरि की महिमा किछु कथनु न जाई ॥ रहाउ ॥
२ कबहू तुरे तुरंग नचावै । कबहू पाइ पनहीओ न पावै ॥
३ कबहू खाट सुपेदी सुवावै । कबहू भूमि पैआरु न पावै ॥
४ भनति नामदेउ इकु नामु निसतारै । जिह गुरु मिलै तिह पारि उतारै ॥

२१६

१ हसत खेलत तेरे देहुरे आइआ । भगति करत नामा पकरि उठाइआ ॥
० हीनडी जात मेरी जादिम राइआ । छीपे के जनमि काहे कउ आइआ ॥ रहाउ ॥
२ लै कमली चलिओ पलटाइ । देहुरै पाछै बैठा जाइ ॥
३ जिउ जिउ नामा हरि गुण उचरै । भगत जनां कउ देहुरा फिरै ॥

२१७

१ घर की नारि तिआगै अंधा । परनारी सिउ घालै धंधा ॥
जैसे सिंबलु देखि सूआ बिगसाना । अंत की बार मूआ लपटाना ॥
० पापी का घरु अगने माहि । जलत रहै मिटवै कब नाहि ॥ रहाउ ॥
२ हरि की भगति न देखै जाइ । मारगु छोडि अमारगि पाइ ॥
मूलहु भूला आवै जाइ । अंमृतु डारि लादि बिखु खाइ ॥
३ जिउ बेस्वा के परै अखारा । कापरु पहिरि करहि सींगारा ॥
पूरे ताल निहाले सास । वा के गले जम का है फास ॥
४ जाके मसतकि लिखिओ करमा । सो भजि परि है गुर की सरना ॥
कहत नामदेउ इहु बीचारु । इन बिधि संतहु उतरहु पारि ॥

२१८

१ सुलतानु पूछे सुनु बे नामा । देखउ राम तुम्हारे कामा ॥
० नामा सुलताने बाधिला । देखउ तेरा हरि बीठुला ॥ रहाउ ॥

१ बिसमिलि गऊ देहु जीवाइ । नातरु गरदनि मारउ ठाइ ॥
३ बादिसाह ऐसी किउ होइ । बिसमिलि कीआ न जीवै कोइ ॥
४ मेरा कीआ कछू न होइ । करिहै रामु होइ है सोइ ॥
५ बादिसाहु चढिओ अहंकारी । गज हसती दीनो चमकारि ॥
६ रुदनु करै नामे की माइ । छोडि राम की न भजहि खुदाइ ॥
७ न हउ तेरा पूंगडा न तू मेरी माइ । पिंडु पडै तउ हरि गुन गाइ ॥
८ करै गजिंदु सुंड की चोट । नामा उबरै हरि की ओट ॥
९ काजी मूलां करहि सलामु । इनि हिंदू मेरा मलिआ मानु ॥
१० बादिसाह बेनती सुनेहु । नामे सर भरि सोना लेहु ॥
११ मालु लेउ तउ दोजकि परउ । दीनु छोडि दुनीआ कउ भरउ ॥
१२ पावहु बेडी हाथहु ताल । नामा गावै गुन गोपाल ॥
१३ गंग जमुन जउ उलटी बहै । तउ नामा हरि करता रहै ॥
१४ सात घडी जब बीती सुणी । अजहु न आइओ त्रिभवन धणी ॥
१५ पाखंतण बाज बजाइला । गरुड चडे गोबिंद आइला ॥
१६ अपने भगत परि की प्रतिपाल । गरुड चढे आए गोपाल ॥
१७ कहहि त धरणि इकोडी करउ । कहहि त ले करि ऊपरि धरउ ॥
१८ कहहि त मुई गऊ देउ जीआइ । सभु कोई देखै पतीआइ ॥
१९ नामा प्रणवै सेलमसेल । गऊ दुहाई बछरा मेलि ॥
२० दूधहि दुहि जब मटुकी भरी । ले बादिसाह के आगे धरी ॥
२१ बादिसाहु महल महि जाइ । अउघट की घट लागी आइ ॥
२२ काजी मुलां बिनती फ़रमाइ । बखसी हिंदू मै तेरी गाइ ॥
२३ नामा कहै सुनहु बादिसाह । इहु किछु पतीआ मुझै दिखाइ ॥
२४ इस पतीआ का इहै परवानु । साचि सीलि चालहु सुलितान ॥
२५ नामदेउ सभ रहिआ समाइ । मिलि हिंदू सभ नामे पहि जाहि ॥
२६ जउ अब की बार न जीवै गाइ । त नामदेव का पतीआ जाइ ॥
२७ नामे की कीरति रही संसारि । भगत जनां ले उधरिआ पारि ॥
२८ सगल कलेस निंदक भइआ खेदु । नामे नाराइन नाही भेदु ॥

२१६

१ जउ गुरदेउ त मिलै मुरारि । जउ गुरदेउ त उतरै पारि ॥
जउ गुरदेउ त बैकुंठ तरै । जउ गुरदेउ त जीवत मरै ॥
सति सति सति सति सति गुरदेव । झूठु झूठु झूठु झूठु आन सभ सेव ॥ रहाउ ॥
२ जउ गुरदेउ त नामु दृड़ावै । जउ गुरदेउ न दहदिस धावै ॥
जउ गुरदेउ पंच ते दूरि । जउ गुरदेउ न मरिबो झूरि ॥

३ जउ गुरदेउ त अंमृत बानी । जउ गुरदेउ त अकथ कहानी ॥
जउ गुरदेउ त अंमृत देह । जउ गुरदेउ नामु जपि लेहि ॥
४ जउ गुरदेउ भवन त्रै सूझै । जउ गुरदेउ ऊच पद बूझै ॥
जउ गुरदेउ त सीसु अकासि । जउ गुरदेउ सदा साबासि ॥
५ जउ गुरदेउ सदा बैरागी । जउ गुरदेउ पर निंदा तिआगी ॥
जउ गुरदेउ बुरा भला एक । जउ गुरदेउ लिलाटहि लेख ॥
६ जउ गुरदेउ कंधु नही हिरै । जउ गुरदेउ देहुरा फिरै ॥
जउ गुरदेउ त छापरि छाई । जउ गुरदेउ सिहज निकसाई ॥
७ जउ गुरदेउ त अठसठि नाइआ । जउ गुरदेउ तनि चक्र लगाइआ ॥
जउ गुरदेउ त दुआदस सेवा । जउ गुरदेउ सभै बिखु मेवा ॥
८ जउ गुरदेउ त संसा टूटै । जउ गुरदेउ त जम ते छूटै ॥
जउ गुरदेउ त भउ जल तरै । जउ गुरदेउ त जनमि न मरै ॥
९ जउ गुरदेउ अठदस बिउहार । जउ गुरदेउ अठारह भार ॥
बिनु गुरदेउ अवर नही जाई । नामदेउ गुर की सरणाई ॥

२२०

१ साहिबु संकटवै सेवकु भजै । चिरंकाल न जीवै दोऊ कुल लजै ॥
तेरी भगति न छोडउ भावै लोगु हसै । चरन कमल मेरे हीअरे बसै ॥ रहाउ ॥
२ जैसे अपने धनहि प्रानी मरनु मांडै । तैसे संत जनां राम नामु न छा ॥
३ गंगा गइआ गोदावरी संसार के कामा । नाराइणु सुप्रसंन होइ त सेवकु नामा ॥

२२१

१ सहज अवलि धूडि मणी गाडी चालती । पीछै तिनका लै करि हांकती ॥
जैसे पनकत थ्रूटिटि हांकती । सरि धोवन चाली लाडुली ॥ रहाउ ॥
२ धोबी धोवै बिरह बिराता । हरि चरन मेरा मनु राता ॥
३ भणति नामदेउ रमि रहिआ । अपने भगत पर करि दइआ ॥

२२२

• दास अनिंन मेरो निज रूप ॥
दरसन निमख ताप त्रई मोचन परसत मुकति करत गृह कूप ॥ रहाउ ॥
१ मेरी बांधी भगतु छडावै बांधै भगतु न छूटै मोहि ॥
एक समै मोकउ गहि बांधै तउ फुनि मोपै जबाबु न होइ ॥

२ मैं गुन बंध सगल की जीवनि मेरी जीवनि मेरे दास ॥
नामदेव जाके जीअ ऐसी तैसी ताकै प्रेम प्रगास ॥

२२३

१ अकुल पुरख इकु चलितु उपाइआ । घटि घटि अंतरि ब्रह्मु लुकाइआ ॥
० जीअ की जोति न जानै कोई । तै मै कीआ सु मालूमु होई ॥ रहाउ ॥
२ जिउ प्रगासिआ माटी कुंभेउ । आप ही करता बीठुलु देउ ॥
३ जीअ का बंधनु करमु बिआपै । जो किछु कीआ सो आपै आपै ॥

२२४

० एकै बीठुला सरणैं जा रे । जनम बायां का दौडा रे ॥
१ तीरथैं तीरथैं कां हींडा रे । लटक्या डोया कां तूंबा रे ॥
२ फूकाचया तुलसी बाहा रे । धू सारीषा पद जोडा रे ॥
३ नांमौं भणैं तूं देव पहा रे । कैसौ भगता चा रिणियां रे ॥

२२५

० पद निरषत कि न जाइ रे दिनां । आप छिपांनौं मन हीं मनां ॥
१ जै तू न डरसि न करसि घाई । तौ तूं निमसि ठांइ कुठांई रे मनां ॥
२ घट भरिलै उदिक चढोई । ऐसैं तूं निह्चल होई रे मंनां ॥
३ नांमदेव कहै सुष सरगै नांहीं । सो सुष भगता माहीं रे मनां ॥

२२४;० एकै। एक १७; एकैं २१; बीठुला। बिठुला १७; बीठुल ४; बीठला २१; सरणैं। सरनैं १७; जनम। जंनम २१; जनमे १७; बायां। बायें १७; बाया ४ ७; का। कां २१; कांइ १७; दौडा। दोडा २१

२२४;१ तीरथैं। तर्थे २१; तीरथैं। तीर्थे २१; कां। का ४ २१; हींडा। हीडा २१; लटक्या। लटकै ७ २१; लटकैं १७; डोया। डोयौ २१; कां। का ४

२२४;२ फूकाचया। फोकटचया २१; फोकाचईया १७; फोचाचया ७; तुलसी। तुलछी ७ २१; बाहा। बहा ४; धू। धू १७; धु ७; सारीषा। सरीषा का १७; पद। ब्यद ४

२२४;३ नांमौं। नांमदेव १७; तूं। तू ४; रे। रै २१; कैसौ। केसौ ४ ७ १७; भगता। भगता १७; रिणियां। रंणियां २१; रणिंयां ४; रणियां ७

२२५;० निरषत। न्रिषत १७; निरषन १; छिपांनौं। छिपानौं १७; मन। रे १७; हीं। - १७

२२५;१ तू। तूं १७; डरसि। डरस्य १७; न। - १७; करसि। करस्य १७; तूं। तू १; निमसि। निमससि १; ठांइ। ठांइं १; कुठांई। ठांइ १; कुठाई १७; मनां। मना १

२२५;२ चढोई। चरोई १; ऐसैं। ऐसा १; मैसैं १७; तूं। तू १; मंनां। मनां १७

२२५;३ नांमदेव। नांम १७; कहै। भणैं १७; सरगै। सुरगैं १७; भगतां। संतनि १७; माहीं। मांहिं १७

२२९

० कुनूं क्रिपा तूंझी होइ ज्यूं आवरी ॥
बिघन व्याधी तेथैं काल कांई करी ॥
१ एक बहूबला महापुरी बलसि या भीतरि ॥
जीवल हो तातारू जेन्हैं धरीला निज करी ॥
२ एक उदेस भूतला तास दीवौ सनमुष भेटिला ॥
नीधंनियां धन धौरी धनाइति कैला ॥
३ हरी दीपावली गुणीं बांणी रेषिला ॥
सुटत सुनौ सरपैं पारधी डंकिला ॥
४ गाइ का पांणधी बाघ झंपाविला ॥
जीवल होता सीहूं तेन्हैं बाघ निरदालीला ॥
५ ऐसी च्यंचर त्रे तुझी नका लेवा देवा ॥
बिश्नदास नांमां बीनवै केसवा ॥

२२९;० कुनूं। कुन्हौं १२; कुनौं १७; कूनूं ४; कवन १; क्रिपा। कुरपा १ २१; क्रु ७; क्रुपा १७; कृपा ४; तूंझी। तुझी १ १२. तूझी ४; होइ। होई ४; दोइ २१; ज्यूं। तुझ १ १२; तूं १७; आवरी। + ४: +ावरी १२; बिघन। बिघंन २१; विघन १; व्याधी। व्याघी २१; तेथैं। तथै २१; कांई। कांई ४ ७ २१; कांइ १२

२२९;१ एक। ऐक १ ४; येक १२; बहूबला। बिहूबला १२; बहूब+ ४; बहूवला १; महापुरी। + ४; पुरी १२; बलसि। बिलसि १२; बलस १; बलसी १७; भीतरि। भींतरि १ ७; भीतरी १२ १७; जीवल। -- ४; तहां जीवल १२ १७; हो। हूं १७; तातारू। तातारु १ २१; जेन्हैं। जीब ४; तेन्हैं १७; तेनैं १२, धरीला। +ीला ४; घरीला २१

२२९;२ एक। ऐक ४; येक १२; उदेस। उधिस १२: उदेस १; भूतला। भूतिला १७; तास। त्या १; दीवौ। दीपक १२; दीयौ १७; दीवो १ २१; दाव ४; सनमुष। +ष ४; संनमुष २१; सनंमुष १; सनमुंष १२; नीधंनियां। नींधंनियां १२ १९: नींधनियां १; नीधन्यंयां २१; नीधनिया ७; धन। - १२; धंन २१; धौरी। - १२; धूंवरी १; धौरी सु ७, धनाइति। धनवंत ७ १२; धनांईति ४; धानाइत १; कैला। कैल+ ४

२२९;३ हरी। - ४; हरि २१; हरे न १७; हरी न १ १२; गुणीं। गुंणी १२; गुंणीं २१: गुणी ४; बांणी। बांणीं १२ १७; वांणीं १; रेषिला। रेषली १२; सुटत। सुटंत १; सुनौ। सुणहैं १; सुनै १२; सुनो १७; सरपैं। अपैं १७; पै १२; सुणौं १

२२९;४ गाइ। गाई ४; का। के १; चै १२ १७; पांणधी। पांणंधी १७; बाघ। वाघ १; झंपाविला। झपाविला १७ २१; जीवल। तहां जीवल १२ १७; होता। हूंता १७; होत ४; हीता २१; सीहूं। सीहू १ ७ १२; तेन्हैं। जेन्हैं ४ ७ २१; तेन्है १; तेनैं १२; बाघ। वाघ १; निरदालीला। निडदाडिला १२; न्रिदालिला १; न्रिदालीला ७: निरदाडिला १७

२२९;५ ऐसी। मैसे १२ १७; मैसी २१; च्यंचर। अचित्र १२; अचत्र चस्यं १७; अच्यंतरि १; च्यंचरं ७; त्रे। चरित्र १२; त्र १७; तुझी। - १२ १७; तूंझी ४ ७; तूझी २१; नका। न्ह ४; निक १२; नक ७ १७ २१; देवा। देवा रांमां ४ ७ २१: बिश्नदास। बिस्नदास ४; विश्नदास १७; दिष्नदास १, नांमां। नांमौं १२; बीनवै। त्रिनवै १; बींनवैं ७; बीनवैं ४; बीनवैं हे १७; यौं प्रणवैं हे १२

२२७

• भाई रे इन नयननि हरि पेषो ॥
हरी की भक्ति साधु की संगति सोई दिन धनि लेख्यो ॥
१ चरन सोई जो नचत प्रेम सो कर जो करै नित पूजा ॥
सीस सोई जो नवै साधु को रसना और न दूजा ॥
२ यह संसार हाट कौ लेखा सब कोउ बनीजहिं आया ॥
जिन जस लादा तिन तस पाया मूरख मूल गवाया ॥
३ आतमराम देह धरि आयो तामैं हरि कौ देखौ ॥
कहत नामदेव बलि बलि जैहो हरि मनि और न लेखौ ॥

२२८

• रुखडी न खाइयो स्वामी रुखडी न खाइयो ॥
हाथ हमारे घिरत कटोरी अपनी बांटा ले जाइयो ॥
१ दौडै दौडै जात स्वामी रोटणियां मुख मांहि ॥
हम तौ दौंडै पहूंच न साकै मेल लेहु गोसाइं ॥
२ घट घट वासी सर्व निवासी पलमें भेष बनाया ॥
कूकर ते ठाकुर भये प्रगटे नामदेव दरसन पाया ॥

२२९

• अस मन लाव राम रसना । तेरो बहुरी न होय जरा मरना ॥
१ जैसे मृगा नाद लव लावै । बान लगे वहि ध्यान लगावै ॥
२ जैसे कीट भृंग मन दीन्ह । आपु सरीखे वा को कीन्ह ॥
३ नामदेव भनै दासन दास । अब न तजैं हरि चरन निवास ॥

२३०

• मोर पिया बिलम्यो परदेस होरी मैं का सौं खेलौं ॥
घरी पहर मोहिं कल न परतु है कहत न कोउ उपदेस ॥
१ झरयो पात बन फूलन लाग्यो मधुकर करत गुंजार ॥
हाहा करौं कंथ घर नाहीं के मोरी सुनै पुकार ॥
२ जा दिन तें पिय गवन कियो है सिंदुरा न पहिरौं मंग ॥
पान फुलेल सबै सुख त्याग्यो तेल न लावों अंग ॥

३ निसु बासर मोहिं नींद न आवै नैन रहे भरपूर ॥
अति दारून मोहिं सवति सतावै पिय मारग बडि दूर ॥
४ दामिनि दमकि घटा घहरानी बिरह उठै घनघोर ॥
चित चातृक ह्वै दादुर बोलै वहि बन बोलत मोर ॥
५ प्रीतम को पतियां लिखि भेजौं प्रेम प्रीति मसि लाय ॥
बेगि मिलो जन नामदेव को जनम अकारथ जाय ॥

२३१

• तू मति बरजै माइ हे मूनैं देहुरै जाता ॥
रांम नांम म्हारै मनि बसै चित चत्रभुजि राता ॥
१ करम छाडि कुकरम करुं तौ तू बरजि हे माई ॥
आदि पुरिष मैं सेइयौ जिंहि यौ सिष्टि उपाई ॥
२ माइ कहै सुंणि पूत रे तुझ बिन घरि क्यौं सरिसी ॥
जिंहि र उपाई मेदनीं सोई चिंता करसी ॥
३ माता बिण बालक किसौ ससिहर बिण रैंणी ॥
दीपक बिण मंदिर किसौ त्यौं म्हे क्रिश्न बिहूंणीं ॥
४ काहू कै मनि क्यौं बसै काहू क्यौं र सुहावै ॥
नांमां कै चिति बीठलौ छीपौं हरि गुंन गावै ॥

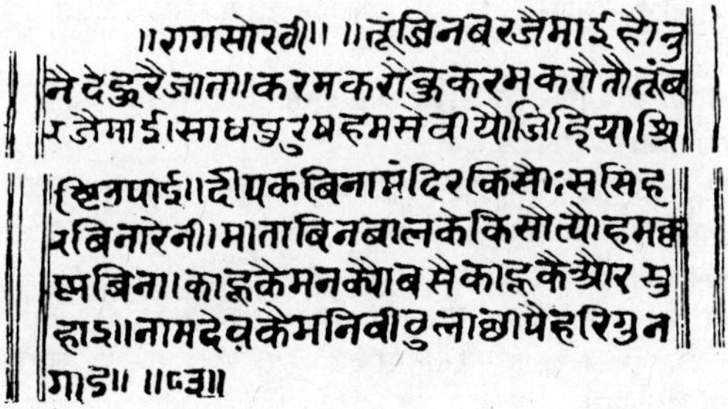

२३२

(See Page No. 128)

२३३

• डोला चै डोल कान्हां जीव चा जीवलु कान्हां ॥
तू आदि चौ समाधी सिध चौ प्रसिध कान्हां ॥
१ तूं बिचार चौ सारू अग्यांन चौ कोठारू कान्हां ॥
तूं आनंद चौ कंदू सुष चौ बिनोदू कान्हां ॥
२ तूं प्रेम चा पूतला नांमों भणैं श्रीगोपाला ॥

२३४

• तुम्ह देवा हरि तुम्ह देवा ॥
मेरे तुम्हही सजन बंधवा ॥
१ आंब बडौ जगनाथ देवा जहां का भगत नांमां ॥
बालपणां कौ मीत मिल्यौ है हंम घरि राघौ पांहुंणा ॥
२ लोग बोलैं नांमां नांमां ए बोल लागै हांमां ॥
अंगुरी दिषायें कुहडा न जीवै मैं कैसैं जीऊं परसोतमां ॥

२३३;• डोला। डोल १; चै। आचै १; जीवलु। जीवल ४; जीवलूं २१; तू। तूं १ २१; समाधी। संमाधी २१; सिध। सिधा २१

२३३;१ सारू। सारुं २१; कोठारू। कुठार २१; कोठार १; आनंद। मानंद ४; बिनोदू। बिनोदी १ २१

२३३;२ भणैं। भंणैं २१; श्रीगोपाला। श्रीपाला १

२३४;• तुम्ह। तुंम १३; तुम १ २०; तुम्ह। तुंम १३; तुम १ २०; मेरे। तु २०; तुम्ह ४; तूंही १३; तुम्हही। मेरे ४ १३ २०; तुम्हे १; तुम्हहीं ७; तुमहीं १६; सजन। सजंणं २१; सजंन २०; सजण १ ७; बंधवा। वंधवा १

२३४;१ आंब। अंम २०; आंव १; बडौ। वडौ १; जगनाथ। जगनांथ २०; जहां। तिहां १; तहां १३; भगत। सेवग २१; बालपणां। बालपना २०; बालपनां १३ १६; वालपणां १ ७; कौ। को २०; मीत। मींत १ ४ ७ १३ २० २१; मिल्यौ। मिंल्यौ १३; है। - १ ४ ७ २१; हरि २०; हंम। हम ७ १६; घरि। घ+ १३; राघौ। गोबिंद १३; राधौ २०; पांहुंणां। पांहुंनां १३; पांहूंणां ४ २०

२३४;२ लोग। जोक १३ २१; बोलैं। बोलै ४ १६ २०; वोलै १; ए। ऐ ४; ये १ १३ २०; बोल। बो २०; वोल १; लागै। लागैं १३ १६ २१; हांमां। हंमां १ २१; अंगुरी। आंगुली १३; दिषायें। दिषांयैं ७ १६; दिषायि १३ २१; दिषांयां २०; कुहडा। कुहड १ २१; कुहडौ २०; कूहड ४; कोह+ १३; न। नही २०; जीवै। जीवैं १३; मैं। मै १३;

३ घाट कालंद्री डोल आछै उपम सोहै भला ॥
नैंन निरषि छीपी मिल्यौ कुटंब नास भैला ॥
४ कंबली पटोलै गांठि परी है कृस्न देव तेरी रावलियां ॥
मूवल बंभन पंग दिषावै षंभ षांऊं तेरो देहुरिया ॥
५ बोलत चालत सरूप आयौ भेष धरें बलिवंडा ॥
नांमां छींपी कौ भाग पलटचौ मिल्यौ रांम मनोहरा ॥

२३५

• न होइ ज्यौ तीरथ ब्रत अस्नांन करीता न होइ ज्यौं कवित परमोध रचीता ॥
न होइ ज्यौ सुघडपणैं गाता जेन्है होइ ज्यौ आतां ॥
ते वेगले च असे ॥
१ न होइ ज्यौं योगा साधणैं न होइ ज्यौ गिरासणैं पवनैं ॥
न होइ ज्यौ इंद्री दवणैं जेन्हैं होइ ज्यौ मनैं ॥
ते वेगले च असे ॥
२ न होइ ज्यौ आतम समाधी न होइ ज्यौ आही कष्ट साधी ॥

कैसैं। क्यूं २१; जीऊं। जीउं १३ २०; जीवूं ४ ७; परसोतमां। प्रसोतमां १३; परसोत्मां १; परसोतंमा २१

२३४;३ घाट। -- १३; बाट २१; कालंद्री। कलंद्री १ २१; आछै। आछैं २०; उपम। -- १३; उपंम २१; वोपम १ ७; वोपमा २०; नैंन। -- १३; नैन २०; छीपी। छींपी १ ४ २०; मिल्यौ। मिल्या १९; कुटंब। -- १३; कटूंब २०; कूटंव १; नास। नांस २०

२३४;४ कंबली। कंमली २०; कंवली १; कव्रली ४; पटोलै। कटोरैं २०; गांठि। गंठि २०; गाठि १९; परी। पडी १ ७ १३ २०; कृस्न। - २०; क्रिस्न १३; क्रिसन १९; क्रिष्न २१; कृष्ण ७; कृष्न १; देव। देवा ४ ७ २०; देवां १३; रावलियां। रावलिया २१; रावलीयां १९ २०; मूवल। मुवल १३; मूव २०; बंभन। बंभण १; ब्रभंन २१; बभन ४; बांम्हन १९; वांभन १३; लंभण २०; पंग। पंक १३, पंगो १९; पग २०; दिषावै। दिषांवै १३; दिषावौ २०; षंभ। षांभ १ १९; षांऊं। पंवौं १३; षांउ ४; षांउं १ २०; षावु २१; देहुरियां। देहुरीगां ४; देहूरीगां २०

२३४;५ बोलत। वोलत १ ४ ७; सरूप। सरुप २१; आयौ। आयौं २०; धरें। धरैं १; धरे १९ २१; बलिवंडा। बलिमंडा ४; बलिमडा २१; वलिवंडा १; नांमां। नांमदेव १३; छींपी। छीपी ४ २१; पलटचौ। पलोट्यौ १३; मिल्यौ। मिल्ययौ १३

२३५;• होइ। होई ४; ब्रत। बरत ४; अस्नांन। अस्नान ४; अश्नान १; करीता। करंतां १; होइ। होई ४; ज्यौं। ज्यौ ४; परमोध। प्रमोध १; रचीता। रचीतां १; होइ। होई ४; सुघडपणैं। सुघडपडैं १; जेन्है। जेन्हैं ४; होइ। होई ४ २१; ज्यौ। जौ २१; आतां। आता १; ते। तेर ४; वेगले। बेगले ४ २१

२३५;१ होइ। होई ४; ज्यौं। ज्यौ ४; योगा। जोग १; साधणैं। साधणै ४; होइ। होई ४; ज्यौ। ज्यौं १; गिरासणैं। गिरासन १; होइ। होई ४; ज्यौ। ज्यूं १; इंद्री। ईंद्री ४; यंद्रियां १; इद्रीय २१; होइ। होई ४; ज्यौ। जौ ४; ते। - ४; वेगले। बेगले ४ २१

२३५;२ होइ। होई ४ २१; ज्यौ। ज्यौं १; आतम। आत्म ४; आसण १; आतंम २१; होइ। होई ४; आही।

न होइ ज्यौ पराक्रंम बुधी जया जया होइ ज्यौ त्रिसुधी ॥
ते वेगले च असे ॥
३ न होइ ज्यौ आकारनैं आगमैं न होइ ज्यौ निरपणैं त्रिगमैं ॥
न होइ ज्यौ षट क्रम साधणैं जेन्हैं होइ ज्यौ ब्रह्मैं ॥
ते वेगले च असे ॥
४ न होइ ज्यौ पुरांण परचीती न होइ ज्यौ देव नी बिगती ॥
न होइ ज्यौ आतम परचीती जया होइ ज्यौ त्रिसुधी ॥
ते वेगले च असे ॥
५ न होइ ज्यौ सुड दरसपणैं न होइ ज्यौ सुचील अंतहकरणैं ॥
न होइ ज्यौ अहो भावहीणैं न होइ ज्यौ एकै केसवा बिनां ॥
बिश्नदास नांमां ॥

२३६

० हरि हरी दून्यूं अष्यर ऊचारी । अरि लटकि बिगारी ॥
१ सौंडणिं धाला पारै दूरि । नांमौं भणैं हवि मंत्र ऊचारी ॥

२३७

० पाया पडूं देव पाया पडूं देवा रांमां ॥
१ जिंम जिंम रूसिजौ तिम तिम गौड । कांन्ह पूरवि मन कोड ॥

अहो १; कष्ट। कस्ट ४; होइ। होई ४ २१; पराक्रंम। प्राक्रंम १; बुधी। बूधी ४; जया। - १; होइ। होई ४ २१; ज्यौ। जौ २१; वेगले। बेग ४; बेगले २१

२३५;३ होइ। होई ४; होइ। होई ४; निरपणैं। निरोपर्णे १; त्रिगमैं। नृगमैं १; न। जेन्हैं २१; होइ। होई ४; षट। षरे ४ २१; क्रम। कंम १, करमैं ४ २१; साधणैं। - ४ २१; जेन्हैं। तेन्हैं २१; होइ। होई ४; ब्रह्मैं। ब्रह्मौ ४; व्रंह्मैं १; वेगले। बेगले ४ २१

२३५;४ होइ। होई ४; पुरांण। पुरंण २१; परचीती। परचाती २१; होइ। होई ४; नी। नीं १; बिगती। विगती १; होइ। होई ४; आतम। आत्म २१; आत्मं १; होइ। होई ४; त्रिसुधी। सुधी ४; वेगले। बेगले ४ २१

२३५;५ होइ। होई ४; सुड। सड २१; सुडु १; होइ। होई ४; अंतहकरणैं। अंतहकरणे १; अतहकरंणैं २१; होइ। होई ४; भावहीणैं। भावहींणें २१; भावहीणौं १; होइ। होई ४; एकै। ऐकै ४ २१; बिनां। बिन २१; विनां १; बिश्नदास। बिसूदास ४; भनैं विश्नदास १; नांमां। नांम ४ २१

२३६;० हरि। हरी १; दून्यूं। दून्हौं १; अष्यर। अक्षिरे १; ऊचारी। उचारी १; लटकि। लटकी ४; बिगारी। विगारी १

२३६;१ सौंडणिं। साइणीं १; दूरि। दूरी १; भणैं। भणे १; मंत्र। जमंत्र १; ऊचारी। उचारी १

२३७;० पाया। पायां १; देव। देवा १; पाया। पायां १

२३७;१ जिंम। जिम १; जिंम। जिम १; रूसिजौ। रूसिज्यौ १; पूरवि। पूरवीले १

२ तार डंडी करी । उभाव तुझैं द्वारैं ॥
३ बीनवैं बिस्नदास नांमां । उपस्यांम कीजै अम्हा ॥

२३८

० सेइये गोपाल राइ अकल निरंजन ॥
भगति कौ दांन दीजै जाचै हो भगत जन ॥
१ जाचै घरां द्रिग दसा सराइचा बैकुंठ सी चित्रसाली ॥
रापत लोक साहिबांन पूरि ले लिषमीं पियारी चंद सूर जाचै दीवला ॥
कंद्रप काल जांनैं बापुला कोटवाल सुक्र सा घरी ॥
ऐसौ राजा है नरहरी ॥
२ जाचै घरां कुलाल वी ब्रह्मां चत्रमुषा दावणां ॥
जिनि बिस्व संसार रचीला जगत्र तणां दातार ॥
जाचै ईस्वर मंत्री बावला तंत मंत अंम्रित भाषिला ॥
पाप पुनि जाचै डांगिया द्वारै चित्र बिचित्र लेषिया ॥
धरमराइ पौली प्रतिहार ऐसौ राजा श्री गोपाल ॥
३ जाचै घरां गांइण चत्रु बेद गंध्रप जन ढाढिया ॥
अष्टादस पुरांण नागरिया सर्ब सास्त्र बहुरूपिया ॥

२३७;२ तार। डाल १; उभाव। ऊभा रही १; तुझैं। तूंझै १

२३७;३ बीनवैं। बिनवैं १; बिस्नदास। विश्नदास १; अम्हा। आम्हा १

२३८;० सेइये। सेविये ८ १६; सेईये ४; सेवीए २१; राइ। राय ४; जाचै। जाचैं ८ १२ २१; हो। हिं २१; जन। जंन २१; जंनं १२

२३८;१ जाचै। साचै ८; जांचै २१; जाकै १२; द्रिग। द्रिगं १६; द्रग ८; दृग ७ १२; दसा। दिंसा ८ १२; दसे १६; सराइचा। सिराइचा ७; सराईचा ४; बैकुंठ। बैकुठ १६; बैकूठ १२; रापत। सप्त १ ७; साहिबांन। सहिबांन १; साहिबांना ४; पूरि। पूजि १६; ले। लै १२; लिषमीं। लिछमीं १२; लिषिमी ४; लछिमी ८; लछिमीं १६; लषमीं २१; जाचै। जाकै ८ १२; जाचैं २१; दीवला। दिवला १; कंद्रप। कंद्रष १२; कोटि १; काल। कपाल १; कला ८ १२ २१; जांनैं। जांणे ४ १२; जाणैं ७ १६; बापुला। बापला १; सुक्र। सुक्रा ८; सुक्रां १२; घरी। धरी ४; षरी १; ऐसौ। असौ ८ १२ २१; असो १६

२३८;२ जाचै। जाचैं १२; कुलाल। कुंलाल २१; वी। बी १ ४; ब्रह्मां। ब्रह्मा ८ १६; ब्रहमां ४ १२; चत्रमुषा। चंत्रमुषा १२; चतुरमुषा ४; चत्रुमुषा ७; चत्रमुषां २१; दावणां। दीवांणां ८; दांवणां १२ २१; दाणव १; जिनि। जिंनिं १२; बिस्व। बिसु १६; जगत्र। जंगत्र २१; जगत १; तणां। तंणां १२; जाचै। जाचैं २१; ईस्वर। ईस्वरं २१; इश्वर ८; मंत्री। - १; मत्री ८; बावला। वावला ४ १२ २१; तंत। तत ८; मंत। मंत्र १; मत ८; अंम्रित। अंमृत १६; अमृत ८; भाषिला। भाषीला १२; पाप। पापु ८; पुनि। पुंन्यि २१; पुंनिं १२; पुंनि १; पुन्यं ४; जाचै। जाचैं १२ २१; डांगिया। डांगीया ४ ७; द्वारै। द्वारौं १२; बिचित्र। बित्र ७; विचित्र १; बचित्र ८ १६; लेषिया। लेषियां २१; धरमराइ। धंमराइ १२; धमराइ ७ ८ २१; धर्मराइ १६; धरमराय ४; प्रतिहार। प्रहिहार ७; प्रतिभार १६; ऐसौ। असौ ८ १२ १६ २१; गोपाल। गोपालं १२

२३८;३ जाचै। जाचैं २१; गांइण। गांईण ४; गांइंण १ १२; गांइणा २१; चत्रु। चत्र १ १२; बेद। बेदा १ ४ २१; गंध्रप। गंध्रब ७; गंधर्प १६; गंद्रप १; जन। जंन १२ २१; अष्टादस। अस्टदस २१; अस्टादस ४; असटादस

तंत मंत बोलै आछिया त्रेता पुरी मंझि काछिया ॥
चंवर ढार जाचै घरि पवनां चेरी सकति जोति ले तीन्यूं भवनां ॥
अंड टूक जाचै बसुमति अैसौ राजा कवलापती ॥
४ जाचै घरां कूरंम सा पालिका सेसनाग सा सेजवालिया ॥
अठारह भार बनासपती मालनी छपन कोटि मेघमाला ॥
जास घरि पणिहारिया नष प्रसेद जाचै सुरसुरी ॥
सात समंद जास बिस्तरी सर्ब जीव जाचै बरतणी ॥
ऐसौ राजा त्रिभुवन धणीं ॥
५ जाचै घरां सनक सनंदन संत कुवार सनकादिक अंबरीष ॥
सुष प्रहिलाद बभीषण हणवंत ॥
नारद धूव ऊधव अक्रूर अनंत कोटि सिध साध ॥
ऐती बरतणि जाचै घरी सकल बियापक अंतरि हरी ॥
नांमदेव प्रणवैं ताकी आंण सकल भगत जाकै नीसांण ॥

सेवीले गोपाल राइ अकुल निरंजन ।
भगति दानु दीजै जाचहि संत जन ॥ रहाउ ॥

१६; पुरांण। पुरांन ८ १२ १६ २१; नागरिया। नांगरिया २१; नागारिया १३; सर्ब। श्रब १ ४ १६ २१; सास्त्र। शास्त्र १३; सासंत्र २१: सासत्र ८ १६; बहुरूपिया। बहुरूपीया ८, मंत। मंत्र १; मत ८; बोलै। बोलैं १६ २१; आछिया। आबिया ७; काछिया। कछिया १; चंवर। चरल १६; चवर १ ७; ढार। ढाल १; ढाले ४; जाचै। जाचैं १२ २१; पवनां। पवन १ ४ १६; चेरी। चडी १; सकति। सक्ति १ २१; ले। - ८; लै १ १३; तीन्यूं। तीन्यौं ७ ८ १६; तीनौं १; भवनां। भवंनां २१; भवन १ ४ १६; अंड। अड १ ८; जाचै। जाकै १ ८; जाचैं २१; बसुमती। बमती ८; बसमती १३, कवलापती। कंवलापती १२ २१

२३८;४ जाचै। जाचैं २१; कूरंम। कूर्म १; कूरम ८ १६, पालिका। पालीका ४; सा। - २१; सेजवालिया। सेजवालियां १३; अठारह। अठार १३; बनासपती। बनांसपती २१; मालनी। मालनि ७: मालनीं १ १६ २१; कोटि। कोडि ७; जास। - १: घरि। - १; घरि पांणीं २१; पणिहारिया। पणिहारियां १३; पनिहारिया ७; पनिहारिगां १; जाचै। जाकै ८ १६: जाचैं २१; सुरसुरी। सुरसरी १ ७; समंद। संमंद २१; समद ८; बिस्तरी। बिसतरी १६; सर्ब। श्रब १ ४ १६ २१; जाचै। जाचैं १ १२ २१; बरतणी। बतंणी २१; बरतणीं १३; बरतणां १ ७ १६; ऐसौ। अैसौ ८ १२ १६ २१; त्रिभुवन। त्रिभुवण २१; त्रिभवण ८; तभुवन १६; धणीं। धंणीं १३ २१; धणी ४ ८

२३८;५ जाचै। जाचैं १३ २१; घरां। घरैं १; सनक। संनक १२ १६ २१; सनंदन। संनदन २१; सनदन ८; संत। संन १; कुवार। कंवार २१; कूंवार १ ४; सनकादिक। सेनकदिक ८; सनकादि १३; अंबरीष। अंमरीष २१; अंब्रीक १३; अंबरीक १६; अब्रीक ८; सुष। सु १; सुक ८ १३; सुष सु ७; प्रहिलाद। प्रहलाद ८; बभीषण। भभीषंण २१; भभीषण ४; बभीषन ८; हणवंत। हंण+ ४; हंणवंत १; हंणवंत २१; हनवंत ८; नारद। नारद २१; धूव। धू १ ८; धू ४; धूव ७; ऊधव। ऊद्धव ४; उधौव २१; अक्रूर। अंकूर ७ १२ २१; अंकूरा ८; अर्कूर ४; अनंत। अंनंत २१; अनत ४ ८; पाहरू। पहरू १६; पहरु ४; ऐती। एती ७ १६; बरतणि। बतणिं १३; बतणि ८; बर्तणि १६; बरतंणिं २१; जाचै। जाचैं १२ २१; घरी। घरि ८; धरी ४ १६; बियापक। बियापिक १; बियापकं २१; अंतरि। अंतर ४; अंतरी ८; प्रणवैं। प्रणवे ४; आंण। आग १६; जाकै। जाकैं २१: जाकौ ८; जाचैं १३; नीसांण। निंसांण १३, नींसांण २१; नींसाण १६

१ जांचै घरि दिगदिसै सराइचा बैकुंठ भवन चित्रसाला ॥
सपत लोक सामानि पूरीअले । जांचै घरि लछिमी कुआरी ॥
चंदु सूरजु दीवडे कउतकु कालु बपुडा ॥
कोटवालु सु करासिरी । सु ऐसा राजा स्री नरहरी ॥
२ जांचै घरि कुलालु ब्रह्मा चतुरमुखु डांव जिनि बिस्व संसारु राचीले ॥
जांकै घरि ईसरु बावला जगत गुरू तत सारखा गिआनु भाखीले ॥
पापु पुंनु जांचै डांगीआ दुआरै चित्र गुपतु लेखीआ ॥
धरमराइ परूली प्रतिहारु । सुो ऐसा राजा स्री गोपालु ॥
३ जांचै घरि गण गंधरब रिखी बपुडे ढाढीआ गावंत आछै ॥
सरब सासत्र बहु रूपीआ अनगरूआ आखाडा मंडलीक बोल बोलहि काछे ॥
चउर ढूल जांचै है पवणु । चेरी सकति जीतिले भवणु ॥
अंड टूक जाचै भसमती । सुो ऐसा राजा त्रिभवण पती ॥
४ जांचै घरि कूरमा पालु सहस्र फनी बासकु सेज वालूआ ॥
अठारह भार बनासपती मालणी छिनवै करोडी मेघ माला पाणी हारीआ ॥
नख प्रसेव जाचै सुरसरी । सपत समुंद जांचै घडथली ॥
एते जीअ जांचै वरतणी । सुो ऐसा राजा त्रिभवण धणी ॥
५ जांचै घरि निकट वरती अरजनु ॥
धू प्रहलादु अंबरीकु नारदु नेजै सिध बुध गण गंधरब बानवै हेला ॥
एते जीअ जांचै हहि घरी । सरब बिआपिक अंतर हरी ॥
प्रणवै नामदेउ तांची आणि । सगल भगत जाचै नीसाणि ॥

२३६

• रांम नांम सुमिरी रे मनां भव बंधन छूटै यातनां ॥
१ रांम नांम भौजल तारिका रांम बांचूं नैंनैंपें आंनका ॥
२ रे मन रांम बिसारिका हीरा कौडी बरै हारि मां ॥
३ रांम नांमां ची करि नाव री ता चढि भौ सागर तिरी ॥
४ रांम नांमां ची मजया गोडी गूंगा की जैसी साकरी ॥
५ रांम नांमां चा करि अभ्यासा रांम नांम सुमिरे नांमदेव दास ॥

२४०

• हरि नांव अंम्रित पषालि मुषां थैं रे।
बहुत ते पांणीं की करै रे ॥

१ आसत्या चा मल लागि लै जिभ्या ॥
ते न छूटति हरि नांव बिगां हो ॥
२ हरि कथा गगिव अस्नांन जला ॥
नांमइया चा स्वांमी ची ऐसी जा हो ॥

२४१

• ऐसै कैसें न मिलंत ते साधू रे ज्यां चा अतरक तरकै न बोधू रे ॥
ज्यां चा निज आंणंद उदबोधू रे ॥
१ ब्रह्म श्रबग तीस दास मिजास आंन नहीं बिसंमि ॥
ते जाणंति अति दूरि गंमि ते भेटति भागि परंम ॥
२ जप तप करवील नुष्टांन धईये धाता धरवील निज ध्यांन ॥
गईए गाता बिबरीरजित ग्यांन ग्यांनां ध्यांनां चा फल ते सजण रे ॥
३ पवनां घालवील पलांण पांऊं चालवील गगन ॥
भूत भवीस कलवील बरतमांन पै त्या साधू चैं न होईल समांन ॥
४ चंद्रा अंमृत सूर्षें सेवील बाहे सागर हेला तरवीली ॥
अस्त जाता रवि धरवील पै त्या साधू ची भट न होईल ॥
५ निज ब्रती चा करावैं निरोधू जीवा सीवा चा भुगावैं आंणंदू ॥
नांमदेव भणै मिलें ते साधू तां चै दरसणैं छूटै भवबंधू ॥

२४२

• बस्त गरीबनि गांम ॥
करुणा स्यंध दींन बे बंधू रहत प्रेम कैं धाम ॥
१ सु मिलत ध्यांन धर्म नहीं रीझत गंमि नाहीं गुण ग्रांम ॥
दींन दुवारि सदा हरि निमसत नांमदेव भणैं उनमांन ॥

२४३

• सुणौ रे अवधू अनभै बांणीं । इन परि पाया अलष बिनांणीं रे ॥

२४०:० अंम्रित। अंमृत ७; पषालि। पषाली ४; मुषां। मुषां ७ २१; थैं। थे ४ ७; बहुत। बहुते २१; पांणीं। पांणी २१; की। कीं ७

२४०:१ आसत्या। आसत्य २१; चा। चां २१; मल। न २१; लै। ले ७; नांव। नांवं ४ २१; हो। - ७

२४०:२ गगिव। गगिवा २१; अस्नान। असनाथ ४ २१; जला। जाला ४ २१; नांमइया। नांमईया ४; नांमां ७; चा। नां ७; स्वांमीं। स्वामीं ७; ऐसी। एही ७; जा। रजा ७; हो। - ७

१ सरोवर सूका कमला फूल्या रे । जल का माछा अगिनें झूल्या रे ॥
२ अगिनि बरिषै अषंड धारा रे । नव पालव भई अठारह भारा रे ॥
३ पांणीं में परबत दह दिसि जलिया रे । दरिया ऊलटि बूंद मैं मिलिया रे ॥
४ अषंड जोतें पतंग मिलिया रे । भणंत नांमदेव संकट टलिया रे ॥

२४४

• सिरजंनहार सुमरि मंन मेरा । पल पल घटै आव मैं तेरा ॥
१ पूजै आयु रहै नहीं पावै । मूरिष काहे न रांमहि गावै ॥
२ कांम क्रोध तजि बिषै बिकारा । राम नांम जपि अम्रित सारा ॥
३ दींन होइ सुक्रित करि लै कोई । अैसा औसर बहुरि न होई ॥
४ निरति सुरति गोबिंद सुष राषी । भणत नांमदेव हरि रस चाषी ॥

२४५

• नांमदे नांमदे साहिब मोरा । मैं भिषारी जंन मांगत तेरा ॥
१ नांव बिनां कही कैसैं जीजै । भाव भक्ति बिसवास स्यौं लीजै ॥
२ नांव बिनां मैं बहु दुष पाया । अंतरि क्रिपा करी रांम राया ॥
३ नांमदेव जंन की पुरवो आसा । न्रिमल नांव मैं दे मोहि बासा ॥

२४६

• म्हारै मंदिर आव हो नरहरी । हूं जावा न देस्यौं नरहरी ॥
१ आगै थकां अगोचर थाइसि । हिरदै थकां म जाइसी हो नरहरी ॥
२ तीनि लोक मैं कहूं न समांनौं । बैसनौं हिरदै समांनौं हो नरहरी ॥
३ अनेक कोटि आगैं उधरिया । धू अबिचल करि राष्यौ हो नरहरी ॥
४ भणंत नांमदेव साहिब मोरा । म्हारौ आवागंवण निंवारि हो नरहरी ॥

२४७

• तू मूझा तूंगा तूं मुझा तूंगा । तूं मुझा कैसें डार देवा ॥
१ कउवा की बिस्टा पीपल उचिस्ठा । घंन चर निकटि गूंचडा भैला ॥
२ सब जग जाईला पैं भगत न जाईला । जनम जमनम नांमदेव नीसांण बाईला ॥
३ प्रणवति नामदेउ इहु जीउ चितवै सु लहै । अमरु होइ सद आकुल रहै ॥

२४८

• ऐसो राम राइ अंतरजामी जैसे दरपन माहि बदन परवानी ॥ रहाउ ॥
१ बसै घटा घट लीप न छीपै बंधन मुकता जातु न दीसै ॥
२ पानी माहि देखु मुखु जैसा नामे को सुआमी बीठुल ऐसा ॥

२४९

१ मन की बिरथा मनु ही जानै कै बूझल आगै कहीऐ ॥
अंतरजामी रामु रवांई मै डरु कैसे चहीऐ ॥
• बेधीअले गोपाल गोसाई । मेरा प्रभु रविआ सरबे ठाई ॥ रहाउ ॥
२ मानै हाटु मानै पाटु मानै है पासारी ॥
मानै बासै नाना भेदी भरमतु है संसारी ॥
३ गुर कै सबदि एहु मनु राता दुबिधा सहजि समाणी ॥
सभो हुकमु हुकमु है आपे निरभउ समतु बीचारी ॥
४ जो जन जानि भजहि पुरखोतमु ताची अबिगतु बाणी ॥
नामा कहै जगजीवनु पाइआ हिरदै अलख बिडाणी ॥

२५०

• तू मेरे तीरथ तू मेरे कासी । बोलगूं रांमहि जो अबिनासी ॥
१ गगनि गंगा भुवनि गंगा । सब बिधि गंगा रांम नांम संगा ॥
२ कोटी तीरथ जौ मन चंगा । रांम कै नांव पषालि लै अंगा ॥
३ नांमदेव भणैं जोगेस्वर सोई । जाकै हिरदै रांम नांम होई ॥

२५१

• अ किवला तैं को को न लूटे । बडे बडे मुनि जन कोई न छूटे ॥
१ तैं लूटचा राजा बलि वांवन । ते र+बि बिगूच्यौ रांवंण ॥
२ तैं कैरू दल सबै सींघारचा । तैं गुर द्रोवंण पितामह मारचा ॥
३ साध संगति मिलि करहु विचारा । नांमदेव नाचै हरि दरबारा ॥

२५२

• सजल जल नीर न दीसै डोला । सघंण घंणवट अमीं चा गोला ॥

१ तलि संसार वरि सरोवर । नीर भरै पणिहारि घरोघर ॥
२ पातालि टिकुली गगन कूवा । बाडी सीचतां माली अंमर हुवा ॥
३ नदी नाव बहै नभि नाभ जोवो री । आंबली चालै तौ नाव भीतरी ॥
४ पाहौ ऐर्णं जलैं जग बुडाला । नांमौं सेवग साहिब चरणैं मुराला ॥

२५३

• मनां सेविया रे हरी नाम ओषदी । जेनैं परम पद पावसी ते ॥
१ सालि पाला कांई सांगसी मजपडा । हरि नांम धडधडा सेवि पारे मना ॥
२ अनेक ओषदी मेलवत का कोडी । हरी नांमैं बोबडी फीटी ले तुझी ॥

२५४

• टाली बाजै टाली बाजै वा । बावै ऐउ दास मनां ॥
१ संसार विष्यापति गहै काउडी । बाई टाली गेली अनं++ली ॥
२ बिदास नामांईया नूं बाई लो टाली । उडाली पाति केली अंत्राली ॥

२५५

• जै जै जै जगदीस हरे । नाम लेत को को न तिरे ॥
१ पतित अजामेल सरणैं आयौ सुत कै हित हरि नांम लियौ ॥
सूवो पढावत गंनिका नारी अधम तिरे तेरे सरणि गये ॥
२ अंबरीष हित चित सौंसुंम स्यौं रटण करत धू अटल करे ॥
सोई जन नांमदेव सुष भरि गायौ नांम लेट को को न तिरे ॥

२५६

• कीजै रे जन मन बैरागी ॥
तन सुभाइ तैसैं ही रहिये हरि हिरदै अनरागी ॥

२५२;० डोला। डौला ४; गोला। गौला ४
२५२;१ वरि। वैरि २१; पणिहारि। पणिहरि २१
२५२;२ टिकुली। टिंकुली २१; सीचतां। सींचतां ४; अंमर। आतीत ४; हुवा। हूवा ४
२५२;३ जोवो। जोवौं २१; आंबली। आबि २१; भीतरी। भींतरी ४
२५२;४ पाहौ। पाहो २१; ऐर्णं। इर्णं २१; जलैं। - २१; जग। ग २१; बुडाला। बूडाला २१; नांमौं। नामी ४; चरणैं। चरंणैं २१

१ श्रीपति गति अंतर की जांनैं तासौं कपट न कीजै ॥
सुध कंवल हरि भजन करहु किं न रांम रसाइंन पीजै ॥
२ सादी भगति भलौ हरि मांनैं बहुत डिंभ नहीं कीजै ॥
नांमदेव कहै अभिमान छाडि करि सब स्यूं दीन रहीजै ॥

२५७

• जीवरा मेरौं गुनहगार । ततो रामु न सुमिरै बारौबार ॥
१ जोनि छाडि जब जुग मै आयौ । लागत पवन षसम बिसरायौ ॥
माया कै रस कहा रे भुलानौ ॥
२ भूले रें मनुषा मलधारी । काम क्रोध तजि जपिलै मुरारी ॥
३ नामा पहरि विनु ते दिन वीते । अंध कूप जल बरषत रीते ॥

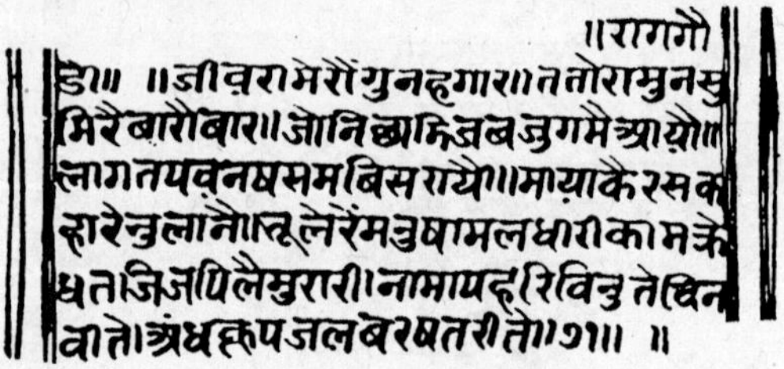
॥रागगौ
डी॥ ॥जीवरा मेरौ गुनहगार॥ ततो रामु न सु
मिरै बारौबार॥ जोनि छाडि जब जुग मै आयो॥
लागत पवन षसम बिसरायो॥ माया कै रस क
हा रे भुलानौ॥ भूले रे मनुषा मलधारी॥ काम क्रो
ध तजि जपिलै मुरारी॥ नामा पहरि विनु ते दिन
वीते॥ अंध कूप जल बरषत रीते॥७१॥ ॥

२५८

• बीठुला देन न जाई माई बीठुला देन न जा माई बीठुल देन न जाई
१ तीनि भुवन को है बलु जाकै वलि पातालि पठायौ ॥
२ निरभौं राजु सुरनि को दीन्हौ । भाग हमारै आयौ ॥
३ विठुल के गुन ऐसे माई । धू निश्चलु जिनि रोप्यौ ॥
४ नामो क स्वामी सीय बहोरी । राज भभीषनु थाप्यौ ॥

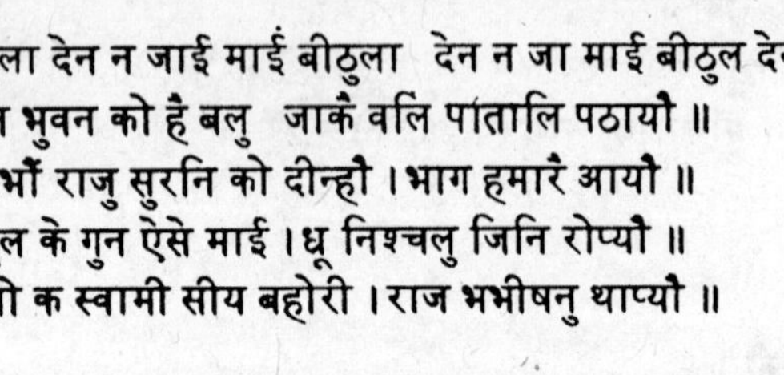
॥रागमारू॥ ॥बीठुला देन न जाई माई वी
ठुला देन न जा माई बीठुल देन न जाई॥ तीनि भु
वन को है बलु जा कै वलि पाताल पठायो॥ नि
रभौ राजु सुरनि को दीन्हो॥ भाग हमारै आयौ॥ वि
ठुल के गुन ऐसे माई॥ धू निश्चलु जिनि रोप्यो॥
नामो क स्वामी सीय बहोरी राज भभीषनु थाप्यो
॥१२३॥

CHAPTER 6

WORD-INDEX

The vast word-index is published as part of the 2 volume *Nirguṇ Bhakti Śabdānukramaṇikā* or *Word-Index of Devotional Hindī Literature* (W.M. Callewaert and B. Op de Beeck, Leuven, 1989). In that publication new editions and reprints are given of the *padas* and/or *sākhīs* of Nāmdev, Kabīr, Raidās, Gorakh, Dādū and Sundardās, along with Word-counts and a complete index with references. The basic purpose of that Word-Index is to make available to scholars parallel passages in *nirguṇ bhakti* literature.

Appendix I

GEYAVIKĀRAS

For a more detailed analysis of the changes brought about by singers, we give in appendix an exhaustive description of these Geyavikāras in the songs of Nāmdev.

Inversions of antarās and lines

We first list the inversions in the songs under *rāg ṭoḍī* (1-47)[1].

The first song of Nāmdev recorded under *ṭoḍī* in the *Guru Granth* has one line found in our song 76, one found in our song 10 and one found in our song 64. For song 5, we find an inverted order of *antarās* in Ms. *a* and Mss. *c/j*. For song 18, under *ṭoḍī* (except for the *Guru Granth,* which has it under *āsā),* an additional *antarā* is found in Mss. *d,a,v, g, j/c* and (with a different reading) in the *Guru Granth.* One *antarā* is omitted in song 20, in Ms. *d.* In song 21, the order is reversed in Ms. *u* (1,3,2,-) --which also drops an *antarā*-- and in Mss. *c/j* (2,1,3,4). In song 22, the order of *antarās* 1,2 is reversed in the Gopāldās *Sarvāṅgī.*

From a study of the irregularities in the versions of song 25, we can clearly see that often not only lines, but also half lines were units the singers could change (for more details, see Ch. 5, critical apparatus). Curious also is the inversion of *antarās* in Ms. *c* (1,3,4,2) and *j* (1,3,2,4). After *antarā* 4, two lines (having a different order of the units) are added in Mss. *u* and *u.* Again, the order of *antarās* is inverted in Ms. *u* for song 26 (2,1) and song 37 (2,1,3,4). In song 42, *antarā* 3 is omitted in Mss. *u, m, p* while in song 47 *antarā* 2 is omitted in Ms. *g.*

In song 48 (the first under *rāg gauḍ)* the order is inverted (1,3,2,4) in Mss. *c/j* and in song 49 we find 2,1,3 in Ms. *a.* In song 50, an *antarā* is added (after 2) in the *Guru Granth.* In Mss. *c/j* the order is 3,2 in song 51. In song 54 (with 5 *antarās) antarā* 2 is dropped and the order of the other lines is changed to 3,4,1,5 in Mss. *c/j.*

Song 59 *(rāg gaur)*

standard	c/j	*GG*
		1
ṭek	*ṭek*	*rahāv*
1	1	2
2	2	2b
3	-	4
4	4	3

(1) For the complete list of *Variations in rāg,* see above, Ch. 2.9.

Antarā 4 is missing in Ms. *u*, which makes 3 the last *antarā*. The omission of the final *antarā* might seem odd, but in this song almost every *antarā* looks like a *bhaṇitā*, giving the poet's name.

Song 61 (*rāg gaur; āsā* in the *GG*)

standard	c/j	*GG*
		1
ṭek	*ṭek*	*rahāv*
1	1	-
2	2	-
3	3	3
4	4	-
5	5	-
6	6	6
7	7	7

The readings of the *Guru Granth* are quite variant from the rather common reading in the Rājasthāni Mss.

Song 62 (*rāg gaur; sāraṅg* in the *GG*)

standard	*GG*
ṭek	*rahāv*
1	3,4
2	-
3	1,2
4	-
5	5,6
6	-

The *antarās* in the *Guru Granth* have 4 lines each, while the others have two-line *antarās*.

Song 63 (*rāg gaur* in all Mss.)

standard	c/j	*GG*
		1
ṭek	*ṭek*	*rahāv*
1	1	2
2	3	3
3	2	4
4	4	-

Song 66 (not in *GG*; all Mss. have it in *rāg gaur*)

standard	Ms. *u*
ṭek	*ṭek*
1	1
2	2
3	3b
4	4

Song 70 (not in *GG*; all have it in *rāg soraṭh*)

standard	c/j	Ms. a
ṭek	*ṭek*	*ṭek*
1	1	3
2	3	2
3	2	1
4	4	4

In song 74 (with 3 *antarās* and uniformly in *soraṭhī*) the order of *antarās* 1,2 and in song 76 (with 4 *antarās* and uniformly in *rāg gauḍī*) the order of *antarās* 2,3 is reversed in Mss. *c/j*. In song 78 (with 4 *antarās* and uniformly in *rāg gauḍī)* the order of *antarās* 2,3 is reversed in the Gopāldās *Sarvāṅgī*. In song 79 (with 4 *antarās* and *rāg gauḍī;* in Ms. *a rāg mālīgauḍī* and in Ms. *u rāg ṭoḍī) antarās* 2,3 are reversed in Mss. *c/j*. In song 84 (which is classified under different *rāgas* and has 2 *antarās)* we find an additional *antarā* after *antarā* 1 in Mss. *c/j*. Interestingly, in song 86 we find an additional *antarā* in Mss. *d, a, g* (not in *c/j)*. The reading of this *antarā* is quite variant in the different manuscripts.

The readings of song 93 (uniformly in *rāmkali;* found in many Mss., not in *GG)* are quite uniform, but the order of *antarās* is not. In Mss. *c/j* the order of *antarās* 1,2 is reversed when compared to the other Mss. In song 94 *(rāg rāmkali* in Mss. *d,a,v,m,p,u,r* and *bhairav* in the *GG)* as in song 91 (see above, Ch. 2.3.a) we notice that smaller units have been interchanged in the different repertoires. In Ms. *a* the last line of *antarā* 1 and the first three of *antarā* 2 are dropped. In the *Guru Granth* the order of the lines of *antarā* is c,d,a,b when compared with the Rājasthānī Mss. Again, in the last *antarā* of the *GG*, the order is c,d,a,b.

In song 95 (with 7 *antarās*, uniformly in *rāg rāmkali;* found in many Mss., not in *GG)* we find additions and omissions: *antarā* 4 is missing in Mss. *a,m,v* and *antarā* 6 is missing in Mss. *a,v,u,g* and *c/j*. We find an additional *antarā* after 5, in several manuscripts (with variant readings).

In song 100 (found in Dādūpanthī collections) one *antarā* is added after 2, in Ms. *a*. In song 109 (also from Dādūpanthī collections) the order of *antarās* 1,2 is reversed in Ms. *u*. Song 111 is found in all the Dādūpanthī collections, uniformly in *rāg basant*, with 4 *antarās;* the order of 1,2 is reversed and *antarā* 3 is dropped in Ms. *a*. The fourth *antarā* is the same in all versions. In song 115 (with uniform *rāg* and readings, except for *antarā* 3) *antarā* 1 becomes the *udgrāha* and an *antarā* is added after 2 in the *Guru Granth*.

In song 117 *(rāg bhairav;* in Ms. *a gaur)* an *antarā* is added after 1 in Ms. *u*. Song 121 is found in all the Rājasthānī collections, under *bhairav*, and with 9 *antarās;* after *antarā* 4 an *antarā* is added in Ms. *u*, while the order of 5,6 is inverted and a line is omitted in *c/j; antarā* 7 is found only in Mss. *u,v,a* and *g*. Song 122 is found in all Rājasthānī Mss., (except *r); antarā* 3 is missing in *c/j*.

For song 125 *(rāg bhairav;* found in all repertoires except Ms. *r)* we see the following pattern:

standard	*GG*
	4
ṭek	*rahāv*
1	-
2	-
3	-
4	-
5	5

In song 135, *antarā* 1 is dropped in Ms. *m*. In Mss. *c/j* the lines of song 136 are different from the 'standard' order: 3ab, 1ab, 2abcd, 1cd, 3cd, and a section of 2b is repeated. Again, in song 137, the order of *antarās* 1,2 is inverted in Mss. *c/j*.

Again, in song 141, the order of *antarās* 3 and 1 is inverted in Mss. *c/j*. The order of the 5 *antarās* in song 142 is different only in Ms. *m*, which has: 1, 4, 2, 3, 5.

Song 195 (relating the miracle of the 'dry bed rescued from the river') is found only in Ms. *d* (1636 AD) and in Ms. *p*, where it has 2 additional *antarās*. Song 206 is found in only three repertoires: (*Pañcavāṇī*) Ms. *a*, the *Guru Granth* (which gives *antarā* 1 as *udgrāha*) and the Fatehpur Ms. For the rather complicated differences in these repertoires, see above, Ch.5, where the three texts are given separately. Song 225 (only in Mss. *a* and *r*) appears under a different *rāg* in each Ms.; the order of the first 2 *antarās* is reversed. For song 233 an *antarā* is added to the refrain in Ms. *d*. Song 234 (with 5 *antarās*) is found in several Mss. (under *rāg rāmkali*) and in Ms. *m* (under *mālīgaur*). The order of *antarās* in Ms. *m* is quite different from the standard: it omits *antarā* 3 and the order is 1,4,2,5.

Fillers

The 'old' song 19 is found in 11 Rājasthānī manuscripts and in the *Guru Granth*. The 16-12 *sār* structure is obvious in the *antarās*, though not in the *ṭek*. In line 2b we note fillers which are different in the different repertoires. If we read *lai* in

ānilai kumbha bhārāilai ūdika (2a)

as a short syllable, we have a 16 *mātrā* structure. Verse 2b

rājakuvāri pulandari

has a smooth 4+4+4 *mātrika* structure. In all the versions we see that 2 *mātrā* fillers have been added to v. 2b (*e*, *ye* and *lā*)[2]. The manuscripts *c/j* have the *stobha* '*lā*' instead of *e*, in an attempt to make the *stobha* rhyme with *lā* in the other lines. The addition of *e* or *lā* turns the 12 *mātrā* line into a 14 *mātrā* line; thus, a stretching of only 2 more *mātrās* is needed to arrive at 16, required for the *āvarta* which the *antarās* clearly point at. This filler reduces the *varṇa-prakarṣa*. What happened with the other 12 *mātrā* lines, where no filler was added? Only musical stretching? It is hard to tell, but it seems likely, for it is hard to imagine what else could have been done. Perhaps the *e* was needed at the end of the line because the syllable with which the line ends, namely an *i* (in *pulandari*), is a short syllable and less suitable for stretching.

Song 20 is another old song, found in most repertoires. For line 1.1 (14 *mātrās*, to be stretched), the singers of the repertoires of Ms. *g* add *je tain* before the line, Mss. *c/j* add *jo*. We must remember that in an

(2) It appears that *e* and *ye* are two versions of the same *stobha*, reminding us of the *Gītagovinda* and the Rājasthānī-Gujarātī songs of the 15th century *Kānhaḍāde Prabandha*. This filler is rare in Nāmdev's songs (see song 135), with the variant spelling *ai*. For the *Gītagovinda*, see the second *aṣṭapadī* "*śritakamalākucamaṇḍal. dhṛtakuṇḍala e*". In his 15th century commentary *Rasikapriyā*, the Mevār king and musicologist Kumbha writes that the syllable *e* was to be used as the basis for a free, purely musical passage: *atra 'e'kārādyālāpo jñeyaḥ*, showing that *e* was a *stobha* (see The Nirnaya Sagar edition, p. 18).
For the *Kānhaḍade Prabandha*, see K.B. Vyās, ed., (published by the Rajasthan Purātattva Mandir, Jaipur, 1953), pp. 95, 195, 60. See also above, Ch. 2.1.

āvarta the addition before the line will actually come at the end in repeated singing.

In song 22 we note the fillers *jau laga* and *tau laga* in several repertoires, before the *ṭek*

rāma nāmai hita na bhayau
merī merī karatā janama gayau.

These additions help to make the meaning more definite, but they also serve a musical need. The first line of the *ṭek* has 13 *mātrās,* which can be smoothened out to 14 if we make the *rā* of *rāma* a *pluta*. Still we are 2 *mātrās* short of the 16 required by the *āvarta*. Both long syllables of the filler of the first line have to be sung short. The second line gives a 18 *mātrā* count, which may be reduced by singing the first *merī* to 2 *mātrās* instead of 4. Other singers seem to have sung both *merī's* to 2 *mātrās* each, so that they could add the *tau lag* to complement *jau lag*. It is actually the first line which needs a filler.

We have a curious phenomenon in song 3, where only line 2 of the *ṭek* has a neat 16 *mātrā* line. But the other lines too can be made to fit this pattern, common to most songs of this group, with some squeezing of syllables. If in

dāsa nāmdeva prema bhagati antari jau jāgai

we leave out *dās nāmdeva,* we again have a good 16 *mātrā* line. This *bhaniṭā* requires 8 (actually 9) *mātrās* for itself. Its addition suggests that the *āvarta* used was of 8 and not 16 *mātrās*. Thus, the final line would have needed 3, not 2, *āvartas*. Add this odd phenomenon -- it makes us think that *dās nāmdeva* is an addition[3] -- to the doubts we already have about the song, and we may perhaps conclude that the song is not of Nāmdev.

In song 51, it is more clear how the filler is something that can be added to a song, something detachable. We read *only* in Mss. *c/j* the filler *bālā*, at the beginning of 0b, and 4b. To the line 4d

mohi ṣei utāro pāra,

we find the filler *ho* added in Ms. *n*. This perhaps also indicates that the 14 *mātrā* lines in this song were actually to be sung to 16 *mātrās*.

In line 1b of song 59 most singers must have stretched the line in singing in order to get the full *āvarta;* in Ms. *u* we find the filler *jyū*, before *bāchā*.

In song 64, most lines have a 16-12 pattern; the 16 *mātrā āvarta* is clear from lines 1a, 1b. In some Mss. the common filler *re* is added in several repertoires. Similar fillers (*re* or *ho*) are found in songs 65, 67, 70 etc., in some manuscripts.

In song 78, we find the filler *re* in an unusual place: the middle of line 2b. Interestingly, we find *sab* instead, in several Mss., while in Ms. *a,* there is no filler at all, giving us a 14 *mātrā* line, perhaps the line as it originally stood.

Song 82 has quite some variants in the different manuscripts. It has a clear 16-12 pattern. In line 0a *aisai* seems to be detachable; instead we read *santo* in Ms. *p* and *bhāī re* in Mss. *u* and *r*.

---

(3) In manuscripts *c* and *j*, the scribes wrote a bar after *dās nāmdev;* this suggests that the singers may have thought of it as an independent unit.

In song 96, line 1d, the filler *jo* (or *je* in some Mss.) was added to reduce the *varṇa-prakarṣa* at the end. The expression *re avadhū* seems to be a filler, not found in all manuscripts, and a few times found only partly. *Re avadhū* is an address found in a Nāth context.

Most often the filler is added at the beginning or at the end of a line. One exception is found in song 78. Another is song 116, found in 3 manuscripts: line 0b may have been a 12 *mātrā* line, where *ho bāp* (see above, song 50) was added. The reason for this hypothesis is that the reading in the repertoire (Ms. *d)* gives *bābā* (another typical filler; see song 94) instead of *ho bāp*. In song 103 many pairs of lines have the 16-14 structure. In line 0b *aru* seems to be added in Mss. *c/j*. Most lines in song 118 are either 16-12 or 16-14 *mātrā* lines; in line 1a we notice an addition of *hī* in the *Guru Granth*. The rest of the song has no signs of a filler, even in lines which could have had one.

In song 131 *ho* is added in many lines, often in all repertoires and we cannot know whether it is a filler. At the end of 0d, however, *ho* is missing in Ms. *j (c* has it). Ms. *a* does not have *in*, showing that perhaps we have two fillers, without which there would be a 12 *mātrā* line. The function of *ho* as a filler is evident in line 1b (a 13 *mātrā* line), where it is found in several manuscripts. In Ms. *u* the filler is *jī* instead. It is interesting to see how in line 2b several alternatives are available: *jī*, or *tau* and *ho*. As in song 19, we notice that *lā* (in the *Guru Granth;* line 2d) acts as a filler. To line 3b (12 *mātrā) ho* or *jī* is added in several repertoires.

In songs 135 and 136 we find the fillers *e* and *re*, at the end of every line. This is suggested by the fact that in some repertoires we read *ye* or *he*, or in others it is dropped. In song 136 *re* is clearly a filler, omitted in Mss. *c/j*. In line 2a the filler *jā sau* (to be read as 2 *mātrās)* is omitted in Mss. *c/j*.
In song 141 *mere* (or *mhāre)* seems to be added as a filler. In line 0b *ho* is added in Ms. *m*. In 0c *re* or *ho* is added, and *mere* in 0d is missing from Ms. *u*. Similar additions and omissions in particular repertoires can be seen in the other lines too.

In song 163 --with a 16 *mātrā* pattern-- we find, amazingly, no filler. Only in later manuscripts (see the edition of Miśra:1964) every 12 *mātrā* line has an additional *re*. In song 164 we have regular 16 *mātrā* lines, along with 8 or 10 *mātrā* lines. In 0c, the 8 (or 9) *mātrā* line is --in some repertoires-- completed with the address *bīṭhalā*. This filler is added a few times more further in the song, always in the same repertoires.

'Varying the beat'

In song 15, line 0a, *bāpa* (or *rāma* in some repertoires) is redundant in a perfect 16 *mātrā* line. But without it, we have too many *gurus*. The introduction of *bāp* adds spice by turning some *gurus* into *laghus;* this must have been welcome, especially in the *ṭek* line which is sung again and again.

In line 3a of song 16 we notice that in two distinct singing traditions *(u* and *c/j)* there is an identical variant: *lā* is added to a line where, apparently, it is not needed:

nirbānai pad koi eka cīnhai.

The line has a good 16 *mātrā* pattern, even without *eka* (or *ka* in Ms. *u*). One obvious reason for adding *lā* is the fact that many lines in the song end that way. But there could also be a 'musical' reason: the addition of *lā* varies the simple and heavy *guru + guru* cadence to a more sprightly *laghu + guru + guru* rhythm.

In song 20 we again have quite uniform readings, except for the filler in line 1a, discussed above. In line 3a

syambhadeva kī sevā jānai

an 'addition' in Ms. *g (je tu)* changes the cadence of 2 *gurus* into *laghus*. Similarly, in song 23, line 1b, *jyū* seems to be added (in Ms. *d*) to break the monotony of the two *gurus* at the end of the line. Such a filler, at the beginning of the line, will in effect be sung at the end. That should render *māḍai* into two *laghus*, adding a *guru* just before the *sam* on *udika*[4].

In song 36, line 1a, *hiradai chipā* may have sounded too plain to some singers; in Ms. *a* a singer inserted *mahī* between the two words. The intention *might* have been to break the cadence and introduce a variation. In song 41, we notice a 8-8 *mātrika* division. In line 0b we find, instead of *abhāgā, abhāg* in two manuscripts, apparently to arrive at a *laghu + pluta + laghu*, to meet the *āvarta* instead of a *laghu* followed by two *gurus*. In three manuscripts *su* is inserted after *bisāryau*, possibly with the idea of uttering the first part of the line as *mai tu bisaryau su;* this breaks the last *guru* into 2 *laghus* and produces a more dramatic movement in the *sam* (if it is taken after 8 *mātrās*) or in the *khālī* if this is not so. A similar phenomenon is seen in song 42, where in one Miśra:1964 manuscript *e* is added after *bolanahār*, in order to break the monotony of the *gurus*.

In song 48 we find a variant line for 1a, with the filler *devā* in repertoires *c/j*. Without this filler we have a good 16 *mātrā* line, similar in metrical pattern to the line found in most repertoires. What then is its purpose? We notice that the final cadence in the *c/j* line has 2 *gurus*. The introduction of *devā* --if it does not change the place of the *sam*-- varies the cadence to *mopai devā;* as a result all *gurus* are read as *laghus*. A similar phenomenon, introduced with a similar purpose, is found in line 3a.

In song 54, 0b, *nara* is inserted before *lājai* in repertoire *p*. In song 56, 0b, a later singer (Miśra:1964) added *hai* after *kaune*. In song 62, the heavy flow of *guru* syllables at the end of line 4b

kanaka kāminī bāndhyau moha

is broken by the addition of *aise* before *kanik*, but only in the *Guru Granth*[5]. In song 76, line 4b, *jāke* which looks like a filler, is actually added to a well-formed 16 *mātrā* line. Evidently, the purpose was to break the *gurus* at the end. This 'addition' is missing in Mss. *c/j*.

(4) The readings here give *udika* and not *ūdika*, but in singing the *u* must have been rendered a *guru*, as the metre demands, especially since *ū* seems to be placed on the *sam*. The vowel on the *sam* tends to be stressed and elongated if there is room to do so, as in this case.

(5) In the 'regular' line, the 4th and 5th *mātrā* are covered by one *guru*. This should not disturb the flow of the *caturasra*, but adds spice to it. Such lines are not uncommon in these songs.

Again, in song 79, line 4a, an 'addition' *(re* after or *nara* before *kahā)* is added in the second part of the line, in some repertoires, with the same purpose.

In song 95 the filler *nārad* has been added in several repertoires (see above), except for line 2b, where it does *not* serve to fill in an empty space. There, in several repertoires, *nārad* is added for an opposite purpose: to break the two *gurus* at the end of the line into four *laghus, pávái nárád.*

In song 97, line 1a, we are not certain if *re avadhū* is a real filler, since it is found in all repertoires. In Ms. *u* the 'addition' *terī* seems to have been brought in to turn all the *gurus* into *laghus.* It would appear that, in song 118, 2a, the original line *might* have been *basudhā basi kīnhī rājā,* to which different 'additions' have been made in different repertoires. In this line there seems to be a tendency, not only to fill in the empty *mātrās* but also to introduce *laghus* into the flow of *gurus.*

In song 122, 0b, all repertoires give an (additional) *hī,* without which the line would have been a well-formed 16 *mātrā* line, consisting only of *gurus.* Besides that, we notice another addition, of *tohi,* only in repertoires *c/j,* at the beginning of the line. In song 132, line 0b does not need the 'filler' *hari kau,* found in all repertoires (except Ms. *a);* the 15 *mātrā* line can easily be stretched to 16 by turning *ā* in *dāsa* into a *pluta.* Otherwise, the song has fine 16 *mātrā* lines, alternating with lines which have 14 *mātrās.* It would look as if *hari kau* is not really a filler, but an 'addition' made to relieve the burden of the *gurus* at the end, breaking them into *laghus.*

Appendix 2

GLOSSARY

Āgam (Skt. *āgama,* lit. 'that which has come down') is the general term for ancient texts of great, almost canonical authority. The term is especially current among Śaivites and Tāntriks. The Āgamas are often referred to along with Nigamas, which are Vedic texts or explanations of the Vedas. To the Sants, the terms probably meant nothing more than 'a sacred text'.

Ajāmil was, according to the Bhāgavat Purāṇ, a high-caste Brahman who lived with a low-caste slave-woman. He was a despicable rogue and made his living through stealing, gambling and cheating. The youngest of his ten sons was called Nārāyān, which is also a name for Viṣṇu. When suddenly Ajāmil died, his mind was on his beloved son Nārāyaṇ. This saved him from the fires of hell, since the messengers of death who had come to drag him away were powerless against one who was thinking of Nārāyān. Ajāmil's story is popular in *bhakti* literature as an example of the great power of the Lord's name.

Anāhad (Skt. *anāhata,* or 'without friction, absence of the act of striking') is often used in the full expression *anāhad nād* or 'the frictionless sound, the sound which sounds without being struck'. The Nāthas, who exercised a great influence on the Sants, believed that the cosmos resounds ceaselessly with the soundless *anāhat nād.* Only the yogī --one who has succeeded in controlling his breath, sexual energy and mind-- can hear it. As one progresses on the path of Haṭh-yoga one becomes open to inner sounds. The first sound one hears is a roar like that of the sea. Gradually the sound becomes subtler: the roar of the sea gives way to the rumble of clouds, which mellows down to the sound of a trumpet, of a cymbal, a conch, a bell, a flute and a vīnā-string until it dissolves completely, turning into the 'soundless' *anāhad.*

Aṣṭa-siddhi. Siddhis are supernatural qualities generally listed as eight:
1. *aṇimā:* the power to assume the size of an atom;
2. *laghimā:* the power to become weightless;
3. *prāptiḥ:* the power to obtain anything at will;
4. *prākāmya:* an irresistible will or command;
5. *mahimā:* the power to increase to any great size;
6. *iṣitva:* the power to rule over anyone;
7. *vaśitva:* the power to control anyone;
8. *kāmāvaśāyitā:* the power to overcome desire.

Aṭhār bhār, lit. 'the eighteen weights'. In Santa literature the phrase is used to denote 'the entire greenery or vegetation of the world'. The phrase has its origins --perhaps unknown to the Sants-- in ancient Indian botany, which describes not only the form and function of plants but also their weight. The total weight of the plant world was said to measure eighteen *bhāras*. One *bhār* was an immensely large unit made up of 38.112.170 smaller units, constituted by the 'weights' of the leaves of different categories of plants. For further details, see A. Nāhṭā, *Aḍhār bhār vanaspati kā vivaraṇ*, in: *Vāradā*, April 1968, 33-35.

Dhruv. The legend of Dhruv is famous in Vaiṣṇav lore. All *bhakti* poets, both *nirguṇ* and *saguṇ* refer to him as an ideal *bhakta*. His story is told in many Purāṇas.

Brahma's son, Manu Svayambhuv, had two sons, Priyavrat and Uttanapād, both great kings. Uttanapād had two wives, Suruci and Sunīti, and two sons, Dhruv and Uttam. Uttam's mother Suruci was her husband's favourite, while Sunīti was badly neglected. One day, at the age of five, Dhruv saw his father in the company of Suruci, with his younger brother Uttam sitting in his lap. Dhruv too wanted to sit there, but his father would not allow it and Suruci disdainfully mocked Dhruv, saying: "If you wish to sit on your father's seat, try first to be born as my son; only my son can sit there". Dhruv ran away crying to his mother Sunīti, who was unable to do anything. She told him that only Lord Viṣṇu could remove his sorrow. Dhruv decided to worship Viṣṇu; he became a mendicant and left his father's capital for the forest. The great sage and famous *bhakta* Nārad heard of this and tried to dissuade the child from this rash step. When he could not succeed, Nārad taught Dhruv the path of *bhakti*. Dhruv came to the Yamunā and began to meditate on Viṣṇu with total concentration, his breath under complete control. As he stopped to breathe the whole world stopped breathing, since Dhruv had become one with Viṣṇu. Fearing that the boy might acquire their power, the gods came to Viṣṇu for help. Viṣṇu set their fears at rest and appeared before Dhruv, who thus had his desires fulfilled. Although he did not want anything else, he was given the boon of 'a seat above all': an abode in the star Dhruv (polar star), which remains stationary, while all other stars move around it.

Elephant. The story of the elephant who was saved by Viṣṇu was very popular in *bhakti* literature. It is narrated in the 8th *skandha* of the Bhāgavat Purāṇ.

An alligator caught an elephant by the foot while he was sporting in a forest lake with other elephants. The elephant could not free himself and as he went down his last sounds were *rrr*, which is half the name of Rām. God saved him.

Hunter. Krishna died at the hands of a hunter while resting under a tree. The hunter mistook Krishna's foot for an animal and shot a fatal arrow. Realising what he had done, the hunter begged for forgiveness. Krishna not only forgave him but sent him to heaven, declaring that what the hunter had done was Krishna's own will. Later commentaries on the Purāṇ add that any contact with Krishna, even that of killing him, will grant salvation.

Kali or Kali-age. The Hindu cyclic view of time divides each full turn of the wheel of time into four ages: Sat, Tretā, Dvāpar and Kali (which is the present age). Sat is the golden age, when *dharma* and morality flourish. Kali, meaning 'strife, quarrel' is the evil age, when morality loses its hold over people. This age began with the death of Krishna.

Meru, or Mahāmeru in the Purāṇas, is believed to be a golden peak in the Himalayas. It is the seat of Śiva, a heavenly region where only the blessed can go. It is so high that it serves as a support for the heavens.

Mārkaṇḍey was one of the most respected sages in ancient times. The power of his austerities and his wisdom was so great that he was granted eternal life: he could live even during *pralay* (the epoch of destruction) and witness the total deluge at the end of each cycle of existence, when every being, even the gods dissolve into a state of virtual non-being.

The Purāṇas tell an intriguing story about Mārkaṇḍey, who wanted to see how Lord Viṣṇu's *māyā* brings about the diversity in creation. This demand looked unreasonable, for if Mārkaṇḍey knew *māyā* he would no longer perceive it. The Purāṇas relate the harrowing experience Mārkaṇḍey went through. For more details, see the Bhāgvat Purāṇ, 12.9.

Moon, see Sun

Nāth. The Nāthas belong to a yogic order of Śaivites whose doctrines and spiritual techniques incorporated elements of Tāntrik thought and practice. Their (legendary) founder is believed to have been Matsyendranāth, who may have lived in the 9th century A.D. The most famous of the Nāthas was Gorakhnāth (floruit 10th century?), whose influence was great in the religious thought and practice of mediaeval India. Many Nāth works --in both Hindī and Sanskrit-- are found in manuscripts of the 17th century. The word *nāth* or 'lord' in the Nāth literature stands both for a perfected yogī or *siddha* such as Matsyendra or Gorakh (tradition names 84 *siddhas)*, and for the highest state of bliss and liberation.

Nav nidhi. The 'nine treasures' are said to be the nine jewels of Kuber, the god of wealth These jewels are named Padma, Mahāpadma, Śankha, Makar, Kacchap, Mukunda, Nanda, Nīl and Kharva. They are also personified as attendants of Kuber or of Lakṣmī, the consort of Viṣṇu and goddess of wealth.

Interestingly, Padma, Mahāpadma etc., are also terms for very large numbers. Padma stands for 1,000 million, Mahāpadma for an even larger number. Śankha stands for 100 billions and Kharva for a figure of 1 followed by 37 zeros. Many Sants were probably unaware of these mathematical details. For them, *nav nidhi* was another word for 'divine treasures'.

Prahlād is, like Dhruv (see above), a legendary Vaiṣṇav *bhakta*. The story of Prahlād is told in many Purāṇas. The version of the story Nāmdev and other Sants had in mind was certainly that of the Bhāgvat Purāṇa.

Prahlād was a son of Hiraṇyakaśipu, a demon king who had subdued the three worlds. Hiraṇyakaśipu was arrogant and thought he was greater than anyone else. When Prahlād was of school age he was sent to the house of Ṣaṇḍa and Amarka, two Brahman teachers. One day Hiraṇyakaśipu wanted to find out how his son was studying and asked him: "Tell me, son, what is it that you consider as good?"

Prahlād replied: "A man should give up all thought of self and ego and seek shelter with Hari. This is the good." Hiraṇyakasipu was startled and vexed with this answer, but he laughed it away as the foolish babblings of a child. He instructed the teachers to be more careful and sent his son back to his studies. Prahlād's teachers tried to draw him away from his inborn inclination toward *bhakti,* but he remained firm in his devotion to Viṣṇu. He even began to preach the doctrine of *bhakti* to his teachers, calling that the highest truth. The Brahmans severely punished the prince and tried to teach him the art of politics.

After some time Hiraṇyakaśipu called Prahlād once again and lovingly asked what he had learnt. In reply Prahlād told his father the various ways for a man to adore and worship Viṣṇu. Prahlād's teachers excused themselves, saying that this was not what they had taught the prince. "Who then is your teacher?" Hiraṇyakaśipu asked. Prahlād: "Men are naturally attached to Viṣṇu, only the deluded are not". Enraged, Hiraṇyakaśipu gave orders to kill Prahlād, but nothing could harm the boy. At the teachers' request Prahlād was then sent back to school. They were convinced the boy was still young and would learn as he grew mature. But Prahlād began to preach his doctrine of *bhakti* to his fellow students. The matter was reported to the king, who asked Prahlād. "On whose strength do you rely when you ignore my orders?" Prahlād: "I rely on Viṣṇu who is not only my strength, but the basis of your strength too". "Where is this Viṣṇu", Hiraṇyakaśipu asked; pointing at a pillar, he said: "If he is everywhere as you say, let him come out of this pillar and save you as I personally cut off your head". Hiraṇyakaśipu unsheathed his sword, but Viṣṇu appeared from the pillar in the form of Nar-hari or Nar-singha (Man-lion) and disemboweled Hiraṇyakaśipu in a fierce battle.

Prayāg is the ancient name for the city of Allahabad. In Prayāg the river Yamunā meets the Gaṅgā. Another river, called the Sarasvatī. is also said to meet the Gaṅgā here, although it remains invisible and is believed to follow a subterranean path. The confluence (Triveṇī) of these three rivers is a very holy site, and millions go to bathe there. In Santa literature Prayāg or Triveṇī was the name for the confluence of three mystic channels in the body, called *iḍā, piṅgalā* and *suṣumnā*. This was an important concept in Tāntrik yoga and in Nāth lore and it greatly influenced the Sants.

Prostitute. The Bhāgvat Purāṇa relates the story of the prostitute named Piṅgalā who turned to God in her disappointment and found peace. See Bh. P., 11th Skandha, 8.

Puruṣ, (lit. 'man'). What is meant by *puruṣ* in poem 100 seems to be similar to the Sāmkhya *puruṣ* who 'stands aloof'. Nāmdev shows awareness of Sāmkhya categories in poems 11, 57, 77 and 97.

Sāmkhya is a system of dualism which accepts two ultimate 'reals', *puruṣ* (pure consciousness) and *prakriti* (the phenomenal world). All creatures are different combinations of the three prime *guṇas* or elements: *sattva, rajas* and *tamas*. *Prakṛti* is dead matter, devoid of all awareness. What gives it a semblance of consciousness, as in the awareness of man, is its closeness to *puruṣ*. Though totally different in nature, *puruṣ* is drawn to *prakrti* and becomes attached to it. Its pure awareness thus becomes phenomenal. It becomes tied to *prakrti*, a tie which must be cut if *puruṣ* is to rest once again in its pure, objectless consciousness.

Sahaj (lit., 'born with, spontaneous, natural') denotes that which is part of oneself, which one does not have to make an effort to obtain. *Sahaj* or *sahaj bhāv* ('the state of *sahaj*') is an important concept in Santa literature. It may be translated as 'absence of conscious or strained endeavour'. A strained effort, according to the Sants (including Nāmdev) leads one away from the true path. Devotion to God should become an innate, spontaneous activity gushing forth like a self-born, natural spring. Effort, they said, was to be directed towards achieving the *sahaj* state which, once achieved, creates an effortless state of ceaseless, unwavering devotion.

Sahasrār cakra, lit. 'the thousand-spoked wheel'. According to Tāntrik yoga, the human body houses both Siva and Śakti. Śiva is the supreme truth, the final state of immortality, freedom and bliss. This state can be reached if Śiva is united with Śakti, the energy which pulsates in every activity, human or cosmic. Siva dwells in the *sahasrār cakra*, which is said to be situated at the top of the skull. It has the form of a thousand-petalled lotus facing downwards. Śakti lies in another *cakra*, called *mūlādhār*, situated near the bottom of the spinal column. Between the *mūlādhār* and the *sahasrār*, at different points along the spine, lie five other centres (*cakras*). With his (physical and) spiritual efforts the yogī must move the Śakti upwards through a subtle vein called *suṣumnā*, which runs through the middle of the spine. Crossing the five *cakras* Śakti is united with Śiva in the *sahasrār cakra*. See also *KV*, p. 130.

Sanak. As a mind-born son of Brahma, this mythical *rishi* was a famous *bhakta*. He and his brothers San, Sanatkumār and Sanandan are also said to be companions or counsellors of Viṣṇu.

Song 165 is largely in Marāṭhī. It is found in printed editions of Nāmdev's *abhangas* where it is ascribed to Viṣṇudās Nāmā[6]. It looks as if the song was borrowed by Rājasthānī singers directly from the Marāṭhī repertoires, but they greatly transformed it. To a Rājasthānī audience the song would have made sense --to whatever extent it did make sense-- only with 'Rājasthānī meanings'. This implies that phrases with a particular meaning in Marāṭhī, probably meant something totally different in Rājasthānī. E.g., *nar līje hvai tānḍe* found in all our manuscripts (except for *luṅje* instead of *līje*). In Marāṭhī this phrase reads as *vānar līṅje hvou ṭhāḍe*. The meanings of the two phrases are different, but in Rājasthān it must have been understood as *nar līje* or *lūṅje hvai ṭānḍe*, however obscure that may be.

We have attempted a translation with this idea in mind, having recourse to the Marāṭhī reading only in one case where the Hindī or Rājasthānī gave us no sense at all.

Besides this, the song uses the code language (*ulaṭ-bānsī*) of the Sants. It is not a straightforward code-language and quite a few

(6) See *Nāmdev Gāthā*, p. 593, No. 2126; p. 608, No. 2181.

words have several meanings. It must have had specific regional meanings too, besides being mixed up with purely poetic expressions where images carry their own suggestive meanings, functioning in ways quite different from a code. One wonders what a Rājasthānī audience made of this[7].

Sun (and Moon). Following the practices current in Tāntrik Buddhism and among the Nāthas, the Sants used ordinary words in a technical, often yogic sense. They had a code which was essential to understand their otherwise puzzling sayings. 'Sun' and 'moon' are such code words.

Tāntrik Kuṇḍalinī Yoga taught that within the human body subtle processes take place which the yogī should know and control. These 'subtle' inner processes have been conceived in terms of centres (see also above, *sahasrār cakra)*, veins and powers. The centres *(cakra)* are situated in different places between the base of the spine to the top of the skull. The lowest centre is called *mūlādhār*, lit. (the 'root base'). It contains a 'power' known as the Sun. This Sun has twelve phases *(kalā)* and its 'heat' causes the inner waters of life or immortality *(amrit)*, which pour down from the Moon above, to evaporate. The Moon has sixteen phases *(kalā)*, but it has no power of its own. When through control of mind and breath the yogī can 'transfer' four *kalās* of the Sun to the Moon, then the Sun and the Moon are in balance and Śiva is united with Śakti. Then also the yogī can drink the waters of immortality.

Surabhī is another name for Kāmdhenu, the wish-fulfilling cow of the gods. It is surprising to find *surabhī* in the metaphor of 'one who can lead across the ocean'.

Trilochan is well-known in Santa literature as an early *bhakta*. He is quoted in the *Guru Granth* and in many Rājasthānī manuscript collections. None of the songs in the *Guru Granth* are found in the Rājasthānī collections. In the *Parcaī* of Trilochan by Anantadās (edition forthcoming), we find no mention of Nāmdev, nor is Trilochan mentioned in the *Nāmdev Parcaī* (see above, Ch. 1.3).

In the *Bhaktamāl* of Nābhādās we read that Nāmdev and Trilochan were co-disciples of Jñāndev of the Viṣṇusvāmī sect *(chappay* 48, p. 342). This seems to have been part of the traditions popular among the Sants and explains why we find songs of Nāmdev addressed to Trilochan.

Vaiṣṇav. The Sants were not Vaiṣṇav in the strict sense: they believed in a formless God, without idol-worship or sectarian denominations. Yet we find frequent references to the need to be a 'Vaiṣṇav'. In Santa literature, it should be noted, the term Vaiṣṇav does not have a sectarian meaning; it means 'a good, saintly person', contrasted with *śākta* or 'low, ungodly person'. We read in Kabīr:

Better is the she-dog of a Vaiṣṇava
than the mother of Śākta:
The one keeps listening to Hari's praise

---

(7) We are gratefully indebted to Prof. S.G. Tulpule, Pune, for his valuable suggestions in interpreting this song.

and the other goes to buy sin[8].

Or

Kabīr, there are no Śāktas,
regard them all as Vaiṣṇava.
But that mouth which utters not the Name of Rām
brings ruin to the body[9].

In both quotations the Vaiṣṇav is a good person, a *bhakta* uttering the name of Rām, as opposed to an evil person who ignores the Name.

We find a few interesting, unknown songs quoted in the anthology of Gopāldās[10]. In the Chapter 'On saintly persons' *(sādh'kau aṅg),* Gopāldās gives a section entitled *baisno mahimā* or The greatness of a Vaiṣṇav'. Along with the famous verse:

nāhi vasāmi vaikuṇṭha yoginām hridaye na ca
madbhakta yatra tisthanti tatra tisthāmi nārada,

we read song 95 of Nāmdev and a song by Bīsau and one by Chaturbhuj. In his song Bīsau emphasizes that a *sajan* (Skt. *sajjana)* and a Vaiṣṇav are identical because they are *bhaktas.*

Let me tell you who is a Vaiṣṇav:
He who keeps Supreme Rām in his heart.
Day after day he drinks from the udder of the Word,
he sees Viṭṭhal in all beings,
he gives up thoughts of lust and greed,
he controls the evil passions,
he looks at living beings like a knower-of-the-Self,
he speaks with a pure tongue and
practices *bhakti* within, ceaselessly,
he does not show it outside and
lives alone or in the company of the good.
He sings the glory of Govind.
The good man never thinks of body or wealth,
he does not fancy the love of a woman.
Bīsau says: the sight of such a Vaiṣṇav
burns up a million sins.

In the next song, by Chaturbhuj, the terms *sādh* and Vaiṣṇav are used in turn and as synonyms. The song is a long tract setting forth the Vaiṣṇav-Sādh ideal, in a *nirguṇ* framework. We translate a few lines only:

He is conscious of nothing, aware of nothing,
keeps Rām in his heart day and night.
He controls the senses and
follows the instructions.
He does not fall into the delusion of 'me' and 'other',
forgives pain and does not give up *dharma:*
These are the characteristics of a *sādhu.*
Seeing him destroys million guilts.

---

(8) *KV,* p.266, in 'True Asceticism', *sākhi* 10.
(9) *KV,* 27, in 'Apprehending the Essence'. For the opposition between Vaiṣṇavas and Śāktas in Kabīr, see *KV,* p. 105-106.
(10) See above, Ch. 2.4.V.

Chaturbhuj, I relate the greatness of a Vaiṣṇav.

The song continues with adjectives and metaphors characteristic for Santa literature: "A Vaiṣṇav brings the Sun and the Moon together in one place", "He realizes his *nirguṇ* essence, and is happy remembering the greatness of Hari". In the same Chapter Gopāldās gives another section, entitled *Siddha ke Lakhyan*.

Appendix 3

BIBLIOGRAPHY

For an extensive bibliography related to Nāmdev, classified chronologically, we refer to Chapter 1.2. In our text, these titles are referred to as e.g. N. Singh:1981.
A bibliographical list of 236 (mainly) Marāṭhī titles has appeared in H.V. INĀMDĀR, ed., *Santa Nāmdev. Kāvyasambhār āṇi Santaparivār,* Pune, 1987, pp. 181-199.

Abbreviations

ALLC: *Association for Literary and Linguistic Computing.*
HSS: *Hindī Shabda Sāgar,* ed. by Shyām Sundar Dās, 11 vols, Vārāṇasī, 1967.
IAVRI: *International Association of the Vrindaban Research Institute,* London.
KG: *Kabīr Granthāvalī,* ed. by P.N. Tivārī, Allahabad, 1961.
KG2: Vaudeville Ch., *Kabīr Granthāvalī,* Pondicherry, 1957.
KV: Vaudeville Ch., *Kabīr I,* Oxford, 1974.
OLA: *Orientalia Lovaniensia Analecta,* Leuven.
OLP: *Orientalia Lovaniensia Periodica,* Leuven.
RSK: *Rājasthānī Sabad Kos,* Sitārām Lālas, 9 vols., Jodhpur, 1967.

Barathvāl P.D., *Gorakh-Bānī,* 3rd ed., Allahabad, 1950.

Belsare M.B., *An etymological Gujurātī-English Dictionary,* (1904), New Delhi, 1981.

W.M. Callewaert:1974,1, *A 17th c. Anthology of Hindī Poetry,* in: OLP,5,1974, 187-196.

W.M. Callewaert:1974,2, *The Anabhay Prabodh of Garībadās,* in: OLP,5,1974, 163-185.

W.M. Callewaert:1977, *Key for Understanding Mystical Literature,* in: OLP,8(1977), 309-330.

W.M. Callewaert:1978, *The Sarvāṅgī of the Dādūpanthī Rajab,* OLA 4, Leuven, 1978.

W.M. Callewaert:1980,1 with L. De Brabandere, *Nirguṇ Literature on Microfilm in Leuven, Belgium,* in: IAVRI Bulletin, London, IX(Dec. 1981), 24-48.

W.M. Callewaert:1984,1, *The Leuven Text-composition System in Indian Alphabets,* in ALLC Bulletin vol.12, 1(1984), 5-8.

M. Lath: The Musical Antecedents of Jayadeva's Gitagovinda', in: ***Jijñāsā: A Journal of the History of Ideas and Culture;*** **published by the Department of History and Indian Culture, University of Rājasthān, Jaipur; vol. 2, no. 1 (Jan. 1975), 21-36**

M. Lath:1978, *A Study of Dattilam. A treatise on the sacred music of Ancient India*, New Delhi, 1978.

Mishra R.C., *Hindī Santo kā ulaṭbānsī Sāhitya.*

Platts J.T., *A Dictionary of Urdū, Classical Hindī and English*, Oxford (1884), 1968.

Rām Sinha et alii, *Dholā-mārū rā Dūhā*, Banāras, 1934.

Sharmā P.H., *Sundar-Granthāvalī*, 2 vols, Calcutta, 1936.

Sharmā S.R., *Dakkhinī Hindī kā gadya aur padya*, Hyderabad, 1962.

Svāmī Mangaldās, ed., *Bakhnā jī kī Vāṇī*, Jaipur, 1937.

Monika Thiel-Horstmann:1983 *Bhakti in Current Research, 1979-1982*, Berlin, 1983.

Varmā V.L., *Rajjab Bāṇī*, Kanpur. 1963.

Appendix 4

THEMATIC INDEX

Appendix 5

NĀMDEV PARCAĪ

WORD-INDEX

In the manuscripts in Rājasthān we found the following *Parcaīs* attributed to Anantadās about the following Sants: Nāmdev, Kabīr, Raidās, Pīpā, Trilocan, Angad and Dhanā From a careful study of these biographies it is clear that the manuscripts (17th century AD) we now have give versions which are different one from the other. The differences are not only due to scribal tampering but also and even more to narrator's creativity. All seven *Parcaīs* have been critically edited and translated into English. In that publication also is given the Word-Index for the complete oeuvre of Anantadās.

Appendix 6

COMPUTER GRAPHS

Programme I gives:

1. the total number of lines in the critical text and in each manuscript.
2. the total number of words in the critical text and in each manuscript.
3. the number of omitted words (represented by hyphens) in each manuscript when compared to the critical text.
4. the number of words that are broken due to the bad condition of the manuscript.
5. the number of 'dialectical' or 'minor' variants in each manuscript; in the input file an asterisk (*) is added to such a string.
6. the number of omitted lines.
7. the number of lines that are missing due to the bad condition of the manuscript.

8-9. additional words or lines (when compared to the critical text); one + represents one missing string; + attached to a word signifies that part of the word is missing.

10-11. the number of words that are half broken due to the bad condition of the manuscript.

12. the number of interpolated words in each manuscript when compared to the critical text.

Graph I.

Total number of lines and words, with number of specific strings

	Ms. ->	f	d	a	u	v	m	p	g	r	c	j	h
1	lines	1984	1481	1544	1243	1390	1478	1511	1306	557	1029	1029	1407
2	words	9571	7056	7262	5814	6603	6940	7087	6263	2529	4938	4939	6644
3	-	0	46	75	59	58	111	41	31	25	88	100	103
4	+	0	111	0	0	0	1	20	0	0	0	0	15
5	*	0	1123	1191	1215	1327	1454	1048	752	329	149	1614	1016
6	--	0	22	11	12	6	19	6	4	3	20	20	12
7	+ +	0	19	0	0	0	0	5	0	0	0	0	0
8	ad.wds	0	0	0	0	0	0	0	0	0	0	0	0
9	a-lines	0	0	0	0	0	0	0	0	0	0	0	0
10	+wds	0	63	0	1	0	0	1	0	0	0	0	9
11	wds+	0	51	0	0	2	2	1	0	0	0	0	7
12	int.wds	0	78	108	84	57	71	71	59	27	113	108	20

Programme II gives the *absolute number of variants* when comparing *two* manuscripts or when comparing a manuscript to the critical text.

Graph II.

Absolute number of variants when comparing two manuscripts.

Ms.f->	d	a	u	v	m	p	g	r	c	j	h
13 wds ms=d	1675	-----									
14 wds ms=a	1651	2149	-----								
15 wds ms=u	1697	2126	2104	-----							
16 wds ms=v	1687	2139	2161	2034	-----						
17 wds ms=m	1883	2303	2418	2218	2154	-----					
18 wds ms=p	1381	2075	2208	2171	2057	2227	-----				
19 wds ms=g	979	1500	1616	1448	1451	1751	1368	-----			
20 wds ms=r	443	798	802	652	815	743	518	522	-----		
21 wds ms=c	1715	1904	1968	1585	1911	1879	1781	1639	700	-----	
22 wds ms=j	2258	2328	2346	1914	2285	2280	2180	2021	805	1912	-----
23 wds ms=h	1640	2170	2268	2141	2165	1965	1915	1613	633	1635	2049

Programme III gives the *relative number of variants* in a manuscript when compared to the critical test. This relative number is obtained by multiplying the absolute number of variants in a manuscript by a factor which relates the total number of words in that manuscript to the total in the critical text. Thus we can compare the relative number of variants in a manuscript. The percentage count of these 'relative' figures is also given.

Graph III.

Relative number of variants when comparing a Ms. to the f-line or critical text.

24 ms <->f	0	2272	2176	2794	2445	2597	1865	1496	1677	3324	4376	2362
25 ms% <->f	0.00	23.74	22.73	29.19	25.55	27.13	19.49	15.63	17.52	34.73	45.72	24.68
		d	a	u	v	m	p	g	r	c	j	h

Programme IV compares only the lines that are common to two manuscripts and gives in graph IV the number of variants shared by two Mss. In brackets is given the total number of words that are identical in the two manuscripts compared. A high score of common variants suggests a close relation between two manuscripts. For each two manuscripts compared, the computer gives

- the number of identical variants
- the percentage of this number in the total amount of identical words in the two manuscripts
- the total number of identical words in two manuscripts.

Of these identical words, the words that are variant from the critical text may suggest a branching off of the two manuscripts. On the basis of these indications an attempt can be made at defining both the 'musical' and the 'scribal' traditions.

	d	a	u	v	m	p	g	r	c	j	h
40 f-l ms = d											
41 (- % -)	0.000										
42 (total)	(5381)										
43 f-l ms = a	0	187									
44 (- % -)	0.000	4.500									
45 (total)	(5606	(4156)									
46 f-l ms = u		152	155								
47 (- % -)	0.000	4.616	4.713								
48 (total)	(4117)	(3293)	(3289)								
49 f-l ms = v	0	248	177	177							
50 (- % -)	.000	5.953	4.596	5.680							
51 (total)	(4916)	(4166)	(3851)	(3116)							
52 f-l ms = m	0	156	185	182	212						
53 (- % -)	0.000	4.221	4.537	5.507	5.772						
54 (total)	(5057)	(3696)	(4078)	(3305)	(3673)						
55 f-l ms = p	0	115	123	128	146	222					
56 (- % -)	0.000	2.804	2.813	3.591	3.791	4.926					
57 (total)	(5706)	(4102)	(4373)	(3564)	(3851)	(4507)					
58 f-l ms = g	0	154	134	96	168	119	162				
59 (- % -)	0.000	4.043	3.470	3.550	4.734	3.388	3.981				
60 (total)	(5284)	(3809)	(3862)	(2704)	(3549)	(3512)	(4069)				
61 f-l ms = r	0	49	48	46	70	75	143	72			
62 (- % -)	0.000	3.040	2.866	4.053	4.353	4.854	7.598	4.265			
63 (total)	(2086)	(1612)	(1675)	(1135)	(1608)	(1545)	(1882)	(1688)			
64 f-l ms = c	0	91	116	133	111	136	102	82	38		
65 (- % -)	0.000	3.785	4.754	7.506	5.101	6.140	4.460	3.507	4.780		
66 (total)	(3223)	(2404)	(2440)	(1772)	(2176)	(2215)	(2287)	(2338)	(795)		
67 f-l ms = j	0	63	104	98	80	99	73	54	30	674	
68 (- % -)	0.000	3.180	5.041	6.773	4.437	5.455	3.864	2.759	4.367	22.296	
69 (total)	(2681)	(1981)	(2063)	(1447)	(1803)	(1815)	(1889)	(1957)	(687)	(3023)	
70 f-l ms = h	0	137	152	168	151	426	275	102	102	147	103
71 (- % -)	0.000	3.709	3.810	5.120	4.262	9.237	5.846	2.898	6.572	6.743	5.819
72 (total)	(5004)	(3694)	(3989)	(3281)	(3543)	(4612)	(4704)	(3520)	(1552)	(2180)	(1770)

Appendix 7

ILLUSTRATIONS

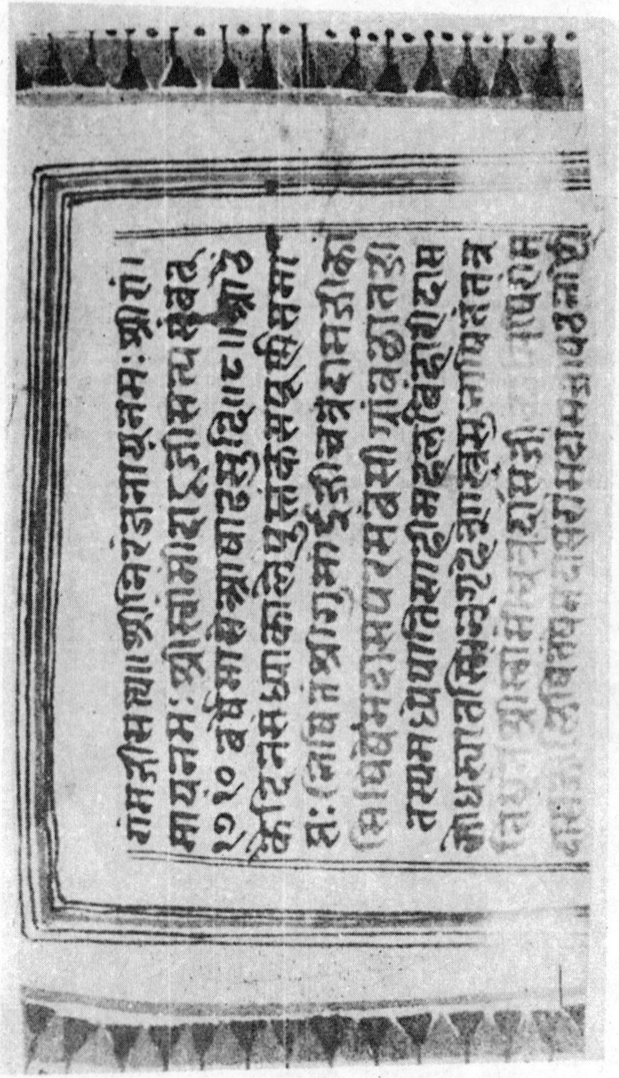

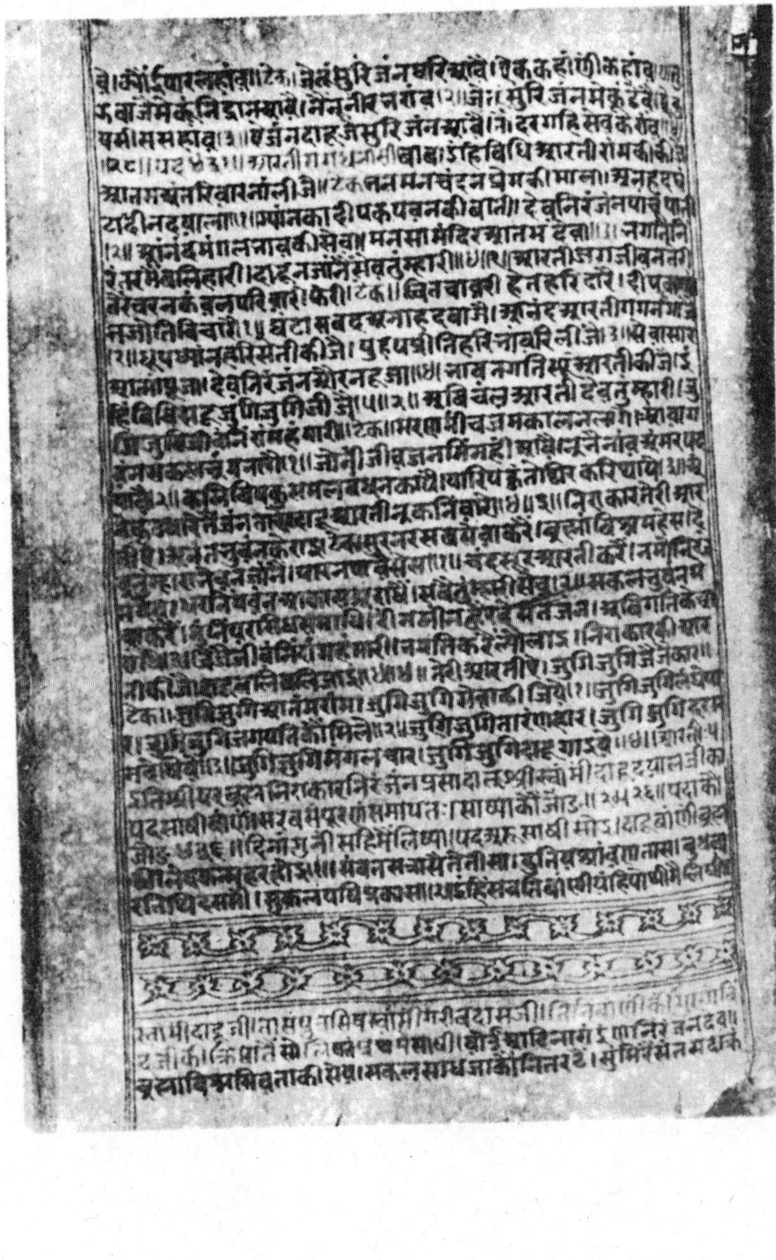

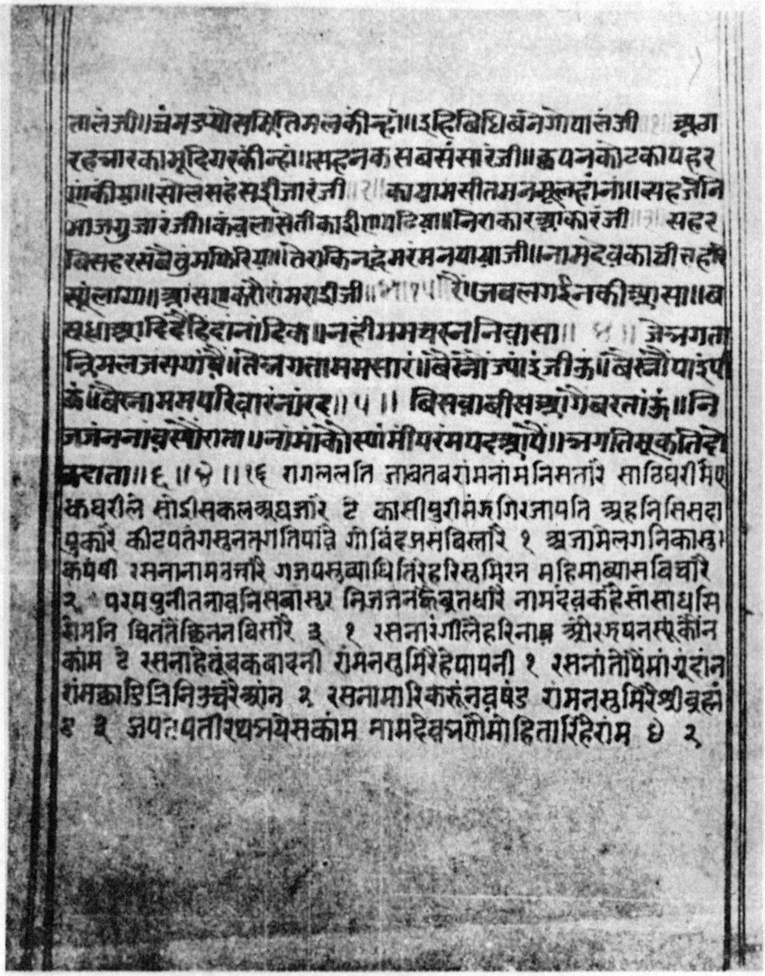

तालेजी॥ चेमहस्योसमितिमलकीन्हो॥ इहिबिधिबनेगोपालजी ॥ ग
रहन्चारकामूंदियरकीन्हो॥ सहनकसबसंसारजी॥ छपनकोटकायहर
गांकीया॥ सोलसहेसइीजारजी ॥ कायामसीतमनमूलतांना॥ सहजैनि
माजगुजारजी॥ कंवलासेतीकाईणपढ़िया॥ निराकारआकारजी ॥ सहर
बिसहरसबेवुसमिरिया॥ तेराकिनहेमरमनयाया॥ जी॥ नामदेवकाचीतहो
ल्लोलाया॥ आसाकरौरामराईजी॥ ॥ रैजबलगइनकीआसा॥ ब
धाआ॥ दिनदिनांदिक॥ नहीममयसनिवासा॥ ॥ जेन्नगत
निमलजसपणे॥ तेनगतामसारं॥ बेस्नोंज्पाइंजीकुं॥ बिस्नोपाइए
कं॥ बेस्नाममपरिवारंनांरद॥ ५ ॥ बिसवाबीसआगेबरतांऊं॥ नि
नजनंनाइसोरामा॥ नामांकोस्वांमीपरमपदआवे॥ जगतिमुकतिदे
रामा॥ ६ ॥ ७ ॥ १६ रागललति तावतबरामनामनिमतारे साठिघरीमिण
कघरीले सोडीसकलअघजारे टे कासीपुरीमंझगिरजापति अहनिसिसदा
पुकारे कीटपतंगखलनजातिपाते गोविंदसमबिस्तारे १ अजामेलगनिकासु
कपंषी रसनानामउधारे गजपसुब्याधितिरहरिसुमिरन महिमाब्यासविचारे
२ परमपुनीतनावनिसबासर निजजनकेब्रतधारे नामदेवकहेसोसाधुसि
रोमनि चितनेछिनविसारे ३ १ रसनारंगीलेहरिनाम श्रीरंगपनसूकौन
कांम टे रसनाहेवकबावनी रांमनसुमिरेहेपापनी १ रसनांतोपैमांगूदांन
रांमछाडिजिनिकहेआंन २ रसनामारिकरूंनवषंड रांमनसुमिरेश्रीब्रह्मं
ड ३ अपतपतीरथसयेसकांम नामदेवजपोमोहितारिहैराम ९ २

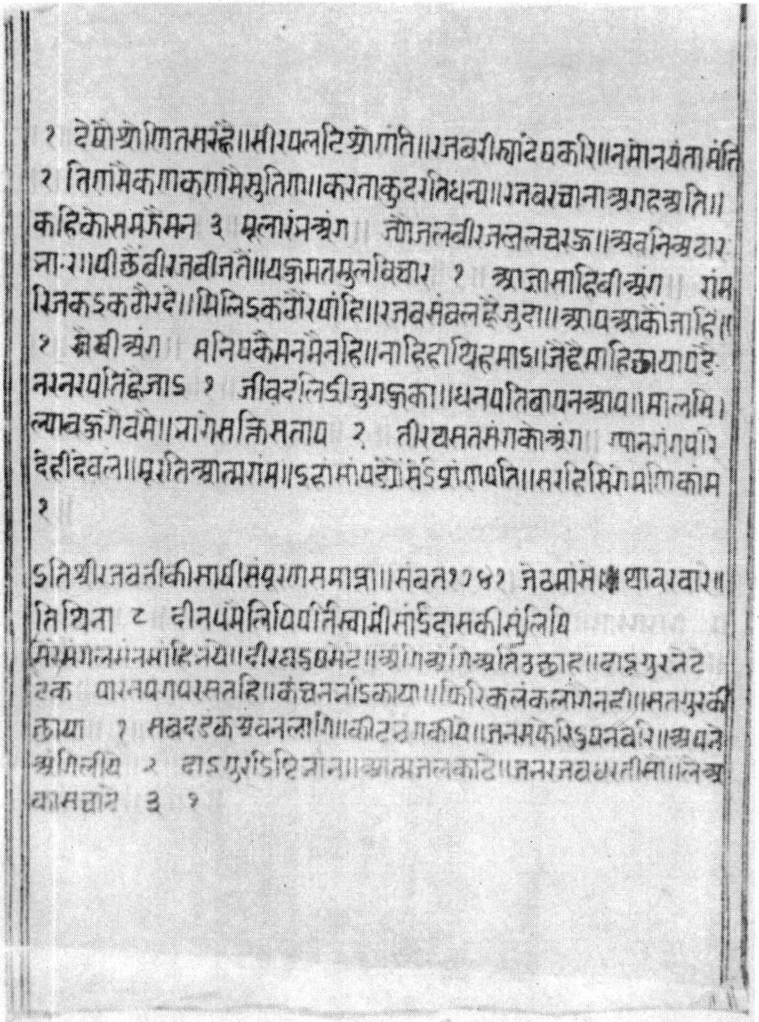

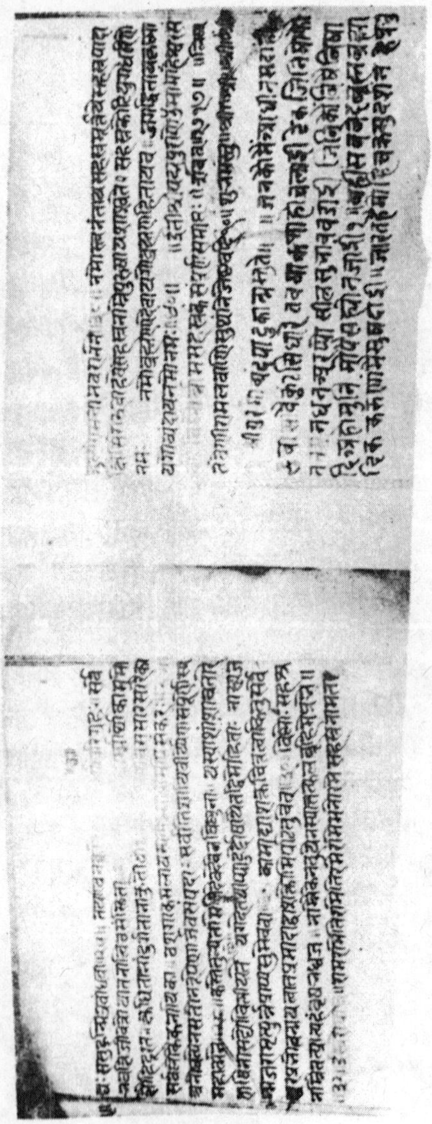

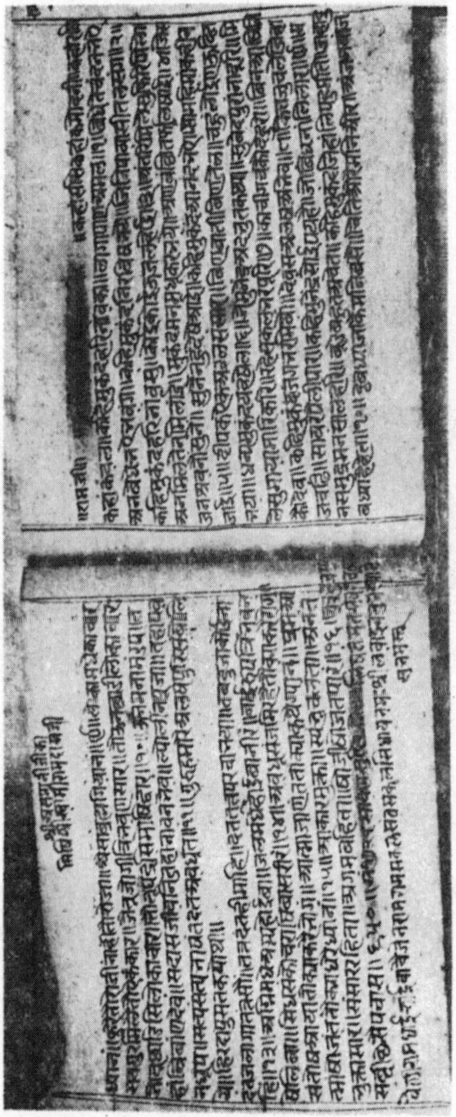

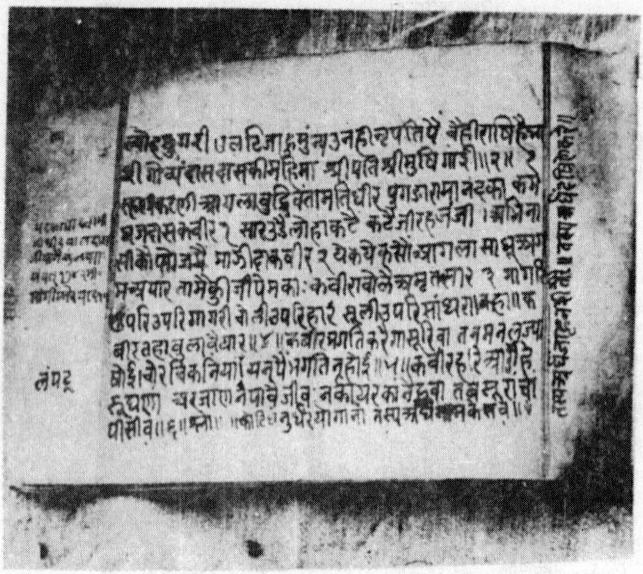

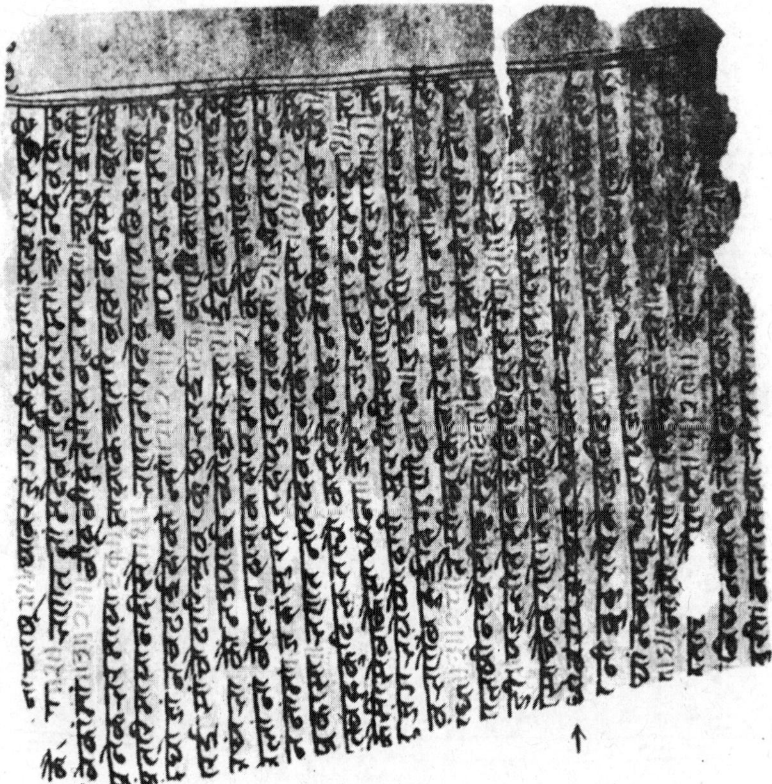

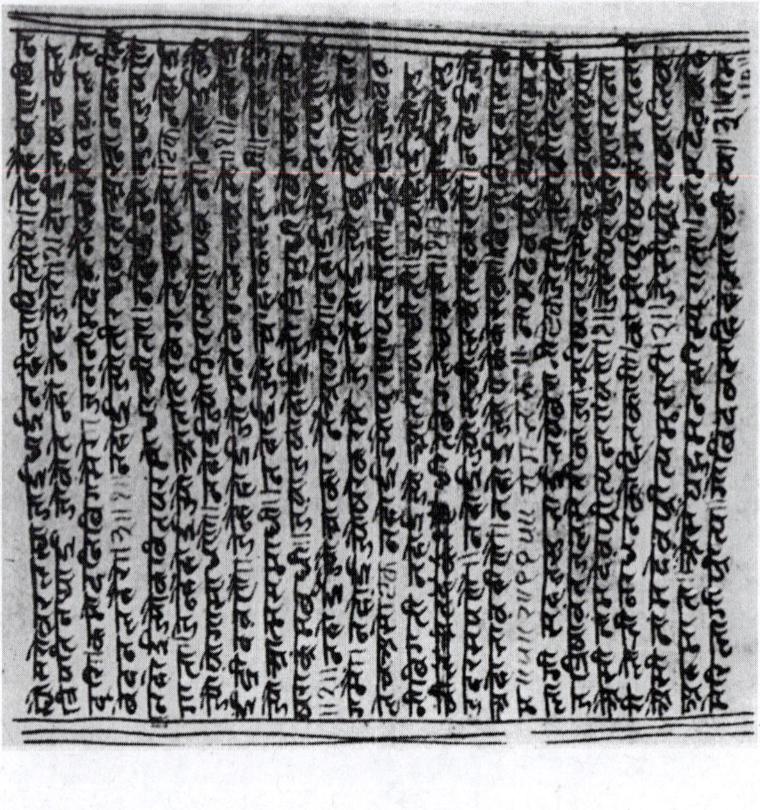